Philosophy
and
Contemporary Issues

Philosophy
and
Contemporary Issues
Ninth Edition

John R. Burr
Milton Goldinger
University of Wisconsin Oshkosh

PEARSON
Prentice
Hall

Upper Saddle River, New Jersey 07458

Library of Congress Cataloging-in-Publication Data

Philosophy and contemporary issues/[edited by] John R. Burr, Milton Goldinger.—9th ed.
   p.cm.
   Includes bibliographical references.
   ISBN 0-13-111256-2
   1. Philosophy.   I. Burr, John Roy   II. Goldinger, Milton

  BD41.P47 2003
  190'.9'04—dc21

                    2003042547

VP, Editorial Director: Charlyce Jones Owen
Senior Acquisitions Editor: Ross Miller
Assistant Editor: Wendy Yurash
Production Editor: Louise Rothman
Editorial Assistant: Carla Worner
Prepress and Manufacturing Buyer: Brian Mackey
Marketing Manager: Claire Bitting
Cover Design Director: Jayne Conte
Cover Design: Kiwi Design
Cover Art: Chuck Carlton, *The Thinker surrounded by gears*, Index Stock Imagery, Inc.

© 2004, 2000, 1996, 1992, 1988 by Pearson Education, Inc.
Upper Saddle River, New Jersey 07458

Printed in the United States of America

10 9 8 7 6 5 4 3

ISBN 0-13-111256-2

Pearson Education Ltd.
Pearson Education Australia Pty., Limited
Pearson Education Singapore, Pte., Ltd.
Pearson Education North Asia Ltd.
Pearson Education Canada, Ltd.
Pearson Educación de Mexico, S.A. de C.V.
Pearson Education – Japan
Pearson Education Malaysia, Pte., Ltd.

Contents

Part Two: God and Religion 103

Part Three: Morality and Society 179

Part Five: Mind and Body   369

Preface

The purpose of this anthology is to show how philosophy illuminates and in some measure helps solve some of the important problems troubling contemporary humankind. The editors intend it to be an introductory text. Unfortunately, many introductory texts in philosophy are flawed by one of two major defects: (1) they are too difficult for the beginning student, or (2) they are too simple for the beginning student. Some introductory philosophy texts are introductory in name only because they demand of the philosophically innocent student a mastery of technical philosophical language and a knowledge of the history of philosophy one could reasonably expect only from a professional philosopher. No wonder students struggling to understand such books become convinced of the truth of the popular view that philosophy is a subject that is wholly unintelligible to all except a few compulsive adepts and is completely irrelevant to life outside the classroom. On the other hand, in an attempt to eliminate excessive philosophical sophistication, other introductory philosophy texts are philosophical in name only because they contain no technical philosophy. Not surprisingly, students reading such books in order to learn about philosophy as a distinct discipline find them hollow and conclude that philosophy is not worth serious study.

In designing the structure of this book, in selecting the readings, in writing the introductions to the various parts, and in choosing the books to be listed in the bibliographies, the editors have striven to produce a work avoiding both defective extremes. Throughout, the guiding aim has been to make philosophy interesting and intelligible to students undertaking their first sustained study of the subject and, above all, to encourage them to engage in philosophizing themselves. To achieve this end, each part of this volume contains pro and con articles on provocative contemporary issues, which in turn raise fundamental philosophical issues. In addition to the material dealing directly with contemporary issues, each part includes other selections discussing at length and in depth some of the philosophical problems raised by the contemporary controversies. Each part closes with a "Problems and Puzzles" section focusing on some deep logical disquietudes embedded in the earlier readings. These problems and puzzles have been chosen not only for their intrinsic fascination but also for their power to lure students into broader philosophical argument. Therefore, each part forms a coherent unit of mutually relevant sections rather than a miscellaneous grouping. Every effort has been made to pick readings as appropriate as possible for the beginning student of philosophy rather than for the advanced or professional student of the subject. Because the editors planned a single volume and not a library, not all philosophical issues, methods, and movements could be included. It should be pointed out also that the readings in one part often will throw light on the material discussed in other parts. Nevertheless, the readings are also numerous and diverse enough to enable individual instructors to select just those they deem most suitable for their courses.

This introductory text is a mutual enterprise, each editor sharing equally in its production and benefiting in the same proportion from the comments and suggestions of his colleague.

This new edition of *Philosophy and Contemporary Issues* is a revision, not a reprint. New readings replace some of those in previous editions, and the introductions have been rewritten accordingly. Changes have been made in the bibliographies. We believe our ninth collaboration has resulted in a fresh edition superior to its eight predecessors.

The editors thank particularly Ross Miller, Editor of Philosophy and Religion at Prentice Hall; Wendy Yurash, Assistant Editor; the faculty of the Forrest R. Polk Library of the University of Wisconsin Oshkosh; the staff of the Oshkosh Public Library; and Terri L. Wouts. Finally we have profited greatly from the thoughtful comments, criticisms, and suggestions of the many users of the previous eight editions of *Philosophy and Contemporary Issues* and take this opportunity to express our appreciation. We especially wish to thank Michael J. Connelly, Longview Community College; Frederick Becker, Illinois Central College; and Carlos Colombetti, Skyline College, for their helpful reviews.

J. R. B.
M. G.

General Introduction

What Philosophy Can Be

Western philosophy has performed many different functions in the course of its long history. Perhaps the most important of these philosophical activities has been the encouragement of intellectual independence. This introductory text, *Philosophy and Contemporary Issues*, focuses on this autonomy-enhancing function of philosophy. But what is intellectual independence? Immanuel Kant (1724–1804), a German philosopher called "great" because his philosophy still profoundly influences what and how educated people think today, succinctly defines it as "Enlightenment." Kant makes clear that Enlightenment is not a set of specific doctrines, a universal system of philosophical truths; rather, Enlightenment is a distinct, active state of being. In his essay "What Is Enlightenment," Kant expresses the essence of Enlightenment, or Intellectual Independence, in the following words:

> Enlightenment is the emergence of man from the immaturity for which he is himself responsible. Immaturity is the inability to use one's understanding without the guidance of another. Man is responsible for his own immaturity, when it is caused, by lack not of understanding, but of the resolution and the courage to use it without the guidance of another. Sapere aude! Have the courage to use your own reason! is the slogan of the Enlightenment.

The first philosophical selection in this book, its overture, is Plato's *Apology*. Kant provides an abstract definition of intellectual autonomy; Plato, the great philosophical artist, gives a vivid, dramatic representation of intellectual autonomy in action. The *Apology* is Plato's account of his teacher Socrates's defense at his trial in Athens in 399 B.C. Socrates has been brought to trial, charged with corrupting the youth and introducing strange gods—in contemporary terms, with being a dangerous subversive. Socrates contends that he is on trial for more than a technical violation of the law. His ideas are on trial; philosophy itself is on trial. The court gives this claim justification when it tells Socrates that he will be acquitted on the condition that he stop philosophizing. Socrates adamantly refuses. His defense becomes a defense of his life of philosophizing.

Socrates defends reason as the supreme authority, as the ultimate court of appeal. He declares that "the unexamined life is not worth living." He vows that the only thing he will follow is reason. Socrates prepares the way for his defense by reminding the jurors that the god Apollo, speaking through the human channel of the Oracle at Delphi, declared that no one is wiser than Socrates. To the ancient Greeks, Apollo, the god of reason, was not a strange god but the son of Zeus, the chief god of the Olympian mythology.[1] To obey one's reason is to obey Apollo.

---

[1]Mythology is someone else's religion.

Socrates's steadfast reliance on his own reason in all things, including religion, is illustrated strikingly by his response to the Oracle at Delphi's declaration about his wisdom. The actual Oracle, a woman called Pythia, would utter weird sounds while in a frenzy. Popular belief held that her words really were those of the god Apollo. Temple priests interpreted her unintelligible utterances to the public. In the *Apology*, Socrates depicts himself as employing his own reason to arrive at his own interpretation of the meaning of what Apollo communicated through the Oracle. While he is convinced that the gods always tell the truth, the meaning of what they say is not self-evident; it must be elicited by rational analysis and observation. Socrates's immediate response to what the Delphic Oracle has said about him is skeptical: how can it be true that Socrates is the wisest of men and yet also true that many men know more than he does? What does Apollo really mean?

Socrates tests the truth of Apollo's statement by questioning others to learn the greater wisdom they claim to possess but which Socrates knows he lacks—only to discover that they really are as ignorant as he is. Socrates concludes that he is wiser than others because he knows that he doesn't know. Self-knowledge is the beginning of wisdom: no one questions, inquires, learns if he believes that he already knows the answers. Socrates sees himself as on a divine mission to ceaselessly question people to prove to them that they don't know the answers—that is, to philosophize. Socrates says that he is not a teacher in the usual sense because he has no set truths or system of doctrines to teach.

Socrates uses his interpretation of the meaning of the Delphic Oracle's pronouncement that there was no one wiser than Socrates to refute those whom he calls "my old accusers" and whom he fears more than he does his present accusers, Meletus, Anytus, and Lycon. Since the childhood of most of those hearing him, these anonymous "old accusers" have slandered him as "a wise man, who speculates about the heavens, and who investigates things that are beneath the earth, and who can make the weaker reason appear the stronger." Socrates indignantly denounces this guilt by association and denies that he is that *kind* of wise man or "sophist." He insists that he is not wise about nature and its workings nor about how to argue persuasively but fallaciously concerning what is good for individuals and communities. Those claiming to be wise about nature have a reputation for being atheists; those claiming to be wise about human affairs are deceivers, who charge tuition for teaching what they do not really know. Socrates is neither. He *is* a wise man or sophist, true enough. But his wisdom is unique; he alone does not believe that he knows what in fact he does not know. Consequently, Socrates, disavowing any knowledge of physical nature (natural science) or of the good life for human beings (social science), declares he is a philo-sophist, a philosopher, a *lover* of wisdom, a *seeker* of wisdom.

Turning next to a refutation of the current accusations that he does not believe in the gods in whom the state believes, but introduces new divinities and that he corrupts the youth, Socrates subjects his present accuser, Meletus, to a brief but devastating cross-examination, a cameo version of what he daily inflicted on anyone willing to talk with him. Illustrating his now famous maieutic method of question and answer in which the philosopher or lover of wisdom questions and the other person claiming to have wisdom answers, Socrates quickly ensnares Meletus in a net of contradictions, thereby revealing Meletus's true ignorance by proving that he does not know what he believes he knows. It is easy to imagine the embarrassment and anger of anyone experiencing the public humiliation of having his lack of wisdom so glaringly exposed to anyone overhearing such a "conversation," and the stinging laughter of the auditors.

Nevertheless, Socrates is not a complete skeptic. Not only does he know that he doesn't know many things, he soon declares that he knows "that it is evil and disgraceful to do wrong, and disobey my superior, whoever he is, whether man or god." Socrates then argues in defense of his philosophical life of ceaseless questioning that the god Apollo in effect commanded him to philosophize or seek wisdom; that a god is a commander superior to any human court or other human authority; and that, therefore, he should obey Apollo and continue to philosophize rather than disobey the god by heeding any order from the court or any other inferior commander to stop philosophizing. If this argument does not demonstrate the wisest course of action to take, then Meletus and the other accusers should educate him by refuting it and so prove that Socrates does not really know what he believes he does instead of forcing him to court and threatening him with punishment. Not even the threat of death can deter Socrates from his rational independence in following the argument wherever it may lead. He asserts that no one knows whether death is a great good or a great evil but he does know that one should avoid a known evil, such as disobeying Apollo and ceasing to philosophize, rather than be intimidated by something that might or might not be evil, such as death.

For the philosopher the most important issue is not whether one lives or dies but whether one is acting as a just or an unjust person would act. Here is impregnable independence. But Socrates goes further and exhorts everyone to make this just or unjust issue paramount in his or her life. Know thyself, Socrates urges, know what is most important. By questioning others and by questioning yourself, discover the good, what is really most important, what you really want as seen by analysis and argument. In short, to love wisdom, to philosophize, is what the Socrates of the *Apology* means by obeying "Apollo, the superior commander," whatever the historical Socrates may have really believed about the existence or non-existence of that deity of the Greek Olympian religion. Socrates is not only a thinker; he is also a reformer. He not only questions himself; he questions everyone, saying: "My good friend, you are a citizen of Athens, a city which is very great and very famous for its wisdom and strength—are you not ashamed of caring so much for the making of money and for fame and prestige when you neither think nor care about wisdom and truth and the improvement of your soul?" Socrates encourages everyone to philosophize, to obey the superior commander. By emulating Socrates you will become a true son or daughter of Apollo.

Philosophy and Contemporary Issues has been designed in the spirit of Socrates. This introductory philosophy text has two main goals: (1) to show students their ignorance and (2) to awaken their desire for wisdom. If it encourages its readers to be intellectually independent, it will have introduced them to philosophy. *Philosophy and Contemporary Issues* is an anthology of writings by many authors, of alleged wisdom from many people said to be wise, on such basic topics as freedom and determinism, God and religion, morality and society, state and society, mind and body, knowledge and science. These range over such traditional fields of philosophy as metaphysics, philosophy of religion, ethics, social and political philosophy, philosophy of mind, epistemology, and philosophy of science. To the beginning student these topics and their technical terms may well seem abstract, remote, even unintelligible. Therefore, each of the six parts of this book includes contemporary issues vigorously, even passionately, discussed by intelligent and educated people who raise such questions as, Are criminals responsible? Should you believe in God on faith alone? Is abortion right or wrong? Should the government censor art? Are men machines? and What is the value of science? Rational attempts to answer these questions inexorably lead to such traditional philosophical subjects as hard determinism, libertarianism, soft determinism, proofs of God's existence, ethical relativism, democracy, individualism, socialism, anarchism, materialism, interactionism, idealism, rationalism, empiricism, and the nature of science. Finally, each of the six parts of this book concludes with some profound, baffling problems and puzzles raised by the previous readings. Rational attempts to answer questions produce more refined questions. Ultimately all important questions end in bafflement. To philosophize is not to be baffled too soon.

Are all of the readings in *Philosophy and Contemporary Issues* examples of genuine wisdom? Hardly. They cannot possibly all be wise because they disagree. The design of this book emphasizes their controversial character in order to awaken readers from their sleep, much as Socrates sought to rouse his fellow Athenians from their dreams. Ultimately each of us is on his or her own. Each of us must dare to ask questions, resolve to use our reason to follow the argument wherever it may lead to discover truth.

To philosophize is no easy task. Socrates's accusers have many contemporary descendants. A prominent American educator has declared:

> There seems to be nothing in the study of chemistry that makes you feel like a superior order of being, but you study Plato and you begin to believe you're a philosopher—and a philosopher should be king. This is a dangerous trend, and it jeopardizes the democratic principles on which this country was founded.[2]

The philosopher Socrates ignored his accusers and steadfastly obeyed the command of Apollo, the god of reason. The philosopher Kant ignored the accusers of his day and called for the courage to use one's own reason. The philosopher Bertrand Russell (1872–1970) interpreted the meaning of Apollo for our own time:

---

[2]Dr. Samuel I. Hayakawa, "The Playboy Panel: Student Revolt," *Playboy*, September 1969, p. 98. Reprinted by permission of *Playboy*.

1. Do not feel certain of anything.
2. Do not think it worthwhile to produce belief by concealing evidence, for the evidence is sure to come to light.
3. Never try to discourage thinking, for you are sure to succeed.
4. When met with opposition, even if it should be from your husband or your children, endeavour to overcome it by argument and not by authority, for a victory dependent upon authority is unreal and illusory.
5. Have no respect for the authority of others, for there are always contrary authorities to be found.
6. Do not use power to suppress opinions you think pernicious, for if you do the opinions will suppress you.
7. Do not fear to be eccentric in opinion, for every opinion now accepted was once eccentric.
8. Find more pleasure in intelligent dissents than in passive agreement, for, if you value intelligence as you should, the former implies a deeper agreement than the latter.
9. Be scrupulously truthful, even when truth is inconvenient, for it is more inconvenient when you try to conceal it.
10. Do not feel envious of the happiness of those who live in a fool's paradise, for only a fool will think that it is happiness.[3]

---

[3]Bertrand Russell, "The Ten Commandments," *The Independent*, June 1965, p. 4. Reprinted by permission of *The Independent*.

1. The Apology

Plato

Plato (427–347 B.C.) was an Athenian aristocrat who early in life came under the influence of Socrates. He wrote more than twenty dialogues, many of which feature his teacher and hero, Socrates. When he was around forty years old, Plato founded the Academy, which was in effect the first university in Europe. So great has been Plato's influence that Alfred North Whitehead said that Western philosophy has been a succession of footnotes to Plato.

Socrates (470–399 B.C.) left no writings. What he says in The Apology *are words attributed to him by Plato. Socrates was neither wealthy nor an aristocrat but a common Athenian whose father was a stonecutter and mother a midwife. Instead of practicing his father's craft, he devoted himself to questioning his fellow citizens in order to learn the wisdom they claimed to possess, only to find they had no wisdom to teach him. The Apology and the Platonic dialogues the* Crito *and the* Phaedo *depict the most famous trial, imprisonment, and death in the West other than that of Jesus Christ.[1]*

Characters—Socrates and Meletus
Scene—The Court of Justice

SOCRATES   I cannot tell what impression my accusers have made upon you, Athenians. For my own part, I know that they nearly made me forget who I was, so believable were they; and yet they have scarcely uttered one single word of truth. But of all their many falsehoods, the one which astonished me most was when they said that I was a clever speaker, and that you must be careful not to let me mislead you. I thought that it was most impudent of them not to be ashamed to talk in that way; for as soon as I open my mouth they will be refuted, and I shall prove that I am not a clever speaker in any way at all—unless, indeed, by a clever speaker they mean a man who speaks the truth. If that is their meaning, I agree with them that I am a much greater orator than they. My accusers, then I repeat, have said little or nothing that is true; but from me you shall hear the whole truth. Certainly you will not hear an elaborate speech, Athenians, dressed up, like theirs, with words and phrases. I will say to you what I have to say,

From Plato, *The Apology*, trans. by Jowett, 3rd edition (Oxford: Oxford University Press) 1896.

[1]There are no alleged facts about the lives of Plato and Socrates that have not been questioned by at least some scholars.

without preparation, and in the words which come first, for I believe that my cause is just; so let none of you expect anything else. Indeed, my friends, it would hardly be seemly for me, at my age, to come before you like a young man with his specious phrases. But there is one thing, Athenians, which I do most earnestly beg and entreat of you. Do not be surprised and do not interrupt with shouts if in my defense I speak in the same way that I am accustomed to speak in the marketplace, at the tables of the money changers, where many of you have heard me, and elsewhere. The truth is this. I am more than seventy years old, and this is the first time that I have ever come before a law court; so your manner of speech here is quite strange to me. If I had been really a stranger, you would have forgiven me for speaking in the language and the fashion of my native country; and so now I ask you to grant me what I think I have a right to claim. Never mind the style of my speech—it may be better or it may be worse—give your whole attention to the question, Is what I say just, or is it not? That is what makes a good judge, as speaking the truth makes a good advocate.

I have to defend myself, Athenians, first against the old false accusations of my old accusers, and then against the later ones of my present accusers. For many men have been accusing me to you, and for very many years, who have not uttered a word of truth; and I fear them more than I fear Anytus and his associates, formidable as they are. But, my friends, those others are still more formidable; for they got hold of most of you when you were children, and they have been more persistent in accusing me untruthfully and have persuaded you that there is a certain Socrates, a wise man, who speculates about the heavens, and who investigates things that are beneath the earth, and who can make the weaker reason appear the stronger. These men, Athenians, who spread abroad this report are the accusers whom I fear; for their hearers think that persons who pursue such inquiries never believe in the gods. Then they are many, and their attacks have been going on for a long time, and they spoke to you when you were at the age most readily to believe them, for you were all young, and many of you were children, and there was no one to answer them when they attacked me. And the most unreasonable thing of all is that I do not even know their names: I cannot tell you who they are except when one happens to be a comic poet. But all the rest who have persuaded you, from motives of resentment and prejudice, and sometimes, it may be, from conviction, are hardest to cope with. For I cannot call any one of them forward in court to cross-examine him. I have, as it were, simply to spar with shadows in my defense, and to put questions which there is no one to answer. I ask you, therefore, to believe that, as I say, I have been attacked by two kinds of accusers—first, by Meletus and his associates, and, then, by those older ones of whom I have spoken. And, with your leave, I will defend myself first against my old accusers; for you heard their accusations first, and they were much more forceful than my present accusers are.

Well, I must make my defense, Athenians, and try in the short time allowed me to remove the prejudice which you have been so long a time acquiring. I hope that I may manage to do this, if it be good for you and for me, and that my defense may be successful; but I am quite aware of the nature of my task, and I know that it is a difficult one. Be the outcome, however, as is pleasing to God, I must obey the law and make my defense.

Let us begin from the beginning, then, and ask what is the accusation which has given rise to the prejudice against me, which was what Meletus relied on when he brought his indictment. What is the prejudice which my enemies have been spreading about me? I must assume that they are formally accusing me, and read their indictment. It would run somewhat in this fashion: Socrates is a wrongdoer, who meddles with inquiries into things beneath the earth and in the heavens, and who makes the weaker reason appear the stronger, and who teaches others these same things. That is what they say; and in the comedy of Aristophanes [*Clouds*] you yourselves saw a man called Socrates swinging round in a basket and saying that he walked the air, and prattling a great deal of nonsense about matters of which I understand nothing, either more or less. I do not mean to disparage that kind of knowledge if there is anyone who is wise about these matters. I trust Meletus may never be able to prosecute me for that. But the truth is, Athenians, I have nothing to do with these matters, and almost all of you are yourselves my witnesses of this. I beg all of you who have heard me discussing, and they are many, to inform your neighbors and tell them if any of you have ever heard me discussing such matters, either more or less. That will show you that the other common stories about me are as false as this one.

But the fact is that not one of these is true. And if you have heard that I undertake to educate men, and make money by so doing, that is not true either, though I think that it would be a fine thing to be able to educate men, as Gorgias of Leontini, and Prodicus of Ceos, and Hippias of Elis do. For each of them, my friends, can go into any city, and persuade the young men to leave the society of their fellow citizens, with any of whom they might associate for nothing, and be only too glad to be allowed to pay money for the privilege of associating with themselves. And I believe that there is another wise man from Paros residing in Athens at this moment. I happened to meet Callias, the son of Hipponicus, a man who has spent more money on sophists than everyone else put together. So I said to him (he has two sons), Callias, if your two sons had been foals or calves, we could have hired a trainer for them who would have made them perfect in the virtue which belongs to their nature. He would have been either a groom or a farmer. But whom do you intend to take to train them, seeing that they are men? Who understands the virtue which belongs to men and to citizens? I suppose that you must have thought of this, because of your sons. Is there such a person, said I, or not? Certainly there is, he replied. Who is he, said I, and where does he come from, and what is his fee? Evenus, Socrates, he replied, from Paros, five minae. Then I thought that Evenus was a fortunate person if he really understood this art and could teach so cleverly. If I had possessed knowledge of that kind, I should have been conceited and disdainful. But, Athenians, the truth is that I do not possess it.

Perhaps some of you may reply: But, Socrates, what is the trouble with you? What has given rise to these prejudices against you? You must have been doing something out of the ordinary. All these stories and reports of you would never have arisen if you had not been doing something different from other men. So tell us what it is, that we may not give our verdict in the dark. I think that that is a fair question, and I will try to explain to you what it is that has raised these prejudices against me and given me this reputation. Listen, then: some of you, perhaps, will think that I am joking, but I assure you that I will tell you the whole truth. I have gained this reputation, Athenians, simply by reason of a certain wisdom. But by what kind of wisdom? It is by just that wisdom which is perhaps human wisdom. In that, it may be, I am really wise. But the men of whom I was speaking just now must be wise in a wisdom which is greater than human wisdom, or else I cannot describe it, for certainly I know nothing of it myself, and if any man says that I do, he lies and speaks to arouse prejudice against me. Do not interrupt me with shouts, Athenians, even if you think that I am boasting. What I am going to say is not my own: I will tell you who says it, and he is worthy of your respect. I will bring the god of Delphi to be the witness of my wisdom, if it is wisdom at all, and of its nature. You remember Chaerephon. From youth upwards he was my comrade; and also a partisan of your democracy, sharing your recent exile and returning with you. You remember, too, Chaerephon's character—how vehement he was in carrying through whatever he took in hand. Once he went to Delphi and ventured to put this question to the oracle—I entreat you again, my friends, not to interrupt me with your shouts—he asked if there was any man who was wiser than I. The priestess answered that there was no one. Chaerephon himself is dead, but his brother here will confirm what I say.

Now see why I tell you this. I am going to explain to you how the prejudice against me has arisen. When I heard of the oracle I began to reflect: What can the god mean by this riddle? I know very well that I am not wise, even the smallest degree. Then what can he mean by saying that I am the wisest of men? It cannot be that he is speaking falsely, for he is a god and cannot lie. For a long time I was at a loss to understand his meaning. Then, very reluctantly, I turned to seek for it in this manner: I went to a man who was reputed to be wise, thinking that there, if anywhere, I should prove the answer wrong, and meaning to point out to the oracle its mistake, and to say, You said that I was the wisest of men, but this man is wiser than I am. So I examined the man—I need not tell you his name, he was a politician—but this was the result, Athenians. When I conversed with him I came to see that, though a great many persons, and most of all he himself, thought that he was wise, yet he was not wise. Then I tried to prove to him that he was not wise, though he fancied that he was; and by so doing I made him indignant, and many of the bystanders. So when I went away, I thought to myself, I am wiser than this man: neither of us knows anything that is really worthwhile, but he thinks that he has knowledge when he has not, while I, having no knowledge, do not think that I have. I seem, at any rate, to be a little wiser than he is on this point: I do not think that I know what I do not know. Next I went to another man who was reputed to be still wiser than the last, with exactly the same result. And there again I made him, and many other men, indignant.

Then I went on to one man after another, seeing that I was arousing indignation every day, which caused me much pain and anxiety. Still I thought that I must set the god's command above everything. So I had to go to every man who seemed to possess any knowledge, and investigate the meaning of the oracle. Athenians, I must tell you the truth; by the god, this was the result of the investigation which I made at the god's bidding: I found that the men whose reputation for wisdom stood highest were nearly the most lacking in it, while others who were looked down on as common people were much more intelligent. Now I must describe to you the wanderings which I undertook, like Heraclean labors, to prove the oracle irrefutable. After the politicians, I went to the poets, tragic, dithyrambic, and others, thinking that there I should find myself manifestly more ignorant than they. So I took up the poems on which I thought that they had spent most pains, and asked them what they meant, hoping at the same time to learn something from them. I am ashamed to tell you the truth, my friends, but I must say it. Almost anyone of the bystanders could have talked about the works of these poets better than the poets themselves. So I soon found that it is not by wisdom that the poets create their works, but by a certain innate power and by inspiration, like soothsayers and prophets, who say many fine things, but who understand nothing of what they say. The poets seemed to me to be in a similar situation. And at the same time I perceived that, because of their poetry, they thought that they were the wisest of men in other matters, too, which they were not. So I went away again, thinking that I had the same advantage over the poets that I had over the politicians.

Finally, I went to the artisans, for I knew very well that I possessed no knowledge at all worth speaking of, and I was sure that I should find that they knew many fine things. And in that I was not mistaken. They knew what I did not know, and so far they were wiser than I. But, Athenians, it seemed to me that the skilled artisans made the same mistake as the poets. Each of them believed himself to be extremely wise in matters of the greatest importance because he was skillful in his own art: and this presumption of theirs obscured their real wisdom. So I asked myself, on behalf of the oracle, whether I would choose to remain as I was, without either their wisdom or their ignorance, or to possess both, as they did. And I answered to myself and to the oracle that it was better for me to remain as I was.

From this examination, Athenians, has arisen much fierce and bitter indignation, and from this a great many prejudices about me, and people say that I am "a wise man." For the bystanders always think that I am wise myself in any matter wherein I refute another. But, my friends, I believe that the god is really wise, and that by this oracle he meant that human wisdom is worth little or nothing. I do not think that he meant that Socrates was wise. He only made use of my name, and took me as an example, as though he would say to men: He among you is the wisest who, like Socrates, knows that in truth his wisdom is worth nothing at all. Therefore I still go about testing and examining every man whom I think wise, whether he be a citizen or a stranger, as the god has commanded me; and whenever I find that he is not wise, I point out to him, on the god's behalf, that he is not wise. I am so busy in this pursuit that I have never had leisure to take any path worth mentioning in public matters or to look after my private affairs. I am in great poverty as the result of my service to the god.

Besides this, the young men who follow me about, who are the sons of wealthy persons and have the most leisure, take pleasure in hearing men cross-examined. They often imitate me among themselves; then they try their hands at cross-examining other people. And, I imagine, they find plenty of men who think that they know a great deal when in fact they know little or nothing. Then the persons who are cross-examined get angry with me instead of with themselves, and say that Socrates is an abomination and corrupts the young. When they are asked, Why, what does he do? what does he teach? they do not know what to say; but, not to seem at a loss, they repeat the stock charges against philosophers, and allege that he investigates things in the air and under the earth, and that he teaches people to disbelieve in the gods, and to make the weaker reason appear the stronger. For, I suppose, they would not like to confess the truth, which is that they are shown up as ignorant pretenders to knowledge that they do not possess. So they have been filling your ears with their bitter prejudices for a long time, for they are ambitious, energetic, and numerous; and they speak vigorously and persuasively against me. Relying on this, Meletus, Anytus, and Lycon have attacked me. Meletus is indignant with me on the part of the poets, Anytus on the part of the artisans and politicians, and Lycon on the part of the orators. And so, as I said at the beginning, I shall be surprised if I am able, in the short time allowed me for my defense, to remove from your minds this prejudice which has grown so strong. What I have told you, Athenians, is the truth: I neither conceal nor do I suppress anything, small or great. Yet I know that it is just this plainness of speech which rouses indignation. But that is only a proof that my words are true, and that the prejudice against me, and the causes of it, are what I have said. And whether you look for them now or hereafter, you will find that they are so.

What I have said must suffice as my defense against the charges of my first accusers. I will try next to defend myself against Meletus, that "good patriot," as he calls himself, and my later accusers. Let us assume that they are a new set of accusers, and read their indictment, as we did in the case of the others. It runs thus. He says that Socrates is a wrong-doer who corrupts the youth, and who does not believe in the gods whom the state believes in, but in other new divinities. Such is the accusation. Let us examine each point in it separately. Meletus says that I do wrong by corrupting the youth. But I say, Athenians, that he is doing wrong, for he is playing a solemn joke by lightly bringing men to trial, and pretending to have zealous interest in matters to which he has never given a moment's thought. Now I will try to prove to you that it is so.

Come here, Meletus. Is it not a fact that you think it very important that the young should be as excellent as possible?

MELETUS It is.

SOCRATES Come then, tell the judges who is it who improves them? You care so much, you must know. You are accusing me, and bringing me to trial, because, as you say, you have discovered that I am the corrupter of the youth. Come now, reveal to the gentlemen who improves them. You see, Meletus, you have nothing to say; you are silent. But don't you think that this is shameful? Is not your silence a conclusive proof of what I say—that you have never cared? Come, tell us, my good sir, who makes the young better citizens?

MELETUS The laws.

SOCRATES That, my friend, is not my question. What man improves the young, who starts with the knowledge of the laws?

MELETUS The judges here, Socrates.

SOCRATES What do you mean, Meletus? Can they educate the young and improve them?

MELETUS Certainly.

SOCRATES All of them? or only some of them?

MELETUS All of them.

SOCRATES By Hera, that is good news! Such a large supply of benefactors! And do the listeners here improve them, or not?

MELETUS They do.

SOCRATES And do the senators?

MELETUS Yes.

SOCRATES Well then, Meletus, do the members of the assembly corrupt the young or do they again all improve them?

MELETUS They, too, improve them.

SOCRATES Then all the Athenians, apparently, make the young into good men except me, and I alone corrupt them. Is that your meaning?

MELETUS Most certainly; that is my meaning.

SOCRATES You have discovered me to be most unfortunate. Now tell me: do you think that the same holds good in the case of horses? Does one man do them harm and everyone else improve them? On the contrary, is it not one man only, or a very few—namely, those who are skilled with horses—who can improve them, while the majority of men harm them if they use them and have anything to do with them? Is it not so, Meletus, both with horses and with every other animal? Of course it is, whether you and Anytus say yes or no. The young would certainly be very fortunate if only one man corrupted them, and every one else did them good. The truth is, Meletus, you prove conclusively that you have never thought about the youth in your life. You exhibit your carelessness in not caring for the very matters about which you are prosecuting me.

Now be so good as to tell us, Meletus, is it better to live among good citizens or bad ones? Answer, my friend. I am not asking you at all a difficult question. Do not the bad harm their associates and the good do them good?

MELETUS Yes.

SOCRATES Is there any man who would rather be injured than benefited by his companions? Answer, my good sir; you are obliged by the law to answer. Does any one like to be injured?

MELETUS Certainly not.

SOCRATES Well then, are you prosecuting me for corrupting the young and making them worse, intentionally or unintentionally?

MELETUS For doing it intentionally.

SOCRATES What, Meletus? Do you mean to say that you, who are so much younger than I, are yet so much wiser than I that you know that bad citizens always do evil, and that good citizens do good, to those with whom they come in contact, while I am so extraordinarily stupid as not to know that, if I make any of my companions evil, he will probably injure me in some way, and as to commit this great evil, as you allege, intentionally? You will not make me believe that, nor anyone else either, I should think. Either I do not corrupt the young at all or, if I do, I do so unintentionally: so that you are lying in either case. And if I corrupt them unintentionally, the law does not call upon you to prosecute me for an error which is unintentional, but to take me aside privately and reprove and instruct me. For, of course, I shall cease from doing wrong involuntarily, as soon as I know that I have been doing wrong. But you avoided associating with me and educating me; instead you bring me up before the court, where the law sends persons, not for instruction, but for punishment.

The truth is, Athenians, as I said, it is quite clear that Meletus has never cared at all about these matters. However, now tell us, Meletus, how do you say that I corrupt the young? Clearly, according to your indictment, by teaching them not to believe in the gods the state believes in, but other new divinities instead. You mean that I corrupt the young by that teaching, do you not?

MELETUS   Yes, most certainly I mean that.

SOCRATES   Then in the name of these gods of whom we are speaking, explain yourself a little more clearly to me and to these gentlemen here. I cannot understand what you mean. Do you mean that I teach the young to believe in some gods, but not in the gods of the state? Do you accuse me of teaching them to believe in strange gods? If that is your meaning, I myself believe in some gods, and my crime is not that of absolute atheism. Or do you mean that I do not believe in the gods at all myself, and I teach other people not to believe in them either?

MELETUS   I mean that you do not believe in the gods in any way whatever.

SOCRATES   You amaze me, Meletus! Why do you say that? Do you mean that I believe neither the sun nor the moon to be gods, like other men?

MELETUS   I swear he does not, judges; he says that the sun is a stone, and the moon earth.

SOCRATES   My dear Meletus, do you think that you are prosecuting Anaxagoras? You must have a very poor opinion of these men, and think them illiterate, if you imagine that they do not know that the works of Anaxagoras of Clazomenae are full of these doctrines. And so young men learn these things from me, when they can often buy places in the theatre for a drachma at most, and laugh at Socrates were he to pretend that these doctrines, which are very peculiar doctrines, too, were his own. But please tell me, do you really think that I do not believe in the gods at all?

MELETUS   Most certainly I do. You are a complete atheist.

SOCRATES   No one believes that, Meletus, not even you yourself. It seems to me, Athenians, that Meletus is very insolent and reckless, and that he is prosecuting me simply out of insolence, recklessness and youthful bravado. For he seems to be testing me, by asking me a riddle that has no answer. Will this wise Socrates, he says to himself, see that I am joking and contradicting myself? or shall I outwit him and everyone else who hears me? Meletus seems to me to contradict himself in his indictment: it is as if he were to say, Socrates is a wrongdoer who does not believe in the gods, but who believes in the gods. But that is mere joking.

Now, my friends, let us see why I think that this is his meaning. Do you answer me, Meletus; and do you, Athenians, remember the request which I made to you at the start, and do not interrupt me with shouts if I talk in my usual way.

Is there any man, Meletus, who believes in the existence of things pertaining to men and not in the existence of men? Make him answer the question, my friends, without these interruptions. Is there any man who believes in the existence of horsemanship and not in the existence of horses? or in flute-playing and not in flute-players? There is not, my friend. If you will not answer, I will tell both you and the judges. But you must answer my next question. Is there any man who believes in the existence of divine things and not in the existence of divinities?

MELETUS   There is not.

SOCRATES   I am very glad that these gentlemen have managed to extract an answer from you. Well then, you say that I believe in divine beings, whether they be old or new ones, and that I teach others to believe in them; at any rate, according to your statement, I believe in divine beings. That you have sworn in your indictment. But if I believe in divine beings, I suppose it follows necessarily that I believe in divinities. Is it not so? It is. I assume that you grant that, as you do not answer. But do we not believe that divinities are either gods themselves or the children of the gods? Do you admit that?

MELETUS   I do.

SOCRATES   Then you admit that I believe in divinities. Now, if these divinities are gods, then, as I say, you are joking and asking a riddle, and asserting that I do not believe in the gods, and at the same time that I do, since I believe in divinities. But if these divinities are the illegitimate children of the gods, either by the nymphs or by other mothers, as they are said to be, then, I ask, what man could believe in the existence of the children of the gods, and not in the existence of the gods? That would be as strange as believing in the existence of the offspring of horses and asses, and not in the existence of horses and asses. You must have indicted me in this manner, Meletus, either to test me or because you could not find any crime that you could accuse me of with truth. But you will never contrive to persuade any man with any sense at all that a belief in divine things and things of the gods does not necessarily involve a belief in divinities, and in the gods, and in heroes.

But in truth, Athenians, I do not think that I need say very much to prove that I have not committed the crime for which Meletus is prosecuting me. What I have said is enough to prove that. But I repeat it is certainly true, as I have already told you, that I have aroused much indignation. That is what will cause my condemnation if I am condemned; not Meletus nor Anytus either, but that prejudice and suspicion of the multitude which have been the destruction of many good men before me, and I think will be so again. There is no fear that I shall be the last victim.

Perhaps someone will say: Are you not ashamed, Socrates, of lead-ing a life which is very likely now to cause your death? I should answer him with justice, and say: My friend, if you think that a man of any worth at all ought to reckon the chances of life and death when he acts, or that he ought to think of anything but whether he is acting rightly or wrongly, and as a good or a bad man would act, you are mistaken. According to you, the demigods who died at Troy would be foolish, and among them the son of Thetis, who thought nothing of danger when the alternative was disgrace. For when his mother—and she was a goddess—addressed him, when he was burning to slay Hector, in this fashion, "My son, if you avenge the death of your comrade Patroclus and slay Hector, you will die yourself, for 'fate awaits you straightaway after Hector's death'"; when he heard this, he scorned danger and death; he feared much more to live a coward and not to avenge his friend. "Let me punish the evil-doer and straightaway die," he said, "that I may not remain here by the beaked ships jeered at, encumbering the earth." Do you suppose that he thought of danger or of death? For this, Athenians, I believe to be the truth. Wherever a man's station is, whether he has chosen it of his own will, or whether he has been placed at it by his commander, there it is his duty to remain and face the danger without thinking of death or of any other thing except dishonor.

When the generals whom you chose to command me, Athenians, assigned me my station at Potidaea and at Amphipolis and at Delium, I remained where they placed me and ran the risk of death, like other men. It would be very strange conduct on my part if I were to desert my station now from fear of death or of any other thing when God has commanded me—as I am persuaded that he has done—to spend my life in searching for wisdom, and in examining myself and others. That would indeed be a very strange thing: then certainly I might with justice be brought to trial for not believing in the gods, for I should be disobeying the oracle, and fearing death and thinking myself wise when I was not wise. For to fear death, my friends, is only to think ourselves wise with-out really being wise, for it is to think that we know what we do not know. For no one knows whether death may not be the greatest good that can happen to man. But men fear it as if they knew quite well that it was the greatest of evils. And what is this but that shameful ignorance of thinking that we know what we do not know? In this matter, too, my friends, perhaps I am different from the multitude; and if I were to claim to be at all wiser than others, it would be because, not knowing very much about the other world, I do not think I know. But I do know very well that it is evil and disgraceful to do wrong, and to disobey my super-ior, whoever he is, whether man or god. I will never do what I know to be evil, and shrink in fear from what I do not know to be good or evil. Even if you acquit me now, and do not listen to Anytus' argument that, if I am to be acquitted, I ought never to have been brought to trial at all, and that, as it is, you are bound to put me to death because, as he said, if I escape, all your sons will be utterly corrupted by practicing what Socrates teaches. If you were therefore to say to me: Socrates, this time we will not listen to Anytus; we will let you go, but on this condition, that you give up this investigation of yours, and philosophy; if you are found following those pursuits again, you shall die. I say, if you offered to let me go on these terms, I should reply: Athenians, I hold you in the highest regard and affection, but I will be persuaded by the god rather than by you; and as long as I have breath and strength I will not give up philosophy and exhorting you and declaring the truth to every one of you whom I meet, saying, as I am accustomed, "My good friend, you are a citizen of Athens, a city which is very great and very famous for its wisdom and strength—are you not ashamed of caring so much for the making of money and for fame and prestige, when you neither think nor care about wisdom and truth and the improvement of your soul?" And if he disputes my words and says that he does care about these things, I shall not at once release him and go away: I shall question him and cross-examine him and test him. If I think that he does not possess virtue, though he says that he does, I shall reproach him for undervaluing the most valuable things, and overvaluing those that are less valuable. This I shall do to everyone whom I meet, young or old, citizen or stranger, but especially to citizens, for they are more nearly akin to me. For know that the god has commanded me to do so. And I think that no greater good has ever befallen you in Athens than my service to the god. For I spend my whole life in going about and persuading you all to give your first and greatest care to the improvement of your souls, and not till you have done that to think of your bodies or your wealth; and telling you that virtue does not come from wealth, but that wealth, and every other good thing which men have, whether in public or in private, comes from virtue. If then I corrupt the youth by this teaching, these things must be harmful; but if any man says that I teach anything else, there is nothing in what he says. And therefore, Athenians, I say, whether you are persuaded by Anytus or not, whether you acquit me or not, be sure I shall not change my way of life; no, not if I have to die for it many times.

Do not interrupt me, Athenians, with your shouts. Remember the request which I made to you, and do not interrupt my words. I think that it will profit you to hear them. I am going to say something more to you, at which you may be inclined to protest, but do not do that. Be sure that if you put me to death, who am what I have told you that I am, you will do yourselves more harm than me. Meletus and Anytus can do me no harm: that is impossible, for I am sure it is not allowed that a good man be injured by a worse. They may indeed kill me, or drive me into exile, or deprive me of my civil rights; and perhaps Meletus and others think those things great evils. But I do not think so. I think it is a much greater evil to do what he is doing now, and to try to put a man to death unjustly. And now, Athenians, I am not arguing in my own defense at all, as you might expect me to do, but rather in yours in order you may not make a mistake about the gift of the god to you by condemning me. For if you put me to death, you will not easily find another who, if I may use a ludicrous comparison, clings to the state as a sort of gadfly to a horse that is large and well-bred but rather sluggish from its size, and needing to be aroused. It seems to me that the god has attached me like that to the state, for I am constantly alighting upon you at every point to rouse, persuade, and reproach each of you all day long. You will not easily find anyone else, my friends, to fill my place; and if you are persuaded by me, you will spare my life. You are indignant, as drowsy persons are, when they are awakened, and, of course, if you are persuaded by Anytus, you could easily kill me with a single blow, and then sleep on undisturbed for the rest of your lives, unless the god in his care for you sends another to rouse you. And you may easily see that it is the god who has given me to your city; for it is not human the way in which I have neglected all my own interests and permitted my private affairs to be neglected now for so many years, while occupying myself unceasingly in your interests, going to each of you privately, like a father or an elder brother, trying to persuade him to care for virtue. There would have been a reason for it, if I had gained any advantage by this, or if I had been paid for my exhortations; but you see yourselves that my accusers, though they accuse me of everything else without shame, have not had the impudence to say that I ever either exacted or demanded payment. Of that they have no evidence. And I think that I have sufficient evidence of the truth of what I say—my poverty.

Perhaps it may seem strange to you that, though I go about giving this advice privately and meddling in others' affairs, yet I do not venture to come forward in the assembly and advise the state. You have often heard me speak of my reason for this, and in many places: it is that I have a certain divine sign, which is what Meletus has caricatured in his indictment. I have had it from childhood. It is a kind of voice which, whenever I hear it, always turns me back from something which I was going to do, but never urges me to act. It is this which forbids me to take part in politics. And I think it does well to forbid me. For, Athenians, it is quite certain that, if I had attempted to take part in politics, I should have perished at once and long ago without doing any good either to you or to myself. And do not be indignant with me for telling the truth. There is no man who will preserve his life for long, either in Athens or elsewhere, if he firmly opposes the multitude, and tries to prevent the commission of much injustice and illegality in the state. He who would really fight for justice must do so as a private citizen, not as an officeholder, if he is to preserve his life, even for a short time.

I will prove to you that this is so by very strong evidence, not by mere words, but by what you value highly, actions. Listen then to what has happened to me, that you may know that there is no man who could make me consent to do wrong from the fear of death, but that I would perish at once rather than give way. What I am going to tell you may be a commonplace in the law court; nevertheless it is true. The only office that I ever held in the state, Athenians, was that of Senator. When you wished to try the ten generals who did not rescue their men after the battle of Arginusae, as a group, which was illegal, as you all came to think afterwards, the tribe Antiochis, to which I belong, held the presidency. On that occasion I alone of all the presidents opposed your illegal action and gave my vote against you. The speakers were ready to suspend me and arrest me; and you were clamoring against me, and crying out to me to submit. But I thought that I ought to face the danger, with law and justice on my side, rather than join with you in your unjust proposal, from fear of imprisonment or death. That was when the state was democratic. When the oligarchy came in, the Thirty sent for me, with four others, to the council-chamber, and ordered us to bring Leon the Salaminian from Salamis, that they might put him to death. They were in the habit of frequently giving similar orders, to many others, wishing to implicate as many as possible in their crimes. But, then, I again proved, not by mere words, but by my actions, that, if I may speak bluntly, I do not care a straw for death; but that I do care very much indeed about not doing anything unjust or impious. That government with all its powers did not terrify me into doing anything unjust; but when we left the council-chamber, the other four went over to Salamis and brought Leon across to Athens; and I went home. And if the rule of the Thirty had not been destroyed soon afterwards, I should very likely have been put to death for what I did then. Many of you will be my witnesses in this matter.

Now do you think that I could have remained alive all these years if I had taken part in public affairs, and had always maintained the cause of justice like an honest man, and had held it a paramount duty, as it is, to do so? Certainly not, Athenians, nor could any other man. But throughout my whole life, both in private and in public, whenever I have had to take part in public affairs, you will find I have always been the same and have never yielded unjustly to anyone; no, not to those whom my enemies falsely assert to have been my pupils. But I was never anyone's teacher. I have never withheld myself from anyone, young or old, who was anxious to hear me discuss while I was making my investigation; neither do I discuss for payment, and refuse to discuss without payment. I am ready to ask questions of rich and poor alike, and if any man wishes to answer me, and then listen to what I have to say, he may. And I cannot justly be charged with causing these men to turn out good or bad, for I never either taught or professed to teach any of them any knowledge whatever. And if any man asserts that he ever learned or heard anything from me in private which everyone else did not hear as well as he, be sure that he does not speak the truth.

Why is it, then, that people delight in spending so much time in my company? You have heard why, Athenians. I told you the whole truth when I said that they delight in hearing me examine persons who think that they are wise when they are not wise. It is certainly very amusing to listen to that. And, I say, the god has commanded me to examine men, in oracles and in dreams and in every way in which the divine will was ever declared to man. This is the truth, Athenians, and if it were not the truth, it would be easily refuted. For if it were really the case that I have already corrupted some of the young men, and am now corrupting others, surely some of them, finding as they grew older that I had given them bad advice in their youth, would have come forward today to accuse me and take their revenge. Or if they were unwilling to do so themselves, surely their relatives, their fathers or brothers, or others, would, if I had done them any harm, have remembered it and taken their revenge. Certainly I see many of them in Court. Here is Crito, of my own deme and of my own age, the father of Critobulus; here is Lysanias of Sphettus, the father of Aeschines; here is also Antiphon of Cephisus, the father of Epigenes. Then here are others whose brothers have spent their time in my company—Nicostratus, the son of Theozotides and brother of Theodotus—and Theodotus is dead, so he at least cannot entreat his brother to be silent; here is Paralus, the son of Demodocus and the brother of Theages; here is Adeimantus, the son of Ariston, whose brother is Plato here; and Aeantodorus, whose brother is Aristodorus. And I can name many others to you, some of whom Meletus ought to have called as witnesses in the course of his own speech; but if he forgot to call them then, let him call them now—I will yield the floor to him—and tell us if he has any such evidence. No, on the contrary, my friends, you will find all these men ready to support me, the corrupter, the injurer, of their relatives, as Meletus and Anytus call me. Those of them who have been already corrupted might perhaps have some reason for supporting me, but what reason can their relatives have who are grown up, and who are uncorrupted, except the reason of truth and justice—that they know very well that Meletus is a liar, and that I am speaking the truth?

Well, my friends, this, and perhaps more like this, is pretty much what I have to say in my defense. There may be some one among you who will be indignant when he remembers how, even in a less important trial than this, he begged and entreated the judges, with many tears, to acquit him, and brought forward his children and many of his friends and relatives in Court in order to appeal to your feelings; and then finds that I shall do none of these things, though I am in what he would think the supreme danger. Perhaps he will harden himself against me when he notices this: it may make him angry, and he may cast his vote in anger. If it is so with any of you—I do not suppose that it is, but in case it should be so—I think that I should answer him reasonably if I said: My friend, I have relatives, too, for, in the words of Homer, "I am not born of an oak or a rock" but of flesh and blood; and so, Athenians, I have relatives, and I have three sons, one of them a lad, and the other two still children. Yet I will not bring any of them forward before you and implore you to acquit me. And why will I do none of these things? It is not from arrogance, Athenians, nor because I lack respect for you—whether or not I can face death bravely is another question—but for my own good name, and for your good name, and for the good name of the whole state. I do not think it right, at my age and with my reputation, to do any thing of that kind. Rightly or wrongly, men have made up their minds that in some way Socrates is different from the mass of mankind. And it will be shameful if those of you who are thought to excel in wisdom, or in bravery, or in any other virtue, are going to act in this fashion. I have often seen men of reputation behaving in an extraordinary way at their trial, as if they thought it a terrible fate to be killed, and as though they expected to live for ever if you did not put them to death. Such men seem to me to bring shame upon the state, for any stranger would suppose that the best and most eminent Athenians, who are selected by their fellow citizens to hold office, and for other honors, are no better than women. Those of you, Athenians, who have any reputation at all ought not to do these things, and you ought not to allow us to do them; you should show that you will be much more ready to condemn men who make the state ridiculous by these pitiful pieces of acting, than men who remain quiet.

But apart from the question of reputation, my friends, I do not think that it is right to entreat the judge to acquit us, or to escape condemnation in that way. It is our duty to convince him by reason. He does not sit to give away justice as a favor, but to pronounce judgment; and he has sworn, not to favor any man whom he would like to favor, but to judge according to law. And, therefore, we ought not to encourage you in the habit of breaking your oaths; and you ought not to allow yourselves to fall into this habit, for then neither you nor we would be acting piously. Therefore, Athenians, do not require me to do these things, for I believe them to be neither good nor just nor pious; and, more especially, do not ask me to do them today when Meletus is prosecuting me for impiety. For were I to be successful and persuade you by my entreaties to break your oaths, I should be clearly teaching you to believe that there are no gods, and I should be simply accusing myself by my defense of not believing in them. But, Athenians, that is very far from the truth. I do believe in the gods as no one of my accusers believes in them: and to you and to God I commit my cause to be decided as is best for you and for me.

(He is found guilty . . .)

I am not indignant at the verdict which you have given, Athenians, for many reasons. I expected that you would find me guilty; and I am not so much surprised at that as at the numbers of the votes. I certainly never thought that the majority against me would have been so narrow. But now it seems that if only thirty votes had changed sides, I should have escaped. So I think that I have escaped Meletus, as it is; and not only have I escaped him, for it is perfectly clear that if Anytus and Lycon had not come forward to accuse me, too, he would not have obtained the fifth part of the votes, and would have had to pay a fine of a thousand drachmae.

So he proposes death as the penalty. Be it so. And what alternative penalty shall I propose to you, Athenians? What I deserve, of course, must I not? What then do I deserve to pay or to suffer for having determined not to spend my life in ease? I neglected the things which most men value, such as wealth, and family interests, and military commands, and popular oratory, and all the political appointments, and clubs, and factions, that there are in Athens; for I thought that I was really too honest a man to preserve my life if I engaged in these matters. So I did not go where I should have done no good either to you or to myself. I went, instead, to each one of you privately to do him, as I say, the greatest of services, and tried to persuade him not to think of his affairs until he had thought of himself and tried to make himself as good and wise as possible, nor to think of the affairs of Athens until he had thought of Athens herself; and to care for other things in the same manner. Then what do I deserve for such a life? Something good, Athenians, if I am really to propose what I deserve; and something good which it would be suitable to me to receive. Then what is a suitable reward to be given to a poor benefactor who requires leisure to exhort you? There is no reward, Athenians, so suitable for him as a public maintenance in the Prytaneum. It is a much more suitable reward for him than for any of you who has won a victory at the Olympic games with his horse or his chariots. Such a man only makes you seem happy, but I make you really happy; and he is not in want, and I am. So if I am to propose the penalty which I really deserve, I propose this—a public maintenance in the Prytaneum.

Perhaps you think me stubborn and arrogant in what I am saying now, as in what I said about the entreaties and tears. It is not so, Athenians; it is rather that I am convinced that I never wronged any man intentionally, though I cannot persuade you of that, for we have discussed together only a little time. If there were a law at Athens, as there is elsewhere, not to finish a trial of life and death in a single day, I think that I could have persuaded you; but now it is not easy in so short a time to clear myself of great prejudices. But when I am persuaded that I have never wronged any man, I shall certainly not wrong myself, or admit that I deserve to suffer any evil, or propose any evil for myself as a penalty. Why should I? Lest I should suffer the penalty which Meletus proposes when I say that I do not know whether it is a good or an evil? Shall I choose instead of it something which I know to be an evil, and propose that as a penalty? Shall I propose imprisonment? And why should I pass the rest of my days in prison, the slave of successive officials? Or shall I propose a fine, with imprisonment until it is paid? I have told you why I will not do that. I should have to remain in prison, for I have no money to pay a fine with. Shall I then propose exile? Perhaps you would agree to that. Life would indeed be very dear to me if I were unreasonable enough to expect that strangers would cheerfully tolerate my discussions and reasonings when you who are my fellow citizens cannot endure them, and have found them so irksome and odious to you that you are seeking now to be relieved of them. No, indeed, Athenians, that is not likely. A fine life I should lead for an old man if I were to withdraw from Athens and pass the rest of my days in wandering from city to city, and continually being expelled. For I know very well that the young men will listen to me wherever I go, as they do here; and if I drive them away, they will persuade their elders to expel me; and if I do not drive them away, their fathers and kinsmen will expel me for their sakes.

Perhaps someone will say, "Why cannot you withdraw from Athens, Socrates, and hold your peace?" It is the most difficult thing in the world to make you understand why I cannot do that. If I say that I cannot hold my peace because that would be to disobey the god, you will think that I am not in earnest and will not believe me. And if I tell you that no better thing can happen to a man than to discuss virtue every day and the other matters about which you have heard me arguing and examining myself and others, and that an unexamined life is not worth living, then you will believe me still less. But that is so, my friends, though it is not easy to persuade you. And, what is more, I am not accustomed to think that I deserve any punishment. If I had been rich, I would have proposed as large a fine as I could pay: that would have done me no harm. But I am not rich enough to pay a fine unless you are willing to fix it at a sum within my means. Perhaps I could pay you a *mina*, so I propose that. Plato here, Athenians, and Crito, and Critobulus, and Apollodorus bid me propose thirty minae, and they will be sureties for me. So I propose thirty minae. They will be sufficient sureties to you for the money.

(He is condemned to death.)

You have not gained very much time, Athenians, and, as the price of it, you will have an evil name for all who wish to revile the state, and they will say that you put Socrates, a wise man, to death. For they will certainly call me wise, whether I am wise or not, when they want to reproach you. If you would have waited for a little while, your wishes would have been fulfilled in the course of nature; for you see that I am an old man, far advanced in years, and near to death. I am saying this not to all of you, only to those who have voted for my death. And to them I have something else to say. Perhaps, my friends, you think that I have been convicted because I was wanting in the arguments by which

I could have persuaded you to acquit me, if, that is, I had thought it right to do or to say anything to escape punishment. It is not so. I have been convicted because I was wanting, not in arguments, but in impudence and shamelessness—because I would not plead before you as you would have liked to hear me plead, or appeal to you with weeping and wailing, or say and do many other things which I maintain are unworthy of me, but which you have been accustomed to from other men. But when I was defending myself, I thought that I ought not to do anything unworthy of a free man because of the danger which I ran, and I have not changed my mind now. I would very much rather defend myself as I did, and die, than as you would have had me do, and live. Both in a lawsuit and in war, there are some things which neither I nor any other man may do in order to escape from death. In battle, a man often sees that he may at least escape from death by throwing down his arms and falling on his knees before the pursuer to beg for his life. And there are many other ways of avoiding death in every danger if a man is willing to say and to do anything. But, my friends, I think that it is a much harder thing to escape from wickedness than from death, for wickedness is swifter than death. And now I, who am old and slow, have been overtaken by the slower pursuer: and my accusers, who are clever and swift, have been overtaken by the swifter pursuer—wickedness. And now I shall go away, sentenced by you to death; and they will go away, sentenced by truth to wickedness and injustice. And I abide by this award as well as they. Perhaps it was right for these things to be so; and I think that they are fairly measured.

And now I wish to prophesy to you, Athenians, who have condemned me. For I am going to die, and that is the time when men have most prophetic power. And I prophesy to you who have sentenced me to death that a far more severe punishment than you have inflicted on me will surely overtake you as soon as I am dead. You have done this thing, thinking that you will be relieved from having to give an account of your lives. But I say that the result will be very different. There will be more men who will call you to account, whom I have held back, though you did not recognize it. And they will be harsher toward you than I have been, for they will be younger, and you will be more indignant with them. For if you think that you will restrain men from reproaching you for not living as you should, by putting them to death, you are very much mistaken. That way of escape is neither possible nor honorable. It is much more honorable and much easier not to suppress others, but to make yourselves as good as you can. This is my parting prophecy to you who have condemned me.

With you who have acquitted me I should like to discuss this thing that has happened, while the authorities are busy, and before I go to the place where I have to die. So, remain with me until I go: there is no reason why we should not talk with each other while it is possible. I wish to explain to you, as my friends, the meaning of what has happened to me. A wonderful thing has happened to me, judges—for you I am right in calling judges. The prophetic sign has been constantly with me all through my life till now, opposing me in quite small matters if I were not going to act rightly. And now you yourselves see what has happened to me—a thing which might be thought, and which is sometimes actually reckoned, the supreme evil. But the divine sign did not oppose me when I was leaving my house in the morning, nor when I was coming up here to the court, nor at any point in my speech when I was going to say anything; though at other times it has often stopped me in the very act of speaking. But now, in this matter, it has never once opposed me, either in my words or my actions. I will tell you what I believe to be the reason. This thing that has come upon me must be a good; and those of us who think that death is an evil must needs be mistaken. I have a clear proof that that is so; for my accustomed sign would certainly have opposed me if I had not been going to meet with something good.

And if we reflect in another way, we shall see that we may well hope that death is a good. For the state of death is one of two things: either the dead man wholly ceases to be and loses all consciousness or, as we are told, it is a change and a migration of the soul to another place. And if death is the absence of all consciousness, and like the sleep of one whose slumbers are unbroken by any dreams, it will be a wonderful gain. For if a man had to select that night in which he slept so soundly that he did not even dream, and had to compare with it all the other nights and days of his life, and then had to say how many days and nights in his life he had spent better and more pleasantly than this night, I think that a private person, nay, even the great King himself, would find them easy to count, compared with the others. If that is the nature of death, I for one count it a gain. For then it appears that all time is nothing more than a single night. But if death is a journey to another place, and what we are told is true—that there are all who have died— what good could be greater than this, my judges? Would a journey not be worth taking, at the end of which, in the other world, we should be released from the self-styled judges here and should find the true judges who are said to sit in judgment below, such as Minos and Rhadamanthus and Aeacus and Triptolemus, and the other demigods who were just in their own lives? Or what would you not give to discuss with Orpheus and Musaeus and Hesiod and Homer? I am willing to die many times if this be true. And for my own part I should find it wonderful to meet there Palamedes, and Ajax, the son of Telamon, and the other men of old who have died through an unjust judgment, and in comparing my experiences with theirs. That I think would be no small pleasure. And, above all, I could spend my time in examining those who are there, as I examine men here, and in finding out which of them is wise, and which of them thinks himself wise when he is not wise. What would we not give, my judges, to be able to examine the leader of the great expedition against Troy, or Odysseus, or Sisyphus, or countless other men and women whom we could name? It would be an infinite happiness to discuss with them and to live with them and to examine them. Assuredly there they do not put men to death for doing that. For besides the other ways in which they are happier than we are, they are immortal, at least if what we are told is true.

And you, too, judges, must face death hopefully, and believe this as a truth that no evil can happen to a good man, either in life or after death. His fortunes are not neglected by the gods; and what has happened to me today has not happened by chance. I am persuaded that it was better for me to die now, and to be released from trouble; and that was the reason why the sign never turned me back. And so I am not at all angry with my accusers or with those who have condemned me to die. Yet it was not with this in mind that they accused me and condemned me, but meaning to do me an injury. So far I may blame them.

Yet I have one request to make of them. When my sons grow up, punish them, my friends, and harass them in the same way that I have harassed you, if they seem to you to care for riches or for any other thing more than virtue; and if they think that they are something when they are really nothing, reproach them, as I have reproached you, for not caring for what they should, and for thinking that they are great men when really they are worthless. And if you will do this, I myself and my sons will have received justice from you.

But now the time has come, and we must go away—I to die, and you to live. Whether life or death is better is known to God, and to God only.

PART ONE

Freedom and Determinism

Introduction

As currently discussed, the issue of whether human behavior is free or determined has been generated by the development of the natural sciences since the sixteenth century. A basic assumption of the evolving sciences was universal causation: that is, the principle that every event has a cause. Further, it was thought that events occurred in orderly patterns, which could be formulated as causal or natural laws. On the basis of these laws and knowledge of the actual causes at work, accurate predictions would be made. In principle, any event could be predicted; it was only the lack of knowledge of the laws or of the present causes that limited prediction. The theory asserting universal causation and total predictability traditionally has been called *determinism*.

For the determinist, human actions are events as predictable as any other type of event. Just as the behavior of water heated to 212 degrees Fahrenheit can be predicted, so, in principle, can the behavior of a person given a million dollars. The determinist would admit that, at the moment, the latter sort of prediction cannot be made reliably because we lack the necessary exact laws of human behavior. Someday, however, the social sciences may find such laws, and correct predictions will become possible.

Determinism is rejected by a group of theorists holding a position called *libertarianism*. Although libertarians present a number of specific criticisms of determinism, most of these objections are concerned primarily with what appears to be a consequence of that position. Libertarians contend that if all actions are the result of causes (and those causes of other causes, and so on), then no actions are ones for which anyone can be held morally responsible. The robber sticking up a bank today does so as a result of a series of causes that can be traced back prior to his birth. His behavior results from such factors as his education, a lack of parental love, and the nutritional quality of the food he ate as a child. In turn, these causes flow from the kind of education his parents received, their lack of parental love, and other such elements. How can the robber justifiably be held responsible or blamed for his behavior? He could not help the way his parents treated him nor the manner in which they were educated. For the libertarian, to be considered responsible for an act is to be free to have acted otherwise; but such freedom apparently cannot exist when all human actions are the predictable outcome of various causes. In "A Brief Defense of Free Will," Tibor Machan denies that all actions are the result of factors beyond our control. Both introspective evidence and ordinary explanations of our conduct support the claim that sometimes we freely cause our own actions. The frequently offered criticism that free will is incompatible with modern science is mistaken, he claims, because science cannot prove that the laws of physics must govern all actions. It is possible that beings could evolve that display initiative and cause their own actions. Finally, determinists must confront some paradoxical consequences; for example, any assessment of the theory would be suspect because the assessment might be the product of a cause that is irrelevant to the truth of the theory.

Hard determinism, a major version of determinism, denies, as does libertarianism, that moral responsibility is compatible with universal causation. Unlike libertarians, however, hard determinists often maintain that the knowledge that no one is morally responsible provides the basis for a satisfactory personal life as well as the ground for a more rational and humane system of interpersonal relationships. For them, the realization that humans are completely determined produces a liberating cessation of worry about the future (since it is out of one's control) and the fortitude to accept whatever befalls one. In dealing with others, one realizes the irrationality of concern about blame, merit, or retribution. In his article "The Delusion of Free Will," Robert Blatchford presents the hard determinists' position. He argues both that there is no free will and that the traditional notions of responsibility are unacceptable. All human actions are ruled by heredity and environment; and, since we are not responsible for either of these, all blame is unjust. Blatchford argues that if the will were free, prediction on the basis of environment and training would be impossible. But since in many cases we can make very reliable predictions about behavior, free will cannot be true. Blatchford also doubts that most supporters of free will really believe in it. If they did, would they try so hard to secure a good environment for their children? The concern for the child's environment indicates a belief that it is of great importance in molding the person.

Not all philosophers have been willing to accept the libertarian claim that determinism erases moral responsibility. Some, defending *soft determinism*, maintain that people can be morally responsible even though their behavior is determined. One argument soft determinists frequently use holds that a person's behavior is free if it is not the result of any compulsion. If you go to the movies because you wish to and are not pressured or coerced by anyone to do so, then your action ordinarily would be called a free one. Of course, your wish is the result of numerous causes swarming in your background. Thus, we have an action that is determined and yet called "free." The soundness of this soft determinist argument depends on the cogency of the analysis of the meaning of "free." W. T. Stace defends soft determinism in his article "The Problem of Free Will." In "What Means This Freedom?" John Hospers raises doubts about the views of soft determinists such as Stace. Hospers describes the usual criteria for assessing moral responsibility, but he doubts that they are useful in dealing with the philosophical concern about the issue. That concern is that our character, which gives rise to our actions, is formed by a variety of hereditary and early childhood influences beyond our control. Given this view of our character, it appears that the way we act, for good or ill, is merely a matter of luck.

A frequently debated problem arising from the conflict between determinists and libertarians involves the proper treatment of criminals. Many determinists argue that any punishment resting on notions of moral blame, retribution, and desert should be replaced by a treatment of criminals that recognizes their lack of responsibility. Thus, such advocates often defend changing the character of society or rehabilitating criminals rather than any sort of traditional punishment. In "An Address Delivered to the Prisoners in the Chicago County Jail," Clarence Darrow maintains that criminals are no more responsible for being in a jail than honest folk are for being outside of one. Since certain factors in our environment cause crime, he is convinced crime would be eliminated if the environment were suitably changed. A more equitable distribution of the wealth would, he believes, eliminate the desire to commit crimes, and so, the need for any jails.

C. S. Lewis, in his article "The Humanitarian Theory of Punishment," asserts that criminals are responsible for their actions and thus deserve punishment. He opposes both those who favor replacing punishment with rehabilitation and those who would use punishment to deter crime. He believes that the methods used to rehabilitate criminals can be harsher and more inhumane than traditional penalties and that the use of punishment to deter crime is open to a variety of moral abuses. He champions punishment on the basis of desert because only this position avoids morally unacceptable consequences and preserves the criminal's dignity as a responsible agent.

The "Problems and Puzzles" section contains two provocative articles. In "Luck Swallows Everything," Galen Strawson, like Hospers, contends that there are good reasons for believing that the kind of person we are is a matter of luck. He argues that we cannot have the kind of freedom needed for moral responsibility. Such freedom would require that we cause our own character, but the result of any attempts to do so would be determined by the character we already possess. Despite the strong arguments against the possession of the kind of freedom that would support genuine moral responsibility, we cannot avoid the conviction that we possess such freedom. Some way is needed to break the impasse between our intuitions that support freedom and the arguments that appear to refute it. In "Fate," Richard Taylor argues that fatalism (that is, the doctrine that whatever happens is and always was unavoidable) is true. He contends that the arguments against this doctrine beg the question and that various attempts to show that determinism differs from fatalism are misguided and futile.

Libertarianism

2. A Brief Defense of Free Will

Tibor Machan

Tibor R. Machan (1939–) is a Research Fellow at the Hoover Institution, Stanford University. He is the author of many books, most recently Initiative: Human Agency & Society *(Hoover Institution Press, 2000), and several hundred scholarly papers.*

The Importance of Having Free Will

This is not a common topic of discussion outside the discipline of philosophy and some other fields. Nevertheless, political economy is related to this philosophical problem in more ways than one. For example, if, say, a certain system of law is just, it is implied that we ought to implement it—even if only gradually, over time. If we claim that aggression is wrong, we implicitly hold that people ought to refrain from it. Indeed, even to say that some argument concerning any topic from logic to astronomy is unsound, we are claiming, implicitly, that one ought not to propose or accept it.

  But as the philosopher Immanuel Kant pointed out, "ought implies can." That means, in part, that only if it is possible to choose to do something can it be the case that it ought to be done. So the very meaningfulness of the advocacy of political ideals implies that free will exists. (The other meaning of "ought implies can" is that some objective standard of human conduct must be identifiable; otherwise one could never do what one ought to do.)

Thus, clearly, it is of some value to explore briefly whether human beings have free will. In connection with the particular principles of classical liberalism, the issue of why respecting individual rights is vital and possible relates to the problem of free will. Individual rights need to be respected because we must have an area of personal responsibility within which to make our choices about our lives or wherein to initiate our own actions. The need for this kind of respect assumes, again, that human beings have free will, that they can make basic choices about their lives, initiate basic conduct, that can turn out to be right or wrong. Furthermore, requiring of people that they respect individual rights also assumes that they possess free will. Otherwise it would make no sense to require such respect from them: something they have no choice about cannot be something they morally ought to and can fail to do.

But there is also the more familiar matter of the issue of personal responsibility concerning everyday conduct, those matters discussed daily in the home, in the press, and on the various media. Not only is there the issue of who is responsible for various good and bad things, but there is also the question of whether most of us are, as so many people seem to believe, in the grip of various forces over which we have no control. This or that addiction—to drugs, sex, violence, power, athletics, or work—is supposed to be our master, with ourselves merely puppets on strings moved about by it.

Yet, only if we have free will does any talk of blaming our parents, politicians, the rich, bureaucrats, and the rest make sense. But there are many people who believe that modern science, including, of course, all the social sciences, leaves no room for such a thing in human life. Where does it stand, then, with the free will issue? It seems to me worth discussing this topic outside the confines of philosophy graduate seminars and encourage some thinking about it on everyone's part. After all, it is a central feature of the political philosophy of liberty that individual citizens in society must not be thwarted in making choices for themselves, in initiating their own thinking and conduct. What does this come to unless they possess free will, the capacity to produce their own behavior?

I want to argue that there is indeed free will. And I'm going to defend the position that free will means that human beings can cause some of what they do, on their own; in other words, what they do is not explainable solely by references to factors that have influenced them, though, of course, their range of options is clearly circumscribed by the world in which they live, by their particular circumstances, capacities, options, talents, etc. My thesis, in other words, is that human beings are able to cause their actions and they are therefore responsible for some of what they do. In a basic sense we all are original actors capable of making novel moves in the world. We are, in other words, initiators of some of our behavior.

The first matter to be noted is that this view is in no way in contradiction to science. Free will is a natural phenomenon, something that emerged in nature with the emergence of human beings, with their kind of minds, namely, minds that can think and be aware of their own thinking.

Nature is complicated and multifaceted. It includes many different sorts of things and one of these is human beings. Such beings exhibit one unique yet natural attribute that other things apparently do not exhibit and that is free will.

I am going to offer eight reasons why a belief in free will makes very good sense. Four of these explain why there can be free will—i.e., why nature does not preclude it. But these do not yet demonstrate that free will exists. That will be the job of the four reasons I will advance next, which will establish that free will actually exists, that it's not just a possibility but an actuality.

Nature's Laws Versus Free Will

First, one of the major objections against free will is that nature is governed by a set of laws, mainly the laws of physics. Everything is controlled by these laws and we human beings are basically more complicated versions of material substances and that therefore whatever governs any other material substance in the universe must also govern human life. Basically, we are subject to the kind of causation every-thing else is. Since nothing else exhibits free will but conforms to causal laws, so must we. Social science is merely looking into the particulars of those causes, but we all know that we are subject to them in any case. The only difference is that we are complicated things, not that we are not governed by the same principles or laws of nature.

.Now, in response I want to point out that nature exhibits innumerable different domains, distinct not only in their complexity but also in the kinds of beings they include.·So it is not possible to rule out ahead of time that there might·be something in nature that exhibits agent causation. This is the phenomenon whereby a thing causes some of its own behavior. So there might be in nature a form of existence that exhibits free will.·Whether there is or is not is something to be discovered, not ruled out by a narrow metaphysics that restricts everything to being just a variation on just one kind of thing. Thus, taking account of what nature is composed of does not at all rule out free will. Yet, simply because of the possibility that there is free will, there may still not be. We consider that a bit later.

Can We Know of Free Will?

Now, another reason why some think that free will is not possible is that the dominant mode of studying, inspecting, or examining nature is what we call "empiricism." In other words, many believe that the only way we know about nature is we observe it with our various sensory organs. But since the sensory organs do not give us direct evidence of such a thing as free will, there really isn't any such thing. Since no observable evidence for free will exists, therefore free will does not exist.

But the doctrine that empiricism captures all forms of knowing is wrong—there are many things that we know not simply through observation but through a combination of observation, inferences, and theory construction. (Consider, even the purported knowledge that empiricism is our form of knowledge is not "known" empirically!)

For one, many features of the universe, including criminal guilt, are detected without eyewitnesses but by way of theories which serve the purpose of best explain-ing what we do have before us to observe. This is true, also, even in the natural sciences. Many of the phenomena or facts in biology, astrophysics, subatomic physics, botany, chemistry—not to mention psychology—consist not of what we see or detect by observation but of what is inferred by way of a theory. And the theory that explains things best—most completely and most consistently—is the best answer to the question as to what is going on.

Free will may well turn out to be in this category. In other words, free will may not be something that we can see directly, but what best explains what we do see in human life. This may include, for example, the many mistakes that human beings make in contrast to the few mistakes that other animals make.' We also notice that human beings do all kinds of odd things that cannot be accounted for in terms of mechanical causation, the type associated with physics. We can examine a person's background and find that some people with bad childhoods turn out to be decent, while others crooks.' And free will comes as a very helpful explanation. For now all we need to consider is that this may well be so, and if empiricism does not allow for it, so much the worse for empiricism. One could know something because it explains something else better than any alternative. And that is not strict empirical knowledge.

Is Free Will Weird?

Another matter that very often counts against free will is that the rest of the beings in nature do not exhibit it. Dogs, cats, lizards, fish, frogs, etc., have no free will and therefore it appears arbitrary to impute it to human beings. Why should we be free to do things when the rest of nature lacks any such capacity? It would be an impossible aberration.

The answer here is similar to what I gave earlier. To wit, there is enough variety in nature—some things swim, some fly, some just lie there, some breathe, some grow, while others do not; so there is plenty of evidence of plurality of types and kinds of things in nature. Discovering that something has free will could be yet another addition to all the varieties of nature.

Let us now consider whether free will actually does exist. I'm going to offer four arguments in support of an affirmative answer.

Are We Determined to Be Determinists—or Not?

There is an argument against determinism to the effect that if we are fully determined in what we think, believe, and do, then of course the belief that determinism is true is also a result of determinism. But the same holds for the belief that determinism is false. There is nothing you can do about whatever you believe—you had to believe it. There is no way to take an independent stance and consider the arguments unprejudiced because of all the various forces making us assimilate the evidence in the world just the way we do. One either turns out to be a determinist or not and in neither case can we appraise the issue objectively because we are predetermined to have a view on the matter one way or the other.

But then, paradoxically, we'll never be able to resolve this debate, since there is no way of obtaining an objective assessment. Indeed, the very idea of scientific or judicial objectivity, as well as of ever reaching philosophical truth, has to do with being free. Thus, if we're engaged in this enterprise of learning about truth and distinguishing it from falsehood, we are committed to the idea that human beings have some measure of mental freedom.

Should We Become Determinists?

There's another dilemma of determinism. The determinist wants us to believe in determinism. In fact, he believes we ought to be determinists rather than believe in this myth called "free will." But, as the saying goes in philosophy, "ought" implies "can." That is, if one ought to believe in or do something, this implies that one has a choice in the matter; it implies that we can make a choice as to whether determinism or free will is a better doctrine. That, then, assumes that we are free. In other words, even arguing for determinism assumes that we are not determined to believe in free will or determinism but that it is a matter of our making certain choices about arguments, evidence, and thinking itself. That's a paradox which troubles a deterministic position.

We Often Know We Are Free!

In many contexts of our lives introspective knowledge is taken very seriously. When you go to a doctor and he asks you, "Are you in pain?" and you say, "Yes," and he says, "Where is the pain?" and you say, "It's in my knee," the doctor doesn't say, "Why, you can't know, this is not public evidence, I will now get verifiable, direct evidence where you hurt." In fact your evidence is very good evidence. Witnesses at trials give evidence as they report about what they have seen, which is introspective evidence: "This indeed is what I have seen or heard." Even in the various sciences people report on what they've read on surveys or seen on gauges or instruments. Thus they are giving us introspective evidence.

Introspection is one source of evidence that we take as reasonably reliable. So what should we make of the fact that a lot of people do say things like, "Damn it, I didn't make the right choice," or "I neglected to do something." They report to us that they have made various choices, decisions, etc., that they intended this or that but not another thing. And they often blame themselves for not having done something; thus they report that they are taking responsibility for what they have or haven't done.

In short, there is a lot of evidence from people all around us of the existence of free choice.

Modern Science Discovers Free Will!

Finally, there is also the evidence of the fact that we do seem to have the capacity for self-monitoring. The human brain has a kind of structure that allows us, so to speak, to govern ourselves. We can inspect our lives; we can detect where we're going; and we can, therefore, change course. And the human brain itself makes it possible. The brain, because of its structure, can monitor itself and as a result we can decide whether to continue in a certain pattern or to change that pattern and go in a different direction. That is the sort of free will that is demonstrable. At least some scientists, for example Roger W. Sperry—in his book *Science and Moral Priority* (Columbia University Press, 1983) and in numerous more technical articles— maintain that there's evidence for free will in this sense. This view depends on a number of points I have already mentioned. It assumes that there can be different causes in nature, so that the higher functioning of the human brain could involve a kind of self-causation. The brain as a system would have to be able to cause some things about the organism's behavior and that depends, of course, on the possibility of there being various kinds of causes.

Precisely the sort of thing Sperry thinks possible is evident in our lives. We make plans and revise them. We explore alternatives and decide to follow one of them. We change a course of conduct we have embarked upon, or continue with it. In other words, there is a locus of individual self-responsibility that is evident in the way in which we look upon ourselves—and the way in which we in fact behave.

Some People Are Determined; Some Are Not.

There clearly are cases of conduct in which some persons behave as they do because they were determined to do so by certain identifiable forces outside of their own control. A brain tumor, a severe childhood trauma, or some other intrusive force sometimes incapacitates people. This is evident in those occasional cases when a person who engaged in criminal behavior is shown to have had no control over what he or she did. Someone who actually had no capacity to control his or her behavior, could not control his or her own thinking or judgment, and was, thus, moved by something other than his own will, cannot be said to possess a bona fide free will.

Those who deny that we have free will simply cannot make sense of our distinction between cases in which one controls one's behavior and those in which one is being moved by forces over which he or she has no control. When we face the latter sort of case, we still admit that the behavior could be good or bad but we deny that it is morally and legally significant—it is more along lines of acts of nature or God by being out of the agent's control. This is also why philosophers who discuss ethics but deny free will have trouble distinguishing between morality and value theory—e.g., utilitarians, Marxists.

The Best Theory Is True.

Finally, what I have alluded to earlier, namely, that when we put all of this together we get a more sensible understanding of the complexities of human life than otherwise—we get a better understanding, for example, of why social engineering and government regulation and regimentation do not work, why there are so many individual and cultural differences, why people can be wrong, why they can disagree with each other, etc. It is because they are free to do so, because they are not set in some pattern the way cats and dogs and orangutans and birds tend to be.

In principle, all of the behavior of these creatures around us can be predicted because they are not creative in a sense that they originate new ideas and behavior, although we do not always know enough about the constitution of these beings and how it would interact with their environment to actually predict what they will do. Human beings produce new ideas and these can introduce new kinds of behavior in familiar situations. This, in part, is what is meant by the fact that different people often interpret their experiences differently. Yet, we can make some predictions about what people will do because they often do make up their minds in a given fashion and stick to their decision over time. This is what we mean when we note that people make commitments, possess integrity, etc. So we can estimate what they are going to do. But even then we do not make certain predictions but only statistically significant ones. Clearly, very often people change their minds and surprise or annoy us. And, if we go to different cultures, they'll surprise us even more. This complexity, diversity, and individuation about human beings is best explained if human beings are free than if they are determined.

Is Free Will Well Founded?

So these several reasons provide a kind of argumentative collage in support of the free will position. Can anyone do better with this issue? I don't know. I think it's best to ask only for what is the best of the various competing theories. Are human beings doing what they do solely as the consequences of forces acting on them? Or do they have the capacity to take charge of their lives, often neglect to do so properly or effectively, make stupid choices? Which supposition explains the human world and its complexities around us?

I think the latter makes much better sense. It explains, much better than do deterministic theories—be they hard or soft—how it is possible that human life involves such a wide range of possibilities, accomplishments as well as defeats, joys as well as sorrows, creation as well as destruction. It explains, also, why in human life there is so much change in language, custom, style, art, and science. Unlike other living beings, for which what is possible is pretty much fixed by instincts and reflexes—even if some extraordinary behavior may be elicited, by way of experiments in laboratories or, at times, in the face of unusual natural developments—people initiate much of what they do, for better and for worse. From their most distinctive capacity of forming ideas and theories, to those of artistic and athletic inventiveness, human beings remake the world without, so to speak, having to do so! And this can make good sense if we understand them to have the distinctive capacity for initiating their own conduct rather than relying on mere stimulation and reaction. It also poses for them certain very difficult tasks, not the least of which is that they cannot expect that any kind of formula or system is going to predictably manage the future of human affairs, such as some of social science seems to hope it will. Social engineering is, thus, not a genuine prospect for solving human problems—only education and individual initiative can do that.

Hard Determinism

3. The Delusion of Free Will

Robert Blatchford

Robert Blatchford (1851–1943) was an English determinist, agnostic, socialist, and crusading social reformer whose writings exerted great influence and were translated into many languages.

The free will delusion has been a stumbling block in the way of human thought for thousands of years. Let us try whether common sense and common knowledge cannot remove it.

Free will is a subject of great importance to us in this case; and it is one we must come to with our eyes wide open and our wits wide awake; not because it is very difficult, but because it has been tied and twisted into a tangle of Gordian knots by twenty centuries full of wordy but unsuccessful philosophers.

The free will party claim that man is responsible for his acts, because his will is free to choose between right and wrong.

We reply that the will is not free, and that if it were free man could not know right from wrong until he was taught.

As to the knowledge of good and evil the free will party will claim that conscience is an unerring guide. But I have already proved that conscience does not and cannot tell us what is right and what is wrong: it only reminds us of the lessons we have learnt as to right and wrong.

The "still small voice" is not the voice of God: it is the voice of heredity and environment.

And now to the freedom of the will.

When a man says his will is free, he means that it is free of all control or interference: that it can over-rule heredity and environment.

We reply that the will is ruled by heredity and environment.

The cause of all the confusion on this subject may be shown in a few words.

When the free will party say that man has a free will, they mean that he is free to act as he chooses to act.

There is no need to deny that. *But what causes him to choose?*

That is the pivot upon which the whole discussion turns.

From *Not Guilty* by Robert Blatchford, Albert and Charles Boni, Inc., 1913. Albert and Charles Boni, Inc.

The free will party seem to think of the will as something independent of the man, as something outside him. They seem to think that the will decides without the control of the man's reason.

If that were so, it would not prove the man responsible. "The will" would be responsible, and not the man. It would be as foolish to blame a man for the act of a "free" will, as to blame a horse for the action of its rider.

But I am going to prove to my readers, by appeals to their common sense and common knowledge, that the will is not free; and that it is ruled by heredity and environment.

To begin with, the average man will be against me. He knows that he chooses between two courses every hour, and often every minute, and he thinks his choice is free. But that is a delusion: his choice is not free. He can choose, and does choose. But he can only choose as his heredity and his environment cause him to choose. He never did choose and never will choose except as his heredity and his environment—his temperament and his training—cause him to choose. And his heredity and his environment have fixed his choice before he makes it.

The average man says, "I know that I can act as I wish to act." But what causes him to wish?

The free will party say, "We know that a man can and does choose between two acts." But what settles the choice?

There is a cause for every wish, a cause for every choice; and every cause of every wish and choice arises from heredity, or from environment.

For a man acts always from temperament, which is heredity, or from training, which is environment.

And in cases where a man hesitates in his choice between two acts, the hesitation is due to a conflict between his temperament and his training, or, as some would express it, "between his desire and his conscience."

A man is practicing at a target with a gun, when a rabbit crosses his line of fire. The man has his eye and his sights on the rabbit, and his finger on the trigger. The man's will is free. If he presses the trigger the rabbit will be killed.

Now, how does the man decide whether or not he shall fire? He decides by feeling, and by reason.

He would like to fire, just to make sure that he could hit the mark. He would like to fire, because he would like to have the rabbit for supper. He would like to fire, because there is in him the old, old hunting instinct, to kill.

But the rabbit does not belong to him. He is not sure that he will not get into trouble if he kills it. Perhaps— if he is a very uncommon kind of man—he feels that it would be cruel and cowardly to shoot a helpless rabbit.

Well. The man's will is free. He can fire if he likes: he can let the rabbit go if he likes. How will he decide? On what does his decision depend?

His decision depends upon the relative strength of his desire to kill the rabbit, and of his scruples about cruelty, and the law.

Not only that, but, if we knew the man fairly well, we could guess how his free will would act before it acted. The average sporting Briton would kill the rabbit. But we know that there are men who would on no account shoot any harmless wild creature.

Broadly put, we may say that the sportsman would will to fire, and that the humanitarian would not will to fire.

Now, as both their wills are free, it must be something outside the wills that makes the difference.

Well. The sportsman will kill, because he is a sportsman: the humanitarian will not kill, because he is a humanitarian.

And what makes one man a sportsman and another a humanitarian? Heredity and environment: temperament and training.

One man is merciful, another cruel, by nature; or one is thoughtful and the other thoughtless, by nature. That is a difference of heredity.

One may have been taught all his life that to kill wild things is "sport"; the other may have been taught that it is inhuman and wrong: that is a difference of environment.

Now, the man by nature cruel or thoughtless, who has been trained to think of killing animals as sport, becomes what we call a sportsman, because heredity and environment have made him a sportsman.

The other man's heredity and environment have made him a humanitarian.

The sportsman kills the rabbit, because he is a sportsman, and he is a sportsman because heredity and environment have made him one.

That is to say the "free will" is really controlled by heredity and environment.

Allow me to give a case in point. A man who had never done any fishing was taken out by a fisherman. He liked the sport, and for some months followed it eagerly. But one day an accident brought home to his mind the cruelty of catching fish with a hook, and he instantly laid down his rod, and never fished again.

Before the change he was always eager to go fishing if invited: after the change he could not be persuaded to touch a line. His will was free all the while. How was it that his will to fish changed to his will not to fish? It was the result of environment. He had learnt that fishing was cruel. The knowledge controlled his will.

But, it may be asked, how do you account for a man doing the thing he does not wish to do?

No man ever did a thing he did not wish to do. When there are two wishes the stronger rules.

Let us suppose a case. A young woman gets two letters by the same post; one is an invitation to go with her lover to a concert, the other is a request that she will visit a sick child in the slums. The girl is very fond of music, and is rather afraid of the slums. She wishes to go to the concert, and to be with her lover; she dreads the foul street and the dirty home, and shrinks from the risk of measles or fever. But she goes to the sick child, and she forgoes the concert. Why?

Because her sense of duty is stronger than her self-love.

Now, her sense of duty is partly due to her nature—that is, to her heredity—but it is chiefly due to environment. Like all of us, this girl was born without any kind of knowledge, and with only the rudiments of a conscience. But she has been well taught, and the teaching is part of her environment.

We may say that the girl is free to act as she chooses, but she *does* act as she has been *taught* that she *ought* to act. This teaching, which is part of her environment, controls her will.

We may say that a man is free to act as he chooses. He is free to act as *he* chooses, but *he* will choose as heredity and environment cause *him* to choose. For heredity and environment have made him that which he is.

A man is said to be free to decide between two courses. But really he is only free to decide in accordance with his temperament and training. . . .

Macbeth was ambitious; but he had a conscience. He wanted Duncan's crown; but he shrank from treason and ingratitude. Ambition pulled him one way, honour pulled him the other way. The opposing forces were so evenly balanced that he seemed unable to decide. Was Macbeth free to choose? To what extent was he free? He was so free that he could arrive at no decision, and it was the influence of his wife that turned the scale to crime.

Was Lady Macbeth free to choose? She did not hesitate. Because her ambition was so much stronger than her conscience that she never was in doubt. She chose as her over-powering ambition compelled her to choose.

And most of us in our decisions resemble either Macbeth or his wife. Either our nature is so much stronger than our training, or our training is so much stronger than our nature, that we decide for good or evil as promptly as a stream decides to run down hill; or our nature and our training are so nearly balanced that we can hardly decide at all.

In Macbeth's case the contest is quite clear and easy to follow. He was ambitious, and his environment had taught him to regard the crown as a glorious and desirable possession. But environment had also taught him that murder, and treason, and ingratitude were wicked and disgraceful.

Had he never been taught these lessons, or had he been taught that gratitude was folly, that honour was weakness, and murder excusable when it led to power, he would not have hesitated at all. It was his environment that hampered his will. . . .

In all cases the action of the will depends upon the relative strength of two or more motives. The stronger motive decides the will; just as the heavier weight decides the balance of a pair of scales. . . .

How, then, can we believe that free will is outside and superior to heredity and environment? . . .

"What! Cannot a man be honest if he choose?" Yes, if he choose. But that is only another way of saying that he can be honest if his nature and his training lead him to choose honesty.

"What! Cannot I please myself whether I drink or refrain from drinking?" Yes. But that is only to say you will not drink because it pleases *you* to be sober. But it pleases another man to drink, because his desire for drink is strong, or because his self-respect is weak.

And you decide as you decide, and he decides as he decides, because you are *you*, and he is *he*; and heredity and environment made you both that which you are.

And the sober man may fall upon evil days, and may lose his self-respect, or find the burden of his trouble greater than he can bear, and may fly to drink for comfort, or oblivion, and may become a drunkard. Has it not been often so?

And the drunkard may, by some shock, or some disaster, or some passion, or some persuasion, regain his self-respect, and may renounce drink, and lead a sober and useful life. Has it not been often so?

And in both cases the freedom of the will is untouched: it is the change in the environment that lifts the fallen up, and beats the upright down.

We might say that a woman's will is free, and that she could, if she wished, jump off a bridge and drown herself. But she cannot *wish*. She is happy, and loves life, and dreads the cold and crawling river. And yet, by some cruel turn of fortune's wheel, she may become destitute and miserable; so miserable that she hates life and longs for death, and *then* she can jump into the dreadful river and die.

Her will was as free at one time as at another. It is the environment that has wrought the change. Once she could not wish to die: now she cannot wish to live.

The apostles of free will believe that all men's wills are free. But a man can only will that which he is able to will. And one man is able to will that which another man is unable to will. To deny this is to deny the commonest and most obvious facts of life. . . .

We all know that we can foretell the action of certain men in certain cases, because we know the men.

We know that under the same conditions Jack Sheppard would steal and Cardinal Manning would not steal. We know that under the same conditions the sailor would flirt with the waitress, and the priest would not; that the drunkard would get drunk, and the abstainer would remain sober. We know that Wellington would refuse a bribe, that Nelson would not run away, that Buonaparte would grasp at power, that Abraham Lincoln would be loyal to his country, that Torquemada would not spare a heretic. Why? If the will is free, how can we be sure, before a test arises, how the will must act?

Simply because we know that heredity and environment have so formed and moulded men and women that under certain circumstances the action of their wills is certain.

Heredity and environment having made a man a thief, he will steal. Heredity and environment having made a man honest, he will not steal.

That is to say, heredity and environment have decided the action of the will, before the time has come for the will to act.

This being so—and we all know that it is so—what becomes of the sovereignty of the will?

Let any man that believes that he can "do as he likes" ask himself *why* he *likes*, and he will see the error of the theory of free will, and will understand why the will is the servant and not the master of the man: for the man is the product of heredity and environment, and these control the will.

As we want to get this subject as clear as we can, let us take one or two familiar examples of the action of the will.

Jones and Robinson meet and have a glass of whisky. Jones asks Robinson to have another. Robinson says, "no thank you, one is enough." Jones says, "all right:

have another cigarette." Robinson takes the cigarette. Now, here we have a case where a man refuses a second drink, but takes a second smoke. Is it because he would like another cigarette, but would not like another glass of whisky? No. It is because he knows that it is *safer* not to take another glass of whisky.

How does he know that whisky is dangerous? He has learnt it—from his environment.

"But he *could* have taken another glass if he wished."

But he could not wish to take another, because there was something he wished more strongly—to be safe.

And why did he want to be safe? Because he had learnt—from his environment—that it was unhealthy, unprofitable, and shameful to get drunk. Because he had learnt—from his environment—that it is easier to avoid forming a bad habit than to break a bad habit when formed. Because he valued the good opinion of his neighbours, and also his position and prospects.

These feelings and this knowledge ruled his will, and caused him to refuse the second glass.

But there was no sense of danger, no well-learned lesson of risk to check his will to smoke another cigarette. Heredity and environment did not warn him against that. So, to please his friend, and himself, he accepted.

Now suppose Smith asks Williams to have another glass. Williams takes it, takes several, finally goes home—as he often goes home. Why?

Largely because drinking is a habit with him. And not only does the mind instinctively repeat an action, but, in the case of drink, a physical craving is set up, and the brain is weakened. It is easier to refuse the first glass than the second; easier to refuse the second than the third; and it is very much harder for a man to keep sober who has frequently got drunk.

So, when poor Williams has to make his choice, he has habit against him, he has a physical craving against him, and he has a weakened brain to think with.

"But, Williams could have refused the first glass."

No. Because in his case the desire to drink, or to please a friend, was stronger than his fear of the danger. Or he may not have been so conscious of the danger as Robinson was. He may not have been so well taught, or he may not have been so sensible, or he may not have been so cautious. So that his heredity and environment, his temperament and training, led him to take the drink, as surely as Robinson's heredity and environment led him to refuse it.

And now, it is my turn to ask a question. If the will is "free," if the conscience is a sure guide, how is it that the free will and the conscience of Robinson caused him to keep sober, while the free will and the conscience of Williams caused him to get drunk?

Robinson's will was curbed by certain feelings which failed to curb the will of Williams. Because in the case of Williams the feelings were stronger on the other side.

It was the nature and the training of Robinson which made him refuse the second glass, and it was the nature and the training of Williams which made him drink the second glass.

What had free will to do with it?

We are told that *every* man has a free will, and a conscience.

Now, if Williams had been Robinson, that is to say if his heredity and his environment had been exactly like Robinson's, he would have done exactly as Robinson did.

It was because his heredity and environment were not the same that his act was not the same.

Both men had free wills. What made one do what the other refused to do?

Heredity and environment. To reverse their conduct we should have to reverse their heredity and environment. . . .

Two boys work at a hard and disagreeable trade. One leaves it, finds other work, "gets on," is praised for getting on. The other stays at the trade all his life, works hard all his life, is poor all his life, and is respected as an honest and humble working man; that is to say, he is regarded by society as Mr. Dorgan was regarded by Mr. Dooley—"he is a fine man, and I despise him."

What causes these two free wills to will so differently? One boy knew more than the other boy. He "knew better." All knowledge is environment. Both boys had free wills. It was in knowledge they differed: environment!

Those who exalt the power of the will, and belittle the power of environment, belie their words by their deeds.

For they would not send their children amongst bad companions or allow them to read bad books. They would not say the children have free will and therefore have power to take the good and leave the bad.

They know very well that evil environment has power to pervert the will, and that good environment has power to direct it properly.

They know that children may be made good or bad by good or evil training, and that the will follows the training.

That being so, they must also admit that the children of other people may be good or bad by training.

And if a child gets bad training, how can free will save it? Or how can it be blamed for being bad? It never had a chance to be good. That they know this is proved by their carefulness in providing their own children with better environment.

As I have said before, every church, every school, every moral lesson is a proof that preachers and teachers trust to good environment, and not to free will, to make children good.

In this, as in so many other matters, actions speak louder than words.

That, I hope, disentangles the many knots into which thousands of learned men have tied the simple subject of free will; and disposes of the claim that man is responsible because his will is free. But there is one other cause of error, akin to the subject, on which I should like to say a few words.

We often hear it said that a man is to blame for his conduct because "he knows better."

It is true that men do wrong when they know better. Macbeth "knew better" when he murdered Duncan. But it is true, also, that we often think a man "knows better," when he does not know better.

For a man cannot be said to know a thing until he believes it. If I am told that the moon is made of green cheese, it cannot be said that I *know* it to be made of green cheese.

Many moralists seem to confuse the words "to know" with the words "to hear."

Jones reads novels and plays opera music on Sunday. The Puritan says Jones "knows better," when he means that Jones has been told that it is wrong to do those things.

But Jones does not know that it is wrong. He has heard someone say that it is wrong, but does not believe it. Therefore it is not correct to say that he knows it.

And, again, as to that matter of belief. Some moralists hold that it is wicked not to believe certain things, and that men who do not believe those things will be punished.

But a man cannot believe a thing he is told to believe: he can only believe a thing which he *can* believe; and he can only believe that which his own reason tells him is true.

It would be no use asking Sir Roger Ball to believe that the earth is flat. He *could not* believe it.

It is no use asking an agnostic to believe the story of Jonah and the whale. He *could not* believe it. He might pretend to believe it. He might try to believe it. But his reason would not allow him to believe it.

Therefore it is a mistake to say that a man "knows better," when the fact is that he has been told "better" and cannot believe what he has been told.

That is a simple matter, and looks quite trivial; but how much ill-will, how much intolerance, how much violence, persecution, and murder have been caused by the strange idea that a man is wicked because *his* reason *cannot* believe that which to another man's reason [is] quite true.

Free will has no power over a man's belief. A man cannot believe by will, but only by conviction. A man cannot be forced to believe. You may threaten him, wound him, beat him, burn him; and he may be frightened, or angered, or pained; but he cannot *believe*, nor can he be made to believe. Until he is convinced.

Now, truism as it may seem, I think it necessary to say here that a man cannot be convinced by abuse, nor by punishment. He can only be convinced by *reason*.

Yes. If we wish a man to believe a thing, we shall find a few words of reason more powerful than a million curses, or a million bayonets. To burn a man alive for failing to believe that the sun goes round the world is not to convince him. The fire is searching, but it does not seem to him to be relevant to the issue. He never doubted that fire would burn; but perchance his dying eyes may see the sun sinking down into the west, as the world rolls on its axis. He dies in his belief. And knows no "better."

Contemporary Issues

*Does Determinism
Eliminate Responsibility?*

4. The Problem of Free Will

W. T. Stace

*Walter Terence Stace (1886–1967) was born in Britain and served in the
British Civil Service in Ceylon before coming to the United States to teach
at Princeton University in 1932. He wrote widely acclaimed books in many
areas of philosophy.*

[A] great problem which the rise of scientific naturalism has created for the modern mind concerns the foundations of morality. The old religious foundations have
largely crumbled away, and it may well be thought that the edifice built upon them
by generations of men is in danger of collapse. A total collapse of moral behavior
is, as I pointed out before, very unlikely. For a society in which this occurred could
not survive. Nevertheless, the danger to moral standards inherent in the virtual
disappearance of their old religious foundations is not illusory.

   I shall first discuss the problem of free will, for it is certain that if there is no
free will there can be no morality. Morality is concerned with what men ought and
ought not to do. But if a man has no freedom to choose what he will do, if whatever
he does is done under compulsion, then it does not make sense to tell him that he
ought not to have done what he did and that he ought to do something different.
All moral precepts would in such case be meaningless. Also if he acts always under
compulsion, how can he be held morally responsible for his actions? How can he,
for example, be punished for what he could not help doing?

   It is to be observed that those learned professors of philosophy or psychology who deny the existence of free will do so only in their professional moments
and in their studies and lecture rooms. For when it comes to doing anything
practical, even of the most trivial kind, they invariably behave as if they and others
were free. They inquire from you at dinner whether you will choose this dish or
that dish. They will ask a child why he told a lie, and will punish him for not having chosen the way of truthfulness. All of which is inconsistent with a disbelief in

free will. This should cause us to suspect that the problem is not a real one; and this, I believe, is the case. The dispute is merely verbal, and is due to nothing but a confusion about the meanings of words. It is what is now fashionably called a semantic problem.

How does a verbal dispute arise? Let us consider a case which, although it is absurd in the sense that no one would ever make the mistake which is involved in it, yet illustrates the principle which we shall have to use in the solution of the problem. Suppose that someone believed that the word "man" means a certain sort of five-legged animal; in short that "five-legged animal" is the correct *definition* of man. He might then look around the world, and rightly observing that there are no five-legged animals in it, he might proceed to deny the existence of men. This preposterous conclusion would have been reached because he was using an incorrect definition of "man." All you would have to do to show him his mistake would be to give him the correct definition; or at least show him that his definition was wrong. Both the problem and its solution would, of course, be entirely verbal. The problem of free will, and its solution, I shall maintain, is verbal in exactly the same way. The problem has been created by the fact that learned men, especially philosophers, have assumed an incorrect definition of free will, and then finding that there is nothing in the world which answers to their definition, have denied its existence. As far as logic is concerned, their conclusion is just as absurd as that of the man who denies the existence of men. The only difference is that the mistake in the latter case is obvious and crude, while the mistake which the deniers of free will have made is rather subtle and difficult to detect.

Throughout the modern period, until quite recently, it was assumed, both by the philosophers who denied free will and by those who defended it, that *determinism is inconsistent with free will*. If a man's actions were wholly determined by chains of causes stretching back into the remote past, so that they could be predicted beforehand by a mind which knew all the causes, it was assumed that they could not in that case be free. This implies that a certain definition of actions done from free will was assumed, namely that they are actions *not* wholly determined by causes or predictable beforehand. Let us shorten this by saying that free will was defined as meaning indeterminism. This is the incorrect definition which has led to the denial of free will. As soon as we see what the true definition is we shall find that the question whether the world is deterministic, as Newtonian science implied, or in a measure indeterministic, as current physics teaches, is wholly irrelevant to the problem.

Of course there is a sense in which one can define a word arbitrarily in any way one pleases. But a definition may nevertheless be called correct or incorrect. It is correct if it accords with a *common usage* of the word defined. It is incorrect if it does not. And if you give an incorrect definition, absurd and untrue results are likely to follow. For instance, there is nothing to prevent you from arbitrarily defining a man as a five-legged animal, but this is incorrect in the sense that it does not accord with the ordinary meaning of the word. Also it has the absurd result of leading to a denial of the existence of men. This shows that *common usage is the criterion for deciding whether a definition is correct or not*. And this is the principle which I shall apply to free will. I shall show that indeterminism is not what is meant by the phrase "free will" *as it is commonly used*. And I shall attempt to discover the correct definition by inquiring how the phrase is used in ordinary conversation.

Here are a few samples of how the phrase might be used in ordinary conversation. It will be noticed that they include cases in which the question whether a man acted with free will is asked in order to determine whether he was morally and legally responsible for his acts.

JONES   I once went without food for a week.

SMITH   Did you do that of your own free will?

JONES   No. I did it because I was lost in a desert and could find no food.

But suppose that the man who had fasted was Mahatma Gandhi. The conversation might then have gone:

GANDHI   I once fasted for a week.

SMITH   Did you do that of your own free will?

GANDHI   Yes. I did it because I wanted to compel the British Government to give India its independence.

Take another case. Suppose that I had stolen some bread, but that I was as truthful as George Washington. Then, if I were charged with the crime in court, some exchange of the following sort might take place:

JUDGE   Did you steal the bread of your own free will?

STACE   Yes. I stole it because I was hungry.

Or in different circumstances the conversation might run:

JUDGE   Did you steal of your own free will?

STACE   No. I stole because my employer threatened to beat me if I did not.

At a recent murder trial in Trenton some of the accused had signed confessions, but afterwards asserted that they had done so under police duress. The following exchange might have occurred:

JUDGE   Did you sign the confession of your own free will?

PRISONER   No. I signed it because the police beat me up.

Now suppose that a philosopher had been a member of the jury. We could imagine this conversation taking place in the jury room.

FOREMAN OF THE JURY   The prisoner says he signed the confession because he was beaten, and not of his own free will.

PHILOSOPHER   This is quite irrelevant to the case. There is no such thing as free will.

FOREMAN   Do you mean to say that it makes no difference whether he signed because his conscience made him want to tell the truth or because he was beaten?

PHILOSOPHER   None at all. Whether he was caused to sign by a beating or by some desire of his own—the desire to tell the truth, for example—in either case his signing was causally determined, and therefore in neither case did he act of his own free will. Since there is no such thing as free will, the question whether he signed of his own free will ought not to be discussed by us.

The foreman and the rest of the jury would rightly conclude that the philosopher must be making some mistake. What sort of a mistake could it be? There is only one possible answer. The philosopher must be using the phrase "free will" in some peculiar way of his own which is not the way in which men usually use it when they wish to determine a question of moral responsibility. That is, he must be using an incorrect definition of it as implying action not determined by causes. Suppose a man left his office at noon, and were questioned about it. Then we might hear this:

JONES   Did you go out of your own free will?
SMITH   Yes. I went out to get my lunch.

But we might hear:

JONES   Did you leave your office of your own free will?
SMITH   No. I was forcibly removed by the police.

We have now collected a number of cases of actions which, in the ordinary usage of the English language, would be called cases in which people have acted of their own free will. We should also say in all these cases that they *chose* to act as they did. We should also say that they could have acted otherwise, if they had chosen. For instance, Mahatma Gandhi was not compelled to fast; he chose to do so. He could have eaten if he had wanted to. When Smith went out to get his lunch, he chose to do so. He could have stayed and done some work, if he had wanted to. We have also collected a number of cases of the opposite kind. They are cases in which men were not able to exercise their free will. They had no choice. They were compelled to do as they did. The man in the desert did not fast of his own free will. He had no choice in the matter. He was compelled to fast because there was nothing for him to eat. And so with the other cases. It ought to be quite easy, by an inspection of these cases, to tell what we ordinarily mean when we say that a man did or did not exercise free will. We ought therefore to be able to extract from them the proper definition of the term. Let us put the cases in a table:

Free Acts	**Unfree Acts**
Gandhi fasting because he wanted to free India.	The man fasting in the desert because there was no food.
Stealing bread because one is hungry.	Stealing because one's employer threatened to beat one.
Signing a confession because one wanted to tell the truth.	Signing because the police beat one.
Leaving the office because one wanted one's lunch.	Leaving because forcibly removed.

It is obvious that to find the correct definition of free acts we must discover what characteristic is common to all the acts in the left-hand column, and is, at the same time, absent from all the acts in the right-hand column. This characteristic which all free acts have, and which no unfree acts have, will be the defining characteristic of free will.

Is being uncaused, or not being determined by causes, the characteristic of which we are in search? It cannot be, because although it is true that all the acts in the right-hand column have causes, such as the beating by the police or the absence of food in the desert, so also do the acts in the left-hand column. Mr. Gandhi's fasting was caused by his desire to free India, the man leaving his office by his hunger, and so on. Moreover there is no reason to doubt that these causes of the free acts were in turn caused by prior conditions, and that these were again the results of causes, and so on back indefinitely into the past. Any physiologist can tell us the causes of hunger. What caused Mr. Gandhi's tremendously powerful desire to free India is no doubt more difficult to discover. But it must have had causes. Some of them may have lain in peculiarities of his glands or brain, others in his past experiences, others in his heredity, others in his education. Defenders of free will have usually tended to deny such facts. But to do so is plainly a case of special pleading, which is unsupported by any scrap of evidence. The only reasonable view is that all human actions, both those which are freely done and those which are not, are either wholly determined by causes, or at least as much determined as other events in nature. It may be true, as the physicists tell us, that nature is not as deterministic as was once thought. But whatever degree of determinism prevails in the world, human actions appear to be as much determined as anything else. And if this is so, it cannot be the case that what distinguishes actions freely chosen from those which are not free is that the latter are determined by causes while the former are not. Therefore, being uncaused or being undetermined by causes must be an incorrect definition of free will.

What, then, is the difference between acts which are freely done and those which are not? What is the characteristic which is present to all the acts in the left-hand column and absent from all those in the right-hand column? Is it not obvious that, although both sets of actions have causes, the causes of those in the left-hand column are *of a different kind* from the causes of those in the right-hand column?

The free acts are all caused by desires, or motives, or by some sort of internal psychological states of the agent's mind. The unfree acts, on the other hand, are all caused by physical forces or physical conditions, outside the agent. Police arrest means physical force exerted from the outside; the absence of food in the desert is a physical condition of the outside world. We may therefore frame the following rough definitions. *Acts freely done are those whose immediate causes are psychological states in the agent. Acts not freely done are those whose immediate causes are states of affairs external to the agent.*

It is plain that if we define free will in this way, then free will certainly exists, and the philosopher's denial of its existence is seen to be what it is—nonsense. For it is obvious that all those actions of men which we should ordinarily attribute to the exercise of their free will, or of which we should say that they freely chose to do them, are in fact actions which have been caused by their own desire, wishes, thoughts, emotions, impulses, or other psychological states.

In applying our definition we shall find that it usually works well, but that there are some puzzling cases which it does not seem exactly to fit. These puzzles can always be solved by paying careful attention to the ways in which words are used, and remembering that they are not always used consistently. I have space for only one example. Suppose that a thug threatens to shoot you unless you give him your wallet, and suppose that you do so. Do you, in giving him your wallet, do so of your own free will or not? If we apply our definition, we find that you acted freely, since the immediate cause of the action was not an actual outside force but the fear of death, which is a psychological cause. Most people, however, would say that you did not act of your own free will but under compulsion. Does this show that our definition is wrong? I do not think so. Aristotle, who gave a solution of the problem of free will substantially the same as ours (though he did not use the term "free will") admitted that there are what he called "mixed" or borderline cases in which it is difficult to know whether we ought to call the acts free or compelled. In the case under discussion, though no actual force was used, the gun at your forehead so nearly approximated to actual force that we tend to say the case was one of compulsion. It is a borderline case.

Here is what may seem like another kind of puzzle. According to our view an action may be free though it could have been predicted beforehand with certainty. But suppose you told a lie, and it was certain beforehand that you would tell it. How could one then say, "You could have told the truth"? The answer is that it is perfectly true that you could have told the truth *if* you had wanted to. In fact you would have done so, for in that case the causes producing your action, namely your desires, would have been different, and would therefore have produced different effects. It is a delusion that predictability and free will are incompatible. This agrees with common sense. For if, knowing your character, I predict that you will act honorably, no one would say when you do act honorably, that this shows you did not do so of your own free will.

Since free will is a condition of moral responsibility, we must be sure that our theory of free will gives a sufficient basis for it. To be held morally responsible for one's actions means that one may be justly punished or rewarded, blamed or praised, for them. But it is not just to punish a man for what he cannot help doing. How can it be just to punish him for an action which it was certain beforehand that he would do? We have not attempted to decide whether, as a matter of fact, all events, including human actions, are completely determined. For that question is irrelevant to the problem of free will. But if we assume for the purposes of argument that complete determinism is true, but that we are nevertheless free, it may then be asked whether such a deterministic free will is compatible with moral responsibility. For it may seem unjust to punish a man for an action which it could have been predicted with certainty beforehand that he would do.

But that determinism is incompatible with moral responsibility is as much a delusion as that it is incompatible with free will. You do not excuse a man for doing a wrong act because, knowing his character, you felt certain beforehand that he would do it. Nor do you deprive a man of a reward or prize because, knowing his goodness or his capabilities, you felt certain beforehand that he would win it.

Volumes have been written on the justification of punishment. But so far as it affects the question of free will, the essential principles involved are quite simple. The punishment of a man for doing a wrong act is justified, either on the ground that it will correct his own character, or that it will deter other people from doing similar acts. The instrument of punishment has been in the past, and no doubt still is, often unwisely used, so that it may often have done more harm than good. But that is not relevant to our present problem. Punishment, if and when it is justified, is justified only on one or both of the grounds just mentioned. The question then is how, if we assume determinism, punishment can correct character or deter people from evil actions.

Suppose that your child develops a habit of telling lies. You give him a mild beating. Why? Because you believe that his personality is such that the usual motives for telling the truth do not cause him to do so. You therefore supply the missing cause, or motive, in the shape of pain and the fear of future pain if he repeats his untrustful behavior. And you hope that a few treatments of this kind will condition him to the habit of truth-telling, so that he will come to tell the truth without the infliction of pain. You assume that his actions are determined by causes, but that the usual causes of truth-telling do not in him produce their usual effects. You therefore supply him with an artificially injected motive, pain and fear, which you think will in the future cause him to speak truthfully.

The principle is exactly the same where you hope, by punishing one man, to deter others from wrong actions. You believe that the fear of punishment will cause those who might otherwise do evil to do well.

We act on the same principle with non-human, and even with inanimate, things, if they do not behave in the way we think they ought to behave. The rose bushes in the garden produce only small and poor blooms, whereas we want large and rich ones. We supply a cause which will produce large blooms, namely fertilizer. Our automobile does not go properly. We supply a cause which will make it go better, namely oil in the works. The punishment for the man, the fertilizer for the plant, and the oil for the car, are all justified by the same principle and in the same way. The only difference is that different kinds of things require different kinds of causes to make them do what they should. Pain may be the appropriate remedy to apply, in certain cases, to human beings, and oil to the machine. It is, of course, of no use to inject motor oil into the boy or to beat the machine.

Thus we see that moral responsibility is not only consistent with determinism, but requires it. The assumption on which punishment is based is that human behavior is causally determined. If pain could not be a cause of truth-telling there would be no justification at all for punishing lies. If human actions and volitions were uncaused, it would be useless either to punish or reward, or indeed to do anything else to correct people's bad behavior. For nothing that you could do would in any way influence them. Thus moral responsibility would entirely disappear. If there were no determinism of human beings at all, their actions would be completely unpredictable and capricious, and therefore irresponsible. And this is in itself a strong argument against the common view of philosophers that free will means being undetermined by causes.

5. What Means This Freedom?

John Hospers

*John Hospers (1918–) is an emeritus professor at the University
of Southern California. He has made important contributions to a variety
of philosophical issues. His introductory textbooks on ethics and analytic
philosophy have been widely used.*

As a preparation for developing my own views on the subject, I want to mention
a factor that I think is of enormous importance and relevance: namely, unconscious
motivation. There are many actions—not those of an insane person (however the
term "insane" be defined), nor of a person ignorant of the effects of his action, nor
ignorant of some relevant fact about the situation, nor in any obvious way mentally
deranged—for which human beings in general and the courts in particular are
inclined to hold the doer responsible, and for which, I would say, he should not be
held responsible. The deed may be planned, it may be carried out in cold calculation, it may spring from the agent's character and be continuous with the rest of his
behavior, and it may be perfectly true that he could have done differently *if* he had
wanted to; nonetheless his behavior was brought about by unconscious conflicts
developed in infancy, over which he had no control and of which (without training
in psychiatry) he does not even have knowledge. He may even *think* he knows why
he acted as he did, he may *think* he has conscious control over his actions, he may
even *think* he is fully responsible for them; but he is not. Psychiatric casebooks
provide hundreds of examples. The law and common sense, though puzzled sometimes by such cases, are gradually becoming aware that they exist; but at this early
stage countless tragic blunders still occur because neither the law nor the public in
general is aware of the genesis of criminal actions. The mother blames her daughter
for choosing the wrong men as candidates for husbands; but though the daughter
thinks she is choosing freely and spends a considerable amount of time "deciding"
among them, the identification with her sick father, resulting from Oedipal fantasies
in early childhood, prevents her from caring for any but sick men, twenty or thirty
years older than herself. Blaming her is beside the point; she cannot help it, and
she cannot change it. Countless criminal acts are thought out in great detail; yet
the participants are (without their own knowledge) acting out fantasies, fears,
and defenses from early childhood, over whose coming and going they have no
conscious control.

Now, I am not saying that none of these persons should be in jails or asylums.
Often society must be protected against them. Nor am I saying that people should

From John Hospers, "What Means This Freedom?" in *Determinism and Freedom in the Age of Modern
Science*, edited by Sidney Hook (New York University Press, 1958). Reprinted by permission.

cease the practices of blaming and praising, punishing and rewarding; in general these devices are justified by the results—although very often they have practically no effect; the deeds are done from inner compulsion, which is not lessened when the threat of punishment is great. I am only saying that frequently persons we think responsible are not properly to be called so; we mistakenly think them responsible because we assume they are like those in whom no unconscious drive (toward this type of behavior) is present, and that their behavior can be changed by reasoning, exhorting, or threatening.

I

I have said that these persons are not responsible. But what is the criterion for responsibility? Under precisely what conditions is a person to be held morally responsible for an action? Disregarding here those conditions that have to do with a person's *ignorance* of the situation or the effects of his action, let us concentrate on those having to do with his "inner state." There are several criteria that might be suggested:

1. The first idea that comes to mind is that responsibility is determined by the presence or absence of *premeditation*—the opposite of "premeditated" being, presumably, "unthinking" or "impulsive." But this will not do—both because some acts are not premeditated but responsible, and because some are premeditated and not responsible.

Many acts we call responsible can be as unthinking or impulsive as you please. If you rush across the street to help the victim of an automobile collision, you are (at least so we would ordinarily say) acting responsibly, but you did not do so out of premeditation; you saw the accident, you didn't think, you rushed to the scene without hesitation. It was like a reflex action. But you acted responsibly: unlike the knee jerk, the act was the result of past training and past thought about situations of this kind; that is why you ran to help instead of ignoring the incident or running away. When something done originally from conviction or training becomes habitual, it becomes *like* a reflex action. As Aristotle said, virtue should become second nature through habit: a virtuous act should be performed *as if* by instinct; this, far from detracting from its moral worth, testifies to one's mastery of the desired type of behavior; one does not have to make a moral effort each time it is repeated.

There are also premeditated acts for which, I would say, the person is not responsible. Premeditation, especially when it is so exaggerated as to issue in no action at all, can be the result of neurotic disturbance or what we sometimes call an emotional "block," which the person inherits from long-past situations. In Hamlet's revenge on his uncle (I use this example because it is familiar to all of us), there was no lack, but rather a surfeit, of premeditation; his actions were so exquisitely premeditated as to make Freud and Dr. Ernest Jones look more closely to find out what lay behind them. The very premeditation camouflaged unconscious motives of which Hamlet himself was not aware. I think this is an important point, since it seems that the courts often assume that premeditation is a criterion of responsibility. If failure to kill his uncle had been considered a crime, every court in the land would have convicted Hamlet. Again: a woman's decision to stay with her husband in spite of endless "mental cruelty" is, if she is the victim of an unconscious masochistic "will to punishment," one for which she is not responsible; she is the victim and not the agent, no matter how profound her conviction that she is the agent; she is caught in a masochistic web (of complicated genesis) dating back to babyhood, perhaps a repetition of a comparable situation involving her own parents, a repetition-compulsion that, as Freud said, goes "beyond the pleasure principle." Again: a criminal whose crime was carefully planned step by step is usually considered responsible, but as we shall see in later examples, the over-whelming impulse toward it, stemming from an unusually humiliating ego defeat in early childhood, was as compulsive as any can be.

2. Shall we say, then, that a person is not responsible for his act unless he can *defend it with reasons*? I am afraid that this criterion is no better than the previous one. First, intellectuals are usually better at giving reasons than nonintellectuals, and according to this criterion would be more responsible than persons acting from moral conviction not implemented by reasoning; yet it is very doubtful whether we should want to say that the latter are the more responsible. Second, the giving of reasons itself may be suspect. The reasons may be rationalizations camouflaging unconscious motives of which the agent knows nothing. Hamlet gave many reasons for not doing what he felt it was his duty to do: the time was not right, his uncle's soul might go to heaven, etc. His various "reasons" contradicted one another, and if an overpowering compulsion had not been present, the highly intellectual Hamlet would not have been taken in for a moment by these rationalizations. The real reason, the Oedipal conflict that made his uncle's crime the accomplishment of his own deepest desire, binding their fates into one and paralyzing him into inaction, was unconscious and of course unknown to him. One's intelligence and reasoning power do not enable one to escape from unconsciously motivated behavior; it only gives one greater facility in rationalizing that behavior; one's intelligence is simply used in the interests of the neurosis—it is pressed into service to justify with reasons what one does quite independently of the reasons.

If these two criteria are inadequate, let us seek others.

3. Shall we say that a person is responsible for his action unless it is the *result of unconscious forces* of which he knows nothing? Many psychoanalysts would probably accept this criterion. If it is not largely reflected in the language of responsibility as ordinarily used, this may be due to ignorance of fact: most people do not know that there are such things as unconscious motives and unconscious conflicts causing human beings to act. But it may be that if they did, perhaps they would refrain from holding persons responsible for certain actions.

I do not wish here to quarrel with this criterion of responsibility. I only want to point out the fact that if this criterion is employed a far greater number of actions will be excluded from the domain of responsibility than we might at first suppose. Whether we are neat or untidy, whether we are selfish or unselfish, whether we provoke scenes or avoid them, even whether we can exert our powers of will to change our behavior—all these may, and often do, have their source in our unconscious life.

4. Shall we say that a person is responsible for his act unless it is *compelled*? Here we are reminded of Aristotle's assertion (*Nicomachean Ethics*, Book III) that a person is responsible for his act except for reasons of either ignorance or compulsion. Ignorance is not part of our problem here (unless it is unconsciously induced ignorance of facts previously remembered and selectively forgotten—in which case the forgetting is again compulsive), but compulsion is. How will compulsion do as a criterion? The difficulty is to state just what it means. When we say an act is compelled in a psychological sense, our language is metaphorical—which is not to say that there is no point in it or that, properly interpreted, it is not true. Our actions are compelled in a literal sense if someone has us in chains or is controlling our bodily movements. When we say that the storm compelled us to jettison the cargo of the ship (Aristotle's example), we have a less literal sense of compulsion, for at least it is open to us to go down with the ship. When psychoanalysts say that a man was compelled by unconscious conflicts to wash his hands constantly, this is also not a literal use of "compel"; for nobody forced his hands under the tap. Still, it is a typical example of what psychologists call *compulsive* behavior: it has unconscious causes inaccessible to introspection, and moreover nothing can change it—it is as inevitable for him to do it as it would be if someone were forcing his hands under the tap. In this it is exactly like the action of a powerful external force; it is just as little within one's conscious control.

In its area of application this interpretation of responsibility comes to much the same as the previous one. And this area is very great indeed. For if we cannot be held responsible for the infantile situations (in which we were after all passive victims), then neither, it would seem, can we be held responsible for compulsive actions occurring in adulthood that are inevitable consequences of those infantile situations. And, psychiatrists and psychoanalysts tell us, actions fulfilling this description are characteristic of all people some of the time and some people most of the time. Their occurrence, once the infantile events have taken place, is inevitable, just as the explosion is inevitable once the fuse has been lighted; there is simply more "delayed action" in the psychological explosions than there is in the physical ones.

(I have not used the word "inevitable" here to mean "causally determined," for according to such a definition every event would be inevitable if one accepted the causal principle in some form or other; and probably nobody except certain philosophers uses "inevitable" in this sense. Rather, I use "inevitable" in its ordinary sense of "cannot be avoided." To the extent, therefore, that adult neurotic manifestations *can* be avoided, once the infantile patterns have become set, the assertion that they are inevitable is not true.)

5. There is still another criterion, which I prefer to the previous ones, by which a man's responsibility for an act can be measured: the degree to which that act can (or could have been) *changed by the use of reasons.* Suppose that the man who washes his hands constantly does so, he says, for hygienic reasons, believing that if he doesn't do so he will be poisoned by germs. We now convince him, on the best medical authority, that his belief is groundless. Now, the test of his responsibility is whether the changed belief will result in changed behavior. If it does not, as with the compulsive hand washer, he is not acting responsibly, but if it does, he is. It is

not the *use* of reasons, but their *efficacy in changing behavior*, that is being made the criterion of responsibility. And clearly in neurotic cases no such change occurs; in fact, this is often made the defining characteristic of neurotic behavior: it is unchangeable by any rational considerations.

II

I have suggested these criteria to distinguish actions for which we can call the agent responsible from those for which we cannot. Even persons with extensive knowledge of psychiatry do not, I think, use any one of these criteria to the exclusion of the others; a conjunction of two or more may be used at once. But however they may be combined or selected in actual application, I believe we can make the distinction along some such lines as we have suggested.

But is there not still another possible meaning of "responsibility" that we have not yet mentioned? Even after we have made all the above distinctions, there remains a question in our minds whether we are, in the final analysis, *responsible for any of our actions at all*. The issue may be put this way: How can anyone be responsible for his actions, since they grow out of his character, which is shaped and molded and made what it is by influences—some hereditary, but most of them stemming from early parental environment—that were not of his own making or choosing? This question, I believe, still troubles many people who would agree to all the distinctions we have just made but still have the feeling that "this isn't all." They have the uneasy suspicion that there is a more ultimate sense, a "deeper" sense, in which we are *not* responsible for our actions, since we are not responsible for the character out of which those actions spring.

Let us take as an example a criminal who, let us say, strangled several persons and is himself now condemned to die in the electric chair. Jury and public alike hold him fully responsible (at least they utter the words "he is responsible"), for the murders were planned down to the minutest detail, and the defendant tells the jury exactly how he planned them. But now we find out how it all came about; we learn of parents who rejected him from babyhood, of the childhood spent in one foster home after another, where it was always plain to him that he was not wanted; of the constantly frustrated early desire for affection, the hard shell of nonchalance and bitterness that he assumed to cover the painful and humiliating fact of being unwanted, and his subsequent attempts to heal these wounds to his shattered ego through defensive aggression.

> The criminal is the most passive person in this world, helpless as a baby in his motorically inexpressible fury. Not only does he try to wreak revenge on the mother of the earliest period of his babyhood; his criminality is based on the inner feeling of being incapable of making the mother even feel that the child seeks revenge on her. The situation is that of a dwarf trying to annoy a giant who superciliously refuses to see these attempts. . . . Because of his inner feeling of being a dwarf, the criminotic uses, so to speak, dynamite. Of that the giant must take cognizance. True, the "revenge"

harms the avenger. He may be legally executed. However, the primary inner aim of forcing the giant to acknowledge the dwarf's fury is fulfilled.[1]

The poor victim is not conscious of the inner forces that exact from him this ghastly toll; he battles, he schemes, he revels in pseudoaggression, he is miserable, but he does not know what works within him to produce these catastrophic acts of crime. His aggressive actions are the wriggling of a worm on a fisherman's hook. And if this is so, it seems difficult to say any longer, "He is responsible." Rather we shall put him behind bars for the protection of society, but we shall no longer flatter our feeling of moral superiority by calling him personally responsible for what he did.

Let us suppose it were established that a man commits murder only if, sometime during the previous week, he has eaten a certain combination of foods—say, tuna fish salad at a meal also including peas, mushroom soup, and blueberry pie. What if we were to track down the factors common to all murders committed in this country during the last twenty years and found this factor present in all of them, and only in them? The example is of course empirically absurd; but may it not be that there is *some* combination of factors that regularly leads to homicide, factors such as are described in general terms in the above quotation? (Indeed the situation in the quotation is less fortunate than in our hypothetical example, for it is easy to avoid certain foods once we have been warned about them, but the situation of the infant is thrust on him; something has already happened to him once and for all, before he knows it has happened.) When such specific factors are discovered, won't they make it clear that it is foolish and pointless, as well as immoral, to hold human beings responsible for crimes? Or, if one prefers biological to psychological factors, suppose a neurologist is called in to testify at a murder trial and produces X-ray pictures of the brain of the criminal; anyone can see, he argues, that the *cella turcica* was already calcified at the age of nineteen; it should be a flexible bone, growing, enabling the gland to grow.[2] All the defendant's disorders might have resulted from this early calcification. Now, this particular explanation may be empirically false; but who can say that no such factors, far more complex, to be sure, exist?

When we know such things as these, we no longer feel so much tempted to say that the criminal is responsible for his crime; and we tend also (do we not?) to excuse him—not legally (we still confine him to prison) but morally; we no longer call him a monster or hold him personally responsible for what he did. Moreover, we do this in general, not merely in the case of crime: "You must excuse Grandmother for being irritable; she's really quite ill and is suffering some pain all the time." Or: "The dog always bites children after she's had a litter of pups; you can't blame her for it: she's not feeling well, and besides she naturally wants to defend them." Or: "She's nervous and jumpy, but do excuse her: she has a severe glandular disturbance."

---

[1] Edmund Bergler, *The Basic Neurosis* (New York: Grune and Stratton, 1949), p. 305.
[2] Meyer Levin, *Compulsion* (New York: Simon and Schuster, 1956), p. 403.

Let us note that the more *thoroughly* and *in detail* we know the causal factors leading a person to behave as he does, the more we tend to exempt him from responsibility. When we know nothing of the man except what we see him do, we say he is an ungrateful cad who expects much of other people and does nothing in return, and we are usually indignant. When we learn that his parents were the same way and, having no guilt feelings about this mode of behavior themselves, brought him up to be greedy and avaricious, we see that we could hardly expect him to have developed moral feelings in this direction. When we learn, in addition, that he is not aware of being ungrateful or selfish, but unconsciously represses the memory of events unfavorable to himself, we feel that the situation is unfortunate but "not really his fault." When we know that this behavior of his, which makes others angry, occurs more constantly when he feels tense or insecure, and that he now feels tense and insecure, and that relief from pressure will diminish it, then we tend to "feel sorry for the poor guy" and say he's more to be pitied than censured. We no longer want to say that he is personally responsible; we might rather blame nature or his parents for having given him an unfortunate constitution or temperament.

> In recent years a new form of punishment has been imposed on middle-aged and elderly parents. Their children, now in their twenties, thirties or even forties, present them with a modern grievance: "My analysis proves that *you* are responsible for my neurosis." Overawed by these authoritative statements, the poor tired parents fall easy victims to the newest variations on the scapegoat theory.
>
> In my opinion, this senseless cruelty—which disinters educational sins which had been buried for decades, and uses them as the basis for accusations which the victims cannot answer—is unjustified. Yes, "the truth loves to be centrally located" (Melville), and few parents—since they are human—have been perfect. But granting their mistakes, they acted as *their* neurotic difficulties forced them to act. To turn the tables and declare the children not guilty because of the *impersonal* nature of their own neuroses, while at the same time the parents are *personally* blamed, is worse than illogical; it is profoundly unjust.[3]

And, so it would now appear, neither of the parties is responsible: "they acted as their neurotic difficulties forced them to act." The patients are not responsible for their neurotic manifestations, but then neither are the parents responsible for theirs; and so, of course, for their parents in turn, and theirs before them. It is the twentieth-century version of the family curse, the curse on the House of Atreus.

"But," a critic complains, "it's immoral to exonerate people indiscriminately in this way. I might have thought it fit to excuse somebody because he was born on the other side of the tracks, if I didn't know so many bank presidents who were also born on the other side of the tracks." Now, I submit that the most immoral thing in this situation is the critic's caricature of the conditions of the excuse. Nobody is excused merely because he was born on the other side of the tracks. But if he was born on the

---

[3]Edmund Bergler, *The Superego* (New York: Grune and Stratton, 1952), p. 320.

other side of the tracks *and* was a highly narcissistic infant to begin with *and* was repudiated or neglected by his parents *and* . . . (here we list a finite number of conditions), and if this complex of factors is *regularly* followed by certain behavior traits in adulthood, and moreover *unavoidably* so—that is, they occur no matter what he or anyone else tries to do—then we excuse him morally and say he is not responsible for his deed. If he is not responsible for *A*, a series of events occurring in his babyhood, then neither is he responsible for *B*, a series of things he does in adulthood, provided that *B* inevitably—that is, unavoidably—follows upon the occurrence of *A*. And according to psychiatrists and psychoanalysts, this often happens.

But one may still object that so far we have talked only about neurotic behavior. Isn't nonneurotic or normal or not unconsciously motivated (or whatever you want to call it) behavior still within the area of responsibility? There are reasons for answering "No" even here, for the normal person no more than the neurotic one has caused his own character, which makes him what he is. Granted that neurotics are not responsible for their behavior (that part of it which we call neurotic) because it stems from undigested infantile conflicts that they had no part in bringing about, and that are external to them just as surely as if their behavior had been forced on them by a malevolent deity (which is indeed one theory on the subject); but the so-called normal person is equally the product of causes in which his volition took no part. And if, unlike the neurotic's, his behavior is changeable by rational considerations, and if he has the will power to overcome the effects of an unfortunate early environment, this again is no credit to him; he is just lucky. If energy is available to him in a form in which it can be mobilized for constructive purposes, this is no credit to him, for this too is part of his psychic legacy. Those of us who can discipline ourselves and develop habits of concentration of purpose tend to blame those who cannot, and call them lazy and weak-willed; but what we fail to see is that they literally *cannot* do what we expect; if their psyches were structured like ours, they could, but as they are burdened with a tyrannical superego (to use psychoanalytic jargon for the moment), and a weak defenseless ego whose energies are constantly consumed in fighting endless charges of the superego, they simply cannot do it, and it is irrational to expect it of them. We cannot with justification blame them for their inability, any more than we can congratulate ourselves for our ability. This lesson is hard to learn, for we constantly and naïvely assume that other people are constructed as we ourselves are.

For example: A child raised under slum conditions, whose parents are socially ambitious and envy families with money, but who nevertheless squander the little they have on drink, may simply be unable in later life to mobilize a drive sufficient to overcome these early conditions. Common sense would expect that he would develop the virtue of thrift; he would make quite sure that he would never again endure the grinding poverty he had experienced as a child. But in fact it is not so: the exact conditions are too complex to be specified in detail here, but when certain conditions are fulfilled (concerning the subject's early life), he will always thereafter be a spendthrift, and no rational considerations will be able to change this. He will listen to the rational considerations and see the force of these, but they will not be able to change him, even if he tries; he cannot change his wasteful habits any more than he can lift the Empire State Building with his bare hands. We moralize and plead with him to be thrifty, but we do not see how strong, how utterly overpowering, and how constantly with him, is the opposite drive, which is so easily manageable with us. But he is possessed by the all-consuming, all-encompassing urge to make the world see that he belongs, that he has arrived, that he is just as well off as anyone else, that the awful humiliations were not real, that they never actually occurred, for isn't he now able to spend and spend? The humiliation must be blotted out; and conspicuous, flashy, expensive, and wasteful buying will do this; it shows the world what the world must know! True, it is only for the moment; true, it is in the end self-defeating, for wasteful consumption is the best way to bring poverty back again; but the person with an overpowering drive to mend a lesion to his narcissism cannot resist the avalanche of that drive with this puny rational consideration. A man with his back against the wall and a gun at his throat doesn't think of what may happen ten years hence. (Consciously, of course, he knows nothing of this drive; all that appears to consciousness is its shattering effects; he knows only that he must keep on spending—not why—and that he is unable to resist.) He hasn't in him the psychic capacity, the energy to stem the tide of a drive that at that moment is all-powerful. We, seated comfortably away from this flood, sit in judgment on him and blame him and exhort him and criticize him; but he, carried along by the flood, cannot do otherwise than he does. He may fight with all the strength of which he is capable, but it is not enough. And we, who are rational enough at least to exonerate a man in a situation of "overpowering impulse" when we recognize it to be one, do not even recognize this as an example of it; and so, in addition to being swept away in the flood that childhood conditions rendered inevitable, he must also endure our lectures, our criticisms, and our moral excoriation.

But, one will say, he could have overcome his spendthrift tendencies; some people do. Quite true: some people do. They are lucky. They have it in them to overcome early deficiencies by exerting great effort, and they are capable of exerting the effort. Some of us, luckier still, can overcome them with but little effort; and a few, the luckiest, haven't the deficiencies to overcome. It's all a matter of luck. The least lucky are those who can't overcome them, even with great effort, and those who haven't the ability to exert the effort.

But, one persists, it isn't a matter simply of luck; it *is* a matter of effort. Very well then, it's a matter of effort; without exerting the effort you may not overcome the deficiency. But whether or not you are the kind of person who has it in him to exert the effort is a matter of luck.

All this is well known to psychoanalysts. They can predict, from minimal cues that most of us don't notice, whether a person is going to turn out to be lucky or not. "The analyst," they say, "must be able to use the residue of the patient's unconscious guilt so as to remove the symptom or character trait that creates the guilt. The guilt must not only be present, but *available* for use, *mobilizable*. If it is used up (absorbed) in criminal activity, or in an excessive amount of self-damaging tendencies, then it cannot be used for therapeutic purposes, and the prognosis is negative." Not all philosophers will relish the analyst's way of putting the matter, but at least as a physician he can soon detect whether the patient is lucky or unlucky—and he knows that whichever it is, it *isn't the patient's fault*. The patient's conscious volition cannot remedy the deficiency. Even whether he will co-operate with the analyst is really out of the patient's hands: if he continually projects the denying-mother fantasy on the analyst and unconsciously identifies him always with the cruel, harsh forbidder of the nursery, thus frustrating any attempt at impersonal observation, the sessions are useless; yet if it happens that way, he can't help that either. That fatal projection is not under his control; whether it occurs or not depends on how his unconscious identifications have developed since his infancy. He can try, yes—but the ability to try enough for the therapy to have effect is also beyond his control; the capacity to try more than just so much is either there or it isn't—and either way "it's in the lap of the gods."

The position, then, is this: if we *can* overcome the effects of early environment, the ability to do so is itself a product of the early environment. We did not give ourselves this ability; and if we lack it we cannot be blamed for not having it. Sometimes, to be sure, moral exhortation brings out an ability that is there but not being used, and in this lies its *occasional* utility; but very often its use is pointless, because the ability is not there. The only thing that can overcome a desire, as Spinoza said, is a stronger contrary desire; and many times there simply is no wherewithal for producing a stronger contrary desire. Those of us who do have the wherewithal are lucky.

There is one possible practical advantage in remembering this. It may prevent us (unless we are compulsive blamers) from indulging in righteous indignation and committing the sin of spiritual pride, thanking God that we are not as this publican here. And it will protect from our useless moralizings those who are least equipped by nature for enduring them.

As with responsibility, so with deserts. Someone commits a crime and is punished by the state; "he deserved it," we say self-righteously—as if we were moral and he immoral, when in fact we are lucky and he is unlucky—forgetting that there, but for the grace of God and a fortunate early environment, go we. Or, as Clarence Darrow said in his speech for the defense in the Loeb-Leopold case:

> I do not believe that people are in jail because they deserve to be. . . . I know what causes the emotional life. . . . I know it is practically left out of some. Without it they cannot act with the rest. They cannot feel the moral shocks which safeguard others. Is [this man] to blame that his machine is imperfect? Who is to blame? I do not know. I have never in my life been interested so much in fixing blame as I have in relieving people from blame. I am not wise enough to fix it.[4]

---

[4]Levin, *op. cit.*, pp. 439–40, 469.

The Responsibility
of Criminals

6. An Address Delivered to the Prisoners in the Chicago County Jail

Clarence Darrow

Clarence Seward Darrow (1857–1938) was one of America's outstanding criminal and trial lawyers. Among his famous cases were the Leopold and Loeb murder trial and the Scopes evolution trial in Tennessee. He was an outspoken agnostic and an opponent of traditional penal practices.

If I looked at jails and crimes and prisoners in the way the ordinary person does, I should not speak on this subject to you. The reason I talk to you on the question of crime, its cause and cure, is because I really do not in the least believe in crime. There is no such thing as a crime as the word is generally understood. I do not believe there is any sort of distinction between the real moral condition of the people in and out of jail. One is just as good as the other. The people here can no more help being here than the people outside can avoid being outside. I do not believe that people are in jail because they deserve to be. They are in jail simply because they can not avoid it on account of circumstances which are entirely beyond their control and for which they are in no way responsible.

I suppose a great many people on the outside would say I was doing you harm if they should hear what I say to you this afternoon, but you can not be hurt a great deal anyway, so it will not matter. Good people outside would say that I was really teaching you things that were calculated to injure society, but it's worth while now and then to hear something different from what you ordinarily get from preachers and the like. These will tell you that you should be good and then you will get rich and be happy. Of course we know that people do not get rich by being good, and that is the reason why so many of you people try to get rich some other way, only you do not understand how to do it quite as well as the fellow outside.

There are people who think that everything in this world is an accident. But really there is no such thing as an accident. A great many folks admit that many of the

Reprinted from *Crime and Criminals* by Clarence Darrow, published by Charles H. Kerr & Company, 1902.

people in jail ought not to be there, and many who are outside ought to be in. I think none of them ought to be here. There ought to be no jails, and if it were not for the fact that the people on the outside are so grasping and heartless in their dealings with the people on the inside, there would be no such institutions as jails.

I do not want you to believe that I think all you people here are angels. I do not think that. You are people of all kinds, all of you doing the best you can, and that is evidently not very well—you are people of all kinds and conditions and under all circumstances. In one sense everybody is equally good and equally bad. We all do the best we can under the circumstances. But as to the exact things for which you are sent here, some of you are guilty and some of you are not guilty. Some of you did the particular act because you needed the money. Some of you did it because you are in the habit of doing it, and some of you because you are born to it, and it comes to be as natural as it does, for instance, for me to be good.

Most of you probably have nothing against me, and most of you would treat me the same as any other person would; probably better than some of the people on the outside would treat me, because you think I believe in you and they know I do not believe in them. While you would not have the least thing against me in the world you might pick my pockets. I do not think all of you would, but I think some of you would. You would not have anything against me, but that's your profession, a few of you. Some of the rest of you, if my doors were unlocked, might come in if you saw anything you wanted—not out of any malice to me, but because that is your trade. There is no doubt there are quite a number of people in this jail who would pick my pockets. And still I know this, that when I get outside pretty nearly everybody picks my pocket. There may be some of you who would hold up a man on the street, if you did not happen to have something else to do, and needed the money; but when I want to light my house or my office the gas company holds me up. They charge me one dollar for something that is worth twenty-five cents, and still all these people are good people; they are pillars of society and support the churches, and they are respectable.

When I ride on the street cars, I am held up—I pay five cents for a ride that is worth two and a half cents, simply because a body of men have bribed the city council and the legislature, so that all the rest of us have to pay tribute to them.

If I do not want to fall into the clutches of the gas trust and choose to burn oil instead of gas, then good Mr. Rockefeller holds me up, and he uses a certain portion of his money to build universities and support churches which are engaged in telling us how to be good.

Some of you are here for obtaining property under false pretenses—yet I pick up a great Sunday paper and read the advertisements of a merchant prince—"Shirt waists for 39 cents, marked down from $3.00."

When I read the advertisements in the paper I see they are all lies. When I want to get out and find a place to stand anywhere on the face of the earth, I find that it has all been taken up long ago before I came here, and before you came here, and somebody says, "Get off, swim into the lake, fly into the air; go anywhere, but get off." That is because these people have the police and they have the jails and the judges and the lawyers and the soldiers and all the rest of them to take care of the earth and drive everybody off that comes in their way.

A great many people will tell you that all this is true, but that it does not excuse you. These facts do not excuse some fellow who reaches into my pocket and takes out a five dollar bill; the fact that the gas company bribes the members of the legislature from year to year, and fixes the law, so that all you people are compelled to be "fleeced" whenever you deal with them; the fact that the street car companies and the gas companies have control of the streets and the fact that the landlords own all the earth, they say, has nothing to do with you.

Let us see whether there is any connection between the crimes of the respectable classes and your presence in the jail. Many of you people are in jail because you have really committed burglary. Many of you, because you have stolen something: in the meaning of the law, you have taken some other person's property. Some of you have entered a store and carried off a pair of shoes because you did not have the price. Possibly some of you have committed murder. I can not tell what all of you did. There are a great many people here who have done some of these things who really do not know themselves why they did them. I think I know why you did them—every one of you; you did these things because you were bound to do them. It looked to you at the time as if you had a chance to do them or not, as you saw fit, but still after all you had no choice. There may be people here who had some money in their pockets and who still went out and got some more money in a way society forbids. Now you may not yourselves see exactly why it was you did this thing, but if you look at the question deeply enough and carefully enough you would see that there were circumstances that drove you to do exactly the thing which you did. You could not help it any more than we outside can help taking the positions that we take. The reformers who tell you to be good and you will be happy, and the people on the outside who have property to protect—they think that the only way to do it is by building jails and locking you up in cells on weekdays and praying for you Sundays.

I think that all of this has nothing whatever to do with right conduct. I think it is very easily seen what has to do with right conduct. Some so-called criminals—and I will use this word because it is handy, it means nothing to me—I speak of the criminals who get caught as distinguished from the criminals who catch them—some of these so-called criminals are in jail for the first offenses, but nine-tenths of you are in jail because you did not have a good lawyer and of course you did not have a good lawyer because you did not have enough money to pay a good lawyer. There is no very great danger of a rich man going to jail.

Some of you may be here for the first time. If we would open the doors and let you out, and leave the laws as they are today, some of you would be back tomorrow. This is about as good a place as you can get anyway. There are many people here who are so in the habit of coming that they would not know where else to go. There are people who are born with the tendency to break into jail every chance they get, and they can not avoid it. You can not figure out your life and see why it was, but still there is a reason for it, and if we were all-wise and knew all the facts we could figure it out.

In the first place, there are a good many more people who go to jail in the winter time than in summer. Why is this? Is it because people are more wicked in winter? No, it is because the coal trust begins to get us in its grip in the winter. A few gentlemen take possession of the coal, and unless the people will pay $7 or $8 a ton for something that is worth $3, they will have to freeze. Then there is nothing to do but to break into jail, and so there are many more in jail in the winter than in summer. It costs more for gas in the winter because the nights are longer, and people go to jail to save gas bills. The jails are electric-lighted. You may not know it, but these economic laws are working all the time, whether we know it or do not know it.

There are more people who go to jail in hard times than in good times—few people comparatively go to jail except when they are hard up. They go to jail because they have no other place to go. They may not know why, but it is true all the same. People are not more wicked in hard times. That is not the reason. The fact is true all over the world that in hard times more people go to jail than in good times, and in winter more people go to jail than in summer. Of course it is pretty hard times for people who go to jail at any time. The people who go to jail are almost always poor people—people who have no other place to live first and last. When times are hard then you find large numbers of people who go to jail who would not otherwise be in jail.

Long ago, Mr. Buckle, who was a great philosopher and historian, collected facts and he showed that the number of people who are arrested increased just as the price of food increased. When they put up the price of gas ten cents a thousand I do not know who will go to jail, but I do know that a certain number of people will go. When the meat combine raises the price of beef I do not know who is going to jail, but I know that a large number of people are bound to go. Whenever the Standard Oil Company raises the price of oil, I know that a certain number of girls who are seamstresses, and who work night after night long hours for somebody else, will be compelled to go out on the streets and ply another trade, and I know that Mr. Rockefeller and his associates are responsible and not the poor girls in the jails.

First and last, people are sent to jail because they are poor. Sometimes, as I say, you may not need money at the particular time, but you wish to have thrifty forehanded habits, and do not always wait until you are in absolute want. Some of you people are perhaps plying the trade, the profession, which is called burglary. No man in his right senses will go into a strange house in the dead of night and prowl around with a dark lantern through unfamiliar rooms and take chances of his life if he has plenty of the good things of the world in his own home. You would not take any such chances as that. If a man had clothes in his clothes-press and beefsteak in his pantry, and money in a bank, he would not navigate around nights in houses where he knows nothing about the premises whatever. It always requires experience and education for this profession, and people who fit themselves for it are no more to blame than I am for being a lawyer. A man would not hold up another man on the street if he had plenty of money in his own pocket. He might do it if he had one dollar or two dollars, but he wouldn't if he had as much money as Mr. Rockefeller has. Mr. Rockefeller has a great deal better hold-up game than that.

The more that is taken from the poor by the rich, who have the chance to take it, the more poor people there are who are compelled to resort to these means for a livelihood. They may not understand it, they may not think so at once, but after all they are driven into that line of employment.

There is a bill before the legislature of this State to punish kidnapping children, with death. We have wise members of the Legislature. They know the gas trust when they see it and they always see it,—they can furnish light enough to be seen, and this Legislature thinks it is going to stop kidnapping children by making a law punishing kidnappers of children, with death. I don't believe in kidnapping children, but the Legislature is all wrong. Kidnapping children is not a crime, it is a profession. It has been developed with the times. It has been developed with our modern industrial conditions. There are many ways of making money—many new ways that our ancestors knew nothing about. Our ancestors knew nothing about a billion dollar trust; and here comes some poor fellow who has no other trade and he discovers the profession of kidnapping children.

This crime is born, not because people are bad; people don't kidnap other people's children because they want the children or because they are devilish, but because they see a chance to get some money out of it. You cannot cure this crime by passing a law punishing by death kidnappers of children. There is one way to cure it. There is one way to cure all these offenses, and that is to give the people a chance to live. There is no other way, and there never was any other way since the world began, and the world is so blind and stupid that it will not see. If every man and woman and child in the world had a chance to make a decent, fair, honest living, there would be no jails, and no lawyers and no courts. There might be some persons here or there with some peculiar formation of their brain, like Rockefeller, who would do these things simply to be doing them; but they would be very, very few, and those should be sent to a hospital and treated, and not sent to jail; and they would entirely disappear in the second generation, or at least in the third generation.

I am not talking pure theory. I will just give you two or three illustrations.

The English people once punished criminals by sending them away. They would load them on a ship and export them to Australia. England was owned by lords and nobles and rich people. They owned the whole earth over there, and the other people had to stay in the streets. They could not get a decent living. They used to take their criminals and send them to Australia—I mean the class of criminals who got caught. When these criminals got over there, and nobody else had come, they had the whole continent to run over, and so they could raise sheep and furnish their own meat, which is easier than stealing it; these criminals then became decent, respectable people because they had a chance to live. They did not commit any crimes. They were just like the English people who sent them there, only better. And in the second generation the descendants of those criminals were as good and respectable a class of people as there were on the face of the earth, and then they began building churches and jails themselves.

A portion of this country was settled in the same way, landing prisoners down on the southern coast; but when they got here and had a whole continent to run over and plenty of chances to make a living, they became respectable citizens, making their own living just like any other citizen in the world; but finally these descendants of the English aristocracy, who sent the people over to Australia, found out they were getting rich, and so they went over to get possession of the earth as they always do, and they organized land syndicates and got control of the land and ores, and then they had just as many criminals in Australia as they did in England. It was not because the world had grown bad; it was because the earth had been taken away from the people.

Some of you people have lived in the country. It's prettier than it is here. And if you have ever lived on a farm you understand that if you put a lot of cattle in a field, when the pasture is short they will jump over the fence; but put them in a good field where there is plenty of pasture, and they will be law-abiding cattle to the end of time. The human animal is just like the rest of the animals, only a little more so. The same thing that governs in the one governs in the other.

Everybody makes his living along the lines of least resistance. A wise man who comes into a country early sees a great undeveloped land. For instance, our rich men twenty-five years ago saw that Chicago was small and knew a lot of people would come here and settle, and they readily saw that if they had all the land around here it would be worth a good deal, so they grabbed the land. You can not be a landlord because somebody has got it all. You must find some other calling. In England and Ireland and Scotland less than five percent own all the land there is, and the people are bound to stay there on any kind of terms the landlords give. They must live the best they can, so they develop all these various professions—burglary, picking pockets and the like.

Again, people find all sorts of ways of getting rich. These are diseases like everything else. You look at people getting rich, organizing trusts, and making a million dollars, and somebody gets the disease and he starts out. He catches it just as a man catches the mumps or the measles; he is not to blame, it is in the air. You will find men speculating beyond their means, because the mania of money-getting is taking possession of them. It is simply a disease; nothing more, nothing less. You can not avoid catching it; but the fellows who have control of the earth have the advantage of you. See what the law is; when these men get control of things, they make the laws. They do not make the laws to protect anybody; courts are not instruments of justice; when your case gets into court it will make little difference whether you are guilty or innocent; but it's better if you have a smart lawyer. And you can not have a smart lawyer unless you have money. First and last it's a question of money. Those men who own the earth make the laws to protect what they have. They fix up a sort of fence or pen around what they have, and they fix the law so the fellow on the outside can not get in. The laws are really organized for the protection of the men who rule the world. They were never organized or enforced to do justice. We have no system for doing justice, not the slightest in the world.

Let me illustrate: Take the poorest person in this room. If the community had provided a system of doing justice the poorest person in this room would have as good a lawyer as the richest, would he not? When you went into court you would have just as long a trial, and just as fair a trial as the richest person in Chicago. Your case would not be tried in fifteen or twenty minutes, whereas it would take fifteen days to get through with a rich man's case.

Then if you were rich and were beaten, your case would be taken to the Appellate Court. A poor man can not take his case to the Appellate Court; he has not the price; and then to the Supreme Court, and if he were beaten there he might perhaps go to the United States Supreme Court. And he might die of old age before he got into jail. If you are poor, it's a quick job. You are almost known to be guilty, else you would not be there. Why should any one be in the criminal court if he were not guilty? He would not be there if he could be anywhere else. The officials have no time to look after all these cases. The people who are on the outside, who are running banks and building churches and making jails, they have no time to examine 600 or 700 prisoners each year to see whether they are guilty or innocent. If the courts were organized to promote justice the people would elect somebody to defend all these criminals, somebody as smart as the prosecutor—and give him as many detectives and as many assistants to help, and pay as much money to defend you as to prosecute you. We have a very able man for State's Attorney, and he has many assistants, detectives and policemen without end, and judges to hear the cases—everything handy.

Most of all our criminal code consists in offenses against property. People are sent to jail because they have committed a crime against property. It is of very little consequence whether one hundred people more or less go to jail who ought not to go—you must protect property, because in this world property is of more importance than anything else.

How is it done? These people who have property fix it so they can protect what they have. When somebody commits a crime it does not follow that he had done something that is morally wrong. The man on the outside who has committed no crime may have done something. For instance: to take all the coal in the United States and raise the price two dollars or three dollars when there is no need of it, and thus kill thousands of babies and send thousands of people to the poorhouse and tens of thousands to jail, as is done every year in the United States,—this is a greater crime than all the people in our jails ever committed, but the law does not punish it. Why? Because the fellows who control the earth make the laws. If you and I had the making of the laws, the first thing we would do would be to punish the fellow who gets control of the earth. Nature put this coal in the ground for me as well as for them and nature made the prairies up here to raise wheat for me as well as for them, and then the great railroad companies came along and fenced it up.

Most all of the crimes for which we are punished are property crimes. There are a few personal crimes, like murder—but they are very few. The crimes committed are mostly those against property. If this punishment is right the criminals must have a lot of property. How much money is there in this crowd? And yet you are all here for crimes against property. The people up and down the Lake Shore have not committed crime, still they have so much property they don't know what to do with it. It is perfectly plain why these people have not committed crimes against property; they make the laws and therefore do not need to break them. And in order for you to get some property you are obliged to break the rules of the game. I don't know but what some of you may have had a very nice chance to get rich by carrying the hod for one dollar a day, twelve hours. Instead of taking that nice, easy profession, you are a burglar. If you had been given a chance to be a banker you would rather follow that. Some of you may have had a chance to work as a switchman on a railroad where you know, according to statistics, that you can not live and keep all your limbs more than seven years, and you get fifty dollars or seventy-five dollars a month for taking your lives in your hands, and instead of taking that lucrative position you choose to be a sneak thief, or something like that. Some of you made that sort of choice. I don't know which I would take if I was reduced to this choice. I have an easier choice.

I will guarantee to take from this jail, or any jail in the world, five hundred men who have been the worst criminals and law-breakers who ever got into jail, and I will go down to our lowest streets and take five hundred of the most abandoned prostitutes, and go out somewhere where there is plenty of land, and will give them a chance to make a living, and they will be as good people as the average in the community.

There is a remedy for the sort of condition we see here. The world never finds it out, or when it does find it out it does not enforce it. You may pass a law punishing every person with death for burglary, and it will make no difference. Men will commit it just the same. In England there was a time when one hundred different offenses were punishable with death, and it made no difference. The English people strangely found out that so fast as they repealed the severe penalties and so fast as they did away with punishing men by death, crime decreased instead of increased; that the smaller the penalty the fewer the crimes.

Hanging men in our county jails does not prevent murder. It makes murderers.

And this has been the history of the world. It's easy to see how to do away with what we call crime. It is not so easy to do it. I will tell you how to do it. It can be done by giving the people a chance to live—by destroying special privileges. So long as big criminals can get the coal fields, so long as the big criminals have control of the city council and get the public streets for street cars and gas rights, this is bound to send thousands of poor people to jail. So long as men are allowed to monopolize all the earth, and compel others to live on such terms as these men see fit to make, then you are bound to get into jail.

The only way in the world to abolish crime and criminals is to abolish the big ones and the little ones together. Make fair conditions of life. Give men a chance to live. Abolish the right of the private ownership of land, abolish monopoly, make the world partners in production, partners in the good things of life. Nobody would steal if he could get something of his own some easier way. Nobody will commit burglary when he has a house full. No girl will go out on the streets when she has a comfortable place at home. The man who owns a sweatshop or a department store may not be to blame himself for the condition of his girls, but when he pays them five dollars, three dollars, and two dollars a week, I wonder where he thinks they will get the rest of their money to live. The only way to cure these conditions is by equality. There should be no jails. They do not accomplish what they pretend to accomplish. If you would wipe them out, there would be no more criminals than now. They terrorize nobody. They are a blot upon any civilization, and a jail is an evidence of the lack of charity of the people on the outside who make the jails and fill them with the victims of their greed.

7. The Humanitarian Theory of Punishment

C. S. Lewis

Clive Staples Lewis (1898–1963) was professor of Medieval and Renaissance English at Cambridge University from 1954 until his death. He is most famous for his numerous books and essays that defend various aspects of Christianity.

In England we have lately had a controversy about capital punishment. I do not know whether a murderer is more likely to repent and make a good end on the gallows a few weeks after his trial or in the prison infirmary thirty years later. I do not know whether the fear of death is an indispensable deterrent. I need not, for the purpose of this article, decide whether it is a morally permissible deterrent. Those are questions which I propose to leave untouched. My subject is not Capital Punishment in particular, but that theory of punishment in general which the controversy showed to be almost universal among my fellow-countrymen. It may be called the Humanitarian Theory. Those who hold it think that it is mild and merciful. In this I believe that they are seriously mistaken. I believe that the "Humanity" which it claims is a dangerous illusion and disguises the possibility of cruelty and injustice without end. I urge a return to the traditional or Retributive theory not solely, nor even primarily, in the interests of society but in the interests of the criminals.

According to the Humanitarian theory, to punish a man because he deserves it, and as much as he deserves, is mere revenge, and, therefore, barbarous and immoral. It is maintained that the only legitimate motives for punishing are the desire to deter others by example or to mend the criminal. When this theory is combined, as frequently happens, with the belief that all crime is more or less pathological, the idea of mending tails off into that of healing or curing and punishment becomes therapeutic. Thus it appears at first sight that we have passed from the harsh and self-righteous notion of giving the wicked their deserts to the charitable and enlightened one of tending the psychologically sick. What could be more amiable? One little point which is taken for granted in this theory needs, however, to be made explicit. The things done to the criminal, even if they are called cures, will be just as compulsory as they were in the old days when we called them punishments. If a tendency to steal can be cured by psychotherapy, the thief will no doubt be forced to undergo the treatment. Otherwise, society cannot continue.

My contention is that this doctrine, merciful though it appears, really means that each one of us, from the moment he breaks the law, is deprived of the rights of a human being.

The reason is this. The Humanitarian theory removes from Punishment the concept of Desert. But the concept of Desert is the only connecting link between punishment and justice. It is only as deserved or undeserved that a sentence can be just or unjust. I do not here contend that the question "Is it deserved?" is the only one we can reasonably ask about a punishment. We may very properly ask whether it is likely to deter others and to reform the criminal. But neither of these two last questions is a question about justice. There is no sense in talking about a "just deterrent" or a "just cure." We demand of a deterrent not whether it is just but whether it will deter. We demand of a cure not whether it is just but whether it succeeds. Thus when we cease to consider what the criminal deserves and consider only what will cure him or deter others, we have tacitly removed him from the sphere of justice altogether; instead of a person, a subject of rights, we now have a mere object, a patient, a "case."

The distinction will become clearer if we ask who will be qualified to determine sentences when sentences are no longer held to derive their propriety from the criminal's deserving. On the old view the problem of fixing the right sentence was a moral problem. Accordingly, the judge who did it was a person trained in jurisprudence; trained, that is, in a science which deals with rights and duties, and which, in origin at least, was consciously accepting guidance from the Law of Nature, and from Scripture. We must admit that in the actual penal code of most countries at most times these high originals were so much modified by local custom, class interests, and utilitarian concessions, as to be very imperfectly recognizable. But the code was never in principle, and not always in fact, beyond the control of the conscience of the society. And when (say, in Eighteenth Century England) actual punishments conflicted too violently with the moral sense of the community, juries refused to convict and reform was finally brought about. This was possible because, so long as we are thinking in terms of Desert, the propriety of the penal code, being a moral question, is a question on which every man has a right to an opinion, not because he follows this or that profession, but because he is simply a man, a rational animal enjoying the Natural Light. But all this is changed when we drop the concept of Desert. The only two questions we may now ask about a punishment are whether it deters and whether it cures. But these are not questions on which anyone is entitled to have an opinion simply because he is a man. He is not entitled to an opinion even if, in addition to being a man, he should happen also to be a jurist, a Christian, and a moral theologian. For they are not questions about principle but about matter of fact; and for such *cuiquam in sua arte credendum*.[1] Only the expert "penologist" (let barbarous things have barbarous names), in the light of previous experiment, can tell us what is likely to deter; only the psychotherapist can tell us what is likely to cure. It will be in vain for the rest

---

[1] ["Experts must be believed."–Ed.]

of us, speaking simply as men, to say, "but this punishment is hideously unjust, hideously disproportionate to the criminal's deserts." The experts with perfect logic will reply, "but nobody was talking about deserts. No one was talking about *punishment* in your archaic vindictive sense of the word. Here are the statistics proving that this treatment cures. What is your trouble?"

The Humanitarian theory, then, removes sentences from the hands of jurists whom the public conscience is entitled to criticize and places them in the hands of technical experts whose special sciences do not even employ such categories as Rights or Justice. It might be argued that since this transference results from an abandonment of the old idea of punishment, and therefore, of all vindictive motives, it will be safe to leave our criminals in such hands. I will not pause to comment on the simple minded view of fallen human nature which such a belief implies. Let us rather remember that the "cure" of criminals is to be compulsory; and let us then watch how the theory actually works in the mind of the Humanitarian. The immediate starting point of this article was a letter I read in one of our Leftist weeklies. The author was pleading that a certain sin, now treated by our Laws as a crime, should henceforward be treated as a disease. And he complained that under the present system the offender, after a term in gaol, was simply let out to return to his original environment where he would probably relapse. What he complained of was not the shutting up but the letting out. On his remedial view of punishment the offender should, of course, be detained until he was cured. And of course the official straighteners are the only people who can say when that is. The first result of the Humanitarian theory is, therefore, to substitute for a definite sentence (reflecting to some extent the community's moral judgment on the degree of ill-desert involved) an indefinite sentence terminable only by the word of those experts—and they are not experts in the moral theology nor even in the Law of Nature—who inflict it. Which of us, if he stood in the dock, would not prefer to be tried by the old system?

It may be said that by the continued use of the word Punishment and the use of the verb "inflict" I am misrepresenting the Humanitarians. They are not punishing, not inflicting, only healing. But do not let us be deceived by a name. To be taken without consent from my home and friends; to lose my liberty; to undergo all those assaults on my personality which modern psychotherapy knows how to deliver; to be remade after some pattern of "normality" hatched in a Viennese laboratory to which I never professed allegiance; to know that this process will never end until either my captors have succeeded or I have grown wise enough to cheat them with apparent success—who cares whether this is called Punishment or not? That it includes most of the elements for which any punishment is feared—shame, exile, bondage, and years eaten by the locust—is obvious. Only enormous ill-desert could justify it; but ill-desert is the very conception which the Humanitarian theory has thrown overboard.

If we turn from the curative to the deterrent justification of punishment we shall find the new theory even more alarming. When you punish a man *in terrorem*, make of him an "example" to others, you are admittedly using him as a means to an end; someone else's end. This, in itself, would be a very wicked thing to do. On the classical theory of Punishment it was of course justified on the ground that the man deserved it. That was assumed to be established before any question of "making him an example" arose. You then, as the saying is, killed two birds with one stone; in the process of giving him what he deserved you set an example to others. But take away desert and the whole morality of the punishment disappears. Why, in Heaven's name, am I to be sacrificed to the good of society in this way?—unless, of course, I deserve it.

But that is not the worst. If the justification of exemplary punishment is not to be based on desert but solely on its efficacy as a deterrent, it is not absolutely necessary that the man we punish should even have committed the crime. The deterrent effect demands that the public should draw the moral, "If we do such an act we shall suffer like that man." The punishment of a man actually guilty whom the public think innocent will not have the desired effect; the punishment of a man actually innocent will, provided the public think him guilty. But every modern State has powers which make it easy to fake a trial. When a victim is urgently needed for exemplary purposes and a guilty victim cannot be found, all the purposes of deterrence will be equally served by the punishment (call it "cure" if you prefer) of an innocent victim, provided that the public can be cheated into thinking him guilty. It is no use to ask me why I assume that our rulers will be so wicked. The punishment of an innocent, that is, an undeserving, man is wicked only if we grant the traditional view that righteous punishment means deserved punishment. Once we have abandoned that criterion, all punishments have to be justified, if at all, on other grounds that have nothing to do with desert. Where the punishment of the innocent can be justified on those grounds (and it could in some cases be justified as a deterrent) it will be no less moral than any other punishment. Any distaste for it on the part of a Humanitarian will be merely a hangover from the Retributive theory.

It is, indeed, important to notice that my argument so far supposes no evil intentions on the part of the Humanitarian and considers only what is involved in the logic of his position. My contention is that good men (not bad men) consistently acting upon that position would act as cruelly and unjustly as the greatest tyrants. They might in some respects act even worse. Of all tyrannies a tyranny sincerely exercised for the good of its victims may be the most oppressive. It may be better to live under robber barons than under omnipotent moral busybodies. The robber baron's cruelty may sometimes sleep, his cupidity may at some point be satiated; but those who torment us for our own good will torment us without end for they do so with the approval of their own conscience. They may be more likely to go to Heaven yet at the same time likelier to make a Hell of earth. Their very kindness stings with intolerable insult. To be "cured" against one's will and cured of states which we may not regard as disease is to be put on a level with those who have not yet reached the age of reason or those who never will; to be classed with infants, imbeciles, and domestic animals. But to be punished, however severely, because we have deserved it, because we "ought to have known better," is to be treated as a human person made in God's image.

In reality, however, we must face the possibility of bad rulers armed with a Humanitarian theory of punishment. A great many popular blue prints for a Christian society are merely what the Elizabethans called "eggs in moonshine" because they assume that the whole society is Christian or that the Christians are in control. This is not so in most contemporary States. Even if it were, our rulers would still be fallen men, and, therefore, neither very wise nor very good. As it is, they will usually be unbelievers. And since wisdom and virtue are not the only or the commonest qualifications for a place in the government, they will not often be even the best unbelievers. The practical problem of Christian politics is not that of drawing up schemes for a Christian society, but that of living as innocently as we can with unbelieving fellow-subjects under unbelieving rulers who will never be perfectly wise and good and who will sometimes be very wicked and very foolish. And when they are wicked the Humanitarian theory of Punishment will put in their hands a finer instrument of tyranny than wickedness ever had before. For if crime and disease are to be regarded as the same thing, it follows that any state of mind which our masters choose to call "disease" can be treated as crime; and compulsorily cured. It will be vain to plead that states of mind which displease government need not always involve moral turpitude and do not therefore always deserve forfeiture of liberty. For our masters will not be using the concepts of Desert and Punishment but those of disease and cure. We know that one school of psychology already regards religion as a neurosis. When this particular neurosis becomes inconvenient to government what is to hinder government from proceeding to "cure" it? Such "cure" will, of course, be compulsory; but under the Humanitarian theory it will not be called by the shocking name of Persecution. No one will blame us for being Christians, no one will hate us, no one will revile us. The new Nero will approach us with the silky manners of a doctor, and though all will be in fact as compulsory as the *tunica molesta* or Smithfield or Tyburn, all will go on within the unemotional therapeutic sphere where words like "right" and "wrong" or "freedom" and "slavery" are never heard. And thus when the command is given every prominent Christian in the land may vanish overnight into Institutions for the Treatment of the Ideologically Unsound, and it will rest with the expert Fablers to say when (if ever) they are to re-emerge. But it will not be persecution. Even if the treatment is painful, even if it is life-long, even if it is fatal, that will be only a regrettable accident; the intention was purely therapeutic. Even in ordinary medicine there were painful operations and fatal operations; so in this. But because they are "treatment," not punishment, they can be criticized only by fellow-experts and on technical grounds, never by men as men and on grounds of justice.

Problems and Puzzles

8. Luck Swallows Everything

Galen Strawson

Galen Strawson (1952–   ) is a professor of philosophy at the University of Reading in England. He has written many books and articles on a variety of philosophical issues.

Are we free agents? Can we be morally responsible for what we do? Philosophers distinguish these questions and have all the answers. Some say YES and YES (we are fully free, and wholly morally responsible for what we do). Others say YES and NO (certainly we are free agents—but we cannot be ultimately responsible for what we do). A third group says NO and NO (we are not free agents at all; a fortiori we cannot be morally responsible). A strange minority says NO and YES (we can be morally responsible for what we do even though we are not free agents). This view is rare, but it has a kind of existentialist panache, and appears to be embraced by Wintergreen in Joseph Heller's novel *Closing Time* (1994), as well as by some Protestants.

Who is right? Suppose that tomorrow is a holiday, and that you are wondering what to do. You can climb a mountain or read Lao Tzu. You can restring your mandolin or go to the zoo. At the moment you are reading about free will. You are free to go on reading or stop now. You have started on this sentence, but you don't have to . . . finish it. Right now, as so often in life, you have a number of options. Nothing forces your hand. Surely you are entirely free to choose what to do, and responsible for what you do?

This is what the Compatibilists think. They say YES and YES, and are very influential in the present day. Their name derives from their claim that free will is entirely compatible with determinism—the view that everything that happens in the universe is necessitated by what has already gone before, in such a way that nothing can happen otherwise than it does. Free will, they think, is just a matter of not being constrained or compelled in certain ways that have nothing to do with whether determinism is true or false. "Consider yourself at this moment," they say. "No one is holding a gun to your head. You are not being threatened or manhandled. You are not (surely) drugged, or in chains, or subject to a psychological compulsion like kleptomania, or a post-hypnotic command. So you are wholly free. This is what being a free agent is. It's wholly irrelevant that your character is determined, if indeed it is."

This piece first appeared in *The Times Literary Supplement*, No. 4969, June 26, 1998 pp. 8–10. www.the-tls.co.uk. Reprinted by permission.

"And although things like guns and chains, threats to the life of your children, psychological obsessions, and so on, are standardly counted as constraints that can limit freedom and responsibility, there is another and more fundamental sense in which you are fully free in any situation in which you can choose or act in any way at all—in any situation in which you are not panicked, or literally compelled to do what you do, in such a way that it is not clear that you can still be said to choose or act at all (as when you press a button because your finger is forced down onto it). Consider pilots of hijacked aeroplanes. They usually stay calm. They choose to comply with the hijackers' demands. They act responsibly, as we naturally say. They are able to do other than they do, but they choose not to. They do what they most want to do, all things considered, in the circumstances in which they find themselves; and all circumstances limit one's options in some way. Some circumstances limit one's options much more drastically than others, but it doesn't follow that one isn't free to choose in those circumstances. Only literal compulsion, panic, or uncontrollable impulse really removes one's freedom to choose, and to (try to) do what one most wants to do given one's character or personality. Even when one's finger is being forced down on the button, one can still act freely in resisting the pressure or cursing one's oppressor, and in many other ways."

So most of us are wholly free to choose and act throughout our waking lives, according to the Compatibilists. We are free to choose between the options we perceive to be open to us. (Sometimes we would rather not face options, but are unable to avoid awareness of the fact that we do face them.) One has options even when one is in chains, or falling through space. Even if one is completely paralyzed, one is still free in so far as one is free to choose to think about one thing rather than another. There is, as Sartre observed, a sense in which we are condemned to freedom, not free not to be free.

One may well not be able to do everything one wants—one may want to fly unassisted, vapourize every gun in the United States by an act of thought, or house all those who sleep on the streets of Calcutta by the end of the month—but few have supposed that free will is a matter of being able to do everything one wants. It is, doubtless, a possible view. But according to the Compatibilists, free will is simply a matter of being unconstrained in such a way that one has genuine options and opportunities for action, and is able to choose between them according to what one wants or thinks best. It doesn't matter if one's character, personality, preferences, and general motivational set are entirely determined by things for which one is in no way responsible—by one's genetic inheritance, upbringing, historical situation, chance encounters, and so on.

Even dogs count as free agents, on this view. So Compatibilists have to explain what distinguishes us from dogs—since we don't think that dogs are free in the way we are. Many of them say that it is our capacity for explicitly self-conscious thought. Not because self-consciousness liberates anyone from determinism: if determinism is true, one is determined to have whatever self-conscious thoughts one has, whatever their complexity. The idea is that self-consciousness makes it possible for one to be explicitly aware of oneself as facing choices and engaging in processes of reasoning about what to do, and thereby constitutes one as a radically free agent in a way unavailable to any unself-conscious agent. One's self-conscious deliberative presence in the situation of choice simply trumps the fact—if it is a fact—that one is, in the final analysis, wholly constituted as the sort of person one is by factors for which one is not in any way ultimately responsible.

Some Compatibilists add that human beings are sharply marked off from dogs by their capacity to act for reasons that they explicitly take to be moral reasons. Compatibilism has many variants. According to Harry Frankfurt's version, for example, one has free will if one wants to be moved to action by the motives that do in fact move one to action. On this view, freedom is just a matter of having a personality that is harmonious in a certain way.

The Compatibilists, then, say YES and YES, and those who want to say YES and YES are well advised to follow them, for determinism is unfalsifiable, and may be true. (In the end, contemporary physics gives us no more reason to suppose that determinism is false than to suppose that it is true.) Many, however, think that the Compatibilist account of things does not even touch the real problem of free will. For what is it, they say, to define freedom in such a way that it is compatible with determinism? It is to define it in such a way that an agent can be a free agent even if all its actions throughout its life are determined to happen as they do by events that have taken place before it is born: so that there is a clear sense in which it could not at any point in its life have done otherwise than it did. This, they say, is certainly not free will or moral responsibility. How can one be truly or ultimately morally responsible for what one does if everything one does is ultimately a deterministic outcome of events for whose occurrence one is in no way responsible?

These are the Incompatibilists, and they divide into two groups: the Libertarians, on the one hand, and the No-Freedom theorists or Pessimists, on the other. The Libertarians are up-beat. They say YES and YES, and think the Compatibilists' account of freedom can be improved on. They hold (1) that we do have free will, (2) that free will is not compatible with determinism, and (3) that determinism is therefore false. But they face an extremely difficult task: they have to show how indeterminism (the falsity of determinism) can help with free will, and in particular with moral responsibility.

The Pessimists do not think this can be shown. They agree that free will is not compatible with determinism, but deny that indeterminism can help. They think that free will, of the sort that is necessary for genuine moral responsibility, is provably impossible. They say NO and NO.

They begin by granting what everyone must. They grant that there is a clear, important, compatibilist sense in which we can be free agents (we can be free, when unconstrained, to choose and to do what we want or think best, given how we are). But they insist that this isn't enough: it doesn't give us what we want, in the way of free will. Nor does it give us what we believe we have. But (they continue) it is not as if the Compatibilists have missed something. The truth is that nothing can give us what we think we want, and ordinarily think we have. We cannot be morally responsible, in the absolute, buck-stopping way in which we often unreflectively think we are. We cannot have "strong" free will of the kind that we would need to have, in order to be morally responsible in this way.

One way of setting out the Pessimists' argument is as follows:

1. When you act, you do what you do, in the situation in which you find your-self, because of the way you are.

But then

2. To be truly or ultimately morally responsible for what you do, you must be truly or ultimately responsible for the way you are, at least in certain crucial mental respects. (Obviously you don't have to be responsible for your height, age, sex, and so on.)

But

3. You can't be ultimately responsible for the way you are in any respect at all, so you can't be ultimately responsible for what you do.

For

4. To be ultimately responsible for the way you are, you must have somehow intentionally brought it about that you are the way you are.

And the problem is then this. Suppose

5. You have somehow intentionally brought it about that you are the way you now are, in certain mental respects: suppose you have brought it about that you have a certain mental nature Z, in such a way that you can be said to be ultimately responsible for Z.

For this to be true

6. You must already have had a certain mental nature Y, in the light of which you brought it about that you now have Z. If you didn't already have a mental nature then you didn't have any intentions or preferences, and can't be responsible for the way you now are, even if you have changed.

But then

7. For it to be true that you are ultimately responsible for how you now are, you must be ultimately responsible for having had that nature, Y, in the light of which you brought it about that you now have Z.

So

8. You must have brought it about that you had Y.

But then

9. You must have existed already with a prior nature, X, in the light of which you brought it about that you had Y, in the light of which you brought it about that you now have Z.

And so on. Here one is setting off on a potentially infinite regress. In order for one to be truly or ultimately responsible for how one is in such a way that one can be truly responsible for what one does, something impossible has to be true: there has to be, and cannot be, a starting point in the series of acts of bringing it about that one has a certain nature; a starting point that constitutes an act of ultimate self-origination.

There is a more concise way of putting the point: in order to be ultimately responsible, one would have to be *causa sui*—the ultimate cause or origin of oneself, or at least of some crucial part of one's mental nature. But nothing can be ultimately *causa sui* in any respect at all. Even if the property of being *causa sui* is allowed to belong unintelligibly to God, it cannot plausibly be supposed to be possessed by ordinary finite human beings. "The *causa sui* is the best self-contradiction that has been conceived so far," as Nietzsche remarked in 1886:

> It is a sort of rape and perversion of logic. But the extravagant pride of man has managed to entangle itself profoundly and frightfully with just this nonsense. The desire for "freedom of the will" in the superlative metaphysical sense, which still holds sway, unfortunately, in the minds of the half-educated; the desire to bear the entire and ultimate responsibility for one's actions oneself, and to absolve God, the world, ancestors, chance, and society involves nothing less than to be precisely this *causa sui* and, with more than Baron Munchhausen's audacity, to pull oneself up into existence by the hair, out of the swamps of nothingness.[1]

In fact, nearly all of those who believe in strong free will do so without any conscious thought that it requires ultimate self-origination. But self-origination is the only thing that could actually ground the kind of strong free will that is regularly believed in.

The Pessimists' argument may seem contrived, but essentially the same argument can be given in a more natural form as follows. (A) One is the way one is, initially, as a result of heredity and early experience. (B) These are clearly things for which one cannot be held to be in any way responsible (this might not be true if there were reincarnation, but this would just shift the problem backwards). (C) One cannot at any later stage of one's life hope to accede to ultimate responsibility for the way one is by trying to change the way one already is as a result of heredity and experience. For one may well try to change oneself, but (D) both the particular way in which one is moved to try to change oneself, and the degree of one's success in one's attempt at change, will be determined by how one already is as a result of heredity and

---

[1][Neitzche, F. W., *Beyond Good and Evil*, trans. W. Kaufman (New York: Random House, 1966), Section 21.–Ed.]

experience. And (E) any further changes that one can bring about only after one has brought about certain initial changes will in turn be determined, via the initial changes, by heredity and previous experience. (F) This may not be the whole story, for it may be that some changes in the way one is are traceable to the influence of indeterministic or random factors. But (G) it is absurd to suppose that indeterministic or random factors, for which one is *ex hypothesi* in no way responsible, can in themselves contribute to one's being truly or ultimately responsible for how one is.

The claim, then, is not that people cannot change the way they are. They can, in certain respects (which tend to be exaggerated by North Americans and under-estimated, perhaps, by members of other cultures). The claim is only that people cannot be supposed to change themselves in such a way as to be or become ulti-mately responsible for the way they are, and hence for their actions. One can put the point by saying that in the final analysis the way you are is, in every last detail, a matter of luck—good or bad.

Philosophers will ask what exactly this "ultimate" responsibility is supposed to be. They will suggest that it doesn't really make sense, and try to move from there to the claim that it can't really be what we have in mind when we talk about moral responsibility. It is very clear to most people, however, and one dramatic way to characterize it is by reference to the story of heaven and hell: it is responsi-bility of such a kind that, if we have it, it makes sense to propose that it could be just to punish some of us with torment in hell and reward others with bliss in heaven. It makes sense because what we do is absolutely up to us. The words "makes sense" are stressed because one doesn't have to believe in the story of heaven and hell in order to understand the notion of ultimate responsibility that it is used to illustrate. Nor does one have to believe in it in order to believe in ultimate responsibility (many atheists have done so).

The story is useful because it illustrates the kind of absolute or ultimate respon-sibility that many have supposed—and do suppose—themselves to have. (Another way to characterize it is to say that it exists if punishment and reward can be fair with-out having any pragmatic—or indeed aesthetic—justification.) But one doesn't have to appeal to it when describing the sorts of everyday situations that are primarily influential in giving rise to our belief in ultimate responsibility. Suppose you set off for a shop on the evening of a national holiday, intending to buy a cake with your last ten pound note. Everything is closing down. There is one cake left; it costs ten pounds. On the steps of the shop someone is shaking an Oxfam tin. You stop, and it seems completely clear to you that it is entirely up to you what you do next: you are truly, radically free to choose, in such a way that you will be ultimately respon-sible for whatever you do choose. You can put the money in the tin, or go in and buy the cake, or just walk away. You are not only completely free to choose. You are not free not to choose.

Standing there, you may believe determinism is true: you may believe that in five minutes time you will be able to look back on the situation you are now in and say, of what you will by then have done, "It was determined that I should do that." But even if you do wholeheartedly believe this, it does not seem to touch your current sense of the absoluteness of your freedom and moral responsibility.

One diagnosis of this phenomenon is that one can't really believe that determinism is true, in such situations, and also can't help thinking that its falsity might make freedom possible. But the feeling of ultimate responsibility seems to remain inescapable even if this is not so. Suppose one fully accepts the Pessimists' argument that no one can be *causa sui*, and that one has to be *causa sui* (in certain crucial mental respects) in order to be ultimately responsible for one's actions. This does not seem to have any impact on one's sense of one's radical freedom and responsibility, as one stands there, wondering what to do. One's radical responsibility seems to stem simply from the fact that one is fully conscious of one's situation, and knows that one can choose, and believes that one action is morally better than the other. This seems to be immediately enough to confer full and ultimate responsibility. And yet it cannot really do so, according to the Pessimists. For whatever one actually does, one will do what one does because of the way one is, and the way one is is something for which one neither is nor can be responsible, however self-consciously aware of one's situation one is.

The Pessimists' argument is hard to stomach (even Hitler is let off the hook), and one challenge to it runs as follows. "Look, the reason why one can be ultimately responsible for what one does is that one's self is, in some crucial sense, independent of one's general mental nature (character or motivational structure). Suppose one faces a difficult choice between *A*, doing one's moral duty, and *B*, following one's desires. You Pessimists describe this situation as follows: Given one's mental nature, you say, one responds in a certain way. One is swayed by reasons for and against both *A* and *B*. One tends towards *A* or *B*, and in the end one does one or the other, given one's mental nature, which is something for which one cannot be ultimately responsible. But this description of yours forgets the self—it forgets what one might call 'the agent-self.' As an agent-self, one is in some way independent of one's mental nature. One's mental nature inclines one to do one thing rather than another, but it does not thereby necessitate one to do one thing rather than the other (to use Leibniz's terms). As an agent-self, one incorporates a power of free decision that is independent of all the particularities of one's mental nature in such a way that one can after all count as ultimately morally responsible in one's decisions and actions even though one is not ultimately responsible for any aspect of one's mental nature."

The Pessimists are unimpressed: "Even if one grants the validity of this conception of the agent-self for the sake of argument," they say, "it cannot help. For if the agent-self decides in the light of the agent's mental nature but is not determined by the agent's mental nature, the following question immediately arises: Why does the dear old agent-self decide as it does? The general answer is clear. Whatever it decides, it decides as it does because of the overall way it is, and this necessary truth returns us to where we started: somehow, the agent-self is going to have to get to be responsible for being the way it is, in order for its decisions to be a source of ultimate responsibility. But this is impossible: nothing can be *causa sui* in the required way. Whatever the nature of the agent-self, it is ultimately a matter of luck. Maybe the agent-self decides as it does partly or wholly because of the presence of indeterministic occurrences in the decision process. Maybe, maybe not. It makes no difference, for indeterministic occurrences can never contribute to ultimate moral responsibility."

Some think they can avoid this debate by asserting that free will and moral responsibility are just a matter of being governed by reason—or by Reason with a dignifying capital "R." But being governed by Reason can't be the source of ultimate responsibility. It can't be a property that makes punishment ultimately just or fair for those who possess it, and unfair for those who don't. For to be morally responsible, on this view, is simply to possess one sort of motivational set among others. But if you do possess this motivational set then you are simply lucky—if it is indeed a good thing—while those who lack it are unlucky.

This will be denied. It will be said, truly, that some people struggle to become more morally responsible, and make an enormous effort. Their moral responsibility is then not a matter of luck: it is their own hard won achievement. The Pessimists' reply is immediate. "Suppose you are someone who struggles to be morally responsible, and make an enormous effort. Well, that too is a matter of luck. You are lucky to be someone who has a character of a sort that disposes you to make that sort of effort. Someone who lacks a character of that sort is merely unlucky."

In the end, luck swallows everything: this is one (admittedly contentious) way of putting the point that there can be no ultimate responsibility, given the natural, strong conception of responsibility that was characterized by reference to the story of heaven and hell. Relative to that conception, no punishment or reward is ever ultimately just or fair, however natural or useful or otherwise humanly appropriate it may be or seem.

The free will problem is like a carousel. One starts with the Compatibilist position. . . . But it cannot satisfy our intuitions about moral responsibility. . . . So it seems that an Incompatibilist and indeed Libertarian account of free will is needed, according to which free will requires the falsity of determinism. . . . But any such account immediately triggers the Pessimists' objection that indeterministic occurrences cannot possibly contribute to moral responsibility. . . . For one can hardly be supposed to be more truly morally responsible for one's choices and actions or character if indeterministic or random occurrences have played a part in their causation than if they have not played such a part. . . . But what this shows is that the Incompatibilists' "ultimate" moral responsibility is obviously impossible. . . . But that means that we should return to Compatibilism, since it is the best we can do. . . . But Compatibilism cannot possibly satisfy our intuitions about moral responsibility. . . .

What should we do? Get off the metaphysical merry-go-round, and take up psychology. The principal positions in the traditional debate are clear. No radically new options are likely to emerge after millennia of debate, and the interesting questions that remain are primarily psychological: Why exactly do we believe we have ultimate responsibility of the kind that can be characterized by reference to the story of heaven and hell? What is it like to live with this belief? What are its varieties? How might we be changed by dwelling intensely on the view that ultimate responsibility is impossible?

One reason for the belief has already been given: it has to do with the way we experience choice, as self-conscious agents confronting the Oxfam box and the cake. And this raises the interesting question whether all self-conscious agents who face choices and are fully self-consciously aware of the fact that they do so must experience themselves as having strong free will, or as being radically self-determining? We human beings cannot experience our choices as determined, even if determinism is true, but perhaps this is a human peculiarity, not an inescapable feature of any possible self-conscious agent. And perhaps it is not even universal among human beings: Krishnamurti claims that "a truly intelligent [spiritually advanced] mind simply cannot have choice" because it "can . . . only choose the path of truth. . . . Only the unintelligent mind has free will," and a related thought is expressed by Saul Bellow in *Humboldt's Gift:* "In the next realm, where things are clearer, clarity eats into freedom. We are free on earth because of cloudiness, because of error, because of marvellous limitation." Spinoza extends the point to God, who cannot, he says, "be said . . . to act from freedom of the will."

Other causes of our belief in strong free will have been suggested, apart from the cake and the Oxfam box. Hume stresses our experience of indecision. Kant holds that our experience of moral obligation makes belief in strong free will inevitable. P. F. Strawson argues that our belief in freedom is grounded in certain fundamental natural reactions to other people—such as gratitude and resentment—that we cannot hope to give up. Those who think hard about free will are likely to conclude that the complex moral psychology of the experience of freedom is the most fruitful area of research. New generations, however, will continue to launch themselves onto the old carousel, and the debate is likely to continue for as long as human beings can think, as the Pessimists' argument that we can't possibly have strong free will keeps bumping into the fact that we can't help believing that we do.

The facts are clear, and they have been known for a long time. When it comes to the metaphysics of free will, Andre Gide's remark is apt: "Everything has been said before, but since nobody listens we have to keep going back and beginning all over again." It seems the only freedom that we can have is Compatibilist freedom. If—since—that is not enough for ultimate responsibility, we cannot have ultimate responsibility.

The debate continues, and some have thought that philosophy ought to move on. There is little reason to expect that it will, as new minds are seduced by the problem. And yet the facts are clear. One cannot be ultimately responsible for one's character or mental nature in any way at all. Heracleitus, Novalis, George Eliot, Nietzsche, Henry James, and others are not quite right in so far as they say (in their various ways) that character is destiny; for external circumstances are also part of destiny. But the point seems good, and final, when it comes to the question of ultimate moral responsibility.

9. Fate

Richard Taylor

Richard Taylor (1919–   ), emeritus professor of philosophy at the University of Rochester, has written highly acclaimed books and articles on a variety of philosophical problems.

We are all, at certain moments of pain, threat, or bereavement, apt to entertain the idea of fatalism, the thought that what is happening at a particular moment is unavoidable, that we are powerless to prevent it. Sometimes we find ourselves in circumstances not of our own making, in which our very being and destinies are so thoroughly anchored that the thought of fatalism can be quite overwhelming, and sometimes consoling. One feels that whatever then happens, however good or ill, will be what those circumstances yield, and we are helpless. Soldiers, it is said, are sometimes possessed by such thoughts. Perhaps everyone would feel more inclined to them if they paused once in a while to think of how little they ever had to do with bringing themselves to wherever they have arrived in life, how much of their fortunes and destinies were decided for them by sheer circumstance, and how the entire course of their lives is often set, once and for all, by the most trivial incidents, which they did not produce and could not even have foreseen. If we are free to work out our destinies at all, which is doubtful, we have a freedom that is at best exercised within exceedingly narrow paths. All the important things—when we are born, of what parents, into what culture, whether we are loved or rejected, whether we are male or female, our temperament, our intelligence or stupidity, indeed everything that makes for the bulk of our happiness and misery—all these are decided for us by the most casual and indifferent circumstances, by sheer coincidences, chance encounters, and seemingly insignificant fortuities. One can see this in retrospect if he searches, but few search. The fate that has given us our very being has given us also our pride and conceit, and has thereby formed us so that, being human we congratulate ourselves on our blessings, which we call our achievements; blame the world for our blunders, which we call our misfortunes; and scarcely give a thought to that impersonal fate that arbitrarily dispenses both.

Fatalism and Determinism

Determinism, it will be recalled, is the theory that all events are rendered unavoidable by their causes. The attempt is sometimes made to distinguish this from fatalism by saying that, according to the fatalist, certain events are going to happen *no*

Metaphysics 3/e by Richard Taylor, © 1974. Reprinted by permission of Pearson Education, Inc., Upper Saddle River, NJ.

matter what, or in other words, regardless of causes. But this is enormously contrived. It would be hard to find in the whole history of thought a single fatalist, on that conception of it.

Fatalism is the belief that whatever happens is unavoidable. That is the clearest expression of the doctrine, and it provides the basis of the attitude of calm acceptance that the fatalist is thought, quite correctly, to embody. One who endorses the claim of universal causation, then, and the theory of the causal determination of all human behavior, is a kind of fatalist—or at least he should be, if he is consistent. For that theory, as we have seen, once it is clearly spelled out and not hedged about with unresolved "ifs," does entail that whatever happens is rendered inevitable by the causal conditions preceding it, and is therefore unavoidable. One can indeed think of verbal formulas for distinguishing the two theories, but if we think of a fatalist as one who has a certain attitude, we find it to be the attitude that a thoroughgoing determinist should, in consistency, assume. That some philosophical determinists are not fatalists does not so much illustrate a great difference between fatalism and determinism but rather the humiliation to one's pride that a fatalist position can deliver, and the comfort that can sometimes be found in evasion.

Fatalism with Respect to the Future and the Past

A fatalist, then, is someone who believes that whatever happens is and always was unavoidable. He thinks it is not up to him what will happen a thousand years hence, next year, tomorrow, or the very next moment. Of course he does not pretend always to *know* what is going to happen. Hence, he might try sometimes to read signs and portents, as meteorologists and astrologers do, or to contemplate the effects upon him of the various things that might, for all he knows, be fated to occur. But he does not suppose that whatever happens could ever have really been avoidable.

A fatalist thus thinks of the future in the way we all think of the past, for everyone is a fatalist as he looks *back* on things. To a large extent we know what has happened—some of it we can even remember—whereas the future is still obscure to us, and we are therefore tempted to imbue it, in our imagination, with all sorts of "possibilities." The fatalist resists this temptation, knowing that mere ignorance can hardly give rise to any genuine possibility in things. He thinks of both past and future "under the aspect of eternity," the way God is supposed to view them. We all think of the past this way, as something settled and fixed, to be taken for what it is. We are never in the least tempted to try to modify it. It is not in the least up to us what happened last year, yesterday, or even a moment ago, any more than are the motions of the heavens or the political developments in Tibet. If we are not fatalists, then we might think that past things once *were* up to us, to bring about or prevent, as long as they were still future—but this expresses our attitude toward the future, not the past.

Such is surely our conception of the whole past, whether near or remote. But the consistent fatalist thinks of the future in the same way. We say of past things that they are no longer within our power. The fatalist says they never were.

The Sources of Fatalism

A fatalistic way of thinking most often arises from theological ideas, or from what are generally thought to be certain presuppositions of science and logic. Thus, if God is really all-knowing and all-powerful, it is not hard to suppose that He has arranged for everything to happen just as it is going to happen, that He already knows every detail of the whole future course of the world, and there is nothing left for you and me to do except watch things unfold, in the here or the hereafter. But without bringing God into the picture, it is not hard to suppose, as we have seen, that everything that happens is wholly determined by what went before it, and hence that whatever happens at any future time is the only thing that can then happen, given what precedes it. Or even disregarding that, it seems natural to suppose that there is a body of truth concerning what the future holds, just as there is such truth concerning what is contained in the past, whether or not it is known to any person or even to God, and hence, that everything asserted in that body of truth will assuredly happen, in the fullness of time, precisely as it is described therein.

No one needs to be convinced that fatalism is the only proper way to view the past. That it is also the proper way to view the future is less obvious, due in part, perhaps, to our vastly greater ignorance of what the future holds. The consequences of holding such fatalism are obviously momentous. To say nothing of the consolation of fatalism, which enables a person to view all things as they arise with the same undisturbed mind with which he contemplates even the most revolting of history's horrors, the fatalist teaching also relieves one of all tendency toward both blame and approbation of others and of both guilt and conceit in himself. It promises that a perfect understanding is possible and removes the temptation to view things in terms of human wickedness and moral responsibility. This thought alone, once firmly grasped, yields a sublime acceptance of all that life and nature offer, whether to oneself or one's fellows; and although it thereby reduces one's pride, it simultaneously enhances the feelings, opens the heart, and expands the understanding.

Divine Omniscience

Suppose for the moment, just for the purpose of this discussion, that God exists and is omniscient. To say that God is omniscient means that He knows everything that is true. He cannot, of course, know that which is false. Concerning any falsehood, an omniscient being can know that it is false; but then it is a truth that is known, namely, the truth that the thing in question is a falsehood. So if it is false that the moon is a cube, then God can, like you or me, know that this is false; but He cannot know the falsehood itself, that the moon is a cube.

Thus, if God is omniscient He knows, as you probably do, the date of your birth. He also knows, as you may not, the hour of your birth. Furthermore, God knows, as you assuredly do not, the date of your conception—for there is such a truth, and we are supposing that God knows every truth. Moreover, He knows as you surely do not, the date of your death, and the circumstances thereof—whether at that moment, known already to Him, you die as the result of accident, a fatal malady, suicide, murder, whatever. And, still assuming God exists and knows everything, He knows whether any ant walked across my desk last night, and if so, what ant it was, where it came from, how long it was on the desk, how it came to be there, and so on, to every truth about this insect that there is. Similarly, of course, He knows when some ant will again appear on my desk, if ever. He knows the number of hairs on my head, notes the fall of every sparrow, knows why it fell, and why it was going to fall. These are simply a few of the consequences of the omniscience that we are for the moment assuming. A more precise way of expressing all this is to say that God knows, concerning any statement whatever that anyone could formulate, that it is true, in case it is, and otherwise, that it is false. And let us suppose that God, at some time or other, or perhaps from time to time, vouchsafes some of his knowledge to people, or perhaps to certain chosen persons. Thus prophets arise, proclaiming the coming of certain events, and things do then happen as they have foretold. Of course it is not surprising that they should, on the supposition we are making, namely, that the foreknowledge of these things comes from God, who is omniscient.

The Story of Osmo

Now, then, let us make one further supposition, which will get us squarely into the philosophical issue these ideas are intended to introduce. Let us suppose that God has revealed a particular set of facts to a chosen scribe who, believing (correctly) that they came from God, wrote them all down. The facts in question then turned out to be all the more or less significant episodes in the life of some perfectly ordinary man named Osmo. Osmo was entirely unknown to the scribe, and in fact to just about everyone, but there was no doubt concerning whom all these facts were about, for the very first thing received by the scribe from God, was: "He of whom I speak is called Osmo." When the revelations reached a fairly voluminous bulk and appeared to be completed, the scribe arranged them in chronological order and assembled them into a book. He at first gave it the title *The Life of Osmo, as Given by God*, but thinking that people would take this to be some sort of joke, he dropped the reference to God.

The book was published but attracted no attention whatsoever, because it appeared to be nothing more than a record of the dull life of a very plain man named Osmo. The scribe wondered, in fact, why God had chosen to convey such a mass of seemingly pointless trivia.

The book eventually found its way into various libraries, where it gathered dust until one day a high school teacher in Indiana, who rejoiced under the name of Osmo, saw a copy on the shelf. The title caught his eye. Curiously picking it up and blowing the dust off, he was thunderstruck by the opening sentence: "Osmo is born in Mercy Hospital in Auburn, Indiana, on June 6, 1942, of Finnish parentage, and after nearly losing his life from an attack of pneumonia at the age of five, he is enrolled in the St. James school there." Osmo turned pale. The book nearly fell from his hands. He thumbed back in excitement to discover who had written it.

Nothing was given of its authorship nor, for that matter, of its publisher. His questions of the librarian produced no further information, he being as ignorant as Osmo of how the book came to be there.

So Osmo, with the book pressed tightly under his arm, dashed across the street for some coffee, thinking to compose himself and then examine this book with care. Meanwhile he glanced at a few more of its opening remarks, at the things said there about his difficulties with his younger sister, how he was slow in learning to read, of the summer on Mackinac Island, and so on. His emotions now somewhat quieted, Osmo began a close reading. He noticed that everything was expressed in the present tense, the way newspaper headlines are written. For example, the text read, "Osmo is born in Mercy Hospital," instead of saying he was born there, and it recorded that he quarrels with his sister, is a slow student, is fitted with dental braces at age eight, and so on, all in the journalistic present tense. But the text itself made quite clear approximately when all these various things happened, for everything was in chronological order, and in any case each year of its subject's life constituted a separate chapter and was so titled—"Osmo's Seventh Year," "Osmo's Eighth Year," and so on through the book.

Osmo became absolutely engrossed, to the extent that he forgot his original astonishment, bordering on panic, and for a while even lost his curiosity concerning authorship. He sat drinking coffee and reliving his childhood, much of which he had all but forgotten until the memories were revived by the book now before him. He had almost forgotten about the kitten, for example, and had entirely forgotten its name, until he read, in the chapter called "Osmo's Seventh Year," this observation: "Sobbing, Osmo takes Fluffy, now quite dead, to the garden, and buries her next to the rose bush." Ah yes! And then there was Louise, who sat next to him in the eighth grade—it was all right there. And how he got caught smoking one day. And how he felt when his father died. On and on. Osmo became so absorbed that he quite forgot the business of the day, until it occurred to him to turn to Chapter 26, to see what might be said there, he having just recently turned twenty-six. He had no sooner done so than his panic returned, for lo! what the book said was *true!* That it rains on his birthday for example, that his wife fails to give him the binoculars he had hinted he would like, that he receives a raise in salary shortly thereafter, and so on. Now how in God's name, Osmo pondered, could anyone know that apparently before it had happened? For these were quite recent events, and the book had dust on it. Quickly moving on, Osmo came to this: "Sitting and reading in the coffee shop across from the library, Osmo, perspiring copiously, entirely forgets, until it is too late, that he is supposed to collect his wife at the hairdresser's at four." Oh my god! He had forgotten all about that. Yanking out his watch, Osmo discovered that it was nearly five o'clock—too late. She would be on her way home by now, and in a very sour mood.

Osmo's anguish at this discovery was nothing, though, compared with what the rest of the day held for him. He poured more coffee, and it now occurred to him to check the number of chapters in this amazing book: only twenty-nine! But surely, he thought, that doesn't mean anything. How anyone could have gotten all this stuff down so far was puzzling enough, to be sure, but no one on God's earth could possibly know in advance how long this or that person is going to live. (Only God could know that sort of thing, Osmo reflected.) So he read along; though not without considerable uneasiness and even depression, for the remaining three chapters were on the whole discouraging. He thought he had gotten that ulcer under control, for example. And he didn't see any reason to suppose his job was going to turn out that badly, or that he was really going to break a leg skiing; after all, he could just give up skiing. But then the book ended on a terribly dismal note. It said: "And Osmo, having taken Northwest flight 569 from O'Hare, perishes when the aircraft crashes on the runway at Fort Wayne, with considerable loss of life, a tragedy rendered the more calamitous by the fact that Osmo had neglected to renew his life insurance before the expiration of the grace period." And that was all. That was the end of the book.

So *that's* why it had only twenty-nine chapters. Some idiot thought he was going to get killed in a plane crash. But, Osmo thought, he just wouldn't get on that plane. And this would also remind him to keep his insurance in force.

(About three years later our hero, having boarded a flight for St. Paul, went berserk when the pilot announced they were going to land at Fort Wayne instead. According to one of the flight attendants, he tried to hijack the aircraft and divert it to another airfield. The Civil Aeronautics Board cited the resulting disruptions as contributing to the crash that followed as the plane tried to land.)

Four Questions

Osmo's extraordinary circumstances led him to embrace the doctrine of fatalism. Not quite completely, perhaps, for there he was, right up to the end, trying vainly to buck his fate—trying, in effect, to make a fool of God, though he did not know this, because he had no idea of the book's source. Still, he had the overwhelming evidence of his whole past life to make him think that everything was going to work out exactly as described in the book. It always had. It was, in fact, precisely this conviction that terrified him so.

But now let us ask these questions, in order to make Osmo's experiences more relevant to our own. First, why did he become, or nearly become, a fatalist? Second, just what did his fatalism amount to? Third, was his belief justified in terms of the evidence he had? And finally, is that belief justified in terms of the evidence we have—or in other words, should we be fatalists too?

This last, of course, is the important metaphysical question, but we have to approach it through the others.

Why did Osmo become a fatalist? Osmo became a fatalist because there existed a set of true statements about the details of his life, both past and future, and he came to know what some of these statements were and to believe them, including many concerning the future. That is the whole of it.

No theological ideas entered into his conviction, nor any presuppositions about causal determinism, the coercion of his actions by causes, or anything of this sort. The foundations of Osmo's fatalism were entirely in logic and epistemology, having to do only with truth and knowledge. Ideas about God did not enter in, for he never suspected that God was the ultimate source of those statements. And at no point did he think God was *making* him do what he did. All he was concerned about was that someone seemed somehow to *know* what he had done and was going to do.

What, then, did Osmo believe? He did not, it should be noted, believe that certain things were going to happen to him *no matter what*. That does not express a logically coherent belief. He did not think he was in danger of perishing in an airplane crash even in case he did not get into any airplane, for example, or that he was going to break his leg skiing, whether he went skiing or not. No one believes what he considers to be plainly impossible. If anyone believes that a given event is going to happen, he does not doubt that those things necessary for its occurrence are going to happen too. The expression "no matter what," by means of which some philosophers have sought an easy and even childish refutation of fatalism, is accordingly highly inappropriate in any description of the fatalist conviction.

Osmo's fatalism was simply the realization that the things described in the book were unavoidable.

Of course we are all fatalists in this sense about some things, and the metaphysical question is whether this familiar attitude should not be extended to everything. We know the sun will rise tomorrow, for example, and there is nothing we can do about it. Each of us knows he is sooner or later going to die, too, and there is nothing to be done about that either. We normally do not know just when, of course, but it is mercifully so! For otherwise we would sit simply checking off the days as they passed, with growing despair, like a man condemned to the gallows and knowing the hour set for his execution. The tides ebb and flow, and heavens revolve, the seasons follow in order, generations arise and pass, and no one speaks of taking preventive measures. With respect to those things each of us recognizes as beyond his control, we are of necessity fatalists.

The question of fatalism is simply: Of all the things that happen in the world, which, if any, are avoidable? And the philosophical fatalist replies: None of them. They never were. Some of them only seemed so.

Was Osmo's fatalism justified? Of course it was. When he could sit right there and read a true description of those parts of his life that had not yet been lived, it would be idle to suggest to him that his future might, nonetheless, contain alternative possibilities. The only doubts Osmo had were whether those statements could really be true. But here he had the proof of his own experience, as one by one they were tested. Whenever he tried to prevent what was set forth, he of course failed. Such failure, over and over, of even the most herculean efforts, with never a single success, must surely suggest, sooner or later, that he was *destined* to fail. Even to the end, when Osmo tried so desperately to save himself from the destruction described in the book, his effort was totally in vain—as he should have realized it was going to be had he really known that what was said there was true. No power in heaven or earth can render false a statement that is true. It has never been done, and never will be.

Is the doctrine of fatalism, then, true? This amounts to asking whether our circumstances are significantly different from Osmo's. Of course we cannot read our own biographies the way he could. Only people who become famous ever have their lives recorded, and even so, it is always in retrospect. This is unfortunate. It is too bad that someone with sufficient knowledge—God, for example—cannot set down the lives of great men in advance, so that their achievements can be appreciated better by their contemporaries, and indeed, by their predecessors—their parents, for instance. But mortals do not have the requisite knowledge, and if there are any gods who do, they seem to keep it to themselves.

None of this matters, as far as our own fatalism is concerned. For the important thing to note is that, of the two considerations that explain Osmo's fatalism, only one of them was philosophically relevant, and that one applies to us no less than to him. The two considerations were: (1) there existed a set of true statements about his life, both past and future, and (2) he came to know what those statements were and to believe them. Now the second of these two considerations explains why, as a matter of psychological fact, Osmo became fatalistic, but it has nothing to do with the validity of that point of view. Its validity is assured by (1) alone. It was not the fact that the statements happened to be written down that rendered the things they described unavoidable; that had nothing to do with it at all. Nor was it the fact that, because they had been written, Osmo could read them. His reading them and coming to believe them likewise had nothing to do with the inevitability of what they described. This was ensured simply by there being such a set of statements, whether written or not, whether read by anyone or not, and whether or not known to be true. All that is required is that they should *be* true.

Each of us has but one possible past, described by that totality of statements about us in the past tense, each of which happens to be true. No one ever thinks of rearranging things there; it is simply accepted as given. But so also, each of us has but one possible future, described by that totality of statements about oneself in the future sense, each of which happens to be true. The sum of these constitutes one's biography. Part of it has been lived. The main outlines of it can still be seen, in retrospect, though most of its details are obscure. The other part has not been lived, though it most assuredly is going to be, in exact accordance with the set of statements just referred to. Some of its outlines can already be seen, in prospect, but it is on the whole more obscure than the part belonging to the past. We have at best only premonitory glimpses of it. It is no doubt for this reason that not all of this part, the part that awaits us, is perceived as given, and people do sometimes speak absurdly of altering it—as though what the future holds, as identified by any true statement in the future tense, might after all *not* hold.

Osmo's biography was all expressed in the present tense because all that mattered was that the things referred to were real events; it did not matter to what part of time they belonged. His past consisted of those things that preceded his reading of the book, and he simply accepted it as a given. He was not tempted to revise what was said there, for he was sure it was true. But it took the book to make him realize that his future was also something given. It was equally pointless for him to try to revise what was said there, for it, too, was true. As the past contains what has happened, the future contains what will happen, and neither contains, in addition to these things, various other things that did not and will not happen.

Of course we know relatively little of what the future contains. Some things we know. We know the sun will go on rising and setting, for example, that taxes will be levied and wars will rage, that people will continue to be callous and greedy, and that people will be murdered and robbed. It is only the details that remain to be discovered. But the same is true of the past; it is only a matter of degree. When I meet a total stranger, I do not know, and will probably never know, what his past has been, beyond certain obvious things—that he had a mother, and things of this sort. I know nothing of the particulars of that vast realm of fact that is unique to his past. And the same for his future, with only this difference—that *all* people are strangers to me as far as their futures are concerned, and here I am even a stranger to myself.

Yet there is one thing I know concerning any stranger's past and the past of everything under the sun; namely, that whatever it might hold, there is nothing anyone can do about it now. What has happened cannot be undone. The mere fact that it has happened guarantees this.

And so it is, by the same token, of the future of everything under the sun. Whatever the future might hold, there is nothing anyone can do about it now. What will happen cannot be altered. The mere fact that it is going to happen guarantees this.

The Law of Excluded Middle

The presupposition of fatalism is therefore nothing but the commonest presupposition of all logic and inquiry; namely, that there is such a thing as truth, and that this has nothing at all to do with the passage of time. Nothing *becomes* true or *ceases* to be true; whatever is truth at all simply *is* true.

It comes to the same thing, and is perhaps more precise, to say that every meaningful statement, whether about oneself or anything else, is either true or else it is false; that is, its denial is true. There is no middle ground. The principle is thus appropriately called *the law of excluded middle*. It has nothing to do with what tense a statement happens to express, nor with the question of whether anyone, man or god, happens to know whether it is true or false.

Thus no one knows whether there was an ant on my desk last night, and no one ever will. But we do know that either this statement is true or else its denial is true—there is no third alternative. If we say it *might* be true, we mean only that we do not happen to know. Similarly, no one knows whether or not there is going to be an ant there tonight, but we do know that either it will or else it will not be there.

In a similar way we can distinguish two mutually exclusive but exhaustive classes of statements about any person; namely, the class of all those that are true, and the class of all that are false. There are no others in addition to these. Included in each are statements never asserted or even considered by anyone, but such that, if anyone were to formulate one of them, it would either be a true statement or else a false one.

Consider, then, that class of statements about some particular person—you, let us suppose—each of which happens to be true. Their totality constitutes your biography. One combination of such statements describes the time, place, and circumstances of your birth. Another combination describes the time, place, and circumstances of your death. Others describe in detail the rises and falls of your fortunes, your achievements and failures, your joys and sorrows—absolutely everything that is true of you.

Some of these things you have already experienced, others await you. But the entire biography is there. It is not written, and probably never will be; but it is nevertheless there, all of it. If, like Osmo, you had some way of discovering those statements in advance, then like him you could hardly help becoming a fatalist. But foreknowledge of the truth would not create any truth, nor invest your philosophy with truth, nor add anything to the philosophical foundations of the fatalism that would then be so apparent to you. It would only serve to make it apparent.

Objections

This thought, and the sense of its force, have tormented and frightened people from the beginning, and thinkers whose pride sometimes exceeds their acumen and their reverence for truth have attempted every means imaginable to demolish it. There are few articles of faith upon which virtually everyone can agree, but one of them is certainly the belief in their cherished free will. Any argument in opposition to the doctrine of fate, however feeble, is immediately and uncritically embraced, as though the refutation of fatalism required only the denial of it, supported by reasons that would hardly do credit to a child. It will be worthwhile, therefore, to look briefly at some of the arguments most commonly heard.

1. One can neither foresee the future nor prove that there is any god, or even if there is, that he could know in advance the free actions of men.

The reply to this is that it is irrelevant. The thesis of fatalism rests on no theory of divination and on no theology. These ideas were introduced only illustratively.

2. True statements are not the cause of anything. Statements only entail; they do not cause, and hence threaten no man's freedom.

But this, too, is irrelevant, for the claim here denied is not one that has been made.

3. The whole argument just conflates fact and necessity into one and the same thing, treating as unavoidable that which is merely true. The fact that a given thing is going to happen implies only that it is *going* to happen, not that it *has* to. Someone might still be able to prevent it—though of course no one will.

For example, President Kennedy was murdered. This means it was true that he was going to be murdered. But it does not mean his death at that time and place was unavoidable. Someone *could* have rendered that statement false; though of course no one did.

That is probably the commonest "refutation" of fatalism ever offered. But how strong is the claim that something *can* be done, when in fact it never *has* been done in the whole history of the universe, in spite, sometimes, of the most strenuous efforts? No one has ever rendered false a statement that was true, however hard some have tried. When an attempt, perhaps a heroic attempt, is made to avoid a given calamity, and the thing in question happens anyway, at just the moment and in just the way it was going to happen, we have reason to doubt that it could have been avoided. And in fact great effort was made to save President Kennedy, for example, from the destruction toward which he was heading on that fatal day, a whole legion of bodyguards having no other mission. And it failed. True, we can say that *if* more strenuous precautions had been taken, the event would not have happened. But to this we must add *true*, they were not taken, and hence *true*, they were not going to be taken—and we have on our hands again a true statement of the kind that no man has ever had the slightest degree of success in rendering false.

4. The fatalist argument just rests on a "confusion of modalities." The fact that something is true entails only that its denial is false, not that its denial is impossible. All that is impossible is that both should be true, or both false. Thus, if the president is going to be murdered, it is certainly false that he is not—but not impossible. What is impossible is that he will be both murdered and spared.

Here again we have only a distracting irrelevancy, similar to the point just made. The fatalist argument has nothing to do with impossibility in those senses familiar to logic. It has to do with unavoidability. It is, in other words, concerned with human abilities. The fact that a statement is true does not, to be sure, entail that it is necessary, nor do all false statements express impossibilities. Nonetheless, no one is able to avoid what is truly described, however contingently, in any statement, nor to bring about what is thus falsely described. Nor can anyone convert the one to the other, making suddenly true that which was false, or vice versa. It has never been done, and it never will be. It would be a conceit indeed for someone now to suggest that he, alone among men, might be able to accomplish that feat. This inability goes far beyond the obvious impossibility of making something both true and false at once. No metaphysics turns on that simple point.

5. Perhaps it would be best, then, to discard the presupposition underlying the whole fatalist philosophy; namely, the idea that statements are true in advance of the things they describe. The future is the realm of possibilities, concerning any of which we should neither say it is true that it will happen, nor that it is false.

But, in reply, this desperate move is nothing but arbitrary fiction, resorted to for no other reason than to be rid of the detested doctrine of fatalism. What is at issue here is the very law of excluded middle, which, it is suggested, we shall be allowed to affirm only up to that point at which it threatens something dear. We shall permit it to hold for one part of time, but suddenly retract it in speaking of another, even though the future is continuously being converted to the past through sheer temporal passage.

Most surely, if the statement, made now, that President Kennedy has been murdered, is a true one, then the prediction, made before the event, that he was going to be murdered, was true too. The two statements have exactly the same content, and are in fact one and the same statement, except for the variation of tense. The fact that this statement is more easily known in retrospect than in prospect casts no doubt on its truth but only illustrates a familiar fact of epistemology. A prediction, to be sure, must await fulfillment, but it does not thereupon for the first time acquire its truth. Indeed, had it not been true from the start, it could not have been fulfilled, nor its author congratulated for having it right. Fulfillment is nothing but the occurrence of what is correctly predicted.

The law of excluded middle is not like a blank check into which we can write whatever values we please, according to our preferences. We can no more make ourselves metaphysically free and masters of our destinies by adding qualifications to this law than a poor person can make himself rich just by adding figures to his bankbook. That law pronounces every meaningful statement true, or, if not true, then false. It leaves no handy peg between these two on which one may hang his beloved freedom of will for safekeeping, nor does it say anything whatever about time.

Every single philosophical argument against the teaching of fatalism rests upon the assumption that we are free to pursue and realize various alternative future possibilities—the very thing, of course, that is at issue. When some of these possibilities have become realized and moved on into the past, the supposed alternative possibilities usually appear to have been less real than they had seemed; but this somehow does not destroy the fond notion that they were there. Metaphysics and logic are weak indeed in the face of an opinion nourished by invincible pride, and most people would sooner lose their very souls than be divested of that dignity that they imagine rests upon their freedom of will.

Invincible Fate

We shall say, therefore, of whatever happens that it was going to be that way. And this is a comfort, both in fortune and in adversity. We shall say of him who turns out bad and mean that he was going to; of him who turns out happy and blessed that he was going to; neither praising nor berating fortune, crying over what has been, lamenting what was going to be, or passing moral judgments.

Shall we, then, sit idly by, passively observing the changing scene without participation, never testing our strength and our goodness, having no hand in what happens, or in making things come out as they should? This is a question for which each will find his own answer. Some people do little or nothing with their lives and might as well never have lived, they make such a waste of it. Others do much, and the lives of a few even shine like the stars. But we knew this before we ever began talking about fate. In time we will all know of which sort we were destined to be.

Suggestions for Further Reading

Anthologies

Ekstom, Laura, ed. *Agency and Responsibility*. Boulder, Co.: Westview Press, 2001. A collection of important, recent papers on free will and determinism. These papers will be challenging to the beginning student.

Hook, Sidney, ed. *Determinism and Freedom in the Age of Modern Science*. New York: New York Univ. Press, 1958. A collection of twenty-seven articles that analyze the concepts of determinism and freedom and the significance of these concepts in physics, law, and ethics. Most of the articles will be difficult for the beginning student.

Kane, Robert, ed. *The Oxford Handbook of Free Will*. New York: Oxford Univ. Press, 2002. A collection of previously unpublished papers emphasizing recent developments. A good guide to present-day controversies and research.

Individual Works

Clemens, Samuel. "What Is Man?" in *What Is Man? and Other Essays*. New York: Harper, 1917. An interesting and amusing statement of the determinist position by a famous writer.

Cranston, Maurice. *Freedom: A New Analysis*. London: Longmans, 1953. The latter half of this book is a good discussion of the main positions and a defense of libertarianism.

D'Angelo, Edward. *The Problem of Freedom and Determinism*. Columbia: Univ. of Missouri Press, 1968. A good, clear discussion of the three major positions.

Darrow, Clarence. *Crime: Its Cause and Treatment*. New York: Crowell, 1922. A famous discussion of criminal treatment from the hard determinist viewpoint.

Dennett, Daniel C. *Elbow Room*. Cambridge: MIT Press, 1984. A prominent contemporary philosopher attempts to clarify the notion of free will.

Lamont, Corliss. *Freedom of Choice Affirmed*. New York: Horizon, 1967. A clear statement and defense of libertarianism.

Matson, Floyd W. *The Broken Image*. New York: George Braziller, 1964. A good discussion of how the hard determinist position has affected man's image of himself. There is also an examination of Skinner and other behaviorists in this connection.

O'Connor, D. J. *Free Will*. Garden City, N.Y.: Doubleday, 1971. A careful survey of the main arguments both for and against determinism.

Schopenhauer, Arthur. "Free-Will and Fatalism" in *The Pessimist's Handbook (Parerga und Paralipomena)*. Translated by T. Bailey Saunders, edited by Hazel E. Barnes. Lincoln: Univ. of Nebraska Press, 1964. A concise and forceful defense of fatalism. Schopenhauer, a clear stylist, uses many illustrations drawn from everyday human behavior and world literature in this essay intended for the general reading public.

Taylor, Richard. *Metaphysics*. 4th ed. Englewood Cliffs, N.J.: Prentice Hall, 1992. Chapter Five contains a clearly written attack on hard and soft determinism and a defense of a version of libertarianism.

Thorton, Mark. *Do We Have Free Will?* New York: St. Martin's Press, 1989. An introductory account of the major positions on the free will versus determinism controversy.

Trusted, Jennifer. *Free Will and Responsibility*. Oxford: Oxford Univ. Press, 1984. The clear style and thorough coverage make this an excellent text for undergraduates.

Encyclopedias

Dictionary of the History of Ideas: Studies of Selected Pivotal Ideas. Philip P. Weiner, editor-in-chief. New York: Scribner's, 1973. Substantial and clearly written essays emphasizing the historical development of topics discussed in this part. Designed to inform the non-specialist, each essay concludes with a select bibliography.

Encyclopedia of Philosophy. Paul Edwards, editor-in-chief. New York: Macmillan, 1967. The student will find many worthwhile articles on the subject treated in this part and excellent bibliographies.

Routledge Encyclopedia of Philosophy. Edward Craig, general editor. New York: Routledge, 1998. This ten-volume encyclopedia contains articles on all areas of philosophy and up-to-date bibliographies.

Internet Web Sites

RESEARCH NAVIGATOR (*http://www.researchnavigator.com*). This web site offers three research data bases: Ebsco Academic Journal and Abstract Data Base, *New York Times* Search by Subject Archive, and "Best of the Web" Link Library. In addition, this site provides helpful advice on how to conduct efficient and productive research from choosing a topic to polishing the final draft. Beginning philosophy students probably will find the "Best of the Web" Link Library the most appropriate place to start their research. The free access code necessary to employ Research Navigator can be found in the Prentice Hall Guide to Evaluating Online Resources. If your text did not come with this guide, please go to *www.prenhall.com/contentselect* for information on how you can purchase an access code.

EpistemeLinks (*http://www.epistemelinks.com*). This site provides many links to philosophical resources on the web.

PART TWO

God and Religion

Introduction

A question troubling many students is whether they should believe in religion. One reason for their hesitation simply to follow in the paths of their parents in this matter is their conviction that religion has failed to bring about a better world for humankind. Perhaps an even more important reason is that there appears to be no scientific manner by which the basic religious tenets can be established. The desire that one's beliefs be supported by science has its roots in the movement of Western civilization away from a religious view of the world to a scientific one. The great success of science has led many to the view that we should believe only those things that can be established in a proper scientific manner. Further, the advance of science has certainly tended to undermine any simplistic acceptance of religious doctrines and writings. The scientifically trained no longer accept, for example, the biblical accounts of creation and the Garden of Eden as literally true. Thus, it is easy to understand why so many of today's students are dubious about accepting traditional orthodox religion. In the light of modern science it appears to be a remnant of ancient superstition that will one day be completely replaced by a scientific view of the world.

Contemporary religious thinkers generally deplore the tendency to view science and religion as competing views of the world. For them, religion and science are concerned with different issues. Science is concerned with discovering the laws that are operative in the physical universe, whereas religion is concerned with issues beyond the scope of science, such as the reason for the existence of the universe, the existence of God, and the purpose of life. Since the issues with which religion is concerned are not within the scope of science, it is held to be inappropriate to demand that religious beliefs should be substantiated by scientific facts.

Must religious beliefs be supported by scientific evidence, or is it acceptable to believe without proof? Do the discoveries of modern science show that the views of the major religions are untenable? These are some of the questions that the philosopher seeks to answer about religion. The philosopher's interest in such questions arises out of the fact that religion gives answers to many of humanity's most fundamental questions about themselves and their place in the world. The philosopher wants to know if the answers are true. Thus, in examining religious views, the philosopher is concerned with their accurate assessment rather than their defense or destruction. The readings in this section show that a great diversity of opinion exists among philosophers regarding the truth and value of religion. Some hold that only in a religious framework can a foundation for morality and a meaning to life be found. Others see various religious views as not only false but a great detriment to the happiness of human beings. The student's job is to assess carefully the various positions and arguments to determine which, if any, are sound.

The basic tenet of the major Western religions is that there exists a supernatural being called "God." God is defined as being an all-good, all-knowing, all-powerful creator of the universe. God is viewed as concerned with our affairs rather than being withdrawn and aloof. For the most part, religious believers are convinced that such a God exists without inquiring into the question of scientific or rational proofs for their conviction. Yet many religious theorists believe it important to show, if possible, that the existence of God can be proven or at least shown to be probable on the basis of scientific evidence or other rational arguments. If God's existence could be proven, not only could the skeptics and atheists be converted but many who believe would feel more confident in their belief.

Numerous proofs have been offered for the existence of God. Most are of little interest to philosophers since they are clearly unsound. Typical of these widely used but unsound arguments are the argument from agreement and the argument from Scripture. The *argument from agreement* consists in attempting to show that God exists on the basis of the fact that so many people throughout the world have believed in the existence of God. It is claimed that such a widespread belief cannot be explained on any other basis than the actual existence of God. One problem with arguing in this manner is that it makes the majority opinion the basis of truth, but it is certainly well known that large majorities have been wrong. At one time, there was widespread agreement that the earth was flat. Another difficulty with this argument is that the widespread belief in God can perhaps be explained as the result of superstition, wishful thinking, or fear. If so, the belief in God would not indicate his existence but the psychological characteristics or the lack of scientific knowledge of the majority of humankind. The *argument from Scripture* attempts to prove God's existence on the basis of the fact that we have some writings (Old Testament, New Testament, Koran, and so on) that tell of God. These writings are assumed to have been inspired by God and therefore reliable. The obvious difficulty with attempting to prove God in this manner is that the events recorded in the writings must be proved to be accurate and such proof seems impossible to get. Those who doubt the existence of God will also be doubtful that the Bible was inspired by God and that the events given there are accurately reported.

In the readings that follow, some of the arguments that philosophers have considered plausible are presented. The one that will probably be most familiar to the student is the *argument from design*. According to this argument, the world is so intricately put together to maintain the existence of various types of life that it must have been designed by an extremely rational being. This argument is presented in a simple, straightforward manner in "Seven Reasons Why a Scientist Believes in God" by A. Cressy Morrison, a highly respected American scientist. Morrison argues that life does not exist by chance because the probability of all the necessary factors existing in the proper relationship would be too slight. Also, he claims that the fact that nature is so balanced that no species can conquer all the others indicates that some great intelligence planned the world. The soundness of this argument is attacked in "The Improbability of God" by Richard Dawkins, who argues that the order in the universe comes from a process of evolution by natural selection. He contends that there is strong evidence that complex objects evolved by numerous small steps over a long period of time. Although evolution cannot explain the origin of our universe, Dawkins thinks that the hypothesis that God is the originator is needlessly complex.

In "The Justification of Theism," Richard Swinburne offers a number of reasons to believe in the existence of God. His claim that God offers the simplest and best explanation for the existence and design of the universe has provoked much controversy among contemporary philosophers. Although Swinburne does not follow many other defenders of a designed universe in rejecting the theory of evolution, he believes that the various scientific laws that make evolution possible need a religious explanation. He also contends that miracles and religious experiences support a belief in God. In the absence of any contrary evidence, he believes that testimony about religious experiences should be believed.

In "Does God Exist? Reflections on Disbelief," Kai Nielsen contends that a belief in God is unreasonable. To support his contention, Nielsen not only offers objections to the traditional arguments for God's existence, but also doubts even the meaningfulness of many religious statements. Many statements about God are suspect because no experienceable state of affairs would count for or against them. Religion is not just false for Nielsen, it is harmful; its emphasis on a better life in a future world discourages people from trying to improve this world.

Some philosophers have maintained not only that God's existence is unprovable but also that we can show that God does not exist. The main attempt to show that an all-good, all-powerful God does not exist arises from a consideration of the evil that exists in the world. It seems undeniably true that bad or evil things happen. Hurricanes and floods destroy houses and crops; children are born crippled or deformed; and murderers and thieves plague our cities. The question that must be answered is this: Why does a God who has the power to eliminate such evils allow them to occur? If God is indifferent to or powerless to prevent such evils, then he is not the kind of good and all-powerful being that Western religions worship. Many theologians have argued that all of the things we call evils are allowed to occur by God for some good purpose. To defend this view, one must show that God could not have produced equally good results without these evils.

The existence of evil and its bearing on God's existence are discussed by B. C. Johnson and John Hick. In "God and the Problem of Evil," Johnson examines the traditional explanations of an all-good God's purpose for allowing evil to exist and concludes that these explanations are inadequate. He argues that a careful assessment of the possible alternatives leads to the conclusion that the existence of an all-good God is unlikely. In "The Problem of Evil," John Hick rejects the claim that no adequate explanation for the evil in the world is possible. He argues that evil is allowed to exist because God's purpose for humans in this world is not to provide them with a carefree, happy existence but to continue the process of "soul-making." To achieve full development, humans must experience and learn to overcome the problems that exist in this world.

When confronted with the difficulty of proving the existence of God, many philosophers and theologians fall back on faith as the basis for religious belief. Faith is usually thought of as belief unsupported by evidence. The contention that it is acceptable to believe the claims of religion or any other topic without evidence has not gone unchallenged. In "The Ethics of Belief," W. K. Clifford argues that it is always wrong to believe anything without evidence, since such a belief could either produce some harm or lead the holder to accept too readily other unsupported and potentially harmful beliefs. Our beliefs should be determined by an assessment of the evidence and probabilities involved, not by unfounded hopes and wishes. In contrast to this view of the value of faith, William James argues that belief without evidence is sometimes justified. In "The Will to Believe," James is careful to point out, however, that such belief is justified only in certain types of situations. He does not want to encourage the holding of unsupported beliefs in every instance where evidence is not available. Ultimately, James believes that to withhold belief on an important matter such as religion just because there is insufficient evidence of God's existence would be too cautious. Since withholding belief might cut one off from God's grace, he believes that one should run the risk of error in hopes that one's belief may be true. In assessing James's position, the student should consider whether it rests on a conception of God as a wrathful being. Would James's argument be correct if God would not punish those who do not believe without evidence? Also, it is interesting to decide if there are any areas outside religion where one should believe without evidence.

The "Problems and Puzzles" section contains two articles that raise important issues. In his autobiography, *My Confession*, Leo Tolstoy vividly described how he reached a state of utter despair because he thought that death, which is destructive of everyone and everything one loves, makes confronting and overcoming the problems of living pointless. He believed that life was a "stupid joke" and that the courageous and consistent course to end his despair was to commit suicide. He was saved from suicide and acquired a renewed interest in life only when he returned to his faith in God. His experience convinced him that such faith was the only way to provide life with any significance and value. In "Three Arguments for Nonbelief," Michael Martin presents recent arguments against a belief in God. The *argument from incoherence* attacks the view of God held by most philosophers; the *argument from nonbelief* and the *moral argument* attack the view of God found in the Bible.

Does God Exist?

10. Seven Reasons Why a Scientist Believes in God

A. Cressy Morrison

A. Cressy Morrison (1884–1951) was an astronomer and president of the New York Academy of Sciences from 1938 to 1939. He wrote a number of books on scientific topics, as well as Man Does Not Stand Alone, *from which the following article was condensed.*

We are still in the dawn of the scientific age and every increase of light reveals more brightly the handiwork of an intelligent Creator. In the 90 years since Darwin we have made stupendous discoveries; with a spirit of scientific humility and of faith grounded in the knowledge we are approaching even nearer to an awareness in God.

For myself, I count seven reasons for my faith:

First: *By unwavering mathematical law we can prove that our universe was designed and executed by a great engineering Intelligence.*

Suppose you put ten pennies, marked from one to ten, into your pocket and give them a good shuffle. Now try to take them out in sequence from one to ten, putting back the coin each time and shaking them all again. Mathematically we know that your chance of first drawing number one is one to ten; of drawing one and two in succession, one to 100; of drawing one, two, and three in succession, one in a thousand, and so on; your chance of drawing them all from number one to number ten in succession, would reach the unbelievable figure of one chance in ten billion.

By the same reasoning, so many exacting conditions are necessary for life on the earth that they could not possibly exist in proper relationship by chance. The earth rotates on its axis one thousand miles per hour; if it turned at one hundred miles an hour, our days and nights would be ten times as long as now, and the hot sun would then burn up our vegetation each long day while in the long night any surviving sprout would freeze.

Again, the sun, source of our life, has a surface temperature of 12,000 degrees Fahrenheit, and our earth is just far enough away so that this "eternal fire" warms us *just enough and not too much!* If the sun gave off only one half its present radiation, we would freeze and if it gave half as much more, we would roast.

The slant of the earth, tilted at an angle of 23 degrees, gives us our seasons; if it had not been so tilted, vapors from the ocean would move north and south, piling up for us continents of ice. If our moon was, say, only 50 thousand miles away instead of its actual distance, our tides would be so enormous that twice a day all continents would be submerged; even the mountains would soon be eroded away. If the crust of the earth had been only ten feet thicker, there would be no oxygen, without which animal life must die. Had the ocean been a few feet deeper, carbon dioxide and oxygen would have been absorbed and no vegetable life could exist. Or if our atmosphere had been much thinner, some of the meteors, now burned in space by the millions every day, would be striking all parts of the earth, setting fires everywhere.

Because of these and a host of other examples, there is not one chance in millions that life on our planet is an accident.

Second: *The resourcefulness of life to accomplish its purpose is a manifestation of all-pervading Intelligence.*

What life itself is, no man has fathomed. It has neither weight nor dimensions; but it does have force; a growing root will crack a rock. Life has conquered water, land and air, mastering the elements, compelling them to dissolve and reform their combinations.

Life, the sculptor, shapes all living things; an artist, it designs every leaf of every tree, and colors every flower. Life is a musician and has taught each bird to sing its love songs, the insects to call each other in the music of their multitudinous sounds. Life is a sublime chemist, giving taste to fruits and spices, and perfume to the rose, changing water and carbonic acid into sugar and wood, and, in so doing, releasing oxygen that animals may have the breath of life.

Behold an almost invisible drop of protoplasm, transparent, jellylike, capable of motion, drawing energy from the sun. This single cell, this transparent mistlike droplet, holds within itself the germ of life, and has the power to distribute this life to every living thing, great and small. The powers of this droplet are greater than our vegetation and animals and people, for all life came from it. Nature did not create life; fire-blistered rocks and a saltless sea could not meet the necessary requirements.

Who, then, has put it here?

Third: *Animal wisdom speaks irresistibly of a good Creator who infused instinct into otherwise helpless little creatures.*

The young salmon spends years at sea, then comes back to his own river, and travels up the very side of the river into which flows the tributary where he was born. What brings him back so precisely? If you transfer him to another tributary he will know at once that he is off his course and he will fight his way down and back to the main stream and then turn up against the current to finish his destiny accurately.

Even more difficult to solve is the mystery of eels. These amazing creatures migrate at maturity from all ponds and rivers everywhere—those from Europe across thousands of miles of ocean—all bound for the same abysmal deeps near Bermuda. There they breed and die. The little ones, with no apparent means of knowing anything except that they are in a wilderness of water, nevertheless start back and find their way not only to the very shore from which their parents came but thence to the rivers, lakes or little ponds—so that each body of water is always populated with eels. No American eel has ever been caught in Europe, no European eel in American waters. Nature has even delayed the maturity of the European eel by a year or more to make up for its longer journey. Where does the directing impulse originate?

A wasp will overpower a grasshopper, dig a hole in the earth, sting the grasshopper in exactly the right place so that he does not die but becomes unconscious and lives on as a form of preserved meat. Then the wasp will lay her eggs handily so that her children when they hatch can nibble without killing the insect on which they feed; to them dead meat would be fatal. The mother then flies away and dies; she never sees her young. Surely the wasp must have done all this right the first time and every time, else there would be no wasps. Such mysterious techniques cannot be explained by adaptation; they were bestowed.

Fourth: *Man has something more than animal instinct—the power of reason.*

No other animal has ever left a record of its ability to count to ten, or even to understand the meaning of ten. Where instinct is like a single note of a flute, beautiful but limited, the human brain contains all the notes of all the instruments in the orchestra. No need to belabor this fourth point; thanks to human reason we can contemplate the possibility that we are what we are only because we have received a spark of Universal Intelligence.

Fifth: *Provision for all living is revealed in phenomena which we know today but which Darwin did not know—such as the wonders of genes.*

So unspeakably tiny are these genes that, if all of them responsible for all living people in the world could be put in one place, there would be less than a thimbleful. Yet these ultramicroscopic genes and their companions, the chromosomes, inhabit every living cell and are the absolute keys to all human, animal, and vegetable characteristics. A thimble is a small place in which to put all the individual characteristics of two billions of human beings. However, the facts are beyond question. Well, then—how do genes lock up all the normal heredity of a multitude of ancestors and preserve the psychology of each in such an infinitely small space?

Here evolution really begins—at the cell, the entity which holds and carries the genes. How a few million atoms, locked up as an ultramicroscopic gene, can absolutely rule all life on earth is an example of profound cunning and provision that could emanate only from a Creative Intelligence; no other hypothesis will serve.

Sixth: *By the economy of nature, we are forced to realize that only infinite wisdom could have foreseen and prepared with such astute husbandry.*

Many years ago a species of cactus was planted in Australia as a protective fence. Having no insect enemies in Australia the cactus soon began a prodigious growth; the alarming abundance persisted until the plants covered an area as long and wide as England, crowding inhabitants out of towns and villages, and destroying their farms. Seeking a defense, the entomologists scoured the world; finally they turned up an insect which lived exclusively on cactus, and would eat nothing else. It would breed freely, too; and it had no enemies in Australia. So animal soon conquered vegetable and today the cactus pest has retreated, and with it all but a small protective residue of the insects, enough to hold the cactus in check forever.

Such checks and balances have been universally provided. Why have not fast-breeding insects dominated the earth? Because they have no lungs such as man possesses; they breathe through tubes. But when insects grow large, their tubes do not grow in ratio to the increasing size of the body. Hence there never has been an insect of great size; this limitation on growth has held them all in check. If this physical check had not been provided, man could not exist. Imagine meeting a hornet as big as a lion!

Seventh: *The fact that man can conceive the idea of God is in itself a unique proof.*

The conception of God rises from a divine faculty of man, unshared with the rest of our world—the faculty we call imagination. By its power, man and man alone can find the evidence of things unseen. The vista that power opens up is unbounded; indeed, as man's perfected imagination becomes a spiritual reality, he may discern in all the evidences of design and purpose the great truth that heaven is wherever and whatever; that God is everywhere and in everything but nowhere so close as in our hearts.

It is scientifically as well as imaginatively true, as the Psalmist said: *The heavens declare the glory of God and the firmament showeth His handiwork.*

11. The Improbability of God

Richard Dawkins

Richard Dawkins (1941–   ), a professor at Oxford University, is one of the leading thinkers in modern evolutionary biology. In addition to his achievements in the field of biology, he is well known for his replies to criticisms of the theory of evolution.

Much of what people do is done in the name of God. Irishmen blow each other up in his name. Arabs blow themselves up in his name. Imams and ayatollahs oppress women in his name. Celibate popes and priests mess up people's sex lives in his name. Jewish *shohets* cut live animals' throats in his name. The achievements of religion in past history—bloody crusades, torturing inquisitions, mass-murdering conquistadors, culture-destroying missionaries, legally enforced resistance to each new piece of scientific truth until the last possible moment—are even more impressive. And what has it all been in aid of? I believe it is becoming increasingly clear that the answer is absolutely nothing at all. There is no reason for believing that any sort of gods exist and quite good reason for believing that they do not exist and never have. It has all been a gigantic waste of time and a waste of life. It would be a joke of cosmic proportions if it weren't so tragic.

Why do people believe in God? For most people the answer is still some version of the ancient Argument from Design. We look about us at the beauty and intricacy of the world—at the aerodynamic sweep of a swallow's wing, at the delicacy of flowers and of the butterflies that fertilize them, through a microscope at the teeming life in every drop of pond water, through a telescope at the crown of a giant redwood tree. We reflect on the electronic complexity and optical perfection of our own eyes that do the looking. If we have any imagination, these things drive us to a sense of awe and reverence. Moreover, we cannot fail to be struck by the obvious resemblance of living organs to the carefully planned designs of human engineers. The argument was most famously expressed in the watchmaker analogy of the eighteenth-century priest William Paley. Even if you didn't know what a watch was, the obviously designed character of its cogs and springs and of how they mesh together for a purpose would force you to conclude "that the watch must have had a maker: that there must have existed, at some time, and at some place or other, an artificer or artificers, who formed it for the purpose which we find it actually to answer; who comprehended its construction, and designed its use." If this is true of a comparatively simple watch, how much the more so is it true of the eye, ear, kidney, elbow joint, brain? These beautiful, complex, intricate, and obviously purpose-built structures must have had their own designer, their own watchmaker—God.

First published in *Free Inquiry*, Spring 1998. © Council for Secular Humanism, 1998.

So ran Paley's argument, and it is an argument that nearly all thoughtful and sensitive people discover for themselves at some stage in their childhood. Throughout most of history it must have seemed utterly convincing, self-evidently true. And yet, as the result of one of the most astonishing intellectual revolutions in history, we now know that it is wrong, or at least superfluous. We now know that the order and apparent purposefulness of the living world has come about through an entirely different process, a process that works without the need for any designer and one that is a consequence of basically very simple laws of physics. This is the process of evolution by natural selection, discovered by Charles Darwin and, independently, by Alfred Russel Wallace.

What do all objects that look as if they must have had a designer have in common? The answer is statistical improbability. If we find a transparent pebble washed into the shape of a crude lens by the sea, we do not conclude that it must have been designed by an optician: the unaided laws of physics are capable of achieving this result; it is not too improbable to have just "happened." But if we find an elaborate compound lens, carefully corrected against spherical and chromatic aberration, coated against glare, and with "Carl Zeiss" engraved on the rim, we know that it could not have just happened by chance. If you take all the atoms of such a compound lens and throw them together at random under the jostling influence of the ordinary laws of physics in nature, it is *theoretically* possible that, by sheer luck, the atoms would just happen to fall into the pattern of a Zeiss compound lens, and even that the atoms round the rim should happen to fall in such a way that the name Carl Zeiss is etched out. But the number of other ways in which the atoms could, with equal likelihood, have fallen, is so hugely, vastly, immeasurably greater that we can completely discount the chance hypothesis. Chance is out of the question as an explanation.

This is not a circular argument, by the way. It might seem to be circular because, it could be said, *any* particular arrangement of atoms is, with hindsight, very improbable. As has been said before, when a ball lands on a particular blade of grass on the golf course, it would be foolish to exclaim: "Out of all the billions of blades of grass that it *could* have fallen on, the ball actually fell on this one. How amazingly, miraculously improbable!" The fallacy here, of course, is that the ball had to land somewhere. We can only stand amazed at the improbability of the actual event if we specify it *a priori*: for example, if a blindfolded man spins himself round on the tee, hits the ball at random, and achieves a hole in one. That would be truly amazing, because the target destination of the ball is specified in advance.

Of all the trillions of different ways of putting together the atoms of a telescope, only a minority would actually work in some useful way. Only a tiny minority would have Carl Zeiss engraved on them, or, indeed, *any* recognizable words of any human language. The same goes for the parts of a watch: of all the billions of possible ways of putting them together, only a tiny minority will tell the time or do anything useful. And of course the same goes, *a fortiori*, for the parts of a living body. Of all the trillions of trillions of ways of putting together the parts of a body, only an infinitesimal minority would live, seek food, eat, and reproduce. True, there are many different ways of being alive—at least ten million different ways if we count the number of distinct species alive today—but, however many ways there may be of being alive, it is certain that there are vastly more ways of being dead!

We can safely conclude that living bodies are billions of times too complicated—too statistically improbable—to have come into being by sheer chance. How, then, did they come into being? The answer is that chance enters into the story, but not a single, monolithic act of chance. Instead, a whole series of tiny chance steps, each one small enough to be a believable product of its predecessor, occurred one after the other in sequence. These small steps of chance are caused by genetic mutations, random changes—mistakes really—in the genetic material. They give rise to changes in the existing bodily structure. Most of these changes are deleterious and lead to death. A minority of them turn out to be slight improvements, leading to increased survival and reproduction. By this process of natural selection, those random changes that turn out to be beneficial eventually spread through the species and become the norm. The stage is now set for the next small change in the evolutionary process. After, say, a thousand of these small changes in series, each change providing the basis for the next, the end result has become, by a process of accumulation, far too complex to have come about in a single act of chance.

For instance, it is theoretically possible for an eye to spring into being, in a single lucky step, from nothing: from bare skin, let's say. It is theoretically possible in the sense that a recipe could be written out in the form of a large number of mutations. If all these mutations happened simultaneously, a complete eye could, indeed, spring from nothing. But although it is theoretically possible, it is in practice inconceivable. The quantity of luck involved is much too large. The "correct" recipe involves changes in a huge number of genes simultaneously. The correct recipe is one particular combination of changes out of trillions of equally probable combinations of chances. We can certainly rule out such a miraculous coincidence. But it *is* perfectly plausible that the modern eye could have sprung from something almost the same as the modern eye but not quite: a very slightly less elaborate eye. By the same argument, this slightly less elaborate eye sprang from a slightly less elaborate eye still, and so on. If you assume a *sufficiently large number of sufficiently small differences* between each evolutionary stage and its predecessor, you are bound to be able to derive a full, complex, working eye from bare skin. How many intermediate stages are we allowed to postulate? That depends on how much time we have to play with. Has there been enough time for eyes to evolve by little steps from nothing?

The fossils tell us that life has been evolving on Earth for more than 3,000 million years. It is almost impossible for the human mind to grasp such an immensity of time. We, naturally and mercifully, tend to see our own expected lifetime as a fairly long time, but we can't expect to live even one century. It is 2,000 years since Jesus lived, a time span long enough to blur the distinction between history and myth. Can you imagine a million such periods laid end to end? Suppose we wanted to write the whole history on a single long scroll. If we crammed all of Common Era history into one meter of scroll, how long would the pre-Common Era part of the scroll, back to the start of evolution, be? The answer is that the pre-Common Era part of the scroll would stretch from Milan to Moscow. Think of the implications of this for the quantity of evolutionary change that can be accommodated. All the domestic breeds of dogs—Pekingeses, poodles, spaniels, Saint Bernards, and Chihuahuas—have come from wolves in a time span measured in hundreds or at the most thousands of years: no more than two meters along the road from Milan to Moscow. Think of the quantity of change involved in going from a wolf to a Pekingese; now multiply that quantity of change by a million. When you look at it like that, it becomes easy to believe that an eye could have evolved from no eye by small degrees.

It remains necessary to satisfy ourselves that every one of the intermediates on the evolutionary route, say from bare skin to a modern eye, would have been favored by natural selection; would have been an improvement over its predecessor in the sequence or at least would have survived. It is no good proving to ourselves that there is theoretically a chain of almost perceptibly different intermediates leading to an eye if many of those intermediates would have died. It is sometimes argued that the parts of an eye have to be all there together or the eye won't work at all. Half an eye, the argument runs, is no better than no eye at all. You can't fly with half a wing; you can't hear with half an ear. Therefore there can't have been a series of step-by-step intermediates leading up to a modern eye, wing, or ear.

This type of argument is so naive that one can only wonder at the subconscious motives for wanting to believe it. It is obviously not true that half an eye is useless. Cataract sufferers who have had their lenses surgically removed cannot see very well without glasses, but they are still much better off than people with no eyes at all. Without a lens you can't focus a detailed image, but you can avoid bumping into obstacles and you could detect the looming shadow of a predator.

As for the argument that you can't fly with only half a wing, it is disproved by large numbers of very successful gliding animals, including mammals of many different kinds, lizards, frogs, snakes, and squids. Many different kinds of tree-dwelling animals have flaps of skin between their joints that really are fractional wings. If you fall out of a tree, any skin flap or flattening of the body that increases your surface area can save your life. And, however small or large your flaps may be, there must always be a critical height such that, if you fall from a tree of that height, your life would have been saved by just a little bit more surface area. Then, when your descendants have evolved that extra surface area, their lives would be saved by just a bit more still if they fell from trees of a slightly greater height. And so on by insensibly graded steps until, hundreds of generations later, we arrive at full wings.

Eyes and wings cannot spring into existence in a single step. That would be like having the almost infinite luck to hit upon the combination number that opens a large bank vault. But if you spun the dials of the lock at random, and every time you got a little bit closer to the lucky number the vault door creaked open another chink, you would soon have the door open! Essentially, that is the secret of how evolution by natural selection achieves what once seemed impossible. Things that cannot plausibly be derived from very different predecessors *can* plausibly be derived from only slightly different predecessors. Provided only that there is a sufficiently long series of such slightly different predecessors, you can derive anything from anything else.

Evolution, then, is theoretically *capable* of doing the job that, once upon a time, seemed to be the prerogative of God. But is there any evidence that evolution actually has happened? The answer is yes; the evidence is overwhelming. Millions of fossils are found in exactly the places and at exactly the depths that we should expect if evolution had happened. Not a single fossil has ever been found in any place where the evolution theory would not have expected it, although this *could* very easily have happened: a fossil mammal in rocks so old that fishes have not yet arrived, for instance, would be enough to disprove the evolution theory.

The patterns of distribution of living animals and plants on the continents and islands of the world are exactly what would be expected if they had evolved from common ancestors by slow, gradual degrees. The patterns of resemblance among animals and plants are exactly what we should expect if some were close cousins, and others more distant cousins to each other. The fact that the genetic code is the same in all living creatures overwhelmingly suggests that all are descended from one single ancestor. The evidence for evolution is so compelling that the only way to save the creation theory is to assume that God deliberately planted enormous quantities of evidence to make it *look* as if evolution had happened. In other words, the fossils, the geographical distribution of animals, and so on are all one gigantic confidence trick. Does anybody want to worship a God capable of such trickery? It is surely far more reverent, as well as more scientifically sensible, to take the evidence at face value. All living creatures are cousins of one another, descended from one remote ancestor that lived more than 3,000 million years ago.

The Argument from Design, then, has been destroyed as a reason for believing in a God. Are there any other arguments? Some people believe in God because of what appears to them to be an inner revelation. Such revelations are not always edifying but they undoubtedly feel real to the individual concerned. Many inhabitants of lunatic asylums have an unshakable inner faith that they are Napoleon or, indeed, God himself. There is no doubting the power of such convictions for those that have them, but this is no reason for the rest of us to believe them. Indeed, since such beliefs are mutually contradictory, we can't believe them all.

There is a little more that needs to be said. Evolution by natural selection explains a lot, but it couldn't start from nothing. It couldn't have started until there was some kind of rudimentary reproduction and heredity. Modern heredity is based on the DNA code, which is itself too complicated to have sprung spontaneously into being by a single act of chance. This seems to mean that there must have been some earlier hereditary system, now disappeared, which was simple enough to have arisen by chance and the laws of chemistry and which provided the medium in which a primitive form of cumulative natural selection could get started. DNA was a later product of this earlier cumulative selection. Before this original kind of natural selection, there was a period when complex chemical compounds were built up from simpler ones and before that a period when the chemical elements were built up from simpler elements, following the well-understood laws of physics. Before that, everything was ultimately built up from pure hydrogen in the immediate aftermath of the big bang, which initiated the universe.

There is a temptation to argue that, although God may not be needed to explain the evolution of complex order once the universe, with its fundamental laws of physics, had begun, we do need a God to explain the origin of all things. This idea doesn't leave God with very much to do: just set off the big bang, then sit back and wait for everything to happen. The physical chemist Peter Atkins, in his beautifully written book *The Creation*, postulates a lazy God who strove to do as little as possible in order to initiate everything. Atkins explains how each step in the history of the universe followed, by simple physical law, from its predecessor. He thus pares down the amount of work that the lazy creator would need to do and eventually concludes that he would in fact have needed to do nothing at all!

The details of the early phase of the universe belong to the realm of physics, whereas I am a biologist, more concerned with the later phases of the evolution of complexity. For me, the important point is that, even if the physicist needs to postulate an irreducible minimum that had to be present in the beginning, in order for the universe to get started, that irreducible minimum is certainly extremely simple. By definition, explanations that build on simple premises are more plausible and more satisfying than explanations that have to postulate complex and statistically improbable beginnings. And you can't get much more complex than an Almighty God!

12. The Justification of Theism

Richard Swinburne

Richard Swinburne (1934–   ), a professor at the University of Oxford, is well-known for his defense of theism and various Christian doctrines. He is the author of fourteen books and numerous scholarly articles on religion, philosophy of science, and epistemology.

Why believe that there is a God at all? My answer is that to suppose that there is a God explains why there is a world at all; why there are the scientific laws there are; why animals and then human beings have evolved; why humans have the opportunity to mould their characters and those of their fellow humans for good or ill and to change the environment in which we live; why we have the well-authenticated account of Christ's life, death, and resurrection; why throughout the centuries men have had the apparent experience of being in touch with and guided by God; and so much else. In fact, the hypothesis of the existence of God makes sense of the whole of our experience, and it does so better than any other explanation which can be put forward, and that is the grounds for believing it to be true. This paper seeks to justify this answer, it presents in summary arguments given in more detailed form in my book *The Existence of God*.[1] . . .

I. Inductive Arguments

Each of the phenomena (things in need of explanation) which I have mentioned has formed the starting point of a philosophical argument for the existence of God, but all that philosophers have tried to do is to codify in a rigorous form the vague reasons which many ordinary men have had for believing that there is a God. These arguments seem to me to have a common pattern. Some phenomenon E, which we can all observe, is considered. It is claimed that E is puzzling, strange, not to be expected in the ordinary course of things; but that E is to be expected if there is a God; for God has the power to bring about E and He might well choose to do so. Hence the occurrence of E is reason for supposing that there is a God. E may be a large phenomenon, such as the existence of the Universe, or something a lot smaller, such as our own individual religious experiences.

    The pattern of argument is one much used in science, history, and all other fields of human inquiry. A detective, for example, finds various clues—John's fingerprints

From *Truth: An International, Inter-Disciplinary Journal of Christian Thought*. Volume 3 (1991). Reprinted by permission of Christian Leadership Ministries.

[1]Oxford: Clarendon Press, 1979. The first four sections of this paper are taken from my booklet *Evidence for God*, Christian Evidence Society, London, 1986.

on a burgled safe, John having a lot of money hidden in his house, John being seen near the scene of the burglary at the time when it was committed. He then suggests that these various clues, although they just *might* have other explanations, are not in general to be expected unless John had robbed the safe. That each clue is some evidence that he did rob the safe confirms the hypothesis that John robbed the safe; and the evidence is cumulative—when put together it makes the hypothesis probable.

Let us call arguments of this kind arguments to a good explanation. Scientists use this pattern of argument to argue to the existence of unobservable entities as causes of the phenomena which they observe. For example, at the beginning of the nineteenth century, scientists observed many varied phenomena of chemical interaction, such as that substances combine in fixed ratios by weight to form new substances (for example, hydrogen and oxygen always form water in a ratio by weight of 1:8). They then claimed that these phenomena would be expected if there existed a hundred or so different kinds of atom, particles far too small to be seen, which combined and recombined in certain simple ways. In their turn physicists postulated electrons, protons, and neutrons and other particles in order to account for the behavior of the atoms, as well as for larger-scale observable phenomena; and now postulate quarks in order to explain the behavior of protons, neutrons, and most other particles.

To be good arguments (that is, to provide evidence for their hypothesis), arguments of this kind must satisfy three criteria. First, the phenomena which they cite as evidence must not be very likely to occur in the normal course of things. We saw in the burglary example how the various clues, such as John's fingerprints on the safe, were not much to be expected in the normal course of things. Secondly, the phenomena must be much more to be expected if the hypothesis is true. If John did rob the safe it is *quite* likely that his fingerprints would be found on it. Thirdly, the hypothesis must be simple. That is, it must postulate the existence and operation of *few* entities, few *kinds* of entities, with few *easily* describable properties behaving in mathematically *simple* kinds of ways. We could always postulate many new entities with complicated properties to explain anything which we find. But our hypothesis will only be supported by the evidence if it postulates few entities, which lead us to expect the diverse phenomena which form the evidence. Thus in the detective story example we could suggest that Brown planted John's fingerprints on the safe, Smith dressed up to look like John at the scene of the crime, and without any collusion with the others Robinson hid the money in John's flat. This new hypothesis would lead us to expect the phenomena which we find just as well as does the hypothesis that John robbed the safe. But the latter hypothesis is supported by the evidence whereas the former is not. And this is because the hypothesis that John robbed the safe postulates *one* object— John—doing *one* deed—robbing the safe—which leads us to expect the several phenomena which we find. Scientists always postulate as few new entities (for example, subatomic particles) as are needed to lead us to expect to find the phenomena which we observe; and they postulate that those entities do not behave erratically (behave one way one day, and a different way the next day) but that they behave in accordance with as simple and smooth a mathematical law as is compatible with what is observed. There is an old Latin saying, *simplex sigillum veri*, "The simple is the sign of the true." To be rendered probable by evidence, hypotheses must be simple.

II. Arguments from the Existence and Order of the Universe

My first phenomenon which provides evidence for the existence of God is the existence of the universe for so long as it has existed (whether a finite time or, if it has no beginning, an infinite time). This is something evidently inexplicable by science. For a scientific explanation as such explains the occurrence of one state of affairs S1 in terms of a previous state of affairs S2 and some law of nature which makes states like S2 bring about states like S1. Thus it may explain the planets being in their present positions by a previous state of the system (the Sun and planets being where they were last year) and the operation of Kepler's laws which state that states like the latter are followed a year later by states like the former. But what science by its very nature cannot explain is why there are any states of affairs at all.

My next phenomenon is the operation of the most general laws of nature, that is, the orderliness of nature in conforming to very general laws. What exactly these laws are science may not yet have discovered—perhaps they are the field equations of Einstein's General Theory of Relativity, or perhaps there are some yet more fundamental laws. Now science can explain why one law operates in some narrow area, in terms of the operation of a wider law in the particular conditions of that narrow area. Thus it can explain why Galileo's law of fall holds—that small objects near the surface of the Earth fall with a constant acceleration towards the Earth. Galileo's law follows from Newton's laws, given that the Earth is a massive body far from other massive bodies and the objects on its surface are close to it and small in mass in comparison. But what science by its very nature cannot explain is why there are the most general laws of nature that there are; for, *ex hypothesi*, no wider law can explain their operation.

That there is a Universe and that there are laws of nature are phenomena so general and pervasive that we tend to ignore them. But there might so easily not have been a Universe at all, ever. Or the Universe might so easily have been a chaotic mess. That there is an *orderly* Universe is something very striking, yet beyond the capacity of science ever to explain. Science's inability to explain these things is not a temporary phenomenon, caused by the backwardness of Twentieth Century science. Rather, because of what a *scientific* explanation is, these things will ever be beyond its capacity to explain. For scientific explanations by their very nature terminate with some ultimate natural law and ultimate arrangement of physical things, and the questions which I am raising are why there are natural laws and physical things at all.

However, there is another kind of explanation of phenomena which we use all the time and which we see as a proper way of explaining phenomena. This is what I call personal explanation. We often explain some phenomenon E as brought about by a person P in order to achieve some purpose or goal G. The present motion of my hand is explained as brought about by me for the purpose of writing a philosophical paper. The cup being on the table is explained by a man having put it there for the purpose of drinking out of it. Yet this is a different way of explaining things from the scientific. Scientific explanation involves laws of nature and previous states of affairs. Personal explanation involves persons and purposes. If we cannot give a scientific explanation of the existence and orderliness of the Universe, perhaps we can give a personal explanation.

But why should we think that the existence and orderliness of the Universe have an explanation at all? We seek for an explanation of all things; but we have seen that we have only reason for supposing that we have found one if the purported explanation is simple, and leads us to expect what we find when that is otherwise not to be expected. The history of science shows that we judge that the complex, miscellaneous, coincidental, and diverse need explaining, and that it is to be explained in terms of something simpler. The motions of the planets (subject to Kepler's laws), the mechanical interactions of bodies on Earth, the behavior of pendula, the motions of tides, the behavior of comets, and so forth formed a pretty miscellaneous set of phenomena. Newton's laws of motion constituted a simple theory which led us to expect these phenomena, and so was judged a true explanation of them. The existence of thousands of different chemical substances combining in different ratios to make other substances was complex. The hypothesis that there were only a hundred or so chemical elements of which the thousands of substances were made was a simple hypothesis which led us to expect the complex phenomenon.

Our Universe is a complex thing. There are lots and lots of separate chunks of it. The chunks have each a different finite and not very natural volume, shape, mass, and so forth—consider the vast diversity of the galaxies, stars and planets, and pebbles on the sea shore. Matter is inert and has no powers which it can choose to exert; it does what it has to do. There is a limited amount of it in any region and it has a limited amount of energy and velocity. There is a complexity, particularity, and finitude about the Universe.

The conformity of objects throughout endless time and space to simple laws is likewise something which cries out for explanation. For let us consider what this amounts to. Laws are not things, independent of material objects. To say that all objects conform to laws is simply to say that they all behave in exactly the same way. To say, for example, that the planets obey Kepler's laws is just to say that each planet at each moment of time has the property of moving in the ways that Kepler's laws state. There is therefore this vast coincidence in the behavioral properties of objects at all times and in all places. If all the coins of some region have the same markings, or all the papers in a room are written in the same handwriting, we seek an explanation in terms of a common source of these coincidences. We should seek a similar explanation for that vast coincidence which we describe as the conformity of objects to laws of nature—for example, the fact that all electrons are produced, attract and repel other particles, and combine with them in exactly the same way at each point of endless time and space.

The hypothesis of theism is that the Universe exists because there is a God who keeps it in being and that laws of nature operate because there is a God who brings it about that they do. He brings it about that the laws of nature operate by sustaining in every object in the universe its liability to behave in accord with those laws. He keeps the Universe in being by making the laws such as to conserve the matter of the Universe, that is, by making it the case at each moment that what there was before continues to exist. The hypothesis is a hypothesis that a person brings about these things for some purpose. He acts directly on the Universe, as we act directly on our brains, guiding them to move our limbs (but the Universe is not his body—for he could at any moment destroy it, and act on another universe, or do without a universe). As we have seen, personal explanation and scientific explanation are the two ways we have of explaining the occurrence of phenomena. Since there cannot be a scientific explanation of the existence of the Universe, either there is a personal explanation or there is no explanation at all. The hypothesis that there is a God is the hypothesis of the existence of the simplest kind of person which there could be. A person is a being with *power* to bring about effects, *knowledge* of how to do so, and *freedom* to make choices of which effects to bring about. God is by definition an omnipotent (that is, infinitely powerful), omniscient (that is, all-knowing), and perfectly free person; He is a person of infinite power, knowledge, and freedom; a person to whose power, knowledge, and freedom there are no limits except those of logic. The hypothesis that there exists a being with infinite degrees of the qualities essential to a being of that kind is the postulation of a very simple being. The hypothesis that there is such a God is a much simpler hypothesis than the hypothesis that there is a god who has such and such a limited power. It is simpler in just the same way that the hypothesis that some particle has zero mass or infinite velocity is simpler than the hypothesis that it has 0.32147 of some unit of mass or a velocity of 221,000 km/sec. A finite limitation cries out for an explanation of why there is just that particular limit, in a way that limitlessness does not.

That there should exist anything at all, let alone a universe as complex and as orderly as ours, is exceedingly strange. But if there is a God, it is not vastly unlikely that he should create such a universe. A universe such as ours is a thing of beauty, and a theatre in which men and other creatures can grow and work out their destiny. The orderliness of the Universe makes it a beautiful Universe, but, even more importantly, it makes it a Universe which men can learn to control and change. For only if there are simple laws of nature can men predict what will follow from what—and unless they can do that, they can never change anything. Only if men know that by sowing certain seeds, weeding and watering them, they will get corn, can they develop an agriculture. And men can only acquire that knowledge if there are easily graspable regularities of behavior in nature. So God has good reason to make an orderly Universe and, *ex hypothesi*, being omnipotent, he has the power to do so. So the hypothesis that there is a God makes the existence of the Universe much more to be expected than it would otherwise be, and it is a very simple hypothesis. Hence the arguments from the existence of the Universe and its conformity to simple natural laws are good arguments to an explanation of the phenomena, and provide substantial evidence for the existence of God.

III. The Argument from the Evolution of Animals and Men

The other phenomena which I have mentioned are also phenomena best explained by postulating the existence and creative activity of God, and so add to the cumulative case for His existence. Consider now the evolution of animals and humans. In the middle of the last century Darwin set out his impressive theory of evolution by natural selection to account for the existence of animals and humans. Animals varied in various ways from their parents (some were taller, some shorter, some fatter, some thinner, some had beginnings of a wing, others did not, and so on). Those animals with characteristics which made them best fitted to survive, survived and handed on their characteristics to the next generation. But, although in general resembling their parents, their offspring varied from them, and those variations which best fitted the animal to survive were again the ones most likely to be handed on to another generation. This process went on for millions of years producing the whole range of animals which we have today, each adapted to survive in a different environment. Among the characteristics giving advantage in the struggle for survival was intelligence, and the selections for this characteristic eventually led to the evolution of man. Such is Darwin's account of why we have today animals and men.

As far as it goes, his account is surely right. But there are two crucial matters beyond its scope. First, the evolutionary mechanism which Darwin describes only works because there are certain laws of biochemistry (animals produce many offspring, these vary in various ways from the parents, and so forth) and certain features of the environment (there is a limited amount of food, drink, space, and so on). But why are there these laws rather than other laws? Perhaps because they follow from the most fundamental laws of physics. But the question then arises as to why the fundamental laws of physics are such as to give rise to laws of evolution. If we can answer this question we should do so. There is again available the same simple answer—that there is a God who makes matter behave in accord with such laws in order to produce a world with animals and men. To develop my earlier point—God has an obvious reason for producing men. He wants there to be creatures who can share in His creative work by making choices which affect the world they live in and the other creatures who live in that world. By the way we treat our environment and our bodies, bring up our children and influence our governments, we can make this world beautiful and its other inhabitants happy and knowledgeable; or we can make it ugly and its other inhabitants miserable and ignorant. A good God will seek other beings with whom to share in his activity of creation, of forming, moulding and changing the world. The fact of a mechanism to produce men is evidence of God behind that mechanism.[2]

Secondly, Darwinian theory is concerned only with the physical characteristics of animals and men. Yet men have thoughts and feelings, beliefs and desires, and they make choices. These are events totally different from publicly

---

[2]Recent science has drawn attention to the fact that the initial conditions of the Universe (e.g., the initial velocity of recession of its components) at the time of the "Big Bang," and the physical constants (e.g., the ratio of the electron mass to the neutron mass) occurring in the laws of nature had to lie within very narrow ranges if intelligent life was to evolve. For full-length development of this theme, see J. D. Barrow and F. J. Tipler, *The Anthropic Cosmological Principle* (Oxford: Clarendon Press, 1986); and for a theistic argument developed on the basis of this evidence, see John Leslie, "Anthropic Principle, World Ensemble, Design," *American Philosophical Quarterly* 19 (1982): 141–51.

observable physical events. Physical objects are, physicists tell us, interacting colorless centers of forces; but they act on our senses, which set up electrical circuits in our brains, and these brain events cause us to have sensations (of pain or color, sound or smell), thoughts, desires and beliefs. Mental events such as these are no doubt largely caused by brain events (and vice-versa), but mental events are distinct from brain events—sensations are quite different from electro-chemical disturbances. They are in fact so different—private, colored or noisy, and felt—from public events such as brain events, that it is very, very unlikely indeed that science will ever explain how brain events give rise to mental events (why this brain event causes a red sensation, and that one a blue sensation). Yet brain events do cause mental events; no doubt there are regular correlations between this type of brain event and that type of mental event, and yet no scientific theory can say why there are the particular correlations there are, or indeed any correlations at all (why did not evolution just throw up unfeeling robots?). Yet these correlations which science cannot explain cry out for explanation of another kind. That is available. God brings it about that brain events of certain kinds give rise to mental events of certain kinds in order that animals and men may learn about the physical world, see it as imbued with color and smell making it beautiful, and learn to control it. Brain events caused by different sights, sounds, and smells give rise to different and characteristic sensations and beliefs in order that men may have knowledge of a beautiful physical world and thus have power over it. Darwinism can only explain why some animals are eliminated in the struggle for survival, not why there are animals and men at all with mental lives of sensation and belief; and in so far as it can explain anything, the question inevitably arises why the laws of evolution are as they are. All this theism can explain.

IV. Outline of Arguments from Miracles and Religious Experience

There are many reports of occasional miraculous events, events which violate laws of nature. Some of these reports are no doubt false, spread by unreliable witnesses. No doubt when men have claimed to see others levitate (float on air) or recover instantaneously from some disease, some of these reports are just false. Sometimes, too, when men have reported correctly some very strange event, although it seemed to be a violation of natural law, it was not. Magnetism might once have seemed miraculous to some people, but it is a perfectly orderly scientific phenomenon. But laying aside all such cases, there is, I suggest, a residue of apparently well-authenticated highly unusual events apparently contrary to laws of nature, but such as a God would have reason for bringing about (for example, a spontaneous cure of cancer in answer to much prayer). Above all, there is the supreme reported miracle—the Resurrection of Jesus Christ from the dead. There is no space to discuss here the historical evidence for the Resurrection (or any other reported miracle). My only point here is that in so far as there is good historical evidence of the physical resurrection of Jesus (as I believe that there is), it is evidence of the occurrence of an event which quite clearly violates the laws of nature and so calls for an explanation different from the scientific. That is available: God raised Christ from the dead to signify his acceptance of Christ's atoning sacrifice, to give his stamp of approval to his teaching, to take back Christ to Heaven where he belongs, and thereby to found a church to draw all men to himself.

Theism is able to explain the most general phenomena of science and more particular historical facts, but it is also able to explain our own individual religious experiences. To so many men it has seemed at different moments of their lives that they were aware of God and His guidance. It is a basic principle of knowledge, which I have called the principle of credulity, that we ought to believe that things are as they seem to be, until we have evidence that we are mistaken. If it seems to me that I am seeing a table or hearing my friend's voice, I ought to believe this until evidence appears that I have been deceived. If you say the contrary—never trust appearances until it is proved that they are reliable, you will never have any beliefs at all. For what would show that appearances were reliable, except more appearances? And if you can't trust appearances, you can't trust them either. Just as you must trust your five ordinary senses, so it is equally rational to trust your religious sense. An opponent may say, you trust your ordinary senses (e.g., your sense of sight) because it agrees with the senses of other men—what you claim to see they claim to see; but your religious sense does not agree with the senses of other men (they don't always have religious experiences at all, or of the same kind as you do). However, it is important to realize that the rational man applies the principle of credulity before he knows what other men experience. You rightly trust your senses even if there is no other observer to check them. And if there is another observer who reports that he seems to see what you seem to see, you have thereafter to remember that he did so report, and that means relying on your own memory (again, how things seem) without present corroboration. Anyway, religious experiences often do coincide with those of many others in their general awareness of a power beyond ourselves guiding our lives. If some men do not have our experiences, even when our experiences coincide with those of others, that suggests that the former are blind to religious realities—just as a man's inability to see colors does not show that many of us who claim to see them are mistaken, only that he is color blind. It is basic to human knowledge of the world that we believe things are as they seem to be in the absence of positive evidence to the contrary. Someone who seems to have an experience of God should believe that he does, unless evidence can be produced that he is mistaken. And it is another basic principle of knowledge that those who do not have an experience of a certain type ought to believe many others when they say that they do—again, in the absence of evidence of mass delusion.

The case for the existence of God is a cumulative one. I claim that the existence and continued operation of God (normally through the laws of nature, but sometimes setting them aside) can explain the whole pattern of science and history, and also men's most intimate religious experiences.

13. Does God Exist? Reflections on Disbelief

Kai Nielsen

Kai Nielsen (1926–   ), emeritus professor of philosophy at the University of Calgary, has written on a wide variety of philosophical issues. He is perhaps best known for his analyses of the arguments for atheism and socialism.

Introduction

Religious people in our culture say things like this: "All mighty God we have sinned against you," "The Lord will comfort us," "We will be happy with God in heaven," "To God our lives lie open," "God is our All Mighty and Eternal Father whose realm extends beyond the bounds of space and time," "God will protect us, enlighten us, and liberate us from fear and crippling anxiety," and "God's Kingdom is coming to bring on a new world."

We hear such things repeatedly and wonder whether we have any good reason to believe that they are true or even probably true or whether they can be reasonably believed by properly informed people. Moreover, some of us wonder whether such utterances are sufficiently intelligible to make their acceptance a coherent object of faith. Can we reasonably believe that such claims—and indeed the central claims of Judaism and Christianity as well—make statements which are either true or false?

I believe that we should answer all those questions in the *negative.* Religious belief—or at least belief in God—should be impossible for someone living in our century, who thinks carefully about these matters and who has a tolerable scientific education and good philosophical training. It is not so hard to convolute oneself into religious belief if one has philosophical expertise but little knowledge of the world and it is easy enough to be a believer if one is a scientist and philosophically naive. However, if we have a scientific education and philosophical sophistication, along with a willingness to reflect on such matters, these things, taken together, should undermine religious belief/I want to go some of the way toward showing that this is so and why it is so. I shall principally argue on two fronts. First, familiarly—and only in a sketchy manner—I shall argue in Part I against the various attempts to prove that God exists, that revelation is reliable, that morality requires religious belief, and that God can be known directly in religious experience. The first part of my argument will be to show that none of these apologetic appeals work. I do not claim originality here, but I do claim that what I argue is a good approximation of

First published in *Free Inquiry*, Spring 1981. © 1981 Council for Secular Humanism.

the truth. [Next, I deal with the skeptical perplexities that] turn principally on questions concerning how we might establish the truth or probable truth of the claims of Judaism or Christianity and whether we could reasonably accept them as articles of faith. I shall turn in Part II to the vexed question of whether such religious beliefs could even count as genuine truth-claims. When we examine closely the truth of religion, our concern should gradually turn to questions about the meaning or intelligibility of the key claims of religion. In *some sense*, God-talk is plainly meaningful. Believers and nonbelievers alike know how to use religious vocabulary nondeviantly, but, to put it at first crudely, we can, if we reflect, come to wonder if such talk makes sense. This strikes us immediately when we study primitive religions. Our familiarity with Christian or Jewish discourse may dull our perceptions here. Yet if we try for a moment to look at our own religious talk with the eyes of an anthropologist coming from an alien culture, we should at least begin to feel the strangeness of talk of God in which God is said to be an "omnipresent, almighty Father whose realm extends beyond the bounds of space and time." What is this *realm* beyond space and time? Try to think very literally about this. What are we really doing here? What does "God" or "heaven" denote or stand for? What are you really referring to when you speak of God? What are you worshipping when you worship God? I shall, after I have examined attempts to prove the viability of religious belief, turn to these questions and attempt to show that the very concept of God is of such a low order of intelligibility that belief in him is unjustified. Belief in God is an ideological belief that distorts our understanding of reality. This is not just an innocent distortion. For often, where we have such beliefs or are affected by such beliefs, they distort our lives. They are not, I shall argue, humanly desirable saving myths. In Part III I shall turn to these considerations by briefly considering what interests religion answers to, and what, under certain societal conditions, socially necessary illusions religion secures.

I

In the Middle Ages, it was generally thought that we could quite definitely prove the existence of God. There were a few skeptics, of course, but they were intellectual outcasts, very much in the minority. With the unfolding of the industrial revolution and the deepening effect of the Enlightenment, this intellectual attitude shifted. Hume and Kant came along—Hume an agnostic and Kant a fideistic Christian—and together they provided powerful philosophical arguments designed to show that we could not prove that God exists. Culturally speaking, though the battle took centuries to unwind, Hume and Kant won. Or, whatever the etiology, the *Zeitgeist* shifted in their favor. It is now a philosophical and, in many quarters, even a cultural commonplace to say that we cannot prove that God exists. Reason and observation cannot show the unprejudiced mind, willing to follow the argument and evidence wherever it will go, that there is a God. What Hume and Kant struggled to establish, many of us take as almost a cultural dogma, so that in one sense we have not earned our right to disbelief. Moreover, this disbelief in the proofs is common ground between skeptics and many believers. They, of course, differ over religious commitment, but not over such a common cultural orientation. It is indeed true that from time to time, some philosopher—sometimes even some relatively distinguished philosopher—comes to believe that, after all, one or another of these proofs, usually in some increasingly esoteric version, works, but very few people are convinced.[1] If he is clever enough or has enough weight in his profession, what happens is that his refurbished version of one of the proofs turns out to be a source of intellectual exercise which for a time helps fill the pages of professional philosophical journals and gives people (often people without the slightest interest in religion) who delight in solving puzzles a chance to strut their stuff: to whet their philosophical knives and show their philosophical wares. But, just as the *Zeitgeist* cut against the skeptic in the Middle Ages, so the *Zeitgeist* in our time, Billy Graham notwithstanding, favors skepticism about proofs. Even the appeal to religious experience isn't what it once was.

However, the *Zeitgeist* may not speak the truth and, even if God is on the side of the big battalions, truth isn't a camp follower, so I will turn now to a rapid fire examination of the traditional proofs.[2]

The first arguments I shall consider are arguments that philosophers call arguments of the *ontological* type. They perhaps fascinate philosophers more than any of the other type proofs and would, if correct, be strict demonstrations of the reality of God, making the denial of God's existence into a self-contradiction. The person articulating such an argument claims, as Anselm did in the Middle Ages and Descartes in the seventeenth century, that to conceive of God clearly is to realize that he *must* exist. "God is that than which no greater can be conceived but then God must exist or he would not be the greatest conceivable being."

But to say that God exists is not to amplify our concept of God, it is not to further characterize God, but to say that there is one or that the concept of God has exemplification. Our concept of the greatest conceivable being is not altered by whether or not that concept is exemplified in reality. Its exemplification or lack thereof does not make the *concept* greater. Our concept of God—our concept of the greatest conceivable being—is not altered by whether there is or isn't such a being. So such an ontological argument fails.

Ontological type arguments are not helped by alternatively arguing that God by definition is an eternal being and that an eternal being could not come to exist, just happen to exist, or cease to exist, but exists necessarily. Thus God *must* exist if God is conceivable at all, for a necessary or eternal being cannot cease or even just contingently exist. He must exist necessarily. Thus, if we can conceive of God at all then God must exist. Against this it should be noted that while an eternal being could not come to exist or just cease to exist, it still could *eternally* be the case that there are no eternal beings. Thus to conceive of an eternal being is not to establish that there actually is one. What our conceptualization tells us is that if there is one, he or it exists timelessly.

---

[1]Norman Malcolm's resurrection of the ontological argument is the most striking example. But Charles Hartshorne, Alvin Plantinga, and Richard Taylor have gone off on their own special tangents.

[2]I examine these proofs in some detail in my *Reason and Practice*.

A second type of argument that has also been popular was articulated by Thomas Aquinas in the thirteenth century and repeated in various formulations ever since. Such arguments, often called *"cosmological* arguments," might, rather pretentiously, be referred to as arguments from the matter-of-fact nature of the world. If certain empirical facts actually obtain, so the argument goes, then either (a) God must exist or (b) (and more weakly) the postulation of God is the best explanation of those undeniable facts. The plain facts that Aquinas had in mind are that there are contingent beings or beings who owe their existence to some other beings. He argued there could not be an infinite series of such beings with no noncontingent being who brought them into existence and sustains their existence. For, if there were no such noncontingent being, even now there would be nothing, for something cannot come from nothing. And since such a series must finally come to an end, nothing could have gotten started in the first place or be ultimately sustained or explained, if there were not at least one self-existent, necessary being who owes its existence to no other reality. All other realities are said to depend upon it.

However, this cosmological argument will not do, for it confuses an *infinite* series with a very long *finite* series. Nothing will have to have gotten started or needed a first sustainer in the first place, if the series is genuinely infinite, for an infinite series, no matter of what type, can have no first member. And, while there will be no *ultimate* explanation of why there is anything at all, there is no good reason to believe that we can, let alone must, have explanations *of that type*. That is to say, there are no good grounds for believing that there are, let alone that there must be, such ultimate explanations. In that special sense it need not be the case that there is a reason for everything.

There is a distinctive form of cosmological argument usually tagged "the argument from design." It was very popular in the eighteenth century and remained popular even in Darwin's time. It is probably, in nonphilosophical circles, still the most favored of the attempts to prove—in this case inductively establish—the existence of God. The argument contends that the universe shows an orderliness and design that can be adequately accounted for only by an infinite and perfect designer of the universe, and that being we call God. But the order we observe, which is surely order *in* the universe and not *of* the universe, is such that it hardly evidences the marks of a perfect designer. Rather, if a designer at all, it bears the marks of an apprentice designer or a decrepit designer whose powers and insight were failing. More fundamentally, this familiar Humean point aside, the observed order in the world (universe) does not show or even lend any probability to the claim that the world (universe) is ordered let alone that the world (universe) is designed. Indeed no clear sense has been given to the phrase "The universe is designed." An observed pattern of things, no matter how intricate, does not show that there was or is an orderer or designer.

Since the destructive attacks of Hume and Kant, it has become rather common, *particularly* in certain Protestant circles, to claim that we do not need the proofs, even if we could have them, for we have a much surer way of knowing God, namely through direct religious experience. At least some people, so the claim goes, have an immediate, direct awareness of the reality of God which is so compelling that the person who has the experience cannot deny this reality. But such a claim—at least construed in some tolerably literal way—cannot be right. Perhaps Zeus (if there is a Zeus) could be so encountered, but the God of our developed Judeo-Christian-Islamic religions cannot be so encountered or encountered at all. God is a Pure Spirit, a being "out of time," transcendent to the world. If we just think what those conceptions literally connote, there can be no encountering—meeting—such a being. Any being which could be met with—seen, observed, in any way sensed—would not be the God of the developed Judeo-Christian-Islamic strand. God is supposedly a mysterious infinite being "beyond the world," "beyond space and time." He could not be observed, as Kierkegaard quipped, like a great green parrot. But then what is it to be aware of God, to stand in the presence of God, to experience God?

To experience God, some have said in reply, is to experience (or perhaps experience to the full) one's finitude, to have feelings of dependency, awe, wonder, dread or to feel a oneness and a love and a sense of security, no matter what happens. But these are plainly human experiences, psychological experiences, which can have purely secular readings or interpretations. They can be, as they were by Feuerbach, Freud, and Marx, understood as a distinctive and often a psychologically and socially compelling kind of human reaction to certain conditions of human living. They can readily be fit into a purely secular or scientific world perspective. Why should we multiply conceptions beyond need and say these understandable human experiences are also experiences of God or that they are best explained as experiences of God or as attesting to the reality of God or as showing that somehow we stand in the presence of God? We are not justified in postulating such odd entities unless there is reason to think that the phenomena cannot be adequately explained by reference to less *recherché* realities, which are plainly realities of our familiar spatio-temporal framework. Plainly, such experiences can be explained in natural or secular terms, so there is no warrant for postulating God to account for them.

It is sometimes said, trying to make the argument turn in another direction, that religious experiences are *self-authenticating* experiences and thus we can know, if we actually have them, that they must be experiences of God. But the only experiences which can plausibly be considered self-authenticating—that is, can be plausibly considered experiences which guarantee the reality of what is said to be experienced—are experiences of psychological realities, such as the fact that I am in pain, am tired, or that I now intend to have a drink before I go to bed. But no non-psychological experiences carry this indubitability. I may be perfectly confident that I am seeing an exit sign at the end of the hall and still be mistaken or I may be quite confident that what I hear is the surf breaking and still be mistaken. We may be justifiably confident that we feel anxiety, but we cannot be so confident that we have experienced God. There is no religious experience which guarantees that our experience is an experience of God. This can be asserted without for a moment doubting that some people have religious experiences. The psychological reality of such experience is one thing, that these experiences are actually experiences of God is another.[3]

---

[3]C. B. Martin has powerfully argued these matters in his *Religious Belief*. I have also elaborated these notions in my *Skepticism*.

The cluster of arguments above has a definite skeptical thrust. If these arguments are in the main right, and we recognize them to be right but we are still trying to cling to religious beliefs, we seem at least to be thrown back on a straight appeal to faith. To have religion at all, we must have religion without foundations: Christianity or Judaism without rational grounds. If it is responded that we have foundations rooted solely in religious authority, we should in turn ask: Why should we accept the authority of a given scripture, faith, or religious tradition? Why Jesus rather than Buddha or Mohammed? We need to recognize that there are many faiths, many religious traditions, many alleged revelations. If we look on the matter as social anthropologists would—that is if we are genuinely empirical about religions—we need to count them in the thousands. Why then opt for any particular one? Why claim or believe that a certain religion is the Truth and the Way? And if there is no decent answer to these questions, why go in for any religious faith at all? If there is no proof for the existence of God, no independent way of establishing or making credible his existence, isn't a claim that Christianity is the Truth and the Way both incredibly arrogant, ethnocentric, and arbitrary? Moreover, we must recognize that these different faiths, different religions do not, in various ways, symbolize the same Transcendent reality. They are sometimes radically different. Some do not have anything like a God at all and they by no means say the same thing. Furthermore, there are no nonethnocentric criteria for determining "the higher" and "the lower" religions. And that we have a higher material and scientific culture does not show our superiority in other aspects of culture. It may well be that man cannot judge of the authenticity of a revelation. How is man to judge God's revealed word? But when there is a host of putative revelations all claiming to be genuine, a reasonable person is not justified in claiming that one of these putative revelations is *the* true revelation: the genuine word of God which is to provide us with the Truth and the Way?[4]

Finally, an anguished Christian or Jew, looking for some way of anchoring his claim to religious truth, might *a là* Pascal, claim, absurdity or not, that we need religion to make sense of our tangled lives and to give our morality some foundation. If God is dead, he echoes a Dostoevskian character, nothing matters. But that is false. For God or no God, killing of innocent children, allowing people to starve when it can be prevented, lying simply to further one's convenience, or treating other human beings as means to further one's ends are plainly vile. Whatever philosophical account we give of the wrongness of these things, we know that, if anything is wrong, these things are wrong and that, even in a Godless world, they would still be wrong, and that God's commanding us to do them could not make them right or morally justified. Without God there may be no purpose to life, but life can still be purposeful, be worth living, even if there is no overarching purpose to life. Even if there is no purpose *of* life or purpose *to* life there can be purposes *in* life, e.g., to cure the sick, to achieve racial equality and

---

[4]For further arguments about an appeal to faith and revelation, see my "Can Faith Validate God-talk?," *Theology Today* (July 1963), "Religious Perplexity and Faith," *Crane Review* (Fall 1965), and my "The Primacy of Philosophical Theology," *Theology Today* (July 1970).

social justice, to achieve happiness and a fuller and more varied life for oneself and for those to whom one relates, to achieve love and close human bonds and solidarity. These are the purposes we human beings can have and they can remain intact in a Godless world.[5]

II

If the arguments above have been close to their mark, claims to religious truth are groundless and indeed Holmesless Watsons. There is no reason to think we have any justified religious truth claims at all or that we need to make a religious leap in the dark to give moral endeavor a point or to make sense out of our tangled lives. But troubles for the believer do not end here and indeed what may be the deepest and most characteristic contemporary malaise has not yet even been mentioned. The trouble is traceable to problems about the very meaning of religious utterances and to our religiously dominant nonanthropomorphic conceptions of God. The worry is that God-talk may not come to anything sufficiently coherent to be capable of even making false claims.[6] Reflect back on the religious utterances we mentioned at the outset. A Christian believer says "Almighty God we have sinned against you" or "God's kingdom is coming to bring on a new world and a new man" or "God is our almighty and eternal Father whose realm extends beyond the bounds of space and time." How are we to understand what is being said here or indeed do we understand what is being said? The words are familiar enough, but do they make sense? In the above arguments about truth in religion we have assumed that we have at least a *minimally coherent* set of concepts embedded in our God-talk, but that we just do not know if the claims of religion are true. But it is this very assumption which is now coming under fire. Certain central concepts, including the concept of God, are so problematic that it is questionable whether we can know or reasonably believe or even justifiably take on trust that these concepts can be put to work to make religious claims which are either true or false.

The believer talks of God and claims to pray and confess to God. *Who* or *what* is he praying and confessing to? (If you do these things, ask it as a question for yourselves.) Once we leave an anthromorphic and idolatrous conception of God, where God—as a kind of cosmic Mickey Mouse—is a being among beings, it is unclear to what or to whom we are referring when we use that term. What does "God" denote or stand for? "God," unlike "Hans" or "Erika" or "Mexico," cannot be ostensively defined or taught. As we have seen, it doesn't even make sense to speak of seeing or encountering God. We can't literally be aware of God or stand

---

[5]See here my *Ethics Without God* and my "Linguistic Philosophy and 'The Meaning of Life,'" *Cross-Currents* 14 (Summer 1964).

[6]The claims made here have been developed in my *Contemporary Critiques of Religion* and my *Skepticism*. They are most succinctly made in my "In Defense of Atheism" in *Perspectives in Education, Religion and the Arts*, Howard Kiefer and Milton Munitz (eds.).

in the presence of God. The term "God" can only be introduced intra-linguistically through definite descriptions. It is understandable that we might try to help a person puzzled about what we are talking about in speaking of God. We might try to elucidate how "God" is used in such religious utterances as we have quoted, by introducing the term intra-linguistically via definitive descriptions. We can say, to use some typical examples,

1. "God is the only infinite individual."
2. "God is the maker of the universe."
3. "God is the only ultimate reality upon whom all other realities depend."
4. "God is the only person transcendent to the world."
5. "God is the foundation of the world."
6. "God is the sole self-existent reality upon whom all other realities depend."

We should note, however, that the alleged definite descriptions we introduced to make it possible to answer our question *who* or *what* is God are at least as puzzling as "God." We should ask if we actually understand what they mean. What is it for something to "transcend the world" or to be "an ultimate reality" or "a foundation of the world" or an "infinite individual" or even "the maker of the universe"? These phrases have a cluster of varied and complicated resonances and they are believed to be key elements in Christian cosmologies, but do they have a sufficiently unproblematic meaning for us to understand what we are asserting or denying when we use them? Do we have any idea of what we are talking about or even any understanding of what is being referred to when we use them?

I think it is questionable that we do. To probe and to begin to test that claim, consider someone who says "God is the maker of the universe." Suppose A asserts it (tries to assert it) and B denies it (tries to deny it). That is, A avows it and B refuses to make that avowal. What support could either provide to establish or even to give a somewhat greater probability to his or her view? What *experienceable* states of affairs count *for* one view and *against* the other such that on balance we are justified in claiming greater probability for one view over the other?

It seems that nothing does. But if every actual or possible happening is equally compatible with either claim, then one must wonder what each is asserting. How could one sentence succeed in asserting something different than the other sentence is used to assert? What is one claiming that the other is denying? If that question cannot be answered—and it appears that it cannot—then the alleged assertions really fail genuinely to assert anything. Since such claims purport to assert "grand cosmological facts," the claims are thus unmasked as incoherent conceptions. They don't and can't do what they purport to do. Moreover, it isn't the situation where we just have two theories equally compatible with the available evidence. What we have is one set of putative claims—the religious ones—claiming to assert something thoroughly different, through and through mysterious, and of a quite different order. Yet there are no differences of an experientially specifiable sort between the two accounts. Experientially the believer cannot show what *more* he is asserting, can't elucidate, except in equally perplexing terms, what he means to be saying that the nonbeliever is not, so that the suspicion is very difficult to resist that there is, after all, no nonverbal difference between them.

Some Christians of a rather empiricist bent would accept much of the general thrust, if not the details, of the above arguments.[7] They would agree that the above "definite descriptions" are in reality *Ersatz* descriptions which are as problematic as the concept whose sense or at least whose reference they are trying to secure. However, they would argue that there is another definite description readily available to Christians which is far less problematic and is one of the most basic things we can say about God. Indeed, it is a something that gives the term an empirical anchorage and enables us to describe or characterize God uniquely such that we can answer the question "Who is God?" The definite description in question is this: "God is the being who raised Jesus from the dead." Here we have talk that relates to the spatio-temporal framework we are in and with which we are familiar. It is a description that gives us a sense of who we are talking about when we talk of or to God. Unlike the alleged definite descriptions I trotted out, this one is linked with the spatio-temporal framework in which we live. Moreover, the claim is falsifiable and verifiable (confirmable and disconfirmable). If in some future situation, after the dissolution of our present bodies, we find out that God did not raise Jesus from the dead, we will have discomfirmed our claim. That is to say, if we discover in that world that Jesus is alive and well and all things are subordinate to him, then we will have confirming evidence that God raised Jesus from the dead. If, however, we do not discover this, we will have disconfirming evidence.

We thus have shown, this Christian defense contends, how key strands of God-talk are verifiable and we have given some determinate sense to "God" by showing who it is we are talking about when speaking of God. But, we are not out of the dark woods yet, for "Jesus is alive and all things are subordinate to him" is equally compatible with "God raised Jesus from the dead" and "It is not the case that God raised Jesus from the dead." But then we have not succeeded by that device in distinguishing what counts for one assertion and against the other. But if we cannot do that, we cannot distinguish between what one is asserting and the other denying, so that we cannot—except in a verbal way—distinguish these claims. Moreover, we have trouble with "God raised Jesus from the dead," for while we understand but do not believe that "Peter raised Jesus from the dead," it is not clear what it *means* to speak of *God*, i.e., "a pure spirit," doing such things and it is not clear what (*if* anything) more is asserted by "God raised Jesus from the dead" than by "Jesus rose from the dead." How can "a pure spirit," "a being beyond space" and "out of time" coherently be said to *do* any of these things? How can a being "out of time" and "beyond space" act "in time" to raise up anything and do all that without a body? It looks like language and indeed sense have gone on a holiday. If nothing more is asserted by the employment of "God raised Jesus from the dead" than is asserted by

---

[7]James Moulder pressed something like this against me, though I would not like to saddle him with my particular formulation.

"Jesus rose from the dead," then we do not have anything that atheists could not consistently assert. If something more is intended, then what this additional (more) is must be explained, but this has not been done and it is not evident that it can be done. But in lieu of an answer here this definite description is little, if any, improvement over the *Ersatz* definite descriptions I have given. We are still at a loss to say *who* God is and we cannot *point* either.

If the central thrust of these arguments is correct, then Christianity is wedded to conceptions so problematic that Christian faith is rendered incoherent. (But then, given its guidance and salvation functions, it will be exposed as an ideology. This seems to be the position we are in.) We do not understand what "God" is supposed to refer to and the constituent terms in the supposedly elucidating descriptions are equally puzzling about their referent. And the sentences in which these terms are employed are such that we have no idea whether their truth or falsity is ascertainable. We do not know how to distinguish, except purely verbally, between their assertions and their denials.

III

Let us suppose (in order to continue the argument) that Christianity has been so exposed. Let us now ask what interests it answers to and what socially necessary illusions it secures. How does it serve to block our understanding of the foundations of society and deflect unreasonably our actions as human agents?

Christianity in particular, and religion in general, arises as a response to human suffering, degradation, and exploitation in societies. Faced with this, it develops eschatological hopes for a new time and a new man grounded in a radical transformation of man and social relations such that, when we have shuffled off these moral coils, we will in Heaven at last have a society based not on man's inhumanity to man but on love, in which a genuine classlessness, and in that sense equality, will have been obtained, where there will no longer be any master and slave, and there will be a genuine human flourishing. This, demythologized, is the utopian ideal which Theodor Adorno says should guide our critique of ideology. But in its religious form the hope for a classless and truly human society, through an ideological conjuring trick, has been *projected* into some peculiar never-never land called Heaven. What we have here is a disguised ideologically distorted expression of genuinely human emancipatory interests and enduring human hopes. But, given the repressive and authoritarian nature of our societies, this hope is placed off in "a spiritual world" after "bodily death." Man, in such an ideology, is seen as a sinful, largely selfish, and aggressive creature who must be tamed into giving unto Caesar what is Caesar's and unto God what is God's and who must obey duly constituted authority. The ideology tells us we must learn not to aspire to, let alone seize, what is not "ours" but instead accept our God-given place in society, do our share, and accept God's will unquestionably. We must come to know our station and its duties; we must accept our lot. It is within this framework that we have our various entitlements and our just deserts. We are enjoined to accept a social order whose foundations are built on miracle, mystery, and authority and indeed on an authority which can rightly claim neither a rational nor a morally justified authority. The foundations of society are actually obscured from us and our condition in this world—which need not be so fixed—is made to seem fixed, as a consequence of our fallen nature. Everything, or almost everything is, as the crude image goes, "Pie in the sky by and by."

While there have been, and continue to be, as a tiny minority in the Christian Church, such truly admirable charismatic figures as Dietrich Bonhoeffer, Martin Luther King, Daniel Berrigan, and Beyers Naude, generally and massively, the Christian Church stands, and has for a long time stood, on the side of reaction and repression. (We should remember Luther and the German peasants and not forget the horrible fate of his perhaps equally great contemporary Thomas Muntzer, who did stand with the German peasants.) Suffering, degraded, and exploited human beings have been repeatedly taught to accept their fate as part of God's providential order and have projected to a "Spiritual World" and a "New Time" what could be distinctively human hopes, aspirations, and earthly expectations. Religion has deflected them from going after what they might have collectively struggled to achieve in this world, by instilling in them an attitude of resignation concerning this world and replacing their worldly hopes with eschatological ones concerning another far better but purely "spiritual world" which was to be their reward for the patient acceptance of the evils in this world. One was to accept one's worldly masters here and look to this "new spiritual world" where such exploitation and degradation would finally cease. It is there and only there that they shall overcome.

We should clearly recognize, in this heavenly swindle, the ideological function of such age-old religious apologetics. It was a brilliant inspiration, for it both leaves scope for utopian hopes and effectively pacifies the masses, deflecting them from the struggle to achieve their actual liberation. As Feuerbach saw, the ideals and moral qualities that should properly be made the objects of purely human ideals are projected onto God. As our concept of God is enriched our concept of man is impoverished. Here we have for a people caught in such repressive societies, a socially necessary but still an ideologically distorted false consciousness. Religion cons them into accepting a dehumanizing *status quo*. It sings of man's liberation while helping to forge his chains.

In asking what is to be done, we should answer that we must break the spell of this false consciousness and make the demystified, ideologically unravelled, and utterly secularized positive side of Christian utopian hopes the object of our realistic endeavors. With the ideal of a classless unauthoritarian society before us, a genuine human flourishing for all can be obtained and the maxim of egalitarian justice for a materially enriched society can not only be inscribed on our banners but conditioned in our hearts.[8]

---

[8]Some of the conceptual underpinning for this last section occurs in my "On Speaking of God," *Theoria* 28 (1962), Part Two, "Religious Perplexity and Faith," *Crane Review* (Fall 1965), "God as a Human Projection," *The Lockhaven Review* 1 (1967), and "Religiosity and Powerlessness," *The Humanist* (May/June 1977). I have tried to say what that maxim of egalitarian justice is in my *Equality and Liberty: A Defense of Radical Egalitarianism* (Totowa, NJ: Rowman and Allanheld, 1985).

Contemporary Issues

The Problem of Evil

14. God and the Problem of Evil

B. C. Johnson

B. C. Johnson is a pen name for the author, who wishes to remain anonymous.

Here is a common situation: a house catches on fire and a six-month-old baby is painfully burned to death. Could we possibly describe as "good" any person who had the power to save this child and yet refused to do so? God undoubtedly has this power and yet in many cases of this sort he has refused to help. Can we call God "good"? Are there adequate excuses for his behavior?

First, it will not do to claim that the baby will go to heaven. It was either necessary for the baby to suffer or it was not. If it was not, then it was wrong to allow it. The child's ascent to heaven does not change this fact. If it was necessary, the fact that the baby will go to heaven does not explain why it was necessary, and we are still left without an excuse for God's inaction.

It is not enough to say that the baby's painful death would in the long run have good results and therefore should have happened, otherwise God would not have permitted it. For if we know this to be true, then we know—just as God knows—that every action successfully performed must in the end be good and therefore the right thing to do, otherwise God would not have allowed it to happen. We could deliberately set houses ablaze to kill innocent people and if successful we would then know we had a duty to do it. A defense of God's goodness which takes as its foundation duties known only after the fact would result in a morality unworthy of the name. Furthermore, this argument does not explain why God allowed the child to burn to death. It merely claims that there is some reason discoverable in the long run. But the belief that such a reason is within our grasp must rest upon the additional belief that God is good. This is just to counter evidence against such a belief by assuming the belief to be true. It is not unlike a lawyer defending his client by claiming that the client is innocent and therefore the evidence against him must be misleading—that proof vindicating the defendant will be found

From *The Atheist Debater's Handbook*, by B. C. Johnson, "God and the Problem of Evil," chapter 12, pp. 99–108 (Amherst, NY: Prometheus Books). Copyright © 1981 B. C. Johnson. Reprinted by permission of the publisher.

in the long run. No jury of reasonable men and women would accept such a defense and the theist cannot expect a more favorable outcome.

The theist often claims that man has been given free will so that if he accidentally or purposefully cause fires, killing small children, it is his fault alone. Consider a bystander who had nothing to do with starting the fire but who refused to help even though he could have saved the child with no harm to himself. Could such a bystander be called good? Certainly not. If we could not consider a mortal human being good under these circumstances, what grounds could we possibly have for continuing to assert the goodness of an all-powerful God?

The suggestion is sometimes made that it is best for us to face disasters without assistance, otherwise we would become dependent on an outside power for aid. Should we then abolish modern medical care or do away with efficient fire departments? Are we not dependent on their help? Is it not the case that their presence transforms us into soft, dependent creatures? The vast majority are not physicians or firemen. These people help in their capacity as professional outside sources of aid in much the same way that we would expect God to be helpful. Theists refer to aid from firemen and physicians as cases of man helping himself. In reality, it is a tiny minority of men helping a great many. We can become just as dependent on them as we can on God. Now the existence of this kind of outside help is either wrong or right. If it is right, then God should assist those areas of the world which do not have this kind of help. In fact, throughout history, such help has not been available. If aid ought to have been provided, then God should have provided it. On the other hand, if it is wrong to provide this kind of assistance, then we should abolish the aid altogether. But we obviously do not believe it is wrong.

Similar considerations apply to the claim that if God interferes in disasters, he would destroy a considerable amount of moral urgency to make things right. Once again, note that such institutions as modern medicine and fire departments are relatively recent. They function irrespective of whether we as individuals feel any moral urgency to support them. To the extent that they help others, opportunities to feel moral urgency are destroyed because they reduce the number of cases which appeal to us for help. Since we have not always had such institutions, there must have been a time when there was greater moral urgency than there is now. If such a situation is morally desirable, then we should abolish modern medical care and fire departments. If the situation is not morally desirable, then God should have remedied it.

Besides this point, we should note that God is represented as one who tolerates disasters, such as infants burning to death, in order to create moral urgency. It follows that God approved of these disasters as a means to encourage the creation of moral urgency. Furthermore, if there were no such disasters occurring, God would have to see to it that they occur. If it so happened that we lived in a world in which babies never perished in burning houses, God would be morally obliged to take an active hand in setting fire to houses with infants in them. In fact, if the frequency of infant mortality due to fire should happen to fall below a level necessary for the creation of maximum moral urgency in our real world, God would be justified in setting a few fires of his own. This may well be happening right now, for there is no guarantee that the maximum number of infant deaths necessary for moral urgency are occurring.

All of this is of course absurd. If I see an opportunity to create otherwise nonexistent opportunities for moral urgency by burning an infant or two, then I should *not* do so. But if it is good to maximize moral urgency, then I *should* do so. Therefore, it is not good to maximize moral urgency. Plainly we do not in general believe that it is a good thing to maximize moral urgency. The fact that we approve of modern medical care and applaud medical advances is proof enough of this.

The theist may point out that in a world without suffering there would be no occasion for the production of such virtues as courage, sympathy, and the like. This may be true, but the atheist need not demand a world without suffering. He need only claim that there is suffering which is in excess of that needed for the production of various virtues. For example, God's active attempts to save six-month-old infants from fires would not in itself create a world without suffering. But no one could sincerely doubt that it would improve the world.

The two arguments against the previous theistic excuse apply here also. "Moral urgency" and "building virtue" are susceptible to the same criticisms. It is worthwhile to emphasize, however, that we encourage efforts to eliminate evils; we approve of efforts to promote peace, prevent famine, and wipe out disease. In other words, we do value a world with fewer or (if possible) no opportunities for the development of virtue (when "virtue" is understood to mean the reduction of suffering). If we produce such a world for succeeding generations, how will they develop virtues? Without war, disease, and famine, they will not be virtuous. Should we then cease our attempts to wipe out war, disease, and famine? If we do not believe that it is right to cease attempts at improving the world, then by implication we admit that virtue-building is not an excuse for God to permit disasters. For we admit that the development of virtue is no excuse for permitting disasters.

It might be said that God allows innocent people to suffer in order to deflate man's ego so that the latter will not be proud of his apparently deserved good fortune. But this excuse succumbs to the arguments used against the preceding excuses and we need discuss them no further.

Theists may claim that evil is a necessary by-product of the laws of nature and therefore it is irrational for God to interfere every time a disaster happens. Such a state of affairs would alter the whole causal order and we would then find it impossible to predict anything. But the death of a child caused by an electrical fire could have been prevented by a miracle and no one would ever have known. Only a minor alteration in electrical equipment would have been necessary. A very large disaster could have been avoided simply by producing in Hitler a miraculous heart attack—and no one would have known it was a miracle. To argue that continued miraculous intervention by God would be wrong is like insisting that one should never use salt because ingesting five pounds of it would be fatal. No one is requesting that God interfere all of the time. He should, however, intervene to prevent especially horrible disasters. Of course, the question arises: where does one draw the line? Well, certainly the line should be drawn somewhere this side of infants burning to death. To argue that we do not know where the line should be drawn is no excuse for failing to interfere in those instances that would be called clear cases of evil.

It will not do to claim that evil exists as a necessary contrast to good so that we might know what good is. A very small amount of evil, such as a toothache, would allow that. It is not necessary to destroy innocent human beings.

The claim could be made that God has a "higher morality" by which his actions are to be judged. But it is a strange "higher morality" which claims that what we call "bad" is good and what we call "good" is bad. Such a morality can have no meaning to us. It would be like calling black "white" and white "black." In reply the theist may say that God is the wise Father and we are ignorant children. How can we judge God any more than a child is able to judge his parent? It is true that a child may be puzzled by his parents' conduct, but his basis for deciding that their conduct is nevertheless good would be the many instances of good behavior he has observed. Even so, this could be misleading. Hitler, by all accounts, loved animals and children of the proper race; but if Hitler had had a child, this offspring would hardly have been justified in arguing that his father was a good man. At any rate, God's "higher morality," being the opposite of ours, cannot offer any grounds for deciding that he is somehow good.

Perhaps the main problem with the solutions to the problem of evil we have thus far considered is that no matter how convincing they may be in the abstract, they are implausible in certain particular cases. Picture an infant dying in a burning house and then imagine God simply observing from afar. Perhaps God is reciting excuses in his own behalf. As the child succumbs to the smoke and flames, God may be pictured as saying: "Sorry, but if I helped you I would have considerable trouble deflating the ego of your parents. And don't forget I have to keep those laws of nature consistent. And anyway if you weren't dying in that fire, a lot of moral urgency would just go down the drain. Besides, I didn't start this fire, so you can't blame *me*."

It does no good to assert that God may not be all-powerful and thus not able to prevent evil. He can create a universe and yet is conveniently unable to do what the fire department can do—rescue a baby from a burning building. God should at least be as powerful as a man. A man, if he had been at the right place and time, could have killed Hitler. Was this beyond God's abilities? If God knew in 1910 how to produce polio vaccine and if he was able to communicate with somebody, he should have communicated this knowledge. He must be incredibly limited if he could not have managed this modest accomplishment. Such a God if not dead, is the next thing to it. And a person who believes in such a ghost of a God is practically an atheist. To call such a thing a god would be to strain the meaning of the word.

The theist, as usual, may retreat to faith. He may say that he has faith in God's goodness and therefore the Christian Deity's existence has not been disproved. "Faith" is here understood as being much like confidence in a friend's innocence despite the evidence against him. Now in order to have confidence in a friend one must know him well enough to justify faith in his goodness. We cannot have justifiable faith in the supreme goodness of strangers. Moreover, such confidence must come not just from a speaking acquaintance. The friend may continually assure us with his words that he is good but if he does not act like a good person, we would have no reason to trust him. A person who says he has faith in God's goodness is speaking as if he had known God for a long time and during that time had never seen him do any serious evil. But we know that throughout history God has allowed numerous atrocities to occur. No one can have justifiable faith in the goodness of such a God. This faith would have to be based on a close friendship wherein God was never found to do anything wrong. But a person would have to be blind and deaf to have had such a relationship with God. Suppose a friend of yours had always claimed to be good yet refused to help people when he was in a position to render aid. Could you have justifiable faith in his goodness?

You can of course say that you trust God anyway—that no arguments can undermine your faith. But this is just a statement describing how stubborn you are; it has no bearing whatsoever on the question of God's goodness.

The various excuses theists offer for why God has allowed evil to exist have been demonstrated to be inadequate. However, the conclusive objection to these excuses does not depend on their inadequacy.

First, we should note that every possible excuse making the actual world consistent with the existence of a good God could be used in reverse to make that same world consistent with an evil God. For example, we could say that God is evil and that he allows free will so that we can freely do evil things, which would make us more truly evil than we would be if forced to perform evil acts. Or we could say that natural disasters occur in order to make people more selfish and bitter, for most people tend to have a "me-first" attitude in a disaster (note, for example, stampedes to leave burning buildings). Even though some people achieve virtue from disasters, this outcome is necessary if persons are to react freely to disaster—necessary if the development of moral degeneracy is to continue freely. But, enough; the point is made. Every excuse we could provide to make the world consistent with a good God can be paralleled by an excuse to make the world consistent with an evil God. This is so because the world is a mixture of both good and bad.

Now there are only three possibilities concerning God's moral character. Considering the world as it actually is, we may believe: (*a*) that God is more likely to be all evil than he is to be all good; (*b*) that God is less likely to be all evil than he is to be all good; or (*c*) that God is equally as likely to be all evil as he is to be all good. In case (*a*) it would be admitted that God is unlikely to be all good. Case (*b*) cannot be true at all, since—as we have seen—the belief that God is all evil can be justified to precisely the same extent as the belief that God is all good. Case (*c*) leaves us with no reasonable excuses for a good God to permit evil. The reason is as follows: if an excuse is to be a reasonable excuse, the circumstances it identifies as excusing conditions must be actual. For example, if I run over a pedestrian and my excuse is that the brakes failed because someone tampered with them, then the facts had better bear this out. Otherwise the excuse will not hold. Now if case (*c*) is correct and, given the facts of the actual world, God is as likely to be all evil as he is to be all good, then these facts do not support the excuses which could be made for a good God permitting evil. Consider an analogous example. If my excuse for running over the pedestrian is that my brakes were tampered with, and if the actual facts lead us to believe that it is no more likely that they were tampered with than that they were not, the excuse is no longer reasonable. To make good my excuse, I must show that it is a fact or at least highly probable that my brakes were tampered with—not that it is just a possibility. The same point holds for God. His excuse must not be a possible excuse, but an actual one. But case (*c*), in maintaining that it is just as likely that God is all evil as that he is all good, rules this out. For if case (*c*) is true, then the facts of the actual world do not make it any more likely that God is all good than that he is all evil. Therefore, they do not make it any more likely that his excuses are good than that they are not. But, as we have seen, good excuses have a higher probability of being true.

Cases (*a*) and (*c*) conclude that it is unlikely that God is all good, and case (*b*) cannot be true. Since these are the only possible cases, there is no escape from the conclusion that it is unlikely that God is all good. Thus the problem of evil triumphs over the traditional theism.

15. The Problem of Evil

John Hick

John Hick (1922–   ) is Danforth Professor of the Philosophy of Religion, Emeritus, at the Claremont Graduate University. He has written numerous books and articles on theology and the philosophy of religion.

To many, the most powerful positive objection to belief in god is the fact of evil. Probably for most agnostics it is the appalling depth and extent of human suffering, more than anything else, that makes the idea of a loving Creator seem so implausible and disposes them toward one or another of the various naturalistic theories of religion.

As a challenge to theism, the problem of evil has traditionally been posed in the form of a dilemma: if God is perfectly loving, he must wish to abolish evil; and if he is all-powerful, he must be able to abolish evil. But evil exists; therefore God cannot be both omnipotent and perfectly loving.

Certain solutions, which at once suggest themselves, have to be ruled out so far as the Judaic-Christian faith is concerned.

To say, for example (with contemporary Christian Science), that evil is an illusion of the human mind, is impossible within a religion based upon the stark realism of the Bible. Its pages faithfully reflect the characteristic mixture of good and evil in human experience. They record every kind of sorrow and suffering, every mode of man's inhumanity to man and of his painfully insecure existence in the world. There is no attempt to regard evil as anything but dark, menacingly ugly, heart-rending, and crushing. In the Christian scriptures, the climax of this history of evil is the crucifixion of Jesus, which is presented not only as a case of utterly unjust suffering, but as the violent and murderous rejection of God's Messiah. There can be no doubt, then, that for biblical faith, evil is unambiguously evil, and stands in direct opposition to God's will.

Again, to solve the problem of evil by means of the theory (sponsored for example, by the Boston "Personalist" School) of a finite deity who does the best he can with a material, intractable and coeternal with himself, is to have abandoned the basic premise of Hebrew-Christian monotheism; for the theory amounts to rejecting belief in the infinity and sovereignty of God.

Indeed, any theory which would avoid the problem of the origin of evil by depicting it as an ultimate constituent of the universe, coordinate with good, has been repudiated in advance by the classic Christian teaching, first developed by Augustine, that evil represents the going wrong of something which in itself is good. Augustine holds firmly to the Hebrew-Christian conviction that the

Philosophy of Religion, 1/e by John Hick © 1965. Reprinted by permission of Pearson Education, Inc, Upper Saddle River, NJ.

universe is *good*—that is to say, it is the creation of a good God for a good purpose. He completely rejects the ancient prejudice, widespread in his day, that matter is evil. There are, according to Augustine, higher and lower, greater and lesser goods in immense abundance and variety; but everything which has being is good in its own way and degree, except in so far as it may have become spoiled or corrupted. Evil—whether it be an evil will, an instance of pain, or some disorder or decay in nature has not been set there by God, but represents the distortion of something that is inherently valuable. Whatever exists is, as such, and in its proper place, good; evil is essentially parasitic upon good, being disorder and perversion in a fundamentally good creation. This understanding of evil as something negative means that it is not willed and created by God; but it does not mean (as some have supposed) that evil is unreal and can be disregarded. On the contrary, the first effect of this doctrine is to accentuate even more the question of the origin of evil.

Theodicy,[1] as many modern Christian thinkers see it, is a modest enterprise, negative rather than positive in its conclusions. It does not claim to explain, nor to explain away, every instance of evil in human experience, but only to point to certain considerations which prevent the fact of evil (largely incomprehensible though it remains) from constituting a final and insuperable bar to rational belief in God.

In indicating these considerations it will be useful to follow the traditional division of the subject. There is the problem of *moral evil* or wickedness: why does an all-good and all-powerful God permit this? And there is the problem of the *nonmoral evil* of suffering or pain, both physical and mental: why has an all-good and all-powerful God created a world in which this occurs?

Christian thought has always considered moral evil in its relation to human freedom and responsibility. To be a person is to be a finite center of freedom, a (relatively) free and self-directing agent responsible for one's own decisions. This involves being free to act wrongly as well as to act rightly. The idea of a person who can be infallibly guaranteed always to act rightly is self-contradictory. There can be no guarantee in advance that a genuinely free moral agent will never choose amiss. Consequently, the possibility of wrongdoing or sin is logically inseparable from the creation of finite persons, and to say that God should not have created beings who might sin amounts to saying that he should not have created people.

This thesis has been challenged in some recent philosophical discussions of the problem of evil, in which it is claimed that no contradiction is involved in saying that God might have made people who would be genuinely free and who could yet be guaranteed always to act rightly. A quote from one of these discussions follows:

> If there is no logical impossibility in a man's freely choosing the good on one, or on several occasions, there cannot be a logical impossibility in his freely choosing the good on every occasion. God was not, then, faced with a choice between making innocent automata and making beings who, in acting freely, would sometimes go wrong: there

---

[1]The word "theodicy," from the Greek *theos* (God) and *dike* (righteous), means the justification of God's goodness in the face of the fact of evil.

was open to him the obviously better possibility of making beings who would act freely but always go right. Clearly, his failure to avail himself of this possibility is inconsistent with his being both omnipotent and wholly good.[2]

A reply to this argument is suggested in another recent contribution to the discussion.[3] If by a free action we mean an action which is not externally compelled but which flows from the nature of the agent as he reacts to the circumstances in which he finds himself, there is, indeed, no contradiction between our being free and our actions being "caused" (by our own nature) and therefore being in principle predictable. There is a contradiction, however, in saying that God is the cause of our acting as we do but that we are free beings in relation to God. There is, in other words, a contradiction in saying that God has made us so that we shall of necessity act in a certain way, and that we are genuinely independent persons in relation to him. If all our thoughts and actions are divinely predestined, however free and morally responsible we may seem to be to ourselves, we cannot be free and morally responsible in the sight of God, but must instead be his helpless puppets. Such "freedom" is like that of a patient acting out a series of post-hypnotic suggestions: he appears, even to himself, to be free, but his volitions have actually been predetermined by another will, that of the hypnotist, in relation to whom the patient is not a free agent.

A different objector might raise the question of whether or not we deny God's omnipotence if we admit that he is unable to create persons who are free from risks inherent in personal freedom. The answer that has always been given is that to create such beings is logically impossible. It is no limitation upon God's power that he cannot accomplish the logically impossible, since there is nothing here to accomplish, but only a meaningless conjunction of words—in this case "person who is not a person." God is able to create beings of any and every conceivable kind; but creatures who lack moral freedom, however superior they might be to human beings in other respects, would not be what we mean by persons. They would constitute a different form of life which God might have brought into existence instead of persons. When we ask why God did not create such beings in place of persons, the traditional answer is that only persons could, in any meaningful sense, become "children of God," capable of entering into a personal relationship with their Creator by a free and uncompelled response to his love.

When we turn from the possibility of moral evil as a correlate of man's personal freedom to its actuality, we face something which must remain inexplicable even when it can be seen to be possible. For we can never provide a complete causal explanation of a free act; if we could, it would not be a free act. The origin of moral evil lies forever concealed within the mystery of human freedom.

The necessary connection between moral freedom and the possibility, now actualized, of sin throws light upon a great deal of the suffering which afflicts

---

[2]J. L. Mackie, "Evil and Omnipotence," *Mind* (April 1955), 209.
[3]Flew, in *New Essays on Philosophical Theology*.

mankind. For an enormous amount of human pain arises either from the inhumanity or the culpable incompetence of mankind. This includes such major scourges as poverty, oppression and persecution, war, and all the injustice, indignity, and inequity which occur even in the most advanced societies. These evils are manifestations of human sin. Even disease is fostered to an extent, the limits of which have not yet been determined by psychosomatic medicine, by moral and emotional factors seated both in the individual and in his social environment. To the extent that all of these evils stem from human failures and wrong decisions, their possibility is inherent in the creation of free persons inhabiting a world which presents them with real choices which are followed by real consequences.

We may now turn more directly to the problem of suffering. Even though the major bulk of actual human pain is traceable to man's misused freedom as a sole or part cause, there remain other sources of pain which are entirely independent of the human will, for example, earthquake, hurricane, storm, flood, drought, and blight. In practice it is often impossible to trace a boundary between the suffering which results from human wickedness and folly and that which falls upon mankind from without. Both kinds of suffering are inextricably mingled together in human experience. For our present purpose, however, it is important to note that the latter category does exist and that it seems to be built into the very structure of our world. In response to it, theodicy, if it is wisely conducted, follows a negative path. It is not possible to show positively that each item of human pain serves the divine purpose of good; but, on the other hand, it does seem possible to show that the divine purpose as it is understood in Judaism and Christianity could not be forwarded in a world which was designed as a permanent hedonistic paradise.

An essential premise of this argument concerns the divine purpose in creating the world. The skeptic's assumption is that man is to be viewed as a completed creation and that God's purpose in making the world was to provide a suitable dwelling-place for this fully-formed creature. Since God is good and loving, the environment which he has created for human life to inhabit is naturally as pleasant and comfortable as possible. The problem is essentially similar to that of a man who builds a cage for some pet animal. Since our world, in fact, contains sources of hardship, inconvenience, and danger of innumerable kinds, the conclusion follows that this world cannot have been created by a perfectly benevolent and all-powerful deity.

Christianity, however, has never supposed that God's purpose in the creation of the world was to construct a paradise whose inhabitants would experience a maximum of pleasure and a minimum of pain. The world is seen, instead, as a place of "soul-making" in which free beings, grappling with the tasks and challenges of their existence in a common environment, may become "children of God" and "heirs of eternal life." A way of thinking theologically of God's continuing creative purpose for man was suggested by some of the early Hellenistic Fathers of the Christian Church, especially Irenaeus. Following hints from St. Paul, Irenaeus taught that man has been made as a person in the image of God but has not yet been brought as a free and responsible agent into the finite likeness of God, which is revealed in Christ. Our world, with all its rough edges, is the sphere in which this second and harder stage of the creative process is taking place.

This conception of the world (whether or not set in Irenaeus' theological framework) can be supported by the method of negative theodicy. Suppose, contrary to fact, that this world were a paradise from which all possibility of pain and suffering were excluded. The consequences would be very far-reaching. For example, no could ever injure anyone else: the murderer's knife would turn to paper or his bullets to thin air; the bank safe, robbed of a million dollars, would miraculously become filled with another million dollars (without this device, on however large a scale, proving inflationary); fraud, deceit, conspiracy, and treason would somehow always leave the fabric of society undamaged. Again, no one would ever be injured by accident: the mountain-climber, steeplejack, or playing child falling from a height would float unharmed to the ground; the reckless driver would never meet with disaster. There would be no need to work, since no harm could result from avoiding work; there would be no call to be concerned for others in time of need or danger, for in such a world there could be no real needs or dangers.

To make possible this continual series of individual adjustments, nature would have to work by "special providence" instead of running according to general laws which men must learn to respect on penalty of pain or death. The laws of nature would have to be extremely flexible: sometimes gravity would operate, sometimes not; sometimes an object would be hard and solid, sometimes soft. There could be no sciences, for there would be no enduring world structure to investigate. In eliminating the problems and hardships of an objective environment, with its own laws, life would become like a dream in which, delightfully but aimlessly, we would float and drift at ease.

One can at least begin to imagine such a world. It is evident that our present ethical concepts would have no meaning in it. If, for example, the notion of harming someone is an essential element in the concept of a wrong action, in our hedonistic paradise there could be no wrong actions—nor any right actions in distinction from wrong. Courage and fortitude would have no point in an environment in which there is, by definition, no danger or difficulty. Generosity, kindness, the *agape* aspect of love, prudence, unselfishness, and all other ethical notions which presuppose life in a stable environment, could not even be formed. Consequently, such a world, however well it might promote pleasure, would be very ill adapted for the development of the moral qualities of human personality. In relation to this purpose it would be the worst of all possible worlds.

It would seem, then, that an environment intended to make possible the growth in free beings of the finest characteristics of personal life must have a good deal in common with our present world. It must operate according to general and dependable laws: and it must involve real dangers, difficulties, problems, obstacles, and possibilities of pain, failure, sorrow, frustration, and defeat. If it did not contain the particular trials and perils which—subtracting man's own very considerable contribution—our world contains, it would have to contain others instead.

To realize this is not, by any means, to be in possession of a detailed theodicy. It is to understand that this world, with all its "heartaches and the thousand natural shocks that flesh is heir to," and environment so manifestly not designed for the maximization of human pleasure and the minimization of human pain, may be rather well adapted to the quite different purpose of "soul-making."

16. The Ethics of Belief

W. K. Clifford

William Kingdon Clifford (1845–1879) was a prominent English mathematician and philosopher who made important contributions to the theory of knowledge and the philosophy of science.

A shipowner was about to send to sea an emigrant ship. He knew that she was old, and not over-well built at the first; that she had seen many seas and climes, and often had needed repairs. Doubts had been suggested to him that possibly she was not seaworthy. These doubts preyed upon his mind and made him unhappy; he thought that perhaps he ought to have her thoroughly overhauled and refitted, even though this should put him to great expense. Before the ship sailed, however, he succeeded in overcoming these melancholy reflections. He said to himself that she had gone safely through so many voyages and weathered so many storms that it was idle to suppose she would not come safely home from this trip also. He would put his trust in Providence, which could hardly fail to protect all these unhappy families that were leaving their fatherland to seek for better times elsewhere. He would dismiss from his mind all ungenerous suspicions about the honesty of builders and contractors. In such ways he acquired a sincere and comfortable conviction that his vessel was thoroughly safe and seaworthy; he watched her departure with a light heart, and benevolent wishes for the success of the exiles in their strange new home that was to be; and he got his insurance money when she went down in midocean and told no tales.

What shall we say of him? Surely this, that he was verily guilty of the death of those men. It is admitted that he did sincerely believe in the soundness of his ship; but the sincerity of his conviction can in no wise help him, because *he had no right to believe on such evidence as was before him*. He had acquired his belief not by honestly earning it in patient investigation, but by stifling his doubts. And although in the end he may have felt so sure about it that he could not think otherwise, yet inasmuch as he had knowingly and willingly worked himself into that frame of mind, he must be held responsible for it.

Let us alter the case a little, and suppose that the ship was not unsound after all; that she made her voyage safely, and many others after it. Will that diminish the

Reprinted from *Lectures and Essays* by William K. Clifford, Macmillan & Co., London, 1879.

guilt of her owner? Not one jot. When an action is once done, it is right or wrong forever; no accidental failure of its good or evil fruits can possibly alter that. The man would not have been innocent, he would only have been not found out. The question of right or wrong has to do with the origin of his belief, not the matter of it; not what it was, but how he got it; not whether it turned out to be true or false, but whether he had a right to believe on such evidence as was before him.

There was once an island in which some of the inhabitants professed a religion teaching neither the doctrine of original sin nor that of eternal punishment. A suspicion got abroad that the professors of this religion had made use of unfair means to get their doctrines taught to children. They were accused of wresting the laws of their country in such a way as to remove children from the care of their natural and legal guardians; and even of stealing them away and keeping them concealed from their friends and relations. A certain number of men formed themselves into a society for the purpose of agitating the public about this matter. They published grave accusations against individual citizens of the highest position and character, and did all in their power to injure those citizens in the exercise of their professions. So great was the noise they made, that a Commission was appointed to investigate the facts; but after the Commission had carefully inquired into all the evidence that could be got, it appeared that the accused were innocent. Not only had they been accused on insufficient evidence, but the evidence of their innocence was such as the agitators might easily have obtained, if they had attempted a fair inquiry. After these disclosures the inhabitants of that country looked upon the members of the agitating society, not only as persons whose judgment was to be distrusted, but also as no longer to be counted honorable men. For although they had sincerely and conscientiously believed in the charges they had made, *yet they had no right to believe on such evidence as was before them.* Their sincere convictions, instead of being honestly earned by patient inquiring, were stolen by listening to the voice of prejudice and passion.

Let us vary this case also, and suppose, other things remaining as before, that a still more accurate investigation proved the accused to have been really guilty. Would this make any difference in the guilt of the accusers? Clearly not; the question is not whether their belief was true or false, but whether they entertained it on wrong grounds. They would no doubt say, "Now you see that we were right after all; next time perhaps you will believe us." And they might be believed, but they would not thereby become honorable men. They would not be innocent, they would only be not found out. Every one of them, if he chose to examine himself *in foro conscientiae*, would know that he had acquired and nourished a belief, when he had no right to believe on such evidence as was before him; and therein he would know that he had done a wrong thing.

It may be said, however, that in both of these supposed cases it is not the belief which is judged to be wrong, but the action following upon it. The shipowner might say, "I am perfectly certain that my ship is sound, but still I feel it my duty to have her examined, before trusting the lives of so many people to her." And it might be said to the agitator, "However convinced you were of the justice of your cause and the truth of your convictions, you ought not to have made a public attack upon any man's character until you had examined the evidence on both sides with the utmost patience and care."

In the first place, let us admit that, so far as it goes, this view of the case is right and necessary; right, because even when a man's belief is so fixed that he cannot think otherwise, he still has a choice in regard to the action suggested by it, and so cannot escape the duty of investigating on the ground of the strength of his convictions; and necessary, because those who are not yet capable of controlling their feelings and thoughts must have a plain rule dealing with overt acts.

But this being premised as necessary, it becomes clear that it is not sufficient, and that our previous judgment is required to supplement it. For it is not possible so to sever the belief from the action it suggests as to condemn the one without condemning the other. No man holding a strong belief on one side of a question, or even wishing to hold a belief on one side, can investigate it with such fairness and completeness as if he were really in doubt and unbiased; so that the existence of a belief not founded on fair inquiry unfits a man for the performance of this necessary duty.

Nor is that truly a belief at all which has not some influence upon the actions of him who holds it. He who truly believes that which prompts him to an action has looked upon the action to lust after it, he has committed it already in his heart. If a belief is not realized immediately in open deeds, it is stored up for the guidance of the future. It goes to make a part of that aggregate of beliefs which is the link between sensation and action at every moment of all our lives, and which is so organized and compacted together that no part of it can be isolated from the rest, but every new addition modifies the structure of the whole. No real belief, however trifling and fragmentary it may seem, is ever truly insignificant; it prepares us to receive more of its like, confirms those which resembled it before, and weakens others; and so gradually it lays a stealthy train in our inmost thoughts, which may some day explode into overt action, and leave its stamp upon our character forever.

And no one man's belief is in any case a private matter which concerns himself alone. Our lives are guided by that general conception of the course of things which has been created by society for social purposes. Our words, our phrases, our forms and processes and modes of thought, are common property, fashioned and perfected from age to age; an heirloom which every succeeding generation inherits as a precious deposit and a sacred trust to be handed on to the next one, not unchanged but enlarged and purified, with some clear marks of its proper handiwork. Into this, for good or ill, is woven every belief of every man who has speech of his fellows. An awful privilege, and an awful responsibility, that we should help to create the world in which posterity will live.

In the two supposed cases which have been considered, it has been judged wrong to believe on insufficient evidence, or to nourish belief by suppressing doubts and avoiding investigation. The reason of this judgment is not far to seek; it is that in both these cases the belief held by one man was of great importance to other men. But for as much as no belief held by one man, however seemingly trivial the belief, and however obscure the believer, is ever actually insignificant or without its effect on the fate of mankind, we have no choice but to extend our judgment to all cases of belief whatever. Belief, that sacred faculty which prompts the decisions of our will, and knits into harmonious working all the compacted energies of our being, is ours not for ourselves, but for humanity. It is rightly used on truths which have been established by long experience and waiting toil, and which have stood in the fierce light of free and fearless questioning. Then it helps to bind men together, and to strengthen and direct their common action. It is desecrated when given to unproved and unquestioned statements, for the solace and private pleasure of the believer; to add a tinsel splendor to the plain straight road of our life and display a bright mirage beyond it; or even to drown the common sorrows of our kind by a self-deception which allows them not only to cast down, but also to degrade us. Whoso would deserve well of his fellows in this matter will guard the purity of his belief with a very fanaticism of jealous care, lest at any time it should rest on an unworthy object, and catch a stain which can never be wiped away.

It is not only the leader of men, statesman, philosopher, or poet, that owes this bounded duty to mankind. Every rustic who delivers in the village alehouse his slow, infrequent sentences, may help to kill or keep alive the fatal superstitions which clog his race. Every hard-worked wife of an artisan may transmit to her children beliefs which shall knit society together, or rend it in pieces. No simplicity of mind, no obscurity of station, can escape the universal duty of questioning all that we believe.

It is true that this duty is a hard one, and the doubt which comes out of it is often a very bitter thing. It leaves us bare and powerless where we thought that we were safe and strong. To know all about anything is to know how to deal with it under all circumstances. We feel much happier and more secure when we think we know precisely what to do, no matter what happens, than when we have lost our way and do not know where to turn. And if we have supposed ourselves to know all about anything, and to be capable of doing what is fit in regard to it, we naturally do not like to find that we are really ignorant and powerless, that we have to begin again at the beginning and try to learn what the thing is and how it is to be dealt with—if indeed anything can be learned about it. It is the sense of power attached to a sense of knowledge that makes men desirous of believing, and afraid of doubting.

This sense of power is the highest and best of pleasures when the belief on which it is founded is a true belief, and has been fairly earned by investigation. For then we may justly feel that it is common property, and holds good for others as well as ourselves. Then we may be glad, not that *I* have learned secrets by which I am safer and stronger, but that *we men* have got mastery over more of the world; and we shall be strong, not for ourselves, but in the name of Man and in his strength. But if the belief has been accepted on insufficient evidence, the pleasure is a stolen one. Not only does it deceive ourselves by giving us a sense of power which we do not really possess, but it is sinful, because it is stolen in defiance of our duty to mankind. That duty is to guard ourselves from such beliefs as from a pestilence, which may shortly master our own body and then spread to the rest of the town. What would be thought of one who, for the sake of a sweet fruit, should deliberately run the risk of bringing a plague upon his family and his neighbors?

And, as in other such cases, it is not the risk only which has to be considered; for a bad action is always bad at the time when it is done, no matter what happens afterwards. Every time we let ourselves believe for unworthy reasons, we weaken our power of self-control, of doubting, of judicially and fairly weighing evidence. We all suffer severely enough from the maintenance and support of false beliefs and the fatally wrong actions which they lead to, and the evil born when one such belief is entertained is great and wide. But a greater and wider evil arises when the credulous character is maintained and supported, when a habit of believing for unworthy reasons is fostered and made permanent. If I steal money from any person, there may be no harm done by the mere transfer of possession; he may not feel the loss, or it may prevent him from using the money badly. But I cannot help doing this great wrong towards Man, that I make myself dishonest. What hurts society is not that it should lose its property, but that it should become a den of thieves; for then it must cease to be society. This is why we ought not to do evil that good may come; for at any rate this great evil has come, that we have done evil and are made wicked thereby. In like manner, if I let myself believe anything on insufficient evidence, there may be no great harm done by the mere belief; it may be true after all, or I may never have occasion to exhibit it in outward acts. But I cannot help doing this great wrong toward Man, that I make myself credulous. The danger to society is not merely that it should believe wrong things, though that is great enough; but that it should become credulous, and lose the habit of testing things and inquiring into them; for then it must sink back into savagery.

The harm which is done by credulity in a man is not confined to the fostering of a credulous character in others, and consequent support of false beliefs. Habitual want of care about what I believe leads to habitual want of care in others about the truth of what is told to me. Men speak the truth to one another when each reveres the truth in his own mind and in the other's mind; but how shall my friend revere the truth in my mind when I myself am careless about it, when I believe things because I want to believe them, and because they are comforting and pleasant? Will he not learn to cry, "Peace," to me, when there is no peace? By such a course I shall surround myself with a thick atmosphere of falsehood and fraud, and in that I must live. It may matter little to me, in my cloud-castle of sweet illusions and darling lies; but it matters much to Man that I have made my neighbors ready to deceive. The credulous man is father to the liar and the cheat; he lives in the bosom of this his family, and it is no marvel if he should become even as they are. So closely are our duties knit together, that whoso shall keep the whole law, and yet offend in one point, he is guilty of all.

To sum up: it is wrong always, everywhere, and for anyone, to believe anything upon insufficient evidence.

If a man, holding a belief which he was taught in childhood or persuaded of afterwards, keeps down and pushes away any doubts which arise about it in his mind, purposely avoids the reading of books and the company of men that call in question or discuss it, and regards as impious those questions which cannot easily be asked without disturbing it—the life of that man is one long sin against mankind.

If this judgment seems harsh when applied to those simple souls who have never known better, who have been brought up from the cradle with a horror of doubt, and taught that their eternal welfare depends on what they believe, then it leads to the very serious question. Who hath made Israel to sin? . . .

Inquiry into the evidence of a doctrine is not to be made once for all, and then taken as finally settled. It is never lawful to stifle a doubt; for either it can be honestly answered by means of the inquiry already made, or else it proves that the inquiry was not complete.

"But," says one, "I am a busy man; I have no time for the long course of study which would be necessary to make me in any degree a competent judge of certain questions, or even able to understand the nature of the arguments." Then he should have no time to believe. . . .

17. The Will to Believe

William James

William James (1842–1910) is considered one of America's greatest philosophers. After attending Harvard Medical School, he taught anatomy and physiology at Harvard. Later his interests were primarily in the fields of psychology and philosophy. He is considered one of the main developers of pragmatism.

. . . I have long defended to my own students the lawfulness of voluntarily adopted faith; but as soon as they have got well imbued with the logical spirit, they have as a rule refused to admit my contention to be lawful philosophically, even though in point of fact they were personally all the time chock-full of some faith or other themselves. I am all the while, however, so profoundly convinced that my own position is correct, that your invitation has seemed to me a good occasion to make my statements more clear. Perhaps your minds will be more open than those with which I have hitherto had to deal. I will be as little technical as I can, though I must begin by setting up some technical distinctions that will help us in the end.

Let us give the name of *hypothesis* to anything that may be proposed to our belief; and just as the electricians speak of live and dead wires, let us speak of any hypothesis as either *live* or *dead*. A live hypothesis is one which appeals as a real possibility to him to whom it is proposed. If I ask you to believe in the Mahdi, the notion makes no electric connection with your nature,—it refuses to scintillate with any credibility at all. As an hypothesis it is completely dead. To an Arab, however (even if he be not one of the Mahdi's followers), the hypothesis is among the mind's possibilities: it is alive. This shows that deadness and liveness in an hypothesis are not intrinsic properties, but relations to the individual thinker. They are measured by his willingness to act. The maximum of liveness in an hypothesis means willingness to act irrevocably. Practically, that means belief; but there is some believing tendency wherever there is willingness to act at all.

Next, let us call the decision between two hypotheses an *option*. Options may be of several kinds. They may be—1, *living* or *dead*; 2, *forced* or *avoidable*; 3, *momentous* or *trivial*; and for our purposes we may call an option a *genuine* option when it is of the forced, living, and momentous kind.

1. A living option is one in which both hypotheses are live ones. If I say to you: "Be a theosophist or be a Mohammedan," it is probably a dead option, because for you neither hypothesis is likely to be alive. But if I say: "Be an agnostic or be a

Reprinted from *The Will to Believe and Other Essays in Popular Philosophy* by William James. Published by Longmans, Green (New York, 1896).

Christian," it is otherwise: trained as you are, each hypothesis makes some appeal, however small, to your belief.

2. Next, if I say to you: "Choose between going out with your umbrella or without it," I do not offer you a genuine option, for it is not forced. You can easily avoid it by not going out at all. Similarly, if I say, "Either love me or hate me," "Either call my theory true or call it false," your option is avoidable. You may remain indifferent to me, neither loving nor hating, and you may decline to offer any judgment as to my theory. But if I say, "Either accept this truth or go without it," I put on you a forced option, for there is no standing place outside of the alternative. Every dilemma based on a complete logical disjunction, with no possibility of not choosing, is an option of this forced kind.

3. Finally, if I were Dr. Nansen and proposed to you to join my North Pole expedition, your option would be momentous; for this would probably be your only similar opportunity, and your choice now would either exclude you from the North Pole sort of immortality altogether or put at least the chance of it into your hands. He who refuses to embrace a unique opportunity loses the prize as surely as if he tried and failed. *Per contra*, the option is trivial when the opportunity is not unique, when the stake is insignificant, or when the decision is reversible if it later prove unwise. Such trivial options abound in the scientific life. A chemist finds an hypothesis live enough to spend a year in its verification: he believes in it to that extent. But if his experiments prove inconclusive either way, he is quit for his loss of time, no vital harm being done.

It will facilitate our discussion if we keep all these distinctions well in mind. . . .

The thesis I defend is, briefly stated, this: *Our passional nature not only lawfully may, but must, decide an option between propositions, whenever it is a genuine option that cannot by its nature be decided on intellectual grounds; for to say, under such circumstances, "Do not decide, but leave the question open," is itself a passional decision,—just like deciding yes or no,—and is attended with the same risk of losing the truth.* . . .

Wherever the option between losing truth and gaining it is not momentous, we can throw the chance of *gaining truth* away, and at any rate save ourselves from any chance of *believing falsehood*, by not making up our minds at all till objective evidence has come. In scientific questions, this is almost always the case; and even in human affairs in general, the need of acting is seldom so urgent that a false belief to act on is better than no belief at all. Law courts, indeed, have to decide on the best evidence attainable for the moment, because a judge's duty is to make law as well as to ascertain it, and (as a learned judge once said to me) few cases are worth spending much time over: the great thing is to have them decided on *any* acceptable principle, and got out of the way. But in our dealings with objective nature we obviously are recorders, not makers, of the truth; and decisions for the mere sake of deciding promptly and getting on to the next business would be wholly out of place. Throughout the breadth of physical nature facts are what they are quite independently of us, and seldom is there any such hurry about them that the risks of being duped by believing a premature theory need be faced. The questions here are always trivial options, the hypotheses are hardly living (at any rate not living for us spectators), the choice between believing truth or falsehood is seldom forced. The attitude of sceptical balance is therefore the absolutely wise one if we would escape mistakes. What difference, indeed, does it make to most of us whether we have or have not a theory of the Röntgen rays, whether we believe or not in mind-stuff, or have a conviction about the causality of conscious states? It makes no difference. Such options are not forced on us. On every account it is better not to make them, but still keep weighing reasons *pro et contra* with an indifferent hand.

I speak, of course, here of the purely judging mind. For purposes of discovery such indifference is to be less highly recommended, and science would be far less advanced than she is if the passionate desires of individuals to get their own faiths confirmed had been kept out of the game. . . . On the other hand, if you want an absolute duffer in an investigation, you must, after all, take the man who has no interest whatever in its results: he is the warranted incapable, the positive fool. The most useful investigator, because the most sensitive observer, is always he whose eager interest in one side of the question is balanced by an equally keen nervousness lest he become deceived. Science has organized this nervousness into a regular *technique*, her so-called method of verification; and she has fallen so deeply in love with the method that one may even say she has ceased to care for truth by itself at all. It is only truth as technically verified that interests her. The truth of truths might come in merely affirmative form, and she would decline to touch it. Such truth as that, she might repeat with Clifford, would be stolen in defiance of her duty to mankind. Human passions, however, are stronger than technical rules. "Le coeur a ses raisons," as Pascal says, "que la raison ne connaît pas";[1] and however indifferent to all but the bare rules of the game the umpire, the abstract intellect, may be, the concrete players who furnish him the materials to judge of are usually, each one of them, in love with some pet "live hypothesis" of his own. Let us agree, however, that wherever there is no forced option, the dispassionately judicial intellect with no pet hypothesis, saving us, as it does, from dupery at any rate, ought to be our ideal.

The question next arises: Are there not somewhere forced options in our speculative questions, and can we (as men who may be interested at least as much in positively gaining truth as in merely escaping dupery) always wait with impunity till the coercive evidence shall have arrived? It seems *a priori* improbable that the truth should be so nicely adjusted to our needs and powers as that. In the great boarding-house of nature, the cakes and the butter and the syrup seldom come out so even and leave the plates so clean. Indeed, we should view them with scientific suspicion if they did.

Moral questions immediately present themselves as questions whose solution cannot wait for sensible proof. A moral question is a question not of what sensibly exists, but of what is good, or would be good if it did exist. Science can tell us what exists; but to compare the *worths*, both of what exists and of what does not exist, we must consult not science, but what Pascal calls our heart. Science herself consults her heart when she lays it down that the infinite ascertainment of fact and correction

---

[1][The heart has its reasons that reason does not know.—Ed.]

of false belief are the supreme goods for man. Challenge the statement, and science can only repeat it oracularly, or else prove it by showing that such ascertainment and correction bring man all sorts of other good which man's heart in turn declares. The question of having moral beliefs at all or not having them is decided by our will. Are our moral preferences true or false, or are they only odd biological phenomena, making things good or bad for us, but in themselves indifferent? How can your pure intellect decide? If your heart does not *want* a world of moral reality, your head will assuredly never make you believe in one. Mephistophelian scepticism, indeed, will satisfy the head's play-instincts much better than any rigorous idealism can. Some men (even at the student age) are so naturally cool-hearted that the moralistic hypothesis never has for them any pungent life, and in their supercilious presence the hot young moralist always feels strangely ill at ease. The appearance of knowingness is on their side, of *naiveté* and gullibility on his. Yet, in the inarticulate heart of him, he clings to it that he is not a dupe, and that there is a realm in which (as Emerson says) all their wit and intellectual superiority is no better than the cunning of a fox. Moral scepticism can no more be refuted or proved by logic than intellectual scepticism can. When we stick to it that there *is* truth (be it of either kind), we do so with our whole nature, and resolve to stand or fall by the results. The sceptic with his whole nature adopts the doubting attitude; but which of us is the wiser, Omniscience only knows.

Turn now from these wide questions of good to a certain class of questions of fact, questions concerning personal relations, states of mind between one man and another. *Do you like me or not?*—for example. Whether you do or not depends, in countless instances, on whether I meet you half-way, am willing to assume that you must like me, and show you trust and expectation. The previous faith on my part in your liking's existence is in such cases what makes your liking come. But if I stand aloof, and refuse to budge an inch until I have objective evidence, until you shall have done something apt, as the absolutists say, *ad extorquendum assensum meum*, ten to one your liking never comes. How many women's hearts are vanquished by the mere sanguine insistence of some man that they *must* love him! He will not consent to the hypothesis that they cannot. The desire for a certain kind of truth here brings about that special truth's existence; and so it is in innumerable cases of other sorts. Who gains promotions, boons, appointments, but the man in whose life they are seen to play the part of live hypotheses, who discounts them, sacrifices other things for their sake before they have come, and takes risks for them in advance? His faith acts on the powers above him as a claim, and creates its own verification.

A social organism of any sort whatever, large or small, is what it is because each member proceeds to his own duty with a trust that the other members will simultaneously do theirs. Wherever a desired result is achieved by the co-operation of many independent persons, its existence as a fact is a pure consequence of the precursive faith in one another of those immediately concerned. A government, an army, a commercial system, a ship, a college, an athletic team, all exist on this condition, without which not only is nothing achieved, but nothing is even attempted. A whole train of passengers (individually brave enough) will be looted by a few highwaymen, simply because the latter can count on one another, while each passenger fears that if he makes a movement of resistance, he will be shot before any one else backs him up. If we believed that the whole car-full would rise at once with us, we should each severally rise, and train-robbing would never even be attempted. There are, then, cases where a fact cannot come at all unless a preliminary faith exists in its coming. *And where faith in a fact can help create the fact*, that would be an insane logic which should say that faith running ahead of scientific evidence is the "lowest kind of immorality" into which a thinking being can fall. Yet such is the logic by which our scientific absolutists pretend to regulate our lives!

In truths dependent on our personal action, then, faith based on desire is certainly a lawful and possibly an indispensable thing.

But now, it will be said, these are all childish human cases, and have nothing to do with great cosmical matters, like the question of religious faith. Let us then pass on to that. Religions differ so much in their accidents that in discussing the religious question we must make it very generic and broad. What then do we now mean by the religious hypothesis? Science says things are; morality says some things are better than other things; and religion says essentially two things.

First, she says that the best things are the more eternal things, the overlapping things, the things in the universe that throw the last stone, so to speak, and say the final word. "Perfection is eternal,"—this phrase of Charles Secretan seems a good way of putting this first affirmation of religion, an affirmation which obviously cannot yet be verified scientifically at all.

The second affirmation of religion is that we are better off even now if we believe her first affirmation to be true.

Now, let us consider what the logical elements of this situation are *in case the religious hypothesis in both its branches be really true*. (Of course, we must admit that possibility at the outset. If we are to discuss the question at all, it must involve a living option. If for any of you religion be a hypothesis that cannot, by any living possibility be true, then you need go no farther. I speak to the "saving remnant" alone.) So proceeding, we see, first, that religion offers itself as a *momentous* option. We are supposed to gain, even now, by our belief, and to lose by our nonbelief, a certain vital good. Secondly, religion is a *forced* option, so far as that good goes. We cannot escape the issue by remaining sceptical and waiting for more light, because, although we do avoid error in that way *if religion be untrue*, we lose the good, *if it be true*, just as certainly as if we positively chose to disbelieve. It is as if a man should hesitate indefinitely to ask a certain woman to marry him because he was not perfectly sure that she would prove an angel after he brought her home. Would he not cut himself off from that particular angel-possibility as decisively as if he went and married some one else? Scepticism, then, is not avoidance of option; it is option of a certain particular kind of risk. *Better risk loss of truth than chance of error,*—that is your faith-vetoer's exact position. He is actively playing his stake as much as the believer is; he is backing the field against the religious hypothesis, just as the believer is backing the religious hypothesis against the field. To preach scepticism to us as a duty until "sufficient evidence" for religion be found, is tantamount therefore to telling us, when in presence of the religious hypothesis, that to yield to our fear of its being error is wiser and better than to yield to our hope that it may be true. It is not intellect against all passions, then; it is only intellect with one passion laying down its law. And by what, forsooth, is the supreme wisdom of this passion warranted? Dupery for dupery, what proof is there that dupery through hope is so much worse than dupery through fear? I, for one, can see no proof; and I simply refuse obedience to the scientist's command to imitate his kind of option, in a case where my own stake is important enough to give me the right to choose my own form of risk. If religion be true and the evidence for it be still insufficient, I do not wish, by putting your extinguisher upon my nature (which feels to me as if it had after all some business in this matter), to forfeit my sole chance in life of getting upon the winning side,—that chance depending, of course, on my willingness to run the risk of acting as if my passional need of taking the world religiously might be prophetic and right.

All this is on the supposition that it really may be prophetic and right, and that, even to us who are discussing the matter, religion is a live hypothesis which may be true. Now, to most of us religion comes in a still further way that makes a veto on our active faith even more illogical. The more perfect and more eternal aspect of the universe is represented in our religions as having personal form. The universe is no longer a mere *It* to us, but a *Thou*, if we are religious; and any relation that may be possible from person to person might be possible here. For instance, although in one sense we are passive portions of the universe, in another we show a curious autonomy, as if we were small active centres on our own account. We feel, too, as if the appeal of religion to us were made to our own active good-will, as if evidence might be forever withheld from us unless we met the hypothesis half-way. To take a trivial illustration: just as a man who in a company of gentlemen made no advances, asked a warrant for every concession, and believed no one's word without proof, would cut himself off by such churlishness from all the social rewards that a more trusting spirit would earn,—so here, one who should shut himself up in snarling logicality and try to make the gods extort his recognition willy-nilly, or not get it at all, might cut himself off forever from his only opportunity of making the gods' acquaintance. This feeling, forced on us we know not whence, that by obstinately believing that there are gods (although not to do so would be so easy both for our logic and our life) we are doing the universe the deepest service we can, seems part of the living essence of the religious hypothesis. If the hypothesis *were* true in all its parts, including this one, then pure intellectualism, with its veto on our making willing advances, would be an absurdity; and some participation of our sympathetic nature would be logically required. I, therefore, for one, cannot see my way to accepting the agnostic rules for truth-seeking, or willfully agree to keep my willing nature out of the game. I cannot do so for this plain reason, that *a rule of thinking which would absolutely prevent me from acknowledging certain kinds of truth if those kinds of truth were really there, would be an irrational rule.* That for me is the long and short of the formal logic of the situation, no matter what the kinds of truth might materially be.

I confess I do not see how this logic can be escaped. But sad experience makes me fear that some of you may still shrink from radically saying with me, *in abstracto,* that we have the right to believe at our own risk any hypothesis that is live enough to tempt our will. I suspect, however, that if this is so, it is because you have got away from the abstract logical point of view altogether, and are thinking (perhaps without realizing it) of some particular religious hypothesis which for you is dead. The freedom to "believe what we will" you apply to the case of some patent superstition; and the faith you think of is the faith defined by the schoolboy when he said, "Faith is when you believe something that you know ain't true." I can only repeat that this is misapprehension. *In concerto*, the freedom to believe can only cover living options which the intellect of the individual cannot by itself resolve; and living options never seem absurdities to him who has them to consider. When I look at the religious question as it really puts itself to concrete men, and when I think of all the possibilities which both practically and theoretically it involves, then this command that we shall put a stopper on our heart, instincts, and courage, and *wait*—acting of course meanwhile more or less as if religion were *not* true—till doomsday, or till such time as our intellect and senses working together may have raked in evidence enough,—this command, I say, seems to me the queerest idol ever manufactured in the philosophic cave. Were we scholastic absolutists, there might be more excuse. If we had an infallible intellect with its objective certitudes, we might feel ourselves disloyal to such a perfect organ of knowledge in not trusting to it exclusively, in not waiting for its releasing word. But if we are empiricists, if we believe that no bell in us tolls to let us know for certain when truth is in our grasp, then it seems a piece of idle fantasticality to preach so solemnly our duty of waiting for the bell. Indeed we wait if we will,—I hope you do not think that I am denying that,—but if we do so, we do so at our peril as much as if we believed. In either case *we act*, taking our life in our hands. No one of us ought to issue vetoes to the other, nor should we bandy words of abuse. We ought, on the contrary, delicately and profoundly to respect one another's mental freedom: then only shall we bring about the intellectual republic; then only shall we have that spirit of inner tolerance without which all our tolerance is soulless, and which is empiricism's glory; then only shall we live and let live, in speculative as well as in practical things. . . .

Problems and Puzzles

18. My Confession

Leo Tolstoy

Leo Tolstoy (1828–1910), author of such famous novels as War *and* Peace *and* Anna Karenina, *was also an important social and moral reformer in his native Russia.*

IV

My life came to a standstill. I could breathe, eat, drink, and sleep, and could not help breathing, eating, drinking, and sleeping; but there was no life, because there were no desires the gratification of which I might find reasonable. If I wished for anything, I knew in advance that, whether I gratified my desire or not, nothing would come of it. If a fairy had come and had offered to carry out my wish, I should not have known what to say. If in moments of intoxication I had, not wishes, but habits of former desires, I knew in sober moments that that was a deception, that there was nothing to wish for. I could not even wish to find out the truth, because I guessed what it consisted in. The truth was that life was meaningless. It was as though I had just been living and walking along, and had come to an abyss, where I saw clearly that there was nothing ahead but perdition. And it was impossible to stop and go back, and impossible to shut my eyes, in order that I might not see that there was nothing ahead but suffering and imminent death,—complete annihilation.

What happened to me was that I, a healthy, happy man, felt that I could not go on living,—an insurmountable force drew me on to find release from life. I cannot say that I *wanted* to kill myself.

The force which drew me away from life was stronger, fuller, more general than wishing. It was a force like the former striving after life, only in an inverse sense. I tended with all my strength away from life. The thought of suicide came as naturally to me as had come before the ideas of improving life. That thought was so seductive that I had to use cunning against myself, lest I should rashly execute it. I did not want to be in a hurry, because I wanted to use every effort to disentangle myself: if I should not succeed in disentangling myself, there would always be time for that. And at such times I, a happy man, hid a rope from myself so that

Reprinted from *The Complete Works of Count Tolstoy*, Vol. 13, translated and edited by Leo Wiener. Colonial Press Co., New York and Boston. Copyright, 1904.

I should not hang myself on a cross-beam between two safes in my room, where I was by myself in the evening, while taking off my clothes, and did not go out hunting with a gun, in order not to be tempted by an easy way of doing away with myself. I did not know myself what it was I wanted: I was afraid of life, strove to get away from it, and, at the same time, expected something from it.

All that happened with me when I was on every side surrounded by what is considered to be complete happiness. I had a good, loving, and beloved wife, good children, and a large estate, which grew and increased without any labour on my part. I was respected by my neighbours and friends, more than ever before, was praised by strangers, and, without any self-deception, could consider my name famous. With all that, I was not deranged or mentally unsound,—on the contrary, I was in full command of my mental and physical powers, such as I had rarely met with in people of my age: physically I could work in a field, mowing, without falling behind a peasant; mentally I could work from eight to ten hours in succession, without experiencing any consequences from the strain. And while in such condition I arrived at the conclusion that I could not live, and, fearing death, I had to use cunning against myself, in order that I might not take my life.

This mental condition expressed itself to me in this form: my life is a stupid, mean trick played on me by somebody. Although I did not recognize that "somebody" as having created me, the form of the conception that some one had played a mean, stupid trick on me by bringing me into the world was the most natural one that presented itself to me.

Involuntarily I imagined that there, somewhere, there was somebody who was now having fun as he looked down upon me and saw me, who had lived for thirty or forty years, learning, developing, growing in body and mind, now that I had become strengthened in mind and had reached that summit of life from which it lay all before me, standing as a complete fool on that summit and seeing clearly that there was nothing in life and never would be. And that was fun to him—

But whether there was or was not that somebody who made fun of me, did not make it easier for me. I could not ascribe any sensible meaning to a single act, or to my whole life. I was only surprised that I had not understood that from the start. All that had long ago been known to everybody. Sooner or later there would come diseases and death (they had come already) to my dear ones and to me, and there would be nothing left but stench and worms. All my affairs, no matter what they might be, would sooner or later be forgotten, and I myself should not exist. So why should I worry about all these things? How could a man fail to see that and live,—that was surprising! A person could live only so long as he was drunk; but the moment he sobered up, he could not help seeing that all that was only a deception, and a stupid deception at that! Really, there was nothing funny and ingenious about it, but only something cruel and stupid.

Long ago has been told the Eastern story about the traveller who in the steppe is overtaken by an infuriated beast. Trying to save himself from the animal, the traveller jumps into a waterless well, but at its bottom he sees a dragon who opens his jaws in order to swallow him. And the unfortunate man does not dare climb out, lest he perish from the infuriated beast, and does not dare jump down to the bottom of the well, lest he be devoured by the dragon, and so clutches the twig of a wild bush growing in a cleft of the well and holds on to it. His hands grow weak and he feels that soon he shall have to surrender to the peril which awaits him at either side; but he still holds on and sees two mice, one white, the other black, in even measure making a circle around the main trunk of the bush to which he is clinging, and nibbling at it on all sides. Now, at any moment, the bush will break and tear off, and he will fall into the dragon's jaws. The traveller sees that and knows that he will inevitably perish; but while he is still clinging, he sees some drops of honey hanging on the leaves of the bush, and so reaches out for them with his tongue and licks the leaves. Just so I hold on to the branch of life, knowing that the dragon of death is waiting inevitably for me, ready to tear me to pieces, and I cannot understand why I have fallen on such suffering. And I try to lick that honey which used to give me pleasure; but now it no longer gives me joy, and the white and the black mouse day and night nibble at the branch to which I am holding on. I clearly see the dragon, and the honey is no longer sweet to me. I see only the inevitable dragon and the mice, and am unable to turn my glance away from them. That is not a fable, but a veritable, indisputable, comprehensible truth.

The former deception of the pleasures of life, which stifled the terror of the dragon, no longer deceives me. No matter how much one should say to me, "You cannot understand the meaning of life, do not think, live!" I am unable to do so, because I have been doing it too long before. Now I cannot help seeing day and night, which run and lead me up to death. I see that alone, because that alone is the truth. Everything else is a lie.

The two drops of honey that have longest turned my eyes away from the cruel truth, the love of family and of authorship, which I have called an art, are no longer sweet to me.

"My family—" I said to myself, "but my family, my wife and children, they are also human beings. They are in precisely the same condition that I am in: they must either live in the lie or see the terrible truth. Why should they live? Why should I love them, why guard, raise, and watch them? Is it for the same despair which is in me, or for fullness of perception? Since I love them, I cannot conceal truth from them,—every step in cognition leads them up to this truth. And the truth is death."

"Art, poetry?" For a long time, under the influence of the success of human praise, I tried to persuade myself that that was a thing which could be done, even though death should come and destroy everything, my deeds, as well as my memory of them; but soon I came to see that that, too, was a deception. It was clear to me that art was an adornment of life, a decoy of life. But life lost all its attractiveness for me. How, then, could I entrap others? So long as I did not live my own life, and a strange life bore me on its waves; so long as I believed that life had some sense, although I was not able to express it,—the reflections of life of every description in poetry and in the arts afforded me pleasure, and I was delighted to look at life through this little mirror of art; but when I began to look for the meaning of life, when I experienced the necessity of living myself, that little mirror became either useless, superfluous, and ridiculous, or painful to me. I could no longer console myself with what I saw in the mirror, namely, that my situation was stupid and desperate. It was all right for me to rejoice so long as I believed in the depth of my soul that life had some sense. At that time the play of lights—of the comical, the tragical, the touching, the beautiful, the terrible in life—afforded me amusement. But when I knew that life was meaningless and terrible, the play in the little mirror could no longer amuse me. No sweetness of honey could be sweet to me, when I saw the dragon and the mice that were nibbling down my support.

That was not all. If I had simply comprehended that life had no meaning, I might have known that calmly,—I might have known that that was my fate. But I could not be soothed by that. If I had been like a man living in a forest from which he knew there was no way out, I might have lived; but I was like a man who had lost his way in the forest, who was overcome by terror because he had lost his way, who kept tossing about in his desire to come out on the road, knowing that every step got him only more entangled, and who could not help tossing.

That was terrible. And, in order to free myself from that terror, I wanted to kill myself. I experienced terror before what was awaiting me,—I knew that that terror was more terrible than the situation itself, but I could not patiently wait for the end. No matter how convincing the reflection was that it was the same whether a vessel in the heart should break or something should burst, and all should be ended, I could not wait patiently for the end. The terror of the darkness was too great, and I wanted as quickly as possible to free myself from it by means of a noose or a bullet. It was this feeling that more than anything else drew me on toward suicide. . . .

VII

Having found no elucidation in science, I began to look for it in life, hoping to find it in the men who surrounded me. I began to observe the people such as I, to see how they lived about me and what attitude they assumed to the question that had brought me to the point of despair.

This is what I found in people who were in the same position as myself through their education and manner of life.

I found that for people of my circle there were four ways out from the terrible condition in which we all are.

The first way out is through ignorance. It consists in not knowing, not understanding that life is evil and meaningless. People of this category—mostly women or very young or very dull persons—have not yet come to understand that question of life which presented itself to Schopenhauer, Solomon, and Buddha. They see neither the dragon that awaits them, nor the mice that are nibbling at the roots of the bushes to which they are holding on, and continue to lick the honey. But they lick the honey only till a certain time: something will direct their attention to the dragon and the mice, and there will be an end to their licking. From them I can learn nothing,—it is impossible to stop knowing what you know.

The second way out is through Epicureanism. It consists in this, that, knowing the hopelessness of life, one should in the meantime enjoy such good as there is, without looking either at the dragon or the mice, but licking the honey in the best manner possible, especially if there is a lot of it in one spot. Solomon expresses this way out like this:

"Go thy way, eat thy bread with joy, and drink thy wine. Live joyfully with the wife whom thou lovest all the days of the life of thy vanity, which he hath given thee under the sun, all the days of thy vanity: for that is thy portion in this life, and in thy labour which thou takest under the sun. Whatsoever thy hand findeth to do, do it with thy might; for there is no work, nor device, nor knowledge, nor wisdom, in the grave, whither thou goest."

Thus the majority of the people of our circle support the possibility of life in themselves. The conditions in which they are give them more good than evil, and their moral dullness makes it possible for them to forget that the advantage of their situation is a casual one; that not everybody can have a thousand wives and palaces, like Solomon; that to every man with a thousand wives there are a thousand men without wives, and for every palace there are a thousand people who built it in the sweat of their brows; and that the accident which had made me a Solomon today, will tomorrow make me a slave of Solomon. The dullness of the imagination of these people makes it possible for them to forget that which gave no rest to Buddha,—the inevitableness of sickness, old age, and death, which sooner or later will destroy all those pleasures.

Thus think and feel the majority of men of our time and our manner of life. The fact that some of these people assert that the dullness of their comprehension and imagination is philosophy, which they call positive, in my opinion does not take them out of the category of those who, in order not to see the question, lick the honey. Such people I could not imitate: as I did not possess their dullness of comprehension, I could not artificially reproduce it in myself. Just like any live man, I could not tear my eyes away from the mice and the dragon, having once seen them.

The third way out is through force and energy. It consists in this, that, having comprehended that life is evil and meaningless, one should set out to destroy it. Thus now and then act strong, consistent people. Having comprehended all the stupidity of the joke which has been played upon them, and seeing that the good of the dead is better than that of the living, and that it is better not to be at all, they go and carry this out and at once put an end to that stupid joke, so long as there are means for it: a noose about the neck, the water, a knife to pierce the heart with, railway trains. The number of people of our circle who do so is growing larger and larger. These people commit the act generally at the best period of life, when the mental powers are in full bloom and few habits have been acquired that lower human reason.

I saw that that was the worthiest way out, and I wanted to act in that way.

The fourth way out is through weakness. It consists in this, that, comprehending the evil and the meaninglessness of life, one continues to drag it out, knowing in advance that nothing can come of it. People of this calibre know that death is better than life, but, not having the strength to act reasonably, to make an end to the deception, and to kill themselves, they seem to be waiting for something. This is the way of weakness, for if I know that which is better, which is in my power, why not abandon myself to that which is better? I belonged to that category.

Thus people of my calibre have four ways of saving themselves from the terrible contradiction. No matter how much I strained my mental attention, I saw no other way out but those four. The one way out was not to understand that life was meaningless, vanity, and an evil, and that it was better not to live. I could not help knowing it and, having once learned it, I could not shut my eyes to it. The second way out was to make use of life such as it is, without thinking of the future. I could not do that either. Like Sakya-Muni, I could not go out hunting, when I knew that there was old age, suffering, death. My imagination was too vivid. Besides, I could not enjoy the accident of the moment, which for a twinkling threw enjoyment in my path. The third way out was, having come to see that life was an evil and a foolishness, to make an end of it and kill myself. I comprehended that, but for some reason did not kill myself. The fourth way out was to live in the condition of Solomon, of Schopenhauer,—to know that life was a stupid joke played on me, and yet to live, wash and dress myself, dine, speak, and even write books. That was repulsive and painful for me, but still I persisted in that situation. . . .

XII

I remember, it was early in spring, I was by myself in the forest, listening to the sounds of the woods. I listened and thought all the time of one and the same thing that had formed the subject of my thoughts for the last three years. I was again searching after God.

"All right, there is no God," I said to myself, "there is not such a being as would be, not my concept, but reality, just like my whole life,—there is no such being. And nothing, no miracles, can prove him to me, because the miracles would be my concept, and an irrational one at that.

"But my idea about God, about the one I am searching after?" I asked myself. "Where did that idea come from?" And with this thought the joyous waves of life again rose in me. Everything about me revived, received a meaning; but my joy did not last long,—the mind continued its work.

"The concept of God is not God," I said to myself. "A concept is what takes place within me; the concept of God is what I can evoke or can not evoke in myself. It is not that which I am searching after. I am trying to find that without which life could not be." And again everything began to die around me and within me, and I wanted again to kill myself.

Then I looked at myself, at what was going on within me, and I recalled those deaths and revivals which had taken place within me hundreds of times. I remembered that I lived only when I believed in God. As it had been before, so it was even now: I needed only to know about God, and I lived; I needed to forget and not believe in him, and I died.

What, then are these revivals and deaths? Certainly I do not live when I lose my faith in the existence of God; I should have killed myself long ago, if I had not had the dim hope of finding him. "So what else am I looking for?" a voice called out within me. "Here he is. He is that without which one cannot live. To know God and live is one and the same thing. God is life."

"Live searching after God, and then there will be no life without God." And stronger than ever all was lighted up within me and about me, and that light no longer abandoned me.

Thus I was saved from suicide. When and how this transformation took place in me I could not say. Just as imperceptibly and by degrees as my force of life had waned, and I had arrived at the impossibility of living, at the arrest of life, at the necessity of suicide, just so by degrees and imperceptibly did that force of life return to me. Strange to say, the force of life which returned to me was not a new, but the same old force which had drawn me on in the first period of my life.

I returned in everything to the most remote, the childish and the youthful. I returned to the belief in that will which had produced me and which wanted something of me; I returned to this, that the chief and only purpose of my life was to be better, that is, to live more in accord with that will; I returned to this, that the expression of this will I could find in that which all humanity had worked out for its guidance in the vanishing past, that is, I returned to the faith in God, in moral perfection, and in the tradition which had handed down the meaning of life. There was only this difference, that formerly it had been assumed unconsciously, while now I knew that I could not live without it.

This is what seemed to have happened with me: I do not remember when I was put in a boat, was pushed off from some unknown shore, had pointed out to me the direction toward another shore, had a pair of oars given into my inexperienced hands, and was left alone. I plied my oars as well as I could, and moved on; but the farther I rowed toward the middle, the swifter did the current become which bore me away from my goal, and the more frequently did I come across oarsmen like myself, who were carried away by the current. There were lonely oarsmen, who continued to row; there were large boats, immense ships, full of people; some struggled against the current, others submitted to it. The farther I rowed, the more did I look down the current, whither all those boats were carried, and forget the direction which had been pointed out to me. In the middle of the current, in the crush of the boats and ships which bore me down, I lost my direction completely and threw down the oars. On every side of me sailing vessels and rowboats were borne down the current with merriment and rejoicing, and the people in them assured me and each other that there could not even be any other direction, and I believed them and went down the stream with them. I was carried away, so far away, that I heard the noise of the rapids where I should be wrecked, and saw boats that had already been wrecked there. I regained my senses. For a long time I could not understand what had happened with me. I saw before me nothing but ruin toward which I was rushing and of which I was afraid; nowhere did I see any salvation, and I did not know what to do; but, on looking back, I saw an endless number of boats that without cessation stubbornly crossed the current, and I thought of the shore, the oars, and the direction, and began to make my way back, up the current and toward the shore.

That shore was God, the direction was tradition, the oars were the freedom given me to row toward the shore,—to unite myself with God. Thus the force of life was renewed in me, and I began to live once more.

19. Three Arguments for Nonbelief

Michael Martin

Michael Martin (1932–   ), emeritus professor of philosophy at Boston University, has written books and articles on a variety of philosophical issues. His book Atheism: A Philosophical Justification *has been widely discussed by philosophers and theologians.*

In this essay, I will present three fresh arguments to justify nonbelief in the theistic God usually associated with Christianity and Judaism. First, the Argument from Incoherence shows that the concept of God is like the concept of a round square or a four-sided triangle. Round squares or four-sided triangles cannot exist; neither can God. Second, the Argument from Nonbelief was originally presented by contemporary American philosopher Theodore Drange. Especially relevant to evangelical Christianity and Orthodox Judaism, it maintains that the large amount of nonbelief in the world makes the existence of God improbable. Third is a new Moral Argument for Nonbelief constructed by contemporary Canadian philosopher Raymond Bradley. It turns on the conflict between the view that God would not cause or condone immoral acts and biblical statements in which God does precisely this.

These three arguments are relatively new. Though versions of the Argument from Incoherence are centuries old, the version I present here combines various insights developed mainly over the last twenty-five years. Drange put forth his Argument from Nonbelief in 1998, and Bradley's version of the Moral Argument was published in 2000.

It should be noted that theism can be viewed from both a philosophical perspective and a biblical standpoint. According to the philosophical perspective, God is an all-knowing (omniscient), all-powerful (omnipotent), all-good (omnibenevolent) disembodied being who created the Universe. This view is rather abstract and remote, compared with the more popular concrete concept of God held by ordinary men and women and assumed in the Bible. On the biblical view, God is personal: He can be understood by analogy to a human person, and human beings can enter into a personal relation with Him, petitioning Him in prayer and referring to Him as "Thou."

Let us call the first view the God of the philosophers, and the second view the God of the Bible. In what follows I will touch on both.

The Argument from Incoherence

One good reason not to believe that God exists is that the very concept of God is incoherent, in the same way as is the concept of a round square or the "largest

First published in *Free Inquiry*, Fall 2001. © Council for Secular Humanism, 2001.

number." In accordance with our two perspectives, philosophical and biblical, this argument can be made in two ways:

First, some properties attributed to God in the Bible are inconsistent.[1] For example, God is said to be invisible (Col. 1:15, 1 Tim. 1:17, 6:16), a being that has never been seen (John 1:18, 1 John 4:12). Yet several people in the Bible, among them Moses (Exod. 33:11, 23), Abraham, Isaac, and Jacob (Gen. 12:7, 26:2; Exod. 6:3) report having seen God. God is supposed to have said, "You cannot see my face, for no one can see me and live" (Gen. 32:30). However, Jacob saw God and lived (Gen. 32:30). In some places God is described as merciful,[2] in others as lacking mercy,[3] in some places as a being who repents and changes His mind,[4] in others as a being who never repents and changes His mind,[5] in some places as a being who deceives and causes confusion and evil,[6] and in others as a being who never does,[7] in some places as someone who punishes children for their parents' wrongdoing,[8] and in others as one who never does.[9] So if one takes what the Bible says seriously, God cannot exist.

The Argument from Incoherence can also be made by showing that the attributes specified in philosophical accounts of God are either in conflict with one another, or are internally inconsistent. In my book *Atheism: A Philosophical Justification*, I spend thirty pages analyzing in detail the incoherence connected with the concepts of omniscience, omnipotence, and divine freedom. Here, I only have space to outline the case regarding omniscience.

In one important sense, to say that God is omniscient is to say that God is all-knowing. To say that God is all-knowing entails that He has all knowledge that there is. Now philosophers have usually distinguished three different kinds of knowledge: *propositional, procedural*, and *knowledge by acquaintance*. Propositional knowledge is factual knowledge, the knowledge that something is the case. Procedural knowledge, or knowledge how, is a type of skill, and is not reducible to propositional knowledge.[10] Finally *knowledge by acquaintance* is direct experience with some object, person, or phenomenon.[11] For example, to say "I know Mr. Jones" implies that one has not only detailed propositional knowledge about Mr. Jones, but direct acquaintance with him. Similarly, to say "I know poverty" implies that, beside detailed propositional knowledge of poverty, one has some direct experience of it.

---

[1] I am indebted here to Ted Drange, *Nonbelief and Evil* (Amherst, N.Y.: Prometheus Books, 1998), pp. 80–82.

[2] Psalms 86:5, 100:5, 103:8, 106:1, 136:2. 148: 8–9; Joel 2:13; Mic. 7:18; James 5:11.

[3] Deut. 7:2, 16, 20:16–17; Josh. 6:21, 10:11, 19, 40, 11:6–20; Isa. 6, 19, 15:3; Nah. 1:2; Jer. 13:14; Matt. 8:12, 13:42, 50, 25:30, 41, 46; Mark 3:29; 2 Thes. 1:8-9; Rev. 14:9–11, 21:8.

[4] Gen. 6:6; Exod. 32:14; 1 Sam. 2:30–31, 15:11, 35; 2 Sam. 24:16; 2 Kings 20: 1–6; Psalms 106:45; Jer. 42:10; Amos 7:3; John 3:10.

[5] Num. 23:19; 1 Sam. 15:29; Ezek. 24:14; Mal. 3:6; James 1:17.

[6] Gen. 11:7; Judg. 9:23; 1 Sam. 16:14; Lam. 3:38; 1 Kings 22:22–23; Isa. 45:7; Amos 3:6; Jer. 18:11, 20:7; Ezek. 20:25; 2 Thes. 2:11.

[7] Deut. 32:4; Psalms 25:8, 100:5, 145:9; 1 Col. 14:33.

[8] Gen. 9:22–25; Exod. 20:5, 34:7; Num. 14:18; Deut. 5:9; 2 Sam. 12:14; Isa. 14:21, 65:6–7.

[9] Deut. 24:16; 2 Chron. 25:4; Ezek. 18:20.

[10] For an account of two types of knowledge—knowing how and knowing that—see Israel Scheffler, *Conditions of Knowledge* (Chicago: Scott, Foresman and Co., 1965).

[11] See D. W. Hamlyn, *The Theory of Knowledge* (Garden City, N.Y.: Doubleday, 1970), pp. 104–106.

To say that God is all-knowing, then, is to say that God has all propositional knowledge, all procedural knowledge, *and* all knowledge by acquaintance. This has implications for the existence of God that usually have not been noticed. First, God's omniscience conflicts with His disembodiedness. If God were omniscient, then God would have all knowledge, including, for example, knowledge of how to swim. Yet only a being with a body can have such procedural knowledge—that is, actually possess the *skill* of swimming—and by definition God does not have a body. Therefore, God's attribute of being disembodied and His attribute of being omniscient are in conflict. Thus, if God is both omniscient and disembodied, God does not exist. Since God is both omniscient and disembodied, therefore He does not exist.

The property of being all-knowing also conflicts with certain moral attributes usually attributed to God. If God is omniscient, He has knowledge by acquaintance of all aspects of lust and envy. But one aspect of lust and envy is *having feelings* of lust and envy. However, God is typically conceived as being morally perfect, and His being morally perfect excludes these feelings. Consequently, there is a contradiction in the concept of God. Consequently, God does not exist.[12]

In addition, God's omniscience conflicts with His omnipotence. Since God is omnipotent He cannot experience fear, frustration, and despair.[13] For, in order to have these experiences, one must believe that one is limited in power. But since God is all-knowing and all-powerful, He knows that He is not limited in power. Consequently, He cannot have complete knowledge *by acquaintance* of all aspects of fear, frustration, and despair. On the other hand, since God is omniscient He *must* have this knowledge. So if one takes philosophical accounts of God seriously, God cannot exist.[14]

The Argument from Nonbelief

A second reason for disbelieving in God is the large number of nonbelievers in the world.[15] The Argument from Nonbelief is especially telling against evangelical Christianity, although it has some force against other religions, for example, Orthodox

---

[12]This argument was developed in Michael Martin, "A Disproof of the God of the Common Man," *Question*, 1974, 115–24; Michael Martin, "A Disproof of God's Existence," *Darshana International*, 1970.

[13]Cf. David Blumenfeld, "On the Compossibility of the Divine Attributes," *Philosophical Studies*, 34(1978): 91–103.

[14]Can my arguments be answered? Of course, one could give a different interpretation of God or of the Old Testament. In so doing one would attempt to show that the concept of God is not incoherent. But any such interpretation must not be arbitrary or otherwise problematic. With respect to conflicting biblical passages, a Christian who read an earlier draft of this essay criticized my method of interpretation as neglecting the central themes and concentrating on what he called "legalistic" details. Unfortunately, he did not venture an opinion about how these details are to be reconciled or how one determines the central themes.

Various objections to my abstract philosophical arguments can, of course, be imagined. One might argue that, since it is not logically possible for God to have all knowledge by acquaintance and all knowledge how, God's knowledge should be limited to factual knowledge. The trouble with this reply, however, is that it would be logically impossible for God to have knowledge that it is logically possible for humans to have. The result is paradoxical, to say the least.

[15]See Theodore Drange, *Nonbelief and Evil*. Drange is the first philosopher I know to develop and defend this argument in a systematic way.

Judaism. Evangelical Christianity asserts that (1) God is merciful and all-loving, compassionate and caring towards humanity; (2) The Bible, and *only* the Bible, is *the* source of God's word; (3) God wants all humans to be saved; (4) A necessary condition for being saved is becoming aware of the word of God and accepting it.

Supposing for the sake of the argument that evangelical Christianity is true, it is difficult to understand why there are nearly one billion nonbelievers in the world. How can a merciful God, a God who wants all humans to be saved, *not* provide clear and unambiguous information about His word to humans when having this information is necessary for salvation? Yet, as we know, countless millions of people down through history have not been exposed to the teaching of the Bible. Those who have been were often exposed in superficial and cursory ways that were not conducive to acceptance. Even today there are millions of people who, through no fault of their own, either remain ignorant of the Christian message or, because of shortcomings in their religious education, reject it. One would expect that, if God were rational, He would have arranged things in such a way that there would be more believers.

Here are a few obvious ideas about how God could have done this:

1. God could have made the Bible more plausible. He could have made it free from contradictions, factual errors, and false or ambiguous prophecies.

2. God could have provided people with exposure to the Bible's message, say, by putting Bibles in every household in the world in the occupants' native language.

3. God could have spoken from the heavens in all known languages so that no human could doubt His existence and His message.

4. God could have sent angels disguised as human preachers to spread His word, empowering them to perform unambiguous miracles and works of wonder.

5. God could have implanted a belief in Himself and His message in every person's mind.

6. In recent times, God could have communicated with millions of people by interrupting prime-time television programs to present His message.

Any and all of these methods, and countless others I have not mentioned, would increase the number of believers and presumably the number of saved people. Yet, God has used none of them.

There are a number of defenses against the Argument for Nonbelief that I should briefly mention:

1. *The Free Will Defense*: Theists might argue that God wants His creatures to believe in Him without coercion. The above suggestions, it might be said, involve *making* people believe in God, and that would interfere with their free will.

However, none of my suggestions about how God could increase people's belief in Him limit free will. For example, to provide people with clear and unambiguous evidence of His existence hardly interferes with free will, since they can reject this evidence. Further, in the Bible God is said to have performed spectacular miracles that influenced people to believe in Him. For example, in Exodus 7:5 God performs a miracle to demonstrate to Israelites that He is the true God. Even if God were to implant belief in Himself in people's minds, they could reject the implanted idea. Moreover, it makes no sense to suppose that a rational God would create human beings in His own image, yet expect them to be so irrational as to believe in Him without strong evidence.

2. *The Testing Defense*: Some evangelical Christians rebut the Argument from Nonbelief by saying that the evidence for God is clear and unambiguous, but humans have rejected it because of spiritual defects such as false pride. Those who accept the evidence pass the test; those who do not accept it fail the test.

However, there is no reason to suppose that evidence for God is convincing and that people reject it because of some spiritual defect. A more plausible hypothesis is that the evidence for God is utterly unconvincing. In addition, even if it were convincing, billions of people because of their backgrounds or circumstances have not been exposed to it. Moreover, if the Bible is convincing in principle, and humans have been exposed to it, they may not see that it is true because of faulty reasoning. It is grossly unfair to punish people for not believing in God either because they have not been exposed to His teachings, or because of an error of reasoning.

3. *The Unknown Purpose Defense*: Theists might argue that God has some unknown reason for permitting so many nonbelievers to exist. However, God has properties that make His having an unknown purpose for permitting so much non-belief implausible. Thus, according to evangelical Christianity, God wants humans to love Him. How can He want this, and yet fail to make billions of humans aware of the gospel message, since loving Him presupposes being aware of His message? The appeal to unknown purposes at worst makes God appear irrational, and at best creates a mystery that detracts from the explanatory power of theism.[16]

Bradley's Moral Argument

Bradley presents a moral argument for the nonexistence of God by showing that four basic claims associated with the Bible are in conflict:[17]

1. Any act that God commits, causes, commands, or condones is morally permissible.

2. The Bible reveals to us many of the acts that God commits, causes, commands, or condones.

3. It is morally impermissible for God to commit, cause, command, or condone acts that violate our moral principles.

4. The Bible tells us that God does in fact commit, cause, command, or condone acts that violate our moral principles.

---

[16]Although I do not have time to develop this argument with respect to Orthodox Judaism, it is fairly clear how it would proceed. In Orthodox Judaism the question is, Why are there so many descendants of the Israelites who since the time of Moses have rejected one or more of the following: (1) There exists a being who rules the entire universe; (2) This Being has a chosen people, namely, the Israelites; (3) He gave them a set of laws, the Torah, and He wants them and their descendants to follow it? God could have done many things to bring the wayward Israelites back into the fold but He did not.

[17]See Raymond D. Bradley, "A Moral Argument for Atheism." *The New Zealand Rationalist and Humanist*, Spring 2000, pp. 2–12.

There are great difficulties standing in the way of anyone who wishes to deny any of these claims, yet since they are in conflict, at least one of them *must* be denied. To deny the first claim—that any act of God that commits, commands, and so on is morally permissible—would be to admit that God is immoral or even evil. But this would mean that He is not worthy of worship. To deny the second claim—that the Bible reveals to us many of the acts that God commits, commands, and so on—would be to give up the foundation of religious and moral epistemology. If this claim is false, then how can we know *what* we ought or ought not to do? The Bible, according to theists, is the major source of our knowledge of ethical principles. To deny the third claim—that it is morally impermissible for God to commit, command, and so on acts that violate our moral principle—would mean that it is morally impermissible to perform acts such as deliberately slaughtering innocent men, women, and children; making people cannibalize their friends and family; practicing human sacrifice; or torturing people endlessly for their beliefs. It would be to align God with moral monsters such as Hitler, Stalin, and Pol Pot. No theist who believes the Ten Commandments or the Sermon on the Mount could deny that this third claim is true.

This leaves the last claim. But the Bible states clearly that God does indeed commit, cause, command, and condone acts that violate our moral principles. God drowned the whole human race except Noah and his family.[18] He punished King David for carrying out a census that God himself had ordered, and He followed David's request to punish others by sending a plague that killed 70,000 people.[19] He commanded Joshua to kill old and young, little children and women, the inhabitants of some thirty-one kingdoms.[20] God says in many places that He has made or will make people cannibalize their own children, husbands, wives, parents, and friends because they have disobeyed Him. God condones Jephthah's act sacrificing his only child as a burnt offering.[21] Finally, God will torture a large portion of the human race in Hell for not believing in Jesus.[22]

Can this moral argument be challenged? One possible strategy apologists might use is to re-interpret biblical passages such as those I have cited in a way that renders them morally harmless. Another is to try to show that our moral principles do not apply to the situations previously described, or that they allow exceptions that would acquit God for having broken them.

Consider the first strategy. With respect to God's threatening to make people cannibalize their own friends and relatives, apologists have offered two rationalizations. First, they have argued that God does not carry out the threat. Second, they argue that these are simply predictions of what will befall the Israelites at the hands of their enemies. However, there are problems with both replies. If

---

[18]Gen. 7:23.
[19]2 Sam. 24:1–15.
[20]Josh. Chapter 10.
[21]Judges 11: 10–39.
[22]Rev. 13:8, 14:10–11.

they are threats, since God did not carry them out they are empty; hence, God is unreliable. Moreover, it is hard to see how a good and merciful God can make threats of immoral actions. If they are predictions, then God has said something false. Moreover, in the case of Jeremiah, it is clear that God is not predicting what the Israelites' enemies will do, but what *He* will do.

With respect to the second strategy, it might be argued that there are exceptions to the moral principles against torturing innocent people endlessly, performing child sacrifice, and slaughtering innocent people. For example, it might be suggested that God is exempt from these principles even though they are binding on humans. But this double standard makes God less than holy and not worthy of worship. Another tactic is to invoke the doctrine of original sin, that every human being is born in sin, and argue that God is acting on the overriding principle that sin must be punished. So God has the right to punish us as he sees fit. There are, however, two problems with this reply. One is that the doctrine of original sin is implausible. How can newborn babes be held responsible for an inherited and, in their own cases, unactualized disposition to sin? That point aside, this principle would allow human beings to slaughter anyone they like and justify their actions in terms of the punishment of original sin. If slaughtering newborn babies is morally permissible for God, why not for humans too?

So I see no way out of Bradley's problem for theists. They must give up at least one of the above claims—either that the acts of God are morally permissible, or that the Bible reveals to us what those acts are. If they abandon the first, they give up belief in God's holiness; if they abandon the second, they give up the belief that the Bible is His revelation.

Conclusion

I have presented three arguments here for nonbelief in the theistic God. The Argument from Incoherence provides good reasons for rejecting both the God of the philosophers and the God of the Bible. The Argument from Nonbelief is especially effective against evangelical Christianity and Orthodox Judaism, which base their doctrines mainly on biblical considerations and not on abstract philosophical arguments. The Moral Argument provides good reasons for not believing in the God of the Bible.

It goes without saying that these three arguments do not constitute the entire case for nonbelief. On the one hand, there are other strong arguments that I have not examined here (see my *Atheism*, Part 2). On the other, in addition to the many arguments *for* atheism there are devastating arguments *against* theism; or to put it another way, there are refutations of arguments that claim to show that God does exist. Indeed, I know of no argument for God that stands up under critical scrutiny (see my *Atheism*, Part 1). So, given the arguments for atheism and against theism, I think it can safely be said that the case for nonbelief is extremely strong.

Suggestions for Further Reading

Anthologies

Brody, Baruch A. *Readings in the Philosophy of Religion*. 2nd ed. Englewood Cliffs, N.J.: Prentice Hall, 1991. A comprehensive collection emphasizing contemporary essays in the recent analytical tradition.

Davies, Brian, ed. *Philosophy of Religion: A Guide and Anthology*. New York: Oxford University Press, 2000. A collection of important classical and contemporary writings on the philosophy of religion, together with commentary and introductory material.

Flew, Antony, and Alasdair Macintyre, eds. *New Essays in Philosophical Theology*. London: SCM Press, 1955. A collection of important writings on various aspects of the philosophy of religion. Many of these articles will be difficult for the beginning student.

Hick, John, ed. *The Existence of God*. New York: Macmillan, 1964. A good collection of classical and contemporary writings on the major arguments for the existence of God.

Kaufmann, Walter, ed. *Religion from Tolstoy to Camus*. New York: Harper, 1961. A collection of some of the most important writings on the philosophy of religion.

Pike, Nelson, ed. *God and Evil*. Englewood Cliffs, N.J.: Prentice Hall, 1964. A collection of opposing views and arguments about the problem of evil. There is a good bibliography for the student who wishes to read further on this topic.

Sanders, Steven and David R. Cheney, eds. *The Meaning of Life*. Englewood Cliffs, N.J.: Prentice Hall, 1980. A collection of significant writings on the meaning and value of life.

Individual Works

Abraham, William J. *An Introduction to the Philosophy of Religion*. Englewood Cliffs, N.J.: Prentice Hall, 1985. A readable introduction to the major topics in the philosophy of religion.

Collins, John. *God in Modern Philosophy*. Chicago: Regnery, 1959. A survey of many of the major issues in the philosophy of religion from a Catholic point of view.

Du Noüy, Lecomte. *Human Destiny*. New York: Longmans, 1947. A version of the argument from design. Du Noüy argues that the facts of biology cannot be adequately explained unless the existence of a Designer is accepted.

Hick, John. *Philosophy of Religion*. 4th ed. Englewood Cliffs, N.J.: Prentice Hall, 1989. An excellent brief introduction to the philosophy of religion. The student will find this a valuable guide in organizing the issues raised by the readings in this text.

Hume, David. *Dialogues on Natural Religion*, edited by Norman Kemp Smith. Indianapolis: Bobbs, 1947. A classic discussion of the argument from design. The beginning student will find this difficult but very rewarding.

Mackie, J. L. *The Miracle of Theism*. Oxford: Clarendon Press, 1982. A careful presentation and criticism of the arguments for God's existence.

Matson, Wallace I. *The Existence of God*. Ithaca, N.Y.: Cornell Univ. Press, 1965. An excellent, detailed analysis of the major arguments for the existence of God.

Nielsen, Kai. *Philosophy and Atheism*. Buffalo, N.Y.: Prometheus, 1985. A collection of articles by a contemporary defender of atheism.

Paley, William. *Natural Theology: Selections*, edited by Frederick Ferré. Indianapolis: Bobbs, 1963. The classic statement of the argument from design.

Purtill, Richard L. *Thinking About Religion*. Englewood Cliffs, N.J.: Prentice Hall, 1978. A clear, entertainingly written introduction to the main issues in the philosophy of religion.

Scriven, Michael. *Primitive Philosophy*. New York: McGraw-Hill, 1966. Chapter Four presents an interesting and detailed defense of atheism.

Smith, George H. *Atheism: The Case Against God*. Buffalo, N.Y.: Prometheus, 1979. An analysis and defense of atheism.

Warren, Thomas B., and Wallace I. Matson. *The Warren-Matson Debate on the Existence of God*. Jonesboro, Ark.: National Christian Press, 1978. This debate is especially noteworthy because of Matson's provocative arguments and emotionally moving appeals for tolerance.

Encyclopedias

Dictionary of the History of Ideas: Studies of Selected Pivotal Ideas. Philip P. Weiner, editor-in-chief. New York: Scribner's, 1973. Substantial and clearly written essays emphasizing the historical development of topics discussed in this part. Designed to inform the nonspecialist, each essay concludes with a select bibliography.

Encyclopedia of Philosophy. Paul Edwards, editor-in-chief. New York: Macmillan, 1967. The beginning student will find many worthwhile articles on the subjects treated in this part and excellent bibliographies.

Routledge Encyclopedia of Philosophy. Edward Craig, general editor. New York: Routledge, 1998. This ten-volume encyclopedia contains articles on all areas of philosophy and up-to-date bibliographies.

Internet Web Sites

RESEARCH NAVIGATOR *(http://www.researchnavigator.com)*. This web site offers three research data bases: Ebsco Academic Journal and Abstract Data Base, *New York Times* Search by Subject Archive, and "Best of the Web" Link Library. In addition, this site provides helpful advice on how to conduct efficient and productive research from choosing a topic to polishing the final draft. Beginning philosophy students probably will find the "Best of the Web" Link Library the most appropriate place to start their research. The free access code necessary to employ Research Navigator can be found in the Prentice Hall Guide to Evaluating Online Resources. If your text did not come with this guide, please go to *www.prenhall.com/contentselect* for information on how you can purchase an access code.

EpistemeLinks *(http://www.epistemelinks.com)*. This site provides many links to philosophical resources on the web.

PART THREE

Morality and Society

Introduction

Just about everyone seeks to distinguish right from wrong behavior and to determine what is worthwhile in life. In our society we frequently encounter discussions about the morality of the death penalty, the decline in current moral values, and the injustice done to minority groups. Also, at times, we are faced with personal moral decisions: Should we lie to get out of an unpleasant situation? Should we fight in a war if we think it unjust? Should we cheat on our income tax if we are sure we will not get caught? It is these kinds of questions that produce philosophical speculations about the basis of morality and the good life.

Although philosophers are concerned with the kinds of moral problems we face in daily life, they believe that primary concern should be given to a number of very basic problems that must be answered before it is possible to give a reasoned answer to any other moral issues. *Ethics* is that branch of philosophy that is concerned with finding answers to these basic problems. Some of the problems most often discussed in the study of ethics include the following: Is there a basis for deciding whether any act is right? How can we prove or disprove that there is such a basis? What kinds of things are most worth attaining? When does a person deserve to be praised or blamed? In answering these kinds of questions, the philosopher does not merely give an opinion or list a variety of opinions on the subject but rather attempts to find reasons that will show that a certain answer is correct. The student seeking to get a lot out of the readings must pay close attention to reasons that are offered and attempt to decide which philosophers, if any, have proved their case.

Many students approach ethics with the belief that there is little to be gained from the investigation because they believe that moral standards or principles are merely products of the society in which one lives. They believe that the moral views of people in other societies, no matter how much they differ from one's own, are correct for the people in those societies. Such a view is called *relativism*.

Two kinds of relativism, sociological and ethical, must be distinguished and defined before the topic can be clearly discussed. *Sociological relativism* is the name given to the factual claim that societies sometimes have different ultimate principles. An ultimate principle is one that is used as a basis for defending all other moral judgments and principles. It seems evident that societies do have different moral principles regarding a variety of matters such as marriage, raising the young, and the treatment of women. The crucial point, however, is whether societies that obviously differ in their moral practices also differ in their view of the correct ultimate principle. The observed differences may not indicate differences in ultimate principles but merely the necessity of different behavior to satisfy the same principle. For example, a society with insufficient food to feed everyone might kill the elderly when they are no longer productive in order to save the young. A society with abundant means to care for the elderly would probably consider killing them abhorrent. Yet if the latter society were suddenly to find its means reduced to that of the former, it might well consider the killing of the elderly as a necessity because, like the first society, it too wants to ensure survival of the group.

The belief in sociological relativism has been of great significance because for many it justifies ethical relativism. *Ethical relativism* is the view that there are different but equally correct ultimate principles. This position is opposed to *ethical absolutism*, a theory that holds that there is only one correct ultimate principle or set of principles. The conflict between the ethical absolutist and ethical relativist is of crucial importance. If the relativist is right, it would be necessary to give up the criticism of other societies, and possibly each individual's ultimate moral principles, although one still could criticize the application of those principles.

W. T. Stace's "Ethical Relativism" presents the arguments for and against both ethical relativism and ethical absolutism. He shows that sociological relativism, even if true, would not require a belief in ethical relativism, for the absolutist could claim that those ultimate moral principles contrary to the "true" one were merely mistaken. Further, Stace argues that the consequences of ethical relativism are unacceptable and that ethical absolutism, despite the difficulty of establishing the correct moral principle, is preferable.

Philosophers have presented a number of theories concerning the correct ultimate moral principles. Three of the most prominent views are egoism, utilitarianism, and formalism. The main tenet of *egoism* is that self-interest is the only proper standard of conduct. Egoists deny that they ever have a moral duty to sacrifice their own interests for the interests of others. Egoists may frequently act generously or charitably, but only because they find such acts to be in their own long-term interests. Many egoists defend their position by claiming that everyone is motivated solely by self-interest, and, thus, it would be pointless to urge people to act in a nonegoistic manner. In "The Morality Trap," Harry Browne presents a forceful statement of the egoist position. For him, a person should always strive to produce the best consequences for himself. To achieve this result, two traps must be avoided: the morality trap and the unselfishness trap. The morality trap is the belief that there is some nonegoistic basis (such as God's will or the good of society) on which one should base moral judgments. The unselfishness trap is the belief that one's own happiness should be sacrificed for the happiness of others. If these two traps are avoided, one is on the road to self-fulfillment and personal happiness.

Utilitarianism is a moral theory that holds that right acts are those that produce the greatest happiness. In deciding which acts are right, a utilitarian considers the consequences of all the acts open to him or her and performs the one that would produce the best consequences for everybody concerned. Although many would agree that this is generally a proper procedure, sometimes there is dissatisfaction with some kinds of acts that might turn out to be right on this basis. For example, if it would produce the best results for all concerned, then it would be right to lie, steal, and even murder. Jeremy Bentham's "Utilitarianism" presents a clear statement of the utilitarian position and attempts to work out some of the details required for its implementation. He maintains that in assessing the consequences of various possible acts, we should be concerned with the amounts of pleasure and pain produced and perform only those acts resulting in the most pleasure or the least pain. Bentham believed that the only thing ultimately worthwhile in life is pleasure. Such a view that the good is pleasure is called *hedonism*. The student should realize, however, that a utilitarian need not be a hedonist. He or she could believe that many things besides pleasure, such as intellectual growth, beauty, and integrity, are worthwhile and that these should be considered in assessing possible actions.

Unlike egoists and utilitarians, some moral theorists maintain that the rightness or wrongness of actions is not determined by the consequences produced by the actions. Such a view is called *formalism* in ethical theory. The kinds of ultimate principles that formalists have held have varied widely. One formalist principle that has had great appeal is the golden rule, "Do unto others as you would have others do unto you." In "The Deep Beauty of the Golden Rule," R. M. MacIver defends this rule as the only one that can bring agreement out of the conflicting moral viewpoints because it lays down a procedure to follow in determining proper behavior rather than stating final goals and values. A problem for the student in considering MacIver's view is to decide on what basis the golden rule is being defended. Is MacIver appealing to the utility of accepting it, or is there some other basis of appeal?

An issue receiving increasing interest from moral theorists is the extent to which our environment should be protected. Some theorists want to protect the environment to help humans, but others want to protect it to help plants and nonhuman animals as well as humans. In "People or Penguins: The Case for Optimal Pollution," William Baxter maintains that environmental policies should be concerned only with the welfare of humans. For him, the survival of plants and animals that are not helpful to humans is unimportant. Baxter asserts that because some human goods cannot be achieved without permitting low levels of air and water pollution, the goal should not be to eliminate pollution, but to allow the level needed for the production of the greatest amount of human goods. In "Environmental Values," Peter Singer contends that we should weigh the interests of every creature that can feel pain, not just humans, in forming our environmental policies. This weighing might show that sometimes it is right to harm humans to protect other animals. Efforts to preserve plants or the beauty of our landscape, however, are justified only if they do not harm sentient creatures.

An issue much debated at present is the morality of abortion. Opinions on this issue range from the extreme liberal view that women should be free to end unwanted pregnancies by abortion at any time to the extreme conservative view that all abortions are wrong since they involve killing an innocent person. Relevant to the assessment of the various views on abortion are a variety of metaphysical and moral issues: Is the fetus a human being? If so, when does it become one? Is it ever morally justified intentionally to kill one innocent person to save another? Should fetuses have the same rights as children? The two readings on this issue deal with these fundamental questions. In "An Almost Absolute Value in History," John T. Noonan contends that a fetus should be considered a human being at the moment of conception because at that time the genetic code that determines human potentialities is acquired. Noonan examines and rejects other proposed criteria for determining when a fetus should be considered human. If every fetus possesses full human rights, then abortion involves the taking of a human life. So, for Noonan, abortion would be justified only in those rare instances when the rights of others outweighed the fetus's right to life. In "A Defense of Abortion," Judith Jarvis Thomson argues that even if a fetus is a human being from the moment of conception, abortion is still morally permissible in many cases. She contends that women, having the right to use their bodies as they choose, need not allow a fetus to use it. Although a fetus needs a mother's body, its use of it must depend on the mother's good will.

The "Problems and Puzzles" section contains two provocative articles. In "The Case for Torture," Michael Levin contends that the use of torture should not be so strongly condemned as it is. Since most people would support its use to prevent a disaster, it is not a type of act that is always wrong. Whether or not torture is justified to prevent harmful acts that are not disasters should be determined by a careful assessment of its consequences in a given case. The need to torture a terrorist to obtain information that would save lives is a case in which torture might be justified. In "The Survival Lottery," John Harris argues that a lottery drawing among healthy people whenever organs were needed for transplants could save lives. If killing and taking the organs of one person could save several people, the lottery would be morally justified. Although the possibility of being selected would be frightening, the lottery actually makes people safer since it saves more lives than it takes.

Are Ethical Values Relative?

20. Ethical Relativism

W. T. Stace

Any ethical position which denies that there is a single moral standard which is equally applicable to all men at all times may fairly be called a species of ethical relativity. There is not, the relativist asserts, merely one moral law, one code, one standard. There are many moral laws, codes, standards. What morality ordains in one place or age may be quite different from what morality ordains in another place or age. The moral code of Chinamen is quite different from that of Europeans, that of African savages quite different from both. Any morality, therefore, is relative to the age, the place, and the circumstances in which it is found. It is in no sense absolute.

This does not mean merely—as one might at first sight be inclined to suppose—that the very same kind of action which is *thought* right in one country and period may be *thought* wrong in another. This would be a mere platitude, the truth of which everyone would have to admit. Even the absolutist would admit this—would even wish to emphasize it—since he is well aware that different people have different sets of moral ideas, and his whole point is that some of these sets of ideas are false. What the relativist means to assert is, not this platitude, but that the very same kind of action which *is* right in one country and period may *be* wrong in another. And this, far from being a platitude, is a very startling assertion.

It is very important to grasp thoroughly the difference between the two ideas. For there is reason to think that many minds tend to find ethical relativity attractive because they fail to keep them clearly apart. It is so very obvious that moral ideas differ from country to country and from age to age. And it is so very easy, if you are mentally lazy, to suppose that to say this means the same as to say that no universal moral standard exists,—or in other words that it implies ethical relativity. We fail to see that the word "standard" is used in two different senses. It is perfectly true that, in one sense, there are many variable moral standards. We speak of judging a man by the standard of his time. And this implies that different times have different standards. And this, of course, is quite true. But when the word "standard" is used in this sense it means simply the set of moral ideas current during the period in question. It means what people *think* right, whether as a matter of fact it *is* right or not. On the other hand when the absolutist asserts that there exists a single universal moral "standard," he is not using the word in this sense at all. He means by "standard" what *is* right as distinct from what people merely think right. His point is that although what people think right varies in different countries and periods, yet what actually is right is everywhere and always the same. And it follows that when the ethical relativist disputes the position of the absolutist and denies that any universal moral standard exists he too means by "standard" what actually is right. But it is exceedingly easy, if we are not careful, to slip loosely from using the word in the first sense to using it in the second sense; and to suppose that the variability of moral beliefs is the same thing as the variability of what really is moral. And unless we keep the two senses of the word "standard" distinct, we are likely to think the creed of ethical relativity much more plausible than it actually is.

The genuine relativist, then, does not merely mean that Chinamen may think right what Frenchmen think wrong. He means that what *is* wrong for the Frenchman may *be* right for the Chinaman. And if one enquires how, in those circumstances, one is to know what actually is right in China or in France, the answer comes quite glibly. What is right in China is the same as what people think right in China; and what is right in France is the same as what people think right in France. So that, if you want to know what is moral in any particular country or age all you have to do is ascertain what are the moral ideas current in that age or country. Those ideas are, *for that age or country*, right. Thus what is morally right is identified with what is thought to be morally right, and the distinction which we made above between these two is simply denied. To put the same thing in another way, it is denied that there can be or ought to be any distinction between the two senses of the word "standard." There is only one kind of standard of right and wrong, namely, the moral ideas current in any particular age or country.

Moral right *means* what people think morally right. It has no other meaning. What Frenchmen think right is, therefore, right *for Frenchmen*. And evidently one must conclude—though I am not aware that relativists are anxious to draw one's attention to such unsavoury but yet absolutely necessary conclusions from their creed—that cannibalism is right for people who believe in it, that human sacrifice is right for those races which practice it, and that burning widows alive was right for Hindus until the British stepped in and compelled the Hindus to behave immorally by allowing their widows to remain alive.

When it is said that, according to the ethical relativists, what is thought right in any social group is right for that group, one must be careful not to misinterpret this. The relativist does not, of course, mean that there actually is an objective moral standard in France and a different objective standard in England, and that French and British opinions respectively give us correct information about these different standards. His point is rather that there are no objectively true moral standards at all. There is no single universal objective standard. Nor are there a variety of local objective standards. All standards are subjective. People's subjective feelings about morality are the only standards which exist.

To sum up. The ethical relativist consistently denies, it would seem, whatever the ethical absolutist asserts. For the absolutist there is a single universal moral standard. For the relativist there is no such standard. There are only local, ephemeral, and variable standards. For the absolutist there are two senses of the word "standard." Standards in the sense of sets of current moral ideas are relative and changeable. But the standard in the sense of what is actually morally right is absolute and unchanging. For the relativist no such distinction can be made. There is only one meaning of the word "standard," namely, that which refers to local and variable sets of moral ideas. Or if it is insisted that the word must be allowed two meanings, then the relativist will say that there is at any rate no actual example of a standard in the absolute sense, and that the word as thus used is an empty name to which nothing in reality corresponds; so that the distinction between the two meanings becomes empty and useless. Finally—though this is merely saying the same thing in another way—the absolutist makes a distinction between what actually is right and what is thought right. The relativist rejects this distinction and identifies what is moral with what is thought by certain human beings or groups of human beings. . . .

I shall now proceed to consider, first, the main arguments which can be urged in favour of ethical relativity, and secondly, the arguments which can be urged against it. . . . The first is that which relies upon the actual varieties of moral "standards" found in the world. It was easy enough to believe in a single absolute morality in older times when there was no anthropology, when all humanity was divided clearly into two groups, Christian peoples and the "heathen." Christian peoples knew and possessed the one true morality. The rest were savages whose moral ideas could be ignored. But all this is changed. Greater knowledge has brought greater tolerance. We can no longer exalt our own morality as alone true, while dismissing all other moralities as false or inferior. The investigations of anthropologists have shown that there exist side by side in the world a bewildering variety of moral codes. On this topic endless volumes have been written, masses of evidence piled up. Anthropologists have ransacked the Melanesian Islands, the jungles of New Guinea, the steppes of Siberia, the deserts of Australia, the forests of central Africa, and have brought back with them countless examples of weird, extravagant, and fantastic "moral" customs with which to confound us. We learn that all kinds of horrible practices are, in this, that, or the other place, regarded as essential to virtue. We find that there is nothing, or next to nothing, which has always and everywhere been regarded as morally good by all men. Where then is our universal morality? Can we, in face of all this evidence, deny that it is nothing but an empty dream?

This argument, taken by itself, is a very weak one. It relies upon a single set of facts—the variable moral customs of the world. But this variability of moral ideas is admitted by both parties to the dispute, and is capable of ready explanation upon the hypothesis of either party. The relativist says that the facts are to be explained by the non-existence of any absolute moral standard. The absolutist says that they are to be explained by human ignorance of what the absolute moral standard is. And he can truly point out that men have differed widely in their opinions about all manner of topics—including the subject-matters of the physical sciences—just as much as they differ about morals. And if the various different opinions which men have held about the shape of the earth do not prove that it has no one real shape, neither do the various opinions which they have held about morality prove that there is no one true morality.

Thus the facts can be explained equally plausibly on either hypothesis. There is nothing in the facts themselves which compels us to prefer the relativistic hypothesis to that of the absolutist. And therefore the argument fails to prove the relativist conclusion. If that conclusion is to be established, it must be by means of other considerations.

This is the essential point. But I will add some supplementary remarks. The work of the anthropologists, upon which ethical relativists seem to rely so heavily, has as matter of fact added absolutely nothing *in principle* to what has always been known about the variability of moral ideas. Educated people have known all along that the Greeks tolerated sodomy, which in modern times has been regarded in some countries as an abominable crime; that the Hindus thought it a sacred duty to burn their widows; that trickery, now thought despicable, was once believed to be a virtue; that terrible torture was thought by our own ancestors only a few centuries ago to be a justifiable weapon of justice; that it was only yesterday that western peoples came to believe that slavery is immoral. Even the ancients knew very well that moral customs and ideas vary—witness the writings of Herodotus. Thus the principle of the variability of moral ideas was well understood long before modern anthropology was ever heard of. Anthropology has added nothing to the knowledge of this principle except a mass of new and extreme examples of it drawn from very remote sources. But to multiply examples of a principle already well known and universally admitted adds nothing to the argument which is built upon that principle. The discoveries of the anthropologists have no doubt been of the highest importance in their own sphere. But in my considered opinion they have thrown no new light upon the special problems of the moral philosopher.

Although the multiplication of examples has no logical bearing on the argument, it does have an immense *psychological* effect upon people's minds. These masses of anthropological learning are impressive. They are propounded in the sacred name of "science." If they are quoted in support of ethical relativity—as they often are—people *think* that they must prove something important. They bewilder and over-awe the simple-minded, batter down their resistance, make them ready to receive humbly the doctrine of ethical relativity from those who have acquired a reputation by their immense learning and their claims to be "scientific." Perhaps this is why so much ado is made by ethical relativists regarding the anthropological evidence. But we must refuse to be impressed. We must discount all this mass of evidence about the extraordinary moral customs of remote peoples. Once we have admitted—as everyone who is instructed must have admitted these last two thousand years without any anthropology at all—the principle that moral ideas vary, all this new evidence adds nothing to the argument. And the argument itself proves nothing for the reasons already given. . . .

The second argument in favour of ethical relativity is also a very strong one. And it does not suffer from the disadvantage that it is dependent upon the acceptance of any particular philosophy such as radical empiricism. It makes its appeal to considerations of a quite general character. It consists in alleging that no one has ever been able to discover upon what foundation an absolute morality could rest, or from what source a universally binding moral code could derive its authority.

If, for example, it is an absolute and unalterable moral rule that all men ought to be unselfish, from whence does this *command* issue? For a command it certainly is, phrase it how you please. There is no difference in meaning between the sentence "You ought to be unselfish" and the sentence "Be unselfish." Now a command implies a commander. An obligation implies some authority which obliges. Who is this commander, what this authority? Thus the vastly difficult question is raised of *the basis of moral obligation*. Now the argument of the relativist would be that it is impossible to find any basis for a universally binding moral law; but that it is quite easy to discover a basis for morality if moral codes are admitted to be variable, ephemeral, and relative to time, place, and circumstance.

In this book I am assuming that it is no longer possible to solve this difficulty by saying naively that the universal moral law is based upon the uniform commands of God to all men. There will be many, no doubt, who will dispute this. But I am not writing for them. I am writing for those who feel the necessity of finding for morality a basis independent of particular religious dogmas. And I shall therefore make no attempt to argue the matter.

The problem which the absolutist has to face, then, is this. The religious basis of the one absolute morality having disappeared, can there be found for it any other, any secular, basis? If not, then it would seem that we cannot any longer believe in absolutism. We shall have to fall back upon belief in a variety of perhaps mutually inconsistent moral codes operating over restricted areas and limited periods. No one of these will be better, or more true, than any other. Each will be good and true for those living in those areas and periods. We shall have to fall back, in a word, on ethical relativity.

For there is no great difficulty in discovering the foundations of morality, or rather of moralities, if we adopt the relativist hypothesis. Even if we cannot be quite certain *precisely* what these foundations are—and relativists themselves are not entirely agreed about them—we can at least see in a general way the *sort* of foundations they must have. We can see that the question on this basis is not in principle impossible to answer—although the details may be obscure; while, if we adopt the absolutist hypothesis—so the arguments runs—no kind of answer is conceivable at all. . . .

This argument is undoubtedly very strong. It *is* absolutely essential to solve the problem of the basis of moral obligation if we are to believe in any kind of moral standards other than those provided by mere custom or by irrational emotions. It is idle to talk about a universal morality unless we can point to the source of its authority—or at least to do so is to indulge in a faith which is without rational ground. To cherish a blind faith in morality may be, for the average man whose business is primarily to live aright and not to theorize, sufficient. Perhaps it is his wisest course. But it will not do for the philosopher. His function, or at least one of his functions, is precisely to discover the rational grounds of our everyday beliefs—if they have any. Philosophically and intellectually, then, we cannot accept belief in a universally binding morality unless we can discover upon what foundation its obligatory character rests.

But in spite of the strength of the argument thus posed in favour of ethical relativity, it is not impregnable. For it leaves open one loop-hole. It is always possible that some theory, not yet examined, may provide a basis for a universal moral obligation. The argument rests upon the negative proposition that *there is no theory which can provide a basis for a universal morality*. But it is notoriously difficult to prove a negative. How can you prove that there are no green swans? All you can show is that none have been found so far. And then it is always possible that one will be found tomorrow. . . .

It is time that we turned our attention from the case in favour of ethical relativity to the case against it. Now the case against it consists, to a very large extent, in urging that, if taken seriously and pressed to its logical conclusion, ethical relativity can only end in destroying the conception of morality altogether, in undermining its practical efficacy, in rendering meaningless many almost universally accepted truths about human affairs, in robbing human beings of any incentive to strive for a better world, in taking the life-blood out of every ideal and every aspiration which has ever ennobled the life of man. . . .

First of all, then, ethical relativity, in asserting that the moral standards of particular social groups are the only standards which exist, renders meaningless all propositions which attempt to compare these standards with one another in respect to their moral worth. And this is a very serious matter indeed. We are accustomed to think that the moral ideas of one nation or social group may be "higher" or "lower" than those of another. We believe, for example, that Christian ethical ideals are nobler than those of the savage races of central Africa. Probably most of us would think that the Chinese moral standards are higher than those of the inhabitants of New Guinea. In short we habitually compare one civilization with another and judge the sets of ethical ideas to be found in them to be some better, some worse. The fact that such judgments are very difficult to make with any justice, and that they are frequently made on very superficial and prejudiced grounds, has no bearing on the question now at issue. The question is whether such judgments have any *meaning*. We habitually assume that they have.

But on the basis of ethical relativity they can have none whatever. For the relativist must hold that there is no *common* standard which can be applied to the various civilizations judged. Any such comparison of moral standards implies the existence of some superior standard which is applicable to both. And the existence of any such standard is precisely what the relativist denies. According to him the Christian standard is applicable only to Christians, the Chinese standard only to Chinese, the New Guinea standard only to the inhabitants of New Guinea.

What is true of comparisons between the moral standards of different races will also be true of comparisons between those of different ages. It is not unusual to ask such questions as whether the standard of our own day is superior to that which existed among our ancestors five hundred years ago. And when we remember that our ancestors employed slaves, practiced barbaric physical tortures, and burnt people alive, we may be inclined to think that it is. At any rate we assume that the question is one which has meaning and is capable of rational discussion. But if the ethical relativist is right, whatever we assert on this subject must be totally meaningless. For here again there is no common standard which could form the basis of any such judgments.

This in its turn implies that the whole notion of moral *progress* is a sheer delusion. Progress means an advance from lower to higher, from worse to better. But on the basis of ethical relativity it has no meaning to say that the standards of this age are better (or worse) than those of a previous age. For there is no common standard by which both can be measured. Thus it is nonsense to say that the morality of the New Testament is higher than that of the Old. And Jesus Christ, if he imagined that he was introducing into the world a higher ethical standard than existed before his time, was merely deluded. . . .

I come now to a second point. Up to the present I have allowed it to be taken tacitly for granted that, though judgments comparing different races and ages in respect of the worth of their moral codes are impossible for the ethical relativist, yet judgments of comparison between individuals living within the same social group would be quite possible. For individuals living within the same social group would presumably be subject to the same moral code, that of their group, and this would therefore constitute, as between these individuals, a common standard by which they could both be measured. We have not here, as we had in the other case, the difficulty of the absence of any common standard of comparison. It should therefore be possible for the ethical relativist to say quite meaningfully that President Lincoln was a better man than some criminal or moral imbecile of his own time and country, or that Jesus was a better man than Judas Iscariot.

But is even this minimum of moral judgment really possible on relativist grounds? It seems to me that it is not. For when once the whole of humanity is abandoned as the area covered by a single moral standard, what smaller areas are to be adopted as the *loci* of different standards? Where are we to draw the lines of demarcation? We can split up humanity, perhaps,—though the procedure will be very arbitrary—into races, races into nations, nations into tribes, tribes into families, families into individuals. Where are we going to draw the *moral* boundaries? Does the *locus* of a particular moral standard reside in a race, a nation, a tribe, a family, or an individual? Perhaps the blessed phrase "social group" will be dragged in to save the situation. Each such group, we shall be told, has its own moral code which is, for it, right. But what *is* a "group"? Can any one define it or give its boundaries? This is the seat of that ambiguity in the theory of ethical relativity to which reference was made on an earlier page.

The difficulty is not, as might be thought, merely an academic difficulty of logical definition. If that were all, I should not press the point. But the ambiguity has practical consequences which are disastrous for morality. No one is likely to say that moral codes are confined within the arbitrary limits of the geographical divisions of countries. Nor are the notions of race, nation, or political state likely to help us. To bring out the essentially practical character of the difficulty let us put it in the form of concrete questions. Does the American nation constitute a "group" having a single moral standard? Or does the standard of what I ought to do change continuously as I cross the continent in a railway train? Do different States of the Union have different moral codes? Perhaps every town and village has its own peculiar standard. This may at first sight seem reasonable enough. "In Rome do as Rome does" may seem as good a rule in morals as it is in etiquette. But can we stop there? Within the village are numerous cliques having their own set of ideas. Why should not each of these claim to be bound only by its own special and peculiar moral standards? And if it comes to that, why should not the gangsters of Chicago claim to constitute a group having its own morality, so that its murders and debaucheries must be viewed as "right" by the only standard which can legitimately be applied to it? And if it be answered that the nation will not tolerate this, that may be so. But this is to put the foundation of right simply in the superior force of the majority. In that case whoever is stronger will be right, however monstrous his ideas and actions. And if we cannot deny to any set of people the right to have its own morality, is it not clear that, in the end, we cannot even deny this right to the individual? Every individual man and woman can put up, on this view, an irrefutable claim to be judged by no standard except his or her own.

If these arguments are valid, the ethical relativist cannot really maintain that there is anywhere to be found a moral standard binding upon anybody against his will. And he cannot maintain that, even within the social group, there is a common standard as between individuals. And if that is so, then even judgments to the effect that one man is morally better than another become meaningless. All moral valuation thus vanishes. There is nothing to prevent each man from being a rule unto himself. The result will be moral chaos and the collapse of all effective standards. . . .

But even if we assume that the difficulty about defining moral groups has been surmounted, a further difficulty presents itself. Suppose that we have now definitely decided what are the exact boundaries of the social group within which a moral standard is to be operative. And we will assume—as is invariably done by relativists themselves—that this group is to be some actually existing social community such as a tribe or nation. How are we to know, even then, what actually *is* the moral standard within that group? How is anyone to know? How is even a member of the group to know? For there are certain to be within the group—at least this will be true among advanced peoples—wide differences of opinion as to what is right, what wrong. Whose opinion, then, is to be taken as representing *the* moral standard of the group? Either we must take the opinion of the majority within the group, or the opinion of some minority. If we rely upon the ideas of the majority, the results will be disastrous. Wherever there is found among a people a small band of select spirits, or perhaps one man, working for the establishment of higher and nobler ideals than those commonly accepted by the group, we shall be compelled to hold that, for that people at that time, the majority are right, and that the reformers are wrong and are preaching what is immoral. We shall have to maintain, for example, that Jesus was preaching immoral doctrines to the Jews. Moral goodness will have to be equated always with the mediocre and sometimes with the definitely base and ignoble. If on the other hand we said that the moral standard of the group is to be identified with the moral opinions of some minority, then what minority is this to be? We cannot answer that it is to be the minority composed of the best and most enlightened individuals of the group. This would involve us in a palpably vicious circle. For by what standard are these individuals to be judged the best and the most enlightened? There is no principle by which we could select the right minority. And therefore we should have to consider every minority as good as every other. And this means that we should have no logical right whatever to resist the claim of the gangsters of Chicago—if such a claim were made—that their practices represent the highest standards of American morality. It means in the end that every individual is to be bound by no standard save his own.

The ethical relativists are great empiricists. *What* is the actual moral standard of any group can only be discovered, they tell us, by an examination on the ground of the moral opinions and customs of that group. But will they tell us how they propose to decide, when they get to the ground, which of the many moral opinions they are sure to find there is *the* right one in that group? To some extent they will be able to do this for the Melanesian Islanders—from whom apparently all lessons in the nature of morality are in future to be taken. But it is certain that they cannot do it for advanced peoples whose members have learnt to think for themselves and to entertain among themselves a wide variety of opinions. They cannot do it unless they accept the calamitous view that the ethical opinion of the majority is always right. We are left therefore once more with the conclusion that, even within a particular social group, anybody's moral opinion is as good as anybody else's, and that every man is entitled to be judged by his own standards.

Finally, not only is ethical relativity disastrous in its consequences for moral theory. It cannot be doubted that it must tend to be equally disastrous in its impact upon practical conduct. If men come really to believe that one moral standard is as good as another, they will conclude that their own moral standard has nothing special to recommend it. They might as well then slip down to some lower and easier standard. It is true that, for a time, it may be possible to hold one view in theory and to act practically upon another. But ideas, even philosophical ideas, are not so ineffectual that they can remain for ever idle in the upper chambers of the intellect. In the end they seep down to the level of practice. They get themselves acted on.

How Should We Behave?

21. The Morality Trap

Harry Browne

Harry Browne (1933–) is an ardent supporter of free enterprise and the author of several books on finance and investment.

I. The Morality Trap

The Morality Trap is the belief that you must obey a moral code created by someone else.

This trap is a variation of the Identity Trap in that it leads you to try to be something other than yourself. It's an easy trap to get caught in and an easy way to lose your freedom.

Morality is a powerful word. Perhaps even more powerful is the word *immoral*. In an attempt to avoid being labeled *immoral*, many people allow themselves to be manipulated by others.

What Is Morality? At the same time, the concept of morality is very vague. What is it? Where does it come from? What purpose does it serve? How is it determined?

My dictionary defines *morality* as "Moral quality or character; rightness or wrongness, as of an action." Well then, let's refer to the definition of *moral*, which is: "Related to, serving to teach, or in accordance with, the principles of right and wrong."

Now we're getting somewhere; all we need is a definition of *right*. And I suppose you can guess what *that* is: "In accordance with justice, law, morality, etc."[1]

Unfortunately, this definitional merry-go-round is typical of the common understanding of morality. You should do something because it's "right"—but *by what standard?*

It seems to me that there are three different kinds of morality. I call them *personal*, *universal*, and *absolute*. By looking at each of them, I think we can get a clearer idea of what morality is and how it can be useful in helping you to achieve your freedom.

Reprinted from *How I Found Freedom in an Unfree World*, © 1997 ISBN 0-9656036-7-9 by Harry Browne, by permission of Collier Associates, P.O. Box 20149, West Palm Beach, FL 33416 USA.

[1] *Webster's New World Dictionary of the American Language*, 1966 edition: World Publishing Company, New York.

Personal Morality We've seen that you act in ways that you hope will bring the best consequences to you. And the "best consequences" are those that bring you happiness.

You always have to consider the consequences of your actions; they're the point of anything you do. However, any given act will undoubtedly cause *many* consequences. You may see that a particular action will produce a consequence you want, but you might also be aware that it could produce other consequences that you don't want. . . .

Since you're always seeking numerous different goals, you try to foresee the ways in which something immediately desirable might get in the way of other things that are ultimately more desirable. You try to consider more than just what's immediately in front of you. You're placing things in a broader context.

Obviously, you can't expect to foresee *all* the consequences of a given act, but you can try to see all the significant ones. In some cases . . . there are obvious consequences that immediately rule out a proposed course of action.

In other cases, more subtle possibilities will be recognized after a few minutes' thought. But there will also be cases in which you won't be aware of the specific consequences until *after* you've acted and begun to experience them.

Code of Conduct Because you can't foresee all the specific consequences of what you do, there's a need to have some generalized rules available that can help keep you out of situations that could be troublesome. Those rules can be valuable if they do two things: (1) steer you away from potential disasters; and (2) remind you of the things you must do to satisfy your most important long-term desires.

The basic question is: "How can I get something I want without hurting my chances for other things that are more important to me?"

It is this generalized, long-term attitude that underlies an individual's basic code of conduct. And when we speak of morality, I can't think of any other sensible reason to be concerned about the subject. Its purpose is to keep you aimed in the direction you most want to go.

Personal morality is an attempt to consider all the relevant consequences of your actions.

"Relevant" means those consequences that will affect *you*. How your actions affect others is only important insofar as that, in turn, affects you.

A personal morality is basic to your overall view of how you'll find happiness. . . .

And it's important that you form it yourself. No one else (including me) is qualified to tell you how to live. A realistic morality has to consider many personal factors: your emotional nature, abilities, strengths, weaknesses, and, most important, your goals.

Your code of conduct has to be consistent with your goals so that you don't do anything that would make those goals unattainable. A code devised by someone else will necessarily be based upon the goals *he* believes possible and desirable.

To be useful, a morality shouldn't include rules for every possible situation. It shouldn't be concerned with minor questions involving only immediate consequences. It's devised to prevent big problems for you and to keep you aimed toward the ultimate goals that mean the most to you. Moral questions are concerned only with matters that involve large consequences.

There's a difference, for instance, between investing three dollars in a movie that might prove to be a dud and investing your life savings in a risky business venture. There's also a difference between tasting a different food that's commonly eaten (such as snails) and sampling toadstools in the forest. The first might cause a stomachache; the second could poison you.

A useful morality will prevent you from doing things that might take years to correct, while keeping you aimed in the direction of the things that are most important to you.

And since such matters are an outgrowth of your own personal values, it's obvious that no one else can create your morality for you.

A *personal morality* is the attempt to consider all the relevant consequences of your actions. This is only one of three common types of moralities, however.

Universal Morality   The second type is a morality that is meant to apply to everyone in the world. A *universal morality* is one that's supposed to bring happiness to anyone who uses it.

When you're exposed to the ideas of someone who has apparently done well with his own life, it's easy to conclude that he has all the final answers. His reasoning makes sense to you; he has results to show for his ideas. What further proof could you need to demonstrate that he knows how to live?

He probably *does* know how to live—*his* life. It would be foolish not to consider the ideas such a person offers. But it would also be foolish to expect that, as intelligent as he may be, he could have answers that apply to every life in the world.

His ideas have worked for him because he's been wise enough to develop ideas that are consistent with his own nature. He hasn't tried to live by the standards created by others; he's found his own. And that's vitally important.

You must do the same thing, too—if you want your code of conduct to work that well for you. Your rules have to consider everything that's unique about you— your emotions, your aptitudes, your weak points, your hopes and fears. . . .

A *universal morality* is a code of conduct that is presumed to bring happiness to anyone who uses it. I don't believe there can be such a thing. The differences between individuals are far too great to allow for anything but the most general kinds of rules.

Absolute Morality   There's a third kind of morality. The first two are attempts to help you achieve happiness—one self-directed and the other coming from someone else. The third type is the opposite of this. An *absolute morality* is a set of rules to which an individual is expected to *surrender* his own happiness.

There are two main characteristics of an absolute morality:

1. It presumably comes from *an authority outside of the individual*. It comes from someone or somewhere more important than the individual himself.

2. It proposes that the individual should be "moral" *regardless of the consequences to himself*. In other words, doing what is "right" is more important than one's own happiness.

These two characteristics intertwine, so we'll consider them together.

Absolute morality is the most common type of morality, and it can be pretty intimidating. You can be made to appear "selfish," "whim-worshipping," "egotistic," "hedonistic," or "ruthless," if you merely assert that your own happiness is the most important thing in your life.

But what could be more important than your happiness? It's said that an authoritarian moral code is necessary to protect society. But who is society? Isn't it just a large group of people, each of whom has differing ideas concerning how one should live?

And if an individual is required to give up his own happiness, of what value is society to him?

It's also suggested that God commanded that we live by certain rules. But who can be sure he knows exactly when and how and what God said and what he meant? And even if that could be established once and for all, what would be the consequences to the individual if he acted otherwise? How do we know?

And if the code did come from God, it still had to be handled by human beings on its way to you. Whatever the absolute morality may be, you're relying upon someone else to vouch for its authority.

Suppose you use a holy book as your guide. I haven't yet seen one that doesn't have some apparent contradictions regarding conduct in it. Those contradictions may disappear with the proper interpretation; but who provides the interpretation? You'll do it yourself or you'll select someone to provide it for you. In either case, *you* have become the authority by making the choice.

There's no way someone else can become your authority; ultimately the decision will be yours in choosing the morality you'll live by—even if you choose to cite someone else (you've chosen) as the authority for your acts.

And there's no way you can ignore the consequences to yourself; a human being naturally acts in terms of consequences.

What happens, however, is that other people introduce consequences that they hope will influence you. They say that your "immoral" acts will: "prevent you from going to heaven"—or "cause other people to disapprove of you"—or "destroy society and cause chaos, and it will all be your fault."

Once again, however, it will be *you* deciding for yourself whether any of these consequences will result and whether any of them are important to you.

The absolute morality fails on its two important characteristics. Even if you choose to believe there's a higher authority, you are the authority who chooses what it is and what it is telling you to do. And since you'll always be considering consequences, even if you try to fix it so that you aren't, it's important to deliberately recognize the consequences and decide which ones are important to you. . . .

The Trap   The Morality Trap is the belief that you must obey a moral code created by someone else. If you're acting in ways you hope will satisfy someone else's concept of what is moral, chances are you're using an ill-suited code of conduct—one that won't lead you to what you want and that may trap you in commitments and complications that can only cause you unhappiness. So in terms of the trap, *what* you do isn't as significant as *why* you do it.

You're in the trap if you hand a very important dollar to a beggar because "it's wrong to be selfish." Or if you continue to deal respectfully with someone who's made trouble for you because "to forgive is divine."

You're in the trap if you allow yourself to be drafted because "you have a duty to your country." Or if you prohibit drinking in your home because "it would weaken the moral fiber of society." Or if you send your children to Sunday school even though you aren't religious, because "you should give them a moral upbringing."

You might have very good reasons for any of these actions. But if you do them *only* in obedience to moral clichés, you're in the Morality Trap. . . .

Your Morality   You are responsible for what happens to you (even if someone else offers to accept that responsibility), because you're the one who'll experience the consequences of your acts.

You are the one who decides what is right and what is wrong—no matter what meaning others may attach to those words. You don't have to obey blindly the dictates that you grew up with or that you hear around you now. Everything can be challenged, *should* be challenged, examined to determine its relevance to you and what you want.

As you examine the teachings of others, you may find that some of it is very appropriate to you, but much of it may be meaningless or even harmful. The important thing is to carefully reappraise any moral precept that has been guiding your actions.

As you examine each of the rules you've been living by, ask yourself:

—Is this rule something that *others* have devised on behalf of "society" to restrain individuals? Or have *I* devised it in order to make my life better for myself?

—Am I acting by an old, just-happens-to-be-there morality? Or is it something I've personally determined from the knowledge of who I am and what I want?

—Are the rewards and punishments attached to the rules vague and intangible? Or do the rules point to specific happiness I can achieve or unhappiness I can avoid?

—Is it a morality I've accepted because "someone undoubtedly knows the reason for it"? Or is it one I've created because *I* know the reason for it?

—Is it a morality that's currently "in style" and accepted by all those around me? Or is it a morality specifically tailored to *my* style?

—Is it a morality that's aimed *at* me and *against* my self-interest? Or is it a morality that's *for* me and comes *from* me?

All the answers must come from you—not from a book or a lecture or a sermon. To assume that someone once wrote down the final answers for your morality is to assume that the writer stopped growing the day he wrote the code. Don't treat him unfairly by thinking that he couldn't have discovered more and increased his own understanding after he'd written the code. And don't forget that what he wrote was based upon what *he* saw.

No matter how you approach the matter, *you* are the sovereign authority who makes the final decisions. The more you realize that, the more your decisions will fit realistically with your own life. . . .

II. The Unselfishness Trap

The Unselfishness Trap is the belief that you must put the happiness of others ahead of your own.

Unselfishness is a very popular ideal, one that's been honored throughout recorded history. Wherever you turn, you find encouragement to put the happiness of others ahead of your own—to do what's best for the world, not for yourself.

If the ideal is sound, there must be something unworthy in seeking to live your life as you want to live it.

So perhaps we should look more closely at the subject—to see if the ideal *is* sound. For if you attempt to be free, we can assume that someone's going to consider that to be selfish.

We saw . . . that each person always acts in ways he believes will make him feel good or will remove discomfort from his life. Because everyone is different from everyone else, each individual goes about it in his own way.

One man devotes his life to helping the poor. Another one lies and steals. Still another person tries to create better products and services for which he hopes to be paid handsomely. One woman devotes herself to her husband and children. Another one seeks a career as a singer.

In every case, the ultimate motivation has been the same. Each person is doing what *he* believes will assure his happiness. What varies between them is the *means* each has chosen to gain his happiness.

We could divide them into two groups labeled "selfish" and "unselfish," but I don't think that would prove anything. For the thief and the humanitarian each have the same motive—to do what he believes will make him feel good.

In fact, we can't avoid a very significant conclusion: *Everyone is selfish.* Selfishness isn't really an issue, because everyone selfishly seeks his own happiness.

What we need to examine, however, are the means various people choose to achieve their happiness. Unfortunately, some people oversimplify the matter by assuming that there are only two basic means: sacrifice yourself for others or make them sacrifice for you. Happily, there's a third way that can produce better consequences than either of those two.

A Better World? Let's look first at the ideal of living for the benefit of others. It's often said that it would be a better world if everyone were unselfish. But would it be?

If it were somehow possible for everyone to give up his own happiness, what would be the result? Let's carry it to its logical conclusion and see what we find.

To visualize it, let's imagine that happiness is symbolized by a big red rubber ball. I have the ball in my hands—meaning that I hold the ability to be happy. But since I'm not going to be selfish, I quickly pass the ball to you. I've given up my happiness for you.

What will you do? Since you're not selfish either, you won't keep the ball; you'll quickly pass it on to your next-door neighbor. But he doesn't want to be selfish either, so he passes it to his wife, who likewise gives it to her children.

The children have been taught the virtue of unselfishness, so they pass it to playmates, who pass it to parents, who pass it to neighbors, and on and on and on.

I think we can stop the analogy at this point and ask what's been accomplished by all this effort. Who's better off for these demonstrations of pure unselfishness?

How would it be a better world if everyone acted that way? Whom would we be unselfish for? There would have to be a selfish person who would receive, accept, and enjoy the benefits of our unselfishness for there to be any purpose to it. But that selfish person (the object of our generosity) would be living by lower standards than we do.

For a more practical example, what is achieved by the parent who "sacrifices" himself for his children, who in turn are expected to sacrifice themselves for *their* children, etc.? The unselfishness concept is a merry-go-round that has no ultimate purpose. No one's self-interest is enhanced by the continual relaying of gifts from one person to another to another.

Perhaps most people have never carried the concept of unselfishness to this logical conclusion. If they did, they might reconsider their pleas for an unselfish world.

Negative Choices   But, unfortunately, the pleas continue, and they're a very real part of your life. In seeking your own freedom and happiness, you have to deal with those who tell you that you shouldn't put yourself first. That creates a situation in which you're pressured to act negatively—to put aside your plans and desires in order to avoid the condemnation of others.

As I've said before, one of the characteristics of a free man is that he's usually choosing positively—deciding which of several alternatives would make him the happiest; while the average person, most of the time, is choosing which of two or three alternatives will cause him the least discomfort.

When the reason for your actions is to avoid being called "selfish" you're making a negative decision and thereby restricting the possibilities for your own happiness.

You're in the Unselfishness Trap if you regretfully pay for your aunt's surgery with the money you'd saved for a new car, or if you sadly give up the vacation you'd looked forward to in order to help a sick neighbor.

You're in the trap if you feel you're *required* to give part of your income to the poor, or if you think that your country, community, or family has first claim on your time, energy, or money.

You're in the Unselfishness Trap any time you make negative choices that are designed to avoid being called "selfish."

It isn't that no one else is important. You might have a self-interest in someone's well-being, and giving a gift can be a gratifying expression of the affection you feel for him. But you're in the trap if you do such things in order to appear unselfish.

Helping Others   There *is* an understandable urge to give to those who are important and close to you. However, that leads many people to think that indiscriminate giving is the key to one's own happiness. They say that the way to be happy is to make others happy; get your glow by basking in the glow you've created for someone else.

It's important to identify that as a personal opinion. If someone says that giving is the key to happiness, isn't he saying that's the key to *his* happiness?

I think we can carry the question further, however, and determine how efficient such a policy might be. The suggestion to be a giver presupposes that you're able to judge what will make someone else happy. And experience has taught me to be a bit humble about assuming what makes others happy.

My landlady once brought me a piece of her freshly baked cake because she wanted to do me a favor. Unfortunately, it happened to be a kind of cake that was distasteful to me. I won't try to describe the various ways I tried to get the cake plate back to her without being confronted with a request for my judgment of her cake. It's sufficient to say that her well-intentioned favor interfered with my own plans.

And now, whenever I'm sure I know what someone else "needs," I remember that incident and back off a little. There's no way that one person can read the mind of another to know all his plans, goals, and tastes.

You may know a great deal about the desires of your intimate friends. But *indiscriminate* gift-giving and favor-doing is usually a waste of resources—or, worse, it can upset the well-laid plans of the receiver.

When you give to someone else, you might provide something he values—but probably not the thing he considers most important. If you expend those resources for *yourself*, you automatically devote them to what you consider to be most important. The time or money you've spent will most likely create more happiness that way.

If your purpose is to make someone happy, you're more apt to succeed if you make yourself the object. You'll never know another person more than a fraction as well as you can know yourself.

Do you want to make someone happy? Go to it—use your talents and your insight and benevolence to bestow riches of happiness upon the one person you understand well enough to do it efficiently—yourself. I guarantee that you'll get more genuine appreciation from yourself than from anyone else.

Give to you.

Support your local self.

Alternatives   As I indicated earlier in this chapter, it's too often assumed that there are only two alternatives: (1) sacrifice your interests for the benefit of others; or (2) make others sacrifice their interests for you. If nothing else were possible, it would indeed be a grim world.

Fortunately, there's more to the world than that. Because desires vary from person to person, it's possible to create exchanges between individuals in which both parties benefit.

For example, if you buy a house, you do so because you'd rather have the house than the money involved. But the seller's desire is different—he'd rather have the money than the house. When the sale is completed, each of you has received something of greater value than what you gave up—otherwise you wouldn't have entered the exchange. Who, then, has had to sacrifice for the other?

In the same way, your daily life is made up of dozens of such exchanges— small and large transactions in which each party gets something he values more than what he gives up. The exchange doesn't have to involve money; you may be spending time, attention, or effort in exchange for something you value.

Mutually beneficial relationships are possible when desires are compatible. Sometimes the desires are the same—like going to a movie together. Sometimes the desires are different—like trading your money for someone's house. In either case, it's the *compatibility* of the desires that makes the exchange possible.

No sacrifice is necessary when desires are compatible. So it makes sense to seek out people with whom you can have mutually beneficial relationships.

Often the "unselfishness" issue arises only because two people with nothing in common are trying to get along together—such as a man who likes bowling and hates opera married to a woman whose tastes are the opposite. If they're to do things together, one must "sacrifice" his pleasure for the other. So each might try to encourage the other to be "unselfish."

If they were compatible, the issue wouldn't arise because each would be pleasing the other by doing what was in his own self-interest.

An efficiently selfish person *is* sensitive to the needs and desires of others. But he doesn't consider those desires to be demands upon him. Rather, he sees them as *opportunities*—potential exchanges that might be beneficial to him. He identifies desires in others so that he can decide if exchanges with them will help him get what he wants.

He doesn't sacrifice himself for others, nor does he expect others to be sacrificed for him. He takes the third alternative—he finds relationships that are mutually beneficial so that no sacrifice is required.

Please Yourself   Everyone is selfish; everyone is doing what he believes will make himself happier. The recognition of that can take most of the sting out of accusations that you're being "selfish." Why should you feel guilty for seeking your own happiness when that's what everyone else is doing, too?

The demand that you be unselfish can be motivated by any number of reasons: that you'd help create a better world, that you have a moral obligation to be unselfish, that you give up your happiness to the selfishness of someone else, or that the person demanding it has just never thought it out.

Whatever the reason, you're not likely to convince such a person to stop his demands. But it will create much less pressure on you if you realize that it's *his* selfish reason. And you can eliminate the problem entirely by looking for more compatible companions.

To find constant, profound happiness requires that you be free to seek the gratification of your own desires. It means making positive choices.

If you slip into the Unselfishness Trap, you'll spend a good part of your time making negative choices—trying to avoid the censure of those who tell you not to think of yourself. You won't have time to be free.

If someone finds happiness by doing "good works" for others, let him. That doesn't mean that's the best way for you to find happiness.

And when someone accuses you of being selfish, just remember that he's only upset because you aren't doing what *he* selfishly wants you to do.

22. Utilitarianism

Jeremy Bentham

Jeremy Bentham (1748–1832), an English philosopher and political theorist, developed the utilitarian theory as a basis for political and legal reform.

Of the Principle of Utility

I. Nature has placed mankind under the governance of two sovereign masters, *pain* and *pleasure*. It is for them alone to point out what we ought to do, as well as to determine what we shall do. On the one hand the standard of right and wrong, on the other the chain of causes and effects are fastened to their throne. They govern us in all we do, in all we say, in all we think: every effort we can make to throw off our subjection, will serve but to demonstrate and confirm it. In words a man may pretend to abjure their empire: but in reality he will remain subject to it all the while. The *principle of utility* recognises this subjection, and assumes it for the foundation of that system, the object of which is to rear the fabric of felicity by the hands of reason and of law. Systems which attempt to question it deal in sounds instead of sense, in caprice instead of reason, in darkness instead of light.

But enough of metaphor and declamation: it is not by such means that moral science is to be improved.

II. The principle of utility is the foundation of the present work: it will be proper therefore at the outset to give an explicit and determinate account of what is meant by it. By the principle of utility is meant that principle which approves or disapproves of every action whatsoever, according to the tendency which it appears to have to augment or diminish the happiness of the party whose interest is in question: or, what is the same thing in other words, to promote or to oppose that happiness. I say of every action whatsoever; and therefore not only of every action of a private individual, but of every measure of government.

III. By utility is meant that property in any object, whereby it tends to produce benefit, advantage, pleasure, good, or happiness (all this in the present case comes to the same thing) or (what comes again to the same thing) to prevent the happening of mischief, pain, evil, or unhappiness to the party whose interest is considered: if that party be the community in general, then the happiness of the community: if a particular individual, then the happiness of that individual.

IV. The interest of the community is one of the most general expressions that can occur in the phraseology of morals: no wonder that the meaning of it is often lost. When it has a meaning, it is this. The community is a fictitious *body*, composed of the individual persons who are considered as constituting as it were its *members*.

From Jeremy Bentham, *An Introduction to the Principles of Morals and Legislation*. First published in 1789.

The interest of the community then is, what?—the sum of the interests of the several members who compose it.

V. It is in vain to talk of the interest of the community, without understanding what is the interest of the individual. A thing is said to promote the interest, or to be *for* the interest, of an individual, when it tends to add to the sum total of his pleasures: or, what comes to the same thing, to diminish the sum total of his pains.

VI. An action then may be said to be comformable to the principle of utility, or, for shortness sake, to utility (meaning with respect to the community at large), when the tendency it has to augment the happiness of the community is greater than any it has to diminish it.

VII. A measure of government (which is but a particular kind of action, performed by a particular person or persons) may be said to be conformable to or dictated by the principle of utility, when in like manner the tendency which it has to augment the happiness of the community is greater than any which it has to diminish it.

VIII. When an action, or in particular a measure of government is supposed by a man to be conformable to the principle of utility, it may be convenient, for the purposes of discourse, to imagine a kind of law or dictate, called a law or dictate of utility: and to speak of the action in question, as being conformable to such law or dictate.

IX. A man may be said to be a partisan of the principle of utility, when the approbation or disapprobation he annexes to any action, or to any measure, is determined by and proportioned to the tendency which he conceives it to have to augment or to diminish the happiness of the community: or in other words, to its conformity or unconformity to the laws or dictates of utility.

X. Of an action that is conformable to the principle of utility one may always say either that it is one that ought to be done, or at least that it is not one that ought not to be done. One may say also, that it is right it should be done; at least that it is not wrong it should be done: that it is a right action; at least that it is not a wrong action. When thus interpreted, the words *ought*, and *right* and *wrong*, and others of that stamp, have a meaning: when otherwise, they have none.

XI. Has the rectitude of this principle been ever formally contested? It should seem that it had, by those who have not known what they have been meaning. Is it susceptible of any direct proof? it should seem not: for that which is used to prove everything else, cannot itself be proved: a chain of proofs must have their commencement somewhere. To give such proof is as impossible as it is needless.

XII. Not that there is or ever has been that human creature breathing, however stupid or perverse, who has not on many, perhaps on most occasions of his life, deferred to it. By the natural constitution of the human frame, on most occasions of their lives men in general embrace this principle, without thinking of it: if not for the ordering of their own actions, yet for the trying of their own actions, as well as of those of other men. There have been, at the same time, not many, perhaps, even of the most intelligent, who have been disposed to embrace it purely and without reserve. There are even few who have not taken some occasion or other to quarrel with it, either on account of their not understanding always how to apply it, or on account of some prejudice or other which they were afraid to examine into, or could not bear to part with. For such is the stuff that man is made of: in principle and in practice, in a right track and in a wrong one, the rarest of all human qualities is consistency.

XIII. When a man attempts to combat the principle of utility, it is with reasons drawn, without his being aware of it, from that very principle itself. His arguments, if they prove any thing, prove not that the principle is *wrong*, but that, according to the applications he supposes to be made of it, it is *misapplied*. Is it possible for a man to move the earth? Yes, but he must first find out another earth to stand upon.

Of Principles Adverse to That of Utility

I. If the principle of utility be a right principle to be governed by, and that in all cases, it follows from what has been just observed, that whatever principle differs from it in any case must necessarily be a wrong one. To prove any other principle, therefore, to be a wrong one, there needs no more than just to show it to be what it is, a principle of which the dictates are in some point or other different from those of the principle of utility: to state it is to confute it.

II. A principle may be different from that of utility in two ways: 1. By being constantly opposed to it: this is the case with a principle which may be termed the principle of *asceticism*. 2. By being sometimes opposed to it, and sometimes not, as it may happen: this is the case with another, which may be termed the principle of *sympathy* and *antipathy*.

III. By the principle of asceticism I mean that principle, which, like the principle of utility, approves or disapproves of any action, according to the tendency which it appears to have to augment or diminish the happiness of the party whose interest is in question; but in an inverse manner: approving of actions in as far as they tend to diminish his happiness; disapproving of them in as far as they tend to augment it.

IV. It is evident that any one who reprobates any the least particle of pleasure, as such, from whatever source derived, is *pro tanto* a partisan of the principle of asceticism. It is only upon that principle, and not from the principle of utility, that the most abominable pleasure which the vilest of malefactors ever reaped from his crime would be to be reprobated, if it stood alone. The case is, that it never does stand alone; but is necessarily followed by such a quality of pain (or, what comes to the same thing, such a chance for a certain quantity of pain) that the pleasure in comparison of it, is as nothing: and this is the true and sole, but perfectly sufficient, reason for making it a ground for punishment. . . .

X. The principle of utility is capable of being consistently pursued; and it is but tautology to say, that the more consistently it is pursued, the better it must ever be for humankind. The principle of asceticism never was, nor ever can be, consistently pursued by any living creature. Let but one tenth part of the inhabitants of this earth pursue it consistently, and in a day's time they will have turned it into a hell.

XI. Among principles adverse to that of utility, that which at this day seems to have most influence in matters of government, is what may be called the principle of sympathy and antipathy. By the principle of sympathy and antipathy, I mean that principle which approves or disapproves of certain actions, not on account of their tending to augment the happiness, nor yet on account of their tending to diminish the happiness of the party whose interest is in question, but merely because a man finds himself disposed to approve or disapprove of them: holding up that approbation or disapprobation as a sufficient reason for itself, and disclaiming the necessity of looking out for any extrinsic ground. Thus far in the general department of morals: and in the particular department of politics, measuring out the quantum (as well as determining the ground) of punishment, by the degree of the disapprobation.

XII. It is manifest, that this is rather a principle in name than in reality: it is not a positive principle of itself, so much as a term employed to signify the negation of all principle. What one expects to find in a principle is something that points out some external consideration, as a means of warranting and guiding the internal sentiments of approbation and disapprobation: this expectation is but ill fulfilled by a proposition, which does neither more nor less than hold up each of those sentiments as a ground and standard for itself.

XIII. In looking over the catalogue of human actions (says a partisan of this principle) in order to determine which of them are to be marked with the seal of disapprobation, you need but to take counsel of your own feelings: whatever you find in yourself a propensity to condemn, is wrong for that very reason. For the same reason it is also meet for punishment: in what proportion it is adverse to utility, or whether it be adverse to utility at all, is a matter that makes no difference. In that same *proportion* also is it meet for punishment: if you hate much, punish much: if you hate little, punish little: punish as you hate. If you hate not at all, punish not at all; the fine feelings of the soul are not to be overborne and tyrannized by the harsh and rugged dictates of political utility. . . .

XV. It is manifest, that the dictates of this principle will frequently coincide with those of utility, though perhaps without intending any such thing. Probably more frequently than not: and hence it is that the business of penal justice is carried on upon that tolerable sort of footing upon which we see it carried on in common at this day. For what more natural or more general ground of hatred to a practice can there be, than the mischievousness of such practice? What all men are exposed to suffer by, all men will be disposed to hate. It is far yet, however, from being a constant ground: for when a man suffers, it is not always that he knows what it is he suffers by. A man may suffer grievously, for instance, by a new tax, without being able to trace up the cause of his sufferings to the injustice of some neighbour, who has eluded the payment of an old one.

XVI. The principle of sympathy and antipathy is more apt to err on the side of severity. It is for applying punishment in many cases which deserve none: in many cases which deserve some, it is for applying more than they deserve. There is no incident imaginable, be it ever so trivial, and so remote from mischief, from which this principle may not extract a ground of punishment. Any difference in taste: any difference in opinion: upon one subject as well as upon another. No disagreement so trifling which perseverance and altercation will not render serious. Each becomes in the other's eyes an enemy, and, if laws permit, a criminal. This is one of the circumstances by which the human race is distinguished (not much indeed to its advantage) from the brute creation. . . .

XIX. There are two things which are very apt to be confounded, but which it imports us carefully distinguish:—the motive or cause, which, by operating on the mind of an individual, is productive of any act: and the ground or reason which warrants a legislator, or other bystander, in regarding that act with an eye of approbation. When the act happens, in the particular instance in question, to be productive of effects which we approve of, much more if we happen to observe that the same motive may frequently be productive, in other instances, of the like effects, we are apt to transfer our approbation to the motive itself, and to assume, as the just ground for the approbation we bestow on the act, the circumstance of its originating from that motive. It is in this way that the sentiment of antipathy has often been considered as a just ground of action. Antipathy, for instance, in such or such a case, is the cause of an action which is attended with good effects: but this does not make it a right ground of action in that case, any more than in any other. Still farther. Not only the effects are good, but the agent sees beforehand that they will be so. This may make the action indeed a perfect right action: but it does not make antipathy a right ground of action. For the same sentiment of antipathy, if implicitly deferred to, may be, and very frequently is, productive of the very worst effects. Antipathy, therefore, can never be a right ground of action. No more, therefore, can resentment, which, as will be seen more particularly hereafter, is but a modification of antipathy. The only right ground of action, that can possibly subsist, is, after all, the consideration of utility, which, if it is a right principle of action, and of approbation, in any one case, is so in every other. Other principles in abundance, that is, other motives, may be the reasons why such and such an act *has* been done: that is, the reasons or causes of its being done: but it is this alone that can be the reason why it might or ought to have been done. Antipathy or resentment requires always to be regulated, to prevent its doing mischief: to be regulated by what? always by the principle of utility. The principle of utility neither requires nor admits of any other regulator than itself.

Value of a Lot of Pleasure or Pain, How to Be Measured

I. Pleasures then, and the avoidance of pains, are the *ends* which the legislator has in view: it behooves him therefore to understand their *value*. Pleasures and pains are the *instruments* he has to work with: it behooves him therefore to understand their force, which is again, in other words, their value.

II. To a person considered *by himself*, the value of a pleasure or pain considered *by itself*, will be greater or less, according to the four following circumstances:

1. Its *intensity*.
2. Its *duration*.
3. Its *certainty* or *uncertainty*.
4. Its *propinquity* or *remoteness*.

III. These are the circumstances which are to be considered in estimating a pleasure or a pain considered each of them by itself. But when the value of any pleasure or pain is considered for the purpose of estimating the tendency of any *act* by which it is produced, there are two other circumstances to be taken into the account; these are,

5. Its *fecundity*, or the chance it has of being followed by sensations of the *same* kind: that is, pleasures, if it be a pleasure: pains, if it be a pain.
6. Its *purity*, or the chance it has of *not* being followed by sensations of the *opposite* kind: that is, pains, if it be a pleasure: pleasures, if it be a pain.

These two last, however, are in strictness scarcely to be deemed properties of the pleasure or the pain itself; they are not, therefore, in strictness to be taken into the account of the value of that pleasure or that pain. They are in strictness to be deemed properties only of the act, or other event, by which such pleasure or pain has been produced; and accordingly are only to be taken into the account of the tendency of such act or such event.

IV. To a *number* of persons, with reference to each of whom the value of a pleasure or a pain is considered, it will be greater or less, according to seven circumstances: to wit, the six preceding ones; *viz.*

1. Its *intensity*.
2. Its *duration*.
3. Its *certainty* or *uncertainty*.
4. Its *propinquity* or *remoteness*.
5. Its *fecundity*.
6. Its *purity*.

And one other; to wit:

7. Its *extent*, that is, the number of persons to whom it *extends*; or (in other words) who are affected by it.

V. To take an exact account then of the general tendency of any act, by which the interests of a community are affected, proceed as follows. Begin with any one person of those whose interests seem most immediately to be affected by it: and take an account.

1. Of the value of each distinguishable *pleasure* which appears to be produced by it in the *first* instance.
2. Of the value of each *pain* which appears to be produced by it in the *first* instance.
3. Of the value of each pleasure which appears to be produced by it *after* the first. This constitutes the *fecundity* of the first *pleasure* and the *impurity* of the first *pain*.

4. Of the value of each *pain* which appears to be produced by it after the first. This constitutes the *fecundity* of the first *pain*, and the *impurity* of the first *pleasure*.

5. Sum up all the values of all the *pleasures* on the one side, and those of all the *pains* on the other. The balance, if it be on the side of pleasure, will give the *good* tendency of the act upon the whole, with respect to the interests of that *individual* person: if on the side of pain, the *bad* tendency of it upon the whole.

6. Take an account of the *number* of persons whose interests appear to be concerned; and repeat the above process with respect to each. *Sum up* the numbers expressive of the degrees of *good* tendency, which the act has, with respect to each individual, in regard to whom the tendency of it is *good* upon the whole: do this again with respect to each individual, in regard to whom the tendency of it is *good* upon the whole: do this again with respect to each individual, in regard to whom the tendency of it is *bad* upon the whole. Take the *balance*; which, if on the side of *pleasure*, will give the general *good tendency* of the act, with respect to the total number or community of individuals concerned; if on the side of pain, the general *evil tendency*, with respect to the same community.

VI. It is not to be expected that this process should be strictly pursued previously to every moral judgment, or to every legislative or judicial operation. It may, however, be always kept in view: and as near as the process actually pursued on these occasions approaches to it, so near will such process approach to the character of an exact one.

VII. The same process is alike applicable to pleasure and pain, in whatever shape they appear: and by whatever denomination they are distinguished: to pleasure, whether it be called *good* (which is properly the cause or instrument of pleasure) or *profit* (which is distant pleasure, or the cause or instrument of distant pleasure), or *convenience*, or *advantage, benefit, emolument, happiness*, and so forth: to pain, whether it be called *evil* (which corresponds to *good*), or *mischief*, or *inconvenience*, or *disadvantage*, or *loss*, or *unhappiness*, and so forth.

VIII. Nor is this a novel and unwarranted, any more than it is a useless theory. In all this there is nothing but what the practice of mankind, wheresoever they have a clear view of their own interest, is perfectly conformable to. An article of property, an estate in land, for instance, is valuable, on what account? On account of the pleasures of all kinds which it enables a man to produce, and what comes to the same thing the pains of all kinds which it enables him to avert. But the value of such an article of property is universally understood to rise or fall according to the length or shortness of the time which a man has in it: the certainty or uncertainty of its coming into possession: and the nearness or remoteness of the time at which, if at all, it is to come into possession. As to the *intensity* of the pleasures which a man may derive from it, this is never thought of, because it depends upon the use which each particular person may come to make of it; which cannot be estimated till the particular pleasures he may come to derive from it, or the particular pains he may come to exclude by means of it, are brought to view. For the same reason, neither does he think of the *fecundity* or *purity* of those pleasures.

Thus much for pleasure and pain, happiness and unhappiness, in *general*.

23. The Deep Beauty
of the Golden Rule

R. M. MacIver

Robert M. MacIver (1882–1970) was a prominent sociologist and political theorist who maintained a strong interest in a number of philosophical issues.

The subject that learned men call ethics is a wasteland on the philosophical map. Thousands of books have been written on this matter, learned books and popular books, books that argue and books that exhort. Most of them are empty and nearly all are vain. Some claim that pleasure is *the* good; some prefer the elusive and more enticing name of happiness; others reject such principles and speak of equally elusive goals such as self-fulfillment. Others claim that *the* good is to be found in looking away from the self, in devotion to the whole—which whole? in the service of God—whose God?—even in the service of the State—who prescribes the service? Here indeed, if anywhere, after listening to the many words of many apostles, one goes out by the same door as one went in.

The reason is simple. You say: "This is the way you should behave." But I say: "No, that is not the way." You say: "This is right." But I say: "No, that is wrong, and this is right." You appeal to experience. I appeal to experience against you. You appeal to authority: it is not mine. What is left? If you are strong, you can punish me for behaving my way. But does that prove anything except that you are stronger than I? Does it prove the absurd dogma that might makes right? Is the slavemaster right because he owns the whip, or Torquemada because he can send his heretics to the flames?

From this impasse no system of ethical rules has been able to deliver itself. How can ethics lay down final principles of behavior that are not your values against mine, your group's values against my group's?

Which, by the way, does not mean that your rules are any less valid for you because they are not valid for me. Only a person of shallow nature and autocratic leanings would draw that conclusion. For the sake of your integrity you must hold to your own values, no matter how much others reject them. Without *your* values you are nothing. True, you should search them and test them and learn by *your* experience and gain wisdom where you can. Your values are your guides through life but you need to use your own eyes. If I have different guides I shall go another way. So far as we diverge, values are relative as between you and me. But your values cannot be relative for you or mine for me.

Selected excerpts from pages 39–47 from *Moral Principles of Action* (*Science of Culture Series*, Vol 3) by Ruth Nanda Anshen, editor. Copyright 1952 by Harper & Row, Publishers, Inc. Copyright renewed © 1980 by Ruth Nanda Anshen. Reprinted by permission of HarperCollins Publishers, Inc.

That is not here the issue. It is that the relativity of values between you and me, between your group and my group, your sect and my sect, makes futile nearly all learned disquisitions about the first principles of ethics.

By ethics I mean the philosophy of how men should behave in their relations to one another. I am talking about philosophy, not about religion. When you have a creed, you can derive from it principles of ethics. Philosophy cannot begin with a creed, but only with reasoning about the nature of things. It cannot therefore presume that the values of other men are less to be regarded than the values of the proponent. If it does, it is not philosophy but dogma, dogma that is the enemy of philosophy, the kind of dogma that has been the source of endless tyranny and repression.

Can it be a philosophy worth the name that makes a universal of your values and thus rules mine out of existence, where they differ from yours?

How can reasoning decide between my values and yours? Values do not claim truth in any scientific sense; instead they claim validity, rightness. They do not declare what is so but what *should* be so. I cling to my values, you to yours. Your values, some of them, do not hold for me; some of them may be repulsive to me; some of them may threaten me. What then? To what court of reason shall we appeal? To what court that you and I both accept is there any appeal?

The lack of any court is the final *fact* about final values. It is a fundamental fact. It is a terrifying fact. It is also a strangely challenging fact. It gives man his lonely autonomy, his true responsibility. If he has anything that partakes of the quality of a God it comes from this fact. Man has more than the choice to obey or disobey. If he accepts authority he also chooses the authority he accepts. He is responsible not only to others but, more deeply, to himself.

Does all this mean that a universal ethical principle, applicable alike to me and you, even where our values diverge, is impossible? That there is no rule to go by, based on reason itself, in this world of irreconcilable valuations?

There is no rule that can prescribe both my values and yours or decide between them. There is one universal rule, and one only, that can be laid down, on ethical grounds—that is, apart from the creeds of particular religions and apart from the ways of the tribe that falsely and arrogantly universalize themselves.

Do to others as you would have them do to you. This is the only rule that stands by itself in the light of its own reason, the only rule that can stand by itself in the naked, warring universe, in the face of the contending values of men and groups.

What makes it so? Let us first observe that the universal herein laid down is one of procedure. It prescribes a mode of behaving, not a goal of action. On the level of goals, of *final* values, there is irreconcilable conflict. One rule prescribes humility, another pride; one prescribes abstinence, another commends the fleshpots; and so forth through endless variations. All of us wish that *our* principle could be universal; most of us believe that it *should* be, that our *ought* ought to be all men's *ought*, but since we differ there can be, on this level, no possible agreement.

When we want to make our ethical principle prevail we try to persuade others, to "convert" them. Some may freely respond, if their deeper values are near enough to ours. Others will certainly resist and some will seek to persuade us in turn—why shouldn't they? Then we can go no further except by resort to force and fraud. We can, if we are strong, dominate some and we can bribe others. We compromise our own values in doing so and we do not in the end succeed; even if we were masters of the whole world we could never succeed in making our principle universal. We could only make it falsely tyrannous.

So if we look for a principle in the name of which we can appeal to all men, one to which their reason can respond in spite of their differences, we must follow another road. When we try to make our values prevail over those cherished by others, we attack their values, their dynamic of behavior, their living will. If we go far enough we assault their very being. For the will is simply valuation in action. Now the deep beauty of the golden rule is that instead of attacking the will that is in other men, it offers their will a new dimension. "Do as you *would* have others. . . ." As *you* would will others to do. It bids you expand your vision, see yourself in new relationships. It bids you transcend your insulation, see yourself in the place of others, see others in your place. It bids you test your values or at least your way of pursuing them. If you would disapprove that another should treat you as you treat him, the situations being reversed, is not that a sign that, by the standard of your own values, you are mistreating him?

This principle obviously makes for a vastly greater harmony in the social scheme. At the same time it is the only universal of ethics that does not take sides with or contend with contending values. It contains no dogma. It bids everyone follow his own rule, as it would apply *apart* from the accident of his particular fortunes. It bids him enlarge his own rule, as it would apply whether he is up or whether he is down. It is an accident that you are up and I am down. In another situation you would be down and I would be up. That accident has nothing to do with my *final* values or with yours. You have numbers and force on your side. In another situation I would have the numbers and the force. All situations of power are temporary and precarious. Imagine then the situations reversed and that you had a more wonderful power than is at the command of the most powerful, the power to make the more powerful act toward you as you would want him to act. If power is your dream, then dream of a yet greater power—and act out the spirit of your dream.

But the conclusive argument is not in the terms of power. It goes far deeper, down to the great truth that power so often ignores and that so often in the end destroys it, the truth that when you maltreat others you detach yourself from them, from the understanding of them, from the understanding of yourself. You insulate yourself, you narrow your own values, you cut yourself off from that which you and they have in common. And this commonness is more enduring and more satisfying than what you possess in insulation. You separate yourself, and for all your power you weaken yourself. Which is why power and fear are such close companions.

This is the reason why the evil you do to another, you do also, in the end, to yourself. While if you and he refrain from doing evil, one to another—not to speak of the yet happier consequences, of doing positive good—this reciprocity of restraint from evil will redound to the good of both.

That makes a much longer story and we shall not here enter upon it. Our sole concern is to show that the golden rule is the *only* ethical principle, as already defined, that can have clear right of way everywhere in the kind of world we have inherited. It is the only principle that allows every man to follow his own intrinsic values while nevertheless it transforms the chaos of warring codes into a reasonably well-ordered universe.

Let us explain the last statement. What are a man's intrinsic values? Beyond his mere self-seeking every human being needs, and must find, some attachment to a large purpose. These attachments, in themselves and apart from the way he pursues them, are his intrinsic values. For some men they are centered in the family, the clan, the "class," the community, the nation, the "race." It is the warfare of their group-attachments that creates the deadliest disturbances of modern society. For some men the focus of attachment is found in the greater "cause," faith, the creed, the way of life. The conflict of these attachments also unlooses many evils on society and at some historical stages has brought about great devastation.

The greatest evils inflicted by man on man over the face of the earth are wrought not by the self-seekers, the pleasure lovers, or the merely amoral, but by the fervent devotees of ethical principles, those who are bound body and soul to some larger purpose, the nation, the "race," the "masses," the "brethren" whoever they may be. The faith they invoke, whatever it may be, is not large enough when it sets a frontier between the members and the non-members, the believers and the non-believers. In the heat of devotion to that larger but exclusive purpose there is bred the fanaticism that corrodes and finally destroys all that links man to the common humanity. In the name of the cause, they will torture and starve and trample under foot millions on millions of their fellowmen. In its name they will cultivate the blackest treachery. And if their methods fail, as fail in the end they must, they will be ready, as was Hitler, to destroy their own cause or their own people, the chosen ones, rather than accept the reality their blinded purpose denied.

How then can we say that the golden rule does not disqualify the intrinsic values of such people—even of people like Hitler or, say, Torquemada? In the name of his values Torquemada burned at the stake many persons who differed from their fellows mainly by being more courageous, honest, and faithful to their faith. What then were Torquemada's values? He was a servant of the Church and the Church was presumptively a servant of Jesus Christ. It was not the intrinsic values of his creed that moved him and his masters to reject the Christian golden rule. Let us concede they had some kind of devotion to religion. It was the distorted, fanatical way in which they pursued the dimmed values they cherished, it was not the values themselves, to which their inhumanity can be charged.

Let us take the case of Hitler. Apart from his passion for Germany, or the German "folk," he would have been of no account, for evil or for good. That passion of itself, that in his view intrinsic value, might have inspired great constructive service instead of destruction. It was the method he used, and not the values he sought to promote thereby, that led to ruin, his blind trust in the efficacy of ruthless might. Belonging to a "folk" that had been reduced in defeat from strength to humiliation, fed on false notions of history and responsive to grotesque fallacies about a "master race," he conceived the resurgence of Germany in the distorted light of his vindictive imagination. Had Hitler been a member of some small "folk," no more numerous, say, than the population of his native Austria, he might have cherished the same values with no less passion, but his aspirations would have taken a different form and would never have expressed themselves in horror and tragedy.

The golden rule says nothing against Hitler's mystic adoration of the German "race," against any man's intrinsic values. By "intrinsic values" we signify the goals, beyond mere self-seeking, that animate a human being. If your group, your nation, your "race," your church, is for you a primary attachment, continue to cherish it—give it all you have, if you are so minded. But do not use means that are repugnant to the standards according to which you would have others conduct themselves to you and your values. If your nation were a small one, would you not seethe with indignation if some large neighbor destroyed its independence? Where, then, is your personal integrity if, belonging instead to the large nation, you act to destroy the independence of a small one? You falsify your own values, in the longer run you do them injury, when you pursue them in ways that cannot abide the test of the golden rule.

It follows that while this first principle attacks no intrinsic values, no primary attachments of men to goods that reach beyond themselves, it nevertheless purifies every attachment, every creed, of its accidents, its irrelevancies, its excesses, its false reliance on power. It saves every human value from the corruption that comes from the arrogance of detachment and exclusiveness, from the shell of the kind of absolutism that imprisons its vitality.

At this point a word of caution is in order. The golden rule does not solve for us our ethical problems but offers only a way of approach. It does not prescribe our treatment of others but only the spirit in which we should treat them. It has no simple mechanical application and often enough is hard to apply—what general principle is not? It certainly does not bid us treat others as others *want* us to treat them—that would be an absurdity. The convicted criminal wants the judge to set him free. If the judge acts in the spirit of the golden rule, within the limits of the discretion permitted him as judge, he might instead reason somewhat as follows: "How would I feel the judge ought to treat *me* were I in this man's place? What could I—the man I am and yet somehow standing where this criminal stands—properly ask the judge to do for me, to me? In this spirit I shall assess his guilt and his punishment. In this spirit I shall give full consideration to the conditions under which he acted. I shall try to understand *him*, to do what I properly can for him, while at the same time I fulfill my judicial duty in protecting society against the dangers that arise if criminals such as he go free."

"Do to others as you would have others do to you." The disease to which all values are subject is the growth of a hard insulation. "I am right: I have the truth. If you differ from me, you are a heretic, you are in error. *Therefore* while you must allow me every liberty when you are in power I need not, in truth I ought not to, show any similar consideration for you." The barb of falsehood has already begun to vitiate the cherished value. While *you* are in power I advocate the equal rights of all creeds: when I am in power, I reject any such claim as ridiculous. This is the position taken by various brands of totalitarianism, and the communists in particular have made it a favorite technique in the process of gaining power, clamoring for rights they will use to destroy the rights of those who grant them. Religious groups have followed the same line. Roman Catholics, Calvinists, Lutherans, Presbyterians, and others have on occasion vociferously advocated religious liberty where they were in the minority, often to curb it where in turn they became dominant.

This gross inconsistency on the part of religious groups was flagrantly displayed in earlier centuries, but examples are still not infrequent. Here is one. *La Civilita Catholicâ*, a Jesuit organ published in Rome, has come out as follows:

"The Roman Catholic Church, convinced, through its divine prerogatives, of being the only true church, must demand the right for freedom for herself alone, because such a right can only be possessed by truth, never by error. As to other religions, the Church will certainly never draw the sword, but she will require that by legitimate means they shall not be allowed to propagate false doctrine. Consequently, in a state where the majority of the people are Catholic, the Church will require that legal existence be denied to error. . . . In some countries, Catholics will be obliged to ask full religious freedom for all, resigned at being forced to cohabitate where they alone should rightly be allowed to live. . . . The Church cannot blush for her own want of tolerance, as she asserts it in principle and applies it in practice."[1]

Since this statement has the merit of honesty it well illustrates the fundamental lack of rationality that lies behind all such violations of the golden rule. The argument runs: "Roman Catholics know they possess the truth; *therefore* they should not permit others to propagate error." By parity of reasoning why should not Protestants say—and indeed they have often said it—"We know we possess the truth; therefore we should not tolerate the errors of Roman Catholics." Why then should not atheists say: "We know we possess the truth; therefore we should not tolerate the errors of dogmatic religion."

No matter what we believe, we are equally convinced that *we* are right. We have to be. That is what belief means, and we must all believe something. The Roman Catholic Church is entitled to declare that all other religious groups are sunk in error. But what follows? That other groups have not the right to believe they are right? That you have the right to repress them while they have no right to repress you? That they should concede to you what you should not concede to them? Such reasoning is mere childishness. Beyond it lies the greater foolishness that truth is advanced by the forceful suppression of those who believe differently from you. Beyond that lies the pernicious distortion of meanings which claims that liberty is only "the liberty to do right"—the "liberty" for me to do what you think is right. This perversion of the meaning of liberty has been the delight of all totalitarians. And it might be well to reflect that it was the radical Rousseau who first introduced the doctrine that men could be "forced to be free."

How much do they have truth who think they must guard it within the fortress of their own might? How little that guarding has availed in the past! How often it

---

[1]Quoted in the *Christian Century* (June 1948).

has kept truth outside while superstition grew moldy within! How often has the false alliance of belief and force led to civil dissension and the futile ruin of war! But if history means nothing to those who call themselves "Christian" and still claim exclusive civil rights for their particular faith, at least they might blush before this word of one they call their Master: "All things therefore whatsoever ye would that men should do unto you, even so do ye also unto them; for this is the law and the prophets."

Contemporary Issues

The Environment:
How Protected Should
It Be?

24. People or Penguins: The Case for Optimal Pollution

William F. Baxter

William F. Baxter (1929–1998) was a professor at the Stanford University Law School. In addition to his writings on pollution, he published books and articles on a variety of economic and legal issues.

I start with the modest proposition that, in dealing with pollution, or indeed with any problem, it is helpful to know what one is attempting to accomplish. Agreement on how and whether to pursue a particular objective, such as pollution control, is not possible unless some more general objective has been identified and stated with reasonable precision. We talk loosely of having clean air and clean water, of preserving our wilderness areas, and so forth. But none of these is a sufficiently general objective: each is more accurately viewed as a means rather than as an end.

With regard to clean air, for example, one may ask, "how clean?" and "what does clean mean?" It is even reasonable to ask, "why have clean air?" Each of these questions is an implicit demand that a more general community goal be stated—a goal sufficiently general in its scope and enjoying sufficiently general assent among the community of actors that such "why" questions no longer seem admissible with respect to that goal.

If, for example, one states as a goal the proposition that "every person should be free to do whatever he wishes in contexts where his actions do not interfere with the interests of other human beings," the speaker is unlikely to be met with a response of "why." The goal may be criticized as uncertain in its implications or difficult to implement, but it is so basic a tenet of our civilization—it reflects a cultural value so broadly shared, at least in the abstract—that the question "why" is seen as impertinent or imponderable or both.

I do not mean to suggest that everyone would agree with the "spheres of freedom" objective just stated. Still less do I mean to suggest that a society could subscribe to four or five such general objectives that would be adequate in their coverage to serve as testing criteria by which all other disagreements might be measured. One difficulty in the attempt to construct such a list is that each new goal added will conflict, in certain applications, with each prior goal listed; and thus each goal serves as a limited qualification on prior goals.

Without any expectation of obtaining unanimous consent to them, let me set forth four goals that I generally use as ultimate testing criteria in attempting to frame solutions to problems of human organization. My position regarding pollution stems from these four criteria. If the criteria appeal to you and any part of what appears hereafter does not, our disagreement will have a helpful focus: which of us is correct, analytically, in supposing that his position on pollution would better serve these general goals. If the criteria do not seem acceptable to you, then it is to be expected that our more particular judgments will differ, and the task will then be yours to identify the basic set of criteria upon which your particular judgments rest.

My criteria are as follows:

1. The spheres of freedom criterion stated above.
2. Waste is a bad thing. The dominant feature of human existence is scarcity—our available resources, our aggregate labors, and our skill in employing both have always been, and will continue for some time to be, inadequate to yield to every man all the tangible and intangible satisfactions he would like to have. Hence, none of those resources, or labors, or skills, should be wasted—that is, employed so as to yield less than they might yield in human satisfactions.
3. Every human being should be regarded as an end rather than as a means to be used for the betterment of another. Each should be afforded dignity and regarded as having an absolute claim to an evenhanded application of such rules as the community may adopt for its governance.
4. Both the incentive and the opportunity to improve his share of satisfactions should be preserved to every individual. Preservation of incentive is dictated by the "no-waste" criterion and enjoins against the continuous, totally egalitarian redistribution of satisfactions, or wealth; but subject to that constraint, everyone should receive, by continuous redistribution if necessary, some minimal share of aggregate wealth so as to avoid a level of privation from which the opportunity to improve his situation becomes illusory.

The relationship of these highly general goals to the more specific environmental issues at hand may not be readily apparent, and I am not yet ready to demonstrate their pervasive implications. But let me give one indication of their implications. Recently scientists have informed us that use of DDT in food production is causing damage to the penguin population. For the present purposes let us accept that assertion as an indisputable scientific fact. The scientific fact is often asserted as if the correct implication—that we must stop agricultural use of DDT—followed from the mere statement of the fact of penguin damage. But plainly it does not follow if my criteria are employed.

My criteria are oriented to people, not penguins. Damage to penguins, or sugar pines, or geological marvels is, without more, simply irrelevant. One must go further, by my criteria, and say: Penguins are important because people enjoy seeing them walk about rocks; and furthermore, the well-being of people would be less impaired by halting use of DDT than by giving up penguins. In short, my observations about environmental problems will be people-oriented, as are my criteria. I have no interest in preserving penguins for their own sake.

It may be said by way of objection to this position, that it is very selfish of people to act as if each person represented one unit of importance and nothing else was of any importance. It is undeniably selfish. Nevertheless I think it is the only tenable starting place for analysis for several reasons. First, no other position corresponds to the way most people really think and act—i.e., corresponds to reality.

Second, this attitude does not portend any massive destruction of nonhuman flora and fauna, for people depend on them in many obvious ways, and they will be preserved because and to the degree that humans do depend on them.

Third, what is good for humans is, in many respects, good for penguins and pine trees—clean air for example. So that humans are, in these respects, surrogates for plant and animal life.

Fourth, I do not know how we could administer any other system. Our decisions are either private or collective. Insofar as Mr. Jones is free to act privately, he may give such preferences as he wishes to other forms of life: he may feed birds in winter and do with less himself, and he may even decline to resist an advancing polar bear on the ground that the bear's appetite is more important than those portions of himself that the bear may choose to eat. In short my basic premise does not rule out private altruism to competing life-forms. It does rule out, however, Mr. Jones' inclination to feed Mr. Smith to the bear, however hungry the bear, however despicable Mr. Smith.

Insofar as we act collectively on the other hand, only humans can be afforded an opportunity to participate in the collective decisions. Penguins cannot vote now and are unlikely subjects for the franchise—pine trees more unlikely still. Again each individual is free to cast his vote so as to benefit sugar pines if that is his inclination. But many of the more extreme assertions that one hears from some conservationists amount to tacit assertions that they are specially appointed representatives of sugar pines, and hence that their preferences should be weighted more heavily than the preferences of other humans who do not enjoy equal rapport with "nature." The simplistic assertion that agricultural use of DDT must stop at once because it is harmful to penguins is of that type.

Fifth, if polar bears or pine trees or penguins, like men, are to be regarded as ends rather than means, if they are to count in our calculus of social organization, someone must tell me how much each one counts, and someone must tell me how these life-forms are to be permitted to express their preferences, for I do not know either answer. If the answer is that certain people are to hold their proxies, then I want to know how those proxy-holders are to be selected: self-appointment does not seem workable to me.

Sixth, and by way of summary of all the foregoing, let me point out that the set of environmental issues under discussion—although they raise very complex technical questions of how to achieve any objective—ultimately raise a normative question: what *ought* we to do. Questions of *ought* are unique to the human mind and world—they are meaningless as applied to a nonhuman situation.

I reject the proposition that we *ought* to respect the "balance of nature" or to "preserve the environment" unless the reason for doing so, express or implied, is the benefit of man.

I reject the idea that there is a "right" or "morally correct" state of nature to which we should return. The word "nature" has no normative connotation. Was it "right" or "wrong" for the earth's crust to heave in contortion and create mountains and seas? Was it "right" for the first amphibian to crawl up out of the primordial ooze? Was it "wrong" for plants to reproduce themselves and alter the atmospheric composition in favor of oxygen? For animals to alter the atmosphere in favor of carbon dioxide both by breathing oxygen and eating plants? No answers can be given to these questions because they are meaningless questions.

All this may seem obvious to the point of being tedious, but much of the present controversy over environment and pollution rests on tacit normative assumptions about just such nonnormative phenomena: that it is "wrong" to impair penguins with DDT, but not to slaughter cattle for prime rib roasts. That it is wrong to kill stands of sugar pines with industrial fumes, but not to cut sugar pines and build housing for the poor. Every man is entitled to his own preferred definition of Walden Pond, but there is no definition that has any moral superiority over another, except by reference to the selfish needs of the human race.

From the fact that there is no normative definition of the natural state, it follows that there is no normative definition of clean air or pure water—hence no definition of polluted air—or of pollution—except by reference to the needs of man. The "right" composition of the atmosphere is one which has some dust in it and some lead in it and some hydrogen sulfide in it—just those amounts that attend a sensibly organized society thoughtfully and knowledgeably pursuing the greatest possible satisfaction for its human members.

The first and most fundamental step toward solution of our environmental problems is a clear recognition that our objective is not pure air or water but rather some optimal state of pollution. That step immediately suggests the question: How do we define and attain the level of pollution that will yield the maximum possible amount of human satisfaction?

Low levels of pollution contribute to human satisfaction but so do food and shelter and education and music. To attain ever lower levels of pollution, we must pay the cost of having less of these other things. I contrast that view of the cost of pollution control with the more popular statement that pollution control will "cost" very large numbers of dollars. The popular statement is true in some senses, false in others; sorting out the true and false senses is of some importance. The first step in that sorting process is to achieve a clear understanding of the difference between dollars and resources. Resources are the wealth of our nation; dollars are merely claim checks upon those resources. Resources are of vital importance; dollars are comparatively trivial.

Four categories of resources are sufficient for our purposes: At any given time a nation, or a planet if you prefer, has a stock of labor, of technological skill, of capital goods, and of natural resources (such as mineral deposits, timber, water, land, etc.). These resources can be used in various combinations to yield goods and services of all kinds—in some limited quantity. The quantity will be larger if they are combined efficiently, smaller if combined inefficiently. But in either event the resource stock is limited, the goods and services that they can be made to yield are limited; even the most efficient use of them will yield less than our population, in the aggregate, would like to have.

If one considers building a new dam, it is appropriate to say that it will be costly in the sense that it will require x hours of labor, y tons of steel and concrete, and z amount of capital goods. If these resources are devoted to the dam, then they cannot be used to build hospitals, fishing rods, schools, or electric can openers. That is the meaningful sense in which the dam is costly.

Quite apart from the very important question of how wisely we can combine our resources to produce goods and services, is the very different question of how they get distributed—who gets how many goods? Dollars constitute the claim checks which are distributed among people and which control their share of national output. Dollars are nearly valueless pieces of paper except to the extent that they do represent claim checks to some fraction of the output of goods and services. Viewed as claim checks, all the dollars outstanding during any period of time are worth, in the aggregate, the goods and services that are available to be claimed with them during that period—neither more nor less.

It is far easier to increase the supply of dollars than to increase the production of goods and services—printing dollars is easy. But printing more dollars doesn't help because each dollar then simply becomes a claim to fewer goods, i.e., becomes worth less.

The point is this: many people fall into error upon hearing the statement that the decision to build a dam, or to clean up a river, will cost $X million. It is regrettably easy to say: "It's only money. This is a wealthy country, and we have lots of money." But you cannot build a dam or clean a river with $X million—unless you also have a match, you can't even make a fire. One builds a dam or cleans a river by diverting labor and steel and trucks and factories from making one kind of goods to making another. The cost in dollars is merely a shorthand way of describing the extent of the diversion necessary. If we build a dam for $X million, then we must recognize that we will have $X million less housing and food and medical care and electric can openers as a result.

Similarly, the costs of controlling pollution are best expressed in terms of the other goods we will have to give up to do the job. This is not to say the job should not be done. Badly as we need more housing, more medical care, and more can openers, and more symphony orchestras, we could do with somewhat less of them, in my judgment at least, in exchange for somewhat cleaner air and rivers.

But that is the nature of the trade-off, and analysis of the problem is advanced if that unpleasant reality is kept in mind. Once the trade-off relationship is clearly perceived, it is possible to state in a very general way what the optimal level of pollution is. I would state it as follows:

People enjoy watching penguins. They enjoy relatively clean air and smog-free vistas. Their health is improved by relatively clean water and air. Each of these benefits is a type of good or service. As a society we would be well advised to give up one washing machine if the resources that would have gone into that washing machine can yield greater human satisfaction when diverted into pollution control. We should give up one hospital if the resources thereby freed would yield more human satisfaction when devoted to elimination of noise in our cities. And so on, trade-off by trade-off, we should divert our productive capacities from the production of existing goods and services to the production of a cleaner, quieter, more pastoral nation up to—and no further than—the point at which we value more highly the next washing machine or hospital that we would have to do without than we value the next unit of environmental improvement that the diverted resources would create.

Now this proposition seems to me unassailable but so general and abstract as to be unhelpful—at least unadministerable in the form stated. It assumes we can measure in some way the incremental units of human satisfaction yielded by very different types of goods. The proposition must remain a pious abstraction until I can explain how this measurement process can occur. . . . But I insist that the proposition stated describes the result for which we should be striving—and again, that it is always useful to know what your target is even if your weapons are too crude to score a bull's eye.

25. Environmental Values

Peter Singer

Peter Singer (1946–), professor of philosophy at Princeton, has written influential books on numerous philosophical issues. His best-known book, Animal Liberation, *attacks the treatment that animals receive from humans.*

A river tumbles through steep wooded valleys and rocky gorges toward the sea. The state hydroelectricity commission sees the falling water as untapped energy. Building a dam across one of the gorges would provide three years of employment for a thousand people, and longer-term employment for twenty or thirty. The dam would store enough water to ensure that the state could economically meet its energy needs for the next decade. This would encourage the establishment of energy-intensive industry in the state, thus further contributing to employment and economic growth.

The rough terrain of the river valley makes it accessible only to the reasonably fit, but it is nevertheless a favored spot for bushwalking. The river itself attracts the more daring white-water rafters. Deep in the sheltered valleys are stands of Huon pine, thousands of years old. The valleys and gorges are home to many birds and animals, including an endangered species of marsupial mouse found in only one other place in Australia. There may be other rare plants and animals as well, but no one knows, for scientists have yet to investigate the region fully.

Should the dam be built? This is one example of a situation in which we must choose between very different sets of values. The description is clearly reminiscent of the controversy over the proposed dam on the Franklin River, in Tasmania's southwest, although I have not tried to make it exact, and it should be treated as a hypothetical case.[1] Many other examples would have posed the choice between values equally well: logging virgin forests, building a paper mill that will release pollutants into coastal waters, or opening a new mine on the edge of a national park. A different set of examples would raise related, but slightly different, issues: banning the use of CFCs to prevent the depletion of the ozone layer; restricting the use of fossil fuels in an attempt to slow the greenhouse effect; mining uranium, where the issue is not the potential damage to the area around the mine but the hazards of nuclear fuel. My aim in this chapter is to explore the values that underlie debates about these decisions, and the example I have presented can serve as a point of reference for these debates. I shall focus particularly on the values at issue in controversies about the preservation of wilderness, because here the fundamentally

[1]For more on the Franklin Dam, see Peter Singer, *How Are We to Live?: Ethics in an Age of Self-interest* (Amherst, N.Y.: Prometheus Books, 1995), pp. 154–70.

different values of the two parties are most apparent. On controversies like water pollution and the control of greenhouse gases, the difference in values tends to be obscured by scientific debates on what is really happening, what the costs are, and what measures will be effective. When we are talking about flooding a river valley, the choice before us is starkly clear.

In general terms, we can say that those who favor building the dam are valuing employment and a higher per capita income for the state above the preservation of wilderness, of plants and animals (both common ones and members of an endangered species) and of opportunities for outdoor recreational activities. Some fundamental questions of philosophy lie behind this difference of values. In what follows, I shall assume that the values we hold may properly be subjected to rational scrutiny and criticism: they are not simply matters of taste, about which argument is futile.[2] Before we begin to scrutinize the values of those who would have the dam built and those who would not, however, let us briefly investigate the origins of modern attitudes toward the natural world. . . .

Valuing the Future

A virgin forest is the product of all the millions of years that have passed since the beginning of our planet. If it is cut down, another forest may grow up, but the continuity has been broken. The disruption in the natural life cycles of the plants and animals means that the forest will never again be as it would have been had it not been cut. The gains made from cutting the forest—employment, profits for business, export earnings, and cheaper cardboard and paper for packaging—are short-term. Once the forest is cut or drowned, however, the link with the past is gone forever. That may be regretted by every generation that succeeds us on this planet. True wilderness now has a high value because it is already scarce. In the future, and considering the world as a whole, it is bound to become scarcer still. It is for that reason that environmentalists are right to speak of wilderness as a "world heritage." It is something that we have inherited from our ancestors, and that we must preserve for our descendants if they are to have it at all.

In contrast to many more stable, tradition-oriented human societies, our modern political and cultural ethos has great difficulty in recognizing long-term values. It is notorious that politicians rarely look beyond the next election; but even if they do, they will find their economic advisers telling them that anything to be gained in the future should be discounted to such a degree as to make it easy to disregard the long-term future altogether. Economists have been taught to apply a discount rate to all future goods. In other words, a million dollars in twenty years is not worth a million dollars today, even when we allow for inflation. Economists will discount the value of the million dollars by a certain percentage, usually

---

[2]I have defended this assumption elsewhere: see "About Ethics" in Peter Singer, *Practical Ethics* (Cambridge and New York: Cambridge University Press, 2nd ed., 1993), pp. 1–4.

corresponding to real long-term interest rates. This makes economic sense, because if I had a thousand dollars today I could invest it so that it would be worth more, in real terms, in twenty years. But the use of a discount rate means that values gained one hundred years hence rank very low in comparison with values gained today, and values gained one thousand years in the future scarcely count at all. This is not because of any uncertainty about whether there will be human beings or other sentient creatures inhabiting this planet at that time, but merely because of the cumulative effect of the rate of return on money invested now. From the standpoint of the priceless and timeless values we can gain from the wilderness, however, applying a discount rate gives us the wrong answer. There are some things that, once lost, no amount of money can regain. Thus to justify the destruction of an ancient forest on the grounds that it will earn us substantial export income is problematic, even if we could invest that income and increase its value from year to year; for no matter how much we increased its value, it could never buy back the link with the past represented by the forest.

This argument does not show that there can be no justification for cutting any virgin forests, but it does mean that any such justification must take full account of the value of the forests to the generations to come in the more remote future, as well as in the more immediate future. This value will obviously be related to the particular scenic or biological significance of the forest; but as the proportion of true wilderness on the earth dwindles, every part of it becomes significant, because the opportunities for experiencing wilderness become scarce, and the likelihood that a reasonable selection of the major forms of wilderness will be preserved is reduced. Moreover it is not only the people who visit a wilderness who gain from its presence. Popular support for wilderness preservation is far broader than could be the case if only those who visited were in favor of preserving it. It seems that people like to "know that it is there" even if they never see it except on their television sets.

Can we be sure that future generations will appreciate the wilderness? Perhaps they will be happier sitting in air-conditioned shopping malls, playing computer games more sophisticated than any we can imagine. That is possible, but there are several reasons why we should not give this possibility too much weight. First, the trend has been in the opposite direction: the appreciation of wilderness has never been higher than it is today, especially among those nations that have overcome the problems of poverty and hunger and have relatively little wilderness left. Wilderness is valued as something of immense beauty, as a reservoir of scientific knowledge still to be gained, for the unique recreational opportunities that it provides, and because many people just like to know that something natural is still there, relatively untouched by modern civilization. If, as we all hope, future generations are able to provide for the basic needs of most people, we can expect that, for centuries to come, they too will value wilderness for the same reasons that we value it.

Second, arguments for preservation based on the beauty of wilderness are sometimes treated as if they were of little weight because they are merely aesthetic. That is a mistake. We go to great lengths to preserve the artistic treasures of earlier human civilizations. It is difficult to imagine any economic gain that we would be prepared to accept as adequate compensation for the destruction of the paintings in the Louvre, for instance. How should we compare the aesthetic value of a wild river valley or a virgin forest with that of the paintings in the Louvre? Here, perhaps, judgment does become inescapably subjective, so I shall report my own experiences. I have looked at the paintings in the Louvre, and in many of the other great galleries of Europe and the United States. I think I have a reasonable sense of appreciation of the fine arts, yet I have not had, in any museum, experiences that have filled my aesthetic senses in the way that I experience when I walk in a natural setting and pause to survey the view from a rocky peak overlooking a forested valley, or sit by a stream tumbling over moss-covered boulders set among tall green tree-ferns. I do not think that I am alone in this. For many people, wilderness is the source of the greatest feelings of aesthetic appreciation; even nonreligious people tend to describe it in terms of a spiritual experience.

It may nevertheless be true that this appreciation of nature may not be shared by people living a century or two hence. But if wilderness can be the source of such deep joy and satisfaction, that would be a great loss. Moreover, whether future generations value wilderness is up to us; it is, at least, something we can influence. By our preservation of areas of wilderness, we provide an opportunity for generations to come, and by the books and films we produce, we create a culture that can be handed on to our children and their children. If we feel that a walk in the forest, with senses attuned to the appreciation of such an experience, is a more deeply rewarding way to spend a day than playing computer games, or if we feel that to carry one's food and shelter in a backpack for a week while hiking through an unspoiled natural environment will do more to develop character than watching television for an equivalent period, then we ought to encourage future generations to have a feeling for nature; if they end up preferring computer games, we shall have failed.

Finally, if we preserve intact the amount of wilderness that exists now, future generations will at least be able to have the choice of getting up from their computer games and going to see a world that has not been created by human beings. They may like to know that some parts of the world in which they are living are much as they were before we humans developed our fearsome powers of destruction. At present, there are still both wilderness and nonwilderness areas. If we destroy the wilderness, that choice is gone forever. Just as we will spend large sums to preserve cities like Venice, even though future generations conceivably may not be interested in such architectural treasures, so we should preserve wilderness even though it is possible that future generations will care little for it. Thus we will not wrong future generations, as we have been wronged by members of past generations whose thoughtless actions have deprived us of so many possibilities, like the chance of glimpsing the thylacine when walking through Tasmanian forests. We must take care not to inflict equally irreparable losses on the generations to follow us.

Thus a human-centered ethic can be the basis of powerful arguments for what we may call "environmental values." Even from the perspective of such an ethic, economic growth based on the exploitation of irreplaceable resources can be seen as something that brings gains to the present generation, and possibly the next generation or two, at a price that will be paid by every generation to come. The price to be paid by future human beings is too high. But should we limit ourselves to a human-centered ethic? We now need to consider more fundamental challenges to this traditional Western approach to environmental issues.

Is There Value Beyond the Human Species?

Although some debates about significant environmental issues can be conducted by appealing only to the long-term interests of our own species, in any serious exploration of environmental values a central issue will be whether there is anything of intrinsic value beyond human beings. To explore this question we first need to understand the notion of "intrinsic value." Something is of intrinsic value if it is good or desirable in itself; the contrast is with instrumental value, which is value as a means to some other end or purpose. Our own happiness, for example, is of intrinsic value, at least to most of us, in that we desire it for its own sake. Money, on the other hand, is only of instrumental value to us. We want it because of the things we can buy with it, but if we were marooned on a desert island, we would not want it (whereas happiness would be just as important to us on a desert island as anywhere else).

Now consider again for a moment the issue of damming the river described at the beginning of this chapter. Should the decision be made on the basis of human interests alone? If we say that it should, we shall balance the economic benefits for Tasmanians of building the dam against the loss for bushwalkers, scientists, and others, now and in the future, who value the preservation of the river in its natural state. We have already seen that because this calculation includes an indefinite number of future generations, the loss of the wild river is a much greater cost than we might at first imagine. Even so, if we are justified in arguing that the decision whether to dam the river should be made on the basis of values that include, but are not limited to, the interests of human beings, we may have much more to set against the economic benefits for Tasmanians of building the dam. We may take into account the interests of the animals who will die if the valley is drowned; we may give weight to the fact that a species may be lost, that trees that have stood for thousands of years will die, and that an entire local ecosystem will be destroyed; and we may give the preservation of the animals, the species, the trees, and the ecosystem a weight that is independent of the interests of human beings—whether economic, recreational, or scientific—in their preservation.

Here we have a fundamental moral disagreement: a disagreement about what kinds of beings ought to be considered in our moral deliberations. Many people think that once we reach a disagreement of this kind, argument must cease. As I have already briefly indicated, I am more optimistic about the scope of rational argument in ethics. In ethics, even at a fundamental level, there are arguments that should convince any rational person. Take, as an example, a view held by one of the founders of the Western ethical tradition: Aristotle's notorious justification of slavery. Aristotle thought that captured barbarians were "living instruments"—that is, human beings who were not of intrinsic value but existed in order to serve some higher end. That end was the welfare of their Greek captors or owners. He justified this view by arguing that barbarians were less rational than Greeks and, in the hierarchy of nature, the purpose of the less rational is to serve the more rational.[3]

No one now accepts Aristotle's defense of slavery. We reject it for a variety of reasons. We would reject his assumption that non-Greeks are less rational than Greeks, although given the cultural achievements of the different groups at the time, that was by no means an absurd assumption to make. More importantly, from the moral point of view, we reject the idea that the less rational exist in order to serve the more rational. Instead we hold that all humans are equal. We regard racism and slavery based on racism as wrong because they fail to give equal consideration to the interests of all human beings. This would be true whatever the level of rationality or civilization of the slave, and therefore Aristotle's appeal to the higher rationality of the Greeks would not have justified the enslavement of non-Greeks, even if it had been true. Members of the "barbarian" tribes can feel pain, as Greeks can; they can be joyful or miserable, as Greeks can; they can suffer from separation from their families and friends, as Greeks can. To brush aside these needs so that Greeks could satisfy much more minor needs of their own was a great wrong and a blot on Greek civilization. This is something that we would expect all reasonable people to accept, as long as they can view the question from an impartial perspective and are not improperly influenced by having a personal interest in the continued existence of slavery.

Now let us return to the question of the moral status of those who are not humans. We shall consider, first, nonhuman animals. In keeping with the dominant Western tradition, many people still hold that all the nonhuman natural world has value only or predominantly insofar as it benefits human beings. A powerful objection to the dominant Western tradition turns against this tradition an extended version of the objection just made against Aristotle's justification of slavery. Many nonhuman animals are also capable of feeling pain, as humans are; they can certainly be miserable, and perhaps in some cases their lives could also be described as joyful; and members of many mammalian species can suffer from separation from their family group. Is it not therefore a blot on human civilization that we brush aside these needs of nonhuman animals to satisfy minor needs of our own?

Rejecting the dominant Western tradition in this way makes a radical difference to the value basis on which we should consider environmental policy. Into the calculations about damming the river must now go the interests of all the nonhuman animals who live in the area that will be flooded. A few may be able to move to a neighboring area that is suitable, but wilderness is not full of suitable niches awaiting an occupant; if there is territory that can sustain a native animal, it is most likely already occupied. Thus most of them will die: either they will be drowned, or they will starve.

Neither drowning nor starvation is an easy way to die, and the suffering involved in these deaths should, as we have seen, be given no less weight than we would give to an equivalent amount of suffering experienced by human beings.

---

[3]Aristotle, *Politics* (London: Dent, 1926), p. 16.

That, in itself, may be enough to swing the balance against building the dam. What of the fact that the animals will die, apart from the suffering that will occur in the course of dying? Are we also to weigh the deaths of nonhuman animals as equivalent to the deaths of a similar number of human beings? If so, it would seem that almost no development of any area can be justified; even industrial wastelands provide habitat for rodents who will die if the land is built upon. But the argument presented above does not require us to regard the death of a nonhuman animal as morally equivalent to the death of a human being, since humans are capable of foresight and forward planning in ways that nonhuman animals are not. This is surely relevant to the seriousness of death, which, in the case of a human being capable of planning for the future, will thwart these plans, and which thus causes a loss that is different in kind from the loss that death causes to beings incapable even of understanding that they exist over time and have a future. It is also entirely legitimate to take into account the greater sense of loss that humans feel when people close to them die; whether nonhuman animals will feel a sense of loss at the death of another animal will depend on the social habits of the species, but in most cases it is unlikely to be as prolonged, and perhaps not as deep, as the grief that humans feel. These differences between causing death to human beings and to nonhuman animals do not mean that the death of a nonhuman animal should be treated as being of no account. On the contrary, death still inflicts a loss on the animal—the loss of all its future existence, and the experiences that that future life would have contained. When a proposed dam would flood a valley and kill thousands, perhaps millions, of sentient creatures, these deaths should be given great importance in any assessment of the costs and benefits of building the dam.

Let us summarize the conclusions reached so far. We have seen that the dominant Western tradition would restrict environmental values to human interests; but this tradition is based on an indefensible prejudice in favor of the interests of our own species. We share our planet with members of other species who are also capable of feeling pain, of suffering, and of having their lives go well or badly. We are justified in regarding their experiences as having the same kind of value as our own similar experiences. The infliction of suffering on other sentient creatures should be given as much weight as we would give to the infliction of suffering on human beings. The deaths of nonhuman animals, considered independently from the suffering that often accompanies death, should also count, although not as much as the deaths of human beings.

Is There Value Beyond Sentient Beings?

Reverence for Life

The position we have now reached extends the ethic of the dominant Western tradition but in other respects is recognizably of the same type. It draws the boundary of moral consideration around all sentient creatures but leaves other living things outside that boundary. This means that if a valley is to be flooded, we should give weight to the interests of human beings, both present and future, and to the interests of the wallabies, possums, marsupial mice, and birds living there; but the drowning of the ancient forests, the possible loss of an entire species, the destruction of several complex ecosystems, and the blockage of the wild river itself and the loss of those rocky gorges, are factors to be taken into account only insofar as they adversely affect sentient creatures. Is a more radical break with the traditional position possible? Can some or all of these aspects of the flooding of the valley be shown to have intrinsic value, so that they must be taken into account independently of their effects on human beings or nonhuman animals?

To extend an ethic in a plausible way beyond sentient beings is a difficult task. An ethic based on the interests of sentient creatures is on recognizable ground. Sentient creatures have wants and desires. They prefer some states to others. We can therefore, though with much imaginative effort and no guarantee of success, form an idea of what it might be like to be that creature under particular conditions. (The question "What is it like to be a possum drowning?" at least makes sense, even if it is impossible for us to give a more precise answer than "It must be awful.") In reaching moral decisions affecting sentient creatures, we can attempt to add up the effects of different actions on all the sentient creatures affected by the alternative actions open to us. This provides us with at least some rough guide to what might be the right thing to do. But there is *nothing* that corresponds to what it is like to be a tree dying because its roots have been flooded. Once we abandon the interests of sentient creatures as our source of value, where do we find value? What is good or bad for nonsentient creatures, and why does it matter?

It might be thought that as long as we limit ourselves to living things, the answer is not too difficult to find. After all, we know what is good or bad for the plants in our garden: water, sunlight, and compost are good; extremes of heat or cold are bad. The same applies to plants in any forest or wilderness, so why can we not regard their flourishing as good in itself, independently of its usefulness to sentient creatures?

One problem here is that without conscious interests to guide us, we have no way of assessing the relative weights to be given to the flourishing of different forms of life. Is a two-thousand-year-old Huon pine more worthy of preservation than a tussock of grass? Most people will say that it is, but such a judgment seems to have more to do with our feelings of awe for the age, size, and beauty of the tree, or with the length of time it would take to replace it, than with our perception of some intrinsic value in the flourishing of an old tree that is not possessed by a young grass tussock.

If we cease talking in terms of sentience, the boundary between living and inanimate natural objects becomes more difficult to defend. Would it really be worse to cut down an old tree than to destroy a beautiful stalactite that has taken even longer to grow? On what grounds could such a judgment be made? Probably the best-known defense of an ethic that draws the boundaries of ethics around all living things is that of Albert Schweitzer. The phrase he used, "reverence for life," is often quoted; the arguments he offered in support of such a position are less well known. Here is one of the few passages in which he defended his ethic:

> Just as in my own will-to-live there is a yearning for more life, and for that mysterious exaltation of the will which is called pleasure, and terror in face of annihilation and that injury to the will-to-live which is called pain; so the same obtains in all the will-to-live around me, equally whether it can express itself to my comprehension or whether it remains unvoiced.
>
> Ethics thus consists in this, that I experience the necessity of practising the same reverence for life toward all will-to-live, as toward my own. Therein I have already the needed fundamental principle of morality. It is *good* to maintain and cherish life; it is *evil* to destroy and to check life.[4]

A similar view has been defended recently by the contemporary American philosopher Paul Taylor. In his book *Respect for Nature,* Taylor argues that every living thing is "pursuing its own good in its own unique way." Once we see this, we can see all living things "as we see ourselves" and therefore we are ready to place the same value on their existence as we do on our own."[5]

The problem with the defenses offered by both Schweitzer and Taylor for their ethical views is that they use language metaphorically and then argue as if what they had said was literally true. We may often talk about plants "seeking" water or light so that they can survive, and this way of thinking about plants makes it easier to accept talk of their "will to live," or of their "pursuing" of their own good. Once we stop, however, to reflect on the fact that plants are not conscious and cannot engage in any intentional behavior, it is clear that all this language is metaphorical; one might just as well say that a river is pursuing its own good and striving to reach the sea, or that the "good" of a guided missile is to blow itself up along with its target. It is misleading of Schweitzer to attempt to sway us toward an ethic of reverence for all life by referring to "yearning," "exaltation," "pleasure," and "terror." Plants experience none of these.

Moreover, in the case of plants, rivers, and guided missiles, it is possible to give a purely physical explanation of what is happening; and in the absence of consciousness, there is no good reason why we should have greater respect for the physical processes that govern the growth and decay of living things than we have for those that govern nonliving things. This being so, it is at least not obvious why we should have greater reverence for a tree than for a stalactite, or for a single-celled organism than for a mountain; and we can pass silently by Taylor's even more extraordinary claim not merely that we should be ready to respect every living thing but that we should place the same value on the life of every living thing as we place on our own.

---

[4]Albert Schweitzer, *Civilization and Ethics* (part II of *The Philosophy of Civilization*, C. T. Campion, trans., 2nd ed. (London: A. & C. Black, 1929), pp. 246–47.
[5]Paul Taylor, *Respect for Nature* (Princeton, N.J.: Princeton University Press, 1986), pp. 45, 128. My discussion draws on a fine critique of Taylor by Gerald Paske, "The Life Principle: A (metaethical) rejection," *Journal of Applied Philosophy* 6: 219–25 (1989).

Deep Ecology

More than forty years ago the American ecologist Aldo Leopold wrote that there was a need for a "new ethic,"an "ethic dealing with man's relation to land and to the animals and plants which grow upon it." His proposed "land ethic" would enlarge "the boundaries of the community to include soils, waters, plants, and animals, or collectively, the land."[6] The rise of ecological concern in the early 1970s led to a revival of this way of thinking. The Norwegian philosopher Arne Naess wrote a brief but influential article distinguishing between the "shallow" and "deep" forms of ecological thinking. Shallow ecological thinking was limited to the traditional moral framework; those who thought in this way were anxious to avoid pollution to our water supply so that we could have safe water to drink, and they sought to preserve wilderness so that people could continue to enjoy walking through it. Deep ecologists, on the other hand, wanted to preserve the integrity of the biosphere for its own sake, irrespective of the possible benefits to humans that might flow from so doing.[7] . . .

Where the reverence-for-life ethic emphasises individual living organisms, proposals for deep ecology ethics tend to take something larger as the object of value: species, ecological systems, even the biosphere as a whole. Leopold summed up the basis of his new land ethic thus: "A thing is right when it tends to preserve the integrity, stability and beauty of the biotic community. It is wrong when it tends otherwise."[8] In a paper published in 1984, Arne Naess and George Sessions set out several principles for a deep ecological ethic, beginning with the following:

1. The well-being and flourishing of human and non-human Life on Earth have value in themselves (synonyms: intrinsic value, inherent value). These values are independent of the usefulness of the non-human world for human purposes.
2. Richness and diversity of life forms contribute to the realization of these values and are also values in themselves.
3. Humans have no right to reduce this richness and diversity except to satisfy *vital* needs.[9]

Although these principles refer only to life, in the same paper Naess and Sessions say that deep ecology uses the term "biosphere in a more comprehensive non-technical way to refer also to what biologists classify as 'nonliving'; rivers

---

[6]A. Leopold, *A Sand Country Almanac* (New York: Oxford University Press, 1966; first published 1949), pp. 219, 238.
[7]A. Naess, "The Shallow and the Deep, Long-Range Ecology Movement," *Inquiry* 16: 95–100 (1973).
[8]Leopold, op. cit., p. 262.
[9]A. Naess and G. Sessions, "Basic Principles of Deep Ecology," *Ecophilosophy* 6: 3–7 (1984), quoted from D. Bennet and R. Sylvan, "Australian Perspectives on Environmental Ethics: A UNESCO Project" (unpublished, 1989).

(watersheds), landscapes, ecosystems." Sylvan and Plumwood also extend their ethic beyond living things, including in it an obligation "not to jeopardize the well-being of natural objects or systems without good reason."[10]

Behind this application of ethics not only to individuals but also to species and ecosystems lies some form of holism—some sense that the species or ecosystem is not just a collection of individuals but really an entity in its own right. This holism is made explicit in Lawrence Johnson's *A Morally Deep World*, probably the most detailed and carefully argued statement of the case for an ethic of deep ecology yet to appear in print. Lawrence is prepared to talk about the interests of a species in a sense that is distinct from the sum of the interests of each member of the species, and to argue that the interests of a species or an ecosystem ought to be taken into account, with individual interests, in our moral deliberations.

There is, of course, a real philosophical question about whether a species or an ecosystem can be considered the sort of individual that can have interests; and even if it can, the deep ecology ethic will face problems similar to those we identified in considering the idea of the reverence-for-life ethic. For it is necessary not merely that trees, species, and ecosystems can properly be said to have interests, but that they have morally significant interests. We saw in discussing the ethic of reverence for life that one way of establishing that an interest is morally significant is to ask what it would be like for the entity affected to have that interest unsatisfied. This works for sentient beings, but it does not work for trees, species, or ecosystems. There is nothing that corresponds to what it is like to be an ecosystem flooded by a dam. In this respect trees, ecosystems, and species are more like rocks than they are like sentient beings; so the divide between sentient and nonsentient creatures is to that extent a firmer basis for a morally important boundary than the divide between living and nonliving things or holistic entities.

If we were to adopt an ethic that attributed value to nonsentient living things, or to ecosystems as a whole, we would need to have a criterion of what made something more valuable than something else. Naess and Sessions, in common with many other deep ecologists, suggest "richness" and "diversity"; sometimes the term used is "complexity."[11] But what is it for something to be rich, diverse, or complex? Did the introduction of European birds into Australia make our birdlife richer and more diverse? If it could be shown that it did, would that make it a good thing? What if we should discover that allowing effluent from intensive farms to seep into our rivers greatly increases the number of microorganisms that live in them—thus giving rivers a different but more diverse and more complex ecosystem than they had before they were polluted. Does that make the pollution desirable?

---

[10]R. Routley [now R. Sylvan] and V. Routley [now V. Plumwood], "Human Chauvinism and Environmental Ethics" in D. Mannison, M. McRobbie, and R. Routley, eds., *Environmental Philosophy* (Canberra: Australian National University Research School of Social Sciences, 1980).
[11]For a useful survey of the value positions of deep ecologists, see R. Sylvan, *A Critique of Deep Ecology* (Canberra: Australian National University, Department of Philosophy, Discussion Papers in Environmental Philosophy, 12, 1985), p. 53.

To seek intrinsic value in diversity or complexity is a mistake. The reason why we may feel more strongly about destruction of diverse and complex ecosystems than about simpler ones (such as a field of wheat) may be the same as the reason why we feel more strongly about preservation of the ceiling of the Sistine Chapel than we do about the preservation of the ceiling of the Lecture Theatre H_3 at Monash University (which is painted a uniform white). To break up Michelangelo's fresco into handy-sized chunks for sale to tourists would be lucrative, and no doubt the Vatican could put the money to good use in fighting poverty (better use than that usually made of the returns from damming rivers or clearing forests); but would it be right to do so? The objection, in both cases, is to vandalism: the destruction, for short-term gain, of something that has enduring value to sentient beings, is easy to destroy, but once destroyed can never exist again.

If the philosophical basis for a deep ecology ethic is difficult to sustain, this does not mean that the case for the preservation of wilderness is not strong. All it means is that one kind of argument—the argument for the intrinsic value of the plants, species, or ecosystems—is, at best, problematic. We are on surer ground if we confine ourselves to arguments based on the interests of sentient creatures, present and future, human and nonhuman. In my view the arguments grounded on the interests of present and future human beings, and on the interests of the sentient nonhumans who inhabit the wilderness, are quite sufficient to show that, at least in a society where no one needs to destroy wilderness in order to survive, the value of preserving the remaining significant areas of wilderness greatly exceeds the values gained by their destruction.

The Morality of Abortion

26. An Almost Absolute Value in History

John T. Noonan Jr.

John T. Noonan Jr. (1926-) is professor emeritus at the University of California at Berkeley School of Law and a judge on the U.S. Court of Appeals, 9th Circuit (San Francisco). He is the author and editor of many books on social and legal issues.

The most fundamental question involved in the long history of thought on abortion is: How do you determine the humanity of a being? To phrase the question that way is to put in comprehensive humanistic terms what the theologians either dealt with as an explicitly theological question under the heading of "ensoulment" or dealt with implicitly in their treatment of abortion. The Christian position as it originated did not depend on a narrow theological or philosophical concept. It had no relation to theories of infant baptism.[1] It appealed to no special theory of instantaneous ensoulment. It took the world's view on ensoulment as that view changed from Aristotle to Zacchia. There was, indeed, theological influence affecting the theory of ensoulment finally adopted, and, of course, ensoulment itself was a theological concept, so that the position was always explained in theological terms. But the theological notion of ensoulment could easily be translated into humanistic language by substituting "human" for "rational soul"; the problem of knowing when a man is a man is common to theology and humanism.

If one steps outside the specific categories used by the theologians, the answer they gave can be analyzed as a refusal to discriminate among human beings on the basis of their varying potentialities. Once conceived, the being was

[1]According to Glanville Williams (*The Sanctity of Human Life supra* n. 169, at 193), "The historical reason for the Catholic objection to abortion is the same as for the Christian Church's historical opposition to infanticide: the horror of bringing about the death of an unbaptized child." This statement is made without any citation of evidence. As has been seen, desire to administer baptism could, in the Middle Ages, even be urged as a reason for procuring an abortion. It is highly regrettable that the American Law Institute was apparently misled by Williams's account and repeated after him the same baseless statement. See American Law Institute, *Model Penal Code: Tentative Draft No. 9* (1959), p. 148, n. 12.

recognized as man because he had man's potential. The criterion for humanity, thus, was simple and all-embracing: if you are conceived by human parents, you are human.

The strength of this position may be tested by a review of some of the other distinctions offered in the contemporary controversy over legalizing abortion. Perhaps the most popular distinction is in terms of viability. Before an age of so many months, the fetus is not viable, that is, it cannot be removed from the mother's womb and live apart from her. To that extent, the life of the fetus is absolutely dependent on the life of the mother. This dependence is made the basis of denying recognition to its humanity.

There are difficulties with this distinction. One is that the perfection of artificial incubation may make the fetus viable at any time: it may be removed and artificially sustained. Experiments with animals already show that such a procedure is possible. This hypothetical extreme case relates to an actual difficulty: there is considerable elasticity to the idea of viability. Mere length of life is not an exact measure. The viability of the fetus depends on the extent of its anatomical and functional development. The weight and length of the fetus are better guides to the state of its development than age, but weight and length vary. Moreover, different racial groups have different ages at which their fetuses are viable. Some evidence, for example, suggests that Negro fetuses mature more quickly than white fetuses. If viability is the norm, the standard would vary with race and with many individual circumstances.

The most important objection to this approach is that dependence is not ended by viability. The fetus is still absolutely dependent on someone's care in order to continue existence; indeed a child of one or three or even five years of age is absolutely dependent on another's care for existence; uncared for, the older fetus or the younger child will die as surely as the early fetus detached from the mother. The unsubstantial lessening in dependence at viability does not seem to signify any special acquisition of humanity.

A second distinction has been attempted in terms of experience. A being who has had experience, has lived and suffered, who possesses memories, is more human than one who has not. Humanity depends on formation by experience. The fetus is thus "unformed" in the most basic human sense.

This distinction is not serviceable for the embryo which is already experiencing and reacting. The embryo is responsive to touch after eight weeks and at least at that point is experiencing. At an earlier stage the zygote is certainly alive and responding to its environment. The distinction may also be challenged by the rare case where aphasia has erased adult memory: has it erased humanity? More fundamentally, this distinction leaves even the older fetus or the younger child to be treated as an unformed inhuman thing. Finally, it is not clear why experience as such confers humanity. It could be argued that certain central experiences such as loving or learning are necessary to make a man human. But then human beings who have failed to love or to learn might be excluded from the class called man.

A third distinction is made by appeal to the sentiments of adults. If a fetus dies, the grief of the parents is not the grief they would have for a living child. The fetus is an unnamed "it" till birth, and is not perceived as personality until at least the fourth month of existence when movements in the womb manifest a vigorous presence demanding joyful recognition by the parents.

Yet feeling is notoriously an unsure guide to the humanity of others. Many groups of humans have had difficulty in feeling that persons of another tongue, color, religion, sex, are as human as they. Apart from reactions to alien groups, we mourn the loss of a ten-year-old boy more than the loss of his one-day-old brother or his 90-year-old grandfather. The difference felt and the grief expressed vary with the potentialities extinguished, or the experience wiped out; they do not seem to point to any substantial difference in the humanity of baby, boy, or grandfather.

Distinctions are also made in terms of sensation by the parents. The embryo is felt within the womb only after about the fourth month. The embryo is seen only at birth. What can be neither seen nor felt is different from what is tangible. If the fetus cannot be seen or touched at all, it cannot be perceived as man.

Yet experience shows that sight is even more untrustworthy than feeling in determining humanity. By sight, color became an appropriate index for saying who was a man, and the evil of racial discrimination was given foundation. Nor can touch provide the test; a being confined by sickness, "out of touch" with others, does not thereby seem to lose his humanity. To the extent that touch still has appeal as a criterion, it appears to be a survival of the old English idea of "quickening"— a possible mistranslation of the Latin *animatus* used in the canon law. To that extent touch as a criterion seems to be dependent on the Aristotelian notion of ensoulment, and to fall when this notion is discarded.

Finally, a distinction is sought in social visibility. The fetus is not socially perceived as human. It cannot communicate with others. Thus, both subjectively and objectively, it is not a member of society. As moral rules are rules for the behavior of members of society to each other, they cannot be made for behavior toward what is not yet a member. Excluded from the society of men, the fetus is excluded from the humanity of men.[2]

By force of the argument from the consequences, this distinction is to be rejected. It is more subtle than that founded on an appeal to physical sensation, but it is equally dangerous in its implications. If humanity depends on social recognition, individuals or whole groups may be dehumanized by being denied any status in their society. Such a fate is fictionally portrayed in *1984* and has actually been the lot of many men in many societies. In the Roman empire, for example, condemnation to slavery meant the practical denial of most human rights; in the Chinese Communist world, landlords have been classified as enemies of the people and so treated as nonpersons by the state. Humanity does not depend on social recognition, though often the failure of society to recognize the prisoner, the alien, the heterodox as human has led to the destruction of human beings. Anyone conceived by a man and a woman is human. Recognition of this condition by society follows a real event in the objective order, however imperfect and halting

[2] ...Thomas Aquinas gave an analogous reason against baptizing a fetus in the womb: "As long as it exists in the womb of the mother, it cannot be subject to the operation of the ministers of the Church as it is not known to men" (*In sententias Petri Lombardi* 4.6 1.1.2).

the recognition. Any attempt to limit humanity to exclude some group runs the risk of furnishing authority and precedent for excluding other groups in the name of the consciousness or perception of the controlling group in the society.

A philosopher may reject the appeal to the humanity of the fetus because he views "humanity" as a secular view of the soul and because he doubts the existence of anything real and objective which can be identified as humanity. One answer to such a philosopher is to ask how he reasons about moral questions without supposing that there is a sense in which he and the others of whom he speaks are human. Whatever group is taken as the society which determines who may be killed is thereby taken as human. A second answer is to ask if he does not believe that there is a right and wrong way of deciding moral questions. If there is such a difference, experience may be appealed to: to decide who is human on the basis of the sentiment of a given society has led to consequences which rational men would characterize as monstrous.

The rejection of the attempted distinctions based on viability and visibility, experience and feeling, may be buttressed by the following considerations: Moral judgments often rest on distinctions, but if the distinctions are not to appear arbitrary *fiat*, they should relate to some real difference in probabilities. There is a kind of continuity in all life, but the earlier stages of the elements of human life possess tiny probabilities of development. Consider for example, the spermatozoa in any normal ejaculate: There are about 200,000,000 in any single ejaculate, of which one has a chance of developing a zygote. Consider the oocytes which may become ova: there are 100,000 to 1,000,000 oocytes in a female infant, of which a maximum of 390 are ovulated. But once spermatozoon and ovum meet and the conceptus is formed, such studies as have been made show that roughly in only 20 percent of the cases will spontaneous abortion occur. In other words, the chances are about 4 out of 5 that this new being will develop. At this stage in the life of the being there is a sharp shift in probabilities, an immense jump in potentialities. To make a distinction between the rights of spermatozoa and the rights of the fertilized ovum is to respond to an enormous shift in possibilities. For about twenty days after conception the egg may split to form twins or combine with another egg to form a chimera, but the probability of either event happening is very small.

It may be asked, What does a change in biological probabilities have to do with establishing humanity? The argument from probabilities is not aimed at establishing humanity but at establishing an objective discontinuity which may be taken into account in moral discourse. As life itself is a matter of probabilities, as most moral reasoning is an estimate of probabilities, so it seems in accord with the structure of reality and the nature of moral thought to found a moral judgment on the change in probabilities at conception. The appeal to probabilities is the most commonsensical of arguments, to a greater or smaller degree all of us base our actions on probabilities, and in morals, as in law, prudence and negligence are often measured by the account one has taken of the probabilities. If the chance is 200,000,000 to 1 that the movement in the bushes into which you shoot is a man's, I doubt if many persons would hold you careless in shooting; but if the chances are 4 out of 5 that the movement is a human being's, few would acquit you of blame. Would the argument be different if only one out of ten children conceived came to term? Of course this argument would be different. This argument is an appeal to probabilities that actually exist, not to any and all states of affairs which may be imagined.

The probabilities as they do exist do not show the humanity of the embryo in the sense of a demonstration in logic any more than the probabilities of the movement in the bush being a man demonstrate beyond all doubt that the being is a man. The appeal is a "buttressing" consideration, showing the plausibility of the standard adopted. The argument focuses on the decisional factor in any moral judgment and assumes that part of the business of a moralist is drawing lines. One evidence of the nonarbitrary character of the line drawn is the difference of probabilities on either side of it. If a spermatozoon is destroyed, one destroys a being which had a chance of far less than 1 in 200 million of developing into a reasoning being, possessed of the genetic code, a heart and other organs, and capable of pain. If a fetus is destroyed, one destroys a being already possessed of the genetic code, organs, and sensitivity to pain, and one which had an 80 percent chance of developing further into a baby outside the womb who, in time, would reason.

The positive argument for conception as the decisive moment of humanization is that at conception the new being receives the genetic code. It is the genetic information which determines his characteristics, which is the biological carrier of the possibility of human wisdom, which makes him a self-evolving being. A being with a human genetic code is man.

This review of current controversy over the humanity of the fetus emphasizes what a fundamental question the theologians resolved in asserting the inviolability of the fetus. To regard the fetus as possessed of equal rights with other humans was not, however, to decide every case where abortion might be employed. It did decide the case where the argument was that the fetus should be aborted for its own good. To say a being was human was to say it had a destiny to decide for itself which could not be taken from it by another man's decision. But human beings with equal rights often come in conflict with each other, and some decision must be made as whose claims are to prevail. Cases of conflict involving the fetus are different only in two respects: the total inability of the fetus to speak for itself and the fact that the right of the fetus regularly at stake is the right to life itself.

The approach taken by the theologians to these conflicts was articulated in terms of "direct" and "indirect." Again, to look at what they were doing from outside their categories, they may be said to have been drawing lines or "balancing values." "Direct" and "indirect" are spatial metaphors; "line-drawing" is another. "To weigh" or "to balance" values is a metaphor of a more complicated mathematical sort hinting at the process which goes on in moral judgments. All the metaphors suggest that, in the moral judgments made, comparisons were necessary, that no value completely controlled. The principle of double effect was no doctrine fallen from heaven, but a method of analysis appropriate where two relative values were being compared. In Catholic moral theology, as it developed, life even of the innocent was not taken as an absolute. Judgments on acts affecting life issued from a process of weighing. In the weighing, the fetus was always given a value greater than zero, always a value separate and independent from its parents. This valuation was crucial and fundamental in all Christian thought on the subject and marked it off from any approach which considered that only the parents' interests needed to be considered.

Even with the fetus weighed as human, one interest could be weighed as equal or superior; that of the mother in her own life. The casuists between 1450 and 1895 were willing to weigh this interest as superior. Since 1895, that interest was given decisive weight only in the two special cases of the cancerous uterus and the ectopic pregnancy. In both of these cases the fetus itself had little chance of survival even if the abortion were not performed. As the balance was once struck in favor of the mother whenever her life was endangered, it could be so struck again. The balance reached between 1895 and 1930 attempted prudentially and pastorally to forestall a multitude of exceptions for interests less than life.

The perception of the humanity of the fetus and the weighing of fetal rights against other human rights constituted the work of the moral analysts. But what spirit animated their abstract judgments? For the Christian community it was the injunction of Scripture to love your neighbor as yourself. The fetus as human was a neighbor; his life had parity with one's own. The commandment gave life to what otherwise would have been only rational calculation.

The commandment could be put in humanistic as well as theological terms: Do not injure your fellow man without reason. In these terms, once the humanity of the fetus is perceived, abortion is never right except in self-defense. When life must be taken to save life, reason alone cannot say that a mother must prefer a child's life to her own. With this exception, now of great rarity, abortion violates the rational humanist tenet of the equality of human lives.

For Christians the commandment to love had received a special imprint in that the exemplar proposed of love was the love of the Lord for his disciples. In the light given by this example, self-sacrifice carried to the point of death seemed in the extreme situations not without meaning. In the less extreme cases, preference for one's own interests to the life of another seemed to express cruelty or selfishness irreconcilable with the demands of love.

27. A Defense of Abortion[1]

Judith Jarvis Thomson

Judith Jarvis Thomson (1929–), professor of philosophy at Massachusetts Institute of Technology, has written highly acclaimed books and articles on a variety of philosophical issues.

Most opposition to abortion relies on the premise that the fetus is a human being, a person, from the moment of conception. The premise is argued for, but, as I think, not well. Take, for example, the most common argument. We are asked to notice that the development of a human being from conception through birth into childhood is continuous; then it is said that to draw a line, to choose a point in this development and say "before this point the thing is not a person, after this point it is a person" is to make an arbitrary choice, a choice for which in the nature of things no good reason can be given. It is concluded that the fetus is, or anyway that we had better say it is, a person from the moment of conception. But this conclusion does not follow. Similar things might be said about the development of an acorn into an oak tree, and it does not follow that acorns are oak trees, or that we had better say they are. Arguments of this form are sometimes called "slippery slope arguments"—the phrase is perhaps self-explanatory—and it is dismaying that opponents of abortion rely on them so heavily and uncritically.

I am inclined to agree, however, that the prospects for "drawing a line" in the development of the fetus look dim. I am inclined to think also that we shall probably have to agree that the fetus has already become a human person well before birth. Indeed, it comes as a surprise when one first learns how early in its life it begins to acquire human characteristics. By the tenth week, for example, it already has a face, arms and legs, fingers and toes; it has internal organs, and brain activity is detectable.[2] On the other hand, I think that the premise is false, that the fetus is not a person from the moment of conception. A newly fertilized ovum, a newly implanted clump of cells, is no more a person than an acorn is an oak tree. But I shall not discuss any of this. For it seems to me to be of great interest to ask what happens if, for the sake of argument, we allow the premise. How, precisely, are we supposed to get from there to the conclusion that abortion is morally impermissible? Opponents of abortion commonly spend most of their time establishing that the fetus is a person and hardly

Thomson, Judith Jarvis, "A Defense of Abortion," in *Philosophy and Public Affairs*, vol. 1, no. 1. Copyright © 1971 by Princeton University Press, pp. 47–66. Reprinted by permission of Princeton University Press.

[1]I am very much indebted to James Thomson for discussion, criticism, and many helpful suggestions.
[2]Daniel Callahan, *Abortion: Law, Choice and Morality* (New York, 1970), p. 373. This book gives a fascinating survey of the available information on abortion. The Jewish tradition is surveyed in David M. Feldman, *Birth Control in Jewish Law* (New York, 1968), Part 5, the Catholic tradition in John T. Noonan Jr., "An Almost Absolute Value in History," in *The Morality of Abortion*, ed. John T. Noonan Jr. (Cambridge, Mass., 1970).

any time explaining the step from there to the impermissibility of abortion. Perhaps they think the step too simple and obvious to require much comment. Or perhaps instead they are simply being economical in argument. Many of those who defend abortion rely on the premise that the fetus is not a person, but only a bit of tissue that will become a person at birth; and why pay out more arguments than you have to? Whatever the explanation, I suggest that the step they take is neither easy nor obvious, that it calls for closer examination than it is commonly given, and that when we do give it this closer examination we shall feel inclined to reject it.

I propose, then, that we grant that the fetus is a person from the moment of conception. How does the argument go from here? Something like this, I take it. Every person has a right to life. So the fetus has a right to life. No doubt the mother has a right to decide what shall happen in and to her body; everyone would grant that. But surely a person's right to life is stronger and more stringent than the mother's right to decide what happens in and to her body, and so outweighs it. So the fetus may not be killed; an abortion may not be performed.

It sounds plausible. But now let me ask you to imagine this. You wake up in the morning and find yourself back to back in bed with an unconscious violinist. A famous unconscious violinist. He has been found to have a fatal kidney ailment, and the Society of Music Lovers has canvassed all the available medical records and found that you alone have the right blood type to help. They have therefore kidnapped you, and last night the violinist's circulatory system was plugged into yours, so that your kidneys can be used to extract poisons from his blood as well as your own. The director of the hospital now tells you, "Look, we're sorry the Society of Music Lovers did this to you—we would never have permitted it if we had known. But still, they did it, and the violinist now is plugged into you. To unplug you would be to kill him. But never mind, it's only for nine months. By then he will have recovered from his ailment, and can safely be unplugged from you." Is it morally incumbent on you to accede to this situation? No doubt it would be very nice of you if you did, a great kindness. But do you *have* to accede to it? What if it were not nine months, but nine years? Or longer still? What if the director of the hospital says, "Tough luck, I agree, but you've now got to stay in bed, with the violinist plugged into you, for the rest of your life. Because remember this. All persons have a right to life, and violinists are persons. Granted you have a right to decide what happens in and to your body, but a person's right to life outweighs your right to decide what happens in and to your body. So you cannot ever be unplugged from him." I imagine you would regard this as outrageous, which suggests that something really is wrong with that plausible-sounding argument I mentioned a moment ago.

In this case, of course, you were kidnapped; you didn't volunteer for the operation that plugged the violinist into your kidneys. Can those who oppose abortion on the ground I mentioned make an exception for a pregnancy due to rape? Certainly. They can say that persons have a right to life only if they didn't come into existence because of rape; or they can say that all persons have a right to life, but that some have less of a right to life than others, in particular, that those who came into existence because of rape have less. But these statements have a rather unpleasant

Violinist plugged into You

sound. Surely the question of whether you have a right to life at all, or how much of it you have, shouldn't turn on the question of whether or not you are the product of a rape. And in fact the people who oppose abortion on the ground I mentioned do not make this distinction, and hence do not make an exception in case of rape.

Nor do they make an exception for a case in which the mother has to spend the nine months of her pregnancy in bed. They would agree that would be a great pity, and hard on the mother; but all the same, all persons have a right to life, the fetus is a person, and so on. I suspect, in fact, that they would not make an exception for a case in which, miraculously enough, the pregnancy went on for nine years, or even the rest of the mother's life.

Some won't even make an exception for a case in which continuation of the pregnancy is likely to shorten the mother's life; they regard abortion as impermissible even to save the mother's life. Such cases are nowadays very rare, and many opponents of abortion do not accept this extreme view. All the same, it is a good place to begin: a number of points of interest come out in respect to it.

1. Let us call the view that abortion is impermissible even to save the mother's life "the extreme view." I want to suggest first that it does not issue from the argument I mentioned earlier without the addition of some fairly powerful premises. Suppose a woman has become pregnant, and now learns that she has a cardiac condition such that she will die if she carries the baby to term. What may be done for her? The fetus, being a person, has a right to life, but as the mother is a person too, so has she a right to life. Presumably they have an equal right to life. How is it supposed to come out that an abortion may not be performed? If mother and child have an equal right to life, shouldn't we perhaps flip a coin? Or should we add to the mother's right to life her right to decide what happens in and to her body, which everybody seems to be ready to grant—the sum of her rights now outweighing the fetus's right to life?

The most familiar argument here is the following. We are told that performing the abortion would be directly killing[3] the child, whereas doing nothing would not be killing the mother, but only letting her die. Moreover, in killing the child, one would be killing an innocent person, for the child has committed no crime, and is not aiming at his mother's death. And then there are a variety of ways in which this might be continued. (1) But as directly killing an innocent person is always and absolutely impermissible, an abortion may not be performed. Or, (2) as directly killing an innocent person is murder, and murder is always and absolutely impermissible, an abortion may not be performed.[4] Or, (3) as one's duty to refrain

---

[3] The term "direct" in the arguments I refer to is a technical one. Roughly, what is meant by "direct killing" is either killing as an end in itself, or killing as a means to some end, for example, the end of saving someone else's life. See note 6 for an example of its use.

[4] Cf. *Encyclical Letter of Pope Pius XI on Christian Marriage,* St. Paul Editions (Boston, n.d.), p. 32: "However much we may pity the mother whose health and even life is gravely imperiled in the performance of the duty allowed to her by nature, nevertheless what could ever be a sufficient reason for excusing in any way the direct murder of the innocent? This is precisely what we are dealing with here." Noonan (*The Morality of Abortion,* p. 43) reads this as follows: "What cause can ever avail to excuse in any way the direct killing of the innocent? For it is a question of that."

from directly killing an innocent person is more stringent than one's duty to keep a person from dying, an abortion may not be performed. Or, (4) if one's only options are directly killing an innocent person or letting a person die, one must prefer letting the person die, and thus an abortion may not be performed.[5]

Some people seem to have thought that these are not further premises which must be added if the conclusion is to be reached, but that they follow from the very fact that an innocent person has a right to life.[6] But this seems to me to be a mistake, and perhaps the simplest way to show this is to bring out that while we must certainly grant that innocent persons have a right to life, the theses in (1) through (4) are all false. Take (2), for example. If directly killing an innocent person is murder, and thus is impermissible, then the mother's directly killing the innocent person inside her is murder, and thus is impermissible. But it cannot seriously be thought to be murder if the mother performs an abortion on herself to save her life. It cannot seriously be said that she *must* refrain, that she *must* sit passively by and wait for her death. Let us look again at the case of you and the violinist. There you are, in bed with the violinist, and the director of the hospital says to you, "It's all most distressing, and I deeply sympathize, but you see this is putting an additional strain on your kidneys, and you'll be dead within the month. But you *have* to stay where you are all the same. Because unplugging you would be directly killing an innocent violinist, and that's murder, and that's impermissible." If anything in the world is true, it is that you do not commit murder, you do not do what is impermissible, if you reach around to your back and unplug yourself from that violinist to save your life.

The main focus of attention in writings on abortion has been on what a third party may or may not do in answer to a request from a woman for an abortion. This is in a way understandable. Things being as they are, there isn't much a woman can surely do to abort herself. So the question asked is what a third party may do, and what the mother may do, if it is mentioned at all, is deduced, almost as an afterthought, from what it is concluded that third parties may do. But it seems to me that to treat the matter in this way is to refuse to grant to the mother that very status of person which is so firmly insisted on for the fetus. For we cannot simply read off what a person may do from what a third party may do. Suppose you find yourself trapped in a tiny house with a growing child. I mean a very tiny house, and a rapidly growing child—you are already up against the wall of the house and in a few minutes you'll be crushed to death. The child on the other hand won't be crushed to death; if nothing is done to stop him from growing he'll be hurt, but in

---

[5]The thesis in (4) is in an interesting way weaker than those in (1), (2), and (3): they rule out abortion even in cases in which both mother *and* child will die if the abortion is not performed. By contrast, one who held the view expressed in (4) could consistently say that one needn't prefer letting two persons die to killing one.

[6]Cf. the following passage from Pius XII, *Address to the Italian Catholic Society of Midwives*: "The baby in the maternal breast has the right to life immediately from God.—Hence there is no man, no human authority, no science, no medical, eugenic, social, economic or moral 'indication' which can establish or grant a valid juridical ground for a direct deliberate disposition of an innocent human life, that is a disposition which looks to its destruction either as an end or as a means to another end perhaps in itself not illicit.—The baby, still not born, is a man in the same degree and for the same reason as the mother" (quoted in Noonan, *The Morality of Abortion*, p. 45).

the end he'll simply burst open the house and walk out a free man. Now I could well understand it if a bystander were to say, "There's nothing we can do for you. We cannot choose between your life and his, we cannot be the ones to decide who is to live, we cannot intervene." But it cannot be concluded that you too can do nothing, that you cannot attack it to save your life. However innocent the child may be, you do not have to wait passively while it crushes you to death. Perhaps a pregnant woman is vaguely felt to have the status of house, to which we don't allow the right of self-defense. But if the woman houses the child, it should be remembered that she is a person who houses it.

I should perhaps stop to say explicitly that I am not claiming that people have a right to do anything whatever to save their lives. I think, rather, that there are drastic limits to the right of self-defense. If someone threatens you with death unless you torture someone else to death, I think you have not the right, even to save your life, to do so. But the case under consideration here is very different. In our case there are only two people involved, one whose life is threatened, and one who threatens it. Both are innocent: the one who is threatened is not threatened because of any fault, the one who threatens does not threaten because of any fault. For this reason we may feel that we bystanders cannot intervene. But the person threatened can.

In sum, a woman surely can defend her life against the threat to it posed by the unborn child, even if doing so involves its death. And this shows not merely that the theses in (1) through (4) are false; it shows also that the extreme view of abortion is false, and so we need not canvass any other possible ways of arriving at it from the argument I mentioned at the outset.

2. The extreme view could of course be weakened to say that, while abortion is permissible to save the mother's life, it may not be performed by a third party, but only by the mother herself. But this cannot be right either. For what we have to keep in mind is that the mother and the unborn child are not like two tenants in a small house which has, by an unfortunate mistake, been rented to both: the mother *owns* the house. The fact that she does adds to the offensiveness of deducing that the mother can do nothing from the supposition that third parties can do nothing. But it does more than this: it casts a bright light on the supposition that third parties can do nothing. Certainly it lets us see that a third party who says "I cannot choose between you" is fooling himself if he thinks this is impartiality. If Jones has found and fastened on a certain coat, which he needs to keep him from freezing, but which Smith also needs to keep him from freezing, then it is not impartiality that says "I cannot choose between you" when Smith owns the coat. Women have said again and again "This is *my* body!" and they have reason to feel angry, reason to feel that it has been like shouting into the wind. Smith, after all, is hardly likely to bless us if we say to him, "Of course it's your coat, anybody would grant that it is. But no one may choose between you and Jones who is to have it."

We should really ask what it is that says "no one may choose" in the face of the fact that the body that houses the child is the mother's body. It may be simply a failure to appreciate this fact. But it may be something more interesting, namely the sense that one has a right to refuse to lay hands on people, even where it would be just and fair to do so, even where justice seems to require that somebody do so.

Thus justice might call for somebody to get Smith's coat back from Jones, and yet you have a right to refuse to be the one to lay hands on Jones, a right to refuse to do physical violence to him. This, I think, must be granted. But then what should be said is not "no one may choose," but only "*I* cannot choose," and indeed not even this, but "I will not *act*," leaving it open that somebody else can or should, and in particular that anyone in a position of authority, with the job of securing people's rights, both can and should. So this is no difficulty. I have not been arguing that any given third party must accede to the mother's request that he perform an abortion to save her life, but only that he may.

I suppose that in some views of human life the mother's body is only on loan to her, the loan not being one which gives her any prior claim to it. One who held this view might well think it impartiality to say "I cannot choose." But I shall simply ignore this possibility. My own view is that if a human being has any just, prior claim to anything at all, he has a just, prior claim to his own body. And perhaps this needn't be argued for here anyway, since, as I mentioned, the arguments against abortion we are looking at do grant that the woman has a right to decide what happens in and to her body.

But although they do grant it, I have tried to show that they do not take seriously what is done in granting it. I suggest the same thing will reappear even more clearly when we turn away from cases in which the mother's life is at stake, and attend, as I propose we now do, to the vastly more common cases in which a woman wants an abortion for some less weighty reason than preserving her own life.

3. Where the mother's life is not at stake, the argument I mentioned at the outset seems to have a much stronger pull. "Everyone has a right to life, so the unborn person has a right to life." And isn't the child's right to life weightier than anything other than the mother's own right to life, which she might put forward as ground for an abortion?

This argument treats the right to life as if it were unproblematic. It is not, and this seems to me to be precisely the source of the mistake.

For we should now, at long last, ask what it comes to, to have a right to life. In some views having a right to life includes having a right to be given at least the bare minimum one needs for continued life. But suppose that what in fact *is* the bare minimum a man needs for continued life is something he has no right at all to be given? If I am sick unto death, and the only thing that will save my life is the touch of Henry Fonda's cool hand on my fevered brow, then all the same, I have no right to be given the touch of Henry Fonda's cool hand on my fevered brow. It would be frightfully nice of him to fly in from the West Coast to provide it. It would be less nice, though no doubt well meant, if my friends flew out to the West Coast and carried Henry Fonda back with them. But I have no right at all against anybody that he should do this for me. Or again, to return to the story I told earlier, the fact that for continued life that violinist needs the continued use of your kidneys does not establish that he has a right to be given the continued use of your kidneys. He certainly has no right against you that *you* should give him continued use of your kidneys. For nobody has any right to use your kidneys unless you give him such a right; and nobody has the right against you that you shall give him this right—if you do allow him to go on using your kidneys, this is a kindness on your part, and not something he can claim from you as his due. Nor has he any right against anybody else that *they* should give him continued use of your kidneys. Certainly he had no right against the Society of Music Lovers that they should plug him into you in the first place. And if you now start to unplug yourself, having learned that you will otherwise have to spend nine years in bed with him, there is nobody in the world who must try to prevent you, in order to see to it that he is given something he has a right to be given.

Some people are rather stricter about the right to life. In their view, it does not include the right to be given anything, but amounts to, and only to, the right not to be killed by anybody. But here a related difficulty arises. If everybody is to refrain from killing that violinist, then everybody must refrain from doing a great many different sorts of things. Everybody must refrain from slitting his throat, everybody must refrain from shooting him—and everybody must refrain from unplugging you from him. But does he have a right against everybody that they shall refrain from unplugging you from him? To refrain from doing this is to allow him to continue to use your kidneys. It could be argued that he has a right against us that *we* should allow him to continue to use your kidneys. That is, while he had no right against us that we should give him the use of your kidneys, it might be argued that he anyway has a right against us that we shall not now intervene and deprive him of the use of your kidneys. I shall come back to third-party interventions later. But certainly the violinist has no right against you that *you* shall allow him to continue to use your kidneys. As I said, if you do allow him to use them, it is a kindness on your part, and not something you owe him.

The difficulty I point to here is not peculiar to the right to life. It reappears in connection with all the other natural rights; and it is something which an adequate account of rights must deal with. For present purposes it is enough just to draw attention to it. But I would stress that I am not arguing that people do not have a right to life—quite to the contrary, it seems to me that the primary control we must place on the acceptability of an account of rights is that it should turn out in that account to be a truth that all persons have a right to life. I am arguing only that having a right to life does not guarantee having either a right to be given the use of or a right to be allowed continued use of another person's body—even if one needs it for life itself. So the right to life will not serve the opponents of abortion in the very simple and clear way in which they seem to have thought it would.

4. There is another way to bring out the difficulty. In the most ordinary sort of case, to deprive someone of what he has a right to is to treat him unjustly. Suppose a boy and his small brother are jointly given a box of chocolates for Christmas. If the older boy takes the box and refuses to give his brother any of the chocolates, he is unjust to him, for the brother has been given a right to half of them. But suppose that, having learned that otherwise it means nine years in bed with that violinist, you unplug yourself from him. You surely are not being unjust to him, for you gave him no right to use your kidneys, and no one else can have given him any such right. But we have to notice that in unplugging yourself, you are killing him; and violinists, like everybody else, have a right to life, and thus in the view we were

considering just now, the right not to be killed. So here you do what he supposedly has a right you shall not do, but you do not act unjustly to him in doing it.

The emendation which may be made at this point is this: the right to life consists not in the right not to be killed, but rather in the right not to be killed unjustly. This runs a risk of circularity, but never mind: it would enable us to square the fact that the violinist has a right to life with the fact that you do not act unjustly toward him in unplugging yourself, thereby killing him. For if you do not kill him unjustly, you do not violate his right to life, and so it is no wonder you do him no injustice.

But if this emendation is accepted, the gap in the argument against abortion stares us plainly in the face: it is by no means enough to show that the fetus is a person, and to remind us that all persons have a right to life—we need to be shown also that killing the fetus violates its right to life, i.e., that abortion is unjust killing. And is it?

I suppose we may take it as a datum that in a case of pregnancy due to rape the mother has not given the unborn person a right to the use of her body for food and shelter. Indeed, in what pregnancy could it be supposed that the mother has given the unborn person such a right? It is not as if there were unborn persons drifting about the world, to whom a woman who wants a child says "I invite you in."

But it might be argued that there are other ways one can have acquired a right to the use of another person's body than by having been invited to use it by that person. Suppose a woman voluntarily indulges in intercourse, knowing of the chance it will issue in pregnancy, and then she does become pregnant; is she not in part responsible for the presence, in fact the very existence, of the unborn person inside her? No doubt she did not invite it in. But doesn't her partial responsibility for its being there itself give it a right to the use of her body?[7] If so, then her aborting it would be more like the boy's taking away the chocolates, and less like your unplugging yourself from the violinist—doing so would be depriving it of what it does have a right to, and thus would be doing it an injustice.

And then, too, it might be asked whether or not she can kill it even to save her own life: If she voluntarily called it into existence, how can she now kill it, even in self-defense?

The first thing to be said about this is that it is something new. Opponents of abortion have been so concerned to make out the independence of the fetus, in order to establish that it has a right to life, just as its mother does, that they have tended to overlook the possible support they might gain from making out that the fetus is *dependent* on the mother, in order to establish that she has a special kind of responsibility for it, a responsibility that gives it rights against her which are not possessed by any independent person—such as an ailing violinist who is a stranger to her.

On the other hand, this argument would give the unborn person a right to its mother's body only if her pregnancy resulted from a voluntary act, undertaken in

---

[7]The need for a discussion of this argument was brought home to me by members of the Society for Ethical and Legal Philosophy, to whom this paper was originally presented.

full knowledge of the chance a pregnancy might result from it. It would leave out entirely the unborn person whose existence is due to rape. Pending the availability of some further argument, then, we would be left with the conclusion that unborn persons whose existence is due to rape have no right to the use of their mothers' bodies, and thus that aborting them is not depriving them of anything they have a right to and hence is not unjust killing.

And we should also notice that it is not at all plain that this argument really does go even as far as it purports to. For there are cases and cases, and the details make a difference. If the room is stuffy, and I therefore open a window to air it, and a burglar climbs in, it would be absurd to say, "Ah, now he can stay, she's given him a right to the use of her house—for she is partially responsible for his presence there, having voluntarily done what enabled him to get in, in full knowledge that there are such things as burglars, and that burglars burgle." It would be still more absurd to say this if I had had bars installed outside my windows, precisely to prevent burglars from getting in, and a burglar got in only because of a defect in the bars. It remains equally absurd if we imagine it is not a burglar who climbs in, but an innocent person who blunders or falls in. Again, suppose it were like this: people-seeds drift about in the air like pollen, and if you open your windows, one may drift in and take root in your carpets or upholstery. You don't want children, so you fix up your windows with fine mesh screens, the very best you can buy. As can happen, however, and on very, very rare occasions does happen, one of the screens is defective; and a seed drifts in and takes root. Does the person-plant who now develops have a right to the use of your house? Surely not—despite the fact that you voluntarily opened your windows, you knowingly kept carpets and upholstered furniture, and you knew that screens were sometimes defective. Someone may argue that you are responsible for its rooting, that it does have a right to your house, because after all you *could* have lived out your life with bare floors and furniture, or with sealed windows and doors. But this won't do—for by the same token anyone can avoid a pregnancy due to rape by having a hysterectomy, or anyway by never leaving home without a (reliable!) army.

It seems to me that the argument we are looking at can establish at most that there are *some* cases in which the unborn person has a right to the use of its mother's body, and therefore *some* cases in which abortion is unjust killing. There is room for much discussion and argument as to precisely which, if any. But I think we should sidestep this issue and leave it open, for at any rate the argument certainly does not establish that all abortion is unjust killing.

5. There is room for yet another argument here, however. We surely must all grant that there may be cases in which it would be morally indecent to detach a person from your body at the cost of his life. Suppose you learn that what the violinist needs is not nine years of your life, but only one hour: all you need do to save his life is spend one hour in that bed with him. Suppose also that letting him use your kidneys for that one hour would not affect your health in the slightest. Admittedly you were kidnapped. Admittedly you did not give anyone permission to plug him into you. Nevertheless it seems to me plain you *ought* to allow him to use your kidneys for that hour—it would be indecent to refuse.

Again, suppose pregnancy lasted only an hour, and constituted no threat to life or health. And suppose that a woman becomes pregnant as a result of rape. Admittedly she did not voluntarily do anything to bring about the existence of a child. Admittedly she did nothing at all which would give the unborn person a right to the use of her body. All the same it might well be said, as in the newly emended violinist story, that she *ought* to allow it to remain for that hour—that it would be indecent in her to refuse.

Now some people are inclined to use the term "right" in such a way that it follows from the fact that you ought to allow a person to use your body for the hour he needs, that he has a right to use your body for the hour he needs, even though he has not been given that right by any person or act. They may say that it follows also that if you refuse, you act unjustly toward him. This use of the term is perhaps so common that it cannot be called wrong; nevertheless it seems to me to be an unfortunate loosening of what we would do better to keep a tight rein on. Suppose that box of chocolates I mentioned earlier had not been given to both boys jointly, but was given only to the older boy. There he sits, stolidly eating his way through the box, his small brother watching enviously. Here we are likely to say "You ought not to be so mean. You ought to give your brother some of those chocolates." My own view is that it just does not follow from the truth of this that the brother has any right to any of the chocolates. If the boy refuses to give his brother any, he is greedy, stingy, callous—but not unjust. I suppose that the people I have in mind will say it does follow that the brother has a right to some of the chocolates, and thus that the boy does act unjustly if he refuses to give his brother any. But the effect of saying this is to obscure what we should keep distinct, namely the difference between the boy's refusal in this case and the boy's refusal in the earlier case, in which the box was given to both boys jointly, and in which the small brother thus had what was from any point of view clear title to half.

A further objection to so using the term "right" that from the fact that A ought to do a thing for B, it follows that B has a right against A that A do it for him, is that it is going to make the question of whether or not a man has a right to a thing turn on how easy it is to provide him with it; and this seems not merely unfortunate, but morally unacceptable. Take the case of Henry Fonda again. I said earlier that I had no right to the touch of his cool hand on my fevered brow, even though I needed it to save my life. I said it would be frightfully nice of him to fly in from the West Coast to provide me with it, but that I had no right against him that he should do so. But suppose he isn't on the West Coast. Suppose he has only to walk across the room, place a hand briefly on my brow—and lo, my life is saved. Then surely he ought to do it, it would be indecent to refuse. Is it to be said "Ah, well, it follows that in this case she has a right to the touch of his hand on her brow, and so it would be an injustice in him to refuse"? So that I have a right to it when it is easy for him to provide it, though no right when it's hard? It's rather a shocking idea that anyone's rights should fade away and disappear as it gets harder and harder to accord them to him.

So my view is that even though you ought to let the violinist use your kidneys for the one hour he needs, we should not conclude that he has a right to do so—we should say that if you refuse, you are, like the boy who owns all the chocolates and will give none away, self-centered and callous, indecent in fact, but not unjust. And similarly, that even supposing a case in which a woman pregnant due to rape ought to allow the unborn person to use her body for the hour he needs, we should not conclude that he has a right to do so; we should conclude that she is self-centered, callous, indecent, but not unjust, if she refuses. The complaints are no less grave; they are just different. However, there is no need to insist on this point. If anyone does wish to deduce "he has a right" from "you ought," then all the same he must surely grant that there are cases in which it is not morally required of you that you allow that violinist to use your kidneys, and in which he does not have a right to use them, and in which you do not do him an injustice if you refuse. And so also for mother and unborn child. Except in such cases as the unborn person has a right to demand it—and we were leaving open the possibility that there may be such cases—nobody is morally *required* to make large sacrifices, of health, of all other interests and concerns, of all other duties and commitments, for nine years, or even for nine months, in order to keep another person alive.

6. We have in fact to distinguish between two kinds of Samaritan: the Good Samaritan and what we might call the Minimally Decent Samaritan. The story of the Good Samaritan, you will remember, goes like this:

> A certain man went down from Jerusalem to Jericho, and fell among thieves, which stripped him of his raiment, and wounded him, and departed, leaving him half dead.
>
> And by chance there came down a certain priest that way; and when he saw him, he passed by on the other side.
>
> And likewise a Levite, when he was at the place, came and looked on him, and passed by on the other side.
>
> But a certain Samaritan, as he journeyed, came where he was; and when he saw him he had compassion on him.
>
> And went to him, and bound up his wounds, pouring in oil and wine, and set him on his own beast, and brought him to an inn, and took care of him.
>
> And on the morrow, when he departed, he took out two pence, and then gave them to the host, and said unto him, "Take care of him; and whatsoever thou spendest more, when I come again, I will repay thee."
>
> (Luke 10:30–35)

The Good Samaritan went out of his way, at some cost to himself, to help one in need of it. We are not told what the options were, that is, whether or not the priest and the Levite could have helped by doing less than the Good Samaritan did, but assuming they could have, then the fact they did nothing at all shows they were not even Minimally Decent Samaritans, not because they were not Samaritans, but because they were not even minimally decent.

These things are a matter of degree, of course, but there is a difference, and it comes out perhaps most clearly in the story of Kitty Genovese, who, as you will remember, was murdered while thirty-eight people watched or listened, and did nothing at all to help her. A Good Samaritan would have rushed out to give direct assistance against the murderer. Or perhaps we had better allow that it would have been a Splendid Samaritan who did this, on the ground that it would have involved a risk of death for himself. But the thirty-eight not only did not do this, they did not even trouble to pick up a phone to call the police. Minimally Decent Samaritanism would call for doing at least that, and their not having done it was monstrous.

After telling the story of the Good Samaritan, Jesus said "Go, and do thou likewise." Perhaps he meant that we are morally required to act as the Good Samaritan did. Perhaps he was urging people to do more than is morally required of them. At all events it seems plain that it was not morally required of any of the thirty-eight that he rush out to give direct assistance at the risk of his own life, and that it is not morally required of anyone that he give long stretches of his life—nine years or nine months—to sustaining the life of a person who has no special right (we were leaving open the possibility of this) to demand it.

Indeed, with one rather striking class of exceptions, no one in any country in the world is *legally* required to do anywhere near as much as this for anyone else. The class of exceptions is obvious. My main concern here is not the state of the law in respect to abortion, but it is worth drawing attention to the fact that in no state in this country is any man compelled by law to be even a Minimally Decent Samaritan to any person; there is no law under which charges could be brought against the thirty-eight who stood by while Kitty Genovese died. By contrast, in most states in this country women are compelled by law to be not merely Minimally Decent Samaritans, but Good Samaritans to unborn persons inside them. This doesn't by itself settle anything one way or the other, because it may well be argued that there should be laws in this country—as there are in many European countries—compelling at least Minimally Decent Samaritanism.[8] But it does show that there is a gross injustice in the existing state of the law. And it shows also that the groups currently working against liberalization of abortion laws, in fact working toward having it declared unconstitutional for a state to permit abortion, had better start working for the adoption of Good Samaritan laws generally, or earn the charge that they are acting in bad faith.

I should think, myself, that Minimally Decent Samaritan laws would be one thing, Good Samaritan laws quite another, and in fact highly improper. But we are not here concerned with the law. What we should ask is not whether anybody should be compelled by law to be a Good Samaritan, but whether we must accede to a situation in which somebody is being compelled—by nature, perhaps—to be a Good Samaritan. We have, in other words, to look now at third-party interventions. I have been arguing that no person is morally required to make large sacrifices to sustain the life of another who has no right to demand them, and this even where the sacrifices do not include life itself; we are not morally required to be Good Samaritans or anyway Very Good Samaritans to one another. But what if a man cannot extricate himself from such a situation? What if he appeals to us to extricate him? It seems to me plain that there are cases in which we can, cases in which a Good Samaritan would extricate him. There you are, you were kidnapped,

---

[8]For a discussion of the difficulties involved, and a survey of the European experience with such laws, see *The Good Samaritan and the Law*, ed. James M. Ratcliffe (New York 1966).

and nine years in bed with that violinist lie ahead of you. You have your own life to lead. You are sorry, but you simply cannot see giving up so much of your life to the sustaining of his. You cannot extricate yourself, and ask us to do so. I should have thought that—in light of his having no right to the use of your body—it was obvious that we do not have to accede to your being forced to give up so much. We can do what you ask. There is no injustice to the violinist in our doing so.

7. Following the lead of the opponents of abortion, I have throughout been speaking of the fetus merely as a person, and what I have been asking is whether or not the argument we began with, which proceeds only from the fetus's being a person, really does establish its conclusion. I have argued that it does not.

But of course there are arguments and arguments, and it may be said that I have simply fastened on the wrong one. It may be said that what is important is not merely the fact that the fetus is a person, but that it is a person for whom the woman has a special kind of responsibility issuing from the fact that she is its mother. And it might be argued that all my analogies are therefore irrelevant—for you do not have that special kind of responsibility for that violinist, Henry Fonda does not have that special kind of responsibility for me. And our attention might be drawn to the fact that men and women both *are* compelled by law to provide support for their children.

I have in effect dealt (briefly) with this argument in section 4 above; but a (still briefer) recapitulation now may be in order. Surely we do not have any such "special responsibility" for a person unless we have assumed it, explicitly or implicitly. If a set of parents do not try to prevent pregnancy, do not obtain an abortion, and then at the time of birth of the child do not put it out for adoption, but rather take it home with them, then they have assumed responsibility for it, they have given it rights, and they cannot *now* withdraw support from it at the cost of its life because they now find it difficult to go on providing for it. But if they have taken all reasonable precautions against having a child, they do not simply by virtue of their biological relationship to the child who comes into existence have a special responsibility for it. They may wish to assume responsibility for it, or they may not wish to. And I am suggesting that if assuming responsibility for it would require large sacrifices, then they may refuse. A Good Samaritan would not refuse—or anyway, a Splendid Samaritan, if the sacrifices that had to be made were enormous. But then so would a Good Samaritan assume responsibility for that violinist; so would Henry Fonda, if he is a Good Samaritan, fly in from the West Coast and assume responsibility for me.

8. My argument will be found unsatisfactory on two counts by many of those who want to regard abortion as morally permissible. First, while I do argue that abortion is not impermissible, I do not argue that it is always permissible. There may well be cases in which carrying the child to term requires only Minimally Decent Samaritanism of the mother, and this is a standard we must not fall below. I am inclined to think it a merit of my account precisely that it does *not* give a general yes or a general no. It allows for and supports our sense that, for example, a sick and desperately frightened fourteen-year-old schoolgirl, pregnant due to rape, may *of course* choose abortion, and that any law which rules this out is an insane law. And

it also allows for and supports our sense that in other cases resort to abortion is even positively indecent. It would be indecent in the woman to request an abortion, and indecent in a doctor to perform it, if she is in her seventh month, and wants the abortion just to avoid the nuisance of postponing a trip abroad. The very fact that the arguments I have been drawing attention to treat all cases of abortion, or even all cases of abortion in which the mother's life is not at stake, as morally on a par ought to have made them suspect at the outset.

Secondly, while I am arguing for the permissibility of abortion in some cases, I am not arguing for the right to secure the death of the unborn child. It is easy to confuse these two things in that up to a certain point in the life of the fetus it is not able to survive outside the mother's body; hence removing it from her body guarantees its death. But they are importantly different. I have argued that you are not morally required to spend nine months in bed, sustaining the life of that violinist; but to say this is by no means to say that if, when you unplug yourself, there is a miracle and he survives, you then have a right to turn round and slit his throat. You may detach yourself even if this costs him his life; you have no right to be guaranteed his death, by some other means, if unplugging yourself does not kill him. There are some people who will feel dissatisfied by this feature of my argument. A woman may be utterly devastated by the thought of a child, a bit of herself, put out for adoption and never seen or heard of again. She may therefore want not merely that the child be detached from her, but more, that it die. Some opponents of abortion are inclined to regard this as beneath contempt—thereby showing insensitivity to what is surely a powerful source of despair. All the same, I agree that the desire for the child's death is not one which anybody may gratify, should it turn out to be possible to detach the child alive.

At this place, however, it should be remembered that we have only been pretending throughout that the fetus is a human being from the moment of conception. A very early abortion is surely not the killing of a person, and so is not dealt with by anything I have said here.

Problems and Puzzles

28. The Case for Torture

Michael Levin

Michael Levin (1940–) is a professor of philosophy at the City University of New York. He is the author of several books and numerous articles on a variety of philosophical topics.

It is generally assumed that torture is impermissible, a throwback to a more brutal age. Enlightened societies reject it outright, and regimes suspected of using it risk the wrath of the United States.

I believe this attitude is unwise. There are situations in which torture is not merely permissible but morally mandatory. Moreover, these situations are moving from the realm of imagination to fact.

Death

Suppose a terrorist has hidden an atomic bomb on Manhattan Island which will detonate at noon on July 4 unless . . . (here follow the usual demands for money and release of his friends from jail). Suppose, further, that he is caught at 10 A.M. of the fateful day, but—preferring death to failure—won't disclose where the bomb is. What do we do? If we follow due process—wait for his lawyer, arraign him—millions of people will die. If the only way to save those lives is to subject the terrorist to the most excruciating possible pain, what grounds can there be for not doing so? I suggest there are none. In any case, I ask you to face the question with an open mind.

Torturing the terrorist is unconstitutional? Probably. But millions of lives surely outweigh constitutionality. Torture is barbaric? Mass murder is far more barbaric. Indeed, letting millions of innocents die in deference to one who flaunts his guilt is moral cowardice, an unwillingness to dirty one's hands. If *you* caught the terrorist, could you sleep nights knowing that millions died because you couldn't bring yourself to apply the electrodes?

Once you concede that torture is justified in extreme cases, you have admitted that the decision to use torture is a matter of balancing innocent lives against the means needed to save them. You must now face more realistic cases involving more modest numbers. Someone plants a bomb on a jumbo jet. He alone can disarm it, and his demands cannot be met (or if they can, we refuse to set a precedent by yielding to his

Reprinted from *Newsweek*, June 7, 1982, with permission of the author.

threats). Surely we can, we must, do anything to the extortionist to save the passengers. How can we tell 300, or 100, or 10 people who never asked to be put in danger, "I'm sorry, you'll have to die in agony, we just couldn't bring ourselves to . . . "

Here are the results of an informal poll about a third, hypothetical, case. Suppose a terrorist group kidnapped a newborn baby from a hospital. I asked four mothers if they would approve of torturing kidnappers if that were necessary to get their own newborns back. All said yes, the most "liberal" adding that she would administer it herself.

I am not advocating torture as punishment. Punishment is addressed to deeds irrevocably past. Rather, I am advocating torture as an acceptable measure for preventing future evils. So understood, it is far less objectionable than many extant punishments. Opponents of the death penalty, for example, are forever insisting that executing a murderer will not bring back his victim (as if the purpose of capital punishment were supposed to be resurrection, not deterrence or retribution). But torture, in the cases described, is intended not to bring anyone back but to keep innocents from being dispatched. The most powerful argument against using torture as a punishment or to secure confessions is that such practices disregard the rights of the individual. Well, if the individual is all that important—and he is—it is correspondingly important to protect the rights of individuals threatened by terrorists. If life is so valuable that it must never be taken, the lives of the innocents must be saved even at the price of hurting the one who endangers them.

Better precedents for torture are assassination and preemptive attack. No Allied leader would have flinched at assassinating Hitler, had that been possible. (The Allies did assassinate Heydrich.) Americans would be angered to learn that Roosevelt could have had Hitler killed in 1943—thereby shortening the war and saving millions of lives—but refused on moral grounds. Similarly, if nation A learns that nation B is about to launch an unprovoked attack, A has a right to save itself by destroying B's military capability first. In the same way, if the police can by torture save those who would otherwise die at the hands of kidnappers or terrorists they must.

Idealism

There is an important difference between terrorists and their victims that should mute talk of the terrorists' "rights." The terrorist's victims are at risk unintentionally, not having asked to be endangered. But the terrorist knowingly initiated his actions. Unlike his victims, he volunteered for the risks of his deed. By threatening to kill for profit or idealism, he renounces civilized standards, and he can have no complaint if civilization tries to thwart him by whatever means necessary.

Just as torture is justified only to save lives (not extort confessions or recantations), it is justifiably administered only to those *known* to hold innocent lives in their hands. Ah, but how can the authorities ever be sure they have the right malefactor? Isn't there a danger of error and abuse? Won't We turn into Them?

Questions like these are disingenuous in a world in which terrorists proclaim themselves and perform for television. The name of their game is public recognition.

After all, you can't very well intimidate a government into releasing your freedom fighters unless you announce that it is your group that has seized its embassy. "Clear guilt" is difficult to define, but when 40 million people see a group of masked gunmen seize an airplane on the evening news, there is not much question about who the perpetrators are. There will be hard cases where the situation is murkier. Nonetheless, a line demarcating the legitimate use of torture can be drawn. Torture only the obviously guilty, and only for the sake of saving innocents, and the line between Us and Them will remain clear.

There is little danger that the Western democracies will lose their way if they choose to inflict pain as one way of preserving order. Paralysis in the face of evil is the greater danger. Some day soon a terrorist will threaten tens of thousands of lives, and torture will be the only way to save them. We had better start thinking about this.

29. The Survival Lottery

John Harris

John Harris (1946–   ) is a professor in the School of Law at the University of Manchester in England. He has written numerous books and articles on bioethics.

Let us suppose that organ transplant procedures have been perfected; in such circumstances if two dying patients could be saved by organ transplants then, if surgeons have the requisite organs in stock and no other needy patients, but nevertheless allow their patients to die, we would be inclined to say, and be justified in saying, that the patients died because the doctors refused to save them. But if there are no spare organs in stock and none otherwise available, the doctors have no choice, they cannot save their patients and so must let them die. In this case we would be disinclined to say that the doctors are in any sense the cause of their patients' deaths. But let us further suppose that the two dying patients, Y and Z, are not happy about being left to die. They might argue that it is not strictly true that there are no organs which could be used to save them. Y needs a new heart and Z new lungs. They point out that if just one healthy person were to be killed his organs could be removed and both of them be saved. We and the doctors would probably be alike in thinking that such a step, while technically possible, would be out of the question. We would not say that the doctors were killing their patients if they refused to prey upon the healthy to save the sick. And because this sort of surgical Robin Hoodery is out of the question we can tell Y and Z that they cannot be saved, and that when they die they will have died of natural causes and not of the neglect of their doctors. Y and Z do not however agree; they insist that if the doctors fail to kill a healthy man and use his organs to save them, then the doctors will be responsible for their deaths.

Many philosophers have for various reason believed that we must not kill even if by doing so we could save life. They believe that there is a moral difference between killing and letting die. On this view, to kill A so that Y and Z might live is ruled out because we have a strict obligation not to kill but a duty of some lesser kind to save life. A. H. Clough's dictum 'Thou shalt not kill but need'st not strive officiously to keep alive' expresses bluntly this point of view. The dying Y and Z may be excused for not being much impressed by Clough's dictum. They agree that it is wrong to kill the innocent and are prepared to agree to an absolute prohibition against so doing. They do not agree, however, that A is more innocent than they are. Y and Z might go on to point out that the currently acknowledged right

Reprinted from "The Survival Lottery" by John Harris from *Philosophy, Vol. 50, No. 191* (1975). Reprinted with the permission of Cambridge University Press.

of the innocent not to be killed, even where their deaths might give life to others, is just a decision to prefer the lives of the fortunate to those of the unfortunate. A is innocent in the sense that he has done nothing to deserve death, but Y and Z are also innocent in this sense. Why should they be the ones to die simply because they are so unlucky as to have diseased organs? Why, they might argue, should their living or dying be left to chance when in so many other areas of human life we believe that we have an obligation to ensure the survival of the maximum number of lives possible?

Y and Z argue that if a doctor refuses to treat a patient, with the result that the patient dies, he has killed that patient as sure as shooting, and that, in exactly the same way, if the doctors refuse Y and Z the transplants that they need, then their refusal will kill Y and Z, again as sure as shooting. The doctors, and indeed the society which supports their inaction, cannot defend themselves by arguing that they are neither expected, nor required by law or convention, to kill so that lives may be saved (indeed, quite the reverse) since this is just an appeal to custom or authority. A man who does his own moral thinking must decide whether, in these circumstances, he ought to save two lives at the cost of one, or one life at the cost of two. The fact that so called 'third parties' have never before been brought into such calculations, have never before been thought of as being involved, is not an argument against their now becoming so. There are of course, good arguments against allowing doctors simply to haul passers-by off the streets whenever they have a couple of patients in need of new organs. And the harmful side-effects of such a practice in terms of terror and distress to the victims, the witnesses and society generally, would give us further reasons for dismissing the idea. Y and Z realize this and have a proposal, which they will shortly produce, which would largely meet objections to placing such power in the hands of doctors and eliminate at least some of the harmful side-effects.

In the unlikely event of their feeling obliged to reply to the reproaches of Y and Z, the doctors might offer the following argument: they might maintain that a man is only responsible for the death of someone whose life he might have saved, if, in all the circumstances of the case, he ought to have saved the man by the means available. This is why a doctor might be a murderer if he simply refused or neglected to treat a patient who would die without treatment, but not if he could only save the patient by doing something he ought in no circumstances to do—kill the innocent. Y and Z readily agree that a man ought not to do what he ought not to do, but they point out that if the doctors, and for that matter society at large, ought on balance to kill one man if two can thereby be saved, then failure to do so will involve responsibility for the consequent deaths. The fact that Y's and Z's proposal involves killing the innocent cannot be a reason for refusing to consider their proposal, for this would just be a refusal to face the question at issue and so avoid having to make a decision as to what ought to be done in circumstances like these. It is Y's and Z's claim that failure to adopt their plan will also involve killing the innocent, rather more of the innocent than the proposed alternative.

To back up this last point, to remove the arbitrariness of permitting doctors to select their donors from among the chance passers-by outside hospitals, and the tremendous power this would place in doctors' hands, to mitigate worries about side-effects and lastly to appease those who wonder why poor old A should be singled out for sacrifice, Y and Z put forward the following scheme: they propose that everyone be given a sort of lottery number. Whenever doctors have two or more dying patients who could be saved by transplants, and no suitable organs have come to hand through 'natural' deaths, they can ask a central computer to supply a suitable donor. The computer will then pick the number of a suitable donor at random and he will be killed so that the lives of two or more others may be saved. No doubt if the scheme were ever to be implemented a suitable euphemism for 'killed' would be employed. Perhaps we would begin to talk about citizens being called upon to 'give life' to others. With the refinement of transplant procedures such a scheme could offer the chance of saving large numbers of lives that are now lost. Indeed, even taking into account the loss of the lives of donors, the numbers of untimely deaths each year might be dramatically reduced, so much so that everyone's chance of living to a ripe old age might be increased. If this were to be the consequence of the adoption of such a scheme, and it might well be, it could not be dismissed lightly. It might of course be objected that it is likely that more old people will need transplants to prolong their lives than will the young, and so the scheme would inevitably lead to a society dominated by the old. But if such a society is thought objectionable, there is no reason to suppose that a programme could not be designed for the computer that would ensure the maintenance of whatever is considered to be an optimum age distribution throughout the population.

Suppose that inter-planetary travel revealed a world of people like ourselves, but who organized their society according to this scheme. No one was considered to have an absolute right to life or freedom from interference, but everything was always done to ensure that as many people as possible would enjoy long and happy lives. In such a world a man who attempted to escape when his number was up or who resisted on the grounds that no one had a right to take his life, might well be regarded as a murderer. We might or might not prefer to live in such a world, but the morality of its inhabitants would surely be one that we could respect. It would not be obviously more barbaric or cruel or immoral than our own.

Y and Z are willing to concede one exception to the universal application of their scheme. They realize that it would be unfair to allow people who have brought their misfortune on themselves to benefit from the lottery. There would clearly be something unjust about killing the abstemious B so that W (whose heavy smoking has given him lung cancer) and X (whose drinking has destroyed his liver) should be preserved to over-indulge again.

What objections could be made to the lottery scheme? A first straw to clutch at would be the desire for security. Under such a scheme we would never know when we would hear *them* knocking at the door. Every post might bring a sentence of death, every sound in the night might be the sound of boots on the stairs. But, as we have seen, the chances of actually being called upon to make the ultimate sacrifice might be slimmer than is the present risk of being killed on the roads, and most of us do not lie trembling a-bed, appalled at the prospect of being dispatched on the morrow. The truth is that lives might well be more secure under such a scheme.

If we respect individuality and see every human being as unique in his own way, we might want to reject a society in which it appeared that individuals were seen merely as interchangeable units in a structure, the value of which lies in its having as many healthy units as possible. But of course Y and Z would want to know why A's individuality was more worthy of respect than theirs.

Another plausible objection is the natural reluctance to play God with men's lives, the feeling that it is wrong to make any attempt to re-allot the life opportunities that fate has determined, that the deaths of Y and Z would be 'natural', whereas the death of anyone killed to save them would have been penetrated by men. But if we are able to change things, then to elect not to do so is also to determine what will happen in the world.

Neither does the alleged moral difference between killing and letting die afford a respectable way of rejecting the claims of Y and Z. For if we really want to counter proponents of the lottery, if we really want to answer Y and Z and not just put them off, we cannot do so by saying that the lottery involves killing and object to it for that reason, because to do so would, as we have seen, just beg the question as to whether the failure to save as many people as possible might not also amount to killing.

To opt for the society which Y and Z propose would be then to adopt a society in which saintliness would be mandatory. Each of us would have to recognize a binding obligation to give up his own life for others when called upon to do so. In such a society anyone who reneged upon this duty would be a murderer. The most promising objection to such a society, and indeed to any principle which required us to kill A in order to save Y and Z, is, I suspect, that we are committed to the right of self-defence. If I can kill A to save Y and Z then he can kill me to save P and Q, and it is only if I am prepared to agree to this that I will opt for the lottery or be prepared to agree to a man's being killed if doing so would save the lives of more than one other man. Of course there is something paradoxical about basing objections to the lottery scheme on the right of self-defence since, *ex hypothesi*, each person would have a better chance of living to a ripe old age if the lottery scheme were to be implemented. None the less, the feeling that no man should be required to lay down his life for others makes many people shy away from such a scheme, even though it might be rational to accept it on prudential grounds, and perhaps even mandatory on utilitarian grounds. Again, Y and Z would reply that the right of self-defence must extend to them as much as to anyone else; and while it is true that they can only live if another man is killed, they could claim that it is also true that if they are left to die, then someone who lives on does so over their dead bodies.

If might be argued that the institution of the survival lottery has not gone far to mitigate the harmful side-effects in terms of terror and distress to victims, witnesses, and society generally, that would be occasioned by doctors simply snatching passers-by off the streets and disorganizing them for the benefit of the unfortunate. Donors would after all still have to be procured, and this process, however it was carried out, would still be likely to prove distressing to all concerned. The lottery scheme would eliminate the arbitrariness of leaving the life and death decisions to the doctors, and remove the possibility of such terrible power falling into the hands of any individuals, but the terror and distress would remain. The effect of having to apprehend presumably unwilling victims would give us pause. Perhaps only a long period of education or propaganda could remove our abhorrence. What this abhorrence reveals about the rights and wrongs of the situation is however more difficult to assess. We might be inclined to say that only monsters could ignore the promptings of conscience so far as to operate the lottery scheme. But the promptings of conscience are not necessarily the most reliable guide. In the present case Y and Z would argue that such promptings are mere squeamishness, an over-nice self-indulgence that costs lives. Death, Y and Z would remind us, is a distressing experience whenever and to whomever it occurs, so the less it occurs the better. Fewer victims and witnesses will be distressed as part of the side-effects of the lottery scheme than would suffer as part of the side-effects of not instituting it.

Lastly, a more limited objection might be made, not to the idea of killing to save lives, but to the involvement of 'third parties'. Why, so the objection goes, should we not give X's heart to Y or Y's lungs to X, the same number of lives being thereby preserved and no one else's life set at risk? Y's and Z's reply to this objection differs from their previous line of argument. To amend their plan so that the involvement of so called 'third parties' is ruled out would, Y and Z claim, violate their right to equal concern and respect with the rest of society. They argue that such a proposal would amount to treating the unfortunate who need new organs as a class within society whose lives are considered to be of less value than those of its more fortunate members. What possible justification could there be for singling out one group of people whom we would be justified in using as donors but not another? The idea in the mind of those who would propose such a step must be something like the following: since Y and Z cannot survive, since they are going to die in any event, there is no harm in putting their names into the lottery, for the chances of their dying cannot thereby be increased and will in fact almost certainly be reduced. But this is just to ignore everything that Y and Z have been saying. For if their lottery scheme is adopted they are not going to die anyway—their chances of dying are no greater and no less than those of any other participant in the lottery whose number may come up. This ground for confining selection of donors to the unfortunate therefore disappears. Any other ground must discriminate against Y and Z as members of a class whose lives are less worthy of respect than those of the rest of society.

It might more plausibly be argued that the dying who cannot themselves be saved by transplants, or by any other means at all, should be the priority selection group for the computer programme. But how far off must death be for a man to be classified as 'dying'? Those so classified might argue that their last few days or weeks of life are as valuable to them (if not more valuable) than the possibly longer span remaining to others. The problem of narrowing down the class of possible donors without discriminating unfairly against some subclass of society is, I suspect, insoluble.

Such is the case for the survival lottery. Utilitarians ought to be in favour of it, and absolutists cannot object to it on the ground that it involves killing the innocent, for it is Y's and Z's case that any alternative must also involve killing the innocent. If the absolutist wishes to maintain his objection he must point to some morally relevant difference between positive and negative killing. This challenge opens the door to a large topic with a whole library of literature, but Y and Z are dying and do not have time to explore it exhaustively. In their own case the most likely candidate for some feature which might make this moral difference is the malevolent intent of Y and Z themselves. An absolutist might well argue that while no one intends the deaths of Y and Z, no one necessarily wishes them dead, or aims at their demise for any reason, they do mean to kill A (or have him killed). But Y and Z can reply that the death of A is no part of their plan, they merely wish to use a couple of his organs, and if he cannot live without them . . . *tant pis*! None would be more delighted than Y and Z if artificial organs would do as well, and so render the lottery scheme otiose.

One form of absolutist argument perhaps remains. This involves taking an Orwellian stand on some principle of common decency. The argument would then be that even to enter into the sort of 'macabre' calculations that Y and Z propose displays a blunted sensibility, a corrupted and vitiated mind. Forms of this argument have recently been advanced by Noam Chomsky (*American Power and the New Mandarins*) and Stuart Hampshire (*Morality and Pessimism*). The indefatigable Y and Z would of course deny that their calculations are in any sense 'macabre', and would present them as the most humane course available in the circumstances. Moreover they would claim that the Orwellian stand on decency is the product of a closed mind, and not susceptible to rational argument. Any reasoned defence of such a principle must appeal to notions like respect for human life, as Hampshire's argument in fact does, and these Y and Z could make conformable to their own position.

Can Y and Z be answered? Perhaps only by relying on moral intuition, on the insistence that we do feel there is something wrong with the survival lottery and our confidence that this feeling is prompted by some morally relevant difference between our bringing about the death of A and our bringing about the deaths of Y and Z. Whether we could retain this confidence in our intuitions if we were to be confronted by a society in which the survival lottery operated, was accepted by all, and was seen to save many lives that would otherwise have been lost, it would be interesting to know.

There would of course be great practical difficulties in the way of implementing the lottery. In so many cases it would be agonizingly difficult to decide whether or not a person had brought his misfortune on himself. There are numerous ways in which a person may contribute to his predicament, and the task of deciding how far, or how decisively, a person is himself responsible for his fate would be formidable. And in those cases where we can be confident that a person is innocent of responsibility for his predicament, can we acquire this confidence in time to save him? The lottery scheme would be a powerful weapon in the hands of someone willing and able to misuse it. Could we ever feel certain that the lottery was safe from unscrupulous computer programmers? Perhaps we should be thankful that such practical difficulties make the survival lottery an unlikely consequence of the perfection of transplants. Or perhaps we should be appalled.

It may be that we would want to tell Y and Z that the difficulties and dangers of their scheme would be too great a price to pay for its benefits. It is as well to be clear, however, that there is also a high, perhaps an even higher, price to be paid for the rejection of the scheme. That price is the lives of Y and Z and many like them, and we delude ourselves if we suppose that the reason why we reject their plan is that we accept the sixth commandment.

Suggestions for Further Reading

Anthologies

Cahn, Steven M., ed. *Ethics: History, Theory and Contemporary Issues*. New York: Oxford University Press, 2001. A large anthology of important writings on a wide range of ethical problems.

Feinberg, Joel, ed. *The Problem of Abortion*. Belmont, Calif.: Wadsworth, 1973. A collection of some of the best philosophical essays on the abortion controversy.

Glover, Jonathan, ed. *Utilitarianism and Its Critics*. New York: Macmillan, 1990. A well-chosen collection of articles defending and attacking utilitarianism.

Kuhse, Helga, and Peter Singer, *Bioethics*. New York and Oxford: Blackwell Publishing Co., 1999. Many valuable papers in this increasingly important area of ethics.

Moser, Paul K., and Thomas L. Carson, eds. *Moral Relativism*. New York: Oxford Univ. Press, 2000. A collection of important articles devoted solely to the topic of moral relativism.

Regan, Tom, ed. *Matters of life and Death*. 3rd ed. New York: McGraw-Hill, 1993. A collection of original essays on a variety of moral issues.

Singer, Peter, ed. *Ethics*. New York: Oxford Univ. Press, 1994. A collection of essays on the nature and origin of ethics. Many of the selections are from such fields as anthropology, biology, and game theory.

Individual Works

Barnes, Hazel E. *An Existentialist Ethics*. New York: Knopf, 1967. A clear presentation of an existentialist approach to ethics, as well as a consideration and rejection of a number of other contemporary ethical views.

Bedau, Hugo Adam. *Making Moral Choices*. New York: Oxford Univ. Press, 1997. A discussion of possible choices in three difficult cases drawn from history and literature.

Binkley, Luther. *Contemporary Ethical Theories*. New York: Citadel, 1961. A clear discussion of the twentieth-century analytic philosophers' approach to ethics.

Brandt, William. *Ethical Theory*. Englewood Cliffs, N.J.: Prentice Hall, 1959. An excellent but somewhat difficult introduction to ethical theory. Contains excellent bibliographies on almost all major topics in ethical theory.

Fletcher, Joseph. *Situation Ethics: The New Morality*. Philadelphia: Westminster, 1966. A contemporary Christian view of ethics, which stresses love as the basis for decision making in ethics.

Frankena, William. *Ethics*. 2nd ed. Englewood Cliffs, N.J.: Prentice Hall, 1973. Provides a clear, concise statement of the major ethical problems and positions.

Hospers, John. *Human Conduct*. New York: Harcourt, 1982. An excellent, clearly written textbook that is highly recommended for the beginning student.

Norman, Richard. *The Moral Philosophers*. New York: Oxford Univ. Press, 1983. A brief survey of the main figures in the history of ethics.

Rand, Ayn. *The Virtue of Selfishness*. New York: Signet, 1964. An interesting, but at times confusing, defense of egoism by a popular novelist and an intellectual leader of the libertarian movement.

264

Russell, Bertrand. *Human Society in Ethics and Politics*. New York: Simon & Schuster, 1952. A clearly written analysis of a variety of ethical issues by a great modern philosopher.

Singer, Peter. *How Are We to Live?* Amherst, N.Y.: Prometheus Books, 1995. The author argues that an ethical approach to life can be more satisfying and meaningful than a self-centered approach.

Smart, J. J. C., and Bernard Williams *Utilitarianism: For and Against*. London: Cambridge Univ. Press, 1973. Smart gives a detailed description and defense of utilitarianism, and Williams offers a variety of criticisms.

Encyclopedias

Dictionary of the History of Ideas: Studies of Selected Pivotal Ideas. Philip P. Weiner, editor-in-chief. New York: Scribner's, 1973. Substantial and clearly written essays emphasizing the historical development of topics discussed in this part. Designed to inform the nonspecialist, each essay concludes with a select bibliography.

Encyclopedia of Philosophy. Paul Edwards, editor-in-chief. New York: Macmillan, 1967. The student will find many worthwhile articles on the subject treated in this part and excellent bibliographies.

Routledge Encyclopedia of Philosophy. Edward Craig, general editor. New York: Routledge, 1998. This ten-volume encyclopedia contains articles on all areas of philosophy and up-to-date bibliographies.

Internet Web Sites

RESEARCH NAVIGATOR (*http://www.researchnavigator.com*). This web site offers three research data bases: Ebsco Academic Journal and Abstract Data Base, *New York Times* Search by Subject Archive, and "Best of the Web" Link Library. In addition, this site provides helpful advice on how to conduct efficient and productive research from choosing a topic to polishing the final draft. Beginning philosophy students probably will find the "Best of the Web" Link Library the most appropriate place to start their research. The free access code necessary to employ Research Navigator can be found in the Prentice Hall Guide to Evaluating Online Resources. If your text did not come with this guide, please go to *www.prenhall.com/contentselect* for information on how you can purchase an access code.

EpistemeLinks (*http://www.epistemelinks.com*). This site provides many links to philosophical resources on the web.

PART FOUR

State and Society

Introduction

Consider these two situations. It is April 14, late in the evening. Completing your federal income tax form, you discover to your dismay that you owe an additional tax of two hundred dollars to the U.S. government. After triple-checking your return, you sigh and write out a personal check in the amount required. For it is either pay or be fined or perhaps be clapped into jail. Nothing voluntary here. You are being coerced by other human beings; if you do not comply, you will suffer. Muttering, you trudge to the mailbox located on the next block. Returning to your home, a man you've never seen before points a revolver at you and demands that you give him all of your money. Nothing voluntary here, either. Choking down your anger, you give the robber the fifty dollars in your wallet. The story ends somewhat happily. You reach home safe but poorer.

Do these two situations differ in any significant way? Or are they the same except for incidental details? Both involve financial loss and coercion that you would prefer to avoid. Is the government nothing more than a robber on a more ambitious scale? Is the robber really an individual entrepreneur heroically defying a company monopoly? Of course, many would hold that the two situations are not comparable at all. The federal income tax is legitimate, legal, justifiable, whereas robbery is criminal, illegal, unjustifiable. The income tax constitutes a self-assessment; through your elected representatives you've consented to it. You have not consented to be robbed. As a result of the Sixteenth Amendment, the federal income tax is constitutional. Armed robbery is unconstitutional. Certainly armed robbery is undemocratic. The federal income tax possesses a political philosophy to give it rational support; armed robbery remains innocent of any political philosophy justifying it.

The field of political philosophy offers a rich and varied landscape of problems, methods of analysis, and solutions. This section focuses on one problem: Can the democratic state be justified rationally? Can its superiority to other forms of government be shown on rational grounds? All governments, whether allegedly democratic or not, claim to be legitimate. That is to say, they assert that they not only have the allegiance of those subject to their authority but that they also deserve loyalty. Democratic governments are no exception to this generalization. The government of the United States claims not only that its citizens must support it by paying taxes and, if necessary, must protect and defend it by fighting and dying in war; it further holds that American citizens ought to be ready and willing to make these sacrifices. If any individual American citizen or group of American citizens refuses to obey the government, then those in authority not only can use the police power to compel obedience but are justified in doing so.

A legitimate government maintains that its physical authority ultimately rests on moral authority. Governments justify their existence and policies by appealing to a political philosophy. Democratic governments claim to be promoting the political philosophy of democracy. Defending the cause of the Union at Gettysburg, Lincoln did not rest that defense on the threat of force; he declared that the nation was "conceived in liberty and dedicated to the proposition that all men are created equal." A political philosophy, whatever else it may comprise, consists of propositions claiming to be true and consistent with one another. And governments, particularly when their authority is seriously and sharply questioned, picture themselves implementing some political philosophy. Therefore, the political philosophy of democracy is not to be identified with familiar democratic practices such as universal suffrage, the two-party system, political conventions, a president and a congress, specific legislation, and so on; these actual governmental forms and exercises presumably are the most effective means so far devised for translating the abstract propositions of democratic political philosophy into concrete reality. A democratic government is supposed to be democratic political philosophy in action.

Of course, the political philosophy of democracy includes many more propositions than merely one or two basic ones such as that all men are created equal. Any serious political philosophy turns out to be more complex than that in the sense of being composed of a large number of propositions. Incidentally, this fact accounts for the inconsistency, which often exists unnoticed in the crowd, among some of the propositions. However, let us concentrate on the proposition that all men are created equal for the moment in order to facilitate the task of briefly sketching what a philosopher in his or her professional capacity does when he or she scrutinizes a political philosophy. Democratic politicians seek to implement the political philosophy of democracy, espouse principles, and renew people's dedication to those tenets. The philosopher works along different lines. He or she seeks to articulate each and every proposition constituting the political philosophy of democracy and to state them as free from ambiguity, vagueness, and emotional connotations as possible. As Socrates questioned the meaning of the Oracle of Delphi's declaration that no one was wiser than Socrates, the political philosopher searches for the meaning of the proposition "All men are created equal." What does the proposition "All men are created equal" mean? Is this the best statement of the proposition? Each word in the statement of the proposition can be found in the dictionary and the words are combined in a grammatically correct way. Does "created" imply some conception of a divine creation of humanity so that democratic political philosophy would have to include certain theological statements about God and the origin of humankind? Certainly some proponents of democracy have argued that democracy rests on supernatural and revealed religion, that it really is God's will. Some critics of democracy also have agreed with the religious defenders of democracy that it has a divine basis, that democracy is Christian ethics translated into a secular vocabulary. However, these critics have gone on to argue that the soundness and even the sense of Christian ethics are inextricably bound up with acceptance of the whole Christian faith. But in terms of the scientific outlook of the present, the Christian faith changes from truth to myth and so democracy along with it becomes no more than a dream, no matter how appealing. In reply, religious exponents of democracy have contended that the warranted conclusion to draw is that if democracy is to survive and prosper, everyone should "get religion." Our religiously pluralistic society has encouraged defenders of this religious basis of democracy to enlarge that basis beyond Christianity to embrace other religions and, even further, just to embrace religion in general. Further, how is the proposition that each individual is of unique worth to be rendered consistent with the principle that all men are created equal? What is meant by "equality"? Equal talents? Equal incomes? Equality before the law? Equality of opportunity? That every adult citizen who is not obviously insane or mentally challenged can fulfill competently the duties of any elective office? Does "equality" mean all of these, some of these, or none of these? Finally, granted clarity and agreement on the meaning of the proposition "All men are created equal," is the proposition true or false? At least what evidence, were it to be found, would be accepted as falsifying the proposition? Is "All men are created equal" an empirical generalization such as "Water freezes at 32 degrees Fahrenheit"? If it is, then producing one human being created unequal would prove this generalization false. Or is the proposition "All men are created equal" prescriptive, rather than descriptive? Instead of asserting some state of affairs, is the proposition simply the expression of a desire: I, or we, wish that all men were created equal? But, then, if it were prescriptive, the proposition "All men are created equal" would be neither true nor false. A wish is neither true nor false.

The aim in this introduction is not to answer these questions but to suggest the distinctive character of the philosophic approach to political thought, an enterprise consisting in the combination of clarification of concepts, determination of logical consistency, formulation and assessment of criteria of truth and falsity, and the ultimate weighing of the truth claims of the principles espoused to justify political action. Political philosophy is distinct from day-to-day political debate and descriptive accounts of actual political behavior, although they may influence political philosophy and vice versa. Some political philosophies are so comprehensive that they range from offering shrewd practical advice on how to be a successful tyrant or win a revolution to envisioning a total form or way of life covering all aspects of individual and collective human life; from how to win elections or seize control of the state to doctrines about the essence of human nature, the direction of history, and the nature of reality; from maneuvers to metaphysics. Certainly, in terms of speculative boldness and development, political philosophy extends beyond what social scientists would consider genuinely scientific theorizing. This bulging over the boundaries of the strictly scientific often has enhanced the power of political philosophies to elicit an active devotion from millions, which at times is religious in both intensity and endurance. From Plato to Karl Popper, influencing the actions of humanity has been one of the main goals of political philosophers.

For a moment let us return to the cases of paying one's taxes and being robbed. The federal income tax is constitutional and the law of the land, and so presumably it represents the will of a majority of American citizens. Yet there are Americans who do not want, do not consent, to pay income taxes any more than they do to being robbed. What rationally persuasive grounds can be found in democratic political philosophy as to why a dissenting minority should abide by the will of a majority and not seek to do everything possible to successfully evade it? Does a majority vote really reflect the will of a majority of the citizens? Convincing answers to these questions are not as easy to find as one might first suppose. Laws are devised and passed by elected representatives and not by a direct vote of the people. Representatives in government are cultivated constantly by skillful lobbyists representing not the people in general but powerful, wealthy special-interest groups. Before laws can be voted on by a legislature as a whole, they must be reported out of a legislative committee composed only of a small number of legislators. As a result of the seniority system in the U.S. Congress, the powerful leadership roles of these committees often are held by representatives who are reelected many times by a small minority of the American people in districts and states where the candidate faces no significant political opposition. The cost of campaigning for high national office has grown to the point where only wealthy individuals or those who have put themselves heavily in debt to wealthy individuals, corporations, unions, and other groups can afford it. The president of the United States, ostensibly representing all of the American people, is not elected directly by the people. Provided he or she has the necessary number of electoral votes, a candidate can become president of the United States even though he does not gain a majority of the popular vote. Furthermore, a majority of the eligible voters often do not even vote. Finally, few candidates for public office are elected unanimously; voters cast ballots against them by voting for opponents or by abstaining from voting entirely. That is to say, at any given time a considerable number of Americans are opposed to those governing them and do not consider their elected rulers to be representing their will at all.

However, let us suppose that the machinery of democratic government functioned perfectly and infallibly registered the will of the people. Is what the majority believes to be true or good always so? At one time a majority of Europeans believed the earth to be flat. A few generations ago a majority of Americans believed that slavery was right and just. Of course, by sheer overwhelming weight of numbers, a majority could force a dissenting minority to go along with its wishes, however much the minority might disagree silently. But all this would prove is the superior might of the majority, not its superior knowledge or virtue. If a dissenting minority should submit to a majority merely because decision, however arrived at, is better than indecisive drifting, a dictator securely in power could supply the decisiveness in a less inconstant manner than could a vague, shifting majority confused by conflicting propaganda. The quality of a majority decision is the resultant of the quality of the individuals who comprise the majority; for example, a majority composed of stupid people would be more likely to reach foolish decisions than wise ones. Such a majority of poor quality might accidentally produce some wise decisions; nevertheless, fortuitous wisdom hardly seems a very persuasive reason for always accepting the will of the majority. Should not the vote of an intelligent, informed, responsible, civic-minded person count two, three, or more times the vote of some lout who must be dragged out of a saloon on election day and lured to the polls to vote with the promise of a free drink afterwards? Perhaps individuals should earn the privilege of the vote by first making some worthwhile contribution to society or only on the condition that they be self-supporting or have I.Q.s over 80. It has been argued that those who possess more property and more capital hold a greater stake in the fate of the country because they have more to lose than those who possess less, and that, therefore, these wealthier people should determine governmental policy. Those with little or nothing to lose are likely to act selfishly, rashly, and irresponsibly. Wealthy officeholders would be immune to bribes since they don't need more money, already having more than enough.

A rational justification of democracy would be impossible without weighing the merits of alternative forms of government. Everyone is familiar with the *mot* to the effect that democracy is the worst form of government except for all the other forms of government that have been tried. Yet the claimed superior worth of democracy hardly goes uncontested. The political philosophy of socialism, now subscribed to by millions of people, views American democracy as a sham doomed to disappear in the future. The political philosophy of anarchism opposes American democracy because it sees all government as inherently evil.

These foregoing remarks are not intended to settle the issue of the merits of democracy; they are intended to point up the fact that it is a real, vital issue.

In his defense of democracy, Sidney Hook defines his philosophical conception of democracy as including not only a form of political government but also as embracing a way of life. For him democracy as a way of life means "a way of organizing human relationships which embodies a certain complex of moral ideas."

Democracy is not only a political concept; it also is an ethical one. That this is so becomes clear when political democracies are criticized for not being democratic enough. Political democracy really is a means for achieving and securing ethical democracy. The principle of ethical democracy is equality. Political democracy means equality of freedom, but ethical democracy carries the concept of equality far beyond this to whatever is relevant to the effective exercise of equality of freedom. Ethical democracy means social equality, including political, educational, and economic democracy. Hook makes clear that ethical democracy does not mean equality of status or origin but, rather, equality of opportunity, relevant functions, and social participation. He clarifies the meaning of the equality principle in ethical democracy by distinguishing seven misconceptions of the nature of equality and contrasting them with their corresponding correct conceptions.

Of chief concern to philosophers is this question: What are the grounds justifying democracy as opposed to other forms of social organization? Hook argues that democracy as a way of life is a hypothesis capable of repeated empirical test and not a set of absolutely certain dogmas self-evidently valid and right. It should be noted that Hook treats moral ideas themselves as hypotheses capable of being tested by appeal to experience. He then sets forth six grounds he believes justify the superiority of democracy. Finally, Hook argues against three objections to the feasibility of the democratic idea.

"I know no country in which there is so little true independence of mind and freedom of discussion as in America." Although Alexis de Tocqueville made this observation about the United States of 1831–1832, many foreign and domestic critics of American democracy find his observation to be just as true today. But de Tocqueville was not merely an acute and shrewd observer of the events of his time; he also was a political philosopher who worked out the logical implications of concepts. He was convinced that the concept of democracy contained within itself the seeds of a future tyranny. Nevertheless, de Tocqueville did not believe in the inevitability of democracy becoming tyrannical; he was too realistic to think that human life always followed logic. He meant his observation of the America he had visited to warn that unless the growth of democracy were limited, democracy surely would destroy independence of mind and freedom of discussion.

What were the democratic seeds of tyranny de Tocqueville detected? They lurk in the principle of majority rule. In de Tocqueville's philosophy, every social order ultimately rests upon some supreme authority to which every other authority is subordinated. The nature of that supreme authority varies from one society to another. In a democracy it is the will of the majority. Legislators and presidents must stand for election; although amending the Constitution requires more than a majority vote, the people can amend it or even create a new one by calling a constitutional convention. The deadly danger to liberty in a democracy lies in the lack of any subordinate power strong enough to provide an effective check on the will of the majority. Any unlimited power becomes tyrannical and eventually destroys liberty, whether it be that of a monarch or majority opinion. Indeed, de Tocqueville believed that an unrestrained power of majority rule would produce a worse curtailment of independence of mind and freedom of discussion than that of any other kind of unchecked authority. Its tyranny would be so complete and pervasive that it would create a self-imposed censorship. Other kinds of despotism seek to control the body but not the mind; the democratic variety, however, subjugates the mind and leaves the body free to engage in its normal activities. Instead of being jailed, tortured, or executed, citizens of a democracy who dare to utter their disagreement with the opinion of the majority soon find themselves pariahs, blacklisted, denied employment, refused celebrity, and shunned by their former friends and associates. An exile in his or her own country, the democratic rebel falls silent and sinks into a hypocritical servility more demoralizing than that of the courtiers of old. De Tocqueville would not be surprised, however much he might be dismayed, were his ghost to return and see the campus protesters and marchers of the 1960s now turned into pillars of the "establishment" they once so vehemently opposed, the earlier student admirer of Socrates now transformed into an enthusiastic Rotarian. De Tocqueville's concern was heightened by what seemed to him to be the relentless march of democracy to world domination. True he did not foresee every future variation of his theme such as the deliberate manufacture of majority opinion by a host of advertisers, propagandists, politicians, and others skilled in the use of the means of mass communication. If he had, he probably would have predicted the same result: the self-inflicted destruction of independence of mind and freedom of expression. In any event, de Tocqueville hoped that if people were alerted to the tyrannical potentialities of democracy, they might be able to devise effective ways to prevent them from being realized.

According to Ayn Rand, in a genuinely free society is one in which individuals are ends in themselves and society is only the means to "the peaceful, orderly, voluntary co-existence of individuals." Societies and governments are merely groups of individuals, not real entities in addition to individual men and women. Neither governments nor societies possess any rights. The only purpose of government in such societies is to protect individual rights. Individual rights constitute the means to bring society under the control of moral law. In most previous societies just the reverse has been the case because they have been dominated by altruism-collectivism, a doctrine that in effect says that the moral law applies to individuals but not to society. Consequently, these societies have been amoral tyrannies and their individual members sacrificial animals.

Rand identifies her conception of a free society with laissez-faire capitalism. Strictly speaking, human beings have only one right: a right to their own lives. All other rights flow from this basic right, which is not given to them by God or society but is theirs by virtue of their own rational natures. The identification of this right with capitalism appears in Rand's insistence that property rights are necessary to all other rights. A property right is a right to action. While it does not guarantee that anyone will own property, it is "a guarantee that he will own it if he earns it. It is the right to gain, to keep, to use and to dispose of material values." But there is no "economic right" to the property of another; no individual, society, or government has any "right" to compel anyone to surrender any of his or her property to others. Consequently, Rand uncompromisingly opposes all altruist-collectivist doctrines such as the welfare state, socialism, communism, and fascism because she sees them as enemies of freedom or, what for her is the same thing, the right to property.

In presenting his "moral case for socialism," Kai Nielsen clarifies what capitalism and socialism are. In capitalism, productive property or the means of production are privately owned; an individual or a group of individuals rather than the general public owns the property and decides what will be done with it. Socialism means genuine public ownership and control of productive property but not of personal property. Nielsen emphasizes that socialism is *not* state ownership without control of the state and its activities by the public or citizenry at large. As Nielsen sees capitalism and socialism, they are not merely economic organizations; they also are social systems, ways of life. As a social system, capitalism is a class society divided into a class of capitalists and a class of workers. In socialism every able-bodied person is a worker.

In arguing for the superiority of socialism over capitalism, Nielsen expressly compares the "pure" models of democratic socialism and competitive capitalism rather than the actually existing "impure" forms of bureaucratic state socialism and corporate capitalism. However, Nielsen does not believe he is comparing one impossible dream with another equally unobtainable one, because he is convinced that the pure models of socialism and capitalism he is contrasting could be realized. He then argues the moral case that socialism will be more successful than capitalism in sustaining and furthering the fundamental values of freedom and autonomy, equality, justice, rights, and democracy.

Murray N. Rothbard's libertarian anarchism agrees with traditional anarchism in viewing the state or government as the chief enemy of all persons and property. Unlike the traditional anarchist, Rothbard does not advocate the violent overthrow of all governments. According to the libertarian anarchism of Rothbard, the state by its very nature is a robber, enslaver, and murderer. There are no exceptions to this indictment of the state; it applies equally to all governments be they democratic, dictatorial, monarchical, or some other form. States or governments always have considered themselves outside the general moral law, an amoral status often euphemistically called "reasons of state."

Can the state or government be reformed, tamed so that it serves moral ends, puts the welfare of the general citizenry ahead of its own selfish aggrandizement? Could any state ever sincerely promote life, liberty, and the pursuit of happiness? Not without ceasing to be a government. According to Rothbard, all social institutions *except* the state rely on voluntary support and must refrain from violence against others. The government, however, compels support through taxation and imposes its will on citizens under the threat or commission of violence against those who defy its tyranny. People have turned to government to protect themselves against private criminals. But who will protect the people against the greatest criminal of all, the government? Who will guard the guardians? Rothbard answers that no one and no institutional tinkering can or will. Such limitations as constitutions, separation of powers, and majority rule are at best feeble and ultimately are doomed to failure. But are not governments needed to provide at least some rough equality? On the contrary, inequality is a pervasive fact of all human life and social relations because it is a fact of nature. A society of free individuals and groups in which all relations are voluntary and untainted by coercion and in which private property is safe from theft is forever incompatible and irreconcilable with any state or government.

Appealing to the feminist demand for the abolition of sexism and sexual inequality because they are wrong or "lies," some activists and philosophers have called for the prohibition or at least control of pornography. Doing so has brought them into conflict with defenders of the democratic right to freedom of speech. The feminist philosopher Helen E. Longino redefines pornography in terms of the viewpoint of feminism. According to her, the distinguishing trait of pornography is not sexual explicitness, sexual realism, or even the depiction of degrading or abusive sexual behavior, as it has been thought to be in the past and is still believed to be by many in the present, but is the *endorsement* or *approval* of sexual behavior abusive of or degrading to one or more of the participants. For example, depictions of women deriving sexual pleasure from abuse or degradation are pornographic because their enjoyment connotes approval or endorsement of their treatment; pornography affirms that women, solely because they are women, want to be raped, bound, tortured, to be only instruments for providing male sexual satisfaction. But this is a lie about the nature of women and what women want. The truth is that women want to be treated as men's equals, as persons of basic human dignity deserving of respect. Thus, pornography defames and libels women and, by endorsing their unequal sexual treatment, also suggests approval of their oppression socially, economically, and culturally.

But the right to free speech is not a right to libel others. In Longino's view, the right to free speech is not the right to utter whatever one pleases. The rights mentioned in the First Amendment to the Constitution, those of speech, press, religion, and the right to petition, are not absolute but rather are *means* needed to secure liberty. In Longino's interpretation, liberty is not "license" or the freedom to do as one pleases but is "independence" or "the status of a person as independent and equal rather than subservient." But pornography endorses the dependent and unequal status of women or their subservience to men. There is no "right" to pornography. Therefore, the prohibition or control of pornography is not an abridgment of a right of free speech or of any other right.

Jan Narveson claims that the case for banning or strictly controlling pornography is a weak one and marshals his reasons mainly in the form of criticisms of the case for suppressing it. Whereas, traditionally, pornography has been defined as the depiction of sexually stimulating subject matter with the purpose of producing sexual arousal, Narveson recognizes the recent expanding of its meaning to include an alleged connection of sex and violence. To argue that pornography should be prohibited or restricted because it demeans women assumes the premise that whatever demeans people should be prohibited or restricted which, in turn, would justify the censorship of the Old Testament and other works many or most people believe should not be censored. To the argument that pornography should be censored on the ground that it approves falsehoods about women in general—for example, women are inferior to men, women want to be abused or degraded, women enjoy being subservient to men—Narveson replies that falsehood does not justify the suppression of the people who express that falsehood but instead provides an opportunity to refute that falsehood. It must be remembered that to depict falsehood or evil is not necessarily to advocate it. In any event, most people can be exposed to falsehood and evil, including explicit approval of them, without being converted. Audiences seeing the movie *Birth of a Nation* have not joined the Ku Klux Klan. Narveson's antipaternalism sounds in his declaration that people must be presumed capable of making their own decisions and that they are morally responsible. There is an undeniable paternalistic caste to any claim that people must be shielded from something lest it corrupt them. Narveson characterizes what empirical evidence there is that viewing pornography causes people to commit rape and other crimes as "overwhelmingly inconclusive." Instead of curtailing free speech, we should rely on education, particularly the proper instruction of children by their parents.

A moral issue that has recently received increasing attention is what obligation, if any, people in affluent countries have to the poor throughout the world. Since many people in poor countries desire to live in richer countries, immigration policy is an important aspect of this issue. In "Lifeboat Ethics: The Case Against Helping the Poor," Garrett Hardin argues that so long as there is no world government to institute rational control of the world's resources, each nation should protect its citizens against encroachments on their resources by others. He contends that it is unwise either to feed the poor in other countries or to allow unrestricted immigration into our own. Peter Singer, who disagrees with Hardin, contends that it is unjustified to ignore the needy in other countries. In "Insiders and Outsiders," he argues that one way to aid the needy is to open our borders to larger numbers of refugees than we now accept.

In "The Prisoner's Dilemma," the first reading in the "Problems and Puzzles" section, Morton Davis clearly sets forth one of the most intriguing problems of game theory. Indeed, some go so far as to claim that the articulation of this dilemma and the realization that it lies at the heart of many of our social and political problems constitute one of the outstanding intellectual achievements of this century. Critical understanding of social and political philosophies is sharpened by viewing them as attempts to grapple with this dilemma. Davis shows that the prisoner's dilemma is no mere game in the sense of a trivial amusement by amply illustrating how it reappears in setting advertising budgets, conserving water, paying taxes, limiting farm overproduction, dealing with the arms race—indeed, reemerges whenever one must decide how to act in response to the way one believes others will act under a given set of circumstances. In this kind of "game," each player can choose to cooperate with the other player or players by acting as they do or to defect or not act as the other player or players do. Essential to generating the dilemma is a graduated system of rewards and punishments such that the greatest reward or payoff goes to the player who defects when the other player cooperates, the second highest reward or payoff goes to all of the players when all of them cooperate, the second greatest punishment goes to all of the players when all of them defect, and the greatest punishment, or "sucker's payoff," goes to the player who cooperates when the others defect. It should be noted that if one side is to win the greatest reward, the other side must suffer the greatest punishment. Conversely, if everyone is to be spared the greatest punishment, then everyone must forgo the greatest reward. Should one cooperate and thus act for the benefit of all, or should one defect and thus act only for one's selfish interest? What is it rational to do? Davis points out that most people are so repelled by the selfish strategy of defection for which the prisoner's dilemma presents such a compelling argument that they shift the question from "What is the rational strategy?" to "How can cooperation or acting in concert be justified?"

Anthony Downs argues that it is not rational for the individual voter to become well informed, although most citizens would benefit if all of the voters were well informed. Of course, conventional wisdom declares that each individual voter should be as well informed as possible in order to be able to make the most rational decision in voting. However, conventional wisdom fails to reckon with the prisoner's dilemma. When is it rational for the individual voter to expend the time, energy, and money necessary to become well informed? Downs appeals to the economic axiom that it is rational to perform any act when its marginal return exceeds its marginal cost. Applying this axiom to individual voters in a populous country like the United States, Downs reaches the unconventional conclusion that it is irrational for most people to acquire political information for the purpose of voting. In a large electorate any individual's vote is insignificant because of the minuscule probability of that vote's being decisive in determining the outcome of the election. Consequently, the marginal cost of becoming a well-informed voter almost always will outweigh the marginal benefit. Downs admits that this conclusion may not be true for every individual voter, but he claims that it is for most. The alleged voter apathy so often deplored really is voter rationality. Admittedly government would better serve the interests of an informed majority than it would those of an uninformed one. Collectively it is rational for voters to become well informed. Individually it is irrational.

In "Why a High Society Is a Free Society," A. C. Grayling argues for the legalization of heroin, cocaine, marijuana, ecstasy, and their cognates in the sense that they should be available just as nicotine and alcohol presently are. Or else we should be honest and consistent and also make nicotine and alcohol illegal. The good society is a free society and a free society respects the autonomy of its citizens by allowing them to decide for themselves as individuals what is good for them in matters "that principally concern only them." Grayling further argues that the choice to consume or not to consume heroin, cocaine, and other such drugs mainly concerns the individual choosing and not other individuals or society in general. It is not that being high is or should be an end or good in itself. Nor does Grayling contend that currently illegal drugs do no harm. Rather, he maintains that the value of the enhancement of individual autonomy or freedom drug legalization would bring greatly outweighs any minor harms it might produce. Furthermore, legalization of drugs would eliminate the very great harms to individual autonomy and society caused by their present prohibition.

Democracy

30. The Philosophical Presuppositions of Democracy

Sidney Hook

Sidney Hook (1902–1989) was a member of the New York University faculty for many years. He devoted particular attention to social, political, moral, and educational issues. His writings on these topics often appeared in publications with broad circulation. Although a Marxist activist in his early years, he later became most celebrated as a critic of communism and an uncompromising advocate and defender of democracy against all forms of totalitarianism on the basis of an undeviating commitment to freedom and to the pragmatic naturalism of John Dewey.

The principle may be stated in various ways, but for our purposes we may say that a democratic state is one in which the basic decisions of government rest upon the freely given consent of the governed. This obviously is only a beginning. For just as soon as we begin to investigate the conditions which must be present before we grant that a state lives up to this principle, we are carried beyond the sphere of political considerations into the domain of ethics. Thus, if information has been withheld or withdrawn before consent is assessed; if the opposition is muzzled or suppressed so that consent is as unanimous as a totalitarian plebiscite; or if economic sanctions are threatened against a section of the community in the event that consent takes one form or another, we declare that the "spirit" or "logic" or "rationale" of democracy is absent from its political forms. If birth does not give divine right, neither does numbers [sic]. We are all acquainted with situations in which we say that a political democracy has traduced its own ideals. Whenever we criticize existing states which conform to the political definition of democracy on the ground that they are not democratic enough; whenever we point out that Athenian democracy was limited only to free men, or that in some parts of the American South it is limited only to white men, or in some countries it is limited only to men, we are invoking a broader principle of democracy as a controlling reference in our judgments of comparison. This principle is an ethical one.

Sidney Hook, "The Presuppositions of Democracy," *Ethics*, Vol. 52, April, 1942, pp. 275–296. Copyright 1942 by The University of Chicago. Reprinted by permission of The University of Chicago Press.

What is this principle of ethical democracy? It is a principle of equality—an equality not of status or origin but of opportunity, relevant functions, and social participation. The enormous literature and bitter controversy which center around the concept of equality indicate that it is only a little less ambiguous than the concept of democracy. It is necessary, therefore, to block it off from some current notions before developing the argument.

a) The principle of equality is not a *description* of fact about men's physical or intellectual natures. It is a *prescription* or policy of treating men.

b) It is not a prescription to treat men in identical ways who are unequal in their physical or intellectual nature. It is a policy of equality of concern or consideration for men whose different needs may require differential treatment.

c) It is not a mechanical policy of equal opportunity for everyone at *any* time and in *all* respects. A musical genius is entitled to greater opportunities to develop his musical talents than someone who is tone deaf. It is equality of opportunity for all individuals to develop whatever personal and socially desirable talents they possess and to make whatever unique contributions their capacities permit.

d) It is not a demand for absolute uniformity of living conditions or even for arithmetically equal compensation for socially useful work. It demands that, when the productive forces of a society makes [*sic*] possible the gratification of basic human needs (which are, of course, historical variables), no one should be deprived of necessities in order to provide others with luxuries.

e) It is not a policy of restricting the freedom of being different or becoming different. It is a policy of *encouraging* the freedom to be different, restricting only that exercise of freedom which converts talents or possessions into a monopoly that frustrates the emergence of other free personalities.

f) It is not a demand that all people be leaders or that none should be. It does demand that the career of leadership, like all other careers, be open to all whose natural or acquired talents qualify them; that everyone have a say in the process of selecting leaders; that the initiative of leaders operates within a framework of basic laws; and that these laws in turn ultimately rest upon the freely given consent of the persons who constitute the community.

g) It does not make the assumption of sentimental humanitarianism that all men are naturally good. It does assume that men, treated as equals in a community of persons, may become better. The emphasis upon respect for the personality of all individuals, the attitude which treats the personality not as something fixed but as a growing, developing pattern, is unique to the philosophy of democracy.

What I have been trying to show is that the logic of the democrat's position compels him to go beyond the limited conception of political democracy—the equality of freedom—to a broader attitude extending to those other phases of social existence that bear upon the effective exercise of equality of freedom. This in fact has been the historical tendency observable wherever democratic principles and programs are permitted to operate. Perhaps the synoptic phrase "social equality," whose connotations encompass political, educational, and economic democracy, may be taken as the most appropriate expression of the meaning of democracy in the broadest sense.

It is clear that the principle of equality, like any principle of justice, cannot by itself determine what is specifically right or good in each concrete case. But whatever the right is discovered to be, from the point of view of democracy it is the result of an analysis which considers equally the needs of all the persons involved in the situation; and, further, whatever the good is, it becomes better to the extent that it is shared among other members of the community. It is also clear that in concrete situations there will be conflicts between various demands for equality and that in negotiating these conflicts the methods of intelligence are indispensable for a functioning democracy. If empiricism be a generic term for the philosophic attitude which submits *all* claims of fact and value to test by experience, then empiricism as a philosophy is more congenial to a democratic than to an antidemocratic community, for it brings into the open light of criticism the interests in which moral values and social institutions are rooted. Empiricism so conceived is commitment to a procedure, not to a theory of metaphysics.

In this brief account of the nature of democracy as a way of life I have not aimed at an exhaustive analysis of the *forms* in which it may be expressed but have tried to indicate the basic ideals which are involved in the customary usage of the term and in the implications of that usage.

We now come to the problem which is of primary concern to philosophers. What are the grounds on which we can justify our acceptance of democracy in contradistinction to other modes of social life? . . .

Democracy as a hypothesis.—When democracy is taken strictly as a form of political government, its superiority over other forms of government can be established to the extent that it achieves more security, freedom, and co-operative diversity than any of its alternatives. If we test the workings of political democracy by Paul's scheme of virtues or by Nietzsche's, we may perhaps reach another conclusion. So long as there is no dispute about observable effects and so long as we raise no question about the moral ideals by which we evaluate these effects, we have clear sailing.

But, as has already been made plain, by democracy as a way of life we mean a way of organizing human relationships which embodies a certain complex of moral ideals. Can these ideals be treated as hypotheses? The conventional reply has always been that no moral principle can be regarded as a hypothesis, for we must already have certain knowledge of what is good before we can evaluate the consequences of acting upon it. If any position is question-begging, surely this seems to be!

Were this a symposium on value theory, I would devote all my time to developing the general theory of moral ideals as hypotheses. But here I can only barely indicate that the notion is not viciously circular. A moral ideal is a prescription to act in a certain situation or class of situations in determinate ways that will organize the human needs and wants involved so as to fulfil a set of *other* values which are *postulated* as binding in relation to the problem in hand. No more than in other cases of inquiry do we start with an empty head. The cluster of values we bring to the situation is the result of prior experience and reflection. They are not arbitrarily postulated. The consequences of acting upon the hypothesis may lead us to challenge a postulated or assumed value. This in turn can become the subject of a similar investigation. Terminal values are always related to specific contexts; there is no absolute terminal value which is either self-evident or beyond the necessity of justifying itself if its credentials are challenged. There is no vicious infinite regress involved if we take our problems concretely and one at a time. Nor is the procedure narrowly circular. For if, in a long history of raising and solving moral problems, we postulate as a value in solving a later problem a value which had itself to be certified in an earlier problem, this would testify to the presence of a fruitful set of systematically related values in the structure of our moral behavior. New values would emerge, or be discovered, in the course of our attempt to act upon our ideals and from the necessity of mediating the conflict between the postulated values as they bear on concrete human needs in specific situations.

I should like, however, to make the general position take form out of the discussion of the theme before us. That theme is: Why should we treat individuals of unequal talents and endowments as persons who are equally entitled to relevant consideration and care? Short of a treatise I can state only the reasons, without amplification of the concrete needs of the social situation which democracy seeks to meet and the institutional practices by which it must meet them.

a) This method of treating human beings is more successful than any other in evoking a maximum of creative, voluntary effort from all members of the community. Properly implemented it gives all persons a stake in the community and elicits a maximum of intelligent loyalty.

b) It enlarges the scope of our experience by enabling us to acquire insight into the needs, drives, and aspirations of others. Learning to understand how life is organized by other centers of experience is both a challenge and a discipline for our imagination. In aiding the growth of others, we aid our own growth.

c) The willingness to understand another man's point of view without necessarily surrendering to it makes it more likely that different points of view may negotiate their differences and learn to live peacefully with one another. A democratic community cannot be free from strife in a world where inequalities will always exist, but its ethics when intelligently acted upon makes more likely the diminution of strife or its transference to socially harmless forms than is the case when its principle of equality is denied. The consequences are less toadying, less fear, and less duplicity in the equalitarian community than in the nonequalitarian society.

d) In nurturing the capacities of each individual so that they may come to their greatest fulfilment, we can best share our existing stores of truth and beauty and uncover new dimensions in these realms. How can anyone dedicated to the values of science and art consistently oppose a policy which maximizes the possibility of the discovery and widest dispersion of scientific truths and artistic meanings?

e) Regard for the potentialities of all individuals makes for less cruelty of man toward man especially where cruelty is the result of blindness to, or ignorance of, other's needs. A community organized along democratic lines is guilty of cruelty only at those points where it has failed to live up to its own ideals. A totalitarian community is systematically insensitive to the personal needs not only of members of the outlawed scapegoat group but of the majority of its subjects who are excluded from policy-making discussions. At best, there is no way of determining these personal needs except by the interpretation of the dictator and his experts who operate with the dogma that they know the true interests of their subjects better than the subjects themselves. At worst, the dictator assumes not only that he speaks for his subjects but that in some mystic way he feels and thinks for them too. Despite the great limitations—limitations from the point of view of their own ideals—under which the nineteenth- and twentieth-century democracies of the Western world suffered, I think it is indisputable, on the evidence, that by and large their social life, in so far as this was the consequence of policy, displayed less cruelty than the social life of any other historical period.

f) Reasonableness of conclusions, where attitudes and interests conflict, depends upon the degree of mutual consultation and free intellectual communication between the principals involved. The democratic way of life makes possible the widest forms of mutual consultation and communication. Conclusions reached by these processes have a quality that can never be found where conclusions are imposed by force or authority—even if they are our own. Let me illustrate what I mean by taking as an example the enterprise represented by this Association [the American Philosophical Association]. Who among us, desirous as we may be of the possibility of philosophical agreement, would forego the methods of public discussion, criticism, argument, and rejoinder for a philosophical consensus imposed by a Gestapo or a G.P.U. even if by a strange quirk of affairs it was *our* philosophic position that the goon squads of orthodoxy sought to make the way of salvation? Who among us, knowing that outside the threshold of our meeting there stood an individual of strange country, color, or faith, capable of making a contribution to our deliberations, would not open the door to him? These are not rhetorical questions framed to discover philosophical fifth columnists. They are designed to show that the procedures of critical discussion and discovery, which are pre-eminently exhibited in the work of a scientific community, take for granted that national, racial, or religious origins are irrelevant to the logic of the method by which reasonable conclusions are reached. Democracy as a way of life differs from its alternatives in that it makes possible the extension of these methods of reaching reasonable conclusions from the fields of professional science and philosophy to all areas of human experience in which genuine problems arise.

There are other grounds that may be offered in justification of democracy as the most adequate social philosophy for our times. Every one of them, like the foregoing, postulates implicitly or explicitly values or desiderata. But I repeat: these postulates are ultimate only for the problem in hand. They may require justification. When we undertake such justification, we have undertaken a new inquiry into a new problem.

There are two important consequences of approaching democracy in this way. The first is that we avoid the temptation, which is rapidly gaining vogue, of making democracy absolutely valid in and for itself. There are many today who write as if they believe that democracy should prevail even though the heavens fall, and who say in so many words that "to question the validity of democracy is to disbelieve in it" and that we can meet the blind fanatical faith of fascism only with a faith in democracy which is at least just as fanatical. This temptation, it seems to me, must be avoided because, by counterposing subrational dogma to subrational dogma, it prepares the ground for an acceptance of a might makes right morality. Second, those who make of democracy an absolute value, which requires no justification but its inherent rightness, tend to identify this absolute democracy with whatever particular democratic status quo exists. On the other hand, the natural tendency of those who cannot distinguish between social philosophies on the ground of their inherent rightness is to test a social philosophy by the social institutions in which it is embodied. They are, therefore, more attentive to the actual workings and effects of democracy, more historical minded, and less likely to gloss over existing imperfections.

To those who say that human beings will not fight whole-heartedly except for certainties, and emphatically not for a hypothesis which is only probable, the reply must be made that this empirical proposition is highly dubious. Men have fought and do fight vigorously for causes on the basis of preponderant evidence. Vigorous action, indeed, is only desirable when we have first decided what is intelligent action. And intelligent action does not result when we assume that our ideas or ideals simply cannot be wrong. That both intelligence and resoluteness are compatible is clear in fields as far apart as military science and medicine. Once it is decided that the chances of one action are relatively better than another, once it is decided that an operation gives a patient a better chance of surviving than no operation, wisdom demands that the best warranted alternative be pursued with all our heart and all our soul. Let us remember that when we fight for democracy we are not fighting for an ideal which has just been proposed as a merely possible valid ideal for our times; we already have considerable evidence in its behalf, the weight of which, unfortunately too often, is properly evaluated only when democracy is lost or imperiled.

We now turn to the question whether democracy is feasible. We can imagine someone who has accepted the tentative ends by which we evaluate ways of life criticizing us as follows: "If only the assertions made in the previous section could be established as true, the case for democracy would be convincing. But the nature of man as we know him, of history as scientifically understood, and of the larger world we live in precludes the possibility of ever achieving democracy. It runs counter to the facts. Although you may still choose to live or die for democracy, the attempt to realize it, like any attempt to realize an ideal which has no natural basis, will be a ghastly failure. Its natural consequences will be worse than the evils it sets out to cure, and it will subvert the very ideals to which you have appealed in your argument. Democracy is an infirmity of noble but innocent minds who have never understood the world. It is not an intelligent option."

I have time to consider briefly three types of objection to the feasibility of the democratic ideal.

1. The first is based upon its alleged psychological impossibility. It maintains that democracy is too good for men who are essentially evil, fallen creatures, dominated by the lust for power, property, and self. In less theological form it asserts that democracy makes too high a call upon human intelligence and disinterestedness.

It is true that the psychological nature of man is quite relevant to our problem. If most human beings were idiots or infantile or permanently incapable of self-development, the democratic ideal could hardly be defended on plausible grounds. But there is no evidence that most human beings are such, and an intelligent attempt to find out whether they are would require that equalization of social opportunity which is of the essence of democracy. Even without such an experiment, if we surrender the utopian expectation of the complete realization of the democratic ideal and bear in mind that the forms of democracy may be direct as well as indirect and that democracy is compatible with the delegation of powers and responsibilities, the evidence at hand could hardly justify the belief either in universal cretinism or in man's permanent ineducability. Nor do we have to counter with the assertion that men are *infinitely* perfectible to make our option for democracy reasonable. We require merely that they be sufficiently plastic, sufficiently capable of learning, criticism, and improvement, to choose responsibly between alternatives of action whenever—and here lies the rub—they have alternatives of choice. It is only the democratic community which will systematically give them the alternatives of choice on basic decisions. It is not without significance that no free people has ever voluntarily relinquished its democratic forms for a government which openly proclaimed as its aim the establishment of a permanent dictatorship. Principled dictatorships, as distinct from those that come in through the unguarded doors of democracy, always triumph by usurpation. As low as the human estate is today, there is no reason to believe that human beings belong to a psychological species inferior to that of their ancestors. Although history is rich in human stupidities and lost opportunities, in the face of men's achievements in the arts and sciences it would be simply foolish to read history as nothing but the record of human error.

The theological doctrine of man's essentially evil nature metaphorically expresses the truth that he is always limited, always tempted, and never free of his animal origins. But, taken literally, it makes any kind of moral virtue inconceivable except by interposition of divine grace or mystery. Here, too, we do not have to counter with a contrary theological proposition that man is essentially good. He is neither one or the other but becomes good or evil depending upon his society, his habits, and his intelligence.

2. The most powerful arguments against the feasibility of democracy, strangely enough, have been neglected by most social philosophers. These are developed in the writings of Gaetano Mosca, Vilfredo Pareto, and Roberto Michels. Their common thesis, formulated on the basis of vast, detailed studies of political and social history, is that all historical change, whether reform or revolution, consists of the substitution of one ruling minority for another. This rule rests upon three pillars: vital myths which cement human relationships and conceal differences of interest; fraud or manipulation which negotiates differences of interests; and

force which ultimately settles differences of interest. The nature of social organization, they claim, is such that democrats may be victorious but democracy never. So it has been, so it is, and so it will be.

I have elsewhere tried to meet their arguments in detail. But here I content myself with one consideration which points to the self-confessed inadequacy of their position. Despite this alleged law, every one of them admits, explicitly or implicitly, that some forms of society are better than others—and in every case it is the society which has a greater degree of democracy than the others. Thus Mosca, after maintaining the inescapability of minority rule, pays strong tribute to the superiority of parliamentary democracy over all other alternatives.

Three basic errors, it seems to me, vitiate their conclusion. The first is that the amount of freedom and democracy in a society is determined by a law *already known* or, as some would say today, by a historical wave. The truth is that the amount of freedom and democracy in the present and future depends as much upon human willingness to fight for them as upon anything else. The second error is the belief, common not only to these thinkers but to countless others, that human nature is unchangeable. In so far as this is neither a proposition of biology or of theology nor a logical tautology, but refers to psychological and social traits, it can be shown to be false. The third is their confusion between an organizing principle and the individual members of the series organized. Since no identification is possible between the principle of democracy and any one member of the series, they go from the true conclusion that the principle is incompletely realized in any one case to the false conclusion that there are no degrees of realization in the series of cases.

3. The third class of objections to the feasibility of the democratic ideal is derived from alleged cosmic or physicochemical laws which contain the equations of doom for man and all his works. Even granting the validity of such laws, they would hold no matter what society exists, and, therefore, they establish nothing about the relative superiority of one form of society over another. Such laws, as William James already pointed out in a definitive refutation of all views of this type, tell us about the *size* of "energy-rills," not their *significance*.

That the cosmic home of man limits his power, if not his dreams, is of course true. It is a perennial source of his humility before the intractabilities of things and the transient character of what he builds. But it is also true that this limitation is the source of his opportunities and a necessary condition for all achievement. From these truths we cannot infer that nature is the guarantor of man's ideals, certainly not of the democratic ideal. But neither is it the enemy of human ideals. Man's friends and enemies are other men. To forget this is to go from natural piety to superstition. The cosmic scene against which men live out their lives will not be affected by Hitler's victory or defeat. Democracy needs no cosmic support other than the *chance* to make good. That chance it has, because man is part of nature. To ask for more is unreasonable even if it were not unworthy. The way in which man acts upon his chances is additional evidence of the objective possibilities and novelties of existence. In so far as he is caught up in the flux of things, the intelligent democratic man honestly confronts the potentialities of existence, its futurities, its openness, its indeterminateness. He is free of the romantic madness which would seek to outlaw the truths of science and of the quaint conceit, permissible only as poetry, that nature is a democratic republic. He takes the world as science describes it. He employs his knowledge of the world to increase man's power over things, to decrease man's power over man, and to enlarge the fellowship of free and equal persons striving to achieve a more just and happier society.

31. Democratic Tyranny

Alexis de Tocqueville

Alexis de Tocqueville (1805–1859) was a French aristocrat. Although his family suffered under the French Revolution, de Tocqueville was not an embittered foe of democracy but greatly sympathized with democratic ideals, thus making his criticism of them more penetrating and prophetic. In his enduring masterpiece Democracy in America, *he sought to give an honest and objective account of both the strengths and weaknesses of the democratic equality he predicted would conquer the future.*

I am of the opinion that some one social power must always be made to predominate over the others; but I think that liberty is endangered when this power is checked by no obstacles which may retard its course, and force it to moderate its own vehemence.

Unlimited power is in itself a bad and dangerous thing; human beings are not competent to exercise it with discretion, and God alone can be omnipotent, because his wisdom and his justice are always equal to his power. But no power upon earth is so worthy of honour for itself, or of reverential obedience to the rights which it represents, that I would consent to admit its uncontrolled and all-predominant authority. When I see that the right and the means of absolute command are conferred on a people or upon a king, upon an aristocracy or a democracy, a monarchy or a republic, I recognize the germ of tyranny, and I journey onward to a land of more hopeful institutions.

In my opinion the main evil of the present democratic institutions of the United States does not arise, as is often asserted in Europe, from their weakness, but from their overpowering strength; and I am not so much alarmed at the excessive liberty which reigns in that country as at the very inadequate securities which exist against tyranny.

When an individual or a party is wronged in the United States, to whom can he apply for redress? If to public opinion, public opinion constitutes the majority; if to the legislature, it represents the majority, and implicitly obeys its injunctions; if to the executive power, it is appointed by the majority, and remains a passive tool in its hands; the public troops consist of the majority under arms; the jury is the majority invested with the right of hearing judicial cases; and in certain States even the judges are elected by the majority. However iniquitous or absurd the evil of which you complain may be, you must submit to it as well as you can.

If, on the other hand, a legislative power could be so constituted as to represent the majority without necessarily being the slave of its passions; an executive, so as

Reprinted from *Democracy in America*, Part One, Chapter XV, translated by Henry Reeve, 1835.

to retain a certain degree of uncontrolled authority; and a judiciary, so as to remain independent of the two other powers; a government would be formed which would still be democratic without incurring any risk of tyrannical abuse.

I do not say that tyrannical abuses frequently occur in America at the present day, but I maintain that no sure barrier is established against them, and that the causes which mitigate the government are to be found in the circumstances and the manners of the country more than in its laws.

A distinction must be drawn between tyranny and arbitrary power. Tyranny may be exercised by means of the law, and in that case it is not arbitrary; arbitrary power may be exercised for the good of the community at large, in which case it is not tyrannical. Tyranny usually employs arbitrary means, but, if necessary, it can rule without them.

In the United States the unbounded power of the majority, which is favourable to the legal despotism of the legislature, is likewise favourable to the arbitrary authority of the magistrate. The majority has an entire control over the law when it is made and when it is executed; and as it possesses an equal authority over those who are in power and the community at large, it considers public officers as its passive agents, and readily confides the task of serving its designs to their vigilance. The details of their office and the privileges which they are to enjoy are rarely defined beforehand; but the majority treats them as a master does his servants when they are always at work in his sight, and he has the power of directing or reprimanding them at every instant.

In general the American functionaries are far more independent than the French civil officers within the sphere which is prescribed to them. Sometimes, even, they are allowed by the popular authority to exceed those bounds; and as they are protected by the opinion, and backed by the co-operation, of the majority, they venture upon such manifestations of their power as astonish a European. By this means habits are formed in the heart of a free country which may some day prove fatal to its liberties.

It is in the examination of the display of public opinion in the United States that we clearly perceive how far the power of the majority surpasses all the powers with which we are acquainted in Europe. Intellectual principles exercise an influence which is so invisible, and often so inappreciable, that they baffle the toils of oppression. At the present time the most absolute monarchs in Europe are unable to prevent certain notions, which are opposed to their authority, from circulating in secret throughout their dominions, and even in their courts. Such is not the case in America; as long as the majority is still undecided, discussion is carried on; but as soon as its decision is irrevocably pronounced, a submissive silence is observed, and the friends, as well as the opponents, of the measure unite in assenting to its propriety. The reason of this is perfectly clear: no monarch is so absolute as to combine all the powers of society in his own hands, and to conquer all opposition with the energy of a majority which is invested with the right of making and of executing the laws.

The authority of a king is purely physical, and it controls the actions of the subject without subduing his private will; but the majority possesses a power which is physical and moral at the same time; it acts upon the will as well as upon the actions of men, and it represses not only all contest, but all controversy.

I know no country in which there is so little true independence of mind and freedom of discussion as in America. In any constitutional state in Europe every sort of religious and political theory may be advocated and propagated abroad; for there is no country in Europe so subdued by any single authority as not to contain citizens who are ready to protect the man who raises his voice in the cause of truth from the consequences of his hardihood. If he is unfortunate enough to live under an absolute government, the people is upon his side; if he inhabits a free country, he may find a shelter behind the authority of the throne, if he require one. The aristocratic part of society supports him in some countries, and the democracy in others. But in a nation where democratic institutions exist, organized like those of the United States, there is but one sole authority, one single element of strength and of success, with nothing beyond it.

In America, the majority raises very formidable barriers to the liberty of opinion: within these barriers an author may write whatever he pleases, but he will repent it if he ever step beyond them. Not that he is exposed to the terrors of an *auto-da-fé*, but he is tormented by the slights and persecutions of daily obloquy. His political career is closed for ever, since he has offended the only authority which is able to promote his success. Every sort of compensation, even that of celebrity, is refused to him. Before he published his opinions he imagined that he held them in common with many others; but no sooner has he declared them openly than he is loudly censured by his overbearing opponents, while those who think like him, without having the courage to speak, abandon him in silence. He yields at length, oppressed by the daily efforts he has been making, and he subsides into silence, as if he was tormented by remorse for having spoken the truth.

Fetters and headsmen were the coarse instruments which tyranny formerly employed; but the civilization of our age has refined the arts of despotism, which seemed, however, to have been sufficiently perfected before. The excesses of monarchical power had devised a variety of physical means of oppression: the democratic republics of the present day have rendered it as entirely an affair of the mind as that will which it is intended to coerce. Under the absolute sway of an individual despot the body was attacked in order to subdue the soul, and the soul escaped the blows which were directed against it and rose superior to the attempt; but such is not the course adopted by tyranny in democratic republics; there the body is left free, and the soul is enslaved. The sovereign can no longer say, "You shall think as I do on pain of death"; but he says: "You are free to think differently from me, and to retain your life, your property, and all that you possess; but if such be your determination, you are henceforth an alien among your people. You may retain your civil rights, but they will be useless to you, for you will never be chosen by your fellow citizens if you solicit their suffrages, and they will affect to scorn you if you solicit their esteem. You will remain among men, but you will be deprived of the rights of mankind. Your fellow-creatures will shun you like an impure being, and those who are most persuaded of your innocence will abandon you too, lest they should be shunned in their turn. Go in peace! I have given you your life, but it is an existence incomparably worse than death."

Monarchical institutions have thrown an odium upon despotism; let us beware lest democratic republics should restore oppression, and should render it less odious and less degrading in the eyes of the many, by making it still more onerous to the few. . . .

The tendencies to which I have just alluded are as yet very slightly perceptible in political society, but they already begin to exercise an unfavourable influence upon the national character of the Americans. I am inclined to attribute the singular paucity of distinguished political characters to the ever-increasing activity of the despotism of the majority in the United States. When the American Revolution broke out they arose in great numbers, for public opinion then served, not to tyrannize over, but to direct the exertions of individuals. Those celebrated men took a full part in the general agitation of mind common at that period, and they attained a high degree of personal fame, which was reflected back upon the nation, but which was by no means borrowed from it. . . .

In free countries, where every one is more or less called upon to give his opinion in the affairs of state; in democratic republics, where public life is incessantly commingled with domestic affairs, where the sovereign authority is accessible on every side, and where its attention can almost always be attracted by vociferation, more persons are to be met with who speculate upon its foibles and live at the cost of its passions than in absolute monarchies. Not because men are naturally worse in these States than elsewhere, but the temptation is stronger, and of easier access at the same time. The result is a far more extensive debasement of the characters of citizens.

Democratic republics extend the practice of currying favour with the many, and they introduce it into a greater number of classes at once: this is one of the most serious reproaches that can be addressed to them. In democratic States organized on the principles of the American republics, this is more especially the case, where the authority of the majority is so absolute and so irresistible that a man must give up his rights as a citizen, and almost abjure his quality as a human being, if he intends to stray from the track which it lays down.

In that immense crowd which throngs the avenues to power in the United States I found very few men who displayed any of that manly candour and that masculine independence of opinion which frequently distinguished the Americans in former times, and which constitutes the leading feature in distinguished characters, wheresoever they may be found. It seems, at first sight, as if all the minds of the Americans were formed upon one model, so accurately do they correspond in their manner of judging. A stranger does, indeed, sometimes meet with Americans who dissent from these rigorous formularies; with men who deplore the defects of the laws, the mutability and the ignorance of democracy; who even go so far as to observe the evil tendencies which impair the national character, and to point out such remedies as it might be possible to apply; but no one is there to hear these things besides yourself, and you, to whom these secret reflections are confided, are a stranger and a bird of passage. They are very ready to communicate truths which are useless to you, but they continue to hold a different language in public. . . .

Despotism debases the oppressed much more than the oppressor: in absolute monarchies the king has often great virtues, but the courtiers are invariably servile. It is true that the American courtiers do not say "Sire," or "Your Majesty"—a distinction without a difference. They are for ever talking of the natural intelligence of the populace they serve; they do not debate the question as to which of the virtues of their master is pre-eminently worthy of admiration, for they assure him that he possesses all the virtues under heaven without having acquired them, or without caring to acquire them; they do not give him their daughters and their wives to be raised at his pleasure to the rank of his concubines, but, by sacrificing their opinions, they prostitute themselves. Moralists and philosophers in America are not obliged to conceal their opinions under the veil of allegory; but, before they venture upon a harsh truth, they say: "We are aware that the people which we are addressing is too superior to all the weaknesses of human nature to lose the command of its temper for an instant; and we should not hold this language if we were not speaking to men whom their virtues and their intelligence render more worthy of freedom than all the rest of the world." It would have been impossible for the sycophants of Louis XIV to flatter more dexterously. For my part, I am persuaded that in all governments, whatever their nature may be, servility will cower to force, and adulation will cling to power. The only means of preventing men from degrading themselves is to invest no one with that unlimited authority which is the surest method of debasing them.

Governments usually fall a sacrifice to impotence or to tyranny. In the former case their power escapes from them; it is wrested from their grasp in the latter. Many observers, who have witnessed the anarchy of democratic States, have imagined that the government of those States was naturally weak and impotent. The truth is, that when once hostilities are begun between parties, the government loses its control over society. But I do not think that a democratic power is naturally without force or without resources: say rather, that it is almost always by the abuse of its force and the misemployment of its resources that a democratic government fails. Anarchy is almost always produced by its tyranny or its mistakes, but not by its want of strength.

It is important not to confound stability with force, or the greatness of a thing with its duration. In democratic republics, the power which directs society is not stable; for it often changes hands and assumes a new direction. But whichever way it turns, its force is almost irresistible. The governments of the American republics appear to me to be as much centralized as those of the absolute monarchies of Europe, and more energetic than they are. I do not, therefore, imagine that they will perish from weakness.

If ever the free institutions of America are destroyed, that event may be attributed to the unlimited authority of the majority, which may at some future time urge the minorities to desperation, and oblige them to have recourse to physical force. Anarchy will then be the result, but it will have been brought about by despotism. . . .

Capitalism

32. Man's Rights

Ayn Rand

Ayn Rand (1905–1982) was an American author and social critic. In her novels and nonfiction writings she expounded and advocated a philosophy of individualism and rational self-interest. Born in Russia and educated under the Soviets, she rebelled against the doctrines and practices of Soviet communism and at the age of 21 came to America alone and determined to become a writer. In her very popular novel Atlas Shrugged *(1957) she gives the fullest statement of her general philosophy of Objectivism. In the last two decades of her life she presented her philosophy in nonfiction form in such works as* Capitalism: The Unknown Ideal *(1946), which also includes several essays by Alan Greenspan, now chairman of the U.S. Federal Reserve.*

If one wishes to advocate a free society—that is, capitalism—one must realize that its indispensable foundation is the principle of individual rights. If one wishes to uphold individual rights, one must realize that capitalism is the only system that can uphold and protect them. And if one wishes to gauge the relationship of freedom to the goals of today's intellectuals, one may gauge it by the fact that the concept of individual rights is evaded, distorted, perverted and seldom discussed, most conspicuously seldom by the so-called "conservatives."

"Rights" are a moral concept—the concept that provides a logical transition from the principles guiding an individual's actions to the principles guiding his relationship with others—the concept that preserves and protects individual morality in a social context—the link between the moral code of a man and the legal code of a society, between ethics and politics. *Individual rights are the means of subordinating society to moral law.*

Every political system is based on some code of ethics. The dominant ethics of mankind's history were variants of the altruist-collectivist doctrine which subordinated the individual to some higher authority, either mystical or social. Consequently, most political systems were variants of the same statist tyranny, differing only in degree, not in basic principle, limited only by the accidents of tradition, of chaos, of bloody strife and periodic collapse. Under all such systems, morality was a code applicable to the individual, but not to society. Society was placed *outside* the moral law, as its embodiment or source or exclusive interpreter—and the inculcation of self-sacrificial devotion to social duty was regarded as the main purpose of ethics in man's earthly existence.

Since there is no such entity as "society," since society is only a number of individual men, this meant, in practice, that the rulers of society were exempt from moral law; subject only to traditional rituals, they held total power and exacted blind obedience—on the implicit principle of: "The good is that which is good for society (or for the tribe, the race, the nation), and the ruler's edicts are its voice on earth."

This was true of all statist systems, under all variants of the altruist-collectivist ethics, mystical or social. "The Divine Right of Kings" summarizes the political theory of the first—"*Vox populi, vox dei*" of the second. As witness: the theocracy of Egypt, with the Pharaoh as an embodied god—the unlimited majority rule or *democracy* of Athens—the welfare state run by the Emperors of Rome—the Inquisition of the late Middle Ages—the absolute monarchy of France—the welfare state of Bismarck's Prussia—the gas chambers of Nazi Germany—the slaughterhouse of the Soviet Union.

All these political systems were expressions of the altruist-collectivist ethics—and their common characteristic is the fact that society stood above the moral law, as an omnipotent, sovereign whim worshiper. Thus, politically, all these systems were variants of an *amoral* society.

The most profoundly revolutionary achievement of the United States of America was *the subordination of society to moral law*.

The principle of man's individual rights represented the extension of morality into the social system—as a limitation on the power of the state, as man's protection against the brute force of the collective, as the subordination of *might* to *right*. The United States was the first *moral* society in history.

All previous systems had regarded man as a sacrificial means to the ends of others, and society as an end in itself. The United States regarded man as an end in himself, and society as a means to the peaceful, orderly, *voluntary* co-existence of individuals. All previous systems had held that man's life belongs to society, that society can dispose of him in any way it pleases, and that any freedom he enjoys is his only by favor, by the *permission* of society, which may be revoked at any time. The United States held that man's life is his by *right* (which means: by moral principle and by his nature), that a right is the property of an individual, that society as such has no rights, and that the only moral purpose of a government is the protection of individual rights.

A "right" is a moral principle defining and sanctioning a man's freedom of action in a social context. There is only *one* fundamental right (all the others are its consequences or corollaries): a man's right to his own life. Life is a process of self-sustaining and self-generated action; the right to life means the right to engage in self-sustaining and self-generated action—which means: the freedom to take all the actions required by the nature of a rational being for the support, the furtherance, the fulfillment and the enjoyment of his own life. (Such is the meaning of the right to life, liberty and the pursuit of happiness.)

The concept of a "right" pertains only to action—specifically, to freedom of action. It means freedom from physical compulsion, coercion or interference by other men.

Thus, for every individual, a right is the moral sanction of a *positive*—of his freedom to act on his own judgment, for his own goals, by his own *voluntary*, *uncoerced* choice. As to his neighbors, his rights impose no obligations on them except of a *negative* kind: to abstain from violating his rights.

The right to life is the source of all rights—and the right to property is their only implementation. Without property rights, no other rights are possible. Since man has to sustain his life by his own effort, the man who has no right to the product of his effort has no means to sustain his life. The man who produces while others dispose of his product, is a slave.

Bear in mind that the right to property is a right to action, like all the others: it is not the right *to an object* but to the action and the consequences of producing or earning that object. It is not a guarantee that a man *will* earn any property, but only a guarantee that he will own it if he earns it. It is the right to gain, to keep, to use and to dispose of material values.

The concept of individual rights is so new in human history that most men have not grasped it fully to this day. In accordance with the two theories of ethics, the mystical or the social, some men assert that rights are a gift of God—others, that rights are a gift of society. But, in fact, the source of rights is man's nature.

The Declaration of Independence stated that men "are endowed by their Creator with certain unalienable rights." Whether one believes that man is the product of a Creator or of nature, the issue of man's origin does not alter the fact that he is an entity of a specific kind—a rational being—that he cannot function successfully under coercion, and that rights are a necessary condition of his particular mode of survival.

"The source of man's rights is not divine law or congressional law, but the law of identity. A is A—and Man is Man. *Rights* are conditions of existence required by man's nature for his proper survival. If man is to live on earth, it is *right* for him to use his mind, it is *right* to act on his own free judgment, it is *right* to work for his values and to keep the product of his work. If life on earth is his purpose, he has a *right* to live as a rational being: nature forbids him the irrational." (*Atlas Shrugged*)

To violate man's rights means to compel him to act against his own judgment, or to expropriate his values. Basically, there is only one way to do it: by the use of physical force. There are two potential violators of man's rights: the criminals and the government. The great achievement of the United States was to draw a distinction between these two—by forbidding to the second the legalized version of the activities of the first.

The Declaration of Independence laid down the principle that "to secure these rights, governments are instituted among men." This provided the only valid justification of a government and defined its only proper purpose: to protect man's rights by protecting him from physical violence.

Thus the government's function was changed from the role of ruler to the role of servant. The government was set to protect man from criminals—and the

Constitution was written to protect man from the government. The Bill of Rights was not directed against private citizens, but against the government—as an explicit declaration that individual rights supersede any public or social power.

The result was the pattern of a civilized society which—for the brief span of some hundred and fifty years—America came close to achieving. A civilized society is one in which physical force is banned from human relationships—in which the government, acting as a policeman, may use force *only* in retaliation and *only* against those who initiate its use.

This was the essential meaning and intent of America's political philosophy, implicit in the principle of individual rights. But it was not formulated explicitly, nor fully accepted nor consistently practiced.

America's inner contradiction was the altruist-collectivist ethics. Altruism is incompatible with freedom, with capitalism and with individual rights. One cannot combine the pursuit of happiness with the moral status of a sacrificial animal.

It was the concept of individual rights that had given birth to a free society. It was with the destruction of individual rights that the destruction of freedom had to begin.

A collectivist tyranny dare not enslave a country by an outright confiscation of its values, material or moral. It has to be done by a process of internal corruption. Just as in the material realm the plundering of a country's wealth is accomplished by inflating the currency—so today one may witness the process of inflation being applied to the realm of rights. The process entails such a growth of newly promulgated "rights" that people do not notice the fact that the meaning of the concept is being reversed. Just as bad money drives out good money, so these "printing-press rights" negate authentic rights.

Consider the curious fact that never has there been such a proliferation, all over the world, of two contradictory phenomena: of alleged new "rights" and of slave-labor camps.

The "gimmick" was the switch of the concept of rights from the political to the economic realm.

The Democratic Party platform of 1960 summarizes the switch boldly and explicitly. It declares that a Democratic Administration "will reaffirm the economic bill of rights which Franklin Roosevelt wrote into our national conscience sixteen years ago."

Bear clearly in mind the meaning of the concept of *"rights"* when you read the list which that platform offers:

"1. The right to a useful and remunerative job in the industries or shops or farms or mines of the nation.

"2. The right to earn enough to provide adequate food and clothing and recreation.

"3. The right of every farmer to raise and sell his products at a return which will give him and his family a decent living.

"4. The right of every businessman, large and small, to trade in an atmosphere of freedom from unfair competition and domination by monopolies at home and abroad.

"5. The right of every family to a decent home.

"6. The right to adequate medical care and the opportunity to achieve and enjoy good health.

"7. The right to adequate protection from the economic fears of old age, sickness, accidents and unemployment.

"8. The right to a good education."

A single question added to each of the above eight clauses would make the issue clear: *At whose expense?*

Jobs, food, clothing, recreation (!), homes, medical care, education, etc., do not grow in nature. These are man-made values—goods and services produced by men. *Who* is to provide them?

If some men are entitled *by right* to the products of the work of others, it means that those others are deprived of rights and condemned to slave labor.

Any alleged "right" of one man, which necessitates the violation of the rights of another, is not and cannot be a right.

No man can have a right to impose an unchosen obligation, an unrewarded duty or an involuntary servitude on another man. There can be no such thing as "*the right to enslave.*"

A right does not include the material implementation of that right by other men; it includes only the freedom to earn that implementation by one's own effort.

Observe, in this context, the intellectual precision of the Founding Fathers: they spoke of the right to *the pursuit* of happiness—*not* of the right to happiness. It means that a man has the right to take the actions he deems necessary to achieve his happiness; it does *not* mean that others must make him happy.

The right to life means that a man has the right to support his life by his own work (on any economic level, as high as his ability will carry him); it does *not* mean that others must provide him with the necessities of life.

The right to property means that a man has the right to take the economic actions necessary to earn property, to use it and to dispose of it; it does *not* mean that others must provide him with property.

The right of free speech means that a man has the right to express his ideas without danger of suppression, interference or punitive action by the government. It does *not* mean that others must provide him with a lecture hall, a radio station or a printing press through which to express his ideas.

Any undertaking that involves more than one man, requires the *voluntary* consent of every participant. Every one of them has the *right* to make his own decision, but none has the right to force his decision on the others.

There is no such thing as "a right to a job"—there is only the right of free trade, that is: a man's right to take a job if another man chooses to hire him. There is no "right to a home," only the right of free trade: the right to build a home or to buy it. There are no "rights to a 'fair' wage or a 'fair' price" if no one chooses to pay it, to hire a man or to buy his product. There are no "rights of consumers" to milk, shoes, movies or champagne if no producers choose to manufacture such items (there is only the right to manufacture them oneself). There are no "rights" of special groups, there are no "rights of farmers, of workers, of businessmen, of employees, of employers, of the old, of the young, of the unborn." There are only *the Rights of Man*—rights possessed by every individual man and by *all* men as individuals.

Property rights and the right of free trade are man's only "economic rights" (they are, in fact, *political* rights)—and there can be no such thing as "an *economic* bill of rights." But observe that the advocates of the latter have all but destroyed the former.

Remember that rights are moral principles which define and protect a man's freedom of action, but impose no obligations on other men. Private citizens are not a threat to one another's rights or freedom. A private citizen who resorts to physical force and violates the rights of others is a criminal—and men have legal protection against him.

Criminals are a small minority in any age or country. And the harm they have done to mankind is infinitesimal when compared to the horrors—the bloodshed, the wars, the persecutions, the confiscations, the famines, the enslavements, the wholesale destructions—perpetrated by mankind's governments. Potentially, a government is the most dangerous threat to man's rights: it holds a legal monopoly on the use of physical force against legally disarmed victims. When unlimited and unrestricted by individual rights, a government is men's deadliest enemy. It is not as protection against *private* actions, but against governmental actions that the Bill of Rights was written.

Now observe the process by which that protection is being destroyed.

The process consists of ascribing to private citizens the specific violations constitutionally forbidden to the government (which private citizens have no power to commit) and thus freeing the government from all restrictions. The switch is becoming progressively more obvious in the field of free speech. For years, the collectivists have been propagating the notion that a private individual's refusal to finance an opponent is a violation of the opponent's right of free speech and an act of "censorship."

It is "censorship," they claim, if a newspaper refuses to employ or publish writers whose ideas are diametrically opposed to its policy.

It is "censorship," they claim, if businessmen refuse to advertise in a magazine that denounces, insults and smears them.

It is "censorship," they claim, if a TV sponsor objects to some outrage perpetrated on a program he is financing—such as the incident of Alger Hiss being invited to denounce former Vice-President Nixon.

And then there is Newton N. Minow who declares: "There is censorship by ratings, by advertisers, by networks, by affiliates which reject programming offered to their areas." It is the same Mr. Minow who threatens to revoke the license of any station that does not comply with his views on programming—and who claims that *that* is not censorship.

Consider the implications of such a trend.

"Censorship" is a term pertaining only to governmental action. No private action is censorship. No private individual or agency can silence a man or suppress a publication; only the government can do so. The freedom of speech of private individuals includes the right not to agree, not to listen and not to finance one's own antagonists.

But according to such doctrines as the "economic bill of rights," an individual has no right to dispose of his own material means by the guidance of his own convictions—and must hand over his money indiscriminately to any speakers or propagandists, who have a "right" to his property.

This means that the ability to provide the material tools for the expression of ideas deprives a man of the right to hold any ideas. It means that a publisher has to publish books he considers worthless, false or evil—that a TV sponsor has to finance commentators who choose to affront his convictions—that the owner of a newspaper must turn his editorial pages over to any young hooligan who clamors for the enslavement of the press. It means that one group of men acquires the "right" to unlimited license—while another group is reduced to helpless irresponsibility.

But since it is obviously impossible to provide every claimant with a job, a microphone or a newspaper column, *who* will determine the "distribution" of "economic rights" and select the recipients, when the owners' right to choose has been abolished? Well, Mr. Minow has indicated *that* quite clearly.

And if you make the mistake of thinking that this applies only to big property owners, you had better realize that the theory of "economic rights" includes the "right" of every would-be playwright, every beatnik poet, every noise-composer and every nonobjective artist (who have political pull) to the financial support you did not give them when you did not attend their shows. What else is the meaning of the project to spend your tax money on subsidized art?

And while people are clamoring about "economic rights," the concept of political rights is vanishing. It is forgotten that the right of free speech means the freedom to advocate one's views and to bear the possible consequences, including disagreement with others, opposition, unpopularity and lack of support. The political function of "the right of free speech" is to protect dissenters and unpopular minorities from forcible suppression—*not* to guarantee them the support, advantages and rewards of a popularity they have not gained.

The Bill of Rights reads: "Congress shall make no law . . . abridging the freedom of speech, or of the press . . ." It does not demand that private citizens provide a microphone for the man who advocates their destruction, or a passkey for the burglar who seeks to rob them, or a knife for the murderer who wants to cut their throats.

Such is the state of one of today's most crucial issues: *political* rights versus *"economic* rights." It's either-or. One destroys the other. But there are, in fact, no "economic rights," no "collective rights," no "public-interest rights." The term "individual rights" is a redundancy: there is no other kind of rights and no one else to possess them.

Those who advocate *laissez-faire* capitalism are the only advocates of man's rights.

Socialism

33. A Moral Case for Socialism

Kai Nielsen

In North America socialism gets a bad press. It is under criticism for its alleged economic inefficiency and for its moral and human inadequacy. I want here to address the latter issue. Looking at capitalism and socialism, I want to consider, against the grain of our culture, what kind of moral case can be made for socialism.

The first thing to do, given the extensive, and, I would add, inexcusably extensive, confusions about this, is to say what socialism and capitalism are. That done I will then, appealing to a cluster of values which are basic in our culture, concerning which there is a considerable and indeed a reflective consensus, examine how capitalism and socialism fare with respect to these values. Given that people generally, at least in Western societies, would want it to be the case that these values have a stable exemplification in our social lives, it is appropriate to ask the question: which of these social systems is more likely stably to exemplify them? I shall argue, facing the gamut of a careful comparison in the light of these values, that, everything considered, socialism comes out better than capitalism. And this, if right, would give us good reason for believing that socialism is preferable—indeed morally preferable—to capitalism if it also turns out to be a feasible socio-economic system.

What, then, are socialism and capitalism? Put most succinctly, capitalism requires the existence of private *productive* property (private ownership of the means of production) while socialism works toward its abolition. What is essential for socialism is public ownership and control of the means of production and public ownership means just what it says: *ownership by the public*. Under capitalism there is a domain of private property rights in the means of production which are not subject to political determination. That is, even where the political domain is a democratic one, they are not subject to determination by the public; only an individual or a set of individuals who own that property can make the final determination of what is to be done with that property. These individuals make that determination and not citizens at large, as under socialism. In fully developed socialism, by contrast, there is, with respect to productive property, no domain which is not subject to political determination by the public, namely by the citizenry at large. Thus, where this public ownership and control [are] genuine, and not a mask for control by an elite of state

Reprinted from *Critical Review*, Vol. 3, Nos. 3–4, 1989, pp. 542–553, by permission of the author.

bureaucrats, it will mean genuine popular and democratic control over productive property. What socialism is *not* is *state* ownership in the absence of, at the very least, popular sovereignty, i.e., genuine popular control over the state apparatus including any economic functions it might have.

The property that is owned in common under socialism is the means of existence—the productive property in the society. Socialism does not proscribe the ownership of private personal property, such as houses, cars, television sets and the like. It only proscribes the private ownership of the means of production.

The above characterizations catch the minimal core of socialism and capitalism, what used to be called the essence of those concepts. But beyond these core features, it is well, in helping us to make our comparison, to see some other important features which characteristically go with capitalism and socialism. Minimally, capitalism is private ownership of the means of production but it is also, at least characteristically, a social system in which a class of capitalists owns and controls the means of production and hires workers who, owning little or no means of production, sell their labor-power to some capitalist or other for a wage. This means that a capitalist society will be a class society in which there will be two principal classes: capitalists and workers. Socialism by contrast is a social system in which every able-bodied person is, was or will be a worker. These workers commonly own and control the means of production (this is the characteristic form of public ownership). Thus in socialism we have, in a perfectly literal sense, a classless society for there is no division between human beings along class lines.

There are both pure and impure forms of capitalism and socialism. The pure form of capitalism is competitive capitalism, the capitalism that Milton Friedman would tell us is the real capitalism while, he would add, the impure form is monopoly or corporate capitalism. Similarly the pure form of socialism is democratic socialism, with firm workers' control of the means of production and an industrial as well as a political democracy, while the impure form is state bureaucratic socialism.

Now it is a noteworthy fact that, to understate it, actually existing capitalisms and actually existing socialisms tend to be the impure forms. Many partisans of capitalism lament the fact that the actually existing capitalisms overwhelmingly tend to be forms of corporate capitalism where the state massively intervenes in the running of the economy. It is unclear whether anything like a fully competitive capitalism actually exists—perhaps Hong Kong approximates it—and it is also unclear whether many of the actual players in the major capitalist societies (the existing capitalists and their managers) want or even expect that it is possible to have laissez-faire capitalism again (if indeed we ever had it). Some capitalist societies are further down the corporate road than other societies, but they are all forms of corporate, perhaps in some instances even monopoly, capitalism. Competitive capitalism seems to be more of a libertarian dream than a sociological reality or even something desired by many informed and tough-minded members of the capitalist class. Socialism has had a similar fate. Its historical exemplifications tend to be of the impure forms, namely the bureaucratic state socialisms. Yugoslavia is perhaps to socialism what Hong Kong is to capitalism. It is a candidate for what might count as an exemplification, or at least a near approximation, of the pure form.

This paucity of exemplifications of pure forms of either capitalism or socialism raises the question of whether the pure forms are at best unstable social systems and at worse merely utopian ideals. I shall not try directly to settle that issue here. What I shall do instead is to compare *models* with *models*. In asking about the moral case for socialism, I shall compare forms that a not inconsiderable number of the theoretical protagonists of each take to be pure forms but which are still, they believe, historically feasible. But I will also be concerned to ask whether these models—these pure forms—can reasonably be expected to come to have a home. If they are not historically feasible models, then, even if we can make a good theoretical moral case for them, we will have hardly provided a good moral case for socialism or capitalism. To avoid bad utopianism we must be talking about forms which could be on the historical agenda. (I plainly here do not take "bad utopianism" to be pleonastic.)

Setting aside for the time being the feasibility question, let us compare the pure forms of capitalism and socialism—that is to say, competitive capitalism and democratic socialism—as to how they stand with respect to sustaining and furthering the values of freedom and autonomy, equality, justice, rights and democracy. My argument shall be that socialism comes out better with respect to those values.

Let us first look at freedom and autonomy. An autonomous person is a person who is able to set her ends for herself and in optimal circumstances is able to pursue those ends. But freedom does not only mean being autonomous; it also means the absence of unjustified political and social interference in the pursuit of one's ends. Some might even say that it is just the absence of interference with one's ends. Still it is self-direction—autonomy—not non-interference which is *intrinsically* desirable. Non-interference is only valuable where it is an aid to our being able to do what we want and where we are sufficiently autonomous to have some control over our wants.

How do capitalism and socialism fare in providing the social conditions which will help or impede the flourishing of autonomy? Which model society would make for the greater flourishing of autonomy? My argument is (a) that democratic socialism makes it possible for more people to be more fully autonomous than would be autonomous under capitalism; and (b) that democratic socialism also interferes less in people's exercise of their autonomy than any form of capitalism. All societies limit liberty by interfering with people doing what they want to do in some ways, but the restrictions are more extensive, deeper and more undermining of autonomy in capitalism than in democratic socialism. Where there is private ownership of productive property, which, remember, is private ownership of the means of life, it cannot help but be the case that a few (the owning and controlling capitalist class) will have, along with the managers beholden to them, except in periods of revolutionary turmoil, a firm control, indeed a domination, over the vast majority of people in the society. The capitalist class with the help of their managers determines whether workers (taken now as individuals) can work, how they work, on what they work, the conditions under which they work and what is done with what they produce (where they are producers) and what use is made of their skills and the like. As we move to welfare state capitalism—a compromise still favoring capital which emerged out of long and bitter class struggles—the state places some restrictions on some of these powers of capital. Hours, working conditions and the like are controlled in certain ways. Yet whether workers work and continue to work, how they work and on what, what is done with what they produce, and the rationale for their work are not determined by the workers themselves but by the owners of capital and their managers; this means a very considerable limitation on the autonomy and freedom of workers. Since workers are the great majority, such socio-economic relations place a very considerable limitation on human freedom and indeed on the very most important freedom that people have, namely their being able to live in a self-directed manner, when compared with the industrial democracy of democratic socialism. Under capitalist arrangements it simply cannot fail to be the case that a very large number of people will lose control over a very central set of facets of their lives, namely central aspects of their work and indeed in many instances, over their very chance to be able to work.

Socialism would indeed prohibit capitalist acts between consenting adults; the capitalist class would lose its freedom to buy and sell and to control the labor market. There should be no blinking at the fact that socialist social relations would impose some limitations on freedom, for there is, and indeed can be, no society without norms and some sanctions. In any society you like there will be some things you are at liberty to do and some things that you may not do. However, democratic socialism must bring with it an industrial democracy where workers by various democratic procedures would determine how they are to work, on what they are to work, the hours of their work, under what conditions they are to work (insofar as this is alterable by human effort at all), what they will produce and how much, and what is to be done with what they produce. Since, instead of there being "private ownership of the means of production," there is in a genuinely socialist society "public ownership of the means of production," the means of life are owned by everyone and thus each person has a *right* to work: she has, that is, a right to the means of life. It is no longer the private preserve of an individual owner of capital but it is owned in common by us all. This means that each of us has an equal right to the means of life. Members of the capitalist class would have a few of their liberties restricted, but these are linked with owning and controlling capital and are not the important civil and political liberties that we all rightly cherish. Moreover, the limitation of the capitalist liberties to buy and sell and the like would make for a more extensive liberty for many, many more people.

One cannot respond to the above by saying that workers are free to leave the working class and become capitalists or at least petty bourgeoisie. They may indeed all in theory, taken *individually*, be free to leave the working class, but if many in fact try to leave the exits will very quickly become blocked. Individuals are only free on the condition that the great mass of people, taken collectively, are not. We could not have capitalism without a working class and the working class is not free within the capitalist system to cease being wage laborers. We cannot all be capitalists. A people's capitalism is nonsense. Though a petty commodity production system (the family farm writ large) is a logical possibility, it is hardly a stable empirical possibility and, what is most important for the present discussion, such a system would not be a capitalist system. Under capitalism, most of us, if we are to find any work at all, will just have to sell (or *perhaps* "rent" is the better word) our labor power as a commodity. Whether you sell or rent your labor power or, where it is provided, you go on welfare, you will not have much control over areas very crucial to your life. If these are the only feasible alternatives facing the working class, working class autonomy is very limited indeed. But these are the only alternatives under capitalism.

Capitalist acts between consenting adults, if they become sufficiently widespread, lead to severe imbalances in power. These imbalances in power tend to undermine autonomy by creating differentials in wealth and control between workers and capitalists. Such imbalances are the name of the game for capitalism. Even if we (perversely I believe) call a system of petty commodity production capitalism, we still must say that such a socio-economic system is inherently unstable. Certain individuals would win out in this exchanging of commodities and in fairly quick order it would lead to a class system and the imbalances of power—the domination of the many by the few—that I take to be definitive of capitalism. By abolishing capitalist acts between consenting adults, then (but leaving personal property and civil and political liberties untouched), socialism protects more extensive freedoms for more people and in far more important areas of their lives.

So democratic socialism does better regarding the value that epitomizes capitalist pride (*hubris*, would, I think, be a better term), namely autonomy. It also does better, I shall now argue, than capitalism with respect to another of our basic values, namely democracy. Since this is almost a corollary of what I have said about autonomy I can afford to be briefer. In capitalist societies, democracy must simply be *political* democracy. There can in the nature of the case be no genuine or thorough workplace democracy. When we enter the sphere of production, capitalists and not workers own, and therefore at least ultimately control, the means of production. While capitalism, as in some workplaces in West Germany and Sweden, sometimes can be pressured into allowing an ameliorative measure of worker control, once ownership rights are given up, we no longer have private productive property but public productive property (and in that way social ownership): capitalism is given up and we have socialism. However, where worker control is restricted to a few firms, we do not yet have socialism. What makes a system socialist or capitalist depends on what happens across the whole society, not just in isolated firms. Moreover, managers can become very important within capitalist firms, but as long as ownership, including the ability to close the place down and liquidate the business, rests in the hands of capitalists we can have no genuine workplace democracy. Socialism, in its pure form, carries with it, in a way capitalism in any form cannot, workplace democracy. (That some of the existing socialisms are anything but pure does not belie this.)

Similarly, whatever may be said of existing socialisms or at least of some existing socialisms, it is not the case that there is anything in the very idea of socialism that militates against political as well as industrial democracy. Socialists are indeed justly suspicious of some of the tricks played by parliamentary democracy in bourgeois countries, aware of its not infrequent hypocrisy and the limitations of its stress on purely legal and formal political rights and liberties. Socialists are also, without at all wishing to throw the baby out with the bath water, rightly suspicious of any simple reliance on majority rule, unsupplemented by other democratic procedures and safe-guards. But there is nothing in socialist theory that would set it against political democracy and the protection of political and civil rights; indeed there is much in socialism that favors them, namely its stress on both autonomy and equality.

The fact that political democracy came into being and achieved stability within capitalist societies may prove something about conditions necessary for its coming into being, but it says nothing about capitalism being necessary for sustaining it. In Chile, South Africa and Nazi Germany, indeed, capitalism has flourished without the protection of civil and political rights or anything like a respect for the democratic tradition. There is nothing structural in socialism that would prevent it from continuing those democratic traditions or cherishing those political and civil rights. That something came about under certain conditions does not establish that these conditions are necessary for its continued existence. That men initially took an interest in chess does not establish that women cannot quite naturally take an interest in it as well. When capitalist societies with long-flourishing democratic traditions move to socialism there is no reason at all to believe that they will not continue to be democratic. (Where societies previously had no democratic tradition or only a very weak one, matters are more problematic.)

I now want to turn to a third basic value, equality. In societies across the polit-ical spectrum, *moral* equality (the belief that everyone's life matters equally) is an accepted value. Or, to be somewhat cynical about the matter, at least lip service is paid to it. But even this lip service is the compliment that vice pays to virtue. That is to say, such a belief is a deeply held considered conviction in modernized societies, though it has not been at all times and is not today a value held in all societies. This is most evident concerning moral equality.

While this value is genuinely held by the vast majority of people in capital-ist societies, it can hardly be an effective or functional working norm where there is such a diminishment of autonomy as we have seen obtains unavoidably in such societies. Self-respect is deeply threatened where so many people lack effective control over their own lives, where there are structures of domination, where there is alienated labor, where great power differentials and differences in wealth make for very different (and often very bleak) life chances. For not inconsiderable numbers, in fact, it is difficult to maintain self-respect under such conditions unless they are actively struggling against the system. And, given present conditions, fighting the system, particularly in societies such as the United States, may well be felt to be a hopeless task. Under such conditions any real equality of opportunity is out of the question. And the circumstances are such, in spite of what is often said about these states, that equality of condition is an even more remote possibility. But without at least some of these things moral equality cannot even be approximated. Indeed, even to speak of it sounds like an obscene joke given the social realities of our lives.

Although under welfare state capitalism some of the worst inequalities of capitalism are ameliorated, workers still lack effective control over their work, with repercussions in political and public life as well. Differentials of wealth cannot but give rise to differentials in power and control in politics, in the media, in education, in the direction of social life and in what options get seriously debated. The life chances of workers and those not even lucky enough to be workers (whose ranks are growing and will continue to grow under capitalism) are impoverished compared to the life chances of members of the capitalist class and its docile professional support stratum.

None of these equality-undermining features would obtain under democratic socialism. Such societies would, for starters, be classless, eliminating the power and control differentials that go with the class system of capitalism. In addition to political democracy, industrial democracy and all the egalitarian and participatory control that goes with that would, in turn, reinforce moral equality. Indeed it would make it possible where before it was impossible. There would be a commitment under democratic socialism to attaining or at least approximating, as far as it is feasible, equality of condition; and this, where approximated, would help make for real equality of opportunity, making equal life chances something less utopian than it must be under capitalism.

In fine, the very things, as we have seen, that make for greater autonomy under socialism than under capitalism, would, in being more equally distributed, make for greater equality of condition, greater equality of opportunity and greater moral equality in a democratic socialist society than in a capitalist one. These values are values commonly shared by both capitalistically inclined people and those who are socialistically inclined. What the former do not see is that in modern industrial societies, democratic socialism can better deliver these goods than even progressive capitalism.

There is, without doubt, legitimate worry about bureaucratic control under socialism. But that is a worry under any historically feasible capitalism as well, and it is anything but clear that state bureaucracies are worse than great corporate bureaucracies. Indeed, if socialist bureaucrats were, as the socialist system requires, really committed to production for needs and to achieving equality of condition, they might, bad as they are, be the lesser of two evils. But in any event democratic socialism is not bureaucratic state socialism, and there is no structural reason to believe that it must—if it arises in a society with skilled workers committed to democracy—give rise to bureaucratic state socialism. There will, inescapably, be some bureaucracy, but in a democratic socialist society it must and indeed will be controlled. This is not merely a matter of optimism about the will of socialists, for there are more mechanisms for democratic control of bureaucracy within a democratic socialism that is both a political and an industrial democracy, than there can be under even the most benign capitalist democracies—democracies which for structural reasons can never be industrial democracies. If, all that notwithstanding, bureaucratic creepage is inescapable in modern societies, then that is just as much a problem for capitalism as for socialism.

The underlying rationale for production under capitalism is profit and capital accumulation. Capitalism is indeed a marvelous engine for building up the productive forces (though clearly at the expense of considerations of equality and autonomy). We might look on it, going back to earlier historical times, as something like a forced march to develop the productive forces. But now that the productive forces in advanced capitalist societies are wondrously developed, we are in a position to direct them to far more humane and more equitable uses under a socio-economic system whose rationale for production is to meet human needs (the needs of everyone as far as this is possible). This egalitarian thrust, together with the socialist's commitment to attaining, as far as that is possible, equality of condition, makes it clear that socialism will produce more equality than capitalism.

In talking about autonomy, democracy and equality, we have, in effect, already been talking about justice. A society or set of institutions that does better in these respects than another society will be a more just society than the other society.

Fairness is a less fancy name for justice. If we compare two societies and the first is more democratic than the second; there is more autonomy in the first society than in the second; there are more nearly equal life chances in the first society than in the second and thus greater equality of opportunity; if, without sacrifice of autonomy, there is more equality of condition in the first society than in the second; and if there is more moral equality in the first society than in the second, then we cannot but conclude that the first society is a society with more fairness than the second and, thus, that it is the more just society. But this is exactly how socialism comes out vis-à-vis even the best form of capitalism.

A society which undermines autonomy, heels in democracy (where democracy is not violating rights), makes equality impossible to achieve and violates rights cannot be a just society. If, as I contend, that is what capitalism does, and cannot help doing, then a capitalist society cannot be a just society. Democratic socialism, by contrast, does not need to do any of those things, and we can predict that it would not, for there are no structural imperatives in democratic socialism to do so and there are deep sentiments in that tradition urging us not to do so. I do not for a moment deny that there are similar sentiments for autonomy and democracy in capitalist societies, but the logic of capitalism, the underlying structures of capitalist societies—even the best of capitalist societies—frustrate the realization of the states of affairs at which those sympathies aim. A radical democrat with a commitment to human rights, to human autonomy and moral equality and fair equality of opportunity ought to be a democratic socialist and a firm opponent of capitalism—even a capitalism with a human face.

Anarchism

34. The State

Murray N. Rothbard

Murray N. Rothbard (1926–1995) has been hailed as the leading economist of his generation of the "Austrian school" and as one of the most influential theoreticians of the American libertarian movement.

The State as Aggressor

The central thrust of libertarian thought, then, is to oppose any and all aggression against the property rights of individuals in their own persons and in the material objects they have voluntarily acquired. While individual and gangs of criminals are of course opposed, there is nothing unique here to the libertarian creed, since almost all persons and schools of thought oppose the exercise of random violence against persons and property. . . .

But the critical difference between libertarians and other people is not in the area of private crime; the critical difference is their view of the role of the State—the government. For libertarians regard the State as the supreme, the eternal, the best organized aggressor against the persons and property of the mass of the public. All States everywhere, whether democratic, dictatorial, or monarchical, whether red, white, blue, or brown.

The State! Always and ever the government and its rulers and operators have been considered above the general moral law. The "Pentagon Papers" are only one recent instance among innumerable instances in history of men, most of whom are perfectly honorable in their private lives, who lie in their teeth before the public. Why? For "reasons of State." Service to the State is supposed to excuse all actions that would be considered immoral or criminal if committed by "private" citizens. The distinctive feature of libertarians is that they coolly and uncompromisingly apply the general moral law to people acting in their roles as members of the State apparatus. Libertarians make no exceptions. For centuries, the State (or more strictly, individuals acting in their roles as "members of the government") has cloaked its criminal activity in high-sounding rhetoric. For centuries the State has committed mass murder and called it "war"; then ennobled the mass slaughter that "war"

From Murray N. Rothbard, *For a New Liberty*, Macmillan, 1973. Reprinted with permission of the Ludwig von Mises Institute and Laissez Faire Books.

involves. For centuries the State has enslaved people into its armed battalions and called it "conscription" in the "national service." For centuries the State has robbed people at bayonet point and called it "taxation." In fact, if you wish to know how libertarians regard the State and any of its acts, simply think of the State as a criminal band, and all of the libertarian attitudes will logically fall into place.

Let us consider, for example, what it is that sharply distinguishes government from all other organizations in society. Many political scientists and sociologists have blurred this vital distinction, and refer to all organizations and groups as hierarchical, structured, "governmental," etc. Left-wing anarchists, for example, will oppose equally government *and* private organizations such as corporations on the ground that each is equally "elitist" and "coercive." But the "rightist" libertarian is not opposed to inequality, and his concept of "coercion" applies only to the use of violence. The libertarian sees a crucial distinction between government, whether central, state, or local, and all other institutions in society. Or rather, two crucial distinctions. First, every other person or group receives its income by voluntary payment: either by voluntary contribution or gift (such as the local community chest or bridge club), *or* by voluntary purchase of its goods or services on the market (i.e., grocery store owner, baseball player, steel manufacturer, etc.). *Only* the government obtains its income by coercion and violence—i.e., by the direct threat of confiscation or imprisonment if payment is not forthcoming. This coerced levy is "taxation." A second distinction is that, apart from criminal outlaws, *only* the government can use its funds to commit violence against its own or any other subjects; only the government can prohibit pornography, compel a religious observance, or put people in jail for selling goods at a higher price than the government deems fit. Both distinctions, of course, can be summed up as: *only* the government, in society, is empowered to aggress against the property rights of its subjects, whether to extract revenue, to impose its moral code, or to kill those with whom it disagrees. Furthermore, any and all governments, even the least despotic, have always obtained the bulk of their income from the coercive taxing power. And historically, by far the overwhelming portion of all enslavement and murder in the history of the world have come from the hands of government. And since we have seen that the central thrust of the libertarian is to oppose all aggression against the rights of person and property, the libertarian necessarily opposes the institution of the State as the inherent and overwhelmingly the most important enemy of those precious rights.

There is another reason why State aggression has been far more important than private, a reason apart from the greater organization and central mobilizing of resources that the rulers of the State can impose. The reason is the absence of any check upon State depredation, a check that does exist when we have to worry about muggers or the Mafia. To guard against private criminals we have been able to turn to the State and its police; but who can guard us against the State itself? No one. For another critical distinction of the State is that it compels the monopolization of the service of protection; the State arrogates to itself a virtual monopoly of violence and of ultimate decision-making in society. If we don't like the decisions of the State courts, for example, there are no other agencies of protection to which we may turn.

It is true that, in the United States, at least, we have a constitution that imposes strict limits on some powers of government. But, as we have discovered in the past century, no constitution can interpret or enforce itself; it must be interpreted by *men*. And if the ultimate power to interpret a constitution is given to the government's own Supreme Court, then the inevitable tendency is for the Court to continue to place its imprimatur on ever-broader powers for its own government. Furthermore, the highly touted "checks and balances" and "separation of powers" in the American government are flimsy indeed, since in the final analysis all of these divisions are part of the same government and are governed by the same set of rulers.

One of America's most brilliant political theorists, John C. Calhoun, wrote prophetically of the inherent tendency of a State to break through the limits of its written constitution:

> A written constitution certainly has many and considerable advantages, but it is a great mistake to suppose that the mere insertion of provisions to restrict and limit the powers of the government, without investing those for whose protection they are inserted with the means of enforcing their observance, will be sufficient to prevent the major and dominant party from abusing its powers. Being the party in possession of the government, they will . . . be in favor of the powers granted by the constitution and opposed to the restrictions intended to limit them. As the major and dominant parties, they will have no need of these restrictions for their protection. . . .
>
> The minor or weaker party, on the contrary, would take the opposite direction and regard them as essential to their protection against the dominant party. . . . But where there are no means by which they could compel the major party to observe the restrictions, the only resort left them would be a strict construction of the constitution. . . . To this the major party would oppose a liberal construction—one which would give to the words of the grant the broadest meaning of which they were susceptible. It would then be construction against construction—the one to contract and the other to enlarge the powers of the government to the utmost. But of what possible avail could the strict construction of the minor party be, against the liberal interpretation of the major, when the one would have all the powers of the government to carry its construction into effect and the other be deprived of all means of enforcing its construction? In a contest so unequal, the result would not be doubtful. The party in favor of the restrictions would be overpowered. . . . The end of the contest would be the subversion of the constitution . . . the restrictions would ultimately be annulled and the government be converted into one of unlimited powers.
>
> Nor would the division of government into separate and, as it regards each other, independent departments prevent this result . . . as each and all the departments— and, of course, the entire government—would be under the control of the numerical majority, it is too clear to require explanation that a mere distribution of its powers among its agents or representatives could do little or nothing to counteract its tendency to oppression and abuse of powers.[1]

---

[1] John C. Calhoun, *A Disquisition on Government* (New York: Liberal Arts Press, 1953), pp. 25–27.

But why worry about the weakness of limits on governmental power? Especially in a "democracy," in the phrase so often used by American liberals in their heyday before the mid-1960s when doubts began to creep into the liberal utopia: "Are *we* not the government?" In the phrase "we are the government," the useful collective term "we" has enabled an ideological camouflage to be thrown over the naked exploitative reality of political life. For if *we* truly *are* the government, then *anything* a government does to an individual is not only just and not tyrannical; it is also "voluntary" on the part of the individual concerned. If the government has incurred a huge public debt which must be paid by taxing one group on behalf of another, this reality of burden is conveniently obscured by blithely saying that "we owe it to ourselves" (but *who* are the "we" and *who* the "ourselves"?). If the government drafts a man, or even throws him into jail for dissident opinions, then he is only "doing it to himself" and therefore nothing improper has occurred. Under this reasoning, then, Jews murdered by the Nazi government were *not* murdered; they must have "committed suicide," since they *were* the government (which was democratically chosen), and therefore anything the government did to them was only voluntary on their part. But there is no way out of such grotesqueries for those supporters of government who see the State merely as a benevolent and voluntary agent of the public.

And so we must conclude that "we" are *not* the government; the government is *not* "us." The government does not in any accurate sense "represent" the majority of the people, but even if it did, even if 90% of the people decided to murder or enslave the other 10%, this would *still* be murder and slavery, and would not be voluntary suicide or enslavement on the part of the oppressed minority. Crime is crime, aggression against rights is aggression, no matter how many citizens agree to the oppression. There is nothing sacrosanct about the majority; the lynch mob, too, is the majority in its own domain.

But while, as in the lynch mob, the majority can become actively tyrannical and aggressive, the normal and continuing condition of the State is *oligarchic* rule: rule by a coercive elite which has managed to gain control of the State machinery. There are two basic reasons for this: one is the inequality and division of labor inherent in the nature of man, which gives rise to an "Iron Law of Oligarchy" in all of man's activities; and second is the parasitic nature of the State enterprise itself.

We have said that the individualist is not an egalitarian. Part of the reason for this is the individualist's insight into the vast diversity and individuality within mankind, a diversity that has the chance to flower and expand as civilization and living standards progress. Individuals differ in ability and in interest both within and between occupations; and hence, in all occupations and walks of life, whether it be steel production or the organization of a bridge club, leadership in the activity will inevitably be assumed by a relative handful of the most able and energetic, while the remaining majority will form themselves into rank-and-file followers. This truth applies to all activities, whether they are beneficial or malevolent (as in criminal organizations). Indeed, the discovery of the Iron Law of Oligarchy was made by the Italian sociologist Robert Michels, who found that the Social Democratic Party of Germany, despite its rhetorical commitment to egalitarianism, was rigidly oligarchical and hierarchical in its actual functioning.

A second basic reason for the oligarchic rule of the State is its parasitic nature—the fact that it lives coercively off the production of the citizenry. To be successful to its practitioners, the fruits of parasitic exploitation must be confined to a relative minority, otherwise a meaningless plunder of all by all would result in no gains for anyone. Nowhere has the coercive and parasitic nature of the State been more clearly limned than by the great late nineteenth-century German sociologist, Franz Oppenheimer. Oppenheimer pointed out that there are two and only two mutually exclusive means for man to obtain wealth. One, the method of production and voluntary exchange, the method of the free market, Oppenheimer termed the "economic means"; the other, the method of robbery by the use of violence, he called the "political means." The political means is clearly parasitic, for it requires previous production for the exploiters to confiscate, and it subtracts from instead of adding to the total production in society. Oppenheimer then proceeded to define the State as the "organization of the political means"—the systematization of the predatory process over a given territorial area.[2] . . .

If the State is a group of plunderers, *who* then constitutes the State? Clearly, the ruling elite consists at any time of (a) the full-time *apparatus*—the kings, politicians, and bureaucrats who man and operate the State; and (b) the groups who have maneuvered to gain privileges, subsidies, and benefices from the State. The remainder of society constitutes the ruled. It was, again, John C. Calhoun who saw with crystal clarity that, no matter how small the power of government, no matter how low the tax burden or how equal its distribution, the very nature of government creates two unequal and inherently conflicting classes in society: those who, on net, *pay* the taxes (the "tax-payers"), and those who, on net, *live off* taxes (the "tax-consumers"). Suppose that the government imposes a low and seemingly equally distributed tax to pay for building a dam. This very act takes money from most of the public to pay it out to net "tax-consumers": the bureaucrats who run the operation, the contractors and workers who build the dam, etc. . . .

If states have everywhere been run by an oligarchic group of predators, how have they been able to maintain their rule over the mass of the population? The answer, as the philosopher David Hume pointed out over two centuries ago, is that in the long run *every* government, no matter how dictatorial, rests on the support of the majority of its subjects. Now this does not of course render these governments "voluntary," since the very existence of the tax and other coercive powers shows how much compulsion the State must exercise. Nor does the majority support have to be eager and enthusiastic approval; it could well be mere passive acquiescence and resignation. The conjunction in the famous phrase "death and taxes" implies a passive and resigned acceptance to the assumed inevitability of the State and its taxation. . . .

---

[2]Franz Oppenheimer, *The State* (New York: Vanguard Press, 1926), pp. 24–27 and passim.

Contemporary Issues

*Free Speech
and Pornography*

35. Pornography, Oppression, and Freedom: A Closer Look

Helen E. Longino

Helen E. Longino (1944–   ), professor of philosophy and women's studies at the University of Minnesota, is one of the founding editors of Hypatia: A Journal of Feminist Philosophy *and has authored books and articles in the areas of feminist philosophy and philosophy of science.*

I. Introduction

The much-touted sexual revolution of the 1960s and 1970s not only freed various modes of sexual behavior from the constraints of social disapproval, but also made possible a flood of pornographic material. According to figures provided by WAVPM (Women Against Violence in Pornography and Media), the number of pornographic magazines available at newsstands has grown from zero in 1953 to forty in 1977, while sales of pornographic films in Los Angeles alone have grown from $15 million in 1969 to $85 million in 1976.[1]

Traditionally, pornography was condemned as immoral because it presented sexually explicit material in a manner designed to appeal to "prurient interests" or a "morbid" interest in nudity and sexuality, material which furthermore lacked any redeeming social value and which exceeded "customary limits of candor." While these phrases, taken from a definition of "obscenity" proposed in the 1954 American Law Institute's *Model Penal Code*,[2] require some criteria of application to eliminate vagueness, it seems that what is objectionable is the explicit description or representation of bodily parts or sexual behavior for the purpose of inducing sexual

[1]*Women Against Violence in Pornography and Media Newspage*, Vol. II, No. 5, June 1978; and Judith Reisman in *Women Against Violence in Pornography and Media Proposal.*
[2]American Law Institute Model Penal Code, sec. 251.4.

stimulation or pleasure on the part of the reader or viewer. This kind of objection is part of a sexual ethic that subordinates sex to procreation and condemns all sexual interactions outside of legitimated marriage. It is this code which was the primary target of the sexual revolutionaries in the 1960s, and which has given way in many areas to more open standards of sexual behavior.

One of the beneficial results of the sexual revolution has been a growing acceptance of the distinction between questions of sexual mores and questions of morality. This distinction underlies the old slogan, "Make love, not war," and takes harm to others as the defining characteristic of immorality. What is immoral is behavior which causes injury to or violation of another person or people. Such injury may be physical or it may be psychological. To cause pain to another, to lie to another, to hinder another in the exercise of her or his rights, to exploit another, to degrade another, to misrepresent and slander another are instances of immoral behavior. Masturbation or engaging voluntarily in sexual intercourse with another consenting adult of the same or the other sex, as long as neither injury nor violation of either individual or another is involved, [is] not immoral. Some sexual behavior is morally objectionable, but not because of its sexual character. Thus, adultery is immoral not because it involves sexual intercourse with someone to whom one is not legally married, but because it involves breaking a promise (of sexual and emotional fidelity to one's spouse). Sadistic, abusive, or forced sex is immoral because it injures and violates another.

The detachment of sexual chastity from moral virtue implies that we cannot condemn forms of sexual behavior merely because they strike us as distasteful or subversive of the Protestant work ethic, or because they depart from standards of behavior we have individually adopted. It has thus seemed to imply that no matter how offensive we might find pornography, we must tolerate it in the name of freedom from illegitimate repression. I wish to argue that this is not so, that pornography is immoral because it is harmful to people.

II. What Is Pornography?

I define pornography as *verbal or pictorial explicit representations of sexual behavior that*, in the words of the Commission on Obscenity and Pornography, *have as a distinguishing characteristic "the degrading and demeaning portrayal of the role and status of the human female . . . as a mere sexual object to be exploited and manipulated sexually."*[3] In pornographic books, magazines, and films, women are represented as passive and as slavishly dependent upon men. The role of female characters is limited to the provision of sexual services to men. To the extent that women's sexual pleasure is represented at all, it is subordinated to that of men and is never

---

[3] *Report of the Commission on Obscenity and Pornography* (New York: Bantam Books, 1979), p. 239. The Commission, of course, concluded that the demeaning content of pornography did not adversely affect male attitudes toward women.

an end in itself as is the sexual pleasure of men. What pleases women is the use of their bodies to satisfy male desires. While the sexual objectification of women is common to all pornography, women are the recipients of even worse treatment in violent pornography, in which women characters are killed, tortured, gang-raped, mutilated, bound, and otherwise abused, as a means of providing sexual stimulation or pleasure to the male characters. It is this development which has attracted the attention of feminists and been the stimulus to an analysis of pornography in general.[4]

Not all sexually explicit material is pornography, nor is all material which contains representations of sexual abuse and degradation pornography.

A representation of a sexual encounter between adult persons which is characterized by mutual respect is, once we have disentangled sexuality and morality, not morally objectionable. Such a representation would be one in which the desires and experiences of each participant were regarded by the other participants as having a validity and a subjective importance equal to those of the individual's own desire and experiences. In such an encounter, each participant acknowledges the other participant's basic human dignity and personhood. Similarly, a representation of a nude human body (in whole or in part) in such a manner that the person shown maintains self-respect—e.g., is not portrayed in a degrading position—would not be morally objectionable. The educational films of the National Sex Forum, as well as a certain amount of erotic literature and art, fall into this category. While some erotic materials are beyond the standards of modesty held by some individuals, they are not for this reason immoral.

A representation of a sexual encounter which is not characterized by mutual respect, in which at least one of the parties is treated in a manner beneath her or his dignity as a human being, is no longer simple erotica. That a representation is of degrading behavior does not in itself, however, make it pornographic. Whether or not it is pornographic is a function of contextual features. Books and films may contain descriptions or representations of a rape in order to explore the consequences of such an assault upon its victim. What is being shown is abusive or degrading behavior which attempts to deny the humanity and dignity of the person assaulted, yet the context surrounding the representation, through its exploration of the consequences of the act, acknowledges and reaffirms her dignity. Such books and films, far from being pornographic, are (or can be) highly moral, and fall into the category of moral realism.

What makes a work a work of pornography, then, is not simply its representation of degrading and abusive sexual encounters, but its implicit, if not explicit, approval and recommendation of sexual behavior that is immoral, i.e., that physically or psychologically violates the personhood of one of the participants. Pornography, then, is verbal or pictorial material which represents or describes sexual behavior that is degrading or abusive to one or more of the

---

[4]Among recent feminist discussions are Diana Russell, "Pornography: A Feminist Perspective" and Susan Griffin, "On Pornography," *Chrysalis*, Vol. I, No. 4, 1978; and Ann Garry, "Pornography and Respect for Women," *Social Theory and Practice*, Vol. 4, Spring 1978, pp. 395–421.

participants *in such a way as to endorse the degradation*. The participants so treated in virtually all heterosexual pornography are women or children, so heterosexual pornography is, as a matter of fact, material which endorses sexual behavior that is degrading and/or abusive to women and children. As I use the term "sexual behavior," this includes sexual encounters between persons, behavior which produces sexual stimulation or pleasure for one of the participants, and behavior which is preparatory to or invites sexual activity. Behavior that is degrading or abusive includes physical harm or abuse, and physical or psychological coercion. In addition, behavior which ignores or devalues the real interests, desires, and experiences of one or more participants in any way is degrading. Finally, that a person has chosen or consented to be harmed, abused, or subjected to coercion does not alter the degrading character of such behavior.

Pornography communicates its endorsement of the behavior it represents by various features of the pornographic context: the degradation of the female characters is represented as providing pleasure to the participant males and, even worse, to the participant females, and there is no suggestion that this sort of treatment of others is inappropriate to their status as human beings. These two features are together sufficient to constitute endorsement of the represented behavior. The contextual features which make material pornographic are intrinsic to the material. In addition to these, extrinsic features, such as the purpose for which the material is presented—i.e., the sexual arousal/pleasure/satisfaction of its (mostly) male consumers—or an accompanying text, may reinforce or make explicit the endorsement. Representations which in and of themselves do not show or endorse degrading behavior may be put into a pornographic context by juxtaposition with others that are degrading, or by a text which invites or recommends degrading behavior toward the subject represented. In such a case the whole complex—the series of representations or representations with text—is pornographic.

The distinction I have sketched is one that applies most clearly to sequential material—a verbal or pictorial (filmed) story—which represents an action and provides a temporal context for it. In showing the before and after, a narrator or filmmaker has plenty of opportunity to acknowledge the dignity of the person violated or clearly to refuse to do so. It is somewhat more difficult to apply the distinction to single still representations. The contextual features cited above, however, are clearly present in still photographs or pictures that glamorize degradation and sexual violence. Phonograph album covers and advertisements offer some prime examples of such glamorization. Their representations of women in chains (the Ohio Players), or bound by ropes and black and blue (the Rolling Stones) are considered high-quality commercial "art" and glossily prettify the violence they represent. Since the standard function of prettification and glamorization is the communication of desirability, these albums and ads are communicating the desirability of violence against women. Representations of women bound or chained, particularly those of women bound in such a way as to make their breasts, or genital or anal areas vulnerable to any passerby, endorse the scene they represent by the absence of any indication that this treatment of women is in any way inappropriate.

To summarize: Pornography is not just the explicit representation or description of sexual behavior, nor even the explicit representation or description of sexual behavior which is degrading and/or abusive to women. Rather, it is material that explicitly represents or describes degrading and abusive sexual behavior so as to endorse and/or recommend the behavior as described. The contextual features, moreover, which communicate such endorsement are intrinsic to the material; that is, they are features whose removal or alteration would change the representation or description.

This account of pornography is underlined by the etymology and original meaning of the word "pornography." *The Oxford English Dictionary* defines pornography as "Description of the life, manners, etc. of prostitutes and their patrons [from πόρνη (porne) meaning "harlot" and γράφειν (graphein) meaning "to write"]; hence the expression or suggestion of obscene or unchaste subjects in literature or art."[5]

Let us consider the first part of the definition for a moment. In the transactions between prostitutes and their clients, prostitutes are paid, directly or indirectly, for the use of their bodies by the client for sexual pleasure.[6] Traditionally males have obtained from female prostitutes what they could not or did not wish to get from their wives or women friends, who, because of the character of their relation to the male, must be accorded some measure of human respect. While there are limits to what treatment is seen as appropriate toward women as wives or women friends, the prostitute as prostitute exists to provide sexual pleasure to males. The female characters of contemporary pornography also exist to provide pleasure to males, but in the pornographic context no pretense is made to regard them as parties to a contractual arrangement. Rather, the anonymity of these characters makes each one Everywoman, thus suggesting not only that all women are appropriate subjects for the enactment of the most bizarre and demeaning male sexual fantasies, but also that this is their primary purpose. The recent escalation of violence in pornography—the presentation of scenes of bondage, rape, and torture of women for the sexual stimulation of the male characters or male viewers—while shocking in itself, is from this point of view merely a more vicious extension of a genre whose success depends on treating women in a manner beneath their dignity as human beings.

III. Pornography: Lies and Violence Against Women

What is wrong with pornography, then, is its degrading and dehumanizing portrayal of women (and *not* its sexual content). Pornography, by its very nature, requires that women be subordinate to men and mere instruments for the fulfillment of male fantasies. To accomplish this, pornography must lie. Pornography lies when it says that our sexual life is or ought to be subordinate to the service of men, that

---

[5]*The Oxford English Dictionary*, Compact Edition (London: Oxford University Press, 1971), p. 2242.
[6]In talking of prostitution here, I refer to the concept of, rather than the reality of, prostitution. The same is true of my remarks about relationships between women and their husbands or men friends.

our pleasure consists in pleasing men and not ourselves, that we are depraved, that we are fit subjects for rape, bondage, torture, and murder. Pornography lies explicitly about women's sexuality, and through such lies fosters more lies about our humanity, our dignity, and our personhood.

Moreover, since nothing is alleged to justify the treatment of the female characters of pornography save their womanhood, pornography depicts all women as fit objects of violence by virtue of their sex alone. Because it is simply being female that, in the pornographic vision, justifies being violated, the lies of pornography are lies about all women. Each work of pornography is on its own libelous and defamatory, yet gains power through being reinforced by every other pornographic work. The sheer number of pornographic productions expands the moral issue to include not only assessing the morality or immorality of individual works, but also the meaning and force of the mass production of pornography.

The pornographic view of women is thoroughly entrenched in a booming portion of the publishing, film, and recording industries, reaching and affecting not only all who look to such sources for sexual stimulation, but also those of us who are forced into an awareness of it as we peruse magazines at newsstands and record albums in record stores, as we check the entertainment sections of city newspapers, or even as we approach a counter to pay for groceries. It is not necessary to spend a great deal of time reading or viewing pornographic material to absorb its male-centered definition of women. No longer confined within plain brown wrappers, it jumps out from billboards that proclaim "Live X-rated Girls!" or "Angels in Pain" or "Hot and Wild," and from magazine covers displaying a woman's genital area being spread open to the viewer by her own fingers.[7] Thus, even men who do not frequent pornographic shops and movie houses are supported in the sexist objectification of women by their environment. Women, too, are crippled by internalizing as self-images those that are presented to us by pornographers. Isolated from one another and with no source of support for an alternative view of female sexuality, we may not always find the strength to resist a message that dominates the common cultural media.

The entrenchment of pornography in our culture also gives it a significance quite beyond its explicit sexual messages. To suggest, as pornography does, that the primary purpose of women is to provide sexual pleasure to men is to deny that women are independently human or have a status equal to that of men. It is, moreover, to deny our equality at one of the most intimate levels of human experience. This denial is especially powerful in a hierarchical, class society such as ours, in which individuals feel good about themselves by feeling superior to others. Men in our society have a vested interest in maintaining their belief in the inferiority of the female sex, so that no matter how oppressed and exploited by the society in which they live and work, they can feel that they are at least superior to someone or some category of individuals—a woman or women. Pornography, by presenting women as wanton, depraved, and made for the sexual use of men, caters directly

---

[7]This was a full-color magazine cover seen in a rack at the check-out counter of a corner delicatessen.

to that interest.[8] The very intimate nature of sexuality which makes pornography so corrosive also protects it from explicit public discussion. The consequent lack of any explicit social disavowal of the pornographic image of women enables this image to continue fostering sexist attitudes even as the society publicly proclaims its (as yet timid) commitment to sexual equality.

In addition to finding a connection between the pornographic view of women and the denial to us of our full human rights, women are beginning to connect the consumption of pornography with committing rape and other acts of sexual violence against women. Contrary to the findings of the Commission on Obscenity and Pornography a growing body of research is documenting (1) a correlation between exposure to representations of violence and the committing of violent acts generally, and (2) a correlation between exposure to pornographic materials and the committing of sexually abusive or violent acts against women.[9] While more study is needed to establish precisely what the causal relations are, clearly so-called hard-core pornography is not innocent.

From "snuff" films and miserable magazines in pornographic stores to *Hustler*, to phonograph album covers and advertisements, to *Vogue*, pornography has come to occupy its own niche in the communications and entertainment media and to acquire a quasi-institutional character (signaled by the use of diminutives such as "porn" or "porno" to refer to pornographic material, as though such familiar naming could take the hurt out). Its acceptance by the mass media, whatever the motivation, means a cultural endorsement of its message. As much as the materials themselves, the social tolerance of these degrading and distorted images of women in such quantities is harmful to us, since it indicates a general willingness to see women in ways incompatible with our fundamental human dignity and thus to justify treating us in those ways.[10] The tolerance of pornographic representations of the rape, bondage, and torture of women helps to create and maintain a climate more tolerant of the actual physical abuse of women.[11] The tendency on the part of

---

[8]Pornography thus becomes another tool of capitalism. One feature of some contemporary pornography—the use of Black and Asian women in both still photographs and films—exploits the racism as well as the sexism of its white consumers. For a discussion of the interplay between racism and sexism under capitalism as it relates to violent crimes against women, see Angela Y. Davis, "Rape, Racism, and the Capitalist Setting," *The Black Scholar*, Vol. 9, No. 7, April 1978.

[9]Urie Bronfenbrenner, *Two Worlds of Childhood* (New York: Russell Sage Foundation, 1970); H. J. Eysenck and D. K. B. Nias, *Sex, Violence and the Media* (New York: St. Martin's Press, 1978); and Michael Goldstein, Harold Kant, and John Hartman, *Pornography and Sexual Deviance* (Berkeley: University of California Press, 1973); and the papers by Diana Russell, Pauline Bart, and Irene Diamond included in this volume.

[10]This tolerance has a linguistic parallel in the growing acceptance and use of nonhuman nouns such as "chick," "bird," "filly," "fox," "doll," "babe," "skirt," etc., to refer to women, and of verbs of harm such as "fuck," "screw," "bang" to refer to sexual intercourse. See Robert Baker and Frederick Elliston, "'Pricks' and 'Chicks': A Plea for Persons." *Philosophy and Sex* (Buffalo, N.Y.: Prometheus Books, 1975).

[11]This is supported by the fact that in Denmark the number of rapes committed has increased while the number of rapes reported to the authorities has decreased over the past twelve years. See *WAVPM Newspage*, Vol. II, No. 5, June, 1978, quoting M. Harry, "Denmark Today—The Causes and Effects of Sexual Liberty" (paper presented to The Responsible Society, London, England, 1976). See also Eysenck and Nias, *Sex, Violence and the Media* (New York: St. Martin's Press, 1978), pp. 120–124.

the legal system to view the victim of a rape as responsible for the crime against her is but one manifestation of this.

In sum, pornography is injurious to women in at least three distinct ways:

1. Pornography, especially violent pornography, is implicated in the committing of crimes of violence against women.
2. Pornography is the vehicle for the dissemination of a deep and vicious lie about women. It is defamatory and libelous.
3. The diffusion of such a distorted view of women's nature in our society as it exists today supports sexist (i.e., male-centered) attitudes, and thus reinforces the oppression and exploitation of women.

Society's tolerance of pornography, especially pornography on the contemporary massive scale, reinforces each of these modes of injury: By not disavowing the lie, it supports the male-centered myth that women are inferior and subordinate creatures. Thus, it contributes to the maintenance of a climate tolerant of both psychological and physical violence against women.

IV. Pornography and the Law

> Congress shall make no law respecting the establishment of religion, or prohibiting the free exercise thereof; or abridging the freedom of speech, or of the press; or the right of the people peaceably to assemble, and to petition the Government for a redress of grievances.—First Amendment, Bill of Rights of the United States Constitution

Pornography is clearly a threat to women. Each of the modes of injury cited above offers sufficient reason at least to consider proposals for the social and legal control of pornography. The almost universal response from progressives to such proposals is that constitutional guarantees of freedom of speech and privacy preclude recourse to law.[12] While I am concerned about the erosion of constitutional rights and also think for many reasons that great caution must be exercised before undertaking a legal campaign against pornography, I find objections to such a campaign that are based on appeals to the First Amendment or to a right to privacy ultimately unconvincing.

Much of the defense of the pornographer's right to publish seems to assume that, while pornography may be tasteless and vulgar, it is basically an entertainment that harms no one but its consumers, who may at worst suffer from the debasement of their taste; and that therefore those who argue for its control are demanding an unjustifiable abridgment of the rights to freedom of speech of those who

---

[12]Cf. Marshall Cohen, "The Case Against Censorship," *The Public Interest*, No. 22, Winter 1971, reprinted in John R. Burr and Milton Goldinger, *Philosophy and Contemporary Issues* (New York: Macmillan, 1976), and Justice William Brennan's dissenting opinion in *Paris Adult Theater I* v. *Slaton*, 431 U.S. 49.

make and distribute pornographic materials and of the rights to privacy of their customers. The account of pornography given above shows that the assumptions of this position are false. Nevertheless, even some who acknowledge its harmful character feel that it is granted immunity from social control by the First Amendment, or that the harm that would ensue from its control outweighs the harm prevented by its control.

There are three ways of arguing that control of pornography is incompatible with adherence to constitutional rights. The first argument claims that regulating pornography involves an unjustifiable interference in the private lives of individuals. The second argument takes the First Amendment as a basic principle constitutive of our form of government, and claims that the production and distribution of pornographic material, as a form of speech, is an activity protected by that amendment. The third argument claims not that the pornographer's rights are violated, but that others' rights will be if controls against pornography are instituted.

The privacy argument is the easiest to dispose of. Since the open commerce in pornographic materials is an activity carried out in the public sphere, the publication and distribution of such materials, unlike their use by individuals, is not protected by rights to privacy. The distinction between the private consumption of pornographic material and the production and distribution of, or open commerce in it, is sometimes blurred by defenders of pornography. But I may entertain, in the privacy of my mind, defamatory opinions about another person, even though I may not broadcast them. So one might create without restraint—as long as no one were harmed in the course of preparing them—pornographic materials for one's personal use, but be restrained from reproducing and distributing them. In both cases what one is doing—in the privacy of one's mind or basement—may indeed be deplorable, but immune from legal proscription. Once the activity becomes public, however—i.e., once it involves others—it is no longer protected by the same rights that protect activities in the private sphere.[13]

In considering the second argument (that control of pornography, private or public, is wrong in principle), it seems important to determine whether we consider the right to freedom of speech to be absolute and unqualified. If it is, then obviously all speech, including pornography, is entitled to protection. But the right is, in the first place, not an unqualified right: There are several kinds of speech not protected by the First Amendment, including the incitement to violence in volatile circumstances, the solicitation of crimes, perjury and misrepresentation, slander, libel, and false advertising.[14] That there are forms of proscribed speech shows that we accept limitations on the right to freedom of speech if such speech, as do the forms listed, impinges on other rights. The manufacture and distribution of

---

[13]Thus, the right to use such materials in the privacy of one's home, which has been upheld by the United States Supreme Court (*Stanley* v. *Georgia*, 394 U.S. 557), does not include the right to purchase them or to have them available in the commercial market. See also *Paris Adult Theater I* v. *Slaton*, 431 U.S. 49.

[14]The Supreme Court has also traditionally included obscenity in this category. As not everyone agrees it should be included, since as defined by statutes, it is a highly vague concept, and since the grounds accepted by the Court for including it miss the point, I prefer to omit it from this list.

material which defames and threatens all members of a class by its recommenda-tion of abusive and degrading behavior toward some members of that class simply in virtue of their membership in it seems a clear candidate for inclusion on the list. The right is therefore not an unqualified one.

Nor is it an absolute or fundamental right, underived from any other right: If it were there would not be exceptions or limitations. The first ten amendments were added to the Constitution as a way of guaranteeing the "blessings of liberty" men-tioned in its preamble, to protect citizens against the unreasonable usurpation of power by the state. The specific rights mentioned in the First Amendment—those of religion, speech, assembly, press, petition—reflect the recent experiences of the makers of the Constitution under colonial government as well as a sense of what was and is required generally to secure liberty.

It may be objected that the right to freedom of speech is fundamental in that it is part of what we mean by liberty and not a right that is derivative from a right to liberty. In order to meet this objection, it is useful to consider a distinction explained by Ronald Dworkin in his book *Taking Rights Seriously*.[15] As Dworkin points out, the word "liberty" is used in two distinct, if related, senses: as "license," i.e., the freedom from legal constraints to do as one pleases, in some contexts; and as "independence," i.e., "the status of a person as independent and equal rather than subservient," in others. Failure to distinguish between these senses in discus-sions of rights and freedoms is fatal to clarity and understanding.

If the right to free speech is understood as a partial explanation of what is meant by liberty, then liberty is perceived as license: The right to do as one pleases includes a right to speak as one pleases. But license is surely not a condition the First Amendment is designed to protect. We not only tolerate but require legal con-straints on liberty as license when we enact laws against rape, murder, assault, theft, etc. If everyone did exactly as she or he pleased at any given time, we would have chaos if not lives, as Hobbes put it, that are "nasty, brutish, and short." We accept government to escape, not to protect, this condition.

If, on the other hand, by liberty is meant independence, then freedom of speech is not necessarily a part of liberty; rather, it is a means to it. The right to freedom of speech is not a fundamental, absolute right, but one derivative from, possessed in virtue of, the more basic right to independence. Taking this view of liberty requires providing arguments showing that the more specific rights we claim are necessary to guarantee our status as persons "independent and equal rather than subservient." In the context of government, we understand independence to be the freedom of each individual to participate as an equal among equals in the determination of how she or he is to be governed. Freedom of speech in this context means that an indi-vidual may not only entertain beliefs concerning government privately, but may express them publicly. We express our opinions about taxes, disarmament, wars, social-welfare programs, the function of the police, civil rights, and so on. Our right to freedom of speech includes the right to criticize the government and to protest

---

[15]Ronald Dworkin, *Taking Rights Seriously* (Cambridge: Harvard University Press, 1977), p. 262.

against various forms of injustice and the abuse of power. What we wish to protect is the free expression of ideas even when they are unpopular. What we do not always remember is that speech has functions other than the expression of ideas.

Regarding the relationship between a right to freedom of speech and the publication and distribution of pornographic materials, there are two points to be made. In the first place, the latter activity is hardly an exercise of the right to the free expression of ideas as understood above. In the second place, to the degree that the tolerance of material degrading to women supports and reinforces the attitude that women are not fit to participate as equals among equals in the political life of their communities, and that the prevalence of such an attitude effectively prevents women from so participating, the absolute and fundamental right of women to liberty (political independence) is violated.

This second argument against the suppression of pornographic material, then, rests on a premise that must be rejected, namely, that the right to freedom of speech is a right to utter anything one wants. It thus fails to show that the production and distribution of such material is an activity protected by the First Amendment. Furthermore, an examination of the issues involved leads to the conclusion that tolerance of this activity violates the rights of women to political independence.

The third argument (which expresses concern that curbs on pornography are the first step toward political censorship) runs into the same ambiguity that besets the arguments based on principle. These arguments generally have as an underlying assumption that the maximization of freedom is a worthy social goal. Control of pornography diminishes freedom—directly the freedom of pornographers, indirectly that of all of us. But again, what is meant by "freedom"? It cannot be that what is to be maximized is license—as the goal of a social group whose members probably have at least some incompatible interests, such a goal would be internally inconsistent. If, on the other hand, the maximization of political independence is the goal, then that is in no way enhanced by, and may be endangered by, the tolerance of pornography. To argue that the control of pornography would create a precedent for suppressing political speech is thus to confuse license with political independence. In addition, it ignores a crucial basis for the control of pornography, i.e., its character as libelous speech. The prohibition of such speech is justified by the need for protection from the injury (psychological as well as physical or economic) that results from libel. A very different kind of argument would be required to justify curtailing the right to speak our minds about the institutions which govern us. As long as such distinctions are insisted upon, there is little danger of the government's using the control of pornography as precedent for curtailing political speech.

In summary, neither as a matter of principle nor in the interests of maximizing liberty can it be supposed that there is an intrinsic right to manufacture and distribute pornographic material.

The only other conceivable source of protection for pornography would be a general right to do what we please as long as the rights of others are respected. Since the production and distribution of pornography violates the rights of women—to respect and to freedom from defamation, among others—this protection is not available.

V. Conclusion

I have defined pornography in such a way as to distinguish it from erotica and from moral realism, and have argued that it is defamatory and libelous toward women, that it condones crimes against women, and that it invites tolerance of the social, economic, and cultural oppression of women. The production and distribution of pornographic material is thus a social and moral wrong. Contrasting both the current volume of pornographic production and its growing infiltration of the communications media with the status of women in this culture makes clear the necessity for its control. Since the goal of controlling pornography does not conflict with constitutional rights, a common obstacle to action is removed.

Appeals for action against pornography are sometimes brushed aside with the claim that such action is a diversion from the primary task of feminists—the elimination of sexism and of sexual inequality. This approach focuses on the enjoyment rather than the manufacture of pornography, and sees it as merely a product of sexism which will disappear when the latter has been overcome and the sexes are socially and economically equal. Pornography cannot be separated from sexism in this way: Sexism is not just a set of attitudes regarding the inferiority of women but the behaviors and social and economic rules that manifest such attitudes. Both the manufacture and distribution of pornography and the enjoyment of it are instances of sexist behavior. The enjoyment of pornography on the part of individuals will presumably decline as such individuals begin to accord women their status as fully human. A cultural climate which tolerates the degrading representation of women is not a climate which facilitates the development of respect for women. Furthermore, the demand for pornography is stimulated not just by the sexism of individuals but by the pornography industry itself. Thus, both as a social phenomenon and in its effect on individuals, pornography, far from being a mere product, nourishes sexism. The campaign against it is an essential component of women's struggle for legal, economic, and social equality, one which requires the support of all feminists.*

*Many women helped me to develop and crystallize the ideas presented in this paper. I would especially like to thank Michele Farrell, Laura Lederer, Pamela Miller, and Dianne Romain for their comments in conversation and on the first written draft. Portions of this material were presented orally to members of the Society for Women in Philosophy and to participants in the workshops on "What Is Pornography?" at the Conference on Feminist Perspectives on Pornography, San Francisco, November 17, 18, and 19, 1978. Their discussion was invaluable in helping me to see problems and to clarify the ideas presented here.

36. Pornography

Jan Narveson

Jan F. Narveson (1936–   ), professor of philosophy at the University of Waterloo, Ontario, Canada, has written books and articles on ethics and on social and political philosophy.

Pornography is the depiction, by visual, literary, or aural means, of subject-matter intended to be sexually stimulating, when that depiction is for the *purpose* of such stimulation. Pornography is a sort of depictional aphrodisiac. Or at least, that was once the idea. Recently, the depiction of nonsexual violence against people has also come to be described as pornographic. Although we will in general have the sexual type in mind in the following discussion, the connection, or a supposed connection, between violence and sex is a major part of the conceptual concern with this matter, as we will see.

Official suppression, censorship, and/or strict control over the circulation of pornography has been commonplace in our society for a long time, and remains the principal form of current censorship. Movies are rated, some are suppressed, and others altered by their makers in order to avoid the censor's hand. The same has been true of books, at various times, though currently "hate literature" is a more likely target than pornography. The question that concerns us here is whether such interventions are justified.

Liberal vs. Conservative

Standing against censorship is the *liberal* principle: that people should be able to live the sort of life they choose, exercising their own taste (or lack of it), not being subject to the rule of others. In political terms, the liberal holds that the purpose of a commonwealth is the advancement of the several goods of its members, a point that the conservative agrees with. *But* the liberal adds that the goods in question must be good in the view of the individual members of society, rather than in the view of some self-appointed or state-appointed authority. It is in this full sense that the liberal holds that the state exists for the sake of the citizen, and not the other way around. The conservative, by contrast, holds that in some or a lot of cases, certain people—namely those in power or hoping to be in power—know what is good for us, the people. "We are out for your good, to be sure," say they—but it is *they* who will decide what that good is.

The same distinction is applicable to morality. A liberal morality attributes to individuals the right to live as they please, free of interference from others, subject only to such controls as are necessary to uphold the same freedom for all. A conservative morality, by contrast, holds that there are right or wrong ways of life, that it is our duty to steer people, by force if necessary, into the right ones—and away from the wrong ones—and that what is right and wrong is known independently of the values and interests that people actually have. Of course, which values are the right ones is a subject on which views will vary greatly from one conservative to another.

My characterization of conservatism is probably broader than that prevalent in ordinary usage—if there is any such usage. If a society were to force its subjects to read pornography or engage in nonstandard sex acts, on the ground that those were part of the ideal way of life which all should adhere to, then few would call this "conservative," although it would, on my usage, be precisely that—and at least as objectionable to the liberal as would be the prohibition of such things on a similar ground. For present purposes, however, we needn't worry about that. In this discussion, we will simply take the conservative to hold that the depiction of sexual acts with a view to stimulating sexual sensations may properly be suppressed.

Harm

Everyone agrees that we may insist on someone's not doing x if his doing x would be *harmful* to others. The question is, what constitutes harm? The liberal version of the harm principle is that harm consists in physical damage to the body, to one's property, or to one's civil and political rights. This is the version of the harm principle that leaves us maximally free to live our lives as we see fit, with all that that entails, for better or worse. It does not allow mere "damage" to one's beliefs, for instance, to count as a reason for restricting the offending person's liberty.

We will explore the subject of censorship in the light of this principle, asking what kind of restrictions it would approve, if any, and whether there is any justification for principles more congenial than that to would-be censors.

Disgust

It is obvious enough that there can be a rationale for censorship in *conservative* terms: that someone else's activity in some respect is "abhorrent," or "disgusting," or the like, is taken by the conservative to be a sufficient basis for action to prevent the alleged miscreant from carrying on in the offending manner. How would the conservative try to argue for his claims? Presumably he hopes to persuade you that the sort of life you live if you view pornography, say, is one from which you would recoil if you could just view it properly. But what if you don't recoil? That the consumer of pornography doesn't see it as disgusting is taken by the conservative as evidence of his base nature: question-begging arguments are the conservative's stock in trade. They are appeals to our aesthetic sense, or our sense of propriety, but not appeals that can be backed up with further reasons; we must either take it or leave it. In the case of pornography, for instance, we must either just take it or leave it that such pleasures as people might get from viewing pictures of genitalia or of people engaged in sex acts are "bad" pleasures. But if they really are pleasures, it is going to be difficult to convince the pornographer that they are also bad ones.

Public/Private

If someone professing to be liberal in his views wants to support any censorship, he must search for an argument of a different kind. He must show that use of the materials in question visits some genuine harm on someone. But the only "harm" he is usually able to demonstrate is *offense*: some people, such as himself, are offended by the prospect of others viewing this kind of material.

But offense is surely not enough for this purpose. If it were, we would all be at the mercy of everyone else's whims and tastes. In fact, though, there is a tacit assumption at work here that needs to be brought out. No one could seriously think that offense can't *ever* be sufficient cause to justify restrictive activity on the part of the offended person. If you offend me in my living room, for example, then I would certainly be justified, on that account alone, in showing you the door. You might think me unreasonable, and for that matter you might be right; still, I surely have the right to do that. What makes all the difference is whether the space in which the expression takes place is privately owned or not. If it is, then the owner has the authority to decide what will and won't be said on the premises. But if it is not, then we have a problem, for nonprivate property is either just unowned (which is rare) or *public*, in which case the familiar problems of politics set in.

Our question, then, must concern conduct in public areas, those where we encounter each other routinely. The general idea concerning such areas is that everyone has the right to be there, going to and fro as they please. Nobody can "show the door" to anyone, for no individual or small group of individuals owns the place. That, indeed, is just the trouble. If no one has any more right than any other, on what rational principle can we govern interactions? How do we decide who has to give way in a public space, when presumably both have the right to be there?

It's easy enough to give a partial answer to this. For not everything in a public area is public. You and I are not public property. The perimeters of our bodies, at least, define a frontier beyond which other members of the public may not go even if the area we respectively occupy is a public area. Physical attacks against each other's bodies are prohibited on the same ground that verbal attacks within our houses may be prohibited by the owner. But what about verbal attacks in public places?

We can also usefully distinguish between, say, a verbal attack at a volume that is physically painful and one that is only "painful" in some other sense. But that will take us back to the subject of offense. And here it seems we can again hardly deny its relevance in some cases: offensive verbal attacks are not routinely allowable in public, either. There our discourse ought to be peaceable, not intended to offend. The same can be true regarding our appearance, perhaps. To go forth topless in public, as one woman did in a small Canadian city one hot summer's day, is to try to unilaterally impose a standard of dress (or undress) that is likely to offend many. Are we justified in coercively prohibiting such exhibitions? May we say that those who are offended are merely prudish and have no real reason for their offense? I'm inclined to agree with that, in fact, but it is surely a matter on which opinions may legitimately differ. Thus, there is a question whether we would merely be imposing another standard if we insisted that citizens must put up with displays of public nudity. It seems uncomfortably comparable to an earlier example: *requiring* people to engage in sexually deviant behavior.

That it is impossible to please everyone here is illustrated by the interesting case of the devout Muslim woman, who goes forth in public dressed in heavy veil and robes. She is presumably offended by the carefree attire of most of those around her. But one can easily imagine that some women would actually be offended at the Muslim woman's dress, holding that her costume shows a submission to male domination that is beneath human dignity. The Muslim woman and the feminist are then in a zero-sum game: a given kind of attire will offend one of them only if it won't offend the other. In fact, we are inclined to award both of them the right to dress as they please, requiring both to restrain any offense they might feel, this being the price they pay for going forth in public at all. Yet the would-be nudist is required to wear something in the interests of nonoffense, and there is a problem drawing the line. Why should we cater to the offense of the "prude" when we do not do so regarding the Muslim or the feminist?

Privacy and Porn

Actually, pornographic viewing doesn't take place in public either. All that happens in public is that enough information is made available to the public, in the form of advertising (which, in turn, can be discreetly displayed) to enable some of its members to seek out the private locations in which they can pursue their interests. So long as those locations are clearly identifiable, they can also be avoided by those of differing taste. Privatization enables all parties to be satisfied, it seems. And the liberal does not defend the *public* display of pornography.

Or does she? Here we have to distinguish between what the privatization idea would do if it were thoroughly carried out, and what would happen in the real world if we tried to approximate it—that is, between what philosophers call "ideal," or "perfect compliance" theory, and "partial compliance" theory. Total privatization means that all costs and benefits of an act are borne by the agent. No costs are imposed on anyone, and no one benefits at the expense of anyone else.

Now let us return to our problem. Suppose that all acts of reading or viewing satisfy our privacy requirement. Nobody sees anything that she doesn't want to see, nobody reads anything that she doesn't want to read, and nobody reads or sees anything without the consent of whoever provides it (authors, booksellers, movie-house operators, and so on). Is everything just fine, then? The liberal says Yes. But many think not, and we must look carefully at their proposed reasons.

There are two types of objection to be concerned with here. First, there is the view that some material *inherently demeans* certain people. This, some hold, harms those people sufficiently to justify restriction even on liberal terms. And second, there is a concern with the effects of such material on the consumer's subsequent behavior. His viewing of pornography, for instance, stimulates him to go out and rape people.

These two objections are important, because they are addressed by people who at least claim to be sympathetic with liberalism. We must look closely at them.

Demeaning Depictions

The first objection is advanced, for instance, by many feminists against pornography. Women, they say, are demeaned in such material. They are portrayed as inferior, or as slaves of men, or as mere "sex objects" to be used as men wish. Probably some pornographic literature does not do this, but let us suppose that some does. The interesting question is whether this would provide ground for suppression.

Here's an example to think about: in the Old Testament, a good many groups of people in the then Middle East were portrayed as pretty bad lots. The Philistines, for instance, were depicted as a bunch of yahoos who went around beating up on people until at last courageous little David came along and laid their main champion low with a deft application of high (for the times) technology. Are the people who make this charge proposing, then, that we should outlaw reading of the Old Testament? That book is not a "sacred cow," to be sure; yet very few of those who favor suppression of other literature would take kindly to the thought that it should be suppressed too. Obviously, evil can be portrayed without implying approval.

Falsity

It might be said that the depiction of women in pornography nevertheless does imply approval, and that its depiction is false and thereby creates a false image of women in general. Would this be a ground for objection even if true? I find it difficult to see how any other construal can be put on it than this: that what are claimed to be demeaning portrayals, say of women or of Palestinians, are false. Women are not slavish, passive, and mere sex objects; Palestinians aren't cruel and warlike. For after all, if these claims were actually true, then there is at least some question why it would be held wrong to depict them in those ways.

But if that's the claim about pornography, then the trouble is that we are back to the old arguments for censorship so successfully refuted by John Stuart Mill in his famous *Essay on Liberty*. The fact that statement **p** is *false* cannot be used as a ground for suppression of those who would say it, though it does provide an excellent occasion for refuting it.

This isn't the end of the matter, however. There are truths about people which nevertheless may not be broadcast. Your sex life, for example, is not something the details of which I am entitled to know. We suppose, and for excellent reason, that there is a right of privacy that should not be invaded even if the result would be the publication of any number of true statements. However, this charge would not be sustainable against pornography, provided that it was produced within the confines of our privatization restrictions. For after all, the actors in those films are required by our principles to have participated voluntarily in their production, for example by accepting payment large enough to make it worth their while. On the face of it, we don't as yet have a clear case against pornographic portrayals, however demeaning we may think them to be.

Voluntariness

Proponents of the objection we are considering might well respond to this by claiming that the actresses in question did *not* participate voluntarily. But to make good this claim, which is superficially implausible, they have to stretch the notion of voluntariness well beyond its normal usage. The soldiers from an all-volunteer army who were unfortunate enough to have been killed in battle nevertheless did volunteer. They signed up in full knowledge that their work entailed a risk of death. The actress in a pornographic movie knows what sort of customers will leer at the results; it is up to her to consider whether she is willing to assume all sorts of undignified positions, with that expected result, in return for the proferred fee.

It might be complained that it isn't really up to the actress to decide whether to act in a scene that depicts women in that way: if she acts in it, then that is how they are depicted, whether she intends that or not. But is this a valid complaint? No one can make women that way, just by so depicting them. Nor can anyone plausibly claim to know all women; our actress is, after all, just one woman among others, and women differ. And in any case, the porn actress would surely disclaim any such intention, insisting that she is only portraying one particular character of that kind—not women in general. Anyone who thinks that any character in any artistic representation *must* represent everybody is surely going far beyond the intentions of typical artists, as well as supposing something that is quite obviously untrue.

Truth, Falsity, and Harm

Is truth good in itself? Is truth any kind of value at all? And is it a value *for* all? *Is* Society just one big clone of Plato's Academy, after all? Opinions may vary on the first question, but to the third, it is hard to see how the answer could be affirmative. Aristotle claimed that "all men by nature desire to know," but as any elementary school teacher will tell you, this is not at all obvious, especially if it means that everyone's goal in life is to maximize her supply of interesting information about the universe, as compared with other possible goals. That relatively clear conjecture we may pretty confidently dismiss. Moreover, those who don't go in for such exotic amusements are guilty of no moral error.

But on the other hand, we might mean that *falsehood*, or more precisely, the provision of false "information" in response to requests for information, is a *disvalue* for anyone. That is indeed plausible. One cannot act well *on the basis of falsehoods*. If my doing x successfully is contingent on some supposed fact, **p**, and **p** is false, then my action to that extent, and in that respect, misfires. How and why action might be so contingent varies, and may sometimes need explaining. But in typical cases, there's no problem at all: if you want to accomplish goal **G** by performing some act, x, then you are assuming that x is connected to **G**. If someone tells you this and what he says is false, he has put you out, at very least by motivating you to perform a useless action, or worse, by getting you to do something you really don't want. In some cases, the point of not being in error is less clear. Certainly it could be in someone's short-run interest, at least, to deceive someone else, and even perhaps himself, about some limited matter. (Yet even the self-deceiver needs to know what is true in order to persuade himself of what is false; if what he wants to believe were actually true, he could spare himself the trouble of deceiving himself about it!) That truth, in the sense of not being in error about things that matter to you, is generally a value is clear enough.

The question of how falsehoods might harm is rather complex. Here are several pointers and queries.

1. To say, sincerely, what is in fact false is to stand in need of correction, for to be in possession of what is false is likely to be unfortunate or worse. One does better to be refuted. And one has the moral duty to entertain proposed refutations rather than ignore them. To what extent must one do so? That's not easy to estimate; my point is that they shouldn't just be shunted aside, unless one has good antecedent reason for believing them false without further examination.

2. To say what one knows is false is to make oneself liable for consequences. When one's misinformation reasonably motivates others to act badly, with results unfortunate for them or others, then one bears liability for the misfortune and may in principle be sued for damages.

3. What if **A** impugns the reputation of **B** on grounds that are either meaningless, or logically insulated from refutation? For example, suppose **A** claims that **B** is "evil," but that his supposed evil consists in having a certain mysterious, unique, but suitably sinister property? That seems pretty nearly equivalent to falsehood, especially if propagated among gullible people. At any rate, it is not a rational ground of action. Its equivalence to falsehood lies in this: that for any given action, x, by some person, **C**, that has certain effects on person **B**, **C**'s doing x to **B** for the reason that **B** is **F** (where x is evil in our defined sense) is based on a necessarily irrelevant ground. If '**F**' is indefinable, then the "fact" that **B** is

F couldn't be a good reason for treating **B** in any one way as opposed to any other. There is also the problem of assessing responsibility of those who act badly on the basis of this drivel. If **B** assassinates **C** because **B** has been told by **A** that "God ordered it," how do we apportion blame to **B** and **A**? A difficult question, but surely both are to blame.

4. The fact that one dislikes person **B** is, of course, a putatively good reason for having as little as possible to do with him. It can also seem to be a reason, so far as it goes, for performing acts that would violate his rights, of course; but there are then independent reasons against it, overriding mere dislike—that, indeed, is part of the point of calling those things "rights." Nor, of course, is the fact that I dislike **B** any reason, so far as it goes, why *you* should dislike **B**. We do not have a general, basic duty to like each other, of course, but we have a general interest in good relations with all people, so we should not easily indulge in ill-considered dislikings. Still, it does not violate someone's rights if you ultimately dislike that person.

5. Do we harm someone by disliking him? We must be careful to distinguish this from the question whether you might come to harm someone *as a result of* disliking him. That, of course, is common enough. But in those cases, we typically have in mind someone's harming someone in various familiar ways; we don't mean that the very fact of dislike is itself harmful to the other person.

But could it not sometimes be so? We might first point out that one could keep one's dislike to oneself, rather than manifesting it in readily observable ways. It's difficult to see how one could regard the sheer *fact* of someone's dislike, independently of any outward manifestations, as constituting "harm." It isn't impossible, to be sure. We can easily enough imagine someone having a desire that everyone like him, and be wounded if they do not. But we can not credit supposed harms of this type. To do so is to court disaster: everyone is really enslaved to everyone else if we can blame Jones merely for disliking Smith. Does the allegation that pornography demeans women identify a genuine ground of moral objection to it? We have noted that portrayals of some person mistreating others may not be false for clearly this sometimes actually happens. It is the "message"—that this is a good way to treat those others—that we may be concerned about. We certainly don't want anyone believing it. But whether this is a ground for suppressing the message is another question. If we think it is, we must be assuming that the audience for the message is gullible and incapable of properly evaluating claims of that kind, or else that it is evil, in which case the video or picture isn't "convincing" them, but is instead just pandering to or reinforcing a base tendency of character that is already present.

We must in any case distinguish those pornographic materials that are, in effect, "hate literature" from those that are not. Most are surely in the latter category: they depict people sexually carrying on in various ways that plenty of possible viewers would find distasteful, but that the buying audience clearly does not. Nor, characteristically, did the participants. But there is a question about inferring intentions from what one sees on a screen, hears on a soundtrack, or reads in a text.

Those who depict evil are not necessarily advocating it: indeed, one must describe something to condemn it. Many fine movies are devoted almost wholly to depicting evils: the message of such movies is typically that they *are* evils.

Now, it is clear that normal people can witness depictions of evil, and even advocacy of it, without being in any way corrupted by this. Cinema buffs have long been keen on certain cinema classics, such as *Birth of a Nation* and Leni Riefenstahl's depiction of the Third Reich, that are and were intended to be out-and-out exercises in propaganda, without being converted to the KKK or the Nazi party. To suppress such movies on the ground that their message is evil would be absurd, if those audiences are typical. And to assume, in general, that those witnessing pornography must be in fact corrupted by it is to make an assumption that we ought not generally to make about people. People must be generally presumed to have minds of their own, as well as to be responsible for their actions—which brings us to the other major question concerning pornography's effects on the consumer's behavior.

Motivation to Do Evil

The other objection to pornography is that exposure to it induces people to engage in harmful behavior, such as rape. That objection cannot be dismissed along the lines we have just been considering. If it is true that reading x will *cause* **A** to go out and commit murder, rape or something comparably evil, then obviously we have reason to be concerned.

Some reason, yes—but how much? When, if ever, do we have a case for outright censorship arising from possibilities like this? It is important and true that murder and rape, among various other forms of interpersonal assault, are things which no person may do to anyone, under almost any conceivable circumstances. Someone who does this is rightly considered liable for criminal proceedings. And if we knew of any actual *causes* of any of these kinds of activity, such that we could know for certain in advance that a certain person was going to do an act of such a kind, then we would certainly be entitled to prevent that person from carrying out his evil plans. But the trouble is, we do *not* know of any such causes.

We do know that certain ways of treating young people, especially very young ones, drastically reduce the probability that they will end up performing such deeds, while certain others greatly increase it. For example, hardened recidivist criminals, the ones who commit another major crime almost right away upon their release from prison for the last one, it turns out, have almost invariably been brought up in domestic environments characterized by frequent violence, verbal and otherwise, by wildly inconsistent disciplinary practices, and by a pronounced shortage of parental (especially maternal) affection. Readers of this book have probably been fortunate enough to have been brought up in good homes. Even so, not all children from bad homes will end up hardened criminals—merely a lot of them. Virtually 100% of those brought up in "good" homes will not end up like that—but not quite 100%. Should we try to legally require parents to provide good homes for their children? If this could possibly be successful, it would have a drastic effect on the crime rate—virtually eliminating it, it seems. But it is clear that massive failure awaits any legal initiative of this kind.

Now apply that result, from an area where the evidence is strong, to the present one, where it is extremely weak. Is there a connection between witnessing pornographic materials and the likelihood of committing rape? Nobody would claim that there is anything remotely approximating a necessary condition here: millions of people view pornography without being rapists. It is certain that eliminating pornography entirely while leaving other things the same would leave us with plenty of rapists. In some cases, I gather, it might even increase the number: pornography in those cases acts as a substitute for the real thing, satisfying the would-be rapist before he gets out the door. It is very clear that this is an empirical question, and one that is decidedly not easy to answer; the evidence, such as it is, is overwhelmingly inconclusive.

All this requires us to address a further issue: what standards of evidence are we to use? Let us suppose that on the whole, people being exposed to pornography slightly increases the probability that they will later commit rape (and we do not even know that as yet). Now consider a figure we shall call **P**: the probability that a given individual will be a rapist given that he is a pornographer, less the probability that he would have been a rapist even if he hadn't been a pornographer. **P**, in other words, represents the marginal increment in this probability for members of the class of consumers of pornography. Then our question is, what value of **P** would justify depriving the entire class of consumers of pornography of opportunities to view it?

Consider another comparison case. Alcohol is a causative factor in a good many murders and a great many automobile accidents. We may be quite certain that the incidence of murder or criminal negligence among drinkers as compared with what it would be for those same people if they didn't drink is significant—far higher, given what we do know, than **P**. Yet prohibition in the USA was agreed to be a massive failure, and there is a genuine issue whether it would have been justified even if it hadn't been. Depriving everyone of alcohol when only some are induced by its consumption to commit criminal acts punishes the innocent in order to get at the guilty. Is this just?

Most readers will probably feel that the joys of alcohol consumption greatly outweigh those of pornography consumption. Perhaps so—but then, the joys of listening to a Mozart string quintet far outweigh either. Yet I don't think we are justified in requiring people to listen to Mozart; and this is not only because our efforts would no doubt prove a total failure. It is instead because how we shall run our lives is up to those whose lives they are, not to others—even if those others have terrific taste.

Zero Risk?

Some may insist that crimes like rape are so serious a matter that if we can do anything at all to make them less probable, then we should do it. That is a common attitude toward many things as well. But it is wrong—profoundly wrong, in one direction, and absurdly so in another.

To see its absurdity, consider your own case, and the risks you will quite reasonably take in order to gain modest pleasures. The most obvious and spectacular case is presented by smokers, who take a statistically very significant risk of contracting cancer in return for a modest amount of pleasure. But their conduct is perfectly rational (and I say this as a moderately fanatical nonsmoker). Given the choice between a probably longer but smoke-free life and a probably shorter and smoke-filled one, they prefer the latter. It's their choice, so long as they keep the smoke out of the lungs of the nonsmokers. For another example: there are people who voluntarily move to places like New York City from amazingly safe places like Selma, North Dakota, despite the vastly greater likelihood of being killed, mugged, or raped if they do so. They reckon that the more interesting things they can do in New York more than compensate for the increased risks of life in the big city. And again, they are not irrational to reason this way.

Given all this, if we imposed total censorship of pornography, who would lose and what would they lose? Presumably the consumers of porn would lose, and what they would lose are the various pleasures they presumably take in such literature. The overwhelming majority of these people will never rape anybody, and of the tiny minority who would, most would do so whether or not they watched pornography. Thus the innocent consumers of pornography would be penalized for the behavior of the others. And that isn't fair, just as it is not fair that the alcohol consumers among us who do not drive when drunk and do not knife people in heated arguments while inebriated should be deprived of their pleasures in order to protect the world from the others who do.

Indeed, it is perfectly clear that nothing in life is perfectly safe, once one considers the matter carefully. What walk of life has not produced its monsters, its aberrations? Academics who are convinced of some bizarre theory go forth to assassinate innocent people; accountants, preachers, secretaries—you name it: who can sincerely claim to know that the probability that persons in that walk of life will as a consequence of following it go out and do major harm to someone is *zero*? To prohibit these activities on that account would be to commit palpable wrongs now in the interests of preventing vague and remote possible wrongs in the future.

On the Theory of Social Risk

I will now suggest a social cost-benefit assessment for proposals like abolition of pornography. First, assign some definite negative value to the actual committing of one of the acts whose prevention we aim at. Then assign an equal positive value to each case in which the act in question didn't occur, though it otherwise would have. Society has paid itself that much in each successful case. Now assign another value, to the costs of the interferences we make in the interest of preventing the larger disvalues. And now suppose that society pays a compensation to each innocent person whose life is interfered with in this way. Then ask whether this was a good investment of society's time and energy.

Let's admit that it is very difficult to estimate the gains of such a policy. The best one can do would be to compare incidences of rape before and after the massive regime of censorship is installed. Nobody knows what the result would be, but if it is only a tiny diminution of the rate of rape, which is the worst we currently have reason to believe, then we have our result: we will have paid an astronomical amount in the way of lost liberty for a tiny gain in personal security—ten kilos of prevention for one gram of cure. This is not a rational way to run a society.

All in all, we do better to continue our liberal maxim. Every individual person is presumed innocent until proven guilty, and guilt will be proved only by deeds, not by the suspect's choice of reading or viewing matter. Other methods, such as argument, or moral suasion, especially in early childhood, will have to be employed by those wishing to protect the public.

Paternalism

Should we perhaps control what gets exposed to the *immature* eye? It does seem rather difficult to suppose that no sort of "censorship" is admissible in such cases, to be sure. But there are at least three angles from which to view this matter. One focuses on parental control and consent. Some parents will not wish their children to be exposed to certain of what they consider subversive influences—religious or moral, for instance. Another concerns the proper extent of community involvement in the nurturing of children. Particular parents may wish their children not to be exposed to certain material, but what if other parents are happy to expose theirs to it? The community may not arbitrarily rule in favour of one parent and against another.

Finally, there is the possibly distinct question of developmental psychology. Is it possible to know what is truly good for children, ignoring what their parents or other people want for them? These are difficult matters, and it is impossible to deny that what they are exposed to will likely have influence on them. But also, I think, what influences it will have must depend heavily on context. In a home where there is an extremely repressive atmosphere about sexual matters, a child's exposure to certain kinds of pornographic literature might help to turn him into the Montreal mass murderer; and yet, the same literature read by the child of tolerant and supportive parents might produce nothing but wry amusement. Indeed, there is probably little if anything that normal children can read or view in such an atmosphere that would produce serious harm to them in later years.

But here again, a major effort to intervene in the home is likely to be hugely counterproductive. What is likely to be much less so, I think, is a policy of holding parents responsible for the behavior of their children, at the same time encouraging the distribution of advice and information about childcaring. Behind almost every teenager committing a violent crime is a parent who did a lot of things very wrong. It might greatly encourage parents to seek advice on what it was, and how to correct it, if when a teenager committed such a crime, its parents were held liable and required to effect at least partial compensation. (This contrasts with the present rule in Canada, in which not even the teenager himself is held responsible, let alone his parents.)

The point here, then, is that it is difficult to find an independent basis for community restrictions on the reading matter to which even children are to be allowed to be exposed. Parents are not acting primarily as agents for the community when they take charge of their children's upbringing. They are, instead, making their own possibly separate judgments about what makes life good or bad. If that is how things stand even with the case of children, they must stand yet worse with the case of adults.

Summing Up

It is easy to be offended at what we are told is a frequent theme of much pornographic literature, that it depicts women as slaves or willing victims of assorted kinds of mistreatment. But the case for outrightly preventing people from creating and seeing such materials is very weak, even so. Normally all participants have acted voluntarily. And there is considerable room for divergent taste as accounting for much of the denunciation. Finally, we would need good evidence of a very strong causal connection between viewing pornography and being moved to commit actual violence before a case for suppression could become strong. In fact, there is at best extremely weak evidence of any such connection. Society would be wisest to leave intact the right of free speech and expression, and to expect its parents to avert evil tendencies by proper attention and training in their family life rather than by trusting to the censor to nip such tendencies in the bud.

Helping Others: What
Limits to Immigration?

37. Lifeboat Ethics: The Case Against Helping the Poor

Garrett Hardin

Garrett Hardin (1915–   ) is emeritus professor of biology, University of California Santa Barbara. Bioethics, or "tough love ethics" on a biological foundation, is a major interest in all his work. Since his retirement in 1978, he has devoted himself to speaking and writing.

Environmentalists use the metaphor of the earth as a "spaceship" in trying to persuade countries, industries, and people to stop wasting and polluting our natural resources. Since we all share life on this planet, they argue, no single person or institution has the right to destroy, waste, or use more than a fair share of its resources.

But does everyone on earth have an equal right to an equal share of its resources? The spaceship metaphor can be dangerous when used by misguided idealists to justify suicidal policies for sharing our resources through uncontrolled immigration and foreign aid. In their enthusiastic but unrealistic generosity, they confuse the ethics of a spaceship with those of a lifeboat.

A true spaceship would have to be under the control of a captain, since no ship could possibly survive if its course were determined by committee. Spaceship Earth certainly has no captain; the United Nations is merely a toothless tiger, with little power to enforce any policy upon its bickering members.

If we divide the world crudely into rich nations and poor nations, two thirds of them are desperately poor, and only one third comparatively rich, with the United States the wealthiest of all. Metaphorically each rich nation can be seen as a lifeboat full of comparatively rich people. In the ocean outside each lifeboat swim the poor of the world, who would like to get in, or at least to share some of the wealth. What should the lifeboat passengers do?

First, we must recognize the limited capacity of any lifeboat. For example, a nation's land has a limited capacity to support a population, and, as the current energy crisis has shown us, in some ways we have already exceeded the carrying capacity of our land.

Adrift in a Moral Sea

So here we sit, say fifty people in our lifeboat. To be generous, let us assume it has room for ten more, making a total capacity of sixty. Suppose the fifty of us in the lifeboat see 100 others swimming in the water outside, begging for admission to our boat or for handouts. We have several options: we may be tempted to try to live by the Christian ideal of being "our brother's keeper," or by the Marxist ideal of "to each according to his needs." Since the needs of all in the water are the same, and since they can all be seen as "our brothers," we could take them all into our boat, making a total of 150 in a boat designed for sixty. The boat swamps, everyone drowns. Complete justice, complete catastrophe.

Since the boat has an unused excess capacity of ten more passengers, we could admit just ten more to it. But which ten do we let in? How do we choose? Do we pick the best ten, the neediest ten, "first come, first served"? And what do we say to the ninety we exclude? If we do let an extra ten into our lifeboat, we will have lost our "safety factor," an engineering principle of critical importance. For example, if we don't leave room for excess capacity as a safety factor in our country's agriculture, a new plant disease or a bad change in the weather could have disastrous consequences.

Suppose we decide to preserve our small safety factor and admit no more to the lifeboat. Our survival is then possible, although we shall have to be constantly on guard against boarding parties.

While this last solution clearly offers the only means of our survival, it is morally abhorrent to many people. Some say they feel guilty about their good luck. My reply is simple: "Get out and yield your place to others." This may solve the problem of the guilt-ridden person's conscience, but it does not change the ethics of the lifeboat. The needy person to whom the guilt-ridden person yields his place will not himself feel guilty about his good luck. If he did, he would not climb aboard. The net result of conscience-stricken people giving up their unjustly held seats is the elimination of that sort of conscience from the lifeboat.

This is the basic metaphor within which we must work out our solutions. Let us now enrich the image, step by step, with substantive additions from the real world, a world that must solve real and pressing problems of overpopulation and hunger.

The harsh ethics of the lifeboat become even harsher when we consider the reproductive differences between the rich nations and the poor nations. The people inside the lifeboats are doubling in numbers every eighty-seven years; those swimming around outside are doubling, on the average, every thirty-five years, more than twice as fast as the rich. And since the world's resources are dwindling, the difference in prosperity between the rich and the poor can only increase.

As of 1973, the U.S. had a population of 210 million people, who were increasing by 0.8 per cent per year. Outside our lifeboat, let us imagine another 210 million people (say the combined populations of Colombia, Ecuador, Venezuela, Morocco, Pakistan, Thailand, and the Philippines), who are increasing at a rate of 3.3 per cent per year. Put differently, the doubling time for this aggregate population is twenty-one years, compared to eighty-seven years for the U.S.

Multiplying the Rich and the Poor

Now suppose the U.S. agreed to pool its resources with those seven countries, with everyone receiving an equal share. Initially the ratio of Americans to non-Americans in this model would be one-to-one. But consider what the ratio would be after eighty-seven years, by which time the Americans would have doubled to a population of 420 million. By then, doubling every twenty-one years, the other group would have swollen to 3.54 billion. Each American would have to share the available resources with more than eight people.

But, one could argue, this discussion assumes that current population trends will continue, and they may not. Quite so. Most likely the rate of population increase will decline much faster in the U.S. than it will in the other countries, and there does not seem to be much we can do about it. In sharing with "each according to his needs," we must recognize that needs are determined by population size, which is determined by the rate of reproduction, which at present is regarded as a sovereign right of every nation, poor or not. This being so, the philanthropic load created by the sharing ethic of the spaceship can only increase.

The Tragedy of the Commons

The fundamental error of spaceship ethics, and the sharing it requires, is that it leads to what I call "the tragedy of the commons." Under a system of private property, the men who own property recognize their responsibility to care for it, for if they don't they will eventually suffer. A farmer, for instance, will allow no more cattle in a pasture than its carrying capacity justifies. If he overloads it, erosion sets in, weeds take over, and he loses the use of the pasture.

If a pasture becomes a commons open to all, the right of each to use it may not be matched by a corresponding responsibility to protect it. Asking everyone to use it with discretion will hardly do, for the considerate herdsman who refrains from overloading the commons suffers more than a selfish one who says his needs are greater. If everyone would restrain himself, all would be well; but it takes only one less than everyone to ruin a system of voluntary restraint. In a crowded world of less-than-perfect human beings, mutual ruin is inevitable if there are no controls. This is the tragedy of the commons.

One of the major tasks of education today should be the creation of such an acute awareness of the dangers of the commons that people will recognize its many varieties. For example, the air and water have become polluted because they are treated as commons. Further growth in the population, or per-capita conversion of natural resources into pollutants, will only make the problem worse. The same holds true for the fish of the oceans. Fishing fleets have nearly disappeared in many parts of the world; technological improvements in the art of fishing are hastening the day of complete ruin. Only the replacement of the system of the commons with a responsible system of control will save the land, air, water, and oceanic fisheries.

The World Food Bank

In recent years there has been a push to create a new commons called a World Food Bank, an international depository of food reserves to which nations would contribute according to their abilities and from which they would draw according to their needs. This humanitarian proposal has received support from many liberal international groups, and from such prominent citizens as Margaret Mead, U.N. Secretary General Kurt Waldheim, and Senators Edward Kennedy and George McGovern.

A world food bank appeals powerfully to our humanitarian impulses. But before we rush ahead with such a plan, let us recognize where the greatest political push comes from, lest we be disillusioned later. Our experience with the Food for Peace program, or Public Law 480, gives us the answer. This program moved billions of dollars worth of U.S. surplus grain to food-short, population-long countries during the past two decades. But when P.L. 480 first became law, a headline in the business magazine *Forbes* revealed the real power behind it: "Feeding the World's Hungry Millions: How It Will Mean Billions for U.S. Business."

And indeed it did. In the years 1960 to 1970, U.S. taxpayers spent a total of $7.9 billion on the Food for Peace program. Between 1948 and 1970, they also paid an additional $50 billion for other economic-aid programs, some of which went for food and food-producing machinery and technology. Though all U.S. taxpayers were forced to contribute to the cost of P.L. 480, certain special-interest groups gained handsomely under the program. Farmers did not have to contribute the grain; the Government, or rather the taxpayers, bought it from them at full market prices. The increased demand raised prices of farm products generally. The manufacturers of farm machinery, fertilizers, and pesticides benefited by the armers' extra efforts to grow more food. Grain elevators profited from storing the surplus until it could be shipped. Railroads made money hauling it to ports, and shipping lines profited from carrying it overseas. The implementation of P.L. 480 required the creation of a vast Government bureaucracy, which then acquired its own vested interest in continuing the program regardless of its merits.

Extracting Dollars

Those who proposed and defended the Food for Peace program in public rarely mentioned its importance to any of these special interests. The public emphasis was always on its humanitarian effects. The combination of silent selfish interests and highly vocal humanitarian apologists made a powerful and successful lobby for extracting money from taxpayers. We can expect the same lobby to push now for the creation of a World Food Bank.

However great the potential benefit to selfish interests, it should not be a decisive argument against a truly humanitarian program. We must ask if such a program would actually do more good than harm, not only momentarily but also in the long run. Those who propose the food bank usually refer to a current "emergency" or "crisis" in terms of world food supply. But what is an emergency? Although they may be infrequent and sudden, everyone knows that emergencies will occur from time to time. A well-run family, company, organization, or country prepares for the likelihood of accidents and emergencies. It expects them, it budgets for them, it saves for them.

Learning the Hard Way

What happens if some organizations or countries budget for accidents and others do not? If each country is solely responsible for its own well-being, poorly managed ones will suffer. But they can learn from experience. They may mend their ways, and learn to budget for infrequent but certain emergencies. For example, the weather varies from year to year, and periodic crop failures are certain. A wise and competent government saves out of the production of the good years in anticipation of bad years to come. Joseph taught this policy to Pharaoh in Egypt more than 2,000 years ago. Yet the great majority of the governments in the world today do not follow such a policy. They lack either the wisdom or the competence, or both. Should those nations that do manage to put something aside be forced to come to the rescue each time an emergency occurs among the poor nations?

"But it isn't their fault!" some kindhearted liberals argue. "How can we blame the poor people who are caught in an emergency? Why must they suffer for the sins of their governments?" The concept of blame is simply not relevant here. The real question is, what are the operational consequences of establishing a world food bank? If it is open to every country every time a need develops, slovenly rulers will not be motivated to take Joseph's advice. Someone will always come to their aid. Some countries will deposit food in the world food bank, and others will withdraw it. There will be almost no overlap. As a result of such solutions to food shortage emergencies, the poor countries will not learn to mend their ways, and will suffer progressively greater emergencies as their populations grow.

Population Control the Crude Way

On the average, poor countries undergo a 2.5 per cent increase in population each year; rich countries, about 0.8 per cent. Only rich countries have anything in the way of food reserves set aside, and even they do not have as much as they should. Poor countries have none. If poor countries received no food from the outside, the rate of their population growth would be periodically checked by crop failures and famines. But if they can always draw on a world food bank in time of need, their population can continue to grow unchecked, and so will their "need" for aid. In the short run, a world food bank may diminish that need, but in the long run it actually increases the need without limit.

Without some system of worldwide food sharing, the proportion of people in the rich and poor nations might eventually stabilize. The overpopulated poor countries would decrease in numbers, while the rich countries that had room for more people would increase. But with a well-meaning system of sharing, such as a world food bank, the growth differential between the rich and the poor countries will not only persist, it will increase. Because of the higher rate of population growth in the poor countries of the world, 88 per cent of today's children are born poor, and only 12 per cent rich. Year by year the ratio becomes worse, as the fast-reproducing poor outnumber the slow-reproducing rich.

A world food bank is thus a commons in disguise. People will have more motivation to draw from it than to add to any common store. The less provident and less able will multiply at the expense of the abler and more provident, bringing eventual ruin upon all who share in the commons. Besides, any system of "sharing" that amounts to foreign aid from the rich nations to the poor nations will carry the taint of charity, which will contribute little to the world peace so devoutly desired by those who support the idea of a world food bank.

As past U.S. foreign-aid programs have amply and depressingly demonstrated, international charity frequently inspires mistrust and antagonism rather than gratitude on the part of the recipient nation.

Chinese Fish and Miracle Rice

The modern approach to foreign aid stresses the export of technology and advice, rather than money and food. As an ancient Chinese proverb goes: "Give a man a fish and he will eat for a day; teach him how to fish and he will eat for the rest of his days." Acting on this advice, the Rockefeller and Ford Foundations have financed a number of programs for improving agriculture in the hungry nations.

Known as the "Green Revolution," these programs have led to the development of "miracle rice" and "miracle wheat," new strains that offer bigger harvests and greater resistance to crop damage. Norman Borlaug, the Nobel Prize-winning agronomist who, supported by the Rockefeller Foundation, developed "miracle wheat," is one of the most prominent advocates of a world food bank.

Whether or not the Green Revolution can increase food production as much as its champions claim is a debatable but possibly irrelevant point. Those who support this well-intended humanitarian effort should first consider some of the fundamentals of human ecology. Ironically, one man who did was the late Alan Gregg, a vice president of the Rockefeller Foundation. Two decades ago he expressed strong doubts about the wisdom of such attempts to increase food production. He likened the growth and spread of humanity over the surface of the earth to the spread of cancer in the human body, remarking that "cancerous growths demand food; but, as far as I know, they have never been cured by getting it."

Overloading the Environment

Every human born constitutes a draft on all aspects of the environment: food, air, water, forests, beaches, wildlife, scenery, and solitude. Food can, perhaps, be significantly increased to meet a growing demand. But what about clean beaches, unspoiled forests, and solitude? If we satisfy a growing population's need for food, we necessarily decrease its per capita supply of the other resources needed by men.

India, for example, now has a population of 600 million, which increases by 15 million each year. This population already puts a huge load on a relatively impoverished environment. The country's forests are now only a small fraction of what they were three centuries ago, and floods and erosion continually destroy the insufficient farmland that remains. Every one of the 15 million new lives added to India's population puts an additional burden on the environment, and increases the economic and social costs of crowding. However humanitarian our intent, every Indian life saved through medical or nutritional assistance from abroad diminishes the quality of life for those who remain, and for subsequent generations. If rich countries make it possible, through foreign aid, for 600 million Indians to swell to 1.2 billion in a mere twenty-eight years, as their current growth rate threatens, will future generations of Indians thank us for hastening the destruction of their environment? Will our good intentions be sufficient excuse for the consequences of our actions?

My final example of a commons in action is one for which the public has the least desire for rational discussion—immigration. Anyone who publicly questions the wisdom of current U.S. immigration policy is promptly charged with bigotry, prejudice, ethnocentrism, chauvinism, isolationism, or selfishness. Rather than encounter such accusations, one would rather talk about other matters, leaving immigration policy to wallow in the crosscurrents of special interests that take no account of the good of the whole, or the interests of posterity.

Perhaps we still feel guilty about things we said in the past. Two generations ago the popular press frequently referred to Dagos, Wops, Polacks, Chinks, and Krauts, in articles about how America was being "overrun" by foreigners of supposedly inferior genetic stock. But because the implied inferiority of foreigners was used then as justification for keeping them out, people now assume that restrictive policies could only be based on such misguided notions. There are other grounds.

A Nation of Immigrants

Just consider the numbers involved. Our Government acknowledges a net inflow of 400,000 immigrants a year. While we have no hard data on the extent of illegal entries, educated guesses put the figure at about 600,000 a year. Since the natural increase (excess of births over deaths) of the resident population now runs about 1.7 million per year, the yearly gain from immigration amounts to at least 19 per cent of the total annual increase, and may be as much as 37 per cent if we include the estimate for illegal immigrants. Considering the growing use of birth-control devices, the potential effect of educational campaigns by such organizations as Planned Parenthood Federation of America and Zero Population Growth, and the influence of inflation and the housing shortage, the fertility rate of American women may decline so much that immigration could account for all the yearly increase in population. Should we not at least ask if that is what we want?

For the sake of those who worry about whether the "quality" of the average immigrant compares favorably with the quality of the average resident, let us assume that immigrants and native-born citizens are of exactly equal quality, however one defines that term. We will focus here only on quantity; and since our conclusions will depend on nothing else, all charges of bigotry and chauvinism become irrelevant.

Immigration vs. Food Supply

World food banks *move food to the people*, hastening the exhaustion of the environment of the poor countries. Unrestricted immigration, on the other hand, *moves people to the food*, thus speeding up the destruction of the environment of the rich countries. We can easily understand why poor people should want to make this latter transfer, but why should rich hosts encourage it?

As in the case of foreign-aid programs, immigration receives support from selfish interests and humanitarian impulses. The primary selfish interest in unimpeded immigration is the desire of employers for cheap labor, particularly in industries and trades that offer degrading work. In the past, one wave of foreigners after another was brought into the U.S. to work at wretched jobs for wretched wages. In recent years the Cubans, Puerto Ricans, and Mexicans have had this dubious honor. The interests of the employers of cheap labor mesh well with the guilty silence of the country's liberal intelligentsia. White Anglo-Saxon Protestants are particularly reluctant to call for a closing of the doors to immigration, for fear of being called bigots.

But not all countries have such reluctant leadership. Most educated Hawaiians, for example, are keenly aware of the limits of their environment, particularly in terms of population growth. There is only so much room on the islands, and the islanders know it. To Hawaiians, immigrants from the other forty-nine states present as great a threat as those from other nations. At a recent meeting of Hawaiian government officials in Honolulu, I had the ironic delight of hearing a speaker, who like most of his audience was of Japanese ancestry, ask how the country might practically and constitutionally close its doors to further immigration. One member of the audience countered: "How can we shut the doors now? We have many friends and relatives in Japan that we'd like to bring here some day so that they can enjoy Hawaii too." The Japanese-American speaker smiled sympathetically and answered: "Yes, but we have children now, and someday we'll have grandchildren too. We can bring more people here from Japan only by giving away some of the land that we hope to pass on to our grandchildren some day. What right do we have to do that?"

At this point, I can hear U.S. liberals asking: "How can you justify slamming the door once you're inside? You say that immigrants should be kept out. But aren't we all immigrants, or the descendants of immigrants? If we insist on staying, must we not admit all others?" Our craving for intellectual order leads us to seek and prefer symmetrical rules and morals: a single rule for me and everybody else; the same rule yesterday, today, and tomorrow. Justice, we feel, should not change with time and place.

We Americans of non-Indian ancestry can look upon ourselves as the descendants of thieves who are guilty morally, if not legally, of stealing this land from its Indian owners. Should we then give back the land to the now living American descendants of those Indians? However morally or logically sound this proposal may be, I, for one, am unwilling to live by it and I know no one else who is. Besides, the logical consequence would be absurd. Suppose that, intoxicated with a sense of pure justice, we should decide to turn our land over to the Indians. Since all our wealth has also been derived from the land, wouldn't we be morally obliged to give that back to the Indians too?

Pure Justice vs. Reality

Clearly, the concept of pure justice produces an infinite regression to absurdity. Centuries ago, wise men invented statutes of limitations to justify the rejection of such pure justice, in the interest of preventing continual disorder. The law zealously defends property rights, but only relatively recent property rights. Drawing a line after an arbitrary time has elapsed may be unjust, but the alternatives are worse.

We are all the descendants of thieves, and the world's resources are inequitably distributed. But we must begin the journey to tomorrow from the point where we are today. We cannot remake the past. We cannot safely divide the wealth equitably among all peoples so long as people reproduce at different rates. To do so would guarantee that our grandchildren, and everyone else's grandchildren, would have only a ruined world to inhabit.

To be generous with one's own possessions is quite different from being generous with those of posterity. We should call this point to the attention of those who, from a commendable love of justice and equality, would institute a system of the commons, either in the form of a world food bank, or of unrestricted immigration. We must convince them, if we wish to save at least some parts of the world from environmental ruin.

Without a true world government to control reproduction and the use of available resources, the sharing ethic of the spaceship is impossible. For the foreseeable future, our survival demands that we govern our actions by the ethics of a lifeboat, harsh though they may be. Posterity will be satisfied with nothing less.

38. Insiders and Outsiders

Peter Singer

The Shelter

It is February 2002, and the world is taking stock of the damage done by the nuclear war in the Middle East towards the close of the previous year. The global level of radioactivity now and for about eight years to come is so high that only those living in fallout shelters can be confident of surviving in reasonable health. For the rest, who must breathe unfiltered air and consume food and water with high levels of radiation, the prospects are grim. Probably 10 per cent will die of radiation sickness within the next two months; another 30 per cent are expected to develop fatal forms of cancer within five years; and even the remainder will have rates of cancer ten times higher than normal, while the risk that their children will be malformed is fifty times greater than before the war.

The fortunate ones, of course, are those who were far-sighted enough to buy a share in the fallout shelters built by real-estate speculators as international tensions rose in the late 1990s. Most of these shelters were designed as underground villages, each with enough accommodation and supplies to provide for the needs of 10,000 people for twenty years. The villages are self-governing, with democratic constitutions that were agreed to in advance. They also have sophisticated security systems that enable them to admit to the shelter whoever they decide to admit, and keep out all others.

The news that it will not be necessary to stay in the shelters for much more than eight years has naturally been greeted with joy by the members of an underground community called Fairhaven. But it has also led to the first serious friction among them. For above the shaft that leads down to Fairhaven, there are thousands of people who are not investors in a shelter. These people can be seen, and heard, through television cameras installed at the entrance. They are pleading to be admitted. They know that if they can get into a shelter quickly, they will escape most of the consequences of exposure to radiation. At first, before it was known how long it would be until it was safe to return to the outside, these pleas had virtually no support from within the shelter. Now, however, the case for admitting at least some of them has become much stronger. Since the supplies need last only eight years, they will stretch to more than double the number of people at present in the shelters. Accommodation presents only slightly greater problems: Fairhaven was designed to function as a luxury retreat when not needed for a real emergency, and it is equipped with tennis courts, swimming pools, and a large gymnasium. If everyone were to consent to keep fit by doing aerobics in their own living rooms, it would be possible to provide primitive but adequate sleeping space for all those whom the supplies can stretch to feed.

So those outside are now not lacking advocates on the inside. The most extreme, labelled "bleeding hearts" by their opponents, propose that the shelter should admit an additional 10,000 people—as many as it can reasonably expect to feed and house until it is safe to return to the outside. This will mean giving up all luxury in food and facilities; but the bleeding hearts point out that the fate for those who remain on the outside will be far worse.

The bleeding hearts are opposed by some who urge that these outsiders generally are an inferior kind of person, for they were either not sufficiently far-sighted, or else not sufficiently wealthy, to invest in a shelter; hence, it is said, they will cause social problems in the shelter, placing an additional strain on health, welfare, and educational services and contributing to an increase in crime and juvenile delinquency. The opposition to admitting outsiders is also supported by a small group who say that it would be an injustice to those who have paid for their share of the shelter if others who have not paid benefit by it. These opponents of admitting others are articulate, but few; their numbers are bolstered considerably, however, by many who say only that they really enjoy tennis and swimming and don't want to give it up.

Between the bleeding hearts and those who oppose admitting any outsiders, stands a middle group: those who think that, as an exceptional act of benevolence and charity, some outsiders should be admitted, but not so many as to make a significant difference to the quality of life within the shelter. They propose converting a quarter of the tennis courts to sleeping accommodation, and giving up a small public open space that has attracted little use anyway. By these means, an extra 500 people could be accommodated, which the self-styled "moderates" think would be a sensible figure, sufficient to show that Fairhaven is not insensitive to the plight of those less fortunate than its own members.

A referendum is held. There are three proposals: to admit 10,000 outsiders; to admit 500 outsiders; and to admit no outsiders. For which would you vote?

The Real World

Like the issue of overseas aid, the situation of refugees today raises an ethical question about the boundaries of our moral community—not, as in earlier chapters, on grounds of species, stage of development, or intellectual capacities, but on nationality. The great majority of the approximately 15 million refugees in the world today are receiving refuge, at least temporarily, in the poorer and less developed countries of the world. More than 12 million refugees are in the less developed countries of Africa, Asia and Latin America. The effect on a poor country of receiving a sudden influx of millions of refugees can be gauged from the experience of Pakistan during the 1980s, when it was home to 2.8 million Afghan refugees—mainly living in the North West Frontier province. Although Pakistan did get some outside assistance to feed its refugees, the effects of bearing the burden of this refugee population for seven years was easily seen around refugee villages. Whole hillsides were denuded of trees as a result of the collection of wood for fuel for the refugees.

According to Article 14 of the 1948 United Nations Declaration of Human Rights, "Everyone has the right to seek and to enjoy in other countries asylum from persecution." The United Nations High Commission for Refugees was established in 1950 and the commissioner entrusted with the protection of any person who is outside the country of his nationality because of a "well founded fear of persecution by reason of his race, religion, nationality or political opinion, and is unwilling or unable to avail himself of the protection of his own government." This definition was originally designed to meet the dislocation caused by the Second World War in Europe. It is a narrow one, demanding that claims to refugee status be investigated case by case. It has failed to cover the large-scale movements of people in times of war, famine, or civil disturbance that have occurred since.

Less than generous responses to refugees are usually justified by blaming the victim. It has become common to distinguish "genuine refugees" from "economic refugees" and to claim that the latter should receive no assistance. This distinction is dubious, for most refugees leave their countries at great risk and peril to their lives—crossing seas in leaky boats under attack from pirates, or making long journeys over armed borders, to arrive penniless in refugee camps. To distinguish between someone fleeing from political persecution and someone who flees from a land made uninhabitable by prolonged drought is difficult to justify when they are in equal need of a refuge. The UN definition, which would not classify the latter as a refugee, defines away the problem.

What are the possible durable solutions for refugees in the world today? The main options are: voluntary repatriation, local integration in the country they first flee to, and resettlement.

Probably the best and most humane solution for refugees would be to return home. Unfortunately for the majority, voluntary repatriation is not possible because the conditions that caused them to flee have not changed sufficiently. Local settlement, where refugees can remain and rebuild their lives in neighboring countries, is too often impossible because of the inability of poor, economically struggling—and politically unstable—countries to absorb a new population when their indigenous people face a daily struggle for survival. This option works best where ethnic and tribal links cross national frontiers.

The difficulty of achieving either voluntary repatriation or local settlement leaves resettlement in a more remote country as the only remaining option. With the number of refugees needing resettlement reaching dimensions never before experienced, the main response of the industrialized countries has been to institute deterrent policies and close their doors as tight as they can. Admittedly, resettlement can never solve the problems that make refugees leave their homes. Nor is it, of itself, a solution to the world refugee problem. Only about 2 per cent of the world's refugees are permanently resettled. Nevertheless, the resettlement option is a significant one. It provides markedly better lives for a considerable number of individuals, even if not for a large proportion of the total number of refugees.

Resettlement also affects the policies of those countries to which refugees first flee. If such countries have no hope that refugees will be resettled, they know that their burden will grow with every refugee who enters their country. And countries of first refuge are among those least able to support additional people. When the resettlement option tightens, the countries to which refugees first go adopt policies to try to discourage potential refugees from leaving their country. This policy will include turning people back at the border, making the camps as unattractive as possible, and screening the refugees as they cross the border.

Resettlement is the only solution for those who cannot return to their own countries in the foreseeable future and are only welcome temporarily in the country to which they have fled; in other words for those who have nowhere to go. There are millions who would choose this option if there were countries who would take them. For these refugees, resettlement may mean the difference between life and death. It certainly is their only hope for a decent existence.

The *Ex Gratia* Approach

A widely held attitude is that we are under no moral or legal obligation to accept any refugees at all; and if we do accept some, it is an indication of our generous and humanitarian character. Though popular, this view is not self-evidently morally sound. Indeed, it appears to conflict with other attitudes that are, if we can judge from what people say, at least as widely held, including the belief in the equality of all human beings, and the rejection of principles that discriminate on the basis of race or national origin.

All developed nations safeguard the welfare of their residents in many ways—protecting their legal rights, educating their children, and providing social security payments and access to medical care, either universally or for those who fall below a defined level of poverty. Refugees receive none of these benefits unless they are accepted into the country. Since the overwhelming majority of them are not accepted, the overwhelming majority will not receive these benefits. But is this distinction in the way in which we treat residents and nonresidents ethically defensible?

Very few moral philosophers have given any attention to the issue of refugees, even though it is clearly one of the major moral issues of our time and raises significant moral questions about who is a member of our moral community. Take, for example, John Rawls, the Harvard philosopher whose book, *A Theory of Justice*, has been the most widely discussed account of justice since its publication in 1971. This 500-page volume deals exclusively with justice *within* a society, thus ignoring all the hard questions about the principles that ought to govern how wealthy societies respond to the claims of poorer nations, or of outsiders in need.

One of the few philosophers who has addressed this issue is another American, Michael Walzer. His *Spheres of Justice* opens with a chapter entitled "The Distribution of Membership" in which he asks how we constitute the community within which distribution takes place. In the course of this chapter Walzer seeks to justify something close to the present situation with regard to refugee policy. The first question Walzer addresses is: Do countries have the right to close their borders to potential immigrants? His answer is that they do, because without such closure, or at least the power to close borders if desired, distinct communities cannot exist.

Given that the decision to close borders can rightfully be made, Walzer then goes on to consider how it should be exercised. He compares the political community with a club, and with a family. Clubs are examples of the *ex gratis* approach: "Individuals may be able to give good reason why they should be selected, but no one on the outside has a right to be inside." But Walzer considers the analogy imperfect, because states are also a bit like families. They are morally bound to open the doors of their country—not to anyone who wants to come in, perhaps, but to a particular group of outsiders, recognized as national or ethnic "relatives." In this way Walzer uses the analogy of a family to justify the principle of family reunion as a basis for immigration policy.

As far as refugees are concerned, however, this is not much help. Does a political community have the right to exclude destitute, persecuted, and stateless men and women simply because they are foreigners? In Walzer's view the community is bound by a principle of mutual aid and he rightly notes that this principle may have wider effects when applied to a community than when applied to an individual, because so many benevolent actions are open to a community that will only marginally affect its members. To take a stranger into one's family is something that we might consider goes beyond the requirement of mutual aid; but to take a stranger, or even many strangers, into the community is far less burdensome.

In Walzer's view, a nation with vast unoccupied lands—he takes Australia as his example, though by assumption rather than by any examination of Australia's water and soil resources—may indeed have an obligation in mutual aid to take in people from densely populated, famine-stricken lands of Southeast Asia. The choice for the Australian community would then be to give up whatever homogeneity their society possessed, or to retreat to a small portion of the land they occupied, yielding the remainder to those who needed it.

Although not accepting any general obligation on affluent nations to admit refugees, Walzer does uphold the popular principle of asylum. In accordance with this principle, any refugee who manages to reach the shores of another country can claim asylum and cannot be deported back to a country in which he may be persecuted for reasons of race, religion, nationality, or political opinion. It is interesting that this principle is so widely supported, while the obligation to accept refugees is not. The distinction drawn may reflect some of the principles discussed in previous chapters of this book. The principle of proximity clearly plays a role—the person seeking asylum is just physically closer to us than those in other countries. Perhaps our stronger support for asylum rests in part on the distinction between an act (deporting a refugee who has arrived here) and an omission (not offering a place to a refugee in a distant camp). It could also be an instance of the difference between doing something to an identifiable individual, and doing something that we know will have the same effect on someone, but we will never be able to tell on whom it has this effect. A further factor is probably the relatively small number of people who are actually able to arrive in order to seek asylum, in contrast to the much larger number of refugees of whose existence we are aware, although they are far from us. This is the "drops in the ocean" argument that was discussed in connection with overseas aid. We can, perhaps, cope with all the asylum seekers, but no matter how many refugees we admit, the problem will still be there. As in the case of the parallel argument against giving overseas aid, this overlooks the fact that in admitting refugees, we enable specific individuals to live decent lives and thus are doing something that is worthwhile, no matter how many other refugees remain whom we are unable to help.

Moderately liberal governments, prepared to heed at least some humanitarian sentiments, act much as Walzer suggests they should. They hold that communities have a right to decide whom they will admit; the claims of family reunion come first, and those of outsiders from the national ethnic group—should the state have an ethnic identity—next. The admission of those in need is an *ex gratis* act. The right of asylum is usually respected, as long as the numbers are relatively small. Refugees, unless they can appeal to some special sense of political affinity, have no real claim to be accepted, and have to throw themselves on the charity of the receiving country. All of this is in general agreement with immigration policy in the Western democracies. As far as refugees are concerned, the *ex gratis* approach is the current orthodoxy.

The Fallacy of the Current Approach

The current orthodoxy rests on vague and usually unargued assumptions about the community's right to determine its membership. A consequentialist would hold, instead, that immigration policy should be based squarely on the interests of all those affected. Where the interests of different parties conflict, we should be giving equal consideration to all interests, which would mean that more pressing or more fundamental interests take precedence over less fundamental interests. The first step in applying the principle of equal consideration of interests is to identify those whose interests are affected. The first and most obvious group is the refugees themselves. Their most pressing and fundamental interests are clearly at stake. Life in a refugee camp offers little prospect of anything more than a bare subsistence, and sometimes hardly even that. Here is one observer's impression of a camp on the Thai-Cambodian border in 1986. At the time the camp was home for 144,000 people:

> The visit of a foreigner causes a ripple of excitement. People gather round and ask earnestly about the progress of their case for resettlement, or share their great despair at continual rejection by the selection bodies for the various countries which will accept refugees. . . . People wept as they spoke, most had an air of quiet desperation. . . . On rice distribution day, thousands of girls and women mill in the distribution area, receiving the weekly rations for their family. From the bamboo observation tower the ground below was just a swirling sea of black hair and bags of rice hoisted onto heads for the walk home. A proud, largely farming people, forced to become dependent on UN rations of water, tinned fish and broken rice, just to survive.
>
> Most of these people could hope for no significant change in their lives for many years to come. Yet I, along with the others from outside, could get into a car and drive

out of the camp, return to Taphraya or Aran, drink iced water, eat rice or noodles at the roadside restaurant at the corner, and observe life passing by. Those simplest parts of life were invested with a freedom I'd never valued so highly.[1]

At the same time, refugees accepted into another country have a good chance of establishing themselves and leading a life as satisfactory and fulfilling as most of us. Sometimes the interests of the refugees in being accepted are as basic as the interest in life itself. In other cases the situation may not be one of life or death, but it will still profoundly affect the whole course of a person's life.

The next most directly affected group is the residents of the recipient nation. How much they will be affected will vary according to how many refugees are taken, how well they will fit into the community, the current state of the national economy, and so on. Some residents will be more affected than others: some will find themselves competing with the refugees for jobs, and others will not; some will find themselves in a neighborhood with a high population of refugees, and others will not; and this list could be continued indefinitely, too.

We should not assume that residents of the recipient nation will be affected for the worse: the economy may receive a boost from a substantial intake of refugees, and many residents may find business opportunities in providing for their needs. Others may enjoy the more cosmopolitan atmosphere created by new arrivals from other countries: the exotic food shops and restaurants that spring up, and in the long run, the benefits of different ideas and ways of living. One could argue that in many ways refugees make the best immigrants. They have nowhere else to go and must commit themselves totally to their new country, unlike immigrants who can go home when or if they please. The fact that they have survived and escaped from hardship suggests stamina, initiative, and resources that would be of great benefit to any receiving country. Certainly some refugee groups, for instance the Indo-Chinese, have displayed great entrepreneurial vigour when resettled in countries like Australia or the United States.

There are also some other *possible* and more diffuse consequences that we at least need to think about. For example, it has been argued that to take large numbers of refugees from poor countries into affluent ones will simply encourage the flow of refugees in the future. If poor and over-populated countries can get rid of their surplus people to other countries, they will have a reduced incentive to do something about the root causes of the poverty of their people, and to slow population growth. The end result could be just as much suffering as if we had never taken the refugees in the first place.

Consequences also arise from *not* taking significant numbers of refugees. Economic stability and world peace depend on international co-operation based on some measure of respect and trust; but the resource-rich and not over-populated countries of the world cannot expect to win the respect or trust of the poorest and most crowded countries if they leave them to cope with most of the refugee problem as best they can.

---

[1]Rossi Van der Borch, "Impressions of a Refugee Camp," quoted in *Asia Bureau Australia Newsletter*, No. 85 (October–December, 1986).

So we have a complex mix of interests—some definite, some highly speculative—to be considered. Equal interests are to be given equal weight, but which way does the balance lie? Consider a reasonably affluent nation that is not desperately overcrowded, like Australia. (I take Australia merely as an example of a country with which I am familiar; one could, with minor modifications, substitute other affluent nations.) In the early 1990s Australia is admitting about 12,000 refugees a year, at a time when there are several million refugees in refugee camps around the world, many of whom have no hope of returning to their previous country and are seeking resettlement in a country like Australia. Now let us imagine that Australia decides to accept twice as many refugees each year as it has in fact been doing. What can we say are the definite consequences of such a decision, and what are the possible consequences?

The first definite consequence would be that each year 12,000 more refugees would have been out of the refugee camps and settled in Australia, where they could expect, after a few years of struggle, to share in the material comforts, civil rights, and political security of that country. So 12,000 people would have been *very* much better off.

The second definite consequence would have been that each year Australia would have had 12,000 more immigrants, and that these additional immigrants would not have been selected on the basis of possessing skills needed in the Australian economy. They would therefore place an additional demand on welfare services. Some long-term residents of Australia may be disconcerted by the changes that take place in their neighborhood, as significant numbers of people from a very different culture move in. More refugees would make some impact on initial post-arrival services such as the provision of English language classes, housing in the first few months, job placement, and retraining. But the differences would be minor—after all, a decade earlier, Australia had accepted approximately 22,000 refugees a year. There were no marked adverse effects from this larger intake.

At this point, if we are considering the *definite* consequences of a doubled refugee intake, in terms of having a significant impact on the interests of others, we come to a halt. We may wonder if the increased numbers will lead to a revival of racist feeling in the community. We could debate the impact on the Australian environment. We might guess that a larger intake of refugees will encourage others, in the country from which the refugees came, to become refugees themselves in order to better their economic condition. Or we could refer hopefully to the contribution towards international goodwill that may flow from a country like Australia easing the burden of less well-off nations in supporting refugees. But all of these consequences are highly speculative.

Consider the environmental impact of an extra 12,000 refugees. Certainly, more people will put some additional pressure on the environment. This means that the increased number of refugees accepted will be just one item in a long list of factors that includes the natural rate of reproduction; the government's desire to increase exports by encouraging an industry based on converting virgin forests to wood-chips; the subdivision of rural land in scenic areas for holiday houses; the spurt in popularity of vehicles suitable for off-road use; the development of ski resorts in sensitive alpine areas; the use of no-deposit bottles and other containers that increase litter—the list could be prolonged indefinitely.

If as a community we allow these other factors to have their impact on the environment, while appealing to the need to protect our environment as a reason for restricting our intake of refugees to its present level, we are implicitly giving less weight to the interests of refugees in coming to Australia than we give to the interests of Australian residents in having holiday houses, roaring around the countryside in four-wheel-drive vehicles, going skiing, and throwing away their drink containers without bothering to return them for recycling. Such a weighting is surely morally outrageous, so flagrant a violation of the principle of equal consideration of interests that I trust it has only to be exposed in order to be seen as indefensible.

The other arguments are even more problematical. No one can really say whether doubling Australia's intake of refugees would have any effect at all on the numbers who might consider fleeing their own homes; nor is it possible to predict the consequences in terms of international relations. As with the similar argument linking overseas aid with increased population, in a situation in which the definite consequences of the proposed additional intake of refugees are positive, it would be wrong to decide against the larger intake on such speculative grounds, especially since the speculative factors point in different directions.

So there is a strong case for Australia to double its refugee intake. But there was nothing in the argument that relied on the specific level of refugees now being taken by Australia. If this argument goes through, it would also seem to follow that Australia should be taking not an extra 12,000 refugees, but an extra 24,000 refugees a year. Now the argument seems to be going too far, for it can then be reapplied to this new level: Should Australia be taking 48,000 refugees? We can double and redouble the intakes of all the major nations of the developed world, and the refugee camps around the world will still not be empty. Indeed, the number of refugees who would seek resettlement in the developed countries is not fixed, and probably there is some truth in the claim that if all those now in refugee camps were to be accepted, more refugees would arrive to take their places. Since the interests of the refugees in resettlement in a more prosperous country will always be greater than the conflicting interests of the residents of those countries, it would seem that the principle of equal consideration of interests points to a world in which all countries continue to accept refugees until they are reduced to the same standard of poverty and overcrowding as the third world countries from which the refugees are seeking to flee.

Is this a reason for rejecting the original argument? Does it mean that if we follow the original argument through it leads to consequences that we cannot possibly accept; and therefore there must be a flaw in the argument that has led us to such an absurd conclusion? This does not follow. The argument we put forward for doubling Australia's refugee intake does not really imply that the doubled intake should then be redoubled, and redoubled again, ad infinitum. At some point in this process—perhaps when the refugee intake is four times what it now is, or perhaps when it is sixty-four times its present level—the adverse consequences that are now only speculative possibilities would become probabilities or virtual certainties.

There would come a point at which, for instance, the resident community had eliminated all luxuries that imperiled the environment, and yet the basic needs of the expanding population were putting such pressure on fragile ecological systems that a further expansion would do irreparable harm. Or there might come a point at which tolerance in a multicultural society was breaking down because of resentment among the resident community, whose members believed that their children were unable to get jobs because of competition from the hard-working new arrivals; and this loss of tolerance might reach the point at which it was a serious danger to the peace and security of all previously accepted refugees and other immigrants from different cultures. When any such point had been reached, the balance of interests would have swung against a further increase in the intake of refugees.

The present refugee intake might increase quite dramatically before any consequences like those mentioned above were reached; and some may take this as a consequence sufficiently unacceptable to support the rejection of our line of argument. Certainly anyone starting from the assumption that the status quo must be roughly right will be likely to take that view. But the status quo is the outcome of a system of national selfishness and political expediency, and not the result of a considered attempt to work out the moral obligations of the developed nations in a world with 15 million refugees.

It would not be difficult for the nations of the developed world to move closer towards fulfilling their moral obligations to refugees. There is no objective evidence to show that doubling their refugee intake would cause them any harm whatsoever. Much present evidence, as well as past experience, points the other way, suggesting that they and their present population would probably benefit.

But, the leaders will cry, what is moral is not what is politically acceptable! This is a spurious excuse for inaction. In many policy areas, presidents and prime ministers are quite happy to try to convince the electorate of what is right—of the need to tighten belts in order to balance budgets, or to desist from drinking and driving. They could just as easily gradually increase their refugee intakes, monitoring the effects of the increase through careful research. In this way they would fulfill their moral and geopolitical obligations and still benefit their own communities.

Shelters and Refuges

How would you have voted, in the referendum conducted in Fairhaven . . . ? I think most people would have been prepared to sacrifice not just a quarter, but all of the tennis courts to the greater need of those outside. But if you would have voted with the "bleeding hearts" in that situation, it is difficult to see how you can disagree with the conclusion that affluent nations should be taking far, far more refugees than they are taking today. For the situation of refugees is scarcely better than that of the outsiders in peril from nuclear radiation; and the luxuries that we would have to sacrifice are surely no greater.

Problems and Puzzles

39. The Prisoner's Dilemma

Morton D. Davis

Morton David Davis (1930–) is an American mathematician whose research focuses on game theory.

Two men suspected of committing a crime together are arrested and placed in separate cells by the police. Each suspect may either confess or remain silent, and each one knows the possible consequences of his action. These are: (1) If one suspect confesses and his partner does not, the one who confessed turns state's evidence and goes free and the other one goes to jail for twenty years. (2) If both suspects confess, they both go to jail for five years. (3) If both suspects remain silent, they both go to jail for a year for carrying concealed weapons—a lesser charge. We will suppose that there is no "honor among thieves" and each suspect's sole concern is his own self-interest. Under these conditions, what should the criminals do? The game, shown in Figure 5.19, is the celebrated prisoner's dilemma which was originally formulated by A. W. Tucker and which has become one of the classical problems in the short history of game theory.

Let us look at the prisoner's dilemma from the point of view of one of the suspects. Since he must make his decision without knowing what his partner will do, he must consider each of his partner's alternatives and anticipate the effect of each of them on himself.

Suppose his partner confesses; our man must either remain silent and go to jail for twenty years, or confess and go to jail for five. Or, if his partner remains silent, he can serve a year by being silent also, or win his freedom by confessing. Seemingly, in either case, *he is better off confessing!* What, then, is the problem?

Figure 5.19

		SUSPECT *II*	
		CONFESS	DO NOT CONFESS
SUSPECT *I*	CONFESS	(5 yrs., 5 yrs.)	(go free, 20 yrs.)
	DO NOT CONFESS	(20 yrs., go free)	(1 yr., 1 yr.)

Morton D. Davis, "The Prisoner's Dilemma," from *Game Theory: A Nontechnical Introduction* (Revised Edition), New York: Dover Publications, 1997.

The paradox lies in this. Two naive prisoners, too ignorant to follow this compelling argument, are both silent and go to prison for only a year. Two sophisticated prisoners, primed with the very best game-theory advice, confess and are given five years in prison in which to contemplate their cleverness.

We will return to this argument in a moment, but before we do, let's consider the essential elements that characterize this game. Each player has two basic choices: he can act "cooperatively" or "uncooperatively." When all the players act cooperatively, each does better than when all of them act uncooperatively. For any fixed strategy(ies) of the other player(s), a player always does better by playing uncooperatively than by playing cooperatively.

In the following examples, taken from many different contexts, these same basic elements appear.

1. Two different firms sell the same product in a certain market. Neither the product's selling price nor the total combined sales of both companies vary from year to year. What does vary is the portion of the market that each firm captures, and this depends on the size of their respective advertising budgets. For the sake of simplicity, suppose each firm has only two choices: spending $6 million or $10 million. The size of the advertising budget determines the share of the market and, ultimately, the profits of each company, as follows:

If both companies spend $6 million, they each get a $5 million profit. If a company spends $10 million when its competitor spends only $6 million, its profit goes up to $8 million at the expense of its competitor, who now loses $2 million. And if both companies spend $10 million, the extra marketing effort is wasted, since the market is fixed and the relative market position of each company remains the same; consequently, the profit of each company drops to $1 million. No collusion is allowed between the firms. The game is shown in Figure 5.20.

2. There is a water shortage and citizens are urged to cut down on water consumption. If each citizen responds to these requests by considering his or her own self-interest, no one will conserve water. Obviously, any saving by an individual has only a negligible effect on the city's water supply, yet the inconvenience involved

Figure 5.20

| | | CORPORATION *II* | |
		SPEND $6 MILLION	SPEND $10 MILLION
CORPORATION *I*	SPEND $6 MILLION	($5 million, $5 million)	(−$2 million, $8 million)
	SPEND $10 MILLION	($8 million, −$2 million)	($1 million, $1 million)

is very real. On the other hand, if everyone acts in his or her own self-interest, the results will be catastrophic for everyone.

3. If no one paid taxes, the machinery of government would break down. Presumably all citizens would prefer that everyone, including themselves, pay taxes to having no one pay taxes. Better yet, of course, everyone would pay taxes except the individual him- or herself.

4. After several years of overproduction, farmers agree to limit their output voluntarily in order to keep the prices up. But no one farmer produces enough seriously to affect the price, so each starts producing what he or she can and selling it for what it will bring, and once again there is overproduction.

5. Two unfriendly nations are preparing their military budgets. Each nation wants to obtain a military advantage over the other by building a more powerful army, and each spends accordingly. They wind up having the same relative strength, and a good deal poorer.

As we can see from these examples, this kind of problem comes up all the time. For convenience's sake, let us fix our attention on a single game, using the first example, that of two companies setting their advertising budgets. The game will be the same, except for an additional condition. The budget will not be set once but, more realistically, we will assume that it is fixed annually for a certain period of time; say, twenty years. When each company decides on its budgets for any given year, it knows what its competitor spent in the past.

In discussing the prisoner's dilemma, we had decided that if the game is played only once, the prisoners have no choice but to confess. The same line of reasoning applied here leads to the conclusion that the firms should each spend $10 million. But when the game is played repeatedly, the argument loses some of its force. It is still true that if you spend $10 million in a given year, you will always do better than if you spend $6 million *that* year. But if you spend $10 million in one year, you are very likely to induce your competitor to spend $10 million the next year, and that is something you don't want. A more optimistic strategy is to signal your intent to cooperate by spending $6 million and hope your competitor draws the proper inference and does the same. This strategy could lead to a cooperative outcome and in practice often does. But in theory there is a problem.

The argument that spending $6 million in any one year tends to encourage your competitor to spend the same amount the next year is all very well for the first nineteen years, but it clearly breaks down in the twentieth year. In the twentieth year, there is *no next year*. When the firms reach the twentieth year, they are in effect in the same position they are in when they play the game only once. If the firms want to maximize their profits, and we assume that they do, the argument favoring the uncooperative strategy is as compelling now as it was then.

But the argument doesn't end there. Once the futility of cooperating in the twentieth year is recognized, it follows that there is no point in cooperating in the nineteenth year either. And if there is no chance of inducing a cooperative response in the nineteenth year, why cooperate in the eighteenth year? Once you fall into the trap, you fall all the way: there is no point in cooperating in the eighteenth, the seventeenth . . . or the first year either. If you accept the argument supporting the uncooperative strategy in the single instance, it follows that you must play uncooperatively not only in the last of a series but in every individual trial as well.

It is when the prisoner's dilemma is played repeatedly—and not for a fixed number of trials but for an indefinite period—that the cooperative strategy comes into its own. And these are precisely the conditions under which the prisoner's dilemma is often played. Two competing firms know that they won't be in business forever, but they generally have no way of knowing when death, merger, bankruptcy, or some other force will end their competition. Thus the players can't analyze what will happen in the last "play" and then work backward from there, for nobody knows when the last "play" will be. The compelling argument in favor of the uncooperative strategy breaks down, then, and we breathe a sigh of relief.

This is really the point. The prisoner's dilemma has one characteristic that makes it different from the other games that have been discussed. As a rule, when analyzing a game, you are content if you can say what rational players should do and predict what the outcome will be. But in the prisoner's dilemma the uncooperative strategy is so unpalatable that the question most people try to answer is not What strategy should a rational person choose? but How can we justify playing a cooperative strategy?. . .

40. Is It Rational to Be an Informed Voter?

Anthony Downs

Anthony Downs (1930–   ) is an urban economist and real estate consultant in Washington, D.C. He has taught economics and political science at the University of Chicago. Since 1977 he has been a senior fellow at the Brookings Institution, Washington, D.C. His books include An Economic Theory of Democracy, Inside Bureaucracy, Racism in America, *and* Stuck in Traffic.

When information is costly, no decision-maker can afford to know everything that might possibly bear on his decision before he makes it. He must select only a few data from the vast supply in existence and base his decision solely upon them. This is true even if he can procure data without paying for them, since merely assimilating them requires time and is therefore costly.

The amount of information it is rational for a decision-maker to acquire is determined by the following economic axiom: It is always rational to perform any act if its marginal return is larger than its marginal cost. The marginal cost of a "bit" of information is the return forgone by devoting scarce resources—particularly time—to getting and using it. The marginal return from a "bit" is the increase in utility income received because the information enabled the decision-maker to improve his decision. In an imperfectly informed world, neither the precise cost nor the precise return is usually known in advance; but decision-makers can nevertheless employ the rule just stated by looking at expected costs and expected returns.

This reasoning is as applicable to politics as it is to economics. Insofar as the average citizen is concerned, there are two political decisions that require information. The first is deciding which party to vote for; the second is deciding on what policies to exercise direct influence on government policy formation (that is, how to lobby). Let us examine the voting decision first.

Before we do so, it is necessary to recognize that in every society a stream of "free" information is continuously disseminated to all citizens. Though such "free" data take time to assimilate, this time is not directly chargeable to any particular type of decision-making, since it is a necessary cost of living in society. For example, conversation with business associates, small talk with friends, reading the newspaper in a barber shop, and listening to the radio while driving to work are all sources of information which the average man encounters without any particular

Anthony Downs, "An Economic Theory of Political Action in Democracy," *Journal of Political Economy*, Section VII, Vol. 65, No. 2, April, 1957. Copyright 1957 by The University of Chicago. Reprinted by permission of the University of Chicago Press and the author. The title "Is It Rational to Be an Informed Voter?" is the responsibility of the editors.

effort to do so. Therefore, we may consider them part of the "free" information stream and exclude them from the problem of how much information a decision-maker should obtain specifically to improve his decisions.

The marginal return on information acquired for voting purposes is measured by the expected gain from voting "correctly" instead of "incorrectly." In other words, it is the gain in utility a voter believes he will receive if he supports the party which would really provide him with the highest utility income instead of supporting some other party. However, unless his vote actually decides the election, it does not cause the "right" party to be elected instead of a "wrong" party; whether or not the "right" party wins does not depend on how he votes. Therefore, voting "correctly" produces no gain in utility whatsoever; he might as well have voted "incorrectly."

This situation results from the insignificance of any one voter in a large electorate. Since the cost of voting is very low, hundreds, thousands, or even millions of citizens can afford to vote. Therefore, the probability that any one citizen's vote will be decisive is very small indeed. It is not zero, and it can even be significant if he thinks the election will be very close; but, under most circumstances, it is so negligible that it renders the return from voting "correctly" infinitesimal. This is true no matter how tremendous a loss in utility income the voter would experience if the "wrong" party were elected. And if that loss is itself small—as it may be when parties resemble each other closely or in local elections—then the incentive to become well informed is practically nonexistent.

Therefore, we reach the startling conclusion that it is irrational for most citizens to acquire political information for purposes of voting. As long as each person considers the behavior of others as given, it is simply not worthwhile for him to acquire information so as to vote "correctly" himself. The probability that his vote will determine which party governs is so low that even a trivial cost of procuring information outweighs its return. Hence ignorance of politics is not a result of unpatriotic apathy; rather it is a highly rational response to the facts of political life in a large democracy.

This conclusion does not mean that every citizen who is well informed about politics is irrational. A rational man can become well informed for four reasons: (1) he may enjoy being well informed for its own sake, so that information as such provides him with utility; (2) he may believe the election is going to be so close that the probability of his casting the decisive vote is relatively high; (3) he may need information to influence the votes of others so that he can alter the outcome of the election or persuade government to assign his preferences more weight than those of others; or (4) he may need information to influence the formation of government policy as a lobbyist. Nevertheless, since the odds are that no election will be close enough to render decisive the vote of any one person, or the votes of all those he can persuade to agree with him, the rational course of action for most citizens is to remain politically uninformed. Insofar as voting is concerned, any attempt to acquire information beyond that furnished by the stream of "free" data is for them a sheer waste of resources.

The disparity between this conclusion and the traditional conception of good citizenship in a democracy is indeed striking. How can we explain it? The answer is that the benefits which a majority of citizens would derive from living in a society with a well-informed electorate are indivisible in nature. When most members of the electorate know what policies best serve their interests, the government is forced to follow those policies in order to avoid defeat (assuming that there is a consensus among the informed). This explains why the proponents of democracy think citizens should be well informed. But the benefits of these policies accrue to each member of the majority they serve, regardless of whether he has helped bring them about. In other words, the individual receives these benefits whether or not he is well informed, so long as most people are well informed and his interests are similar to those of the majority. On the other hand, when no one else is well informed, he cannot produce these benefits by becoming well informed himself, since a collective effort is necessary to achieve them.

Thus, when benefits are indivisible, each individual is always motivated to evade his share of the cost of producing them. If he assumes that the behavior of others is given, whether or not he receives any benefits does not depend on his own efforts. But the cost he pays does depend on his efforts; hence the most rational course for him is to minimize that cost—in this case, to remain politically ignorant. Since every individual reasons in the same way, no one bears any costs, and no benefits are produced.

The usual way of escaping this dilemma is for all individuals to agree to be coerced by a central agency. Then each is forced to pay his share of the costs, but he knows all others are likewise forced to pay. Thus everyone is better off than he would be if no costs were borne, because everyone receives benefits which (I here assume) more than offset his share of the costs. This is a basic rationale for using coercion to collect revenues for national defense and for many other government operations that yield indivisible benefits.

But this solution is not feasible in the case of political information. The government cannot coerce everyone to be well informed, because "well-informedness" is hard to measure, because there is no agreed-upon rule for deciding how much information of what kinds each citizen "should" have, and because the resulting interference in personal affairs would cause a loss of utility that would probably outweigh the gains to be had from a well-informed electorate. The most any democratic government has done to remedy this situation is to compel young people in schools to take courses in civics, government, and history.

Consequently, it is rational for every individual to minimize his investment in political information, in spite of the fact that most citizens might benefit substantially if the whole electorate were well informed. As a result, democratic political systems are bound to operate at less than maximum efficiency. Government does not serve the interests of the majority as well as it would if they were well informed but they never become well informed. It is collectively rational, but individually irrational, for them to do so; and, in the absence of any mechanism to insure collective action, individual rationality prevails.

41. Why a High Society Is a Free Society

A. C. Grayling

Anthony C. Grayling (1949–   ) is a reader in philosophy at Birkbeck College, University of London, and a Supernumerary Fellow of St. Anne's College, Oxford. He has written and edited many books on philosophy and other subjects. In addition he writes a column for the Guardian *newspaper's "The Last Word" column and is a regular reviewer for the* Literary Review *and the* Financial Times. *For nearly ten years he served as the honorary secretary of the Aristotelian Society, the principal British philosophical association.*

One measure of a good society is whether its individual members have the autonomy to do as they choose in respects that principally concern only them. The debate about heroin, cocaine and marijuana touches precisely on this. In my submission, a society in which such substances are legal and available is a good society not because drugs are in themselves good, but because the autonomy of those who wish to use them is respected. For other and broader reasons, many of them practical, such a society will be a better one.

I have never taken drugs other than alcohol, nicotine, caffeine and medicinal drugs. Of these, I have for many years not taken the two former. I think it is inimical to a good life to be dependent for pleasure and personal fulfilment on substances which gloss or distort reality and interfere with rationality; and yet I believe that heroin, cocaine, marijuana, ecstasy and cognates of these should be legal and available in exactly the same way as nicotine and alcohol.

In logic [there] is no difference between legal and currently illegal drugs. Both are used for pleasure, relief from stress or anxiety, and 'holidaying' from normal life, and both are, in different degrees, dangerous to health. Given this, consistent policy must do one of two things: criminalise the use of nicotine and alcohol, in order to bring them in line with currently illegal substances; or legalise currently illegal substances under the same kinds of regime that govern nicotine and alcohol.

On civil liberties grounds the latter policy is preferable because there is no justification in a good society for policing behaviour unless, in the form of rape, murder, theft, riot or fraud, it is intrinsically damaging to the social fabric, and involves harm to unwilling third parties. Good law protects in these respects; bad law tries to coerce people into behaving according to norms chosen by people who claim to know and to do better than those for whom they legislate. But the imposition of such norms is an injustice. By all means let the disapprovers argue and exhort; giving them the power to coerce and punish as well is unacceptable.

Reprinted from the *Guardian Unlimited Observer: Special Report*, May 19, 2002. Reprinted with permission of the author.

Arguments to the effect that drugs should be kept illegal to protect children fall by the same token. On these grounds, nicotine and alcohol should be banned too. In fact there is greater danger to children from the illegality of drugs.

Almost everyone who wishes to try drugs, does so; almost everyone who wishes to make use of drugs does it irrespective of their legal status. Opponents say legalisation will lead to unrestrained use and abuse. Yet the evidence is that where laws have been relaxed there is little variation in frequency or kind of use.

The classic example is Prohibition in the USA during the 1920s. (The hysteria over alcohol extended to other drugs; heroin was made illegal in the USA in 1924, on the basis of poor research on its health risks and its alleged propensity to cause insanity and criminal behaviour.) Prohibition created a huge criminal industry. The end of Prohibition did not result in a frenzy of drinking, but did leave a much-enhanced crime problem, because the criminals turned to substances which remained illegal, and supplied them instead.

Crime destabilises society. Gangland rivalry, the use of criminal organisations to launder money, to fund terrorism and gun-running, to finance the trafficking of women and to buy political and judicial influence all destabilise the conditions for a good society far beyond such problems as could be created by private individuals' use of drugs. If drugs were legally and safely available through chemist shops, and if their use was governed by the same provisions as govern alcohol purchase and consumption, the main platform for organised crime would be removed, and thereby one large obstacle to the welfare of society.

It would also remove much petty crime, through which many users fund their habit. If addiction to drugs were treated as a medical rather than criminal matter, so that addicts could get safe, regular supplies on prescription, the crime rate would drop dramatically, as argued recently by certain police chiefs.

The safety issue is a simple one. Paracetemol is more dangerous than heroin. Taking double the standard dose of paracetemol, a nonprescription analgesic, can be dangerous. Taking double the standard medical dose of heroin (diamorphine) causes sleepiness and no lasting effects.

A good society should be able to accommodate practices which are not destructive of social bonds (in the way that theft, rape, murder and other serious crimes are), but mainly have to do with private behaviour. In fact, a good society should only interfere in private behaviour in extremis.

Until a century ago, now-criminal substances were legal and freely available. Some (opium in the form of laudanum) were widely used. Just as some people are damaged by misuse of alcohol, so a few were adversely affected by misuses of other drugs. Society as a whole was not adversely affected by the use of drugs; but it was benefited by the fact that it did not burden itself with a misjudged, unworkable and paternalistic endeavour to interfere with those who chose to use drugs.

The place of drugs in the good society is not about the drugs as such, but rather the freedom and the value to individuals and their society of openness to experimentation and alternative behaviours and lifestyles. The good society is permissive, seeking to protect third parties from harm but not presuming to order people to take this or that view about what is in their own good.

Suggestions for Further Reading

Anthologies

Lederer, Laura, and Richard Delgado, eds. *The Price We Pay: The Case Against Racist Speech, Hate Propaganda and Pornography*. New York: Hill and Wang, 1995. In this collection of forty-two essays leading legal scholars, theorists, and activists argue that "First Amendment Absolutism" must not be allowed to infringe on the guarantee of equal protection under the laws and suggest ways to preserve both civil rights and civil liberties.

Pettit, Philip, and Robert E. Goodin, eds. *Contemporary Political Philosophy: An Anthology*. Malden, Mass., and Oxford, U.K.: Blackwell, 1997. This is a useful collection of more technical writings in the field by current political philosophers. This volume and *A Companion to Contemporary Political Philosophy*, Blackwell, 1993, 1995, together provide a systematic introduction to political philosophy as carried on today.

Phillips, Anne, ed. *Feminism and Politics*. New York: Oxford Univ. Press, 1998. This anthology offers twenty articles on a wide range of topics in the area of feminism and politics.

Skoble, Aeon J., and Tibor R. Machan, eds. *Political Philosophy: Essential Selections*. Upper Saddle River, N.J.: Prentice Hall, 1999. The readings in this anthology range in chronological order from the ancient world to the present. Many other collections of readings in political philosophy currently in print confine themselves either to classical sources or to contemporary ones but not to both.

Somerville, John, and Ronald E. Santoni, eds. *Social and Political Philosophy: Readings from Plato to Gandhi*. New York: Doubleday, Anchor, 1963. Extensive selections (in some instances the unabridged work) from some of the most famous and influential writings in social and political thought by philosophers and political leaders.

Stewart, Robert M. *Readings in Social and Political Philosophy*. Oxford: Oxford Univ. Press, 1986, 1996. This is an anthology of classical and contemporary readings in social and political philosophy.

Individual Works

Dworkin, Ronald. "Women and Pornography." *New York Review of Books*, 40:36–42 (Oct., 1993). For a number of years Ronald Dworkin, a philosopher of law, has been criticizing feminist positions on pornography and free speech such as the one expressed by Helen E. Longino. This article is an analysis and evaluation of Catharine MacKinnon's *Only Words* by Dworkin, whom MacKinnon calls the "liberal philosopher-king."

Flew, Antony. *The Politics of Procrustes: Contradictions of Enforced Equality*. Buffalo, N.Y.: Prometheus, 1981. A twentieth-century British philosopher vigorously critiques the philosophical assumptions of socialism and egalitarianism.

Held, Virginia. *Models of Democracy*. Stanford, Calif.: Stanford Univ. Press, 1987. An examination of democracy undertaken by an American philosopher who specializes in social and political philosophy, game theory, and public policy.

Hook, Sidney. *Political Power and Personal Freedom: Critical Studies in Democracy, Communism, and Civil Rights*. New York: Collier, 1962. An American philosopher vigorously analyzes the philosophical assumptions of the major political systems, including democracy, socialism, liberalism, and communism, as well as such issues as limitations to individual freedom, from the standpoint of his interpretation of John Dewey's philosophy.

Hook, Sidney. *Reason, Social Myths, and Democracy*. Amherst, N.Y.: Prometheus Books, 1991. In this work the author defends democracy in terms of a detailed philosophical analysis of democracy and scientific method, the nature of social inquiry, capitalism, Catholicism, and Marxism.

Howe, Irving. *Socialism and America*. New York: Harcourt Brace Jovanovich, 1985. An American socialist defends a form of socialism designed for contemporary America.

Levine, Andrew. *Arguing for Socialism: Theoretical Considerations*. London and Boston: Routledge & Kegan Paul, 1984. The author presents a theoretical defense of a form of socialism suitable for today and the foreseeable future.

MacKinnon, Catharine. *Only Words*. Cambridge, Mass.: Harvard Univ. Press, 1993. A professor of law at the university of Michigan briefly and vigorously argues that pornography is not speech as American law conceives of it but rather is an act of sexual discrimination and harassment that subordinates women to men and thus denies women the equality that is their right.

Macpherson, Crawford B. *The Life and Times of Liberal Democracy*. New York: Oxford Univ. Press, 1977. A brief, clear attempt to set forth the essence of liberal democracy as now conceived.

Nielsen, Kai. *Equality and Liberty: A Defense of Radical Egalitarianism*. Totowa, N.J.: Rowman & Allanheld, a Division of Littlefield, Adams and Company, 1985. A Canadian philosopher defends his version of radical egalitarianism and critiques the liberal egalitarianism of John Rawls, Ronald Dworkin, and others and the individualistic libertarianism of Robert Nozick, Milton Friedman, and others.

Nozick, Robert. *Anarchy, State and Utopia*. New York: Basic Books, 1974. Nozick's conception of the minimal state, or the "nightwatchman" state with the primary function of protection rather than redistribution of wealth, has provoked much discussion.

Oakeshott, Michael. *Rationalism in Politics*. New York: Basic Books, 1962. This work offers a stimulating challenge to liberalism.

Poundstone, William. *Prisoner's Dilemma*. New York: Doubleday, 1992. In a vivid and lively fashion Poundstone tells the history of the discovery of the prisoner's dilemma as a landmark in twentieth-century thought and investigates game theory's far-reaching impact on public policy.

Quinton, Anthony. "Political Philosophy" in *The Oxford History of Western Philosophy*. Edited by Anthony Kenny. New York: Oxford Univ. Press, 1994. A crisp, clear, and felicitously written history of political philosophy and its philosophical problems from ancient Greece and Rome to the present. This essay is recommended highly for the beginning student seeking a comprehensive orientation to the field.

Rand, Ayn. *Capitalism: The Unknown Ideal*. New York: New American Library–Dutton, 1986. In a series of essays the author argues that laissez-faire capitalism is the consequence and application of fundamental philosophical principles.

Raphael, D. D. *Problems of Political Philosophy*. London: Pall Mall, 1970. A clearly written introduction for the beginning student.

Rawls, John. *A Theory of Justice*. Cambridge: Belknap Press of Harvard Univ. Press, 1971. An outstanding systematic work in social and political philosophy by an American philosopher. It has provoked a great deal of discussion. Recommended for the more advanced student.

Reitman, Jeffrey H. *In Defense of Political Philosophy*. New York: Harper, Harper Torchbooks, 1972. The book vigorously argues against R. P. Wolff's *In Defense of Anarchism* (see Wolff, *In Defense of Anarchism*) and for majoritarian democracy.

Rothbard, Murray N. *The Ethics of Liberty*. New York: New York Univ. Press, 1998. In many ways this work provides the fullest exposition and defense of Rothbard's political philosophy.

Sabine, George H. *A History of Political Theory*. 3d ed. New York: Holt, Rinehart & Winston, 1961. 4th ed. revised by Thomas Landon Thorson. Hinsdale, Ill.: Dryden, 1973. This is the classic work with which every student should be familiar.

Singer, Peter. *How Are We to Live?* Amherst, N.Y.: Prometheus Books, 1995. The author argues that an ethical approach to life can be more satisfying and meaningful than a self-centered approach.

Spencer, Herbert. *The Man versus the State*. Edited by Donald Macrae. Baltimore: Penguin, 1969. As a result of the growing conviction that governments have become too strong for the preservation of men's liberties, the writings of the great nineteenth-century champion of laissez-faire individualism against an inherently oppressive state have sparked renewed interest.

Taylor, Richard. *Freedom, Anarchy, and the Law: An Introduction to Political Philosophy*. Englewood Cliffs, N.J.: Prentice Hall, 1973. Beginning and advanced students will find this lucid work stimulating and a pleasure to read.

Wolff, Robert Paul. *In Defense of Anarchism*. New York: Harper, Harper Torchbooks, 1970. This iconoclastic work by an American philosopher has provoked much discussion. (See Reitman, *In Defense of Political Philosophy*.)

Encylopedias

Dictionary of the History of Ideas: Studies of Selected Pivotal Ideas. Philip P. Wiener, editor-in-chief. New York: Scribners, 1973. Substantial and clearly written essays emphasizing the historical development of topics discussed in this part. Designed to inform the nonspecialist, each essay concludes with a select bibliography.

Encyclopedia of Philosophy. Paul Edwards, editor-in-chief. New York: Macmillan, 1967. The student will find many worthwhile articles on the subjects treated in this part and excellent bibliographies.

Philosophy and Public Affairs. Princeton, N.J.: Princeton Univ. Press. A quarterly journal. Philosophers and philosophically inclined writers from various disciplines bring their methods to bear on problems that concern everyone interested in social and political issues.

Routledge Encyclopedia of Philosophy. Edward Craig, general editor. New York: Routledge, 1998. This ten-volume encyclopedia contains articles on all areas of philosophy and up-to-date bibliographies.

Internet Web Sites

RESEARCH NAVIGATOR (*http://www.researchnavigator.com*). This web site offers three research data bases: Ebsco Academic Journal and Abstract Data Base, *New York Times* Search by Subject Archive, and "Best of the Web" Link Library. In addition, this site provides helpful advice on how to conduct efficient and productive research from choosing a topic to polishing the final draft. Beginning philosophy students probably will find the "Best of the Web" Link Library the most appropriate place to start their research. The free access code necessary to employ Research Navigator can be found in the Prentice Hall Guide to Evaluating Online Resources. If your text did not come with this guide, please go to *www.prenhall.com/contentselect* for information on how you can purchase an access code.

EpistemeLinks (*http://www.epistemelinks.com*). This site provides many links to philosophical resources on the web.

PART FIVE

Mind and Body

Introduction

In Karel Čapek's well-known play *R.U.R.* (*Rossum's Universal Robots*), scientists have learned to manufacture robots capable of doing all the manual and intellectual activities humans perform. Humans consider the robots to be lacking a soul since they are nothing more than a machine produced by a complex physical process, and they use the robots in any way that serves human needs. The robots, whose manufacture resulted from a new method of organizing matter, look and act very much like humans except that they lack emotions and feelings, which were purposely omitted to increase productivity. Since the robot's insensitivity to pain often leads to accidents, a scientist at Rossum's robot factory experiments with changes in their formula to give them human emotions. His experiments succeed; but the new, sensitive robots consider themselves to be equal to humans and, frustrated by their inferior status, rebel and destroy their creators.

This play raises the question of whether the robots, though only physical objects, essentially are like the people who created them. The answer to this question can affect our view of ourselves and our place in the world. Humans generally like to consider themselves especially important and unique, but their importance and uniqueness are diminished if they are not significantly different from robots. Also, if humans, like robots, are solely physical, they apparently must act in accord with the natural laws that govern the rest of nature. To preserve human uniqueness and to avoid viewing humans as determined objects, some philosophers claim that humans, unlike machines, possess nonphysical minds. These minds, they contend, enable humans to think and feel in ways that could not be duplicated by any machine. The claim that humans possess minds is very controversial: opponents consider it to be an unverifiable and unnecessary hypothesis, but supporters consider it an important component in their defense of the existence of free will, moral responsibility, and immortality.

The problem of whether humans possess minds and, if so, how the mind is related to the body is called the mind-body problem. One prominent view of reality—*materialism*—holds that the universe consists only of particles of matter moving in space. Thus, materialists consider humans, as all other objects in the universe, to be solely physical. Our ability to reason is attributed to our highly developed nervous system and brain, not to a mind. Since they deny that there are minds, materialists also deny that there is any disembodied personal immortality; for them, all thoughts and feelings cease when the body ceases to function. This sort of materialism should not be confused with a popular use of the term "materialism" to refer to those who have low moral aims or who are primarily concerned with acquiring worldly goods. The metaphysical materialist, who denies the existence of mind, can be quite idealistic and without any special interest in acquiring possessions.

Dualism, which maintains that humans possess both a body and a nonphysical mind, is opposed to materialism. The most widely held form of dualism, the form that is perhaps closest to our ordinary beliefs, is *interactionism*. According to this theory, the mind and body causally affect each other. Thus, mental events, such as thoughts, images, and sensations, produce bodily behavior, and bodily events produce mental occurrences. An example of a mental event causing physical activity would be the thought of a girl friend that causes one to pick up the phone and call her. Feeling pain from stubbing one's toe would be an example of a physical event causing a mental one.

Many philosophers have rejected interactionism because it has difficulty explaining how mental and physical events can causally affect each other. We ordinarily think of causation in terms of one physical event producing another. A simple example would be a moving billiard ball's hitting a second ball and moving it. But how can a thought produce movement in a person's body? And where does the mind act on the body to cause it to move? One might be inclined to say that the mind affects some portion of the brain, but physiologists have found no place where the brain seems to be stimulated by any invisible cause.

Confronted with such difficulties, some dualists have given up interactionism in favor of epiphenomenalism. *Epiphenomenalism* maintains that there are mental events but that that they do not cause any physical activity. Rather than interaction, we have a one-way causal relation: from the body to the mind. This view, too, has been criticized because it fails to explain how a physical event can cause a mental one. Also, the theory leads to the paradoxical result that all our thoughts and reasoning have no effect on our behavior. It is certainly hard to believe that the world would be exactly as it is today had none of people's thoughts about democracy, religion, and morality ever occurred.

In the first group of readings, both materialism and interactionism are defended. In "Materialism," Hugh Elliot rejects any forms of existence other than those envisaged by physics and chemistry. He answers some of the major objections to materialism, especially those concerning the nature of images and the apparent existence of purposive behavior, and criticizes interactionism and epiphenomenalism. In "The Mind as Distinct from the Body," C. E. M. Joad defends interactionism. He argues that the materialist cannot adequately explain purposive behavior or the way in which meaning is apprehended. For him, the mind is an active, creative force, which carries on activities that could not result from the function of the brain. He maintains that a perfect knowledge of a person's brain would fail to tell us what he or she was thinking since different thoughts could result in the same brain state.

Speculation about the nature of mind gives rise to some knotty problems. One problem is that if the mind is distinct from the body, I could not be sure that other people have thoughts and feelings similar to mine. In "The Problem of Other Minds," John Hospers presents the main arguments for and against the claim that the thoughts and feelings of others are similar to our own. He shows not only that there are grounds for doubting that others have mental states, but also that there are grounds for doubting our beliefs about our own mental states. A second problem, dealt with in "Brain Transplants and Personal Identity: A Dialogue," is whether someone who has undergone significant changes can be identified as the same person who existed before the changes. One might, for example, wonder whether a person whose knowledge and memories have been lost in an accident is still the friend you used to know. The dialogue between Godfrey Vesey and Derek Parfit points out the fact that the possibilities of brain transplants and splitting a brain and then placing it into two bodies present special difficulties for deciding the identity of a person.

Although the development of robots has long been a subject for science fiction stories and plays, such as *R.U.R.*, it is becoming a subject of increasing interest to philosophers and scientists as a result of the development of computers. Some theorists maintain that computers will eventually be developed to the point where they can perform all of the rational processes of human beings. With the development of computerized robots, we would have a machine that could do everything a human being can do. In fact, it is argued, such a machine would be a human being, and a human being would have been shown to be nothing more than a machine. But is it possible to develop a machine that can perform all of the "mental" feats of a human being? And if such a machine could be developed, would it still lack something that humans possess? If we produce a machine that can do everything a human being can do, then have we shown that humans are really nothing more than physical objects?

In discussing whether machines can think, Christopher Evans analyzes Alan Turing's famous test for machine intelligence in "Can a Machine Think?" The test, which places a computer and a human behind opaque screens, is designed to prove whether the responses of a computer can be distinguished from those of a human. Turing claimed that computers must be deemed as capable as humans of thought and intelligence if those taking the test cannot determine which is behind each screen. Along with exploring the value of the Turing test, Evans criticizes numerous objections to the possibility of machine intelligence. In contrast to Evans, John Beloff contends that machines can never be developed that can perform all the mental processes of humans. In "Minds or Machines," he argues that machines, unlike humans, lack awareness of what they are doing. Beliefs about human consciousness are supported by introspective evidence, but beliefs about machine consciousness lack any such direct, immediate evidence

The "Problems and Puzzles" section contains two essays on issues related to the mind-body controversy. In the first essay, "The Myth of the Soul," Clarence Darrow contends that the oft-held belief that people's soul, spirit, or mind survives the destruction of their bodies is without foundation. He presents a number of arguments against the likelihood of consciousness surviving death as well as arguments against the religious doctrine of the resurrection of the dead. In concluding his article, he states some doubts about the value of a belief in immortality. He believes that a satisfactory life can be lived without such a belief and that the rejection of a future life will produce a closer kinship with one's fellow humans than could otherwise be achieved. In the second essay, "Parable of the Chinese Room," John Searle maintains that a digital computer is not the same as a mind because its operations are defined syntactically; that is, it responds in specified ways to symbols that are not about anything. A person, unlike a computer, responds to the semantic content of symbols.

Materialism

42. Materialism

Hugh Elliot

Hugh Elliot (1881–1930), editor of the Annual Register, *England, was a champion of modern science and materialism and a student and biographer of Herbert Spencer, the famous nineteenth-century philosopher of evolution.*

The main purpose of the present work is to defend the doctrine of materialism. . . .

The outlines of this system are not new; the main features of it, indeed, have been admittedly associated with scientific progress for centuries past. An age of science is necessarily an age of materialism; ours is a scientific age, and it may be said with truth that we are all materialists now. The main principles which I shall endeavour to emphasize are three.

1. The uniformity of law. In early times events appeared to be entirely hazardous and unaccountable, and they still seem so, if we confine attention purely to the passing moment. But as science advances, there is disclosed a uniformity in the procedure of Nature. When the conditions at any one moment are precisely identical with those which prevailed at some previous moment, the results flowing from them will also be identical. It is found, for instance, that a body of given mass attracts some other body of given mass at a given distance with a force of a certain strength. It is found that when the masses, distances, and other conditions are precisely repeated, the attraction between the bodies is always exactly the same. It is found, further, that when the distance between the bodies is increased the force of their attraction is diminished in a fixed proportion, and this again is found to hold true at all distances at which they may be placed. The force of their attraction again varies in a different but still constant proportion to their masses. And hence results the law of gravitation, by which the force of attraction can be precisely estimated from a knowledge of the masses and distances between any two bodies whatever. A uniformity is established which remains absolute within the experience of Man, and to an equivalent extent the haphazard appearance of events is found to be only an appearance. Innumerable other laws of a similar character are gradually discovered, establishing a sort of nexus between every kind of event. If oxygen and hydrogen in the proportion by weight of eight to one are mixed together, and an electric spark is passed through them, water is formed; and on

From *Modern Science and Materialism* by Hugh Elliot. Published by Longman's, Green and Company, Ltd., 1919.

every occasion where precisely the same conditions are realized precisely the same result ensues. This truth is the basis of the experimental method. If from similar conditions it were possible that dissimilar results should follow on various occasions, then experiments would be useless for advancing knowledge. . . .

2. The denial of teleology. Scientific materialism warmly denies that there exists any such thing as purpose in the Universe, or that events have any ulterior motive or goal to which they are striving. It asserts that all events are due to the interaction of matter and motion acting by blind necessity in accordance with those invariable sequences to which we have given the name of laws. This is an important bond of connection between the materialism of the ancient Greeks and that of modern science. Among all peoples not highly cultivated there reigns a passionate conviction, not only that the Universe as a whole is working out some predetermined purpose, but that every individual part of it subserves some special need in the fulfillment of this purpose. Needless to say, the purpose has always been regarded as associated with human welfare. The Universe, down to its smallest parts, is regarded by primitive superstition as existing for the special benefit of man. To such extreme lengths has this view been carried that even Bernardin de Saint-Pierre, who only died last century, argued that the reason why melons are ribbed is that they may be eaten more easily by families. . . .

When it is alleged that the Universe is purposive, it is assumed that humanity is intimately connected with the purpose. Without that assumption, none but the most transcendental of philosophers would have any interest in maintaining teleology. As the anthropocentric doctrine falls, therefore, the doctrine of teleology must fall with it. This, at all events, is the position taken up by scientific, as indeed by all materialism; it is the position that I hope I shall have little difficulty in defending in the following pages. Nevertheless, however obvious its truth, we must recognize that it involves a profound alteration in the existing mental point of view of the majority of mankind; for most men have as yet not shaken off the habit, which all men necessarily start from, that they themselves, or their family, nation or kind, are in fact, as in appearance, the very centre of the cosmos.

3. The denial of any form of existence other than those envisaged by physics and chemistry, that is to say, other than existences that have some kind of palpable material characteristics and qualities. It is here that modern materialism begins to part company with ancient materialism, and it is here that I expect the main criticisms of opponents to be directed. The modern doctrine stands in direct opposition to a belief in any of those existences that are vaguely classed as "spiritual." To this category belong not only ghosts, gods, souls, *et hoc genus omne*, for these have long been rejected from the beliefs of most advanced thinkers. The time has now come to include also in the condemned list that further imaginary entity which we call "mind," "consciousness," etc., together with its various subspecies of intellect, will, feeling, etc., in so far as they are supposed to be independent or different from material existences or processes.

. . . It seems to the ordinary observer that nothing can be more remotely and widely separated than some so-called "act of consciousness" and a material object. An act of consciousness or mental process is a thing of which we are immediately and indubitably aware: so much I admit. But that it differs in any sort of way from a material process, that is to say, from the ordinary transformations of matter and energy, is a belief which I very strenuously deny. . . .

The proposition which I here desire to advance is that every event occurring in the Universe, including those events known as mental processes, and all kinds of human action or conduct, are expressible purely in terms of matter and motion. If we assume in the primeval nebula of the solar system no other elementary factors beyond those of matter and energy or motion, we can theoretically, as above remarked, deduce the existing Universe, including mind, consciousness, etc., without the introduction of any new factor whatsoever. The existing Universe and all things and events therein may be theoretically expressed in terms of matter and energy, undergoing continuous redistribution in accordance with the ordinary laws of physics and chemistry. If all manifestations within our experience can be thus expressed, as has for long been believed by men of science, what need is there for the introduction of any new entity of spiritual character, called mind? It has no part to play; it is impotent in causation. . . . Now there is an ancient logical precept which retains a large validity: *entia non sunt multiplicanda praeter necessitatem.* It is sometimes referred to as William of Occam's razor, which cuts off and rejects from our theories all factors or entities which are superfluous in guiding us to an explanation. "Mind" as a separate entity is just such a superfluity. I will not deny—indeed I cordially affirm—that it is a direct datum of experience; but there is no direct datum of experience to the effect that it is anything different from certain cerebral processes. . . .

The materialism which I shall advocate, therefore, is centred round three salient points: the uniformity of law, the exclusion of purpose, and the assertion of monism; that is to say, that there exists no kind of spiritual substance or entity of a different nature from that of which matter is composed.

The first of these propositions, otherwise called the Law of Universal Causation, affirms that nothing happens without a cause, and that the same causes under the same conditions always produce the same effects. In order to gain a true comprehension of this law, we have to define what we mean by "cause" and "effect," and what is the nature of the nexus between them. The conception of the Universe from which we start is that of a great system of matter and motion undergoing redistribution according to fixed sequences, which in the terminology of science are called laws. The matter is constantly undergoing transformation from one of its forms into another, and the energy is redistributed and transformed in a corresponding manner. From this primary conception alone, we are able to derive a precise definition of what is meant by cause, a problem which is almost insuperable from any other standpoint. . . . If we regard an event as a momentary phase in the redistribution of matter and motion, then the cause of the event is found in the immediately preceding state of distribution of that same matter and motion. Let us ask, for instance, what is the cause of the sudden appearance of a new fixed star in the heavens. Supposing that there were previously two extinct suns moving rapidly towards each other and coming into collision, we should be making a statement of events which would be recognized as a possibly true "cause." The second event, or "effect," is represented exclusively in terms of matter and motion by the idea of two coalesced and volatilized bodies giving rise to vast quantities of heat and light. And the cause is given merely by stating the previous distribution of that matter and energy which is concerned in the production of the event. The *matter* concerned in the event consisted of two solid bodies at a rapidly diminishing distance from one another. The *energy* consisted of half the product of their momentum and velocity. By the collision the matter contained in the solid bodies underwent that redistribution involved in passing into a gaseous state, with the decomposition of many of its molecules, that is to say, with a rearrangement or redistribution of its atoms. The energy of motion previously contained in the solid bodies underwent at the same time a transformation into heat and light. The sudden light, therefore, is explained, or derives its cause, merely by furnishing a statement of the previous distribution of the matter and energy concerned in its production. . . .

And this leads me to the second problem which I have here to deal with, the problem of teleology. I have hitherto endeavoured to represent the notion of cause and effect in purely materialistic terms, to the exclusion of all metaphysical transcendentalism; to state the relation of cause and effect in terms of the redistribution of matter and motion. I now have to perform the same task for the conception of purpose, and more particularly of human purpose, in order to show how purposiveness may be translated into purely materialistic and mechanical terms; that is to say, how it, too, may be expressed as a phase of the normal process of redistribution of matter and motion under fixed and invariable laws.

At the outset of this inquiry, we have to notice that the word "purpose" is involved in the same vagueness of significance that attends almost all words used in popular speech. In general a word in popular use has to be defined and limited to some precise meaning before it is fit for employment in a philosophical discussion. In the present case the word is commonly employed in at least two meanings, which differ greatly from each other; and this duality of meaning leads to a duality in the derivative conceptions of "teleology," "finalist," "end," etc., which has not infrequently given rise to confusion and error. The two significations may be roughly grouped as intelligent purposiveness and unintelligent purposiveness, and the reduction of each of these to mechanistic terms involves two different lines of analysis. I shall deal first with unintelligent purposiveness.

In this case, the word is usually applied to certain kinds of organic reactions that bear an obvious relation to the requirements of the reacting organism. An *Amoeba* in the water throws out pseudopodia at random in all directions. When one of these pseudopodia comes into contact with some substance suitable for food, the protoplasm streams round and encloses the particle, which is thus incorporated in the body of the *Amoeba* and there digested. The reaction is purposive in the sense that a somewhat complicated series of movements is carried out, which leads to the preservation of the active organism.

In just the same way, when we ascend the animal scale, the sea-anemone spreads it tentacles at large under the surface of the water. On contact with any substance suitable for food the tentacles contract around the substance and draw it into the interior of the sea-anemone. This action is similarly purposive in that it procures the continued existence of the animal. In all animals the common movements and reactions are predominantly of this purposive type. If an object suddenly appears close to our eyes, we involuntarily close them for an instant, and this reaction is obviously purposive, as directed toward the protection of the eyes.

All these instinctive actions are purposive in character, yet equally, without doubt, they are all of the nature of reflex action, working blindly and inevitably to their conclusion. On contact with the tentacle of a sea-anemone, the stimulus thus applied to that tentacle sets up by entirely mechanical procedure organic processes which necessarily result in the observed contractions. Similarly, in the case of the human being, the sudden appearance of a near object causes an impulse to be conveyed down the optic nerve, which immediately and mechanically propagates its effect to the efferent nerves which lead to the muscles that close the eyelids. The same kind of reaction is characteristic of the functions in plants. The turning of flowers towards the light, and all the processes of absorption, transpiration, etc., are, on the one hand, subservient to the life and prosperity of the plant, while, on the other hand, they are blind mechanical reactions to stimuli.

Seeing that a single action may thus be at the same time both purposive and mechanical, it is plain that there can be no antithesis between the two; but that the difference between purposive and blind mechanism arises simply from our point of view, and not from any difference of objective character. Purposive reactions are not different from mechanical reactions, but they *are* mechanical reactions of a certain kind. Not all mechanical reactions are purposive, but all purposive reactions are mechanical; and it remains to determine *what* mechanical actions may be correctly described as purposive, and what are simply blind and meaningless. . . .

I now come to the second class of activities to which the name of purpose is applied, that is to say, cases of activity which bear reference to an end consciously and intelligently foreseen, such as the acts inspired by the conscious will in human beings. These activities are commonly regarded as being in a higher degree teleological than the unintelligent reactions hitherto considered; and in many uses of the word "purpose," reference is intended exclusively to these intelligent anticipations of future events, and to the activities carried out in consequence of such anticipations. In this sense purpose is allied to will, and purposive actions are more or less synonymous with voluntary actions. . . .

We are now in a position to appreciate the true meaning of those acts which are described as intelligently purposive. Being deliberate and reasoned activities, they are as far as possible removed from the simple type of reflex action in which response follows immediately on external stimulus. They belong to the category in which the immediate stimulus is in the brain itself, and is to be regarded as consisting of rearrangements of the matter and energy contained in the nervous substance of the brain. The brain during consciousness can never be still, and its unceasing activities supply the stimulus, not only for purposive, but for all actions of an intellectual character. Now this permanent cerebral activity can be divided into a number of different types, known psychologically by such names as memory, imagination, reason, etc. Although nervous physiology has not yet advanced far enough to enable us to say what are the different kinds of material processes in the brain corresponding to these psychical processes, yet there is no doubt that the psychical distinction is based upon some actual distinction in the corresponding activities occurring in the brain. Among these cerebral processes is that which is known psychologically as a desire for some external object or event, a visualization of some external phenomenon as an end or purpose to be attained. This desire may then act upon efferent nerves and give rise to the activities which we know as purposive. The essence of a purposive action, and the standard by which it is distinguished from other kinds of actions, is that the "end" to which the action leads was previously represented in the brain of the agent, and composes the stimulus of action. The compound stimulus arises, as I have said, from the composition of large numbers of elementary stimuli previously received. It consists psychologically of a faint representation of the sensation which would be vividly presented by the realization of some outward occurrence. And when this faint representation actually functions as a stimulus which innervates the muscles whose contraction brings about the external occurrence represented, we have what is called an action of intelligent purpose. . . .

Intelligent purpose, like unintelligent purpose, is then only a name given to a particular kind of incident in the midst of the eternal redistribution of matter and motion under blind mechanical laws. It is in perfect harmony with that materialistic scheme; it can be stated in terms of the purest mechanism. As the matter and motion undergo their invariable and unalterable redistribution, we naturally find ourselves more interested in some phases of it than in others; and in one class of evolving events we are so interested and we have such frequent occasion to refer to them, that we denominate them by a special name—the name of purposive. By this name we designate the majority of those redistributions which issue from the little whirlpools of matter and energy called organisms, and those factors in particular by which the immediate continuance of such whirlpools is ensured.

I have now dealt with the law of universal causation, and with the doctrine of teleology. It remains only to say a few words about the third main pillar of materialism—the assertion of monism, that is, that there are not two kinds of fundamental existences, material and spiritual, but one kind only. . . . For simplifying the discussion, it will be as well at once to dismiss from consideration all those kinds of spiritual entities imagined by religious believers. The Victorian writers said on this subject nearly all that could be said, and interest now attaches only to those problems of matter and spirit which they left unsolved. I shall, therefore, confine myself to an attempt to reduce the last stronghold of dualism; to ascertain the relation between mind and body; to show that mental manifestations and bodily manifestations are not two different things, as generally supposed, but one and the same thing appearing under different aspects. I shall not attempt to deal with any of the so-called "non-material" existences with the exception of mind; for if mind can be identified with matter, all other kinds of non-material entities must lapse, even those described by religious systems. . . .

We reached the conclusion in a previous chapter that the bodily organism is a complex machine. We found that all its processes and activities are attributable to physico-chemical forces, identical with those which are recognized in the inorganic realm. We learnt that there is no "vital force" or other spiritual interference with the normal physical sequences. If, then, there be a mind, it is reduced to the function of inertly and uselessly accompanying the activities of certain neural elements. This is the doctrine of epiphenomenalism, and it is the last word possible to one who accepts the duality of mind and matter. It is a theory which on the face of it is devoid of verisimilitude. What can be the use of such a shadowy and inefficient entity? What parallel can be found in Nature for the existence of so gratuitous a super-fluity? Moreover, what mechanism, conceivable or inconceivable, could cause it thus to shadow neural processes, which *ex hypothesi* do not produce it? If one such mental state is the cause of the next, how does it happen that it causes the one which is necessary to accompany the actual neural process at the moment? Epiphenom-enalism involves us in a pre-established harmony that is profoundly opposed to the scientific spirit of the twentieth century. The problem, however, is not one that need be discussed on the grounds of *a priori* probability. It is a theory that may be rigidly refuted, and to that task I now turn.

It is a part of the doctrine of epiphenomenalism that a man would to all external appearance be precisely the same whether he was possessed of his epiphe-nomenal mind or not. Conduct, action, expression, would not in the slightest extent be affected were he completely devoid of mind and consciousness; for all these things depend upon material sequences alone. Men are puppets or automata, and we have no further grounds for supposing them to have minds than the fact that we know we have a mind ourselves, and the argument by analogy from ourselves to them. But arguments from analogy are notoriously insecure, and it seems, there-fore, to be quite within the bounds of possibility to the epiphenomenalist that some or all other men may be mindless syntheses of matter. . . .

Now let us assume that such a man actually exists, or, if you prefer, let us assume that physical chemistry has advanced to such a pitch that a man may be syn-thesized in the laboratory, starting from the elements, carbon, nitrogen, etc., of which protoplasm is composed. Let us assume in any case a "synthetic man" with-out a mind, yet indistinguishable by the epiphenomenalist hypothesis from another man identically constituted materially but having a mind. Ask the synthetic man whether he *has* a mind. What will he say? Inevitably he will say yes. For he must say the same thing as the man, identically made, who *has* a mind. Otherwise the same question would set up different responses in the nervous systems of the two, and that is by hypothesis impossible. The sound of the words "have you a mind?" entering the ears of the synthetic man sets up highly complex cerebral associations (which we call grasping their meaning); these associations will, after a short time, culminate in nervous currents to the tongue, lips and larynx, which will be moved in such a way as to produce an audible and intelligent answer. Now this answer must be the same in the case of the man who *has* a mind as in the case of the mind-less man, since their nervous systems are the same. If there was a different vocal response to an identical aural stimulus, then there must in one of them have been some external interference with the physico-chemical sequences. Mind must have broken through the chain of physical causality, and that is contrary to hypothesis.

What can the epiphenomenalist say? That the mindless man is a liar, to say he has a mind? That will not do, for if the two men are objectively identical one cannot be a liar, and the other not; one engaged in deceit, while the other speaks the truth.

The epiphenomenalist is thrown back, therefore, on the assumption that the mind-less man has made a mistake; that he thinks he has a mind, but really has not one; that his nervous constitution is such as to impel him to the conviction that he has a mind when he really has not, to lead him to talk upon psychical phenomena and their differences from matter, and in general to behave exactly as if he knew all about mind and matter, had considered the subject of their relationship, etc.

The example shows, furthermore, that the condition of "knowing one has a mind" is a condition which can be stated and accounted for in rigidly materialistic terms. When the epiphenomenalist himself asserts that he has a mind, the movements of his vocal cords by which he makes that pronouncement are by his own theory led up to by a chain of purely material sequences. He would make just the same pronouncement if he had no mind at all. His claim to possess a mind, therefore, is wholly irrelevant to the real question whether he actually has a mind or not. The events that make him say he has a mind are not the actual possession of a mind, but those cerebral processes which, in epiphenomenalist language, are said to underlie states of consciousness. It is the cerebral processes alone which make him speak, and his utterance, his belief in a mind, furnish testimony alone to the existence of those cerebral processes. Were the mind truly able to compel a belief and an announcement of its own existence, it could only be by breaking through the chain of material bodily sequences, and this is a vitalistic supposition that is ruled out by physiology. The belief in the possession of a mind is a cerebral condition, due, not to the actual possession of a mind, but to definite pre-existing cerebral conditions on the same material plane.

I do not see how epiphenomenalism could be much more effectively refuted. Yet it is the only respectable dualistic theory that is compatible with physiological mechanism. Let me recapitulate for a moment the facts, now before us, upon which we have to establish a theory of the relationship of mind and body.

Physiology has shown that bodily activity of every kind is a product of purely material sequences, into the course of which there is no irruption of any spiritualistic factor. On the dualistic theory, that doctrine is excessively difficult to understand. You move your arm by an act of will, or what seems to be a non-material cause, and yet it is conclusively established that the movement of the arm is due to definite material changes occurring in the brain, and caused by the fixed laws of physics and chemistry in the most determinist fashion. Now, anchoring ourselves firmly to that fact, we are confronted with the problem of where to put the mind. For every mental state there is some corresponding cerebral state; the one appears to be the exact counterpart of the other down to the smallest discoverable particular. Now on the dualistic assumption, there is only one possible hypothesis, namely, that of epiphenomenalism. Or, rather, it is incorrect to call it an hypothesis; for *if* there are two things, mind and body, epiphenomenalism is no more than a statement of the facts established by physiology and psychology. Dualistic physiologists, therefore, are practically forced to accept it. Yet, as I have shown, it is utterly untenable when properly thought out.

We are faced, therefore, by two possible alternatives: (1) to abandon mechanism, (2) to abandon dualism. Now mechanism is physiological theory which is proved. We must hold fast to it therefore at any expense to our metaphysical preconceptions. The only remaining alternative, then, is the abandonment of dualism. . . .

   When once we have got over the shock which monism carries to those accustomed to think in dualistic terms, we find that the great majority of the difficulties of metaphysics fall away. By an act of will I raise my arm. The plain man insists that his will did it; the physiologist knows that it was physico-chemical processes in the brain. The dilemma is at once overcome when the philosopher points out that the will *is* the physico-chemical processes, and that they both mean the same thing. . . . The difficulty of the epiphenomenalist is also solved. He says he has a mind. What makes him say so is not a transcendental "knowledge of having mind," but a certain cerebral state. When we have affirmed the absolute identity of that knowledge with that cerebral state, all difficulties vanish. The mind is the sum-total of cerebral conditions. He says he has a mind; it is the existence of the cerebral conditions which cause him to say so. He says he has a mind because he has cerebral conditions, and his remark is true and intelligible only on the one hypothesis that the mind *is* the cerebral conditions. . . .

   Monism resolves the great biological difficulty as to the origin of consciousness. The biological conclusions as to the origin of life are to the effect that living and organic matter was developed by evolution from non-living and inorganic matter. The evolution of Man from unicellular parentage is a fact. There is little or no reason to doubt that his unicellular ancestor was evolved just as gradually from inorganic matter. Now, says the dualist, we know that the man has a mind. It follows, therefore, either that inorganic matter has a psychical accompaniment, or else that, in the course of evolution, there was a sudden leap: mind was suddenly intruded at some period of Man's past history. Neither of these hypotheses is easy to entertain, or perhaps even practicable to conceive. The doctrine of monism, with its assertion that there are not two ultimate things, but one, causes the difficulty to vanish; for there is then no necessity to introduce a new entity at any period of an organism's evolution. According to our theory, a conscious state is a specific neural functioning. If there is no discontinuity in the evolution of nervous elements from inorganic matter, there is then no discontinuity in the evolution of consciousness.

Interactionism

43. The Mind as Distinct from the Body

C. E. M. Joad

Cyril Edwin Mitchinson Joad (1891–1953) was a prolific English author whose books, articles, and speeches on philosophy exerted broad public appeal in his lifetime.

The issue between those who endeavour to interpret mind action in terms of body action, and those who contend for the unique, distinct, and in some sense independent status of mind, is not capable of definite settlement. . . . The most that can be done is to suggest certain objections that can be and have been brought against the materialist position, . . . and at the same time to indicate a number of independent considerations which seem to demand a different kind of approach to psychology, and a different interpretation of its problems. This interpretation, to put it briefly, insists that a living organism is something over and above the matter of which its body is composed; that it is, in short, an expression of a principle of life, and that life is a force, stream, entity, spirit, call it what you will, that cannot be described or accounted for in material terms; that in human beings this principle of life expresses itself at the level of what is called mind, that this mind is distinct from both body and brain, and, so far from being a mere register of bodily occurrences, is able, acting on its own volition, to produce such occurrences, and that no account of mind action which is given in terms of brain action, gland activity or bodily responses to external stimuli can, therefore, be completely satisfactory. This is the view which in some form or other is held by those who find a materialist explanation of psychology unsatisfactory, and in this chapter we shall be concerned with the reasons for it.

Biological Considerations

Purposiveness
Some of these reasons, and perhaps the most important, are derived in part from regions which lie outside the scope of psychology proper; they belong to biology, and are based on a consideration of the characteristics which all living beings

From *How Our Minds Work* by C. E. M. Joad. Published by Philosophical Library (1947). Reprinted by permission of the publishers.

are found to possess in common. With regard to one of these "alleged" characteristics of living organisms it is necessary to say a few words, since it constitutes a starting point for the method of interpretation with which we shall be concerned in this chapter. The characteristic in question is that to which we give the name of purposiveness, and because of this characteristic it is said that any attempt to interpret the behaviour of living creatures in terms of material response to stimuli must inevitably break down. Purposiveness implies the capacity to be influenced by and to work for a purpose; this in its turn involves the apprehension, whether conscious or unconscious, of some object which lies in the future and which the purpose seeks to achieve; it therefore necessitates the existence of a mind. If, therefore, purposiveness is a true characteristic of living creatures, then we have established a good starting point for our "mental" approach to psychology.

What, therefore, is meant by saying that living creatures are purposive? Primarily, that in addition to those of their movements which may be interpreted as responses to existing situations, they also act in a way which seems to point to the existence of a spontaneous impulse or need to bring about some other situation which does not yet exist. This impulse or need is sometimes known as a conation; a good instance of the sort of thing that is meant is the impulse we feel to maintain the species by obtaining food or seeking a mate. The impulse is chiefly manifested in the efforts a living organism will make to overcome any obstacle which impedes the fulfillment of its instinctive need. It will try first one way of dealing with it and then another, as if it were impelled by some overmastering force which drove it forward to the accomplishment of a particular purpose. Thus the salmon, proceeding up stream, leaping over rocks and breasting the current in order to deposit her spawn in a particular place, is acting in a way which it is difficult to explain in terms of a response to external stimuli. An organism again will seek to preserve the trend of natural growth and development by which alone the purpose of existence will be fulfilled; in its endeavour to reach and to maintain what we may call its natural state or condition, it is capable, if need arises, of changing or modifying its bodily structure. If you take the hydroid plant *Antennularia* and remove it from the flat surface to which it is accustomed to adhere, it will begin to proliferate long wavy roots or fibers in the effort to find something solid to grip, while everybody has heard of the crab's habit of growing a new leg in place of one that has been knocked off.

Activity of this kind seems difficult to explain on materialist lines as the response to a stimulus; it appears rather to be due to the presence of a living, creative impulse to develop in the face of any obstacle in a certain way. That a living organism works as a machine works, by reacting in the appropriate way to the appropriate stimulus, is admitted; all that is contended is that it acts in other ways as well, that these other activities depend not only upon the quality of stimulus received, but upon the intensity of the creature's conative impulse, and that the existence of the impulse is only explicable on the assumption that the creature is animated by the need to fulfill a purpose.

Foresight and Expectation

When we apply this conclusion to human psychology, we are immediately struck by the fact that the individual not only exhibits in common with other organisms this characteristic of purposive behaviour, but is in many cases conscious of the nature of the purpose which inspires his behaviour. The man who studies in order to pass an examination is not only impelled by a push from behind; he is drawn forward by a pull from in front. This pull from in front can only become operative if he can be credited with the capacity to conceive the desirability of a certain state of affairs—namely, the passing of the examination, which does not yet exist; he shows, in other words, foresight and expectation. It is activities of this kind which seem most insistently to involve the assumption of a mind to do the foreseeing and expecting. In other words, the capacity to be influenced by events which lie in the future seems inexplicable on the stimulus-response basis; the *thought* of what does not exist may be allowed to influence the mind, but it is difficult to see how the non-existent can stimulate the body. . . .

The Apprehension of Meaning

An important fact about our mental life is that we are capable of appreciating meaning. A statement of fact written on a piece of paper is, so far as its material content is concerned, merely a number of black marks inscribed on a white background. Considered, then, as a collection of visual, physical stimuli, it is comparatively unimportant; what is important is the meaning which is attached to these marks. If they inform us, for example, that we have received a legacy of ten thousand pounds it is not the black marks on the white background but the meaning they convey that effects a disturbance in our emotional life, sufficiently profound to keep us awake all night. Now the meaning of the marks is obviously not a physical stimulus; it is something immaterial. How, then, is its effect to be explained in terms of bodily responses to physical stimuli, which the mind merely registers? Let us take one or two further examples in order to present the difficulty in a concrete form.

Let us suppose that I am a geometrician and am thinking about the properties of a triangle. As I do not wish at this point to enter into the vexed question of whether *some* physical stimulus is or is not necessary to initiate every chain of reasoning, we will assume that in this case there was a physical stimulus—it may have been a chance remark about Euclid, or the appearance of a red triangular road signpost while I am driving a car—a stimulus which we will call X, which prompted me to embark upon the train of speculations about the triangle. My reasoning proceeds until I arrive at a conclusion, which takes the form of a geometrical proposition expressed in a formula. I carry this formula in my head for a number of days and presently write it down. In due course I write a book, setting forth my formula and giving an account of the reasoning which led me to it. The book is read and understood by A. Presently it is translated into French, and is read and understood by B. Later still I deliver a lecture on the subject which is heard and understood by C. As A, B, and C have each of them understood my formula and the reasoning upon which it is based, we may say that the reasoning process has had for them the same meaning throughout. If it had not, they would not all have reached the same conclusion and understood the same thing by it. Yet in each of the four cases the sensory stimulus was different; for myself it was X, for A it was a number of black marks on a white background, for B a number of different black marks on a white background, and for C a number of vibrations in the atmosphere impinging upon his ear drums. It seems incredible that all these different stimuli should have been able to produce a consciousness of the same meaning, if our respective reactions to them were confined to physical responses (which must in each case have been different) which were subsequently reflected in our minds by a process of mental registration of the different responses. The stimuli being different, the intervention of something possessed of the capacity to grasp the *common* element among these physically different entities alone seems able to account for the facts, but the common element is the meaning, which is immaterial and can be grasped, therefore, only by a mind.

Let us take another example instanced by Professor McDougall:

A man receives a telegram which says "Your son is dead." The visual physical stimulus here is, as before, a collection of black marks on an orange field. The reaction experienced in terms of his bodily behaviour may take the form of a complete cessation of all those symptoms usually associated with life—that is to say, he may faint. When he recovers consciousness his thoughts and actions throughout the whole of the remainder of his life may be completely changed. Now that all these complicated reactions are not constituted by and do not even spring from a response to the *physical* stimulus, may be seen by comparing the reactions of an acquaintance who reads the telegram, and so subjects himself to the same stimulus. Moreover, the omission of a single letter, converting the telegram into "Our son is dead," would cause none of the reactions just described, but might result at most in the writing of a polite letter of condolence.

The independence of the bodily reactions to the physical stimuli actually presented is in these cases very marked, and, unless we are to introduce conceptions such as the intellectual apprehension of the *meaning* of the marks, it seems impossible to explain their effect. Yet such a conception again involves the active intervention of mind.

Synthesizing Power of Mind

This conclusion is reinforced by what we may call the synthesizing power of mind. Synthesizing means putting together, and one of the most remarkable powers that we possess is that of taking a number of isolated sensations and forming them into a whole. We shall have occasion to return to this point at greater length in connection with our account of sensation in the next chapter. For the present we will content ourselves with giving one or two examples of mental synthesis.

Let us consider for a moment the case of aesthetic appreciation. The notes of a symphony considered separately consist merely of vibrations in the atmosphere.

Each note may, when sounded in isolation produce a pleasant sensation, and as one note is struck after another we get a sequence of pleasant sensations. But although this is a sufficient description of the symphony considered as a collection of material events, and of our reactions to these events considered merely in terms of sensations, it is quite clear that we normally think of a symphony as being something more than this. We think of it in fact as a whole, and it is as a whole that it gives what is called aesthetic pleasure. Now in thinking of the symphony in this way our mind is going beyond the mere sequence of pleasant sensations which its individual notes produce, and putting them together into some sort of pattern. If the notes were arranged in a different order, although the actual vibrations which impinged upon our senses would be the same, the pleasurable aesthetic effect would be destroyed.

It seems to follow that our pleasure in a symphony cannot be wholly accounted for, although it may depend upon our physical responses to the stimuli of the individual notes; in order to obtain aesthetic pleasure we must somehow be able to perceive it as more than the sum total of the individual notes—that is, as a whole pattern or arrangement. The pleasure ceases when the *wholeness* of the object perceived is destroyed, as it is, for example, by the transposition of certain notes. We may compare the difference between the physical sensations which are our responses to the visual stimuli of the colours and canvas of which a picture is composed, with our synthesized perception of a picture as a work of art.

We must conclude, then, that we possess the power of realizing external objects not merely as collections of physical stimuli, which of course they are, but as wholes in which the actual sensory elements are combined to form a single object of a higher order. This faculty of combining or putting together seems to involve the existence not only of a mind, but of a mind of an active, creative type which is able to go out beyond the raw material afforded by our bodily sensations, and to apprehend ideal objects as wholes which are more than the collection of physical events which compose their constituent parts.

Summary of Argument

The conclusion to which the arguments of this chapter appear to point is that, in addition to the body and brain, the composition of the living organism includes an immaterial element which we call mind; that this element, although it is in very close association with the brain, is more than a mere glow or halo surrounding the cerebral structure, the function of which is confined to reflecting the events occurring in the structure; that, on the contrary, it is in some sense independent of the brain, and in virtue of its independence is able in part to direct and control the material constituents of the body, using them to carry out its purposes in relation to the external world of objects, much as a driver will make use of the mechanism of his motorcar. Mind so conceived is an active, dynamic, synthesizing force; it goes out beyond the sensations provided by external stimuli and arranges them into patterns, and it seems to be capable on occasion of acting without the provocation of bodily stimuli to set it in motion. It is, in other words, creative, that is, it carries on activities which even the greatest conceivable extension of our physiological knowledge would not enable us to infer from observing the brain. How, then, are we to conceive of the relationship of the mind to the brain?

An actor in a play of Shakespeare not only speaks words, but makes gestures, so that if you were completely deaf you would still be able to infer something of what the play was about from seeing the gestures. It is obvious, however, that there is much more in the play than the pantomime of the players. There are, for example, the words, the characters, the plot, and the poetry. Now to use a simile of the philosopher Bergson, the brain is the organ of pantomime. If you were to observe a man's brain you would know just as much of his thoughts as found vent in gestures. You would know, in other words, all that his thoughts imply in the way of actions or the beginnings of actions,[1] but the thoughts themselves would escape you just as the words and meaning of the play would escape the deaf spectator. This is what is meant by saying that the mind overflows the brain. If our knowledge of both psychology and physiology were perfect, we should be able to describe the movements of the brain without observing it, provided we had complete understanding of a man's state of mind; but we should not from the most minute and thorough inspection of the brain be able to tell what the man was thinking, since just as one gesture of the actor may stand for many different thoughts, so one state of the brain may represent any one of a host of states of mind.

---

[1]Among the beginnings of actions may be mentioned those movements of the larynx which are involved in talking.

Contemporary Issues

*Personal Identity
and Other Minds*

44. The Problem of Other Minds

John Hospers

When my finger is cut and bleeding, I know that I have a pain in the most direct way possible: I feel it. I do not *infer* from my behavior or anything else that I feel pain, I am *directly* aware of it—what philosophers sometimes call "immediate acquaintance." But when *your* finger is cut and bleeding, I do not know in the same way that you are feeling pain. I *infer* it from the fact that I see the blood and hear you saying that it hurts, and so on, but I do not feel your pain. (I may feel great empathy toward you, and feel distressed at the thought that you are in pain, but that still isn't feeling your pain in the way I feel my own pain when my finger is cut.) It seems to be impossible for me to feel your pain, or for you to feel mine. We are each aware of our own experiences, and no one else's. . . .

Thus, even if it is granted that I can know you're in pain, I still can't *feel* your pain, or think your thoughts, or experience your worry. If you tell me what you're worried about ("There's a hurricane on the way"), I too may feel worried; but even so, I feel my worry and you feel yours. There are two worries going on here, yours and mine, and I can't experience yours any more than you can experience mine. In fact, it would seem to be a necessary truth that I can't experience your experiences and you can't experience mine.

But is it a necessary truth? Suppose that the laws of physiology were different, and that we consider two persons, A and B. When A is cut with a knife, B feels pain, and when B is cut, A feels pain. Wouldn't that be a case of A feeling B's pain, and B A's pain? We might *say* that it is; if "my pain" means "the pain felt in my body," the answer would be yes. But in another sense the answer would be no. A might feel pain when B's body is injured and B feel pain when A's body is injured; this would be a very peculiar kind of world: I might say to you, "Don't get hit over the head today, I don't want to have that headache again." Still, wouldn't I be having *my* pain—but feeling it when your body was injured—just as you would still be feeling your pain when my body was injured? The causal conditions of having pain would be different in such a world, but I would still have my pain and you would have yours. "My pain" is *the pain I feel*—regardless of the causal conditions under which it was felt; even if I feel the pain when your finger is cut, it would still be my pain, because I am the one who has the pain.

It seems, then, that "I feel your pain" and "You feel my pain" are not just empirically impossible—contrary to biological laws—but logically impossible; it would involve saying that I feel a pain that is not mine but yours. Experiences, including pains, are essentially private; I could not have your pain any more than a circle could be square. In that case, however, I cannot possibly *verify* that you are in pain; I can verify only what your facial expression is and, if necessary, supplement that with a lie-detector test and a brainscan. But I cannot feel your pain myself. By such means I may be able to discover what thoughts or feelings you are having— even to know (at least in the weak sense of "know") *that* you are feeling so-and-so. But knowing *that* you are having a certain feeling is not at all the same as feeling it myself. If I know you well I may be able to say truly, "I know just what you're going through," but that's not the same thing as feeling it myself. I may empathize strongly with you and even feel pain when you are in pain, but the pain I feel is still mine and the pain you feel is yours.

Can I verify the proposition that you are feeling pain? Not if verifying means having all the evidence, or even the best possible evidence, which would be feeling it. At best I can verify that you behave in a certain way, and respond in a certain way to a lie-detector test.

Perhaps then all I mean by saying that you are in pain is that you behave in a certain way and respond to lie-detector tests and so on. But this view is absurdly implausible. If you have just cut yourself badly and I see your agonized behavior, do I, in saying that you feel pain, mean only that you behave *as if* you felt pain? Surely I mean that your behavior is an *indication* that you feel pain—and when I say that you are in pain I mean to say exactly the same thing about you that I am saying about myself when I say that I am in pain. The only difference between "I am in pain" and "You are in pain" is the personal pronoun. *What* I am saying about me and about you is exactly the same in the two cases. The question is, How can I verify the pain in your case, as I can do so immediately in my own?

"Well, at least I can *confirm* that you are feeling pain." Surely the fact that you cry out after having been cut is a good *confirmation* to me that you are in pain. Sometimes when you cry out you may be play-acting, but with careful observation I can confirm that too.

Many would be content with confirmation rather than verification. But a skeptic can pursue the question further: How do I know that you have pains or any other experiences at all? How do I know that you experience pain or pleasure or have sensations or thoughts or feelings of any kind? Could you not be a cleverly rigged-up automaton, wound up like a top every morning to go through certain complicated motions every day, but all the while experiencing nothing at all? True, you give answers to mathematical questions faster than I do; but so do computers when they have been programmed to do so. How do I know that you are not a fancy computer, having no more feelings or thoughts than the computers scientists build? If you were one, programmed to go through just the motions that you do, how would I ever know the difference? You would do the same things, say the same things, every bit of your behavior would be the same—so how could I tell? I can tell that you feel pain only from the symptoms from which I make the inference—but what if the symptoms were the same? If I don't believe that a computer has feelings, and if you behaved just as a computer does (the computer too can exhibit pain behavior and even say that it is in pain), what reason would I have for saying that you experience pain but the computer doesn't? Your behavior is all I can confirm, and I have no evidence that there is anything else beyond that. I have never even once felt your pain; for all that I know, your pain may be a myth.

To counter this alarming possibility, the *argument from analogy* is often invoked. When my finger is cut (A), I feel pain (B); therefore, I infer that when your finger is cut (A'), you feel pain (B'). That doesn't confer certainty on the statement that you feel pain, but doesn't it make your feeling quite probable? After all, you behave as I do when I feel pain; you too are composed of skin, bones, nerves, and blood vessels—just as I am. So can't I infer by analogy (similarity) that if I feel pain when cut, so do you?

The trouble is that as an argument from analogy, this seems a weak one. Suppose I see a set of boxes stored in someone's garage. I open one box and find that it is full of books. I don't open any of the rest, but I say, "Since all the boxes look pretty much alike, I infer that they all contain books." Admittedly this wouldn't be a very safe inference, and you wouldn't bet much on it. The boxes might contain anything—trinkets, papers, children's toys. If you open only one box, you're not in a very good position to say that they all contain books. Your position would be much better if you had opened all the boxes but one, found that they contained books, and then inferred that probably the last box would contain books also. An argument from analogy based on only one case is a pretty poor argument.

But isn't that exactly the position we are in with regard to other minds? In my own case, I have (1) my behavior and (2) my feeling pain. But in every other case, I have only the behavior to go by. So am I not in the position of the person who concludes that all the boxes contain books, on the slender basis of finding that one box contains books?

Yet I am much more confident that you feel pain when your finger is cut, than I am that all the boxes contain books after examining the contents of only one box. Why is this? Is this just an irrational conclusion, a prejudice? Or is it my belief that you have feelings based on something other than a weak argument from analogy?

Consider the following three statements:

1. I ask you, "Where is the book I lent you?"
2. You understand my question and think for a moment.
3. You utter the words, "I'm sorry—I forgot it, I left it at home."

The first statement is a report of words emanating from my mouth; these I not only utter but can hear myself uttering. The third statement is also something I can hear; your lips move and you utter the words. The problem is with the second statement. How do I know it is true, since I can't experience your thoughts? John Stuart Mill wrote,

> I conclude that other human beings have feelings like me because, first, they have bodies like me, which I know in my own case, to be the antecedent condition of feelings; and because secondly, they exhibit the acts, and other outward signs, which in my own case I know from experience to be caused by feelings. . . . In the case of other human beings I have the evidence of my senses for the first and last links of the series, but not for the intermediate link. I find, however, that the sequence between the first and last is as regular and constant in those other cases as it is in mine. In my own case I know that the first link produces the last through the intermediate link, and could not produce it without. Experience, therefore, obliges me to conclude that there must be an intermediate link; which must either be the same in others as in myself, or a different one; I must either believe them to be alive, or to be automatons; and by believing them to be alive, that is, by supposing the link to be of the same nature as in the case of which I have experience, and which is in all other respects similar, I bring other human beings, as phenomena, under the same generalizations which I know by experience to be the true story of my own existence.[1]

Particularly impressive is the fact that I ask someone a question and then from that person's lips emanate words which answer the very question I asked. How would this be possible if the other body doesn't have a mind that understands the question? To understand the question must he not have consciousness like me? Surely, the belief that he has consciousness like me is *the best explanation* of his ability to answer my questions.

Many would rest content with this answer, believing the problem of other minds to be solved. But there are a few bothersome questions that have been raised about this account.

1. How did we ever learn to use words like "pain" and "anger"—and other words we use—in talking about our "inner states"? As children we learned to use words by having them uttered by parents, accompanied typically by acts of pointing: "That's a chair," "That's a car." But of course you can't point to pain or anger. So how does the child learn to use the language of sensations and feelings? How did we ourselves learn to use the words correctly? How did words like "pain" become part of a *public language?*

Suppose you have some special feeling whenever you see, say, a mountain gorge. You might give a name to that peculiar sensation, and use it again if you had that same peculiar sensation another time. But thus far the name would not be part of a public language; you could use it only in "communing with yourself." You might try to communicate this special feeling to others, but others might be quite uncomprehending as to what you meant. But the word "pain" is not the same.

---

[1]John Stuart Mill, *An Examination of Sir William Hamilton's Philosophy*, 6th ed. (London: Longmans Green, 1889), pp. 243–244.

You learned to use that word from seeing your parents and other people use it: And to use it correctly you didn't need to feel their pains, or even to feel pain yourself. It was only necessary to observe the occasions on which they used the word—what their behavior was like when they used it, and by doing so you became able to use it yourself. If your father cut his finger and said that it hurt, and later you cut your finger, you could say the same thing of yourself—and presumably the feeling you had when this happened would be one you would identify as "pain."

This is not to say, then, that you have no "inner episodes" such as sensations of pain, but that you can learn to identify something as pain only by observing behavior that accompanies the use of the word. The child did not begin with her own case, as the argument from analogy seems to assume. She learned it as she learned any word in a public language, by observing the contexts in which other people used it. Thus, even though you can feel only your own pain, as a child you could learn how to use the word "pain" without having felt it. And you would recognize what you feel as being pain because of the similarity of the context to that of others when they spoke of pain. How else, it would be asked, would we learn the meaning of terms like "anger," "hope," "dread," and countless others?

2. We have argued thus far that you can know that you are in pain, and that your pain report is about as certain as a statement can be. But this too has been questioned.

Suppose that an encephalograph was constructed to test whether your reports that you are in pain are true; the machine is designed to test your pain level. What if you sincerely report that you are in pain, but this report conflicts with the evidence of the encephalograph? Should it be concluded that you are not telling the truth when you say you are in pain?

"Not at all," one might well exclaim, "I *know* whether I feel a pain. If the machine says I'm not, then it's the machine that's making the mistake. After all, *I* know whether I have a pain or not—I feel it! The machine only provides an indirect test—one that can be mistaken if the machine malfunctions."

> However good the evidence may be, such a physiological theory can never be used to show the sufferer that he was mistaken in thinking that he had a pain. . . . The sufferer's epistemological authority must therefore be better than the best physiological theory can ever be.[2]

But wait: How does Jones know that he is using the word "pain" correctly? Has he any *criteria* for the use of the term? He feels what he feels, but perhaps he is misdescribing what he feels in calling it a pain. Or perhaps he can describe it rightly once it is recognized for what it is, but he doesn't recognize it for what it is, in much the same way that a person may think she sees someone else in the room when she is only seeing her image in a mirror.

---

[2]Kurt Baier, "Smart on Sensations," *Australian Journal of Philosophy* (1962): 57.

> The encephalograph says that the brain-process constantly correlated with pain-reports occurs in Jones's brain. However, although he exhibits pain-behavior, Jones thinks that he does not feel pain. . . . Now is it that he does not know that *pain* covers what you feel when you are burned as well as what you feel when you are stuck, struck, etc.? Or is it that he really does not feel pain when he is burned? Suppose we tell Jones that what he feels when he is burned is *also* called "pain." Suppose he then admits that he does feel *something*, but insists that what he feels is quite *different* from what he feels when he is stuck, struck, etc. Where does Jones go from here? Has he failed to learn the language properly, or is he correctly (indeed infallibly) reporting that he has different sensations than those normally had in the situation in question?[3]

If the certainty of a sincere pain report is thus cast in doubt, some alarming skeptical possibilities now confront us. Would one sincere pain report—if at odds with the machine report—be enough to break down at one blow well-confirmed scientific theories? Can our certainty about our pains possibly be shaken by such questions as "Does she really know which sensations are called pains?" and "Is she a good judge of whether she is in pain or not?" Can the truth of a pain report *never* be overridden by evidence from other sources?

Consider another kind of case. You say, "It's hot in this room." But you look at the thermometer and it reads 55°; you check other thermometers and they all say the same. Are you sure you are right and the thermometers wrong? In this case we say the thermometers are right and that it isn't hot in the room, you just *feel* hot; perhaps you have a slight fever. Here we trust the thermometer and not your individual judgment. Why not do the same in trusting the encephalogram rather than your individual pain report?

"But this is different," one might say. Instead of saying it's hot in the room, you should say that you *feel* hot—no one will doubt that this is true. You do have a heat experience, no one is doubting the truth of your report that you *feel* hot; it's just that this time your heat experience doesn't correspond to the actual temperature. But in the case of the pain report, how can we deny that the person is feeling pain? If *you* are the one who has the pain, won't you say without hesitation that the encephalograph is mistaken? Aren't *you* the final judge of whether you feel pain? Isn't this one case that's absolutely clear and unshakable?

But some philosophers have questioned even this. We learn the word "pain"—like other words—in certain behavioral and environmental contexts; that's how we come to recognize pain when we feel it, and to name it correctly. However,

> Now suppose that these public criteria (for "knowing how to use 'pain'") change as physiology and technology progress. Suppose, in particular, that we find it convenient to speed up the learning of contrastive observation predicates (such as "painful" "tickling," etc.) by supplying children with portable encephalographs-cum-teaching-machines which, whenever the appropriate brain-process occurs, murmur the

---

[3]Richard Rorty, "Mind-Body Identity, Privacy, and Categories," *Review of Metaphysics* 19 (1965): 24–25.

appropriate term in their ears. Now "appropriate brain-process" will start out by meaning "brain-process constantly correlated with sincere utterances of 'I'm in pain' by people taught the use of 'pain' in the old rough-and-ready way." But soon it will come to mean, "the brain-process which we have always programmed the machine to respond to with a murmur of 'pain' ". . . . Given this situation, it would make sense to say things like "You say you are in pain, and I'm sure you are sincere, but you can see for yourself that your brain is not in the state to which you were trained to respond to with 'Pain,' so apparently the training did not work, and you do not yet understand what pain is." In such a situation, our "inability to be mistaken" about our pains would remain, but our "final epistemological authority" on the subject would be gone, for there would be a standard procedure for overriding our reports.[4]

The question is, however, whether such first-person reports can be overridden in this way. The person reporting the experience may be lying, or may be misreporting the experience by using words incorrectly. But if neither of these things is taking place, how can the person be mistaken? Some would contend that the first-person report is not coherent with the physical evidence, and that if the physical evidence is considerable, the first-person report, lacking coherence with the other propositions, must be rejected. But others would contend that if the physical evidence is not coherent with the first-person report, then it is the physical evidence that should be rejected and the first-person report that should be maintained.

[4]Ibid.

45. Brain Transplants and Personal Identity: A Dialogue

Derek Parfit and Godfrey Vesey

Derek Parfit (1942–   ) teaches philosophy at Oxford University. He has made outstanding contributions to ethical theory and the problem of personal identity.

Godfrey Vesey (1923–   ) teaches philosophy at the Open University in England. He has published books on a variety of philosophical topics.

Brain Transplants

In 1973 in the *Sunday Times* there was a report of how a team from the Metropolitan Hospital in Cleveland under Dr. R. J. White had successfully transplanted a monkey's head on to another monkey's body.[1] Dr. White was reported as having said, "Technically a human head transplant is possible," and as hoping that "it may be possible eventually to transplant *parts* of the brain or other organs inside the head."

The possibility of brain transplants gives rise to a fascinating philosophical problem. Imagine the following situation:

> Two men, a Mr. Brown and a Mr. Robinson, had been operated on for brain tumours and brain extractions had been performed on both of them. At the end of the operations, however, the assistant inadvertently put Brown's brain in Robinson's head, and Robinson's brain in Brown's head. One of these men immediately dies, but the other, the one with Robinson's body and Brown's brain, eventually regains consciousness. Let us call the latter "Brownson." Upon regaining consciousness Brownson exhibits great shock and surprise at the appearance of his body. Then, upon seeing Brown's body, he exclaims incredulously "That's me lying there!" Pointing to himself as he says "This isn't my body; the one over there is!" When asked his name he automatically replies "Brown." He recognizes Brown's wife and family (whom Robinson had never met), and is able to describe in detail events in Brown's life, always describing them as events in his own life. Of Robinson's past life he evinces no knowledge at all. Over a period of time he is observed to display all of the personality traits, mannerisms, interests, likes and dislikes, and so on, that had previously characterized Brown, and to act and talk in ways completely alien to the old Robinson.[2]

"Brain Transplants and Personal Identity" from *Philosophy in the Open* edited by Godfrey Vesey, Open University Press, 1974.

[1]*Sunday Times* (London: December 9, 1973), p. 13.
[2]Sydney Shoemaker, *Self-Knowledge and Self-Identity* (New York: Cornell University Press, 1963).

The next step is to suppose that Brown's brain is not simply transplanted whole into someone else's brainless head, but is divided in two and half put into each of *two* other people's brainless heads. The same memory having been coded in many parts of the cortex, they *both* then say they are Brown, are able to describe events in Brown's life as if they are events in their own lives, etc. What should we say now?

The implications of this case for what we should say about personal identity are considered by Derek Parfit in a paper entitled "Personal Identity." Parfit's own view is expressed in terms of a relationship he calls "psychological continuity." He analyses this relationship partly in terms of what he calls "q-memory" ("q" stands for "quasi"). He sketches a definition of "q-memory" as follows:

> I am q-remembering an experience if (1) I have a belief about a past experience which seems in itself like a memory belief, (2) someone did have such an experience, and (3) my belief is dependent upon this experience in the same way (whatever that is) in which a memory of an experience is dependent upon it.[3]

The significance of this definition of q-memory is that two people can, in theory, q-remember doing what only one person did. So two people can, in theory, be psychologically continuous with one person.

Parfit's thesis is that there is nothing more to personal identity than this "psychological continuity." This is *not* to say that whenever there is a sufficient degree of psychological continuity there is personal identity, for psychological continuity could be a one-two, or "branching," relationship, and we are able to speak of "identity" only when there is a one-one relationship. It *is* to say that a common belief—in the special nature of personal identity—is mistaken.

In the discussion that follows I began by asking Parfit what he thinks of this common belief. Derek Parfit is a Fellow of All Souls, Oxford.

Personal Identity

VESEY   Derek, can we begin with the belief that you claim most of us have about personal identity? It's this: whatever happens between now and some future time either I shall still exist or I shan't. And any future experience will either be my experience or it won't. In other words, personal identity is an all or nothing matter: either I survive or I don't. Now what do you want to say about that?

PARFIT   It seems to me just false. I think the true view is that we can easily describe and imagine large numbers of cases in which the question, "Will

[3]Derek Parfit, "Personal Identity," *The Philosophical Review*, Vol. 80, p. 15.

the future person be me—or someone else?," is both a question which doesn't have any answer at all, and there's no puzzle that there's no answer.

VESEY   Will you describe one such case?

PARFIT   One of them is the case discussed in the correspondence material, the case of division in which we suppose that each half of my brain is to be transplanted into a new body and the two resulting people will both seem to remember the whole of my life, have my character and be psychologically continuous with me in every way. Now in this case of division there were only three possible answers to the question, "What's going to happen to *me*?" And all three of them seem to me open to very serious objections. So the conclusion to be drawn from the case is that the question of what's going to happen to me, just doesn't have an answer. I think the case also shows that that's not mysterious at all.

VESEY   Right, let's deal with these three possibilities in turn.

PARFIT   Well, the first is that I'm going to be both of the resulting people. What's wrong with that answer is that it leads very quickly to a contradiction.

VESEY   How?

PARFIT   The two resulting people are going to be different people from each other. They're going to live completely different lives. They're going to be as different as any two people are. But if they're different people from each other it can't be the case that I'm going to be both of them. Because if I'm both of them, then one of the resulting people is going to be the same person as the other.

VESEY   Yes. They can't be different people and be the same person, namely me.

PARFIT   Exactly. So the first answer leads to a contradiction.

VESEY   Yes. And the second?

PARFIT   Well, the second possible answer is that I'm not going to be both of them but just one of them. This doesn't lead to a contradiction, it's just wildly implausible. It's implausible because my relation to each of the resulting people is exactly similar.

VESEY   Yes, so there's no reason to say that I'm one rather than the other?

PARFIT   It just seems absurd to suppose that, when you've got exactly the same relation, one of them is identity and the other is nothing at all.

VESEY   It does seem absurd, but there are philosophers who would say that sort of thing. Let's go on to the third.

PARFIT   Well, the only remaining answer, if I'm not going to be both of them or only one of them, is that I'm going to be neither of them. What's wrong with this answer is that it's grossly misleading.

VESEY   Why?

PARFIT   If I'm going to be neither of them, then there's not going to be anyone in the world after the operation who's going to be me. And that implies, given the way we now think, that the operation is as bad as death. Because if there's going to be no one who's going to be me, then I cease to exist. But it's obvious on reflection that the operation isn't as bad as death. It isn't bad in any way at all. That this is obvious can be shown by supposing that when they do the operation only one of the transplants succeeds and only one of the resulting people ever comes to consciousness again.

VESEY   Then I think we would say that this person is me. I mean we'd have no reason to say that he wasn't.

PARFIT   On reflection I'm sure we would all think that I would survive as that one person.

VESEY   Yes.

PARFIT   Yes. Well, if we now go back to the case where both operations succeed . . .

VESEY   Where there's a double success . . .

PARFIT   It's clearly absurd to suppose that a double success is a failure.

VESEY   Yes.

PARFIT   So the conclusion that I would draw from this case is firstly, that to the question, "What's going to happen to me?," there's no true answer.

VESEY   Yes.

PARFIT   Secondly, that if we decide to say one of the three possible answers, what we say is going to obscure the true nature of the case.

VESEY   Yes.

PARFIT   And, thirdly, the case isn't in any way puzzling. And the reason for that is this. My relation to each of the resulting people is the relation of full psychological continuity. When I'm psychologically continuous with only one person, we call it identity. But if I'm psychologically continuous with two future people, we can't call it identity. It's puzzling because we know exactly what's going to happen.

VESEY   Yes, could I see if I've got this straight? Where there is psychological continuity in a one-one case, this is the sort of case which we'd ordinarily talk of in terms of a person having survived the operation, or something like that.

PARFIT   Yes.

VESEY   Now what about when there is what you call psychological continuity— that's to say, where the people seem to remember having been me and so on—in a one-two case? Is this survival or not?

PARFIT   Well, I think it's just as good as survival, but the block we have to get over is that we can't say that anyone in the world after the operation is going to be me.

VESEY   No.

PARFIT   Well, we can say it but it's very implausible. And we're inclined to think that if there's not going to be anyone who is me tomorrow, then I don't survive. What we need to realize is that my relation to each of those two people is just as good as survival. Nothing is missing at all in my relation to both of them, as compared with my relation to myself tomorrow.

VESEY   Yes.

PARFIT   So here we've got survival without identity. And that only seems puzzling if we think that identity is a further fact over and above psychological continuity.

VESEY   It is very hard not to think of identity being a further fact, isn't it?

PARFIT   Yes, I think it is. I think that the only way to get rid of our temptation to believe this is to consider many more cases than this one case of division. Perhaps I should give you another one. Suppose that the following is going to happen to me. When I die in a normal way, scientists are going to map the states of all the cells in my brain and body and after a few months they will have constructed a perfect duplicate of me out of organic matter. And this duplicate will wake up fully psychologically continuous with me, seeming to remember my life with my character, etc.

VESEY   Yes.

PARFIT   Now in this case, which is a secular version of the Resurrection, we're very inclined to think that the following question arises and is very real and very important. The question is, "Will that person who wakes up in three months be me or will he be some quite other person who's merely artificially made to be exactly like me?"

VESEY   It does seem to be a real question. I mean in the one case, if it is going to be me, then I have expectations and so on, and in the other case, where it isn't me, I don't.

PARFIT   I agree, it seems as if there couldn't be a bigger difference between it being me and it being someone else.

VESEY   But you want to say that the two possibilities are in fact the same?

PARFIT   I want to say that those two descriptions, "It's going to be me" and "It's going to be someone who is merely exactly like me," don't describe different outcomes, different courses of events, only one of which can happen. They are two ways of describing one and the same course of events. What I mean by that perhaps could be shown if we take an exactly comparable case involving not a person but something about which I think we're not inclined to have a false view.

VESEY   Yes.

PARFIT   Something like a club. Suppose there's some club in the nineteenth century . . .

VESEY The Sherlock Holmes Club or something like that?

PARFIT Yes, perhaps. And after several years of meeting it ceases to meet. The club dies.

VESEY Right.

PARFIT And then two of its members, let's say, have emigrated to America, and after about fifteen years they get together and they start up a club. It has exactly the same rules, completely new membership except for the first two people, and they give it the same name. Now suppose someone came along and said: "There's a real mystery here, because the following question is one that must have an answer. But how can we answer it?" The question is, "Have they started up the very same club—is it the same club as the one they belonged to in England—or is it a completely new club that's just exactly similar?"

VESEY Yes.

PARFIT Well, in that case we all think that this man's remark is absurd; there's no difference at all. Now that's my model for the true view about the case where they make a duplicate of me. It seems that there's all the difference in the world between its being me and its being this other person who's exactly like me. But if we think there's no difference at all in the case of the clubs, why do we think there's a difference in the case of personal identity, and how can we defend the view that there's a difference?

VESEY I can see how some people would defend it. I mean, a dualist would defend it in terms of a soul being a simple thing, but . . .

PARFIT Let me try another case which I think helps to ease us out of this belief we're very strongly inclined to hold.

VESEY Go on.

PARFIT Well, this isn't a single case, this is a whole range of cases. A whole smooth spectrum of different cases which are all very similar to the next one in the range. At the start of this range of cases you suppose that the scientists are going to replace one per cent of the cells in your brain and body with exact duplicates.

VESEY Yes.

PARFIT Now if that were to be done, no one has any doubt that you'd survive. I think that's obvious because after all you can *lose* one per cent of the cells and survive. As we get further along the range they replace a larger and larger percentage of cells with exact duplicates, and of course at the far end of this range, where they replace a hundred per cent, then we've got my case where they just make a duplicate out of wholly fresh matter.

VESEY Yes.

PARFIT Now on the view that there's all the difference in the world between its being me and its being this other person who is exactly like me, we ought in consistency to think that in some case in the middle of the range, where, say, they're going to replace fifty per cent, the same question arises: Is it going to be me or this completely different character? I think that even the most convinced dualist who believes in the soul is going to find this range of cases very embarrassing, because he seems committed to the view that there's some crucial percentage up to which it's going to be him and after which it suddenly ceases to be him. But I find that wholly unbelievable.

VESEY   Yes. He's going to have to invent some sort of theory about the relation of mind and body to get round this one. I'm not quite sure how he would do it. Derek, could we go on to a related question? Suppose that I accepted what you said, that is, that there isn't anything more to identity than what you call psychological continuity in a one-one case. Suppose I accept that, then I would want to go on and ask you, well, what's the philosophical importance of this?

PARFIT   The philosophical importance is, I think, that psychological continuity is obviously, when we think about it, a matter of degree. So long as we think that identity is a further fact, one of the things we're inclined to think is that it's all or nothing, as you said earlier. Well, if we give up that belief and if we realize that what matters in my continued existence is a matter of degree, then this does make a difference in actual cases. All the cases that I've considered so far are of course bizarre science fiction cases. But I think that in actual life it's obvious on reflection that, to give an example, the relations between me now and me next year are much closer in every way than the relation between me now and me in twenty years. And the sorts of relations that I'm thinking of are relations of memory, character, ambition, intention—all of those. Next year I shall remember much more of this year than I will in twenty years. I shall have a much more similar character. I shall be carrying out more of the same plans, ambitions and, if that is so, I think there are various plausible implications for our moral beliefs and various possible effects on our emotions.

VESEY   For our moral beliefs? What have you in mind?

PARFIT   Let's take one very simple example. On the view which I'm sketching it seems to me much more plausible to claim that people deserve much less punishment, or even perhaps no punishment, for what they did many years ago as compared with what they did very recently. Plausible because the relations between them now and them many years ago when they committed the crime are so much weaker.

VESEY   But they are still the people who are responsible for the crime.

PARFIT   I think you say that because even if they've changed in many ways, after all it was just as much they who committed the crime. I think that's true, but on the view for which I'm arguing, we would come to think that it's a completely trivial truth. It's like the following truth: it's like the truth that all of my relatives are just as much my relatives. Suppose I in my will left more money to my close relatives and less to my distant relatives; a mere pittance to my second cousin twenty-nine times removed. If you said, "But that's clearly unreasonable because all of your relatives are just as much your relatives," there's a sense in which that's true but it's obviously too trivial to make my will an unreasonable will. And that's because what's involved in kinship is a matter of degree.

VESEY   Yes.

PARFIT   Now, if we think that what's involved in its being the same person now as the person who committed the crime is a matter of degree, then the truth that it was just as much him who committed the crime, will seem to us trivial in the way in which the truth that all my relatives are equally my relatives is trivial.

VESEY   Yes. So you think that I should regard myself in twenty years' time as like a fairly distant relative of myself?

PARFIT   Well, I don't want to exaggerate; I think the connections are much closer.

VESEY   Suppose I said that this point about psychological continuity being a matter of degree—suppose I said that this isn't anything that anybody denies?

PARFIT   I don't think anybody does on reflection deny that psychological continuity is a matter of degree. But I think what they may deny, and I think what may make a difference to their view, if they come over to the view for which I'm arguing—what they may deny is that psychological continuity is all there is to identity. Because what I'm arguing against is this further belief which I think we're all inclined to hold even if we don't realize it. The belief that however much we change, there's a profound sense in which the changed us is going to be just as much us. That even if some magic wand turned me into a completely different sort of person—a prince with totally different character, mental powers—it would be just as much me. That's what I'm denying.

VESEY   Yes. This is the belief which I began by stating, and I think that if we did lose that belief that would be a change indeed.

Are People Machines?

46. Can a Machine Think?

Christopher Evans

Christopher Evans (1931–1979) was an experimental psychologist and computer scientist. He wrote several books on various aspects of psychology.

In the early years of the second world war when the British began, in ultra-secret, to put together their effort to crack German codes, they set out to recruit a team of the brightest minds available in mathematics and the then rather novel field of electronic engineering. Recruiting the electronic whizzes was easy, as many of them were to be found engrossed in the fascinating problem of radio location of aircraft— or radar as it later came to be called. Finding mathematicians with the right kind of obsessive brilliance to make a contribution in the strange field of cryptography was another matter. In the end they adopted the ingenious strategy of searching through lists of young mathematicians who were also top-flight chess players. As a result of a nationwide trawl an amazing collection of characters were billeted together in the country-house surroundings of Bletchley Park, and three of the most remarkable were Irving John Good, Donald Michie, and Alan Turing. . . .

If contemporary accounts of what the workers at Bletchley were talking about in their few moments of spare time can be relied on, many of them were a bit over-optimistic if anything. Both Good and Michie believed that the use of electronic computers such as Colossus[1] would result in major advances in mathematics in the immediate post-war era and Turing was of the same opinion. All three (and one or two of their colleagues) were also confident that it would not be long before machines were exhibiting intelligence, including problem-solving abilities, and that their role as simple number-crunchers was only one phase in their evolution. Although the exact substance of their conversations, carried long into the night when they were waiting for the test results of the first creaky Colossus prototypes, has softened with passage of time, it is known the topic of machine intelligence loomed very large. They discussed, with a *frisson* of excitement and unease, the peculiar ramifications of the subject they were pioneering and about which the rest of the world knew (and still knows) so little. Could there ever be a machine which

[1]An early computer that was first used in 1943.–Ed.

was able to solve problems that no human could solve? Could a computer ever beat a human at chess? Lastly, could a machine *think?*

Of all the questions that can be asked about computers none has such an eerie ring. Allow a machine intelligence perhaps, the ability to control other machines, repair itself, help us solve problems, compute numbers a million fold quicker than any human; allow it to fly airplanes, drive cars, superintend our medical records and even, possibly, give advice to politicians. Somehow you can see how a machine might come to do all these things. But that it could be made to perform that apparently exclusively human operation known as *thinking* is something else, and something which is offensive, alien and threatening. Only in the most *outré* forms of science fiction, stretching back to Mary Shelley's masterpiece *Frankenstein*, is the topic touched on, and always with a sense of great uncertainty about the enigmatic nature of the problem area.

Good, Michie and their companions were content to work the ideas through in their spare moments. But Turing—older, a touch more serious and less cavalier—set out to consider things in depth. In particular he addressed himself to the critical question: Can, or could, a machine think? The way he set out to do this three decades ago and long before any other scientists had considered it so cogently, is of lasting interest. The main thesis was published in the philosophical journal *Mind* in 1950. Logically unassailable, when read impartially it serves to break down any barriers of uncertainty which surround this and parallel questions. Despite its classic status the work is seldom read outside the fields of computer science and philosophy, but now that events in computer science and in the field of artificial intelligence are beginning to move with the rapidity and momentum which the Bletchley scientists knew they ultimately would, the time has come for Turing's paper to achieve a wider public.

Soon after the war ended and the Colossus project folded, Turing joined the National Physical Laboratory in Teddington and began to work with a gifted team on the design of what was to become the world's most powerful computer, ACE. Later he moved to Manchester, where, spurred by the pioneers Kilburn, Hartee, Williams and Newman, a vigorous effort was being applied to develop another powerful electronic machine. It was a heady, hard-driving time, comparable to the state of events now prevailing in microprocessors, when anyone with special knowledge rushes along under immense pressure, ever conscious of the feeling that whoever is second in the race may as well not have entered it at all. As a result Turing found less time than he would have hoped to follow up his private hobbies, particularly his ideas on computer game-playing—checkers, chess and the ancient game of Go—which he saw was an important sub-set of machine intelligence.

Games like chess are unarguably intellectual pursuits, and yet, unlike certain other intellectual exercises, such as writing poetry or discussing the inconsistent football of the hometown team, they have easily describable rules of operation. The task, therefore, would seem to be simply a matter of writing a computer program which "knew" these rules and which could follow them when faced with moves offered by a human player. Turing made very little headway as it happens, and the first chess-playing programs which were scratched together in the late '40s and early '50s were quite awful—so much so that there was a strong feeling that this kind of project was not worth pursuing, since the game of chess as played by an "expert" involves some special intellectual skill which could never be specified in machine terms.

Turing found this ready dismissal of the computer's potential to be both interesting and suggestive. If people were unwilling to accept the idea of a machine which could play games, how would they feel about one which exhibited "intelligence," or one which could "think"? In the course of discussions with friends Turing found that a good part of the problem was that people were universally unsure of their definitions. What exactly did one mean when one used the word "thought"? What processes were actually in action when "thinking" took place? If a machine was created which *could* think, how would one set about testing it? The last question, Turing surmised, was the key one, and with a wonderful surge of imagination spotted a way to answer it, proposing what has in computer circles come to be known as "The Turing Test for Thinking Machines." In the next section, we will examine that test, see how workable it is, and also try to assess how close computers have come, and will come, to passing it.

When Turing asked people whether they believed that a computer could think, he found almost universal rejection of the idea—just as I did when I carried out a similar survey almost thirty years later. The objections I received were similar to those that Turing documented in his paper "Computing Machinery and Intelligence,"[2] and I will summarize them here, adding my own comments and trying to meet the various objections as they occur.

First there is the Theological Objection. This was more common in Turing's time than it is now, but it still crops up occasionally. It can be summed up as follows: "Man is a creation of God, and has been given a soul and the power of conscious thought. Machines are not spiritual beings, have no soul and thus must be incapable of thought." As Turing pointed out, this seems to place an unwarranted restriction on God. Why shouldn't he give machines souls and allow them to think if he wanted to? On one level I suppose it is irrefutable: if someone chooses to define thinking as something that *only* Man can do and that *only* God can bestow, then that is the end of the matter. Even then the force of the argument does seem to depend upon a confusion between "thought" and "spirituality," upon the old Cartesian dichotomy of the ghost in the machine. The ghost presumably does the thinking while the machine is merely the vehicle which carries the ghost around.

Then there is the Shock/Horror Objection, which Turing called the "Heads in the Sand Objection." Both phrases will do though I prefer my own. When the subject of machine thought is first broached, a common reaction goes something like this: "What a horrible idea! How could any scientist work on such a monstrous development? I hope to goodness that the field of artificial intelligence doesn't advance a step further if its end-product is a thinking machine!" The attitude is not very logical—and it is not really an argument why it *could* not happen, but rather the expression of a heartfelt wish that it never will!

---

[2]Published in *Mind*, Vol. LIX (October, 1950).—Ed.

The Extra-sensory Perception Objection was the one that impressed Turing most, and impresses me least. *If* there were such a thing as extra-sensory perception and *if* it were in some way a function of human brains, then it could well also be an important constituent of thought. By this token, in the absence of any evidence proving that computers are telepathic, we would have to assume that they could never be capable of thinking in its fullest sense. The same argument applies to any other "psychic" or spiritual component of human psychology. I cannot take this objection seriously because there seems to me to be no evidence which carries any scientific weight that extra-sensory perception does exist. The situation was different in Turing's time, when the world-renowned parapsychology laboratory at Duke University in North Carolina, under Dr. J. B. Rhine, was generating an enormous amount of material supposedly offering evidence for telepathy and precognition. This is not the place to go into the long, and by no means conclusive, arguments about the declining status of parapsychology, but it is certainly true that as far as most scientists are concerned, what once looked like a rather good case for the existence of telepathy, etc., now seems to be an extremely thin one. But even if ESP *is* shown to be a genuine phenomenon, it is, in my own view, something to do with the transmission of information from a source point to a receiver and ought therefore to be quite easy to reproduce in a machine. After all, machines can communicate by radio already, which is, effectively, ESP and is a far better method of long-distance communication than that possessed by any biological system.

The Personal Consciousness Objection is, superficially, a rather potent argument which comes up in various guises. Turing noticed it expressed particularly cogently in a report, in the *British Medical Journal* in 1949, on the Lister Oration for that year, which was entitled "The Mind of Mechanical Man." It was given by a distinguished medical scientist, Professor G. Jefferson. A short quote from the Oration will suffice:

> Not until a machine can write a sonnet or compose a concerto *because of thoughts and emotions felt*, and not by the chance fall of symbols, could we agree that machine equals brain—that is, not only write it but *know that it had written it*. No mechanism could feel (and not merely artificially signal, an easy contrivance) pleasure at its successes, grief when its valves fuse, be warmed by flattery, be made miserable by its mistakes, be charmed by sex, be angry or depressed when it cannot get what it wants.

The italics, which are mine, highlight what I believe to be the fundamental objection: the output of the machine is more or less irrelevant, no matter how impressive it is. Even if it wrote a sonnet—and a very good one—it would not mean much unless it had written it as the result of "thoughts and emotions felt," and it would also have to "know that it had written it." This could be a useful "final definition" of one aspect of human thought—but how would you establish whether or not the sonnet was written with "emotions"? Asking the computer would not help for, as Professor Jefferson realized, there would be no guarantee that it was not simply *declaring* that it had felt emotions. He is really propounding the extreme solipsist position and should, therefore, apply the same rules to humans. Extreme solipsism is logically irrefutable ("I am the only real thing; all else is illusion") but it is so unhelpful a view of the universe that most people choose to ignore it and decide that when people say they are thinking or feeling they may as well believe them. In other words, Professor Jefferson's objection could be over-ridden if you *became* the computer and experienced its thoughts (if any)—only then could you really *know*. His objection is worth discussing in some depth because it is so commonly heard in one form or another, and because it sets us up in part for Turing's resolution of the machine-thought problem, which we will come to later.

The Unpredictability Objection argues that computers are created by humans according to sets of rules and operate according to carefully scripted programs which themselves are sets of rules. So if you wanted to, you could work out exactly what a computer was going to do at any particular time. It is, in principle, totally predictable. *If* you have all the facts available you *can* predict a computer's behavior because it follows rules, whereas there is no way in which you could hope to do the same with a human *because he is not behaving according to a set of immutable rules.* Thus there is an essential difference between computers and humans, so (the argument gets rather weak here) thinking, because it is unpredictable and does not blindly follow rules, must be an essentially human ability.

There are two comments: firstly, computers are becoming so complex that it is doubtful their behavior could be predicted even if everything was known about them—computer programmers and engineers have found that one of the striking characteristics of present-day systems is that they constantly spring surprises. The second point follows naturally: humans are *already* in that super-complex state and the reason that we cannot predict what they do is *not* because they have no ground rules but because (a) we don't know what the rules are, and (b) even if we did know them they would still be too complicated to handle. At best, the unpredictability argument is thin, but it is often raised. People frequently remark that there is always "the element of surprise" in a human. I have no doubt that that is just because *any* very complex system is bound to be surprising. A variant of the argument is that humans are capable of error whereas the "perfect" computer is not. That may well be true, which suggests that machines are superior to humans, for there seems to be little point in having any information-processing system, biological or electronic, that makes errors in processing. It would be possible to build a random element into computers to make them unpredictable from time to time, but it would be a peculiarly pointless exercise.

The "See How Stupid They Are" Objection will not need much introduction. At one level it is expressed in jokes about computers that generate ridiculous bank statements or electricity bills; at another and subtler level, it is a fair appraisal of the computer's stupendous weaknesses in comparison with Man. "How could you possibly imagine that such backward, limited things could ever reach the point where they could be said to think?" The answer, as we have already pointed out, is that they may be dumb now but they have advanced at a pretty dramatic rate and show every sign of continuing to do so. Their present limitations may be valid when arguing whether they could be said to be capable of thinking *now* or in the *very* near future, but it has no relevance to whether they would be capable of thinking at some later date.

The "Ah But It Can't Do That" Objection is an eternally regressing argument which, for a quarter of a century, computer scientists have been listening to, partially refuting, and then having to listen to all over again. It runs: "Oh yes, you can obviously make a computer do so and so—you have just demonstrated that, but of course you will never be able to make it do such and such." The such and such may be anything you name—once it was play a good game of chess, have a storage capacity greater than the human memory, read human hand-writing or understand human speech. Now that these "Ah buts" have (quite swiftly) been overcome, one is faced by a new range: beat the world human chess champion, operate on parallel as opposed to serial processing, perform medical diagnosis better than a doctor, translate satisfactorily from one language to another, help solve its own software problems, etc. When these challenges are met, no doubt it will have to design a complete city from scratch, invent a game more interesting than chess, admire a pretty girl/handsome man, work out the unified field theory, enjoy bacon and eggs, and so on. I cannot think of anything more silly than developing a computer which could enjoy bacon and eggs, but there is nothing to suggest that, provided enough time and money was invested, one could not pull off such a surrealistic venture. On the other hand, it might be *most* useful to have computers design safe, optimally cheap buildings. Even more ambitious (and perhaps comparable to the bacon and egg project but more worthwhile) would be to set a system to tackle the problem of the relationship between gravity and light, and my own guess is that before the conclusion of the long-term future (before the start of the twenty-first century), computers will be hard at work on these problems and will be having great success.

The "It Is Not Biological" Objection may seem like another version of the theological objection—only living things could have the capacity for thought, so nonbiological systems could not possibly think. But there is a subtle edge that requires a bit more explanation. It is a characteristic of most modern computers that they are discrete state machines, which is to say that they are digital and operate in a series of discrete steps—on/off. Now the biological central nervous system may not be so obviously digital, though there is evidence that the neurone, the basic unit of communication, acts in an on/off, all or nothing way. But if it turned out that it were *not*, and operated on some more elaborate strategy, then it is conceivable that "thought" might only be manifest in things which had switching systems of this more elaborate kind. Put it another way: it might be possible to build digital computers which were immensely intelligent, but no matter how intelligent they became they would never be able to *think*. The argument cannot be refuted at the moment, but even so there is no shred of evidence to suppose that only non-digital systems can think. There may be other facets of living things that make them unique from the point of view of their capacity to generate thought, but none that we can identify, or even guess at. This objection therefore is not a valid one at present, though in the event of some new biological discovery, it may became so.

The Mathematical Objection is one of the most intriguing of the ten objections, and is the one most frequently encountered in discussions with academics. It is based on a fascinating exercise in mathematical logic propounded by the Hungarian Kurt Gödel. To put it rather superficially, Gödel's theorem shows that within any sufficiently powerful logical system (which could be a computer operating according to clearly defined rules), statements can be formulated which can neither be proved nor disproved *within the system*. In his famous 1936 paper, Alan Turing restructured Gödel's theorem so that it could apply specifically to machines. This effectively states that no matter how powerful a computer is, there are bound to be certain tasks that it cannot tackle on its own. In other words, you could not build a computer which could solve *every* problem no matter how well it was programmed; or, if you wanted to carry the thing to the realms of fancy, no computer (or any other digital system) could end up being God.

Gödel's theorem, and its later refinements by Alonzo Church, Bertrand Russell and others, is interesting to mathematicians, not so much because it assumes an implicit limitation to machine intelligence, but because it indicates a limitation to mathematics itself. But the theorem has been used, incorrectly, by critics of machine intelligence to "prove" that computers could never reach the same intellectual level as Man. The weakness of the position is that it is based on the assumption that the human brain is not a formal logical system. But such evidence as we have suggests very strongly that it is and will, therefore, be bound by the same Gödel-limitations as are machines. There is also a tweak in the tail. While the theorem admittedly states that no system *on its own* can completely tackle its own problems—"understand itself"—it does *not* imply that the areas of mystery could not be tackled by some other system. No individual human brain could solve its own problems or fully "know itself," but with the assistance of other brains these deficiencies might be corrected. Equally, and significantly, problem areas associated with complex computer systems could be solved totally and absolutely by other computer systems, provided that *they* were clever enough.

The last of the ten arguments against the concept of a thinking machine has become known as Lady Lovelace's Objection. . . . In its modern form this comes up as, "A Computer cannot do anything that you have not programmed it to." The objection is so fundamental and so widely accepted that it needs detailed discussion.

In the most absolute and literal sense, this statement is perfectly correct and applies to any machine or computer that has been made or that could be made. According to the rules of the universe that we live in, nothing can take place without a prior cause; a computer will not spring into action without something powering it and guiding it on its way. In the case of the various tasks that a computer performs, the "cause"—to stretch the use of the word rather—is the program or sets of programs that control these tasks. Much the same applies to a brain: it, too, must come equipped with sets of programs which cause it to run through its repertoire of tasks. This might seem to support Lady Lovelace, at least to the extent that machines "need" a human to set them up, but it would also seem to invalidate the argument that this constitutes an essential difference between computers and people. But is there not still a crucial difference between brains and computers? No matter how sophisticated computers are, must there not always have been a human being to *write* its programs? Surely the same does not have to be said for humans?

To tackle this we need to remember that all brains, human included, are equipped at birth with a comprehensive collection of programs which are common to all members of a species and which are known as instincts. These control respiration, gastric absorption, cardiac activity, and, at a behavioral level, such reflexes as sucking, eyeblink, grasping and so on. There may also be programs which "cause" the young animal to explore its environment, exercise its muscles, play and so on. Where do these come from? Well, they are acquired over an immensely long-winded trial-and-error process through the course of evolution. We might call them permanent software ("firmware" is the phrase used sometimes by computer scientists) and they correspond to the suites of programs which every computer has when it leaves the factory, and which are to do with its basic running, maintenance, and so on.

In addition to this, all biological computers come equipped with a bank of what might best be described as raw programs. No one has the faintest idea whether they are neurological, biochemical, electrical or what—all we know is that they *must* exist. They start being laid down the moment the creature begins to interact with the world around it. In the course of time they build up into a colossal suite of software which ultimately enables us to talk, write, walk, read, enjoy bacon and eggs, appreciate music, think, feel, write books, or come up with mathematical ideas. These programs are useful only to the owner of that particular brain, vanish with his death and are quite separate from the "firmware."

If this seems too trivial a description of the magnificent field of human learning and achievement, it is only because anything appears trivial when you reduce it to its bare components: a fabulous sculpture to a quintillion highly similar electrons and protons, a microprocessor to a million impurities buried in a wafer of sand, the human brain into a collection of neurones, blood cells and chemical elements. What is not trivial is the endlessly devious, indescribably profound way in which these elements are structured to make up the whole. The real difference between the brain and most existing computers is that in the former, data acquisition and the initial writing and later modification of the program is done by a mechanism within the brain itself, while in the latter, the software is prepared outside and passed to the computer in its completed state. But I did use the word "most." In recent years increasing emphasis has been placed on the development of "adaptive" programs—software which can be modified and revised on the basis of the program's interaction with the environment. In simple terms these could be looked upon as "programs which learn for themselves," and they will, in due course, become an important feature of many powerful computer systems.

At this point the sceptic still has a few weapons in his armoury. The first is generally put in the form of the statement: "Ah, but even when computers *can* update their own software and acquire new programs for themselves, they will still only be doing this because of Man's ingenuity. Man may no longer actually write the programs, but had he not invented the idea of the self-adaptive program in the first place none of this could have happened." This is perfectly true but has little to do with whether or not computers could think, or perform any other intellectual exercise. It could place computers eternally in our debt, and we may be able to enjoy a smug sense of pride at having created them, but it offers no real restriction on their development.

The sceptic may also argue that no matter how clever or how intelligent you make computers, they will never be able to perform a creative task. Everything they do will inevitably spring from something they have been taught, have experienced or is the subject of some preexisting program. There are two points being made here. One is that computers could never have an original or creative thought. The other is that the seeds of everything they do, no matter how intelligent, lie in their existing software. To take the second point first: again one is forced to say that the same comment applies to humans. Unless the argument is that some of Man's thoughts or ideas come from genuine inspiration—a message from God, angels, or spirits of the departed—no one can dispute that all aspects of our intelligence evolve from preexisting programs and the background experiences of life. This evolution may be enormously complex and its progress might be impossible to track, but any intellectual flowering arises from the seeds of experience planted in the fertile substrate of the brain.

There still remains the point about creativity, and it is one that is full of pitfalls. Before making any assumptions about creativity being an *exclusive* attribute of Man, the concept has to be defined. It is not enough to say "write a poem," "paint a picture" or "discuss philosophical ideas," because it is easy enough to program computers to do all these things. The fact that their poems, paintings and philosophical ramblings are pretty mediocre is beside the point: it would be just as unfair to ask them to write, say, a sonnet of Shakespearian calibre or a painting of da Vinci quality and fail them for lack of creativity as it would be to give the same task to the man in the street. Beware too of repeating the old saying, "Ah, but you have to program them to paint, play chess and so on," for the same is unquestionably true of people. Try handing a twelve-month-old baby a pot of paint or a chessboard if you have any doubts about the need for some measure of learning and experience.

Obviously a crisper definition of creativity is required, and here is one that is almost universally acceptable: If a person demonstrates a skill which has never been demonstrated before and which was not specifically taught to him by someone else, or in the intellectual domain provides an *entirely novel* solution to a problem—a solution which was not known to any other human being—then they can be said to have done something original or had an original or creative thought. There may be other forms of creativity of course, but this would undeniably be an example of it in action. There is plenty of evidence that humans are creative by this standard and the history of science is littered with "original" ideas which humans have generated. Clearly, until a computer also provides such evidence, Lady Lovelace's Objection still holds, at least in one of its forms.

But alas for the sceptics. This particular barrier has been overthrown by computers on a number of occasions in the past few years. A well-publicized one was the solution, by a computer, of the venerable "four colour problem." This has some mathematical importance, and can best be expressed by thinking of a two-dimensional map featuring a large number of territories, say the counties of England or the states of the USA. Supposing you want to give each territory a colour, what is the minimum number of colours you need to employ to ensure that no two territories of the same colour adjoin each other?

After fiddling around with maps and crayons, you will find that the number seems to come out at four, and no one has ever been able to find a configuration where five colours are required, or where you can always get away with three. Empirically, therefore, four is the answer—hence the name of the problem. But if you attempt to demonstrate this mathematically and *prove* that four colours will do for any conceivable map, you will get nowhere. For decades mathematicians have wrestled with this elusive problem, and from time to time have come up with a "proof" which in the end turns out to be incomplete or fallacious. But the mathematical world was rocked when in 1977 the problem was handed over to a computer, which attacked it with a stupendous frontal assault, sifting through huge combinations of possibilities and eventually demonstrating, to every mathematician's satisfaction, that four colours would do the trick. Actually, although this is spectacular testimony to the computer's creative powers, it is not really the most cogent example, for its technique was block-busting rather than heuristic (problem solving by testing hypotheses). It was like solving a chess problem by working out every possible combination of moves, rather than by concentrating on likely areas and experimenting with them. A better, and much earlier, demonstration of computer originality came from a program which was set to generate some totally new proofs in Euclidean geometry. The computer produced a completely novel proof of the well-known theorem which shows that the base angles of an isosceles triangle are equal, by flipping the triangles through 180 degrees and declaring them to be congruent. Quite apart from the fact that it had not before been known to Man, it showed such originality that one famous mathematician remarked, "If any of my students had done that, I would have marked him down as a budding genius."

And so Lady Lovelace's long-lasting objection can be overruled. We have shown that computers can be intelligent, and that they can even be creative—but we have not yet proved that they can, or ever could, *think*.

Now, what do we mean by the word "think"?

Towards the Ultra-Intelligent Machine

The most common objections raised to the notion of thinking machines are based on misunderstandings of fairly simple issues, or on semantic confusions of one kind or another. We are still left with the problem of defining the verb "to think," and in this section we will attempt to deal with this, or at least to discuss one particular and very compelling way of dealing with it. From this position we shall find ourselves drifting inevitably into a consideration of the problem of creating thinking machines, and in particular to the eerie concept of the Ultra-Intelligent Machine.

Most people believe that they know what they mean when they talk about "thinking" and have no difficulty identifying it when it is going on in their own heads. We are prepared to believe other human beings think because we have experience of it ourselves and accept that it is a common property of the human race. But we cannot make the same assumption about machines, and would be sceptical if one of them told us, no matter how persuasively, that it too was thinking. But sooner or later a machine will make just such a declaration and the question then will be, how do we decide whether to believe it or not?

When Turing tackled the machine-thought issue, he proposed a characteristically brilliant solution which, while not entirely free from flaws, is nevertheless the best that has yet been put forward. The key to it all, he pointed out, is to ask what the signs and signals are that humans give out, from which we infer that *they* are thinking. It is clearly a matter of *what kind of conversation we can have with them*, and has nothing to do with what kind of face they have and what kind of clothes they wear. Unfortunately physical appearances automatically set up prejudices in our minds, and if we were having a spirited conversation with a microprocessor we might be very sceptical about its capacity for thought, simply because it did not look like any thinking thing we had seen in the past. But we *would* be interested in what it had to say; and thus Turing invented his experiment or test.

Put a human—the judge or tester—in a room where there are two computer terminals, one connected to a computer, the other to a person. The judge, of course, does not know which terminal is connected to which, but can type into either terminal and receive typed messages back on them. Now the judge's job is to decide, by carrying out conversations with the entities on the end of the respective terminals, *which is which*. If the computer is very stupid, it will immediately be revealed as such and the human will have no difficulty identifying it. If it is bright, he may find that he can carry on quite a good conversation with it, though he may ultimately spot that it must be the computer. If it is exceptionally bright and has a wide range of knowledge, he may find it impossible to say whether it is the computer he is talking to or the person. In this case, Turing argues, the computer will have passed the test and could for all practical purposes be said to be a thinking machine.

The argument has a simple but compelling force: if the intellectual exchange we achieve with a machine is indistinguishable from that we have with a being we *know* to be thinking, then we are, to all intents and purposes, communicating with another thinking being. This, by the way, does not imply that the personal experience, state of consciousness, level of awareness or whatever, of the entity is going to be the same as that experienced by a human when he or she thinks, so the test is not for these particular qualities. They are not, in any case, the parameters which concern the observer.

At first the Turing Test may seem a surprising way of looking at the problem, but it is an extremely sensible way of approaching it. The question now arises: Is any computer at present in existence capable of passing the test?—And if not, how long is it likely to be before one comes along? From time to time one laboratory or another claims that a computer has had at least a pretty good stab at it. Scientists using the big computer conferencing systems (each scientist has a terminal in his office and is connected to his colleagues via the computer, which acts as host and general message-sorter) often find it difficult to be sure, for a brief period of time at least, whether they are talking to the computer or to one of their colleagues. On one celebrated occasion at MIT, two scientists had been chatting via the network when one of them left the scene without telling the other, who carried on a cheery conversation with the computer under the assumption that he was talking to his friend. I have had the same spooky experience when chatting with computers which I have programmed myself, and often find their answers curiously perceptive and unpredictable.

To give another interesting example: in the remarkable match played in Toronto in August 1978 between the International Chess Master David Levy, and the then computer chess champion of the world, Northwestern University's "Chess 4.7," the computer made a number of moves of an uncannily "human" nature. The effect was so powerful that Levy subsequently told me that he found it difficult to believe that he was not facing an outstanding human opponent. Few chess buffs who looked at the move-by-move transcripts of the match were, without prior knowledge, able to tell which had been made by the computer and which by the flesh-and-blood chess master. David Levy himself suggested that Chess 4.7 had effectively passed the Turing Test.

It would be nice to believe that I had been present on such an historic occasion, but this did not constitute a proper "pass." In the test as Turing formulated it, the judge is allowed to converse with either of his two mystery entities on any topic that he chooses, and he may use any conversational trick he wants. Furthermore he can continue the inquisition for as long as he wants, always seeking some clue that will force the computer to reveal itself. Both the computer and the human can lie if they want to in their attempts to fool the tester, so the answers to questions like "Are you the computer?" or "Do you watch much television?" will not give much away. Obviously any computer with a chance in hell of passing the test will have to have a pretty substantial bank of software at its disposal, and not just be extremely bright in one area. Chess 4.7 for example might look as though it was thinking if it was questioned about chess, or, better still, invited to play the game, but switch the area of discourse to human anatomy, politics or good restaurants and it would be shown up as a dunderhead.

As things stand at present, computers have quite a way to go before they jump the hurdle so cleverly laid out for them by Turing. But this should not be taken as providing unmitigated comfort for those who resist the notion of advanced machine intelligence. It should now be clear that the difference, in intellectual terms, between a human being and a computer is one of degree and not of kind.

Turing himself says in his *Mind* paper that he feels computers will have passed the test before the turn of the century, and there is little doubt that he would dearly have liked to live long enough to be around on the splendiferous occasion when "machine thinking" first occurred.

47. Minds or Machines

John Beloff

John Beloff (1920–) is a retired professor of psychology at the University of Edinburgh in Scotland. He is best known for his defense of dualism and his writings on parapsychology.

The attempt to understand the workings of the mind using mechanical models and analogies is as old as psychology itself. An entirely new chapter began, however, around the middle of this century with the advent of the computer. For the first time we had now to reckon with the fact that machines could perform tasks which had hitherto depended on human ingenuity. From then on the temptation to take the computer as the model for our own cognitive processes became even harder to resist. Yet the time has come to ask ourselves whether this computational metaphor as it has been called might not be more misleading than illuminating. Much will depend on whether we believe that a living mind has properties that distinguish it from any conceivable artifact that might be designed to simulate its output. What in this paper I shall refer to as the "strong claim" is the claim put forward by some proponents of artificial intelligence that nothing essential differentiates the human mind from a possible mind-like machine so that a perfect simulation of human mental activity using the hardware of a computer would in fact amount to an exemplification of such activity. This strong claim carries with it the corollary that there is no theoretical limit to what a machine could be expected to do.

It is clear that the claim we are to consider is a bold one and yet it has already received widespread endorsement from eminent contemporary philosophers and psychologists. Nor should this surprise us. Behavioristic and physicalistic theories of mind have been a recurrent feature of twentieth-century philosophy and psychology at any rate in the English-speaking world. Such theories purport to cut the ground from under the obvious objection which the claim might otherwise encounter, namely that while minds are conscious machines are not. For, if mental processes are nothing over and above the workings of the brain conceived as a self-regulating physical system there seems to be no reason, other than practical limitations in our engineering techniques, why mental processes should not be exemplified in an artifact. On the traditional dualistic account, of course, mental events were taken to indicate the interaction between an immaterial mind and a material brain and, so long as this view prevailed the scope of A.I. was clearly restricted. Thus, the strong claim is closely bound up with the perennial mind-body problem and our assessment of it will depend on the position we take on that issue.

From *Truth: An International, Inter-Disciplinary Journal of Christian Thought.* Volume 2 (1988). Reprinted by permission of Christian Leadership Ministries.

The current theory of mind that is most congenial to the strong claim is that which goes by the name of Functionalism. . . . Briefly, it is the contention of a Functionalist that a mental event is to be understood in terms of the function that it performs with reference to a given system or organism. For example, for a Functionalist, a given sensation is not something that is to be defined ostensively in terms of its peculiar quality but rather by reference to the sort of behavioral discriminations that it makes possible.

Thus a pain should not in the first instance be thought of as some special kind of private event but as that which brings about avoidance or escape reactions. Likewise, thinking should not be regarded as a process going on in some private arena to which the thinker alone has access but as the process that brings about problem-solving or other such objective achievements and, in the same vein, a Functionalist analysis can be provided for desiring, intending, believing, expecting and so on across the board for each instance of what traditionally comes under the heading of the mental. The novelty of the Functionalist position is that it is neutral with respect to the composition of the system with whose operations one is concerned. That the system in question should be made of neurons rather than wires and transistors, that it should be a living organism rather than an artifact, is, for Functionalism, a matter of indifference since the concept of the mental is to be defined in terms of function not in terms of the nature of the system in which it originates. In this respect it differed from other earlier physicalistic theories of mind. Thus, according to "Central State Materialism" mental events had to be identified with events in the brain or central nervous system. This implied that brain tissues had some special property that could not necessarily be attributed to inanimate systems. It follows that Functionalism is easier to reconcile with our "strong claim" than any version of mind-brain identity theory.

The crucial question we have next to ask is whether Functionalism is, in fact, a tenable position with respect to the mind-body problem[.] Given its illustrious credentials one hesitates to say no. Nevertheless this is the answer that I propose to make and which I shall endeavour to justify. It transpires that Functionalism falls at the first post inasmuch as it disregards certain facts that are universally acknowledged, at least by everyone who does not happen to be committed to some bizarre philosophical thesis. Consider those objects of introspection which philosophers sometimes refer to as "qualia" or which in ordinary parlance we might call conscious sensations. The fact is that these entities can be recognized and described by those who experience them independently of the function, if any, that they may perform in our behavior or mental life. Indeed, in certain types of passive experience, say in contemplation, it is arguable whether they have any observable consequences but they are none the less real and definite for all that. In short, Functionalism cannot be the whole truth about the nature of mental events. Nevertheless, the Functionalist might well plead that the sacrifice of the qualia is a small price to pay for the advantages which his philosophy offers in the wider context of the continuing debate about the compatibility of artificial and natural intelligence. So, rather than digging in our heels over the issue of qualia, let us move on to something much closer to the heart of this controversy, namely the nature of thinking itself.

Such plausibility as attaches to the strong claim derives from the fact that computers solve complex problems often more successfully and always more rapidly than the unaided human intellect. This is a remarkable fact which familiarity tends to make us take too much for granted. There was a time when the very idea that a machine might be able to compete on the intellectual plane with a rational human being would have been regarded as too fantastic or absurd to merit serious consideration. During the early 19th century a certain showman toured Europe and the United States with what was billed as a chess-playing automaton. People would be invited to challenge the "Turk," as the robot figure was nicknamed, and usually they were beaten. Naturally the shrewder onlookers suspected that a human operator was concealed somewhere inside the contraption but the concealment was done with such cunning that the audience would go away thoroughly bemused. The fame of this invention gave rise to a fair amount of controversy that found its way into print over the question of whether, in principle, it was possible to build a machine that was capable of thinking and reasoning. One of those who was fascinated by his encounter with the "Turk" was the American writer Edgar Allan Poe.[1]

Nowadays, of course, we would not be very surprised if we were to read in our newspaper one day that the new world chess champion was not Kasparaov nor yet Karpov but some chess-playing program with a fancy name conceived in some laboratory of A.I. For the fact is that we have learned to accept the principle that any rule-governed activity that can be precisely formalized can be simulated with a computer program. And even though in chess, thanks to the vast number of possible combinations, one cannot compute an infallible minimax strategy as one can for simpler board games, the use of appropriate heuristics has made possible increasingly powerful chess-playing programs. If, therefore, what we mean by thinking is finding solutions to problems or answers to questions then we already have all the evidence we need to say that machines can think. But is that all there is to thinking? No one would be tempted to say, for example, of a chess-manual that it thinks or of a textbook that gave the answers to the exercises it set. Yet, when all is said and done, a computer program is no more than a glorified book even if the manner in which we interact with the computer is more reminiscent of the way we might interrogate a fellow human. But, if there is more to thinking than just information-processing in the widest sense, what is that something extra?

The answer, I submit, is plain enough when we turn to our own experience of being engaged in thinking. The least that we would require before we were ready to say of something that it was thinking is that it should be aware of what it is doing, that it should know what it was thinking about, that it should recognize when it has reached a conclusion and that, in general, it should have

---

[1]This episode is discussed at length by David Fryer in his *Wheels within Wheels* (Unpublished Ph.D. Thesis; Edinburgh, 1978) see Chap. 6 "Opinions on Pinions: An Eighteenth Century Turing Game." The inventor of the machine was von Kempelen, a brilliant mechanician who was a court councillor at the court of Empress Maria Theresa of Austria. It was there that the machine was first demonstrated in 1769. It was later taken on tour by the showman Maelzel. Poe published his reflections on it in the *Southern Literary Messenger* for April 1836. Maelzel had a chess-player among his entourage which gave rise to speculations as to who might have been the "ghost" in his machine.

insight into what is going on. So the question is, can a machine have experiences of the sort which this implies? Admittedly one cannot prove that this cannot be the case but, at the same time, there is not the slightest reason for supposing that it does. Since the information-processing that is performed by a machine is wholly explicable in physicalistic terms it would be entirely gratuitous and fanciful to credit it with consciousness as this would imply. One could argue that, if we understood exactly how our own brains were constructed and knew the complete sensory input to which we have been exposed then we could explain our own thinking along physicalistic lines without needing to invoke conscious awareness. That is as may be. The point, however, is that, in the human case, we do have one instance where it is no longer a question of whether thinking is reflected in consciousness because we know, in a way that leaves no opening to doubt, that this is so, namely when we ourselves are the thinker. For it makes no sense to doubt whether we are conscious since doubting, as Descartes would have said, implies that one is conscious. It is true we cannot prove that other human beings are conscious when they think, logically speaking they might be insentient automata, that is the classic problem of "other minds," the inescapable possibility that the solipsistic nightmare might be true. But neither is there the slightest reason to suppose that we might be unique in this very fundamental way when, in most superficial respects, we are so similar to our fellow beings. In the case of the artifact, on the contrary, there is no reason to think and every reason to doubt that consciousness supervenes when information-processing is going on. Thus the situation as between minds and machines is in this respect by no means symmetrical. Defenders of the strong claim have tried to restore a degree of symmetry by proposing a law of emergence such that, once a given system attains a certain level of complexity and sophistication, it is deemed to be conscious. But it is difficult to see what evidence could be adduced to support such a law when the only known instance where consciousness supervenes is the human one. Moreover a study of brain activity suggests that there can be no simple relationship between brain processes and conscious experience since an important segment of our thinking, including perhaps the critical stages of problem solving, proceeds at an unconscious level.

One of the current cliches about mind and brain is that the brain corresponds to the hardware of a computer while the mind corresponds to its software, that is, to the way in which it is programmed. It is an analogy that is very much in accord with the Functionalist standpoint. A closer examination of the analogy, however, reveals certain confusions. We may compare the description of a computer as an information-processing device with the description of a chair as an item of furniture. The designation in both cases is appropriate and unexceptionable but we must not forget that it specifies the use to which the object is put. Hence, if we were to banish from the scene all potential users there could be neither information-processors nor items of furniture although, of course, computers and chairs would continue to exist as physical objects. Indeed one could imagine a computer, after the ultimate holocaust, continuing to print out information it was programmed to supply for as long as the electricity supply held out. And yet all that would be happening, in this instance, from an objective or ontological standpoint, is that electrical impulses would be passing through its circuitry. The point of this illustration is to bring out the distinction between the functional account of some entity, how it is used, what it is designed to do, etc., and an ontological account, what it consists of, what goes on inside it, etc. The basic deficiency of the Functionalist account of mind which allows for the comparison of mind with a computer program is that a program is a program only so long as there is a potential user; a mind, on the other hand, exists in its own right, my subjective experiences exist for me whether or not they have any implications for anyone else. We may conclude that Functionalism can at best account for the functional aspect of mental life. It can provide no warrant for the strong claim that there is no essential difference between a machine and a mind.

But where does that leave what we called the corollary of the strong claim to the effect that in terms of achievement, at any rate, nothing was in principle beyond the capacity of an artificial intelligence? Having reconciled ourselves to the advent of an artificial world chess champion, have we any reason to doubt the future advent of artificial geniuses of all kinds or of the ultraintelligent robot such as the science fiction writers have taught us to envisage? Stated thus I do not think there can be a definitive answer to this question. For the question here is no longer whether such machines will resemble minds but rather whether they will be able to do everything and more than the human mind could do. But what *a priori* principle could we invoke to set an upper limit to the advances of technology in any direction, be it in transport, in manufacture or in information technology? Whether one is optimistic or skeptical about technological progress will depend on which of the various relevant factors one takes into account. An optimist about progress in the field of A.I. will no doubt take heart from the rapid advances that have already been achieved. A skeptic, on the other hand, is likely to dwell on the unevenness of the progress that has so far been made. He may point out that where A.I. has scored its most spectacular successes has been in just such tasks as chess-playing which lend themselves most effectively to formal analysis. Where it has been less successful has been in connection with those skills that are so central in human life, the use of natural language, pattern recognition, the exercise of creative imagination and so on. What lesson can we draw from this comparison?

There is a question which at first sounds odd because we so rarely perceive it as a problem. It is the stark question as to why we should have minds at all. If thinking is an activity of the brain alone, why should we not have evolved with brains such as we now possess but without minds? We might even speculate that we would have been even more efficient from the biological point of view if our brain processes were free from any risk of interference from consciousness. However, we know that somehow and at some point in time consciousness emerged and it is a reasonable presumption that it did so because a conscious organism was more effective than one devoid of consciousness. In that case it is meaningful to inquire what specifically consciousness might contribute to thinking which brain activity alone could not have done. It is a question which William James asked himself in opposition to the scientific materialists of his day who took an epiphenomenal view of the nature of consciousness and he speculated about a possible answer.[2] It now seems more plausible than ever that mind is responsible for just those aspects of thinking that are lacking in computer simulations, notably the intuitive insights on which we constantly rely but which cannot be reduced to any set of explicit rules or the voluntary aspects of thinking such as attending to the task in hand and striving to attain its fulfillment.

Thus we come back again to the mind-body problem. We already noted that any solution that rests upon a denial of consciousness is a non-starter. This leaves us with two viable contenders. Either consciousness is an entirely superfluous feature of the world which might just as well have run its course as a closed physical system without ever becoming the object of awareness, since there would then have been no conscious observers only anthropoid robots going through the motions of observing, or, alternatively, consciousness could be taken to represent the incidence of mind when it intervenes in the physical world at the juncture that we call the brain. This is the dualist interactionist view of the mind-brain relationship and, if I am right in believing that it is the correct alternative, then it follows that an artificial brain necessarily lacks one vital ingredient of a natural brain, namely its link with the non-physical mind or psyche that activates or animates it. How far this imposes a break on the potential achievements of artificial brains may be a matter for trial and error but it does weaken the assumptions on which the strong claim is based.

There is a further consideration that leads one to doubt the strong claim. There exists a body of evidence that suggests that the mind has certain transcendental powers that cannot be explained in physicalistic terms and are independent of the constraints of time and space. I allude here to what parapsychologists have called "psi phenomena," those transactions between the individual and the external world that do not appear to be mediated by any of the known sensorimotor channels. Of course there is at present no obligation to accept such evidence at face value. The phenomena in question are so unstable and so marginal that, even after a hundred years of psychical research, no conclusive demonstration or unequivocal experiment can be cited to prove that they exist. Nevertheless, my impression, as one who has made a special study of the field, is that it would be unwise and short-sighted to ignore such evidence as of no account. At the very least there remains a real possibility that the evidence may be valid and it is, after all, the only empirical evidence which, if valid, would decisively sway opinion in favor of the dualist position. And, if we do take such evidence into account, then it represents another barrier to the pretensions of the A.I. enthusiast as indeed Turing himself recognized when, in his 1950 paper, he introduced the concept of an imitation game.[3]

---

[2]The school of psychology associated with James came to be known as the functionalists on account of their insistence on the efficacy of mind as a force in nature. However, unlike the present day Functionalists who are closer to the behaviorists, the original functionalists were dualists like James.

[3]See A. M. Turing "Computing Machinery and Intelligence," *Mind* 59, 1950. This classic paper has been reprinted many times in various compilations, most recently by D. R. Hoftstadter and D. C. Dennett (Eds.) in their *The Mind's I: Fantasies and Reflections on Self and Soul* with a commentary by the editors.

In my talk I have dwelt on the limitations of A.I. because it was this negative aspect that struck me as being philosophically the most interesting. I hope that, in doing so, I have not given the impression that I do not care about or value the positive achievements of this youthful science. I would like to add, therefore, that psychology is always liable to stagnate unless it can draw sustenance from developments in allied sciences and, in my lifetime, no other developments have made a profounder impact on psychology, more especially cognitive psychology, than those of A.I. What may eventually come of this we can only surmise but it can hardly fail to be of importance. It is my belief that the most important lesson we are likely to learn from A.I. is precisely what mind is not. It should enable us to see more clearly the distinction between the purely mechanical aspects of thinking which are presumably mediated for us by the brain, and what is intrinsically and irreducibly mental. Perhaps we shall even be able to lay down a general principle to the effect that whatever can be fully automated in a machine does not pertain to the mind.

Problems and Puzzles

48. The Myth of the Soul

Clarence Darrow

believability
belief

There is, perhaps, no more striking example of the credulity of man than the widespread belief in immortality. This idea includes not only the belief that death is not the end of what we call life, but that personal identity involving memory persists beyond the grave. So determined is the ordinary individual to hold fast to this belief that, as a rule, he refuses to read or to think upon the subject lest it cast doubt upon his cherished dream. Of those who may chance to look at this contribution, many will do so with the determination not to be convinced, and will refuse even to consider the manifold reasons that might weaken their faith. I know that this is true, for I know the reluctance with which I long approached the subject and my firm determination not to give up my hope. Thus the myth will stand in the way of a sensible adjustment to facts.

Even many of those who claim to believe in immortality still tell themselves and others that neither side of the question is susceptible of proof. Just what can these hopeful ones believe that the word "proof" involves? The evidence against the persistence of personal consciousness is as strong as the evidence of gravitation, and much more obvious. It is as convincing and unassailable as the proof of the destruction of wood or coal by fire. If it is not certain that death ends personal identity and memory, then almost nothing that man accepts as true is susceptible of proof.

The beliefs of the race and its individuals are relics of the past. Without careful examination, no one can begin to understand how many of man's cherished opinions have no foundation in fact. The common experience of all men should teach them how easy it is to believe what they wish to accept. Experienced psychologists know perfectly well that if they desire to convince a man of some idea, they must first make him *want* to believe it. There are so many hopes, so many strong yearnings and desires attached to the doctrine of immortality that it is practically impossible to create in any mind the wish to be mortal. Still, in spite of strong desires, millions of people are filled with doubts and fears that will not down. After all, is it not better to look the question squarely in the face and find out whether we are harboring a delusion?

It is customary to speak of a "belief in immortality." First, then, let us see what is meant by the word "belief." If I take a train in Chicago at noon, bound for

This essay originally appeared in *The Forum* (1928). It is reprinted with the permission of the Estate of Clarence Darrow.

New York, I believe I will reach that city the next morning. I believe it because I have been to New York. I have read about the city, I have known many other people who have been there, and their stories are not inconsistent with any known facts in my own experience. I have even examined the timetables, and I know just how I will go and how long the trip will take. In other words, when I board the train for New York, I believe I will reach that city because I have *reason* to believe it.

But if I am told that next week I shall start on a trip to Goofville; that I shall not take my body with me; that I shall stay for all eternity: Can I find a single fact connected with my journey—the way I shall go, the part of me that is to go, the time of the journey, the country I shall reach, its location in space, the way I shall live there— or anything that would lead to a rational belief that I shall really make the trip? Have I ever known anyone who has made the journey and returned? If I am really to believe, I must try to get some information about all these important facts.

But people hesitate to ask questions about life after death. They do not ask, for they know that only silence comes out of the eternal darkness of endless space. If people really believed in a beautiful, happy, glorious land waiting to receive them when they died; if they believed that their friends would be waiting to meet them; if they believed that all pain and suffering would be left behind: Why should they live through weeks, months, and even years of pain and torture while a cancer eats its way to the vital parts of the body? Why should one fight off death? Because he does *not* believe in any real sense: he only hopes. Everyone knows that there is no real evidence of any such state of bliss; so we are told not to search for proof. We are to accept through faith alone. But every thinking person knows that faith can only come through belief. Belief implies a condition of mind that accepts a certain idea. This condition can be brought about only by evidence. True, the evidence may be simply the unsupported statement of your grandmother; it may be wholly insufficient for reasoning men; but, good or bad, it must be enough for the believer or he could not believe.

Upon what evidence, then, are we asked to believe in immortality? There is no evidence. One is told to rely on faith, and no doubt this serves the purpose so long as one can believe blindly whatever he is told. But if there is no evidence upon which to build a positive belief in immortality, let us examine the other side of the question. Perhaps evidence can be found to support a positive conviction that immortality is a delusion.

The belief in immortality expresses itself in two different forms. On the one hand, there is a belief in the immortality of the "soul." This is sometimes interpreted to mean simply that the identity, the consciousness, the memory of the individual persists after death. On the other hand, many religious creeds have formulated a belief in "the resurrection of the body"—which is something else again. It will be necessary to examine both forms for this belief in turn.

The idea of continued life after death is very old. It doubtless had its roots back in the childhood of the race. In view of the limited knowledge of primitive man, it was not unreasonable. His dead friends and relatives visited him in dreams and visions and were present in his feeling and imagination until they were forgotten. Therefore the lifeless body did not raise the question of dissolution, but rather of duality. It was thought that man was a dual being possessing a body and a soul as separate entities, and that when a man died, his soul was released from his body to continue its life apart. Consequently, food and drink were placed upon the graves of the dead to be used in the long journey into the unknown. In modified forms, this belief in the duality of man persists to the present day.

But primitive man had no conception of life as having a beginning and an end. In this he was like the rest of the animals. Today, everyone of ordinary intelligence knows how life begins, and to examine the beginnings of life leads to inevitable conclusions about the way life ends. If man has a soul, it must creep in somewhere during the period of gestation and growth.

All the higher forms of animal life grow from a single cell. Before the individual life can begin its development, it must be fertilized by union with another cell; then the cell divides and multiplies until it takes the form and pattern of its kind. At a certain regular time the being emerges into the world. During its term of life millions of cells in its body are born, die, and are replaced until, through age, disease, or some catastrophe, the cells fall apart and the individual life is ended.

It is obvious that but for the fertilization of the cell under right conditions, the being would not have lived. It is idle to say that the initial cell has a soul. In one sense it has life; but even that is precarious and depends for its continued life upon union with another cell of the proper kind. The human mother is the bearer of probably ten thousand of one kind of cell, and the human father of countless billions of the other kind. Only a very small fraction of these result in human life. If the unfertilized cells of the female and the unused cells of the male are human beings possessed of souls, then the population of the world is infinitely greater than has ever been dreamed. Of course no such idea as belief in the immortality of the germ cells could satisfy the yearnings of the individual for a survival of life after death.

If that which is called a "soul" is a separate entity apart from the body, when, then, and where and how was this soul placed in the human structure? The individual began with the union of two cells, neither of which had a soul. How could these two soulless cells produce a soul? I must leave this search to the metaphysicians. When they have found the answer, I hope they will tell me, for I should really like to know.

We know that a baby may live and fully develop in its mother's womb and then, through some shock at birth, may be born without life. In the past, these babies were promptly buried. But now we know that in many cases, where the bodily structure is complete, the machine may be set to work by artificial respiration or electricity. Then it will run like any other human body through its allotted term of years. We also know that in many cases of drowning, or when some mishap virtually destroys life without hopelessly impairing the body, artificial means may set it in motion once more, so that it will complete its term of existence until the final catastrophe comes. Are we to believe that somewhere around the stillborn child and somewhere in the vicinity of the drowned man there hovers a detached soul waiting to be summoned back into the body by a pulmotor? This, too, must be left to the metaphysicians.

The beginnings of life yield no evidence of the beginnings of a soul. It is idle to say that the something in the human being which we call "life" is the soul itself, for the soul is generally taken to distinguish human beings from other forms of life. There is life in all animals and plants, and at least potential life in inorganic matter. This potential life is simply unreleased force and matter—the great storehouse from which all forms of life emerge and are constantly replenished. It is impossible to draw the line between inorganic matter and the simpler forms of plant life, and equally impossible to draw the line between plant life and animal life, or between other forms of animal life and what we human beings are pleased to call the highest form. If the thing which we call "life" is itself the soul, then cows have souls; and, in the very nature of things, we must allow souls to all forms of life and to inorganic matter as well.

Life itself is something very real, as distinguished from the soul. Every man knows that his life had a beginning. Can one imagine an organism that has a beginning and no end? If I did not exist in the infinite past, why should I, or could I, exist in the infinite future? "But," say some, "your consciousness, your memory may exist even after you are dead. This is what we mean by the soul." Let us examine this point a little.

I have no remembrance of the months that I lay in my mother's womb. I cannot recall the day of my birth nor the time when I first opened my eyes to the light of the sun. I cannot remember when I was an infant, or when I began to creep on the floor, or when I was taught to walk, or anything before I was five or six years old. Still, all of these events were important, wonderful, and strange in a new life. What I call my "consciousness," for lack of a better word and a better understanding, developed with my growth and the crowding experiences I met at every turn. I have a hazy recollection of the burial of a boy soldier who was shot toward the end of the Civil War. He was buried near the schoolhouse when I was seven years old. But I have no remembrance of the assassination of Abraham Lincoln, although I must then have been eight years old. I must have known about it at the time, for my family and my community idolized Lincoln, and all America was in mourning at his death. Why do I remember the dead boy soldier who was buried a year before? Perhaps because I knew him well. Perhaps because his family was close to my childish life. Possibly because it came to me as my first knowledge of death. At all events, it made so deep an impression that I recall it now.

"Ah, yes," say the believers in the soul, "what you say confirms our own belief. You certainly existed when these early experiences took place. You were conscious of them at the time, even though you are not aware of it now. In the same way, may not your consciousness persist after you die, even though you are not now aware of the fact?"

On the contrary, my fading memory of the events that filled the early years of my life leads me to the opposite conclusion. So far as these incidents are concerned, the mind and consciousness of the boy are already dead. Even now, am I fully alive? I am seventy-one years old. I often fail to recollect the names of some of those I knew full well. Many events do not make the lasting impression that they once did. I know that it will be only a few years, even if my body still survives decay, when few important matters will even register in my mind. I know how it is with the old. I know that physical life can persist beyond the time when the mind can fully function. I know that if I live to an extreme old age, my mind will fail. I shall eat and drink and go to my bed in an automatic way. Memory—which is all that binds me to the past—will already be dead. All that will remain will be a vegetative existence; I shall sit and doze in the chimney corner, and my body will function in a measure even though the ego will already be practically dead. I am sure that if I die of what is called "old age," my consciousness will gradually slip away with my failing emotions; I shall no more be aware of the near approach of final dissolution than is the dying tree.

In primitive times, before men knew anything about the human body or the universe of which it is a part, it was not unreasonable to believe in spirits, ghosts, and the duality of man. For one thing, celestial geography was much simpler then. Just above the earth was a firmament in which the stars were set, and above the firmament was heaven. The place was easy of access, and in dreams the angels were seen going up and coming down on a ladder. But now we have a slightly more adequate conception of space and the infinite universe of which we are so small a part. Our great telescopes reveal countless worlds and planetary systems which make our own sink into utter insignificance in comparison. We have every reason to think that beyond our sight there is endless space filled with still more planets, so infinite in size and number that no brain has the smallest conception of their extent. Is there any reason to think that in this universe, with its myriads of worlds, there is no other life so important as our own? Is it possible that the inhabitants of the earth have been singled out for special favor and endowed with souls and immortal life? Is it at all reasonable to suppose that any special account is taken of the human atoms that forever come and go upon this planet?

If man has a soul that persists after death, that goes to a heaven of the blessed or to a hell of the damned, where are these places? It is not so easily imagined as it once was. How does the soul make its journey? What does immortal man find when he gets there, and how will he live after he reaches the end of endless space? We know that the atmosphere will be absent; that there will be no light, no heat—only the infinite reaches of darkness and frigidity. In view of modern knowledge, can any one *really believe* in the persistence of individual life and memory?

There are those who base their hope of a future life upon the resurrection of the body. This is a purely religious doctrine. It is safe to say that few intelligent men who are willing to look obvious facts in the face hold any such belief. Yet we are seriously told that Elijah was carried bodily to heaven in a chariot of fire, and that Jesus arose from the dead and ascended into heaven. The New Testament abounds in passages that support this doctrine. St. Paul states the tenet over and over again. In the fifteenth chapter of First Corinthians he says: "If Christ be preached that he rose from the dead, how say some among you that there is no resurrection of the dead? . . . And if Christ be not risen, then is our preaching vain. . . . For if the dead rise not, then is not Christ raised." The Apostles' Creed says: "I believe in the resurrection of the body." This has been carried into substantially all the orthodox creeds; and while it is more or less minimized by neglect and omission, is still a cardinal doctrine of the orthodox churches.

Two thousand years ago, in Palestine, little was known of man, of the earth, or of the universe. It was then currently believed that the earth was only four thousand years old, that life had begun anew after the deluge about two thousand years before, and that the entire earth was soon to be destroyed. Today it is fairly well established that man has been upon the earth for a million years. During that long stretch of time the world has changed many times; it is changing every moment. At least three or four ice ages have swept across continents, driving death before them, carrying human beings into the sea or burying them deep in the earth. Animals have fed on man and on each other. Every dead body, no matter whether consumed by fire or buried in the earth, has been resolved into its elements, so that the matter and energy that once formed human beings has fed animals and plants and other men. As the great naturalist, Fabre, has said: "At the banquet of life each is in turn a guest and a dish." Thus the body of every man now living is in part made from the bodies of those who have been dead for ages.

Yet we are still asked to believe in the resurrection of the body. By what alchemy, then, are the individual bodies that have successfully fed the generations of men to be separated and restored to their former identities? And if I am to be res-urrected, what particular *I* shall be called from the grave, from the animals and plants and the bodies of other men who shall inherit this body I now call my own? My body has been made over and over, piece by piece, as the days went by, and will continue to be so made until the end. It has changed so slowly that each new cell is fitted into the living part, and will go on changing until the final crisis comes. Is it the child in the mother's womb or the tottering frame of the old man that shall be brought back? The mere thought of such a resurrection beggars reason, ignores facts, and enthrones blind faith, wild dreams, hopeless hopes, and cowardly fears as sovereign of the human mind.

Some of those who profess to believe in the immortality of man—whether it be of his soul or his body—have drawn what comfort they could from the modern scientific doctrine of the indestructibility of matter and force. This doctrine, they say, only confirms in scientific language what they have always believed. This, however, is pure sophistry. It is probably true that no matter or force has ever been or ever can be destroyed. But it is likewise true that there is no connection whatever between the notion that personal consciousness and memory persist after death and the scientific theory that matter and force are indestructible. For the scientific theory carries with it a corollary, that the forms of matter and energy are constantly changing through an endless cycle of new combinations. Of what possible use would it be, then, to have a consciousness that was immortal, but which, from the moment of death, was dispersed into new combinations so that no two parts of the original identity could ever be reunited again?

These natural processes of change, which in the human being take the forms of growth, disease, senility, death, and decay, are essentially the same as the process by which a lump of coal is disintegrated in burning. One may watch the lump of coal burning in the grate until nothing but ashes remains. Part of the coal goes up the chimney in the form of smoke; part of it radiates through the house as heat; the residue lies in the ashes on the hearth. So it is with human life. In all forms of life nature is engaged in combining, breaking down, and recombining her store of energy and matter into new forms. The thing we call "life" is nothing other than a state of equilibrium which endures for a short span of years between the two opposing tendencies of nature—the one that builds up, and the one that tears down. In old age, the tearing-down process has already gained the ascendency, and when death intervenes, the equilibrium is finally upset by the complete stoppage of the building-up process, so that nothing remains but complete disintegration. The energy thus released may be converted into grass or trees or animal life; or it may lie dormant until caught up again in the crucible of nature's laboratory. But whatever happens, the man—the *You* and the *I*—like the lump of coal that has been burned, is gone, irrevocably dispersed. All the King's horses and all the King's men cannot restore it to its former unity.

The idea that man is a being set apart, distinct from all the rest of nature, is born of man's emotions, of his loves and hates, of his hopes and fears, and of the primitive conceptions of undeveloped minds. The *You* or the *I* which is known to our friends does not consist of an immaterial something called a "soul" which cannot be conceived. We know perfectly well what we mean when we talk about this *You* and this *Me*: and it is equally plain that the whole fabric that makes up our separate personalities is destroyed, dispersed, disintegrated beyond repair by what we call "death."

Those who refuse to give up the idea of immortality declare that nature never creates a desire without providing the means for its satisfaction. They likewise insist that all people, from the rudest to the most civilized, yearn for another life. As a matter of fact, nature creates many desires which she does not satisfy; most of the wishes of men meet no fruition. But nature does not create any emotion demanding a future life. The only yearning that the individual has is to keep on living—which is a very different thing. This urge is found in every animal, in every plant. It is simply the momentum of a living structure: or, as Schopenhauer put it, "the will to live." What we long for is a continuation of our present state of existence, not an uncertain reincarnation in a mysterious world of which we know nothing.

All men recognize the hopelessness of finding any evidence that the individual will persist beyond the grave. As a last resort, we are told that it is better that the doctrine be believed even if it is not true. We are assured that without this faith, life is only desolation and despair. However that may be, it remains that many of the conclusions of logic are not pleasant to contemplate; still, so long as men think and feel, at least some of them will use their faculties as best they can. For if we are to believe things that are not true, who is to write our creed? Is it safe to leave it to any man or organization to pick out the errors that we must accept? The whole history of the world has answered this question in a way that cannot be mistaken.

And after all, is the belief in immortality necessary or even desirable for man? Millions of men and women have no such faith; they go on with their daily tasks and feel joy and sorrow without the lure of immortal life. The things that really affect the happiness of the individual are the matters of daily living. They are the companionship of friends, the games and contemplations. They are misunderstandings and cruel judgments, false friends and debts, poverty and disease. They are our joys in our living companions and our sorrows over those who die. Whatever our faith, we mainly live in the present—in the here and now. Those who hold the view that man is mortal are never troubled by metaphysical problems. At the end of the day's labor we are glad to lose our consciousness in sleep; and intellectually, at least, we look forward to the long rest from the stresses and storms that are always incidental to existence.

When we fully understand the brevity of life, its fleeting joys and unavoidable pains; when we accept the fact that all men and women are approaching an inevitable doom: the consciousness of it should make us more kindly and considerate of each other. This feeling should make men and women use their best efforts to help their fellow travellers on the road, to make the path brighter and easier as we journey on. It should bring a closer kinship, a better understanding, and a deeper sympathy for the wayfarers who must live a common life and die a common death.

49. Parable of the Chinese Room

John Searle

John Searle (1932–   ), professor of philosophy at the University of California–Berkeley, is well known for his writings on the philosophy of mind and the philosophy of language. In recent years his views on artificial intelligence have produced extensive controversy.

Though we do not know in detail how the brain functions, we do know enough to have an idea of the general relationships between brain processes and mental processes. Mental processes are caused by the behaviour of elements of the brain. At the same time, they are realised in the structure that is made up of those elements. I think this answer is consistent with the standard biological approaches to biological phenomena. Indeed, it is a kind of commonsense answer to the question, given what we know about how the world works. However, it is very much a minority point of view. The prevailing view in philosophy, psychology, and artificial intelligence is one which emphasises the analogies between the functioning of the human brain and the functioning of digital computers. According to the most extreme version of this view, the brain is just a digital computer and the mind is just a computer program. One could summarise this view—I call it "strong artificial intelligence" or "strong AI"—by saying that the mind is to the brain, as the program is to the computer hardware.

This view has the consequence that there is nothing essentially biological about the human mind. The brain just happens to be one of an indefinitely large number of different kinds of hardware computers that could sustain the programs which make up human intelligence. On this view, any physical system whatever that had the right program with the right inputs and outputs would have a mind in exactly the same sense that you and I have minds. So, for example, if you made a computer out of old beer cans powered by windmills; if it had the right program, it would have to have a mind. And the point is not that for all we know it might have thoughts and feelings, but rather that it must have thoughts and feelings, because that is all there is to having thoughts and feelings: implementing the right program.

Most people who hold this view think we have not yet designed programs which are minds. But there is pretty much general agreement among them that it's only a matter of time until computer scientists and workers in artificial intelligence design the appropriate hardware and programs which will be the equivalent of human brains and minds. These will be artificial brains and minds which are in every way the equivalent of human brains and minds.

Reprinted by permission of the publishers from *Minds, Brains and Science*, by John Searle, pp. 28–38, Cambridge, Mass.: Harvard University Press, Copyright © 1984 by John R. Searle.

Many people outside of the field of artificial intelligence are quite amazed to discover that anybody could believe such a view as this. So, before criticising it, let me give you a few examples of the things that people in this field have actually said. Herbert Simon of Carnegie-Mellon University says that we already have machines that can literally think. There is no question of waiting for some future machine, because existing digital computers already have thoughts in exactly the same sense that you and I do. Well, fancy that! Philosophers have been worried for centuries about whether or not a machine could think, and now we discover that they already have such machines at Carnegie-Mellon. Simon's colleague Alan Newell claims that we have now discovered (and notice that Newell says "discovered" and not "hypothesized" or "considered the possibility," but we have *discovered*) that intelligence is just a matter of physical symbol manipulation; it has no essential connection with any specific kind of biological or physical wetware or hardware. Rather, any system whatever that is capable of manipulating physical symbols in the right way is capable of intelligence in the same literal sense as human intelligence of human beings. Both Simon and Newell, to their credit, emphasise that there is nothing metaphorical about these claims; they mean them quite literally. Freeman Dyson is quoted as having said that computers have an advantage over the rest of us when it comes to evolution. Since consciousness is just a matter of formal processes, in computers these formal processes can go on in substances that are much better able to survive in a universe that is cooling off than beings like ourselves made of our wet and messy materials. Marvin Minsky of MIT says that the next generation of computers will be so intelligent that we will "be lucky if they are willing to keep us around the house as household pets." My all-time favourite in the literature of exaggerated claims on behalf of the digital computer is from John McCarthy, the inventor of the term "artificial intelligence." McCarthy says even "machines as simple as thermostats can be said to have beliefs." And indeed, according to him, almost any machine capable of problem-solving can be said to have beliefs. I admire McCarthy's courage. I once asked him: "What beliefs does your thermostat have?" And he said: "My thermostat has three beliefs—it's too hot in here, it's too cold in here, and it's just right in here." As a philosopher, I like all these claims for a simple reason. Unlike most philosophical theses, they are reasonably clear, and they admit of a simple and decisive refutation. It is this refutation that I am going to undertake in this chapter.

The nature of the refutation has nothing whatever to do with any particular stage of computer technology. It is important to emphasize this point because the temptation is always to think that the solution to our problems must wait on some as yet untreated technological wonder. But in fact, the nature of the refutation is completely independent of any state of technology. It has to do with the very definition of a digital computer, with what a digital computer is.

It is essential to our conception of a digital computer that its operations can be specified purely formally; that is, we specify the steps in the operation of the computer in terms of abstract symbols—sequences of zeroes and ones printed on a tape, for example. A typical computer "rule" will determine that when a machine is in a certain state and it has a certain symbol on its tape, then it will perform a certain operation such as erasing the symbol or printing another symbol and then enter another state such as moving the tape one square to the left. But the symbols have no meaning; they have no semantic content; they are not about anything. They have to be specified purely in terms of their formal or syntactical structure. The zeroes and ones, for example, are just numerals; they don't even stand for numbers. Indeed, it is this feature of digital computers that makes them so powerful. One and the same type of hardware, if it is appropriately designed, can be used to run an indefinite range of different programs. And one and the same program can be run on an indefinite range of different types of hardwares.

But this feature of programs, that they are defined purely formally or syntactically, is fatal to the view that mental processes and program processes are identical. And the reason can be stated quite simply. There is more to having a mind than having formal or syntactical processes. Our internal mental states, by definition, have certain sorts of contents. If I am thinking about Kansas City or wishing that I had a cold beer to drink or wondering if there will be a fall in interest rates, in each case my mental state has a certain mental content in addition to whatever formal features it might have. That is, even if my thoughts occur to me in strings of symbols, there must be more to the thought than the abstract strings, because strings by themselves can't have any meaning. If my thoughts are to be *about* anything, then the strings must have a *meaning* which makes the thoughts about those things. In a word, the mind has more than a syntax, it has a semantics. The reason that no computer program can ever be a mind is simply that a computer program is only syntactical, and minds are more than syntactical. Minds are semantical, in the sense that they have more than a formal structure, they have a content.

To illustrate this point I have designed a certain thought-experiment. Imagine that a bunch of computer programmers have written a program that will enable a computer to simulate the understanding of Chinese. So, for example, if the computer is given a question in Chinese, it will match the question against its memory, or data base, and produce appropriate answers to the questions in Chinese. Suppose for the sake of argument that the computer's answers are as good as those of a native Chinese speaker. Now then, does the computer, on the basis of this, understand Chinese, does it literally understand Chinese, in the way that Chinese speakers understand Chinese? Well, imagine that you are locked in a room, and in this room are several baskets full of Chinese symbols. Imagine that you (like me) do not understand a word of Chinese, but that you are given a rule book in English for manipulating these Chinese symbols. The rules specify the manipulations of the symbols purely formally, in terms of their syntax, not their semantics. So the rule might say: "Take a squiggle-squiggle sign out of basket number one and put it next to a squoggle-squoggle sign from basket number two." Now suppose that some other Chinese symbols are passed into the room, and that you are given further rules for passing back Chinese symbols out of the room. Suppose that unknown to you the symbols passed into the room are called "questions" by the people outside the room, and the symbols you pass back out of the room are called "answers to the questions." Suppose, furthermore, that the programmers are so good at designing the programs and that you are so good at manipulating the symbols, that very soon your answers are indistinguishable from those of a native Chinese speaker. There you are locked in your room shuffling your Chinese symbols and passing out Chinese symbols in response to incoming Chinese symbols. On the basis of the situation as I have described it, there is no way you could learn any Chinese simply by manipulating these formal symbols.

Now the point of the story is simply this: by virtue of implementing a formal computer program from the point of view of an outside observer, you behave exactly as if you understood Chinese, but all the same you don't understand a word of Chinese. But if going through the appropriate computer program for understanding Chinese is not enough to give *you* an understanding of Chinese, then it is not enough to give *any other digital computer* an understanding of Chinese. And again, the reason for this can be stated quite simply. If you don't understand Chinese, then no other computer could understand Chinese because no digital computer, just by virtue of running a program, has anything that you don't have. All that the computer has, as you have, is a formal program for manipulating uninterpreted Chinese symbols. To repeat, a computer has a syntax, but no semantics. The whole point of the parable of the Chinese room is to remind us of a fact that we knew all along. Understanding a language, or indeed, having mental states at all, involves more than just having a bunch of formal symbols. It involves having an interpretation, or a meaning attached to those symbols. And a digital computer, as defined, cannot have more than just formal symbols because the operation of the computer, as I said earlier, is defined in terms of its ability to implement programs. And these programs are purely formally specifiable—that is, they have no semantic content.

We can see the force of this argument if we contrast what it is like to be asked and to answer questions in English, and to be asked and to answer questions in some language where we have no knowledge of any of the meanings of the words. Imagine that in the Chinese room you are also given questions in English about such things as your age or your life history, and that you answer these questions. What is the difference between the Chinese case and the English case? Well again, if like me you understand no Chinese and you do understand English, then the difference is obvious. You understand the questions in English because they are expressed in symbols whose meanings are known to you. Similarly, when you give the answers in English you are producing symbols which are meaningful to you. But in the case of the Chinese, you have none of that. In the case of the Chinese, you simply manipulate formal symbols according to a computer program, and you attach no meaning to any of the elements.

Various replies have been suggested to this argument by workers in artificial intelligence and in psychology, as well as philosophy. They all have something in common; they are all inadequate. And there is an obvious reason why they have to be inadequate, since the argument rests on a very simple logical truth, namely, syntax alone is not sufficient for semantics, and digital computers insofar as they are computers have, by definition, a syntax alone.

I want to make this clear by considering a couple of the arguments that are often presented against me.

Some people attempt to answer the Chinese room example by saying that the whole system understands Chinese. The idea here is that though I, the person in the room manipulating the symbols do not understand Chinese, I am just the central processing unit of the computer system. They argue that it is the whole system, including the room, the baskets full of symbols and the ledgers containing the programs and perhaps other items as well, taken as a totality, that understands Chinese. But this is subject to exactly the same objection I made before. There is no way that the system can get from the syntax to the semantics. I, as the central processing unit, have no way of figuring out what any of these symbols means; but then neither does the whole system.

Another common response is to imagine that we put the Chinese understanding program inside a robot. If the robot moved around and interacted causally with the world, wouldn't that be enough to guarantee that it understood Chinese? Once again the inexorability of the semantics-syntax distinction overcomes this manoeuvre. As long as we suppose the robot has only a computer for a brain then, even though it might behave exactly as if it understood Chinese, it would still have no way of getting from the syntax to the semantics of Chinese. You can see this if you imagine that I am the computer. Inside a room in the robot's skull I shuffle symbols without knowing that some of them come in to me from television cameras attached to the robot's head and others go out to move the robot's arms and legs. As long as all I have is a formal computer program, I have no way of attaching any meaning to any of the symbols. And the fact that the robot is engaged in causal interactions with the outside world won't help me to attach any meaning to the symbols unless I have some way of finding out about the fact. Suppose the robot picks up a hamburger and this triggers the symbol for hamburger to come into the room. As long as all I have is the symbol with no knowledge of its causes or how it got there, I have no way of knowing what it means. The causal interactions between the robot and the rest of the world are irrelevant unless those causal interactions are represented in some mind or other. But there is no way they can be if all that the so-called mind consists of is a set of purely formal, syntactical operations.

It is important to see exactly what is claimed and what is not claimed by my argument. Suppose we ask the question that I mentioned at the beginning: "Could a machine think?" Well, in one sense, of course, we are all machines. We can construe the stuff inside our heads as a meat machine. And of course, we can all think. So, in one sense of "machine," namely that sense in which a machine is just a physical system which is capable of performing certain kinds of operations, in that sense, we are all machines, and we can think. So, trivially, there are machines that can think. But that wasn't the question that bothered us. So let's try a different formulation of it. Could an artefact think? Could a man-made machine think? Well, once again, it depends on the kind of artefact. Suppose we designed a machine that was molecule-for-molecule indistinguishable from a human being. Well then, if you can duplicate the causes, you can presumably duplicate the effects. So once again, the answer to that question is, in principle at least, trivially yes. If you could build a machine that had the same structure as a human being, then presumably that machine would be able to think. Indeed, it would be a surrogate human being. Well, let's try again.

The question isn't: "Can a machine think?" or "Can an artefact think?" The question is: "Can a digital computer think?" But once again we have to be very careful in how we interpret the question. From a mathematical point of view, anything whatever can be described as *if* it were a digital computer. And that's because it may be described as instantiating or implementing a computer program. In an utterly trivial sense, the pen that is on the desk in front of me can be described as a digital computer. It just happens to have a very boring computer program. The program says: "Stay there." Now since in this sense, anything whatever is a digital computer, because anything whatever can be described as implementing a computer program, then once again, our question gets a trivial answer. Of course our brains are digital computers, since they implement any number of computer programs. And of course our brains can think. So once again, there is a trivial answer to the question. But that wasn't really the question we were trying to ask. The question we wanted to ask is this: "Can a digital computer, as defined, think?" That is to say: "Is instantiating or implementing the right computer program with the right inputs and outputs, sufficient for, or constitutive of, thinking?" And to this question, unlike its predecessors, the answer is clearly "no." And it is "no" for the reason that we have spelled out, namely, the computer program is defined purely syntactically. But thinking is more than just a matter of manipulating meaningless symbols, it involves meaningful semantic contents. These semantic contents are what we mean by "meaning."

It is important to emphasize again that we are not talking about a particular stage of computer technology. The argument has nothing to do with the forthcoming, amazing advances in computer science. It has nothing to do with the distinction between serial and parallel processes, or with the size of programs, or the speed of computer operations, or with computers that can interact causally with their environment, or even with the invention of robots. Technological progress is always grossly exaggerated, but even subtracting the exaggeration, the development of computers has been quite remarkable, and we can reasonably expect that even more remarkable progress will be made in the future. No doubt we will be much better able to simulate human behaviour on computers than we can at present, and certainly much better than we have been able to in the past. The point I am making is that if we are talking about having mental states, having a mind, all of these simulations are simply irrelevant. It doesn't matter how good the technology is, or how rapid the calculations made by the computer are. If it really is a computer, its operations have to be defined syntactically, whereas consciousness, thoughts, feelings, emotions, and all the rest of it involve more than a syntax. Those features, by definition, the computer is unable to *duplicate* however powerful may be its ability to *simulate*. The key distinction here is between duplication and simulation. And no simulation by itself ever constitutes duplication.

What I have done so far is give a basis to the sense that those citations I began this talk with are really as preposterous as they seem. There is a puzzling question in this discussion though, and that is: "Why would anybody ever have thought that computers could think or have feelings and emotions and all the rest of it?" After all, we can do computer simulations of any process whatever that can be given a formal description. So, we can do a computer simulation of the flow of money in the British economy, or the pattern of power distribution in the Labour party. We can do computer simulation of rain storms in the home counties, or warehouse fires in East London. Now, in each of these cases, nobody supposes that the computer simulation is actually the real thing; no one supposes that a computer simulation of a storm will leave us all wet, or a computer simulation of a fire is likely to burn the house down. Why on earth would anyone in his right mind suppose a computer simulation of mental processes actually had mental processes? I don't really know the answer to that, since the idea seems to me, to put it frankly, quite crazy from the start. But I can make a couple of speculations.

First of all, where the mind is concerned, a lot of people are still tempted to some sort of behaviourism. They think if a system behaves as if it understood Chinese, then it really must understand Chinese. But we have already refuted this form of behaviourism with the Chinese room argument. Another assumption made by many people is that the mind is not a part of the biological world, it is not a part of the world of nature. The strong artificial intelligence view relies on that in its conception that the mind is purely formal; that somehow or other, it cannot be treated as a concrete product of biological processes like any other biological product. There is in these discussions, in short, a kind of residual dualism. AI partisans believe that the mind is more than a part of the natural biological world; they believe that the mind is purely formally specifiable. The paradox of this is that the AI literature is filled with fulminations against some view called "dualism," but in fact, the whole thesis of strong AI rests on a kind of dualism. It rests on a rejection of the idea that the mind is just a natural biological phenomenon in the world like any other. . . .

Suggestions for Further Reading

Anthologies

Chalmers, David J., ed. *Philosophy of Mind*. New York: Oxford Univ. Press, 2002. A collection of outstanding papers on the philosophy of mind. The articles are difficult but worthwhile reading.

Edwards, Paul, ed. *Immortality*. Amherst, N.Y.: Prometheus Books, 1997. A collection of many of the best articles on immortality and the related philosophical issues of personal identity and the nature of mind.

Flew, Anthony, ed. *Body, Mind, and Death*. New York: Macmillan, 1966. Some important articles on the mind-body problem from Plato to the present day. The introduction and annotated bibliography are excellent.

Hofstadter, Douglas R., and Daniel Dennett, eds. *The Mind's I*. New York: Basic Books, 1981. Twenty-seven articles on artificial intelligence and the nature of mind, with extensive comments by the editors.

Stich, Stephen P., and Ted A. Warfield, eds. *The Blackwell Guide to the Philosophy of Mind*. Oxford: Blackwell Publishing, 2002. A collection of original essays by prominent philosophers on important topics in the philosophy of mind.

Individual Works

Adler, Mortimer. *The Difference of Man and the Difference It Makes*. Cleveland: World, 1967. The relation of the problem of the existence of mind to the issue of how men differ from animals. There is also a good discussion of whether men differ essentially from computing machines.

Beloff, John. *The Existence of Mind*. New York: Citadel, 1964. An examination of the arguments for and against dualism.

Brown, Geoffrey. *Minds, Brains, and Machines*. New York: St. Martin's Press, 1989. An introductory account of the major positions on the mind-body controversy and a discussion of the possibility of thinking machines.

Churchland, Paul. *Matter and Consciousness*. Cambridge, Mass.: MIT Press, 1984. A clear introduction to the mind-body controversy.

Dennett, Daniel C. *Brainstorms*. Montgomery, Vt.: Bradford Books, 1978. A series of provocative articles dealing with various aspects of the mind-body controversy.

Dreyfus, Hubert, and Stuart Dreyfus. *Mind Over Machine*. New York: Macmillan, 1986. An attack on the claim that computers can duplicate human intelligence.

Ducasse, C. J. *Nature, Mind, and Death*. LaSalle, Ill.: Open Court, 1951. A good discussion of the mind-body problem and its relation to the question of immortality.

Gardner, Howard. *The Mind's New Science*. New York: Basic Books, 1985. An explanation of the new field of cognitive science, which is closely tied to the mind-body controversy and artificial intelligence.

Hospers, John. *An Introduction to Philosophical Analysis*, 3d ed. Englewood Cliffs, N.J.: Prentice Hall, 1988. Chapter Six presents a clear account of the mind-body controversy.

Shaffer, Jerome. *Reality, Knowledge, and Value*. New York: Random, 1971. Chapters Eight to Fourteen provide a very readable account of the main issues in the mind-body controversy.

Taylor, Richard. *Metaphysics*, 4th ed. Englewood Cliffs, N.J.: Prentice Hall, 1992. Chapters Two to Four provide a clear discussion of the mind-body controversy and a defense of materialism.

Encyclopedias

Dictionary of the History of Ideas: Studies of Selected Pivotal Ideas. Philip P. Weiner, editor-in-chief. New York: Scribners, 1973. Substantial and clearly written essays emphasizing the historical development of topics discussed in this part. Designed to inform the nonspecialist, each essay concludes with a select bibliography.

Encyclopedia of Philosophy. Paul Edwards, editor-in-chief. New York: Macmillan, 1967. The student will find many worthwhile articles on the subject treated in this part and excellent bibliographies.

Routledge Encyclopedia of Philosophy. Edward Craig, general editor. New York: Routledge, 1998. This ten-volume encyclopedia contains articles on all areas of philosophy and up-to-date bibliographies.

Internet Web Sites

RESEARCH NAVIGATOR (*http://www.researchnavigator.com*). This web site offers three research data bases: Ebsco Academic Journal and Abstract Data Base, *New York Times* Search by Subject Archive, and "Best of the Web" Link Library. In addition, this site provides helpful advice on how to conduct efficient and productive research from choosing a topic to polishing the final draft. Beginning philosophy students probably will find the "Best of the Web" Link Library the most appropriate place to start their research. The free access code necessary to employ Research Navigator can be found in the Prentice Hall Guide to Evaluating Online Resources. If your text did not come with this guide, please go to *www.prenhall.com/contentselect* for information on how you can purchase an access code.

EpistemeLinks (*http://www.epistemelinks.com*). This site provides many links to philosophical resources on the web.

PART SIX

Knowledge and Science

Introduction

All human beings want knowledge, admire it, even revere it. Platitudinous as this statement may appear, it is certainly ambiguous. No doubt this accounts for the fact that so many people think the statement true. For knowledge as something sought, as a value, suggests two quite different things: (1) knowledge as a good or end-in-itself independent of any use to which it may be put; (2) knowledge as a means necessary for the securing of some other value. We call those who dedicate themselves to the disinterested pursuit of knowledge, to the free play of ideas, "intellectuals," or "theoreticians." In this sense, philosophers traditionally have seen themselves and have been seen by others as superintellectuals, as the theoretician's theoretician. Historical legend has it that the first philosopher known to us, Thales of Miletus in Asia Minor (circa 585 B.C.), afflicted with the reproaches of his fellow citizens that he was a man of knowledge but also a poor man (and so what worth did knowledge have?), used his knowledge of nature to predict that the next crop of olives would be a bumper one. Keeping the practical results of his knowledge to himself, as would become a hardheaded businessman, Thales then bought up all of the olive presses in the region, thereby securing a monopoly for himself. When the unusually abundant harvest of olives duly took place, Thales rented out his olive presses at a high price and so made a large amount of money by cornering the market. Philosophers could make money if they wanted to do so, he reportedly declared, but willingly were poor because they valued knowledge above everything else, even wealth. No doubt Thales would never enroll in a business school; however, if he did, he would earn all A's.

Socrates refused to accept money for his teaching, not wishing to be financially dependent on anyone. (No wonder he scorned politicians.) Socrates distrusted wealth; for of what use is wealth but to stimulate and delight the senses, so sapping one's rational energies and distracting one's reason from the pursuit of truth. Refusing to stop asking questions as the price of life and freedom, condemned to death, drinking the hemlock, dying, Socrates has become a symbol of the fearless and unrelenting search for knowledge despite the opposition of the ignorant majority. The god Apollo announced that Socrates was the wisest man in Greece. Aristotle, the most influential philosopher in the Western world and the first great biologist, conceived man's highest destiny, because man is the only animal possessing reason, to be the full and unimpeded functioning of that reason, sheer knowing for its own sake. In knowing, man comes closest to being a god. If there are gods, knowing would be the only activity compatible with their exalted status. Practical activities, such as healing broken legs or multiplying loaves and fishes, would be beneath divine dignity. In the seventeenth century, the philosopher Spinoza equated God and Nature. In the glow of his own "intellectual love of God," Spinoza revealed how knowing the unchanging truth for its own sake can elicit all of the traditional religious emotions of devotion to what is greater and worthier than one's self and how knowing for its own sake can satisfy the old religious yearning for triumph over devouring time and for unshakable peace. The pursuit of knowledge as the ultimate Good thus emits cosmic, religious echoes. The devotees of knowing for its own sake have moved with a priestly mien whether they wore the toga or the white laboratory coat of the modern scientist. In our day Albert Einstein is the symbol of the philosopher-scientist, the pure Knower, the inspired theoretician—Einstein, with the massive brow, the lined face, the flowing white hair suggesting a symphony conductor or other artist, and the luminous eyes through which the universe gazes into you.

Nevertheless, the pursuit of knowledge for its own sake evokes the supreme allegiance of only a small minority of Americans and people in other countries. The great majority value knowledge as technique, as know-how, as a necessary means to other more important values, such as excitement and amusement. Over a century ago, a Jewish prophet, who had read Greek and German philosophy, wrote that until his day philosophers had been content to understand the world but that the real task of philosophy was to change the world. Most Americans and all thoroughly modern people of other countries agree with Marx. The great majority of contemporary men and women prize knowledge as power, science as technology, as a kind of magic that works, a cornucopia pouring forth an unending and swelling stream of wealth with its attendant power and luxury. A small minority of intellectuals excepted, most contemporaries know very well what they want—wealth, power, luxury. For them, the problem concerns means: how to produce wealth, power, luxury, and all things dependent on them ever more abundantly. If the cost of that production means a polluted environment, chemically fouled lakes and streams, dying wildlife, and degraded human life, so far we have been willing to pay that cost. And should that cost become exorbitant, even deadly, we are sustained by the faith that the cure for the ills of technology is a bigger and better technology.

Only because science has shown itself so fecund in producing these goods and in progressively eliminating undesirable side effects has it been allowed to develop to its present level. For science, particularly on its theoretical side as a pursuit of knowledge for its own sake, was and is one of the most subversive agents ever invented by humans. It is no coincidence that controversy whirls around the figures of Copernicus, Galileo, Darwin, Einstein, and Freud like black clouds rumbling with thunder and flashing with lightning. They symbolize the disturbing fact that science constantly shows us that the world and humans really are quite different from what most people thought they were. Hence, for most people the value of knowing for its own sake must be subordinated to other values. Millions of Americans drive automobiles and at the same time reject the proposition that a human being is a mammal. The pursuit of knowledge is splendid, but such an enterprise must be compatible with national security. Of course we must hold all of our theories tentatively, but we "know" that any average American is superior in every way to any foreigner.

This ambiguity of knowledge as an end for its own sake and as a means to realizing other values provides the humus out of which philosophical reflection on knowledge and science grows. Hence, philosophers study and discuss what they technically call *epistemology*: the investigation of the origin, nature, methods, and limits of knowledge. Philosophers wonder about and often answer such questions as: What is the nature of knowledge? What criteria distinguish genuine knowledge from the spurious article? Does all knowledge come from sense experience, or can our reason know that certain propositions must be true independently of sense experience? What is science? What is the scientific method? Is there *a* scientific method? Is all knowledge that is worthy of the name produced by science and science alone? Is there anything that science cannot find out? More radically, can we know anything at all, or is it all merely a matter of shifting opinions, what we call "knowledge" being merely those illusions, or perhaps even delusions, agreed upon?

Underlying questions concerning the nature of science and such contemporary issues as skepticism and the value of science is a profound philosophical dispute: Rationalism *versus* Empiricism. Rationalism is the doctrine that reason alone is a source of knowledge and is independent of sense experience. Empiricism is the doctrine that *all* knowledge comes from sense experience. Rationalism and Empiricism contradict each other. The propositions that "Some of our knowledge does not derive from sense experience" and that "All of our knowledge does derive from sense experience" cannot both be true nor both be false. But which proposition is true and which one is false?

René Descartes, often called the father of modern philosophy, sought intellectual certainty. For Descartes, genuinely to know something is to be unable to doubt its truth. Hence, he searches for propositions that he cannot doubt. In "Meditations I and II," he gives an account of his search and its result. Descartes resolves to examine the principles on which depend all that he once believed, only to discover that there is not one principle whose truth he cannot doubt. He finds that he can doubt the reliability of his senses, the existence of his physical body and senses, the existence of an external world. Indeed, he can doubt whether he presently is awake or asleep. Descartes goes further. Might there not be an "evil genius" who is systematically deceiving him so that all that he formerly believed is false, even his belief that two plus three makes five? Yet Descartes snatches certainty from the jaws of doubt. He finds it to be self-evidently true that he is a being that thinks. Nothing could be more clear and distinct to his reason. He cannot doubt that he is doubting; to doubt his existence is to affirm it. In its Latin expression as *cogito ergo sum*, "I think, therefore I am" has become the most famous principle of all modern philosophy. Descartes now possesses criteria of certainty: Whatever is perfectly clear and distinct to his reason cannot be doubted and so must be true. Applying these criteria, Descartes proceeds to discover other truths such as the existence of extended substance or matter. For rationalists like Descartes, all knowledge is expressible in self-evident propositions or their consequences.

As Friedrich Paulsen points out, empiricism claims that all of our knowledge about the world is derived from sense experience. Our reason alone cannot reveal what does or does not exist. The empiricist distinguishes two basic kinds of science, differing in nature and method: purely formal or conceptual sciences, such as logic and mathematics, and objective sciences, such as physics and psychology. The former kind gives us certainty but tells us nothing about matters of fact. From what is logically possible (i.e., not self-contradictory) alone, nothing can be deduced about what exists. The other kind, the objective sciences, gives us probabilities only, not certainties, but does tell us about matters of fact. Friedrich Paulsen then proceeds to a more detailed account, from the empiricist standpoint, of the differences in nature and method between the formal or conceptual sciences and the objective or empirical sciences. At the close of the selection, Paulsen infers a more general conclusion from empiricism: We can have no absolute or certain knowledge of matters of fact. Then is knowledge about existence impossible? According to empiricism, such knowledge is possible if we will relinquish the rationalist demand that knowledge be certain or beyond all doubt.

It has been said that the question of why there is something rather than nothing at all fuels the engine of metaphysics and keeps it churning out theories of reality. A. C. Grayling makes clear that the question of how any knowledge is possible at all fuels the motor of epistemology and keeps it producing theories of knowledge. Philosophical skepticism is the persistent asking of the question of how any knowledge at all is possible. The philosophical skeptic is not asking how knowledge of any particular thing or event is possible but how *any* knowledge, no matter what it is alleged to be knowledge of, no matter what its alleged object or content, is possible. Questioning the truthfulness of a politician, doubting the existence of extraterrestrial intelligence, and distrusting the objectivity of the media are not examples of philosophical skepticism. Philosophical skepticism is the fundamental questioning of the very *possibility* of any knowledge of anything. As Grayling notes, the skeptic observes that we can have the very best possible evidence for a belief and yet the conjunction of the evidence and the falsity of that belief do not result in a contradiction. If there were a contradiction, then there would be knowledge and the skeptic would be refuted. There seems to be an unbridgeable gap between evidence and belief; and hence we can never *know* whether any belief is true. Grayling further emphasizes that in order to understand fully the nature, point, and power of skeptical arguments, one must realize that philosophical skepticism is not a claim to knowledge but a challenge to any claim to know. It is the sense in which Socrates was a skeptic; he took no fee for teaching because he had nothing to teach. He wanted others to teach him; and so he went about not merely asking his fellow Athenians what they believed but insisting that they justify their beliefs, only to find out that none (with the exception of the craftsmen's narrow knowledge of their own crafts) could do so. No skeptic worth his or her salt would hold the obvious self-contradiction of claiming to know knowledge is impossible. Indeed, for the philosophical skeptic to claim to know anything at all would be self-contradictory. The skeptic does not assert any claim to knowledge; the burden of proof falls on the knower not the skeptic. The philosophical skeptic says, "I do not claim knowledge is possible; I do not claim knowledge is impossible; I merely insist you convince me *you* can justify or prove what *you* claim to be true. And, of course, it's not my fault if you can't succeed in doing so."

After a brief historical sketch of the history of skepticism in philosophy and analysis of the nature of skeptical arguments, Grayling distinguishes two kinds of skeptical arguments: those appealing to error, delusion, and dreams and those appealing to perception and perceptual relativities. Together, these two kinds of arguments constitute a serious and even fundamental challenge to both rationalism and empiricism and to science to the extent it relies on both theories of knowledge. However, to attempt to refute these skeptical arguments directly and on a one-by-one basis would, Grayling contends, be doomed to failure. And for two reasons. First, these arguments are most powerful when they are understood, not as claims that knowledge is impossible, but as requests to justify our claims to knowledge. Second, all these arguments are methodological or "maieutic" in the Socratic sense (Socrates claimed to be an "intellectual midwife" who prodded others to think and thus give birth to the ideas latent in them). Taken together the skeptical arguments perform the valuable service of revealing what is necessary for a sound epistemology or theory of knowledge. But is there a way to demonstrate that knowledge is possible? How can the challenge of skeptical arguments be met successfully? Grayling concludes by indicating what would refute the skeptic's arguments.

"The Detective as Scientist" by Irving M. Copi, an outstanding contemporary logician, provides a clear and authoritative outline of the structure or logic of the process of inquiry that we have come to call "science" or "the scientific method," which has proved so increasingly successful since the seventeenth century. Copi's description reveals how scientific inquiry fruitfully combines elements from philosophical skepticism, rationalism, and empiricism without basing itself wholly on any one of those positions alone.

However, science is not only a problem-solving enterprise; it is a cultural phenomenon of enormous and growing importance. Deprived of science and scientific technologies, our lives would be transformed out of all recognition. Success breeds criticism. The achievement of science is no exception. We may live in a scientific age, as many claim or complain; nonetheless, critics and powerful enemies of science abound in contemporary life and, some fear, steadily mount in numbers and influence. They challenge the value of science, accuse it of doing more harm than good, and champion other methods of obtaining the truth as superior to that of science. In "The Limits and the Value of Scientific Method," two eminent American philosophers of science, Morris Cohen and Ernest Nagel, defend science as "the finest flower and test of a liberal civilization" against its critics and foes.

In "Can Science Prove That God Does Not Exist?" Theodore Schick Jr. argues that it can. What is meant by "proof" constitutes the crux of the matter. First, there is proof in the sense of logical possibility and impossibility. A concept or proposition is logically possible if its denial is not a self-contradiction; however, if its denial is self-contradictory, then it is logically impossible. For example, round squares are logically impossible because a round square would be round and not round and square and not square. The concept of a purple cow, on the other hand, is logically possible. What is logically possible may or may not exist; what is logically impossible does not and cannot exist. The proposition that "round squares exist" must be false because it involves a contradiction. Hence, the contradictory of "round squares exist" must be true, that is, the proposition "round squares do not exist" must be true. (To say that two propositions are contradictory means that both of them cannot be true and both of them cannot be false.) Schick contends that the proposition "No one can prove an unrestricted negative," that is, that something does not exist anywhere, involves a self-contradiction and so must be false. The proposition "No one can prove an unrestricted negative" is itself an unrestricted negative. Consequently it must be true that it is logically possible to prove an unrestricted negative. Of course what is logically possible may or may not exist; someone may or may not succeed in proving an unrestricted negative. Applying this logical analysis to the concept of God, Schick charges that some concepts of God may well be logical impossibilities. If this is correct, such Gods so conceived cannot exist.

But what if a concept of the nature of God is logically possible? Can it be proven that such a logically possible being does not exist? This brings us to what Schick calls a second sense of proof or proof beyond a reasonable doubt. The nonexistence of something is proven beyond a reasonable doubt if the assumption of its existence is not necessary to explain some phenomenon. The existence of a tiny, invisible singer and combo in your boom box is not necessary to explain why music comes out of it. So we can conclude there is no tiny, invisible singer and combo in your boom box. Schick points out that science in this way has proven the nonexistence of many things once thought to exist such as phlogiston, the planet Vulcan, and so on. The ever increasing success of science in explaining phenomena without appealing to the hypothesis that God exists in this sense proves God does not exist, that atheism is true. Furthermore, naturalistic (atheistic) explanations are superior to supernatural (theistic) ones because the former better meet criteria of theoretical adequacy such as simplicity, number of assumptions made, and so on. In order to prove that science will *never* be able to explain something, theists would have to prove an unrestricted negative, and it already has been shown that to do so is a logical impossibility.

In rebuttal of Schick, Bobby Treat maintains that "Science Cannot Prove that God Does Not Exist." According to Treat, the proposition "God exists" does not belong in any scientific theory because such a proposition cannot be disproven. No predictions that can be checked by observation follow from the theistic hypothesis; if there are no such predictions, then obviously they never can be falsified. On the basis of the theory that this white stuff on the table is sugar, one can predict that it will taste sweet and will dissolve in water. If the white stuff does not taste sweet and does not dissolve, then one has good grounds for abandoning the theory as not useful. In the same manner science has discarded the phlogiston and other theories. But the theistic hypothesis does not fit this pattern of empirical testability; consequently, science cannot disprove God's existence nor can science prove it true. Does this mean that the proposition "God exists" must be false? No, it *might* be true. Science is irrelevant to proving or disproving God's existence.

In "A Consumer's Guide to Pseudoscience," the physicist James S. Trefil seeks not only to distinguish unorthodox science from pseudoscience but also to offer the "consumer" or scientific person helpful tips on how to tell the difference. To confuse unorthodox science with pseudoscience would be to throw the baby of new ideas out with the bathwater of error. Novel ideas should be taken seriously; pseudoscientific ones should not be. Professional scientists assume this sound attitude. Trefil offers a brief checklist to aid us in appropriately adopting the same stance.

How does one distinguish genuine science from pseudoscience or "baloney" as Carl Sagan derisively dubbed it? Must one be a scientist to tell one from the other reliably? Michael Shermer briefly describes ten tests or questions to ask when confronted with some allegedly scientific claim. These tests or questions to be employed in differentiating genuine science from pseudoscience do not require some special expertise; whether scientist or not, any intelligent person should be able to apply them successfully. By and large, there is nothing strange or esoterically technical about Shermer's ten questions. They possess a common-sense character. However, we must remind ourselves again and again to be common-sensical, particularly when moved by some strong emotion such as fear or hope. Sometimes the difference between science and pseudoscience is sharp and clear; Shermer remarks that the big bang cosmology should be given a 0.9 probability of being true and UFO reports a probability of merely 0.1. However, the demarcation between science and pseudoscience is not always so stark. Shermer recognizes that the boundary separating the two can be vague, fuzzy, indistinct. Science shades into speculation and speculation into pseudoscience. Scientists themselves may disagree as to whether some claim is scientific or pseudoscientific. Shermer believes that his ten questions or tests will be of particular help when one finds oneself in the speculative gray area between science and pseudoscience. Patiently and persistently seeking answers to his questions should provide maximum protection against embracing something later proven to have been pseudoscience.

In the first reading in the "Problems and Puzzles" section, John Hospers carefully distinguishes which conceptions of time travel are logically possible and which are logically impossible. The former do not involve a contradiction; the latter do. It is certainly possible to remain in the present and yet *imagine* ourselves in some remote past or future era. Historians do it; science fiction authors do it. Such imaginary time travel is both empirically possible and a fact. However, literal conceptions of time travel would be logically impossible. Hospers argues that it would be logically impossible to be one and the same person living in two different centuries at one and the same time; to live in the past and interact with it and at the same time to live in the present and interact with it would be contradictory. The past without you in it and the past with you in it would not be the same past. To travel backward in time literally and change the past would be logically impossible. The past is what has happened. But to change the past would be to make what has happened not to have happened. If the past could be changed, it would not be the past. Literal travel into the future also involves contradictions. One can state a logically impossible concept in words; the rub is that there is nothing for the words to describe. The fact that people continue to hold logically impossible conceptions of time travel shows the need for careful philosophical analysis.

Sextus Empiricus claims that a criterion of truth or a principle or standard by which to judge something true or false is undiscoverable. Any attempt to find such a criterion must result ultimately in an infinite regression. The truth of propositions is established either by assertion or by proof. Sheer assertion must be rejected because for every assertion there is a contradictory assertion. Therefore, we are driven to seek a criterion or standard by which to judge the assertions. But why should we accept the criterion? We cannot do so on the basis of assertion alone because that justification already has failed. If we try to judge asserted disagreeing criteria, we must then search for another criterion and so on without end. We cannot appeal to any characteristics of those making assertions such as age, intelligence, or agreement with the majority because they are unreliable bases for determining who speaks truly and who does not. Can a criterion or standard be established by proof rather than bare assertion? Sextus Empiricus claims that every attempt at proof must fail. How can we know any proof is sound or unsound? We cannot merely assert that a proof is sound or unsound because we have appealed to proof as the result of the inadequacy of assertion. We need a criterion or standard of proof. Yet we cannot justify the proof by the criterion and then justify the criterion by the proof or vice versa without plunging into a vicious circle of reasoning. But we cannot appeal to yet another criterion or standard without encountering the same pitfall of viciously circular reasoning and being driven on to yet another criterion or standard ad infinitum. Sextus Empiricus is not maintaining that all propositions are true or that all are false. What he is maintaining is that it is impossible for us to determine which are true and which are false.

Rationalism

50. Meditations I and II

René Descartes

René Descartes (1596–1650), inventor of analytic geometry and one of the greatest of French philosophers, has affected profoundly the problems, methods, and solutions of modern philosophy.

Meditation I

Of the Things of Which We May Doubt   Several years have now elapsed since I first became aware that I had accepted, even from my youth, many false opinions for true, and that consequently what I afterwards based on such principles was highly doubtful; and from that time I was convinced of the necessity of undertaking once in my life to rid myself of all the opinions I had adopted, and of commencing anew the work of building from the foundation, if I desired to establish a firm and abiding super structure in the sciences. But as this enterprise appeared to me to be one of great magnitude, I waited until I had attained an age so mature as to leave me no hope that at any stage of life more advanced I should be better able to execute my design. On this account, I have delayed so long that I should henceforth consider I was doing wrong were I still to consume in deliberation any of the time that now remains for action. Today, then, since I have opportunely freed my mind from all cares, and am happily disturbed by no passions, and since I am in the secure possession of leisure in a peaceable retirement, I will at length apply myself earnestly and freely to the general overthrow of all my former opinions. But, to this end, it will not be necessary for me to show that the whole of these are false—a point, perhaps, which I shall never reach; but as even now my reason convinces me that I ought not the less carefully to withhold belief from what is not entirely certain and indubitable, than from what is manifestly false, it will be sufficient to justify the rejection of the whole if I shall find in each some ground for doubt. Nor for this purpose will it be necessary even to deal with each belief individually, which would be truly an endless labour; but, as the removal from below of the foundation necessarily involves the downfall of the whole edifice, I will at once approach the criticism of the principles on which all my former beliefs rested.

From *The Meditations and Selections from the Principles of René Descartes*, translated by John Veitch, The Open Court Publishing Co., La Salle, Illinois, 1905.

All that I have, up to this moment, accepted as possessed of the highest truth and certainty, I received either from or through the senses. I observed however, that these sometimes misled us; and it is the part of prudence not to place absolute confidence in that by which we have even once been deceived.

But it may be said, perhaps that, although the senses occasionally mislead us respecting minute objects, and such as are so far removed from us as to be beyond the reach of close observation, there are yet many other of their information (presentations), of the truth of which it is manifestly impossible to doubt; as for example, that I am in this place, seated by the fire, clothed in a winter dressing-gown, that I hold in my hands this piece of paper, with other intimations of the same nature. But how could I deny that I possess these hands and this body, and withal escape being classed with persons in a state of insanity, whose brains are so disordered and clouded by dark bilious vapours as to cause them pertinaciously to assert that they are monarchs when they are in the greatest poverty; or clothed in gold and purple when destitute of any covering; or that their head is made of clay, their body of glass, or that they are gourds? I should certainly be not less insane than they, were I to regulate my procedure according to examples so extravagant.

Though this be true, I must nevertheless here consider that I am a man, and that, consequently, I am in the habit of sleeping, and representing to myself in dreams those same things, or even sometimes others less probable, which the insane think are presented to them in their waking moments. How often have I dreamt that I was in these familiar circumstances,—that I was dressed, and occupied this place by the fire, when I was lying undressed in bed? At the present moment, however, I certainly look upon this paper with eyes wide awake; the head which I now move is not asleep; I extend this hand consciously and with express purpose, and I perceive it; the occurrences in sleep are not so distinct as all this. But I cannot forget that, at other times, I have been deceived in sleep by similar illusions; and, attentively considering those cases, I perceive so clearly that there exist no certain marks by which the state of waking can ever be distinguished from sleep, that I feel greatly astonished; and in amazement I almost persuade myself that I am now dreaming.

Let us suppose, then, that we are dreaming, and that all these particulars—namely, the opening of the eyes, the motion of the head, the forth putting of the hands—are merely illusions; and even that we really possess neither an entire body nor hands such as we see. Nevertheless, it must be admitted at least that the objects which appear to us in sleep are, as it were, painted representations which could not have been formed unless in the likeness of realities; and, therefore, that those general objects, at all events,—namely, eyes, a head, hands, and an entire body—are not simply imaginary, but really existent. For, in truth, painters themselves, even when they study to represent sirens and satyrs by forms the most fantastic and extraordinary, cannot bestow upon them natures absolutely new, but can only make a certain medley of the members of different animals; or if they chance to imagine something so novel that nothing at all similar has ever been before, and such as is, therefore, purely fictitious and absolutely false, it is at least certain that the colours of which this is composed are real.

And on the same principle, although these general objects, viz. a body, eyes, a head, hands, and the like, be imaginary, we are nevertheless absolutely necessitated to admit the reality at least of some other objects still more simple and universal than these, of which, just as of certain real colours, all those images of things, whether true and real, or false and fantastic, that are found in our consciousness, are formed.

To this class of objects seem to belong corporeal nature in general and its extension; the figure of extended things, their quantity or magnitude, and their number, as also the place in, and the time during which they exist, and other things of the same sort. We will not, therefore, perhaps reason illegitimately if we conclude from this that Physics, Astronomy, Medicine, and all the other sciences that have for their end the consideration of composite objects, are indeed of a doubtful character; but that Arithmetic, Geometry, and the other sciences of the same class, which regard merely the simplest and most general objects, and scarcely inquire whether or not these are really existent, contain somewhat that is certain and indubitable; for whether I am awake or dreaming, it remains true that two and three makes five, and that a square has but four sides; nor does it seem possible that truths so apparent can ever fall under a suspicion of falsity or incertitude.

Nevertheless, the belief that there is a God who is all-powerful, and who created me, such as I am, has, for a long time, obtained steady possession of my mind. How, then, do I know that he has not arranged that there should be neither earth, nor sky, nor any extended thing, nor figure, nor magnitude, nor place, providing at the same time, however, for the rise in me of the perceptions of all these objects, and the persuasion that these do not exist otherwise than as I perceive them? And further, as I sometimes think that others are in error respecting matters of which they believe themselves to possess a perfect knowledge, how do I know that I am not also deceived each time I add together two and three, or number the sides of a square, or form some judgment still more simple, if more simple indeed can be imagined? But perhaps Deity has not been willing that I should be thus deceived, for He is said to be supremely good. If, however, it were repugnant to the goodness of Deity to have created me subject to constant deception, it would seem likewise to be contrary to this goodness to allow me to be occasionally deceived; and yet it is clear that this is permitted. Some, indeed, might perhaps be found who would be disposed rather to deny the existence of a Being so powerful than to believe that there is nothing certain. But let us for the present refrain from opposing this opinion, and grant that all which is here said of a Deity is fabulous; nevertheless in whatever way it be supposed that I reached the state in which I exist, whether by fate, or chance, or by an endless series of antecedents and consequents, or by any other means, it is clear (since to be deceived and to err is a certain defect) that the probability of my being so imperfect as to be the constant victim of deception, will be increased exactly in proportion as the power possessed by the cause, to which they assign my origin, is lessened. To these reasonings I have assuredly nothing to reply, but am constrained at last to avow that there is nothing of all that I formerly believed to be true of which it is impossible to doubt, and that not through thoughtlessness or levity, but from cogent and maturely considered reasons; so that henceforward, if I desire to discover anything certain, I ought not the less carefully to refrain from assenting to those same opinions than to what might be shown to be manifestly false.

But it is not sufficient to have made these observations; care must be taken likewise to keep them in remembrance. For those old and customary opinions perpetually recur—long and familiar usage giving them the right to occupying my mind, even almost against my will, and subduing my belief; nor will I lose the habit of deferring to them and confiding in them so long as I shall consider them to be what in truth they are, viz., opinions to some extent doubtful, as I have already shown, but still highly probable, and such as it is much more reasonable to believe than deny. It is for this reason I am persuaded that I shall not be doing wrong, if, taking an opposite judgment of deliberate design, I become my own deceiver, by supposing, for a time, that all those opinions are entirely false and imaginary, until at length, having thus balanced my old by my new prejudices, my judgment shall no longer be turned aside by perverted usage from the path that may conduct to the perception of truth. For I am assured that, meanwhile, there will arise neither peril nor error from this course, and that I cannot for the present yield too much distrust, since the end I now seek is not action but knowledge.

I will suppose, then, not that Deity, who is sovereignly good and the fountain of truth, but that some malignant demon, who is at once exceedingly potent and deceitful, has employed all his artifice to deceive me; I will suppose that the sky, the air, the earth, colours, figures, sounds, and all external things, are nothing better than the illusions of dreams, by means of which this being has laid snares for my credulity; I will consider myself as without hands, eyes, flesh, blood, or any of the senses, and as falsely believing that I am possessed of these; I will continue resolutely fixed in this belief, and if indeed by this means it be not in my power to arrive at the knowledge of truth, I shall at least do what is in my power, viz., suspend my judgment, and guard with settled purpose against giving my assent to what is false, and being imposed upon by this deceiver, whatever be his power and artifice.

But this undertaking is arduous, and a certain indolence insensibly leads me back to my ordinary course of life; and just as the captive, who, perchance, was enjoying in his dreams an imaginary liberty; when he begins to suspect that it is but a vision, dreads awakening, and conspires with the agreeable illusions that the deception may be prolonged; so I, of my own accord, fall back into the train of my former beliefs, and fear to arouse myself from my slumber, lest the time of laborious wakefulness that would succeed this quiet rest, in place of bringing any light of day, should prove inadequate to dispel the darkness that will arise from the difficulties that have now been raised.

Meditation II

Of the Nature of the Human Mind; and That It Is More Easily Known Than the Body   The Meditation of yesterday has filled my mind with so many doubts, that it is no longer in my power to forget them. Nor do I see, meanwhile, any principle on which they can be resolved; and, just as if I had fallen all of a sudden into very deep water, I am so greatly disconcerted as to be unable either to plant my feet firmly on the bottom or sustain myself by swimming on the surface, I will, nevertheless, make an effort, and try anew the same path on which I had entered yesterday, that is, proceed by casting aside all that admits of the slightest doubt, not less than if I had discovered it to be absolutely false; and I will continue always in this track until I shall find something that is certain, or at least, if I can do nothing more, until I shall know with certainty that there is nothing certain. Archimedes, that he might transport the entire globe from the place it occupied to another, demanded only a point that was firm and immovable; so also, I shall be entitled to entertain the highest expectations, if I am fortunate enough to discover only one thing that is certain and indubitable.

I suppose, accordingly, that all the things which I see are false (fictitious); I believe that none of those objects which my fallacious memory represents ever existed; I suppose that I possess no senses; I believe that body, figure, extension, motion, and place are merely fictions of my mind. What is there, then, that can be esteemed true? Perhaps this only, that there is absolutely nothing certain.

But how do I know that there is not something different altogether from the objects I have now enumerated, of which it is impossible to entertain the slightest doubt? Is there not a God, or some being, by whatever name I may designate him, who causes these thoughts to arise in my mind? But why suppose such a being, for it may be I myself am capable of producing them? Am I, then, at least not something? But I before denied that I possessed senses or a body; I hesitate, however, for what follows from that? Am I so dependent on the body and the senses that without these I cannot exist? But I had the persuasion that there was absolutely nothing in the world, that there was no sky and no earth, neither minds nor bodies; was I not, therefore, at the same time, persuaded that I did not exist? Far from it; I assuredly existed, since I was persuaded. But there is I know not what being, who is possessed at once of the highest power and the deepest cunning, who is constantly employing all his ingenuity in deceiving me. Doubtless, then, I exist, since I am deceived; and, let him deceive me as he may, he can never bring it about that I am nothing, so long as I shall be conscious that I am something. So that it must, in fine, be maintained, all things being maturely and carefully considered, that this proposition, I am, I exist, is necessarily true each time it is expressed by me, or conceived in my mind.

But I do not yet know with sufficient clearness what I am, though assured that I am; and hence, in the next place, I must take care, lest perchance I inconsiderately substitute some other object in room of what is properly myself, and thus wander from truth, even in that knowledge which I hold to be of all others the most certain and evident. For this reason, I will now consider anew what I formerly believed myself to be, before I entered on the present train of thought; and of my previous opinion I will retrench all that can in the least be invalidated by the grounds of doubt I have adduced, in order that there may at length remain nothing but what is certain and indubitable. What then did I formerly think I was? Undoubtedly I judged that I was a man. But what is a man? Shall I say a rational animal? Assuredly not; for it would be necessary forthwith to inquire into what is meant by animal, and what by rational, and thus, from a single question, I should insensibly glide into others, and these more difficult than the first; nor do I now possess enough of leisure to warrant me in wasting my time amid subtleties of this sort. I prefer here to attend to the thoughts that sprung up of themselves in my mind, and were inspired by my own nature alone, when I applied myself to the consideration of what I was. In the first place, then, I thought that I possessed a countenance, hands, arms, and all the fabric of members that appears in a corpse, and which I called by the name of body. It further occurred to me that I was nourished, that I walked, perceived, and thought, and all those actions I referred to the soul, but what the soul itself was I either did not stay to consider, or, if I did, I imagined that it was something extremely rare and subtile, like wind, or flame, or ether, spread through my grosser parts. As regarded the body, I did not even doubt of its nature, but thought I distinctly knew it, and if I had wished to describe it according to the notions I then entertained, I should have explained myself in this manner: By body I understand all that can be terminated by a certain figure; that can be comprised in a certain place, and so fill a certain space as therefrom to exclude every other body; that can be perceived either by touch, sight, hearing, taste, or smell; that can be moved in different ways, not indeed of itself, but by something foreign to it by which it is touched and from which it receives the impression; for the power of self-motion, as likewise that of perceiving and thinking, I held as by no means pertaining to the nature of body; on the contrary, I was somewhat astonished to find such faculties existing in some bodies.

But as to myself, what can I now say that I am, since I suppose there exists an extremely powerful, and, if I may so speak, malignant being, whose whole endeavours are directed towards deceiving me? Can I affirm that I possess any one of all those attributes of which I have lately spoken as belonging to the nature of body? After attentively considering them in my own mind, I find none of them that can properly be said to belong to myself. To recount them were idle and tedious. Let us pass, then, to the attributes of the soul. The first mentioned were the powers of nutrition and walking; but, if it be true that I have no body, it is true likewise that I am capable neither of walking nor of being nourished. Perception is another attribute of the soul; but perception too is impossible without the body: besides, I have frequently during sleep, believed that I perceived objects which I afterwards observed I did not in reality perceive. Thinking is another attribute of the soul; and here I discover what properly belongs to myself. This alone is inseparable from me. I am—I exist: this is certain; but how often? As often as I think; for perhaps it would even happen, if I should wholly cease to think, that I should at the same time altogether cease to be. I now admit nothing that is not necessarily true: I am therefore, precisely speaking, only a thinking thing, that is, a mind, understanding, or reason,—terms whose signification was before unknown to me. I am, however, a real thing, and really existent; but what thing? The answer was, a thinking thing. The question now arises, am I aught besides? I will stimulate my imagination with a view to discover whether I am not still something more than a thinking being. Now it is plain I am not the assemblage of members called the human body; I am not a thin and penetrating air diffused through all these members, or wind, or flame, or vapour, or breath, or any of all the things I can imagine; for I supposed that all these were not, and, without changing the supposition, I find that I still feel assured of my existence.

But it is true, perhaps, that those very things which I suppose to be nonexistent, because they are unknown to me, are not in truth different from myself whom I know. This is a point I cannot determine, and do not now enter into any dispute regarding it (I can only judge of things that are known to me: I am conscious that I exist, and I who know that I exist inquire into what I am. It is, however, perfectly certain that the knowledge of my existence, thus precisely taken, is not dependent on things, the existence of which is as yet unknown to me: and consequently it is not dependent on any of the things I can feign in imagination. Moreover, the phrase itself, I frame an image, reminds me of my error; for I should in truth frame one if I were to imagine myself to be anything, since to imagine is nothing more than to contemplate the figure or image of a corporeal thing; but I already know that I exist, and that it is possible at the same time that all those images, and in general all that relates to the nature of body, are merely dreams or chimeras. From this I discover that it is not more reasonable to say, I will excite my imagination that I may know more distinctly what I am, than to express myself as follows: I am now awake and perceive something real; but because my perception is not sufficiently clear, I will of express purpose go to sleep that my dreams may represent to me the object of my perception with more truth and clearness. And, therefore, I know that nothing of all that I can embrace in imagination belongs to the knowledge which I have of myself, and that there is need to recall with the utmost care the mind from this mode of thinking, that it may be able to know its own nature with perfect distinctness.

But what, then, am I? A thinking thing, it has been said. But what is a thinking thing? It is a thing that doubts, understands, conceives, affirms, denies, wills, refuses, that imagines also, and perceives. Assuredly it is not little, if all these properties belong to my nature. But why should they not belong to it? Am I not that very being who now doubts of almost everything; who, for all that, understands and conceives certain things; who affirms one alone as true, and denies the others; who desires to know more of them, and does not wish to be deceived; who imagines many things, sometimes even despite his will; and is likewise percipient of many, as if through the medium of the senses? Is there nothing of all this as true as that I am, even although I should be always dreaming, and although he who gave me being employed all his ingenuity to deceive me? Is there also any one of these attributes that can be properly distinguished from my thought, or that can be said to be separate from myself? For it is of itself so evident that it is I who doubt, I who understand, and I who desire, that it is here unnecessary to add anything by way of rendering it more clear. And I am as certainly the same being who imagines; for, although it may be (as I before supposed) that nothing I imagine is true) still the power of imagination does not cease really to exist in me and to form part of my thought. In fine, I am the same being who perceives, that is, who apprehends certain objects as by the organs of sense, since, in truth, I see light, hear a noise, and feel heat. But it will be said that these presentations are false, and that I am dreaming. Let it be so. At all events it is certain that I seem to see light, hear a noise, and feel heat; this cannot be false, and this is what in me is properly called perceiving, which is nothing else than thinking) From this I begin to know what I am with somewhat greater clearness and distinctness than heretofore.

But, nevertheless, it still seems to me, and I cannot help believing, that corporeal things, whose images are formed by thought, which fall under the senses, and are examined by the same, are known with much greater distinctness than that I know not what part of myself which is not imaginable; although, in truth, it may seem strange to say that I know and comprehend with greater distinctness things whose existence appears to me doubtful, that are unknown, and do not belong to me, than others of whose reality I am persuaded, that are known to me, and appertain to my proper nature; in a word, than myself. But I see clearly what is the state of the case. My mind is apt to wander, and will not yet submit to be restrained within the limits of truth. Let us therefore leave the mind to itself once more, and, according to it every kind of liberty, permit it to consider the objects that appear to it from without, in order that, having afterwards withdrawn it from these gently and opportunely, and fixed it on the consideration of its being and the properties it finds in itself, it may then be the more easily controlled.

Let us now accordingly consider the objects that are commonly thought to be the most easily, and likewise the most distinctly known, viz., the bodies we touch and see; not, indeed, bodies in general, for these general notions are usually somewhat more confused, but one body in particular. Take, for example, this piece of wax; it is quite fresh, having been but recently taken from the bee-hive; it has not yet lost the sweetness of the honey it contained; it still retains somewhat of the odour of the flowers from which it was gathered; its colour, figure, size, are apparent to the sight, it is hard, cold, easily handled; and sounds when struck upon with the finger. In fine, all that contributes to make a body as distinctly known as possible, is found in the one before us. But, while I am speaking, let it be placed near the fire—what remained of the taste exhales, the smell evaporates, the colour changes, its figure is destroyed, its size increases, it becomes liquid, it grows hot, it can hardly be handled, and, although struck upon, it emits no sound. Does the same wax still remain after this change? It must be admitted that it does remain; no one doubts it, adjudges otherwise. What, then, was it I knew with so much distinctness in the piece of wax? Assuredly, it could be nothing of all that I observed by means of the senses, since all the things that fell under taste, smell, sight, touch, and hearing are changed, and yet the same wax remains. It was perhaps what I now think, viz., that this wax was neither the sweetness of honey, the pleasant odour of flowers, the whiteness, the figure, nor the sound, but only a body that a little before appeared to me conspicuous under these forms, and which is now perceived under others. But, to speak precisely, what is it that I imagine when I think of it in this way? Let it be attentively considered, and, retrenching all that does not belong to the wax, let us see what remains. There certainly remains nothing, except something extended, flexible, and movable. But what is meant by flexible and movable? Is it not that I imagine that the piece of wax, being round, is capable of becoming square, or of passing from a square into a triangular figure? Assuredly such is not the case, because I conceive that it admits of an infinity of similar changes; and I am, moreover, unable to compass this infinity by imagination, and consequently this conception which I have of the wax is not the product of the faculty of imagination. But what now is this extension? Is it not also unknown? For it becomes greater when the wax is melted, greater when it is boiled, and greater still when the heat increases; and I should not conceive clearly and according to truth, the wax as it is, if I did not suppose that the piece we are considering admitted even of a wider variety of extension that I ever imagined. I must, therefore, admit that I cannot even comprehend by imagination what the piece of wax is, and that it is the mind alone which perceives it. I speak of one piece in particular; for, as to wax in general, this is still more evident. But what is the piece of wax that can be perceived only by the understanding or mind? It is certainly the same which I see, touch, imagine; and, in fine, it is the same which, from the beginning, I believed it to be. But (and this it is of moment to observe) the perception of it is neither an act of sight, of touch, nor of imagination, and never was either of these, though it might formerly seem so, but is simply an intuition of the mind, which may be imperfect and confused, as it formerly was, or very clear and distinct, as it is at present, according as the attention is more or less directed to the elements which it contains, and of which it is composed.

But, meanwhile, I feel greatly astonished when I observe the weakness of my mind, and its proneness to error. For although, without at all giving expression to what I think, I consider all this in my own mind, words yet occasionally impede my progress, and I am almost led into error by the terms of ordinary language. We say, for example, that we see the same wax when it is before us, and not that we judge it to be the same from its retaining the same colour and figure: whence I should forthwith be disposed to conclude that the wax is known by the act of sight, and not by the intuition of the mind alone, were it not for the analogous instance of human beings passing on in the street below, as observed from a window. In this case I do not fail to say that I see the men themselves, just as I say that I see the wax; and yet what do I see from the window beyond hats and cloaks that might cover artificial machines, whose motions might be determined by springs? But I judge that there are human beings from these appearances, and thus I comprehend, by the faculty of judgment alone which is in the mind, what I believed I saw with my eyes.

The man who makes it his aim to rise to knowledge superior to the common, ought to be ashamed to seek occasions of doubting from the vulgar forms of speech: instead, therefore, of doing this, I shall proceed with the matter in hand, and inquire whether I had a clearer and more perfect perception of the piece of wax when I first saw it, and when I thought I knew it by means of the external sense itself, or, at all events, by the common sense, as it is called, that is, by the imaginative faculty; or whether I rather apprehend it more clearly at present, after having examined with greater care, both what it is, and in what way it can be known. It would certainly be ridiculous to entertain any doubt on this point. For what, in that first perception, was there distinct? What did I perceive which any animal might not have perceived? But when I distinguish the wax from its exterior forms, and when, as if I had stripped it of its vestments, I consider it quite naked, it is certain, although some error may still be found in my judgement, that I cannot, nevertheless, thus apprehend it without possessing a human mind.

But, finally, what shall I say of the mind itself, that is, of myself? For as yet I do not admit that I am anything but mind. What, then! I who seem to possess so distinct an apprehension of the piece of wax,—do I not know myself, both with greater truth and certitude, and also much more distinctly and clearly? For if I judge that the wax exists because I see it, it assuredly follows, much more evidently, that I myself am or exist, for the same reason: for it is possible that what I see may not in truth be wax, and that I do not even possess eyes with which to see anything; but it cannot be that when I see, or, which comes to the same thing, when I think I see, I myself who think am nothing. So likewise, if I judge that the wax exists because I touch it, it will still also follow that I am; and if I determine that my imagination or any other cause, whatever it be, persuades me of the existence of the wax, I will still draw the same conclusion. And what is here remarked of the piece of wax, is applicable to all the other things that are external to me. And further, if the notion or perception of wax appeared to me more precise and distinct, after that not only sight and touch, but many other causes besides, rendered it manifest to my apprehension, with how much greater distinctness must I not know myself, since all the reasons that contribute to the knowledge of the nature of wax, or of any body whatever, manifest still better the nature of my mind? And there are besides so many other things in the mind itself that contribute to the illustration of its nature, that those dependent on the body, to which I have here referred, scarcely merit to be taken into account.

But in conclusion, I find I have insensibly reverted to the point I desired; for, since it is now manifest to me that bodies themselves are not properly perceived by the senses nor by the faculty of imagination, but by the intellect alone; and since they are not perceived because they are seen and touched, but only because they are understood or rightly comprehended by thought, I readily discover that there is nothing more easily or clearly apprehended than my own mind. But because it is difficult to rid one's self so promptly of an opinion to which one has been long accustomed, it will be desirable to tarry for some time at this stage, that, by long continued meditation, I may more deeply impress upon my memory this new knowledge

Empiricism

51. Empiricism

Friedrich Paulsen

Friedrich Paulsen (1846–1908) was professor of philosophy and pedagogy at the University of Berlin. His Introduction to Philosophy, *translated from the third German edition by the American philosopher Frank Thilly, went through a total of twenty-three editions. Its clarity, felicity of style, learning without pedantry, and humane common sense helped make Paulsen's book a standard introductory philosophy text in Germany and the United States.*

The fundamental conception of empiricism is: There are *two kinds of sciences, differing in nature and method*—purely *conceptual sciences*, like *mathematics*, and *objective sciences*, like physics and psychology. Rationalism errs in recognizing only *one* form of science, the mathematical, and in attempting to fashion all sciences after its pattern. That is an impossible undertaking; the sciences dealing with matters of fact, natural and mental sciences, wholly differ from mathematics in content and method.[1]

It is characteristic of mathematics that it makes no assertions concerning the existence and behavior of reality, but deals solely with deductions from notions. Geometry does not say: This figure is a circle; this body is a sphere, and its motion has the form of an ellipse but: Such and such consequences follow from the definition of the circle and the sine. Whoever accepts the definition must also accept its deductions; he is bound by logic to do so. It is wholly immaterial whether or not anything exists corresponding to the notion.

The case is quite different in the other group of sciences, which deal with objects. Physics and psychology aim to inform us how things act which exist independently of our notions. How can we know anything about them? Empiricism answers: Only by experience. It is absolutely impossible to discover from the notion of water and of heat what will happen when the thermometer falls to zero or rises to one hundred degrees; or to infer from the concept of the body what will occur if it is deprived of its support. Only by perception do we learn that it will fall under such circumstances; the concept does not help us in the least. Not even the most perfect intellect, says Hume, the intellect of Adam before the fall, could have told him

From *Introduction to Philosophy* by Friedrich Paulsen, second American edition from the third German edition. Henry Holt and Company, New York, 1895.

[1]The distinction between demonstrative and experimental knowledge founded on perception is fundamental to the entire fourth book of Locke's *Essay*, which is in reality the principal part of the work. The distinction is, however, not accurately defined. The clear and logical exposition of this difference forms the starting-point of Hume's *Enquiry* (Section IV and Section XII, conclusion).

that if he should happen to fall into the water, he would sink and be suffocated. Nay, it could not even reveal to him what would happen were a body in motion to collide with one at rest. Nor can psychology deduce from an absolute notion of the soul that it feels and desires, reasons and infers, or foresee that air-waves will arouse a sensation of sound, or pressure upon the eye, sensations of light, or a blow in the face, a feeling of anger. All these facts are known by experience only.

Locke[2] began these reflections. He attempts to prove that all our notions are derived from experience. In the first book of the *Essay Concerning the Human Understanding* he undertakes to show, with hypercritical thoroughness, that men do not come into the world with innate ideas; a fact of which perhaps no philosopher, least of all Descartes, needed to be apprised. The real opposition between them is a different one. Descartes claims that it is as possible to form notions in physics and psychology as in mathematics, the validity or truth of which is proved by their inner possibility. Locke denies it. The definition of the body: *corpus est res mere extensa* (body is essentially extension), or the definition: *mens est res mere cogitans* (mind is essentially thinking), may be logically possible; it may be clearly and distinctly conceivable, but that by no means establishes its validity: We may have as clear and distinct a conception of a golden mountain. The truth of the notions of all sciences that deal with facts is based solely on the perception of such facts and connections. Hence it follows that the definitions of sciences of fact cannot be as fixed and final as mathematical concepts; they may be enlarged and modified by further observation. Our notion of *gold* is the result of all previous observations concerning this body: It has such and such a color, a particular specific gravity, and reacts in a certain way upon mechanical, chemical, and thermal influences. Further observations may possibly discover new qualities. It is also possible that we may become acquainted with a body having all the qualities of gold but a somewhat higher or lower melting-point. We should in that event extend our notion sufficiently to admit this difference. The mathematical concept, however, is final: A figure in which the radii are not quite equal is not a circle; a line that touches a circle at more than one point is not a tangent. The same remarks apply to the notions on which Descartes aims to base physics and psychology; they are not final or mathematical, but provisional and empirical. Descartes explains: A body is a thing whose essence consists in states of consciousness (*cogitatio*) for I can clearly and distinctly conceive such a thing. Of course I can; but should experience show that this extended thing also thinks, at least occasionally, or that this thinking being also sets bodies in motion, could I not also conceive that? And in that case would it be advisable to retain the above definitions? Evidently not. For then they would be inadequate to explain actual facts. Hence all concepts concerning matters of fact are provisional notions, they are constantly changing in order to fit the facts yielded by observation. Such notions make a demonstrative procedure like mathematics impossible.

Locke often insists that mathematics is the most perfect form of knowledge. He deplores the fact that this kind of knowledge (which outside of mathematics is

---

[2][John Locke (1632–1704) was an English philosopher and empiricist.—Ed.]

possible only in morals) is restricted to so narrow a field. Nevertheless we must confess that the sciences of fact like physics, chemistry, and psychology cannot be treated according to the mathematical method; observation and experiment are necessary here.

Hume[3] continued and completed these reflections. His examination of the *notion of cause and effect* forms the cardinal point in his brief and simple but thoughtful *Inquiry Concerning Human Understanding.* The law of causality had always been the chief support of rationalism. It was supposed that the effect could be deduced from the cause; the relation existing between cause and effect is the same as that existing between ground and consequent: *sequi = causari.* Hume shows that this is an error. Inference according to the law of causality is entirely different from concluding according to the logical law of contradiction. The relation between cause and effect is no logical relation at all, discoverable by pure thought. In physics and psychology such phenomena are said to be causally related as they invariably succeed each other in time. The perception of succession in time is all that is really observed here; at any rate, an *inner connection* of phenomena, a necessity that binds them together, is not a matter of observation. I perceive that a certain state follows upon a given state; I expect the same event to succeed it the next time it occurs. Here we have the beginning of the causal conception. We find it in animals; they too learn from experience, and in the manner indicated: A certain succession is perceived in events; at the recurrence of the first, the second is expected or anticipated. The function is more highly developed in man; not every perceived succession leads us to expect its return; we gradually learn to separate the constant causal relations existing between phenomena from the accidental and dissoluble connections. But the principle is the same in either case. It is absolutely impossible to discover the effect from the notion of the cause by logical inference. Take the simplest example. The motion of a body in a given period of time is the cause of the same movement during the succeeding period. This is in no wise discoverable by a logical inference. From the proposition that a certain body moves with a certain velocity per second, and in a certain direction, no logical conclusion follows, except the falseness of its opposite. Nothing whatever can be deduced as to what is going to happen during the *next* second. On the ground of previous observations, I *expect* this body to pass through an equal space with the same velocity and in the same direction, during the ensuing period of time. But this expectation is not a *necessity of thought,* like a mathematical proposition. It is also conceivable that the movement should cease of its own accord, either suddenly or gradually, or that it should turn off in any direction whatever. Past experience has invariably taught us that things behave in the manner stated in the law of inertia, but it is not a logical necessity that the future should resemble the past. Moreover, says Hume,—and that is his most general proposition,—there is absolutely no fact the non-existence of which would not be conceivable or logically possible. The non-existence of any body, the invalidity of any natural law, is conceivable, for the non-existence of the entire world is conceivable.

---

[3][David Hume (1711–1776) was a Scottish philosopher, empiricist, and skeptic.—Ed.]

Hence it follows: In the sciences concerning matters of fact like physics and psychology there are no *truths that are strictly universal and necessary*. These sciences contain propositions that are *only probably universal*. Each one is true with the tacit proviso: Subject to correction by subsequent experience. The propositions of mathematics are absolutely universal and necessary. No observation can shake or change the proposition that the sum of the angles of a plane triangle is equal to two right angles; it is implied in the notions themselves as their logically necessary consequence. On the other hand, there is no proposition in physics or psychology that can be said to possess such necessity. Nor is the causal law itself an exception; the proposition that there is absolute regularity in the succession of natural phenomena has presumptive validity only. It is also conceivable or logically possible that phenomena should occur that stand in no relation whatever to all antecedent and all consequent phenomena. We should call such phenomena miracles. Hence miracles are undoubtedly possible, just as possible to thought as facts that may be explained by our laws of nature, *i.e.,* inserted into the natural connection of things according to rules. The question is not a question of possibility, but one of fact. Have facts been observed that would have to be regarded as miracles? Hume raises serious objections to the assertion. According to him the theory that the alleged miracles are explainable, if not physically, psychologically at least, has such great probability that it may be regarded as practically certain. It is a matter of such common experience that human testimony rests on voluntary or involuntary deception, that it seems much more plausible for us to explain an alleged miracle in this way than to abandon the fundamental principle of all natural science, the universal reign of law in nature. This presupposition is, of course, not logically necessary, but has been so often confirmed by facts and has, upon close observation, been so often verified even in the case of alleged miracles, that we have the right, on *a priori* grounds, to doubt new miracles.

That is the epistemology of empiricism. . . . The question at stake in the controversy between rationalism and empiricism is: Do we possess an *a priori* or rational knowledge of objects? Rationalism answers in the affirmative: By pure thought we reach an absolute knowledge of things that cannot be acquired through the senses. Empiricism denies the statement: We gain a knowledge of objects solely by perception, whence it follows that we have no absolute knowledge. . . .

Scepticism

52. Scepticism

A. C. Grayling

Introduction

In both the ordinary and the philosophical senses, a sceptic is one who, at least unless he is shown satisfactory reason why he should do otherwise, doubts some proposition, belief, or theory. Sceptical considerations are immensely important for philosophical inquiry into questions about knowledge. For these purposes the characterization just given is too general as it stands, so a more careful explanation of scepticism is needed, together with an account of the reasons that prompt it.

In the general business of life a sceptical attitude is healthy when it aims at testing the grounds for claims upon our credence, by whomever they are made. It is of course impractical to be sceptical about everything; ordinarily we have to take on trust a great deal of what others say. Society could not function unless most people were taken to be honest, and most information reliable, most of the time. But there are cases where it is appropriate, even necessary, to be sceptical; where the responsible course is to question a given claim and to assess the case offered in its support. A barrister in a court of law, or a voter listening to politicians on the hustings, has a duty to do so.

In philosophy the study and use of sceptical arguments belongs to epistemology, and in one sense might be said to define it. One of the chief concerns of epistemology is to determine how we can be sure that the means we employ to acquire knowledge are adequate. A powerful way to show what is required is to look carefully at sceptical challenges to our knowledge-acquiring endeavours, challenges which reveal or allege ways in which they can go wrong. If we are able to identify and meet them, we will have achieved a primary epistemological aim.

Scepticism is often described as the claim that nothing is—or, more strongly, can be—known. But this is a bad characterization, because if we know or can know nothing, then we do not or cannot know that we know nothing, and so the claim is trivially self-defeating. It is more telling to premise the view of scepticism given in the previous paragraph: as a challenge directed at knowledge-claims made in some field of inquiry, the form and nature of the challenge varying with the field in question, but in general taking the form of a request for the justification available in support of the knowledge-claims at issue, together with the reasons that motivate

Reprinted from *Philosophy I: A Guide Through the Subject*, edited by A. C. Grayling (1998) by permission of Oxford Univ. Press. © The University of London, 1995, 1998.

such a request—standardly, that certain considerations indicate that the assumed justification might be inadequate to its task. To conceive of scepticism like this is to see it as more philosophically troubling than if it is described as a positive thesis asserting our ignorance or incapacity for knowledge.

If therefore scepticism consists in asking 'How do you know?', and if it advances points which suggest that ordinary standards of justification for our epistemic claims are vulnerable in various ways, then it makes a serious demand on us. But if it consists in assertions that we do not know this or that, then it is a positive claim in need of a supporting case, about which we are entitled to be sceptical in our turn. And if it consists in a denial that we know anything at all, it is merely self-defeating and ignorable.

A Historical Sketch

Pessimism about the prospects for scientific progress—using 'science' in the broadest sense to mean theoretical knowledge of the world—so infected some among the philosophers of antiquity that they developed distinctive sceptical viewpoints. Pyrrho of Elis (*c.* 360–270 B.C.) and his followers argued that because inquiry is both unproductive and vexing, given the difficulty of determining whether the arguments for any proposition are better or worse than those against, one should suspend judgement altogether, for only thus will the important goal—shared by most philosophical schools of the time—of achieving *ataraxia* (peace of mind) be realizable.

Less radically, the successors of Plato in his Academy, although they agreed with Pyrrho that certainty must elude us, tempered this view with a recognition of the need to accept life's demands, and therefore argued that we should accept whatever proposition or theory is more probable than its competitors. They did not think it a practical possibility to 'suspend judgement', as the Pyrrhonists recommended. The various views of these thinkers are collectively known as Academic scepticism.

In the later part of the Renaissance, with religious certainties under attack and new ideas abroad, some of the sceptical considerations discussed by the Academics and Pyrrhonians acquired a special significance, most notably in the work of René Descartes (1596–1650); for they proved useful as tools in the highly consequential matter of investigating the nature of knowledge and the proper means of getting it. In Descartes's day practitioners of astronomy and astrology, chemistry and alchemy, medicine and magic were often the same people in each or all cases, so there was an urgent need for a way of distinguishing those inquiries that might yield genuine knowledge from those that merely yield nonsense. In his *Meditations* Descartes accordingly identified epistemology as an essential preliminary to science, and sought to establish the grounds of certainty as a preparation for the study of physics and mathematics. As a sharp way of effecting that task Descartes adapted some of the traditional sceptical arguments. His contribution in this respect is so significant that, until recently, epistemology—and in particular the task of refuting scepticism—has occupied a central place in philosophy. The arguments he used are discussed later.

The Nature of Sceptical Arguments

Sceptical arguments exploit certain contingent psychological facts about the ways we acquire, test, remember, and reason about our beliefs. Since knowledge consists in belief which at very least is true and, in a way to be defined, properly justified, any problem which infects the acquisition and employment of beliefs about a given subject-matter threatens our claims to knowledge in respect of that subject-matter.

The contingent psychological facts in question are those relating to the nature of perception, the normal human vulnerability to error, and the existence of states of mind—for example, dreaming and delusion—which can be subjectively indistinguishable from those we take to be appropriate for acquiring knowledge, but which are not so. By appealing to these considerations the sceptic aims to show that there are significant questions to be answered about the degree of confidence we are entitled to repose in our standard ways of getting knowledge.

The considerations appealed to by the sceptic between them pose problems for epistemologists of both the 'rationalist' and the 'empiricist' schools of thought. This division into competing views about knowledge is somewhat crude, but is a useful way of marking the difference between those who hold that the main instrument in the acquisition of knowledge is reason, and those who hold that it is experience. A rationalist might typically emphasize reason because in his view the objects of knowledge are propositions which are eternally, immutably, and necessarily true, for example the propositions of mathematics and logic; and these, he says, can only be arrived at by thought. An empiricist might typically hold that all genuine knowledge of the world must be learned through empirical experience, by means of the five senses (and their extension via telescopes, microscopes, and other instruments). The rationalist need not deny that empirical awareness is an important adjunct of our rational faculties, nor the empiricist that reason is an important adjunct of empirical investigation; both will, however, hold that the primary, chief, or final means to knowledge is respectively one or the other.

The refinements and details of debates about these matters merit more detailed examination than can be given here. For present purposes the point is that scepticism is a problem for both schools of thought. For both, possibilities of error and delusion pose a challenge. For the empiricist in particular, to these must be added problems about perception and perceptual consciousness.

Sceptical Arguments: Error, Delusion, and Dreams

The arguments from error and delusion are simply stated. Consider the error argument first. We are fallible creatures; we sometimes make mistakes. If, however, we are ever to be able to claim to know some proposition p, we must be able to exclude the possibility that at the time of claiming to know p we are in error. But since we typically or at least frequently do not realize, as we make an error in claiming to know p, that we are indeed making an error, we are not justified in making such a claim.

The same applies when a person is the subject of delusion, illusion, or hallucination. Sometimes one who experiences one or other of these states does not know that he is doing so, and takes himself to be having veridical experiences. But although he thinks he is in a state which lends itself to his being justified in claiming to know a given *p*, he is not so. In such a case he does not know what he claims to know. So in order for anyone to claim knowledge of some *p*, he must be able to exclude the possibility that he is the subject of such states.

This pattern of argument is at its most familiar in the 'dream argument' of Descartes. One way of sketching it is as follows. When I sleep I sometimes dream, and when I dream I often do not know I am dreaming. So I can have experiences which appear to be veridical waking experiences on the basis of which I take myself to be entitled to claim knowledge of such-and-such. But because I am dreaming, I do not in fact know such-and-such; I merely dream that I do. Might I not be dreaming now? If I cannot exclude the possibility that I am now, at this moment, dreaming, I am unable to claim knowledge of the things I at this moment take myself to know. For example, it seems to me that I am writing this at a pair of French windows opened to a garden, with recorded music playing in the room behind me. But because I might be dreaming that this is so, I cannot claim to know it.

In these arguments the possibility of error, delusion, or dreaming acts as a 'defeater' to knowledge-claims. The pattern is: If one knows *p*, then nothing is acting to subvert one's entitlement to know it. But one can seem to oneself fully entitled to claim to know some *p*, and in fact not be so, as the foregoing considerations show. So our claims to knowledge are in need of better grounds than we standardly take ourselves to have. We must find a way of defeating the defeaters.

Sceptical Arguments: Perception and Perceptual Relativities

The arguments sketched in the preceding paragraphs equally threaten both rationalist and empiricist views about the sources of knowledge. Further considerations which trouble the empiricist arise from the nature and limitations of sensory experience.

Our best current model of perception tells us something like the following. Light reflects from the surfaces of objects in the physical environment and passes into the eyes, where it irritates the cells of the retinas in such a way that impulses are triggered in the optic nerves. The nerves convey the impulses to the part of the cerebral cortex which processes visual data, where they stimulate certain sorts of brain activity. As a result, in ways yet mysterious to science and philosophy, coloured motion pictures arise in the consciousness of the subject of these events, representing the world outside his head. This remarkable transaction, *mutatis mutandis*, is repeated in the other sensory pathways of hearing, smell, taste, and touch, although in these cases it is not of course coloured motion pictures which result from the impingement of the world upon the subject's sensitive membranes, but music and conversation, flavours and scents, textures and temperatures.

The sceptic can use this model to make another application of the defeater argument. He points out that the complex causal story thus told is one which might be interrupted at any point along its length in problematic ways. The experiences which we say result from the interaction of our sense organs and the world might occur in us for other reasons. They might occur when, as noted above, we dream or suffer hallucinations; or, to take fancy further, they might be produced in us by a deity, or by a mad scientist who has wired our brains to a computer. From the subjective point of view there might be no way of telling the difference. So unless we find means of excluding these possibilities, says the sceptic, we are not entitled to claim knowledge of what we standardly take ourselves to know.

But these same considerations about perception might prompt sceptical challenge by a different route. Only a little reflection shows that some of the properties we seem to perceive in objects are in fact not 'in the objects themselves' but are the artefact of the perceptual relation. The colour, taste, smell, sound, and texture of objects vary according to the condition of the perceiver or the conditions under which they are perceived. The standard examples are legion. Grass is green in daylight, grey or black at night; tepid water feels warm to a cold hand, cool to a hot hand; objects look large from close by, small from far away; the sides of a table look parallel from above, but coverge when looked at from one end. And so on. These perceptual relativities are invoked by the sceptic to raise questions not just about whether perception is a reliable source of information about the world, but, further, whether the world can properly be said to exist independently of perception at all. For what if the properties by whose means we detect the presence of objects—their colours, textures, shapes, and the rest—cannot be described apart from their being objects of perception? Only consider the old conundrum whether a sound is made by something that falls to the ground with no sentient beings present to hear it do so. If there is no ear to hear, there is no sound, only at best the conditions—vibrating airwaves—which might cause sound to be heard if there were eardrums, aural nerves, and the rest to be affected by them.

What these considerations suggest to the sceptic is that perceivers are in something like this case: Imagine a person wearing a helmet of the type worn by motorbike-riders, with the big difference that it has no visor, so that the wearer cannot see out. And imagine that a camera, a microphone, and other sensors affixed to the top of the helmet transmit pictures, sounds, and related information to the helmet's interior. And suppose finally that it is impossible for the wearer to remove the helmet to check whether the information passed to its interior faithfully represents the exterior world; the wearer has to rely on the intrinsic character of the information available inside the helmet to judge its reliability. He knows that the information sometimes comes from sources other than the exterior world, as in dreams and delusions; he has deduced that the equipment affixed to the helmet works upon the incoming data and changes it, for example adding colours, scents, and sounds to its picture of what intrinsically has none of these properties (at very least, in those forms); and he knows that his beliefs about what lies outside the helmet rest on the inferences he draws from the information available inside it, and that his inferences are only as good as his fallible, error-prone capacities allow them to be. Given all this, asks the sceptic, have we not a job of work to do to justify our claims to knowledge?

Methodological and Problematic Scepticism

Before reflecting on these arguments and inspecting some ways of responding to them, it is helpful to note one fact and to draw one distinction. The fact is that sceptical arguments are not best dealt with by attempts at direct refutation on a one-by-one basis. The distinction is one between—broadly speaking—two ways in which scepticism can be employed in epistemology. It is important to note both this fact and this distinction because otherwise the prima-facie implausibility of most sceptical arguments will mislead one into ignoring their significance.

Attempted refutation of sceptical arguments singly and directly is futile for two very good reasons. One is that they are at their strongest not when they seek to prove an agniological result—that is, one which positively affirms that we are ignorant about some subject-matter—but when they ask us to justify our claims to knowledge. A challenge to justify is not a claim or a theory, and cannot be refuted; it can only be accepted or ignored. Since the sceptic offers reasons why justification is needed, the response might be to inspect those reasons to see whether the challenge needs response. This indeed is one good response to scepticism. Where the reasons are cogent, the next good response is to try to meet the challenge thus posed.

The second good reason is that the whole range of sceptical arguments taken together has maieutic status. Literally 'maieusis' means midwifery, that is, the practice of aiding childbirth. Whatever has maieutic status is whatever helps something else into being. To say that sceptical considerations are maieutic is to say that they together bring into the light what is needed for a satisfactory theory of knowledge. If one could refute, or show to be ungrounded, one or another particular sceptical argument, it would leave others in place still demanding that we give a positive account of knowledge.

These points can be simply illustrated by a consideration of Gilbert Ryle's attempt to refute the argument from error by a 'polar concept' argument. There cannot be counterfeit coins, Ryle observes, unless there are genuine ones, nor crooked paths unless there are straight paths, nor tall men unless there are short men. Many concepts come in pairs which are polar opposites of one another, and these conceptual polarities are such that one cannot grasp either pole unless one grasps its opposite at the same time. Now, 'error' and 'getting it right' are conceptual polarities. If one understands the concept of error, one understands the concept of getting it right. But to understand this latter concept is to be able to apply it. So our very grasp of the concept of error implies that we sometimes get things right.

Ryle takes the error sceptic to be claiming that, for all we know, we might always be in error. Accordingly his argument—that if we understand the concept of error, we must sometimes get things right—is aimed at refuting the intelligibility of claiming that we might always be wrong. But of course the error sceptic is not claiming this. He is simply asking how, given that we sometimes make mistakes, we can rule out the possibility of being in error on any given occasion of judgement—say, at this present moment. But the sceptic need not concede to the more general claims Ryle makes, namely, that for any conceptual polarity, both poles must be understood, and, further, to understand a concept is to know how to apply it, and for it to be applicable is for it actually to be applied (or to have been applied). This last move is question-begging enough, but so is the claim about conceptual polarities itself. For the sceptic can readily cite cases of conceptual polarities—those denoted, for example, by the expressions 'perfect-imperfect', 'mortal-immortal', 'finite-infinite'—where it is by no means clear that the more exotic poles apply to anything, or even that we really understand them (taking a term and attaching a negative prefix to it does not guarantee that we have grasped an intelligible concept).

These thoughts suggest that sceptical arguments, even if singly they appear implausible, jointly invite a serious response; which is what, in large measure, epistemology seeks to offer. But there is still the matter of the distinction to be explained, and here a brief rehearsal of Descartes's use of sceptical arguments proves useful.

Descartes's aim is to find something of which he can be certain as a basis for knowledge. To find certainty he needs to exclude whatever admits of the least taint of doubt, however absurd that doubt, for only then will what is truly indubitable be revealed. In the first *Meditation* he embarks on this task by borrowing some sceptical arguments from antiquity. First he cites the fact that we can be misled in perception. But this is not a thoroughgoing enough scepticism, for even if we make perceptual mistakes, there is much that we can still claim to know. So he next considers the possibility that on any given occasion of taking oneself to know something, one might be dreaming. This sceptical consideration catches more in its net, but is still not enough, for even in dreams we can know things; arithmetical truths, for example. So to get as swingeing a consideration as possible Descartes introduces the 'evil demon' hypothesis, in which the supposition is that, with respect to everything about which one can possibly be misled, an evil demon is indeed misleading one. Famously, what such a being cannot mislead one about is that, whenever one thinks 'I exist', this proposition is true.

It is vital to note that Descartes's use of these arguments is purely methodological. The remainder of the *Meditations* is devoted to showing that we know a great deal, because the fact (as he unsuccessfully attempts to prove) that there is a good deity ensures that, providing we use our faculties correctly, whatever we clearly and distinctly perceive to be true will indeed be true—for a good deity, unlike an evil one, would not wish us to embrace ignorance. So Descartes is by no means a sceptic, nor does he think the sceptical arguments, least of all the one employed as a device to set aside as many beliefs as possible, are persuasive. The 'method of doubt' is merely a tool.

Descartes's successors, however, were far more impressed by the sceptical arguments he employed than by the response he gave to them. They accepted his diagnosis of the problem, but not the cure. So for the tradition of epistemological thinking after his time these and allied sceptical arguments were not mere

methodological devices, but problems requiring solution. Hence the distinction
I draw between methodological and problematic scepticism.

It is clear that there are sceptical considerations which have merely methodological utility, and are not genuinely problematic, because they do not represent a
stable and cogent challenge to our ordinary epistemological standards. The 'evil
demon' device is a case in point. Since the hypothesis that there is such a thing is
about as arbitrary and groundless as a hypothesis can get, it does not merit being
taken seriously otherwise than as a tactic to make a point. But considerations about
perception, error, delusion, and dreams raise more interesting and troubling general
issues, and it is these which merit examination.

Two things might be noted about Descartes's discussion. First, his quest for
certainty is arguably misconceived. Certainty is a psychological state that one can
be in independently of whether one is right or wrong. For example, one can be
certain that such-and-such a horse will win the Derby, and yet lose one's money. The
falsity of a belief is no bar to one's feeling certain that it is true. Descartes's intention was of course to identify means of recognizing which of our beliefs are true, but
he led himself into talking of certainty because—and this is the second point—he
assumed that epistemology's task is to provide individuals with a way of knowing,
from their own subjective viewpoints, that they are in possession of knowledge
rather than error. His inquiry begins from the private data of an individual
consciousness and attempts to work outward to knowledge of what lies beyond,
securing a guarantee for itself *en route*. Almost all of Descartes's successors in
epistemology, up to and including Bertrand Russell and A. J. Ayer in the twentieth
century, unquestioningly accepted this perspective upon their task. In this respect
at least they are all Cartesians. And . . . , it is for this reason that they all found it
difficult to meet the sceptical challenge.

Some Responses to Scepticism: The 'Gap'

The general effect of sceptical challenges is to suggest that we suffer an epistemic
plight, which is that we can possess the very best possible evidence for believing
some p, and yet be wrong. Stated more formally, scepticism comes down to the
observation that there is nothing contradictory in the conjunction of statements s
embodying our best grounds for a given belief p with the falsity of p: schematically,
$(s \ \& \ \sim p)$ is not a contradiction.

Scepticism thus epitomized can informatively be represented as the opening
of a gap between, on the one hand, the evidence any putative knower has for the
knowledge-claims he makes, and, on the other hand, those claims themselves.
Responses to scepticism variously take the form of attempts either to bridge that gap
or to close it. The standard perceptual model, in which our beliefs are formed by sensory interaction with the world, postulates a causal bridge across the gap; but that
bridge is alleged to be vulnerable to sceptical sabotage, so without support a causal
story is insufficient. Descartes, as noted, identified the epistemological task as the
need to identify a guarantee—call it X—which, added to our ordinary grounds for

belief, renders them proof against scepticism and thus transforms belief into knowledge. His candidate for X was the goodness of a deity; rejecting this candidate sets
us the task of finding an alternative. If an X cannot be found to support a bridge
across the sceptical gap, an option is to try closing the gap—or more accurately, to
show against the sceptic that there is in fact no gap at all. Both the quest for X and
the closing of the gap have constituted major epistemological endeavours against
scepticism in modern philosophy. In brief, some of these endeavours are as follows.

Descartes's immediate successors, as mentioned, were unpersuaded by his
attempt to bridge the gap by appeal to a theistic X. John Locke made covert use of a
weaker version of Descartes's view by saying that sceptical threats to the causal story
can be ignored because 'the light that is set up in us shines bright enough for all our
purposes'. For Locke's own purposes it does not matter whether the light was set up
by God or nature; the point is that there is something X—the light—that provides a
ground for regarding our ordinary knowledge-acquiring means as adequate.

Others, not content with such unsatisfactory moves, looked elsewhere for X,
and claimed to find it in the thought that our system of beliefs has foundations
in the form of basic self-justifying or self-evident beliefs which, in conjunction
with the evidence we ordinarily have for making knowledge-claims, secure them
against sceptical attack. This approach has given rise to a debate in which some
participants attempt to make the notion of 'foundations' plausible, while others
reject it in favour of so-called 'coherence' theories of knowledge, which have it that
beliefs mutually support one another without resting on a privileged base, the
ground for rejecting which is that no satisfactory candidate for foundations can,
so it is claimed, be identified. . . .

Concluding Remarks

Two points in this brief survey of scepticism merit special emphasis. Scepticism
defines one of the central problems in epistemology, namely, the need to demonstrate how knowledge is possible. This is done—if it can be done—by meeting the
challenge to show that sceptical considerations do not after all defeat our best
epistemic endeavours. Implicit in this characterization are two important claims:
first, that scepticism is best understood as a *challenge*, not as an agniological *claim*
that we do or can know nothing; and secondly, that the best way to respond to
scepticism is not by attempting to refute it on an argument-by-argument basis, but
by showing how we know.

The Nature of Science

53. The Detective as Scientist

Irving M. Copi

Irving M. Copi (1917–2002), an American professor of philosophy, wrote extensively and lucidly on logic, scientific method, and the philosophy of language.

... A perennial favorite in this connection is the detective, whose problem is not quite the same as that of the pure scientist, but whose approach and technique illustrate the method of science very clearly. The classical example of the astute detective who can solve even the most baffling mystery is A. Conan Doyle's immortal creation, Sherlock Holmes. Holmes, his stature undiminished by the passage of time, will be our hero in the following account:

1. The Problem

Some of our most vivid pictures of Holmes are those in which he is busy with magnifying glass and tape measure, searching out and finding essential clues which had escaped the attention of those stupid bunglers, the "experts" of Scotland Yard. Or those of us who are by temperament less vigorous may think back more fondly on Holmes the thinker, "... who, when he had an unsolved problem upon his mind, would go for days, and even for a week, without rest, turning it over, rearranging his facts, looking at it from every point of view until he had either fathomed it or convinced himself that his data were insufficient."[1] At one such time, according to Dr. Watson:

> He took off his coat and waistcoat, put on a large blue dressing-gown, and then wandered about the room collecting pillows from his bed and cushions from the sofa and armchairs. With these he constructed a sort of Eastern divan, upon which he perched himself cross-legged, with an ounce of shag tobacco and a box of matches laid out in front of him. In the dim light of the lamp I saw him sitting there, an old briar pipe between his lips, his eyes fixed vacantly upon the corner of the ceiling, the blue smoke

[1]*The Man with the Twisted Lip.*

curling up from him, silent, motionless, with the light shining upon his strong-set aquiline features. So he sat as I dropped off to sleep, and so he sat when a sudden ejaculation caused me to wake up, and I found the summer sun shining into the apartment. The pipe was still between his lips, the smoke still curling upward, and the room was full of a dense tobacco haze, but nothing remained of the heap of shag which I had seen upon the previous night.[2]

But such memories are incomplete. Holmes was not always searching for clues or pondering over solutions. We all remember those dark periods—especially in the earlier stories—when, much to the good Watson's annoyance, Holmes would drug himself with morphine or cocaine. That would happen, of course, between cases. For when there is no mystery to be unraveled, no man in his right mind would go out to look for clues. Clues, after all, must be clues for something. Nor could Holmes, or anyone else, for that matter, engage in profound thought unless he had something to think about. Sherlock Holmes was a genius at solving problems, but even a genius must have a problem before he can solve it. All reflective thinking, and this term includes criminal investigation as well as scientific research, is a problem-solving activity, as John Dewey and other pragmatists have rightly insisted. There must be a problem felt before either the detective or the scientist can go to work.

Of course the active mind sees problems where the dullard sees only familiar objects. One Christmas season Dr. Watson visited Holmes to find that the latter had been using a lens and forceps to examine " . . . a very seedy and disreputable hard-felt hat, much the worse for wear, and cracked in several places."[3] After they had greeted each other, Holmes said of it to Watson, "I beg that you will look upon it not as a battered billycock but as an intellectual problem."[4] It so happened that the hat led them into one of their most interesting adventures, but it could not have done so had Holmes not seen a problem in it from the start. A problem may be characterized as a fact or group of facts for which we have no acceptable explanation, which seem unusual, or which fail to fit in with our expectations or preconceptions. It should be obvious that *some* prior beliefs are required if anything is to appear problematic. If there are no expectations there can be no surprises.

Sometimes, of course, problems came to Holmes already labeled. The very first adventure recounted by Dr. Watson began with the following message from Gregson of Scotland Yard:

My Dear Mr. Sherlock Holmes:
    There has been a bad business during the night at 3, Lauriston Gardens, off the Brixton Road. Our man on the beat saw a light there about two in the morning, and as the house was an empty one, suspected that something was amiss. He found the door open, and in the front room, which is bare of furniture, discovered the body of a gentleman, well dressed, and having cards in his pocket bearing the name of "Enoch

---

[2]Ibid.
[3]*The Adventure of the Blue Carbuncle.*
[4]Ibid.

J. Drebber, Cleveland, Ohio, U.S.A." There had been no robbery, nor is there any evidence as to how the man met his death. There are marks of blood in the room, but there is no wound upon his person. We are at a loss as to how he came into the empty house; indeed, the whole affair is a puzzler. If you can come round to the house any time before twelve, you will find me there. I have left everything *in statu quo* until I hear from you. If you are unable to come, I shall give you fuller details, and would esteem it a great kindness if you would favour me with your opinion.

Yours faithfully,

Tobias Gregson[5]

Here was a problem indeed. A few minutes after receiving the message, Sherlock Holmes and Dr. Watson "were both in a hansom, driving furiously for the Brixton Road."

2. Preliminary Hypotheses

On their ride out Brixton way, Holmes "prattled away about Cremona fiddles and the difference between a Stradivarius and an Amati." Dr. Watson chided Holmes for not giving much thought to the matter at hand, and Holmes replied: "No data yet . . . . It is a capital mistake to theorize before you have all the evidence. It biases the judgment."[6] This point of view was expressed by Holmes again and again. On one occasion he admonished a younger detective that "The temptation to form premature theories upon insufficient data is the bane of our profession."[7] Yet for all of his confidence about the matter, on this one issue Holmes was completely mistaken. Of course one should not reach a *final judgment* until a great deal of evidence has been considered, but this procedure is quite different from *not theorizing*. As a matter of fact, it is strictly impossible to make any serious attempt to collect evidence unless one *has* theorized beforehand. As Charles Darwin, the great biologist and author of the modern theory of evolution, observed: ". . . all observation must be for or against some view, if it is to be of any service." The point is that there are too many particular facts, too many data in the world, for anyone to try to become acquainted with them all. Everyone, even the most patient and thorough investigator, must pick and choose, deciding which facts to study and which to pass over. He must have some working hypothesis for or against which to collect relevant data. It need not be a *complete* theory, but at least the rough outline must be there. Otherwise how could one decide what facts to select for consideration out of the totality of all facts, which is too vast even to begin to sift?

Holmes' actions were wiser than his words in this connection. After all, the words were spoken in a hansom speeding towards the scene of the crime. If Holmes really had no theory about the matter, why go to Brixton Road? If facts and data

[5]*A Study in Scarlet.*
[6]Ibid.
[7]*The Valley of Fear.*

were all that he wanted, any old facts and any old data, with no hypotheses to guide him in their selection, why should he have left Baker Street at all? There were plenty of facts in the rooms at 221-B, Baker Street. Holmes might just as well have spent his time counting all the words on all the pages of all the books there, or perhaps making very accurate measurements of the distances between each separate pair of articles of furniture in the house. He could have gathered data to his heart's content and saved himself cab fare into the bargain!

It may be objected that the facts to be gathered at Baker Street have nothing to do with the case, whereas those which awaited Holmes at the scene of the crime were valuable clues for solving the problem. It was, of course, just this consideration which led Holmes to ignore the "data" at Baker Street and hurry away to collect those off Brixton Road. It must be insisted, however, that the greater relevance of the latter could not be *known* beforehand but only conjectured on the basis of previous experience with crimes and clues. It was in fact a *hypothesis* which led Holmes to look in one place rather than another for his facts, the hypothesis that there was a murder, that the crime was committed at the place where the body was found, and that the murderer had left some trace or clue which could lead to his discovery. Some such hypothesis is always required to guide the investigator in his search for relevant data, for in the absence of any preliminary hypothesis, there are simply too many facts in this world to examine. The preliminary hypothesis ought to be highly tentative, and it must be based on previous knowledge. But a preliminary hypothesis is as necessary as the existence of a problem for any serious inquiry to begin.

It must be emphasized that a preliminary hypothesis, as here conceived, need not be a complete solution to the problem. The hypothesis that the man was murdered by someone who had left some clues to his identity on or near the body of his victim was what led Holmes to Brixton Road. This hypothesis is clearly incomplete: it does not say who committed the crime, or how it was done, or why. Such a preliminary hypothesis may be very different from the final solution to the problem. It will never be complete: it may be a tentative explanation of only part of the problem. But however partial and however tentative, a preliminary hypothesis is required for any investigation to proceed.

3. Collecting Additional Facts

Every serious investigation begins with some fact or group of facts which strike the investigator as problematic and which initiate the whole process of inquiry. The initial facts which constitute the problem are usually too meagre to suggest a wholly satisfactory explanation for themselves, but they will suggest—to the competent investigator—some preliminary hypotheses which lead him to search out additional facts. These additional facts, it is hoped, will serve as clues to the final solution. The inexperienced or bungling investigator will overlook or ignore all but the most obvious of them; but the careful worker will aim at completeness in his examination of the additional facts to which his preliminary hypotheses had led. Holmes, of course, was the most careful and painstaking of investigators.

Holmes insisted on dismounting from the hansom a hundred yards or so from their destination and approached the house on foot, looking carefully at its surroundings and especially at the pathway leading up to it. When Holmes and Watson entered the house, they were shown the body by the two Scotland Yard operatives, Gregson and Lestrade. ("There is no clue," said Gregson. "None at all," chimed in Lestrade.) But Holmes had already started his own search for additional facts, looking first at the body:

> . . . his nimble fingers were flying here, there, and everywhere, feeling, pressing, unbuttoning, examining. . . . So swiftly was examination made, that one would hardly have guessed the minuteness with which it was conducted. Finally, he sniffed the dead man's lips, and then glanced at the soles of his patent leather boots.[8]

Then turning his attention to the room itself.

> . . . he whipped a tape measure and large round magnifying glass from his pocket. With these two implements he trotted noiselessly about the room, sometimes stopping, occasionally kneeling, and once lying flat upon his face. So engrossed was he with his occupation that he appeared to have forgotten our presence, for he chattered away to himself under his breath the whole time, keeping up a running fire of exclamations, groans, whistles, and little cries, suggestive of encouragement and of hope. As I watched him I was irresistibly reminded of a pure-blooded, well-trained fox-hound as it dashes backward and forward through the covert, whining in its eagerness, until it comes across the lost scent. For twenty minutes or more he continued his researches, measuring with the most exact care the distance between marks which were entirely invisible to me, and occasionally applying his tape to the walls in an equally incomprehensible manner. In one place he gathered up very carefully a little pile of gray dust from the floor and packed it away in an envelope. Finally he examined with his glass the word upon the wall, going over every letter of it with the most minute exactness. This done, he appeared to be satisfied, for he replaced his tape and his glass in his pocket.
>
> "They say that genius is an infinite capacity for taking pains," he remarked with a smile. "It's a very bad definition, but it does apply to detective work."[9]

One matter deserves to be emphasized very strongly. Steps 2 and 3 are not completely separable but are usually very intimately connected and interdependent. True enough, we require a preliminary hypothesis to begin any intelligent examination of facts, but the additional facts may themselves suggest new hypotheses, which may lead to new facts, which suggest still other hypotheses, which lead to still other additional facts, and so on. Thus having made his careful examination of the facts available in the house off Brixton Road, Holmes was

---

[8] *A Study in Scarlet.*
[9] Ibid.

led to formulate a further hypothesis which required the taking of testimony from the constable who found the body. The man was off duty at the moment, and Lestrade gave Holmes the constable's name and address.

> Holmes took a note of the address.
>
> "Come along, Doctor," he said: "we shall go and look him up. I'll tell you one thing which may help you in the case," he continued, turning to the two detectives. "There has been murder done, and the murderer was a man. He was more than six feet high, was in the prime of life, had small feet for his height, wore coarse, square-toed boots and smoked a Trichinopoly cigar. He came here with his victim in a four-wheeled cab, which was drawn by a horse with three old shoes and one new one on his off fore-leg. In all probability the murderer had a florid face, and the fingernails of his right hand were remarkably long. These are only a few indications, but they may assist you."
>
> Lestrade and Gregson glanced at each other with an incredulous smile.
>
> "If this man was murdered, how was it done?" asked the former.
>
> "Poison," said Sherlock Holmes curtly, and strode off.[10]

4. Formulating the Hypothesis

At some stage or other of his investigation, any man—whether detective, scientist, or ordinary mortal—will get the feeling that he has all the facts needed for his solution. He has his "2 and 2," so to speak, but the task still remains of "putting them together." At such a time Sherlock Holmes might sit up all night, consuming pipe after pipe of tobacco, trying to think things through. The result or end product of such thinking, if it is successful, is a hypothesis which accounts for all the data, both the original set of facts which constituted the problem, and the additional facts to which the preliminary hypotheses pointed. The actual discovery of such an explanatory hypothesis is a process of creation, in which imagination as well as knowledge is involved. Holmes, who was a genius at inventing hypotheses, described the process as reasoning "backward." As he put it,

> Most people if you describe a train of events to them, will tell you what the result would be. They can put those events together in their minds, and argue from them that something will come to pass. There are few people, however, who, if you told them a result, would be able to evolve from their own inner consciousness what the steps were which led up to that result.[11]

Here is Holmes' description of the process of formulating an explanatory hypothesis. However that may be, when a hypothesis has been proposed, its evaluation

---

[10]Ibid.
[11]Ibid.

must be along the lines that were sketched in Section III [omitted here]. Granted its relevance and testability, and its compatibility with other well-attested beliefs, the ultimate criterion for evaluating a hypothesis is its predictive power.

5. Deducing Further Consequences

A really fruitful hypothesis will not only explain the facts which originally inspired it, but will explain many others in addition. A good hypothesis will point beyond the initial facts in the direction of new ones whose existence might otherwise not have been suspected. And of course the verification of those further consequences will tend to confirm the hypothesis which led to them. Holmes' hypothesis that the murdered man had been poisoned was soon put to such a test. A few days later the murdered man's secretary and traveling companion was also found murdered. Holmes asked Lestrade, who had discovered the second body, whether he had found anything in the room which could furnish a clue to the murderer. Lestrade answered, "Nothing," and went on to mention a few quite ordinary effects. Holmes was not satisfied and pressed him, asking, "And was there nothing else?" Lestrade answered, "Nothing of any importance," and named a few more details, the last of which was "a small chip ointment box containing a couple of pills." At this information,

> Sherlock Holmes sprang from his chair with an exclamation of delight.
> "The last links," he cried, exultantly. "My case is complete."
> The two detectives stared at him in amazement.
> "I have now in my hands," my companion said, confidently, "all the threads which have formed such a tangle. . . . I will give you a proof of my knowledge. Could you lay your hands upon those pills?"
> "I have them," said Lestrade, producing a small white box . . . [12]

On the basis of his hypothesis about the original crime, Holmes was able to predict that the pills found at the scene of the second crime must contain poison. Here deduction has an essential role in the process of any scientific or inductive inquiry. The ultimate value of any hypothesis lies in its predictive or explanatory power, which means that additional facts must be deducible from an adequate hypothesis. From his theory that the first man was poisoned and that the second victim met his death at the hands of the same murderer, Holmes inferred that the pills found by Lestrade must be poison. His theory, however sure he may have felt about it, was only a theory and needed further confirmation. He obtained that confirmation by testing the consequences deduced from the hypothesis and finding them to be true. Having used deduction to make a prediction, his next step was to test it.

---

[12]Ibid.

6. Testing the Consequences

The consequences of a hypothesis, that is, the predictions made on the basis of that hypothesis, may require various means for their testing. Some require only observation. In some cases, Holmes needed only to watch and wait—for the bank robbers to break into the vault, in the "Adventure of the Redheaded League," or for Dr. Roylott to slip a venomous snake through a dummy ventilator, in the "Adventure of the Speckled Band." In the present case, however, an experiment had to be performed.

Holmes asked Dr. Watson to fetch the landlady's old and ailing terrier, which she had asked to have put out of its misery the day before. Holmes then cut one of the pills in two, dissolved it in a wineglass of water, added some milk, and

> . . . turned the contents of the wineglass into a saucer and placed it in front of the terrier, who speedily licked it dry. Sherlock Holmes's earnest demeanour had so far convinced us that we all sat in silence, watching the animal intently, and expecting some startling effect. None such appeared, however. The dog continued to lie stretched upon the cushion, breathing in a laboured way, but apparently neither the better nor the worse for its draught.
>
> Holmes had taken out his watch, and as minute followed minute without result, an expression of the utmost chagrin and disappointment appeared upon his features. He gnawed his lip, drummed his fingers upon the table, and showed every other symptom of acute impatience. So great was his emotion that I felt sincerely sorry for him, while the two detectives smiled derisively, by no means displeased at this check which he had met.
>
> "It can't be a coincidence," he cried, at last springing from his chair and pacing wildly up and down the room: "it is impossible that it should be a mere coincidence. The very pills which I suspected in the case of Drebber are actually found after the death of Stangerson. And yet they are inert. What can it mean? Surely my whole chain of reasoning cannot have been false. It is impossible! And yet this wretched dog is none the worse. Ah, I have it! I have it!" With a perfect shriek of delight he rushed to the box, cut the other pill in two, dissolved it, added milk, and presented it to the terrier. The unfortunate creature's tongue seemed hardly to have been moistened in it before it gave a convulsive shiver in every limb, and lay as rigid and lifeless as if it had been struck by lightning.
>
> Sherlock Holmes drew a long breath, and wiped the perspiration from his forehead.[13]

By the favorable outcome of his experiment, Holmes' hypothesis had received dramatic and convincing confirmation.

7. Application

The detective's concern, after all, is a practical one. Given a crime to solve, he has not merely to explain the facts but to apprehend and arrest the criminal. The latter involves making application of his theory, using it to predict where the criminal

---

[13]Ibid.

can be found and how he may be caught. He must deduce still further consequences from the hypothesis, not for the sake of additional confirmation but for practical use. From his general hypothesis Holmes was able to infer that the murderer was acting the role of a cabman. We have already seen that Holmes had formed a pretty clear description of the man's appearance. He sent out his army of "Baker Street Irregulars," street urchins of the neighborhood, to search out and summon the cab driven by just that man. The successful "application" of this hypothesis can be described again in Dr. Watson's words A few minutes after the terrier's death,

> . . . there was a tap at the door, and the spokesman of the street Arabs, young Wiggins, introduced his insignificant and unsavoury person.
>
> "Please, sir," he said touching his forelock, "I have the cab downstairs."
>
> "Good boy," said Holmes, blandly. "Why don't you introduce this pattern at Scotland Yard?" he continued, taking a pair of steel handcuffs from a drawer. "See how beautifully the spring works. They fasten in an instant."
>
> "The old pattern is good enough," remarked Lestrade, "if we can only find the man to put them on."
>
> "Very good, very good," said Holmes, smiling. "The cabman may as well help me with my boxes. Just ask him to step in, Wiggins."
>
> I was surprised to find my companion speaking as though he were about to set out on a journey, since he had not said anything to me about it. There was a small portmanteau in the room, and this he pulled out and began to strap. He was busily engaged at it when the cabman entered the room.
>
> "Just give me a help with this buckle, cabman," he said, kneeling over his task, and never turning his head.
>
> The fellow came forward with a somewhat sullen, defiant air, and put down his hands to assist. At that instant there was a sharp click, the jangling of metal, and Sherlock Holmes sprang to his feet again.
>
> "Gentlemen," he cried, with flashing eyes, "let me introduce you to Mr. Jefferson Hope, the murderer of Enoch Drebber and of Joseph Stangerson."[14]

Here we have a picture of the detective as scientist, reasoning from observed facts to a testable hypothesis which not only explains the facts but permits of practical application.

[14]Ibid.

54. The Limits and the Value of Scientific Method

Morris R. Cohen and Ernest Nagel

Morris Raphael Cohen (1880–1947), American philosopher and logician, was professor of philosophy at the College of the City of New York for many years, then at the University of Chicago. He was a tireless champion of reason, scientific naturalism, and liberalism against all forms of irrationalism, supernaturalism, and dogmatism.

Ernest Nagel (1901–1985), an internationally known American philosopher of science, was university professor emeritus, Columbia University, when he died. From 1955 to 1966 he was John Dewey Professor of Philosophy at the same institution. Like Morris Cohen, he was an unwavering defender of reason, scientific naturalism, and liberalism.

The desire for knowledge for its own sake is more widespread than is generally recognized by anti-intellectualists. It has its roots in the animal curiosity which shows itself in the cosmological questions of children and the gossip of adults. No ulterior utilitarian motive makes people want to know about the private lives of their neighbors, the great, or the notorious. There is also a certain zest which makes people engage in various intellectual games or exercises in which one is required to find out something. But while the desire to know is wide, it is seldom strong enough to overcome the more powerful organic desires, and few indeed have both the inclination and the ability to face the arduous difficulties of scientific method in more than one special field. The desire to know is not often strong enough to sustain critical inquiry. Men generally are interested in the results, in the story or romance of science, not in the technical methods whereby these results are obtained and their truth continually is tested and qualified. Our first impulse is to accept the plausible as true and to reject the uncongenial as false. We have not the time, inclination, or energy to investigate everything. Indeed, the call to do so is often felt as irksome and joy-killing. And when we are asked to treat our cherished beliefs as mere hypotheses, we rebel as violently as when those dear to us are insulted. This provides the ground for various movements that are hostile to rational scientific procedure (though their promoters do not often admit that it is science to which they are hostile).

Mystics, intuitionists, authoritarians, voluntarists, and factionalists are all trying to undermine respect for the rational methods of science. These attacks have always met with wide acclaim and are bound to continue to do so, for they strike a responsive note in human nature. Unfortunately they do not offer any reliable alternative method for obtaining verifiable knowledge. The great French writer Pascal opposed to logic the spirit of subtlety or finesse (*esprit géometrique and esprit de finesse*) and urged that the heart has its reasons as well as the mind, reasons that cannot be accurately formulated but which subtle spirits apprehend none the less. Men as diverse as James Russell Lowell and George Santayana are agreed that:

"The soul is oracular still,"

and

"It is wisdom to trust the heart . . .
To trust the soul's invincible surmise."

Now it is true that in the absence of omniscience we must trust our soul's surmise; and great men are those whose surmises or intuitions are deep or penetrating. It is only by acting on our surmise that we can procure the evidence in its favor. But only havoc can result from confusing a surmise with a proposition for which there is already evidence. Are all the reasons of the heart sound? Do all oracles tell the truth? The sad history of human experience is distinctly discouraging to any such claim. Mystic intuition may give men absolute subjective certainty, but can give no proof that contrary intuitions are erroneous. It is obvious that when authorities conflict we must weigh the evidence in their favor logically if we are to make a rational choice. Certainly, when a truth is questioned it is no answer to say, "I am convinced," or, "I prefer to rely on this rather than on another authority." The view that physical science is no guide to proof, but is a mere fiction, fails to explain why it has enabled us to anticipate phenomena of nature and to control them. These attacks on scientific method receive a certain color of plausibility because of some indefensible claims made by uncritical enthusiasts. But it is of the essence of scientific method to limit its own pretension. Recognizing that we do not know everything, it does not claim the ability to solve all of our practical problems. It is an error to suppose, as is often done, that science denies the truth of all unverified propositions. For that which is unverified today may be verified tomorrow. We may get at truth by guessing or in other ways. Scientific method, however, is concerned with verification. Admittedly the wisdom of those engaged in this process has not been popularly ranked as high as that of the sage, the prophet, or the poet. Admittedly, also, we know of no way of supplying creative intelligence to those who lack it. Scientists, like all other human beings, may get into ruts and apply their techniques regardless of varying circumstances. There will always be formal procedures which are fruitless. Definitions and formal distinctions may be a sharpening of tools without the wit to use them properly, and statistical information may conform to the highest technical standards and yet be irrelevant and inconclusive. Nevertheless, scientific method is the only way to increase the general body of tested and verified truth and to eliminate arbitrary opinion. It is well to clarify our ideas by asking for the precise meaning of our words, and to try to check our favorite ideas by applying them to accurately formulated propositions.

In raising the question as to the social need for scientific method, it is well to recognize that the suspension of judgment which is essential to that method is difficult or impossible when we are pressed by the demands of immediate action. When my house is on fire, I must act quickly and promptly—I cannot stop to consider the possible causes, nor even to estimate the exact probabilities involved in the various alternative ways of reacting. For this reason, those who are bent upon some specific course of action often despise those devoted to reflection; and certain ultra-modernists seem to argue as if the need for action guaranteed the truth of our decision. But the fact that I must either vote for candidate X or refrain from doing so does not of itself give me adequate knowledge. The frequency of our regrets makes this obvious. Wisely ordered society is therefore provided with means for deliberation and reflection *before* the pressure of action becomes irresistible. In order to assure the most thorough investigation, all possible views must be canvassed, and this means toleration of views that are *prima facie* most repugnant to us.

In general the chief social condition of scientific method is a widespread desire for truth that is strong enough to withstand the powerful forces which made us cling tenaciously to old views or else embrace every novelty because it is a change. Those who are engaged in scientific work need not only leisure for reflection and material for their experiments, but also a community that respects the pursuit of truth and allows freedom for the expression of intellectual doubt as to its most sacred or established institutions. Fear of offending established dogmas has been an obstacle to the growth of astronomy and geology and other physical sciences; and the fear of offending patriotic or respected sentiment is perhaps one of the strongest hindrances to scholarly history and social science. On the other hand, when a community indiscriminately acclaims every new doctrine the love of truth becomes subordinated to the desire for novel formulations.

On the whole it may be said that the safety of science depends on there being men who care more for the justice of their methods than for any results obtained by their use. For this reason it is unfortunate when scientific research in the social field is largely in the hands of those not in a favorable position to oppose established or popular opinion.

We may put it the other way by saying that the physical sciences can be more liberal because we are sure that foolish opinions will be readily eliminated by the shock of facts. In the social field, however, no one can tell what harm may come of foolish ideas before the foolishness is finally, if ever, demonstrated. None of the precautions of scientific method can prevent human life from being an adventure, and no scientific investigator knows whether he will reach his goal. But scientific method does enable large numbers to walk with surer step. By analyzing the possibilities of any step or plan, it becomes possible to anticipate the future and adjust ourselves to it in advance. Scientific method thus minimizes the shock of novelty and the uncertainty of life. It enables us to frame policies of action and of moral judgment fit for a wider outlook than those of immediate physical stimulus or organic response.

Scientific method is the only effective way of strengthening the love of truth. It develops the intellectual courage to face difficulties and to overcome illusions that are pleasant temporarily but destructive ultimately. It settles differences without any external force by appealing to our common rational nature. The way of science, even if it is up a steep mountain, is open to all. Hence, while sectarian and partisan faiths are based on personal choice or temperament and divide men, scientific procedure unites men in something nobly devoid of all pettiness. Because it requires detachment, disinterestedness, it is the finest flower and test of a liberal civilization.

Contemporary Issues

*Can Science
Disprove God?*

55. Can Science Prove That God Does Not Exist?

Theodore Schick Jr.

Theodore William Schick Jr. (1952–   ) is professor of philosophy at Muhlenberg College. He is the co-author of How to Think About Weird Things. *He has written extensively on the interrelation of science and religion.*

"No one can prove an unrestricted negative" is the reply usually given to those who claim that science can prove that God does not exist. An unrestricted negative is a claim to the effect that something doesn't exist anywhere. Since no one can exhaustively examine every place in the universe, the reply goes, no one can conclusively establish the nonexistence of anything.

The principle that no one can prove an unrestricted negative, however, is itself an unrestricted negative. It says, in effect, that there are no proofs of unrestricted negatives. But, if there are no proofs of unrestricted negatives, then no one can prove that no one can prove an unrestricted negative. And if no one can prove that no one can prove an unrestricted negative, then it must be logically possible to prove an unrestricted negative. So the claim that no one can prove a universal negative is self-refuting—if it's true, it's false. What I intend to show here is not only that unrestricted negatives can be proven, but that a number of them have been proven.

Parmenides realized over 2,500 years ago that anything that involves a logical contradiction cannot exist. We know that there are no married bachelors, no square circles, and no largest number because these notions are self-contradictory. They violate the most fundamental law of logic—the law of noncontradiction—which says that nothing can both have a property and lack it at the same time. So one way to prove a universal negative is to show that the notion of a thing is inconsistent.

To prove that God does not exist, then, one only has to demonstrate that the concept of God is inconsistent. Traditional theism defines God as a supreme

From *Free Inquiry*, Winter, 2000/01, Vol. 21, No. 1. Reprinted by permission of *Free Inquiry*.

being—a being than which none greater can be conceived, as St. Anselm would have it. We know, however, that there is no supreme number because such a notion involves a logical contradiction. Every number is such that the number 1 can be added to it. If there were a supreme number, it would be such that the number 1 can and cannot be added to it, and that's impossible. Many believe that the notion of a supreme being is just as incoherent as the notion of a supreme number.

Consider, for example, the claim that god is all-good and thus both perfectly merciful and perfectly just. If he is perfectly just, he makes sure that everyone gets exactly what's coming to them. If he is perfectly merciful, he let's everyone off. But he can't do both. So the notion of a supreme being may be internally inconsistent. This is just one of many inconsistencies that have been found in the traditional concept of God. For a more complete review of them, see Theodore Drange, "Incompatible-Properties Arguments: A Survey" in *Philo* (Fall/Winter 1998). Theists, of course, will claim that, properly understood, there is no contradiction. What if they're right? What if it's logically possible for the God of traditional theism to exist? Does that mean that one cannot prove that he does not exist? No, for in order to prove that something does not exist, one need not show that it is logically impossible. One need only show that it is epistemically unnecessary—that it is required to explain anything. Science has proven the nonexistence of many things in this way, such as phlogiston, the luminiferous ether, and the planet Vulcan. Scientific proofs, unlike logical proofs, do not establish their conclusions beyond any possibility of doubt. But they are proofs nonetheless, for they establish their conclusions beyond a reasonable doubt and that is all that is needed to justify them.

Phlogiston, the luminiferous ether, and the planet Vulcan are theoretical entities that were postulated in order to explain various phenomena. Phlogiston was postulated to explain heat, the luminiferous ether was postulated to explain the propagation of light waves through empty space, and Vulcan was postulated to explain the perturbations in the orbit of Mercury. Science has shown, however, that these phenomena can be explained without invoking these entities. By demonstrating that these entities are not needed to explain anything, science has proven that they do not exist.

God is a theoretical entity that is postulated by theists to explain various phenomena, such as the origin of the universe, the design of the universe, and the origin of living things. Modern science, however, can explain all of these phenomena without postulating the existence of God.[1] In the words of Laplace, science has no need of that hypothesis.[2] By demonstrating that God is not needed to explain anything, science has proven that there is no more reason to believe in the existence of God than to believe in the existence of phlogiston, the luminiferous ether, or

---

[1]See, for example, Richard Dawkins, *Climbing Mount Improbable* (New York: W.W. Norton, 1996); Stephen Hawking, *A Brief History of Time* (New York: Bantam, 1998); Lee Smolin, *The Life of the Cosmos* (London: Oxford, 1997).

[2]When the French physicist Pierre Simon de Laplace explained his theory of the universe to Napoleon, Napoleon is said to have asked, "Where does God fit into your theory?" to which Laplace replied, "I have no need of that hypothesis."

Vulcan. This may explain why more than 90% of the world's top scientists disbelieve or doubt the existence of God.[3]

Scientists prefer natural explanations to supernatural ones, not because of any metaphysical bias on their part, but because natural explanations produce more understanding than supernatural ones. As Plato realized, to say that God did it is not to explain anything, but simply to offer an excuse for not having an explanation.[4]

The goodness of an explanation is determined by how much understanding it produces, and the amount of understanding produced by an explanation is determined by how well it systematizes and unifies our knowledge. The extent to which an explanation systematizes and unifies our knowledge can be measured by various criteria of adequacy such as simplicity (the number of assumptions made), scope (the types of phenomena explained), conservatism (fit with existing theory), and fruitfulness (ability to make successful novel predictions).

Supernatural explanations are inherently inferior to natural ones because they do not meet the criteria of adequacy as well. For example, they are usually less simple because they assume the existence of at least one additional type of entity. They usually have less scope because they don't explain how the phenomena in question are produced and thus they raise more questions than they answer. They are usually less conservative because they imply that certain natural laws have been violated. And they are usually less fruitful because they don't make any novel predictions. That is why scientists avoid them.

The realization that the traditional God of theism is not needed to explain anything—that there is nothing for him to do—has led a number of theologians to call for the rejection of this notion of God. In *Why Believe in God?* Michael Donald Goulder argues that the only intellectually respectable position on the God question is atheism.[5] In *Why Christianity Must Change or Die*, Reverend Spong, former Episcopal Bishop of New Jersey, argues that the traditional theistic conception of God must be replaced by one grounded in human relationships and concerns.[6] Both agree with Stephen J. Gould that religion should not be in the business of trying to explain the world.[7]

What if there was no plausible natural explanation for some phenomena? Would that justify the claim that God caused it? No, for our inability to provide a natural explanation may simply be due to our ignorance of the operative natural forces. Many phenomena that were once attributed to supernatural beings such as earthquakes, volcanoes, and disease can now be explained in purely natural terms. As St. Augustine realized, apparent miracles are not contrary to nature but contrary to our knowledge of nature.[8]

[3]E. J. Larson and L. Witham, "Leading Scientists Still Reject God," *Nature* 394 (July 23, 1998).
[4]Plato, *Cratylus*, 426 a.
[5]Michael Donald Goulder, *Why Believe in God?* (London: SCM Press, 1983).
[6]John Shelby Spong, *Why Christianity Must Change or Die* (San Francisco: Harper, 1999).
[7]Stephen J. Gould, *Rock of Ages: Science and Religion in the Fullness of Life* (New York: Ballantine, 1999).
[8]St. Augustine, *The City of God*, XXI, 8.

Given the inherent inferiority of supernatural explanations and the incompleteness of our knowledge, theists would be justified in offering a supernatural explanation for a phenomenon only if they could prove that it is in principle impossible to provide a natural explanation of it. In other words, to undermine the scientific proof for the nonexistence of God, theists have to prove an unrestricted negative, namely, that no natural explanation of a phenomenon will be found. And that, I believe, is an unrestricted negative that no theist will ever be able to prove.

56. Science Cannot Prove That God Does Not Exist

Bobby Treat

Bobby Ray Treat (1952–   ) received his doctorate in Management Science and Information Systems. He is a retired U.S. Air Force major, having served as a computer programmer and personnel analyst. Recently, he was principal research scientist at the Battelle Memorial Institute, Arlington, Virginia.

I thoroughly enjoyed reading Theodore Schick's "Can Science Prove that God Does Not Exist?" (*FI*, Winter 2000/01). He made some good points and compelling arguments, and I largely agree with his point of view. It is puzzling, however, that a professor of philosophy could make some of the logical blunders he committed to paper.

We've long heard the maxim that "You can't prove a negative," but it obviously isn't true without qualification. Dr. Schick says the maxim is equivalent to saying "There are no proofs of unrestricted negatives," but the maxim itself is an unrestricted negative, hence if it is true it cannot be proven, and so it cannot be true. (His argument in a nutshell.)

Without getting into what, exactly, an "unrestricted negative" may be, the major flaw in Dr. Schick's argument is that a statement *can* be true even though it cannot be proven. In fact, mathematician Kurt Gödel proved that *no* logical system that includes ordinary arithmetic can be both *consistent* (free of contradictions) and *complete* (including a proof for every true statement). In a very real and immediate sense, Gödel's work puts limits on the power of logic to settle questions.

There is a process for dealing with statements that may be true but cannot be proven. First, in order to positively identify such a statement, we have to show that we get a consistent system both by (a) assuming the statement as an axiom, or by (b) assuming the statement's negation as an axiom. Second, we choose one of these two new systems, whichever is more useful. This illustrates a principle that might be stated simply as, "Feel free to use any consistent system you please, so long as it is useful to you." It also illustrates that two consistent systems can be contradictory to each other.

Now, as to the question of God's existence. To reach a system in which God exists, we have two options. We may take God as an axiom, or (if possible) we can prove God's existence from other axioms. I believe the second to be impossible, but what about the first option? To be specific, I'll state the axiom this way: "God exists as a personal (male) entity who created the Universe and its physical laws, and

From *Free Inquiry*, Summer, 2001, Vol. 21, No. 3. Reprinted by permission of *Free Inquiry*.

who continues to control it as He sees fit." How well will this axiom, and systems built upon it, hold up under scrutiny?

As Dr. Schick points out, there are criteria for judging logical systems and their axioms, including what he called simplicity, scope, conservatism, and "fruitfulness." Contrary to Dr. Schick's opinion, I suggest the "God axiom" is wonderfully simple, magnificently broad in scope, and completely consistent with existing theory (hence conservative). The complaint that the God axiom is "supernatural" is spurious: if Nature is ruled minute by minute by a personal God, if physical laws can change at any moment, and if they sometimes do, then the God axiom, however much we may dislike it, is precisely "natural," because nothing else correctly describes nature.

However, the axiom doesn't lead to successful new predictions (is not fruitful). Worse, it undermines the predictive power of any system it is added to.

Electromagnetic theory (for instance) predicts a multitude of observable and (as yet) unobservable events, relationships, and effects. It is precisely by making such predictions that a theory opens itself up to disproof. If the electromagnetic theory predicts something different from what occurs in nature, observation calls theory into question, so that we may correct or abandon erroneous theory. (When this happens, we've abandoned a theory because it wasn't useful—not because it wasn't "true.")

Adding the God axiom leads to no new contradictions, since other laws are presumed to be created and enforced by God. But it leaves us unable to predict, unless we know what "He sees fit." So long as God sees fit, our televisions will continue to function, but the instant He doesn't any longer, they will fail.

Electromagnetic laws can change at any moment, and we'll be forced to discover new ones if we can. If the laws never change, that doesn't prove there's no God available to change them: He simply hasn't chosen to do so. The God axiom can hide in the system indefinitely, immune to any challenge, while making all predictions forever contingent upon something very like a prayer. Because there's nothing we can predict, there's no potential for an observation that could contradict predictions made in the system, and hence invalidate the system.

Nonetheless, showing that an assumption makes for poor theory is not the same as disproving it. Despite Dr. Schick's statements to the contrary, science doesn't disprove a statement by showing no necessity for it. Science disproves by finding contradictions. The God axiom doesn't belong in scientific theory precisely *because* it can't be disproven. The question naturally arises, then: What if it is true?

That would be a very sad state of affairs, for reasons I've already alluded to. It would make meaningless what we call science, and make blind beggars of us all. It is for that reason—not because the God axiom is "supernatural"—that I might stubbornly reject it even if it could be proven. Frequently, in discussions with my younger brother (a fundamentalist Christian), I've pointed out that, even if he's entirely right, even if he could prove it to me, I still would not be interested in what he's selling. I have no need of it, it would not make me happy, and I object to the unspeakably *vicious* argument that I *must* believe in order to save my soul from eternal torture. (To be fair, my brother doesn't make that argument; Christianity is founded on it nonetheless.)

Atheists are not, after all, ruled by reason. Logic doesn't give one a reason to get up in the morning. We have feelings, such as pride, dignity, and the love of figuring things out. However logical we wish to appear, the reason we're willing to argue the question is that life based on the God axiom (like theory that includes it) is not *useful* to us.

Science and Pseudoscience

57. A Consumer's Guide to Pseudoscience

James S. Trefil

James S. Trefil (1938–   ) is Clarence J. Robinson Professor of Physics at George Mason University. He has written extensively on scientific topics and on science and society for the general public.

I have mixed feelings about the current boom in things parascientific—movies like *Star Wars* and *Close Encounters of the Third Kind*, TV shows about weekly UFO landings, and books about spaceships that descended to earth in prehistoric times. As a physicist, I realize that today's flights of fancy may well be tomorrow's scientific orthodoxy. But it worries me that a public ill equipped to distinguish between razzle-dazzle and sound speculation is swallowing whole many pseudoscientific notions that strike me as silly at best and as a species of intellectual junk food at worst.

My concern here is not, incidentally, altogether cool and disinterested; I still brood about the time several years ago when my son, then ten, was watching a TV "documentary" about ancient civilizations that had been visited by extraterrestrials. When I ventured something mildly skeptical about the show, my son turned on me and cried, "But didn't you *see*? They *proved* it!"

Repeated experiences like this with my children, my students, and my contemporaries have left me convinced that the world could use a kind of do-it-yourself guide to getting one's bearings in the Alice-in-Wonderland realm of unorthodox scientific claims. Before launching into this guide, however, I'd like to make some general remarks about off-beat claims and mention some concrete examples.

As I said above, it's important to realize that unorthodox views are not alien to conventional science. When you come down to it, every accepted scientific principle started out in life as an unorthodox thought in the mind of one man. It follows, then, that in every living science there is a frontier area where new basic principles are being sought and where innovative ideas can gain a hearing. In my own field of physics there are several frontier areas, the most wide-open one being the study of elementary particles (the subatomic objects that in some way contain the key to

From *The Saturday Review*, April 29, 1978. Reprinted by permission of the *Saturday Review* and the author.

the ultimate structure of matter). So newness in itself is not now and never has been a basis for the rejection of an idea by the scientific community.

One can visualize the situation in science in terms of concentric circles: At the *center* is that body of time-tested, universally accepted ideas that are set forth in school and college texts. The first circle out from the center is the *frontier*, which interacts constantly with the center, feeding it new ideas that the center, after lengthy testing, adopts and assimilates.

If we move beyond the frontier region of a science, however, we come to a hazy outer circle area that I like to call the *fringe*. The fringe is characterized by a scarcity of hard data and by a general fuzziness of ideas that make the average scientist very uncomfortable. It is a zone in which neither accepted scientific writ nor reasonable extrapolations of scientific knowledge seem to apply. For these reasons, it is an area that scientists generally prefer to avoid.

Yet the fringe has its uses, for it feeds ideas to the frontier, much as the frontier feeds ideas to the center. Fifty years ago, the notion that we should attempt to communicate with extraterrestrial intelligences would most emphatically have been a fringe concept. Yet today this idea has moved into the more respectable frontier circle. (Incidentally, this move illustrates an important point about the ideas contained within both the fringe and the frontier. The soundest, most useful of them keep gravitating inward, ring by ring, toward the orthodox center.)

Now there is only one thing that will make the average scientist more uneasy than talking about what lies beyond his particular frontier and that is having someone express doubts about the validity of ideas that he considers to be established at the center of his discipline and therefore no longer open to question. For example, in the time of Isaac Newton the law of gravity was a frontier subject, but now it is regarded as a principle that has been validated by centuries of experiment and use. This law has passed from the frontier of science and is firmly ensconced within the vital center. Anyone who suggests that the law ought to be abandoned or modified is not going to get a sympathetic hearing unless he presents a very convincing argument.

The progression of scientific ideas from frontier circle to "center" acceptance isn't always smooth. The germ theory of disease and the theory of continental drift are examples of ideas that were considered too "fringy" when they were first introduced. Only long, often acrimonious campaigns won them official recognition.

There have of course been thousands of fringe ideas that never made it to the frontier and thousands of frontier ideas that never gained centrist respectability. The basic problems, then, that anyone, scientist or layman, faces when confronted with a new theory are how to decide where it belongs on the concentric-circle scale and how to determine its chances of eventual acceptance.

In making such judgments, scientists have to keep two criteria in mind: A new idea may be rejected because it is too far beyond the frontier—for instance, too fringy and unprovable; or it may be rejected because it is too far behind the frontier—for instance, a clumsy, complicated way of accomplishing ends already being accomplished by simple, efficient, economical centrist theories. Thus, an overly elaborate, hard-to-prove, Rube Goldberg-like notion could be rejected because it might be at once too fringy and too inefficient in comparison with well-established centrist theories.

With this framework in mind, let's look at some current offbeat theories and the problems they pose for the citizen who is wondering whether to accept or reject their striking claims.

Velikovsky and *Worlds in Collision*

In 1950 Immanuel Velikovsky, a Russian-born psychoanalyst, published a book called *Worlds in Collision* that touched off a minor tempest among astronomers and served as a model for an entire generation of pseudoscientific writing. The premise of his work was that the recent history of our solar system has been marked by a series of catastrophic events and that these events are faithfully recorded in ancient writings. Thus, according to Velikovsky the planet we now know as Venus was ejected from Jupiter about 5,000 years ago (an event recorded in Greek mythology). Thereafter, Venus wandered about the solar system as a comet, experiencing several close encounters with our earth before settling into its present orbit. One of these encounters coincided with the parting of the Red Sea for the Israelites and another, with the stopping of the rotation of the earth for the benefit of the ancient Hebrew leader Joshua. Both of these events and other "catastrophes" too numerous to mention are recorded in the Old Testament.

To substantiate these claims, Velikovsky cited examples from other legends about massive floods and about days when the sun stood still in the sky. He also used the ancient writings to predict the properties of the planets. For example, since the manna that fell on the Israelites during their wanderings in the desert was supposed to have been material from the Venusian comet, he predicted that hydrocarbons (or many carbohydrates—the distinction between the two isn't clear in the book) would be found in the Venusian atmosphere. He also predicted that Venus would be found to be "candescent."

When these claims were made, very little was known about planetary science, so they could be classified as fringe ideas. At the same time, they required that known physical laws (such as the conservation of energy) had to have been violated at some time in the past or the events Velikovsky described would have been impossible. Thus, the scientific community rejected his thesis because his ideas were both too far ahead of and too far behind the frontier. (Velikovsky's followers also claim that a group of professors tried to suppress publication of the book. If this is true, I can only say that professors have less clout now than in the early Fifties.)

Velikovsky's claims are set forth in a book that runs to 389 pages in the paperback edition. Faced with this avalanche of fact and hypothesis, what is the reader supposed to do? Well, in Velikovsky's case we're lucky because his book caused so much furor that a number of refutations have been written. The most recent of these refutations is the published proceedings of a symposium held in 1973 by the American Association for the Advancement of Science (AAAS) (Donald Goldsmith, ed., "Scientists Confront Velikovsky," Cornell University Press, 1977). A quick look at the *Reader's Guide to Periodical Literature* or at the card catalog of a public library will turn up other books and articles contra Velikovsky. The counterarguments fall into three categories: questions of fact, questions of logical consistency, and questions of alternative explanations.

Let's take the category of factual questions. As we noted above, Velikovsky claimed flatly that hydrocarbon-based manna from Venus fell upon the Israelites during their desert wanderings. Yet National Aeronautics and Space Administration space probes have turned up no evidence of hydrocarbons in the atmosphere of Venus—although once a scientist was misquoted as saying that an early probe did find such evidence—and the temperature of the planet is about what you'd expect on the basis of the greenhouse effect. (Certainly it's not hot enough to make the surface candescent.) Such evidence helps to clear the air, but it's hardly the kind of knowledge that most of us would have at our fingertips. In keeping with my goal of providing a do-it-yourself system for analyzing theories then, I'll have to turn to the other two categories, logical consistency and alternative explanations.

About logical consistency: If you look over Velikovsky's argument, it becomes apparent that the central point is his idea that ancient writings are supposed to be taken as literal, eyewitness accounts of celestial events. Fair enough. But when I read the Bible's account of the Israelites' wanderings, I find that the manna fell from heaven daily *except for the Sabbath*. Now I can imagine a comet whose tail contains edible material, and I can even conceive of this edible material falling only on one small area of the earth for an extended period, but I cannot for the life of me imagine a comet that keeps the Sabbath. That doesn't seem to me "logically consistent." This sort of example can be multiplied ad infinitum by anyone who looks seriously into the thousands of statements in *Worlds in Collision*.

In the same way—and here we come to the category of alternative explanations—we can ask if it's really necessary to suspend the laws of nature in order to explain the accounts of natural disasters in ancient writings. Isn't there some less complicated way of interpreting these phenomena? Surely disaster is one experience that has been shared, at one time or another, by the entire human race. And of course, the idea that ancient writers never took liberties with facts in order to achieve literary effect is a notion that doesn't stand scrutiny very well. If it did, we'd be faced with trying to explain why ancient writers were so different from their modern counterparts.

Erich von Daniken and *Chariots of the Gods*

If there is ever a prize established for the most rhetorical questions per page, Erich von Daniken will win it hands down. Using this device, he theorizes that mythological references to flying gods actually refer to extraterrestrial visitors to earth and that many of the achievements of ancient civilizations were realized with the help of advanced technology made available by ancient space-faring astronauts. Because so many claims are made in a short space of time, the reader's rational circuits overload and he just floats along. Being unable to challenge every claim, he is reduced to the state of challenging none.

The way to cope with this blizzard of assertions and rhetorical questions (which is fairly common in pseudoscientific writing) is to resist the temptation of allowing the verbal avalanche to bury you. Instead, pick out one or two claims and look into them thoroughly. For example, here's a quote from von Daniken about the Egyptian pyramids:

> Is it really a coincidence that the height of the pyramids multiplied by a thousand million corresponds approximately to the distance between the earth and the sun? Is it a coincidence that a meridian running through the pyramids divides continents and oceans into two exactly equal halves? Is it coincidence that the area of the base of the pyramid divided by twice its height gives the celebrated figure $\pi = 3.14159$? Is it coincidence that calculations of the weight of the earth were found and is it also coincidence that the rocky ground on which the structure stands is carefully and accurately leveled?

Confronted with a paragraph like this, it would be an unusual reader who would not become intimidated and move on to the next paragraph, carrying with him the definite impression that the Egyptians could never have built the pyramids without outside help—even though this claim is not made explicitly. But instead, let's stop for a moment. There are five claims made in this paragraph, and checking all of them could occupy the better part of a day. Few people would want to spend that much time investigating one paragraph in a book full of such paragraphs.

So let's not. Let's pick one claim at random and check it out. For example, in Volume 18 of the *Encyclopaedia Britannica* (Plastics–Razin) I find the information that the pyramids were originally built to be 146.59 meters high and to have a square base of 230 meters to a side. A quick check shows that the claim about π can't be right (actually, any student in a freshman physics class could have told us that you can't get a dimensionless number like π when you divide an area by a height). In the interest of fairness, though, I tried a few combinations and came up with the fact that twice the length of a side of the Pyramid of Cheops divided by the structure's height is 3.138, which differs from π by only 0.1 percent. Assuming that this is what von Daniken meant, doesn't this bit of research confirm the claim implicit in his rhetorical question?

Not necessarily. Let's take the idea one step farther. If the ancient astronauts intended to have this number be exactly π, it means they mismeasured the side of the pyramid by 0.1 percent. (For reference, 0.1 percent of 230 meters is about 9 inches.) A check through some books on surveying at the library revealed that run-of-the-mill commercial surveying is usually accurate to .01 percent (10 times more precise than the measurements done at the pyramid). A call to a man who teaches surveying yielded the information that beginning college-level surveying students routinely get an accuracy of 0.05 percent; not commercial quality but still better than that at the pyramid. What I found therefore was that although an accuracy of 0.1 percent sounds very good, it is actually pretty poor by modern standards. (As an interesting aside, it turns out that all of the dimensions of the pyramid were surveyed with about this accuracy.)

So what do we have? Either the numbers quoted by von Daniken are the result of the Egyptians' building to plan as best they could, or we have a race of ancient astronauts who could assemble and operate a spaceship but who would have flunked freshman surveying. Take your pick.

This example illustrates one important weapon in the consumer's arsenal. If you ignore an author's invitation to slide over a series of glib claims and instead take a few statements and follow them to their logical conclusion, you can get a pretty good idea of how much weight should be given to the claims that you don't verify. In the case of von Daniken's rhetorical questions, this probably isn't much.

The pyramid-measuring example also brings up a question that is frequently asked about the pseudosciences: If they're wrong, why aren't they refuted by reputable scientists? The answer is that it would simply take too much time. It took me the better part of a morning to chase down this claim, and an exhaustive analysis of even a single chapter in this one book would take months. Very few scientists have this much time to spare for a project that will not advance their professional standing in any way and that will in all likelihood gain them nothing but a lot of crank mail. They prefer to remain silent (though disapproving) and will only do something if they are irritated beyond endurance (as they eventually were in the case of Velikovsky).

ETI and UFO Phenomena

If I had been writing this article 10 years ago, the field of extraterrestrial intelligence (ETI) and unidentified flying objects (UFOs) would have been relegated to the farthest reaches of the fringe. The whole thing reeked of little green men and bug-eyed monsters, and the Condon report had pretty well established that the great majority of UFO sightings could be assigned a perfectly natural (although sometimes complex) explanation. There seemed to be nothing more to say on the subject.

In the past few years, however, a number of developments have occurred to alter this picture. Astronomers have started to give serious thought to the idea that radio telescopes might be able to "listen in" on signals from other planetary systems. In fact, the search for evidence of ETI has already begun with existing telescopes, and proposals are in the wind to build new ones just for this purpose. In a sense, the interest in ETI constitutes a success story in which a formerly unacceptable idea has moved into the realm of serious scientific consideration.

Although the UFO phenomenon hasn't achieved this sort of status, in recent years a few reputable scientists have been willing to look into UFO sightings to see if there might be something there beyond optical illusion. The results to date are not impressive, but the fact that some scientists are willing to take the time to examine the question is itself significant. I know it may sound terribly elitist to say so, but one of the best indicators of the soundness of a new idea is the willingness of scientists to devote their time to developing it.

Most scientists aren't wealthy, so about the only things they can invest in their career are the time and effort that go into research. Like an investor looking through stock offerings, each scientist has to make a judgment as to where his energies should go to produce the maximum return. Thus, when a scientist passes up "sure thing" conventional research to devote his time to something like listening with a radio telescope for extraterrestrial signals, he's doing the equivalent of putting his money where his mouth is.

Of course, the presence of reputable scientists in a field doesn't guarantee that the ideas being investigated will turn out to be right. On the other hand, there are a lot of conventional research projects that don't prove out either. So although the ETI-UFO subject still has a very fringy flavor to it, the past few years have seen some parts of it move tentatively into the legitimate frontier area of conventional science.

Pyramid Power

This whole pyramid-power business is so far out that I wasn't going to deal with it at all. I changed my mind when I saw the following ad in the catalog of a respected scientific-supplies company:

> CAN THE GREAT PYRAMID UNLOCK THE MYSTERIES OF ENERGY & AGING? . . . Did the ancient Egyptians build Cheops's Pyramid in such a way that the laws of nature are contradicted? Some people have been using exact scale models of the pyramids and are claiming all kinds of things . . . meat doesn't rot, razor blades stay sharp, things don't rust, and other strange phenomena. All these claims are based on energy resonating in an exact scale model of Cheops's Pyramid oriented to magnetic North

From this ad, it's clear we're dealing with something firmly established behind the frontier. Oh well, back to Volume 18 of the *Britannica* for the pyramid dimensions. Assemble, as I did, a cardboard pyramid. Put a piece of hamburger inside and line the pyramid up with a compass. Wait a few days. Whew!

Do-It-Yourself Checklist

On the basis of the foregoing examples, I think we can now try to list general techniques that anyone can use when confronted with the next plausibly presented arguments for God-only-knows-what new idea. Here are some useful questions to ask:

Are the facts really what the author says they are? Further (and more to the point), has someone already been sufficiently irritated by the author's claims to answer this question for you?

Some of the "facts" presented in any argument just might be wrong, but it's not always convenient to check them out yourself. It's always easier if someone else does the work. For example, trying to run down all the half-truths, rumors, and inaccuracies about the Bermuda Triangle would be a prodigious task. Fortunately, you don't have to do it because it's been done and the results published by Lawrence Kusche in *The Bermuda Triangle Mystery—Solved* (Harper & Row, 1975). In a similar vein, the proceedings of the AAAS symposium mentioned previously give a pretty good overall critique of Velikovsky, so you don't have to go searching around for scattered articles.

Therefore the first thing to do is to check your local library listings on the subject you want to look into.

Is the author trying to overload your circuits?

Although Erich von Daniken is the best (or worst) example of this technique of bludgeoning the reader into quiescence, all such authors that I have read use it. The only defense against the ploy is to pick out a few statements made about a field you know something of and look into them thoroughly. The chances are that if the author hasn't gotten those right, he hasn't done too good a job on the material you don't check.

Given the author's facts, is there a simpler explanation of them?

If I had to pick the single failing that characterizes pseudoscientific theories, I would choose their tendency *to propose complex solutions to simple problems*. We have already seen in the case of Velikovsky that the existence of old manuscripts describing cataclysmic events can easily be explained in terms of shared human experiences and of the known tendency of writers to exaggerate. What are we to do then when given the choice between revising almost the whole body of physics and astronomy and accepting as literal truth "facts" that may be only-too-human exaggerations? It seems to me that the most sensible path is to take the explanation that does the least amount of damage to other ideas.

I can't resist mentioning another example of how this criterion works. In the ancient-astronaut documentary mentioned earlier, there was an episode in which a subterranean vault with painted walls was shown. The announcer made a big point of claiming that there was no evidence of soot (such as a torch would have left) anywhere in the vault. The program's conclusion was that the ancient Egyptians must have had access to electric lights and hence had been visited by extraterrestrials.

Now, even assuming that it is correct that this chamber was put together without any soot being left behind by the workmen, does it necessarily follow that the Egyptians were visited by astronauts? Putting it another way, if you were an Egyptian engineer, could you think of a way to get a chamber built without leaving deposits of soot? A few minutes' reflection turns up (1) washing the soot off after the work is finished, (2) sinking a shaft to the chamber to let smoke out and light in, (3) doing it all with mirrors.

The interested citizen should always take a little time to play devil's advocate on such questions because the penchant for ignoring the very existence of a simpler explanation of the facts—an explanation that doesn't require a wildly complicated set of theories—is the besetting weakness of almost all pseudoscience.

Does the whole thing boil down to being unable to prove a negative?

It is impossible to prove that there are no unicorns. All we can prove is that we've found none so far. If the end result of a long argument (the "bottom line," if you prefer) is nothing more than the statement that a particular theory can't be disproved, you are probably safe putting it in the same class as unicorns.

Are established scientists putting time in on the phenomenon?

In the case of UFOs and ETIs, discussed above, one element in our considerations was the fact that a number of reputable scientists have been willing to bet their valuable time that the idea has something to it. While this doesn't guarantee that an idea is right, it does mean that someone has looked into it thoroughly and has come up with the conclusion that it's worth looking into a little more.

Having said this, let me hasten to add a caveat. There is no proposition on God's green earth so silly that it can't find at least one Ph.D. to support it. If you're going to use this criterion in judging a theory, find out who the scientists are. A quick check in *American Men and Women of Science* or in *Who's Who* will give you some idea of the credentials of the person involved. If you want a standard of comparison, look up Peter Sturrock, of Stanford University—he's one of the people with sound credentials who are investigating UFO sightings these days.

Finally, you have to realize that this "credentials" criterion is only one of several you should use in making a judgment. If the theory sounds fishy to you, if you feel that the conclusions are unreasonable, and if the arguments of the scientists don't convince you, then so be it. In the final analysis, you have to make up your own mind anyway.

Can you test the theory yourself?

If you have a mechanical turn of mind, you can occasionally check out a claim yourself, as I did with the pyramid-power test.

Ask such simple questions as those on the checklist when you're reading the next book that reveals the secret of the ages—they will help you decide whether you're looking at a genuine scientific breakthrough or at just another addition to the fringe. There are two areas in which such questioning will be of little help, however, and we might as well get them straight right now. If outright fraud is involved—as it is reputed to have been in the famous "demonstration" by Uri Geller at the Stanford Research Institute—going through this sort of questioning will do you little good. There is no way that fraud can be detected secondhand by the layman, and there is probably no one more ill equipped than the average scientist to deal with outright duplicity. Also, the test questions really don't apply to writings that are specifically nonrational, such as the mystical and drug-oriented books that were so common a few years ago. Such books aren't playing the same game as those by the pseudoscientists and therefore can't be judged by the same rules.

No discussion of pseudoscience would be complete without some comment on its social implications. I am well aware that many of my colleagues regard modern pseudoscience as the forerunner of an antirational swing in our society and denounce it in terms that are worthy of that doom-crying German philosopher Oswald Spengler. I feel that this is something of an overreaction. Pseudoscience has been around at least as long as (and perhaps even longer than) conventional science. Perhaps it serves some deep need of human beings to believe that there is still some mystery—something unknown—left in life. Maybe the unknown thrives because people like to see the pompous scientific establishment discomfited ("Okay, Mr. Know-it-all, explain *this* one"). Or maybe it's just that P. T. Barnum was right about a sucker being born every minute. None of these interpretations constitutes a threat to conventional science.

After all, Luigi Galvani's "animal electricity" cures in the nineteenth century didn't impair the development of the science of electricity. Mme. Blavatsky's theosophy certainly had little effect on American science. And despite the apocalyptic terms with which it was greeted, it would be hard to show that Velikovsky's *Worlds in Collision* has had much of an effect on modern astronomy. At its worst, pseudoscience is a minor inconvenience of the cocktail party variety; and at its best, it is good entertainment. I certainly make no apology for the fact that I enjoyed reading Velikovsky and von Daniken, even though I think they are wrong.

On balance, I'd say the best attitude to have toward pseudoscience is the one reflected in the story (probably apocryphal) about the time Groucho Marx attended a séance. After the usual hand holding, table thumping, and light dimming, the medium announced in funereal tones that she was now in contact with the spirit world and that the participants could ask any questions they liked: Nothing, she said, was hidden from the spirits. Without hesitation, Groucho shot back, "What's the capital of North Dakota?"

A Compact (and Highly Personal) Guide to the Frontier and the Fringe Beyond

 *Immanuel Velikovsky and *Worlds in Collision*: The space program has pretty well taken the shine off this one.

 ***ESP: Started life on the far fringe but is moving toward respectability as more hard data is collected.

 **UFOs: This old favorite is moving up in the rankings on the basis of new interest by a few scientists, but it could move down again just as fast.

 *Ancient Astronauts: If the UFOs are here now, they may have been here before, but that doesn't mean one of their crews built the pyramids.

 ****Extraterrestrial Intelligence: There's a reasonable amount of effort and (more important) money going into listening for signals from space. So this subject has pretty well moved into the frontier regions of astronomy.

****Is moving into a respectable frontier position.
***Still does not have wide acceptance, but it's moving that way.
**Probably will never amount to anything, but you might want to keep an eye on it.
*Forget it.

*Bermuda Triangle: It turns out there are no more mysterious disappearances than you'd expect for an ocean area often hit by hurricanes and other storms.

*Lost Atlantis: Another group that didn't build the pyramids.

**Water Witching (Dowsing): Ordinarily I'd give this one star, but a student recently showed me not only that he could locate an underground water pipe but that I could too. There's probably a neurological explanation.

*Pollen Power: Pollen collected by honeybees is supposed to be very healthful. But since the pollen is taken from the bees before they go into the hives, why not just eat the flowers and eliminate the middleman?

***Acupuncture: It shouldn't work, but it seems to.

*Biorhythms: People are marketing calculators that will allow you to keep separate track of your three cycles (mental, emotional, physical) according to your birth date. But statistical studies show as many successes at the low points as at the high. Another numerological fad.

*Horoscopes, Phrenology, and Palmistry: These can be fun if you don't take them too seriously.

*Perpetual Motion Machines: Interest in these devices, the ultimate in energy saving, has dropped considerably since the patent office began requiring a working model with each application.

*Fingertip Reading: A few years ago the Russians caused quite a stir when they announced that they had found a woman who could read with her fingertips while blindfolded. Various professors at American universities promptly made headlines by claiming they too had located women fingertip readers. When the blindfolds were improved according to instructions from stage magicians, the powers mysteriously vanished, both here and in the U.S.S.R.

**Bigfoot, the Abominable Snowman, and All That: Undoubtedly there's a measure of hoaxing here, but the discovery of something like these creatures wouldn't violate any scientific principles.

*Loch Ness Monster: The failures of searches in a small place have pretty well ruled this one out. I draw this conclusion with regret because I was rooting for Nessie.

*Psychic Phenomena a la Uri Geller: As far as the various key-bending, spoon-twisting, and remote-reading tricks are concerned, I'll believe them when they are done in front of a panel that includes at least one magician.

58. Baloney Detection: How to Draw Boundaries Between Science and Pseudoscience

Michael Shermer

Michael Shermer (1954–   ) is founding publisher of Skeptic *magazine and author of the* Borderlands of Science *as well as other works on science and pseudoscience and scepticism.*

When lecturing on science and pseudoscience at colleges and universities, I am inevitably asked, after challenging common beliefs held by many students, "Why should we believe you?" My answer: "You shouldn't."

I then explain that we need to check things out for ourselves and, short of that, at least to ask basic questions that get to the heart of the validity of any claim. This is what I call baloney detection, in deference to Carl Sagan, who coined the phrase "Baloney Detection Kit." To detect baloney—that is, to help discriminate between science and pseudoscience—I suggest 10 questions to ask when encountering any claim.

1. *How reliable is the source of the claim?* Pseudoscientists often appear quite reliable, but when examined closely, the facts and figures they cite are distorted, taken out of context or occasionally even fabricated. Of course, everyone makes some mistakes. And as historian of science Daniel Kevles showed so effectively in his book *The Baltimore Affair*, it can be hard to detect a fraudulent signal within the background noise of sloppiness that is a normal part of the scientific process. The question is, Do the data and interpretations show signs of intentional distortion? When an independent committee established to investigate potential fraud scrutinized a set of research notes in Nobel laureate David Baltimore's laboratory, it revealed a surprising number of mistakes. Baltimore was exonerated because his lab's mistakes were random and nondirectional.

2. *Does this source often make similar claims?* Pseudoscientists have a habit of going well beyond the facts. Flood geologists (creationists who believe that Noah's flood can account for many of the earth's geologic formations) consistently make outrageous claims that bear no relation to geological science. Of course, some great

thinkers do frequently go beyond the data in their creative speculations. Thomas Gold of Cornell University is notorious for his radical ideas, but he has been right often enough that other scientists listen to what he has to say. Gold proposes, for example, that oil is not a fossil fuel at all but the by-product of a deep, hot biosphere (microorganisms living at unexpected depths within the crust). Hardly any earth scientists with whom I have spoken think Gold is right, yet they do not consider him a crank. Watch out for a pattern of fringe thinking that consistently ignores or distorts data.

3. *Have the claims been verified by another source?*   Typically pseudoscientists make statements that are unverified or verified only by a source within their own belief circle. We must ask, Who is checking the claims, and even who is checking the checkers? The biggest problem with the cold fusion debacle, for instance, was not that Stanley Pons and Martin Fleischman were wrong. It was that they announced their spectacular discovery at a press conference before other laboratories verified it. Worse, when cold fusion was not replicated, they continued to cling to their claim. Outside verification is crucial to good science.

4. *How does the claim fit with what we know about how the world works?*   An extraordinary claim must be placed into a larger context to see how it fits. When people claim that the Egyptian pyramids and the Sphinx were built more than 10,000 years ago by an unknown, advanced race, they are not presenting any context for that earlier civilization. Where are the rest of the artifacts of those people? Where are their works of art, their weapons, their clothing, their tools, their trash? Archaeology simply does not operate this way.

5. *Has anyone gone out of the way to disprove the claim, or has only supportive evidence been sought?*   This is the confirmation bias, or the tendency to seek confirmatory evidence and to reject or ignore disconfirmatory evidence. The confirmation bias is powerful, pervasive and almost impossible for any of us to avoid. It is why the methods of science that emphasize checking and rechecking, verification and replication, and especially attempts to falsify a claim, are so critical.

When exploring the borderlands of science, we often face a "boundary problem" of where to draw the line between science and pseudoscience. The boundary is the line of demarcation between geographies of knowledge, the border defining countries of claims. Knowledge sets are fuzzier entities than countries, however, and their edges are blurry. It is not always clear where to draw the line. . . . Continuing with the baloney-detection questions, we see that in the process we are also helping to solve the boundary problem of where to place a claim.

6. *Does the preponderance of evidence point to the claimant's conclusion or to a different one?*   The theory of evolution, for example, is proved through a convergence of evidence from a number of independent lines of inquiry. No one fossil, no one piece of biological or paleontological evidence has "evolution" written on it; instead tens of thousands of evidentiary bits add up to a story of the evolution

of life. Creationists conveniently ignore this confluence, focusing instead on trivial anomalies or currently unexplained phenomena in the history of life.

7. *Is the claimant employing the accepted rules of reason and tools of research, or have these been abandoned in favor of others that lead to the desired conclusion?* A clear distinction can be made between SETI (Search for Extraterrestrial Intelligence) scientists and UFOlogists. SETI scientists begin with the null hypothesis that ETIs do not exist and that they must provide concrete evidence before making the extraordinary claim that we are not alone in the universe. UFOlogists begin with the positive hypothesis that ETIs exist and have visited us, then employ questionable research techniques to support that belief, such as hypnotic regression (revelations of abduction experiences), anecdotal reasoning (countless stories of UFO sightings), conspiratorial thinking (governmental cover-ups of alien encounters), low-quality visual evidence (blurry photographs and grainy videos), and anomalistic thinking (atmospheric anomalies and visual misperceptions by eyewitnesses).

8. *Is the claimant providing an explanation for the observed phenomena or merely denying the existing explanation?* This is a classic debate strategy—criticize your opponent and never affirm what you believe to avoid criticism. It is next to impossible to get creationists to offer an explanation for life (other than "God did it"). Intelligent Design (ID) creationists have done no better, picking away at weaknesses in scientific explanations for difficult problems and offering in their stead "ID did it." This stratagem is unacceptable in science.

9. *If the claimant proffers a new explanation, does it account for as many phenomena as the old explanation did?* Many HIV/AIDS skeptics argue that lifestyle causes AIDS. Yet their alternative theory does not explain nearly as much of the data as the HIV theory does. To make their argument, they must ignore the diverse evidence in support of HIV as the causal vector in AIDS while ignoring the significant correlation between the rise in AIDS among hemophiliacs shortly after HIV was inadvertently introduced into the blood supply.

10. *Do the claimant's personal beliefs and biases drive the conclusions, or vice versa?* All scientists hold social, political and ideological beliefs that could potentially slant their interpretations of the data, but how do those biases and beliefs affect their research in practice? Usually during the peer-review system, such biases and beliefs are rooted out, or the paper or book is rejected.

Clearly, there are no foolproof methods of detecting baloney or drawing the boundary between science and pseudoscience. Yet there is a solution: science deals in fuzzy fractions of certainties and uncertainties, where evolution and big bang cosmology may be assigned a 0.9 probability of being true, and creationism and UFOs a 0.1 probability of being true. In between are borderland claims: we might assign superstring theory a 0.7 and cryonics a 0.2. In all cases, we remain open-minded and flexible, willing to reconsider our assessments as new evidence arises. This is, undeniably, what makes science so fleeting and frustrating to many people; it is, at the same time, what makes science the most glorious product of the human mind.

Problems and Puzzles

59. Time Travel: Possible or Impossible?

John Hospers

"Is it logically possible to go back in time—say, to 3000 B.C., and help the Egyptians build the pyramids?"

We must be very careful about this one. We can speak quite easily and literally about going backward and forward in space, and it is tempting to use the same language about time as we do about space, and assume that time-language is meaningful in all the same contexts as is space-language. But, as we shall see, this is a dangerous assumption. Let us also be clear that when we talk about "going back to 3000 B.C." we mean it *literally*; taken in a figurative sense, there is no problem, for we certainly can and do *imagine* ourselves being at far distant places in space and at various eras in time. We can *imagine* ourselves being there as the pyramids were being built. "But if we can *imagine* it, then surely it's logically possible. If we can't imagine it, that doesn't show that it isn't logically possible (our powers of imagination may be limited), but if we *can* imagine it, then it is logically possible, and we can imagine this as clearly as we can imagine anything. In fact, H. G. Wells did imagine it in *The Time Machine*, and every reader imagines it with him." But let us be quite clear about what we are imagining. We can imagine ourselves as having been born in a different era[1] and being with the Egyptians building the pyramids. But can we imagine ourselves *now*, in the 20th century A.D., *being* (not merely in our imagination) in 3000 B.C.? How can we be in the 20th century A.D. and the 30th century B.C. *at the same time*? Here already is one contradiction. We cannot *be* in the 20th century A.D. and *not* in the 20th century A.D. (for example, in some other century, like the 30th century B.C.) at the same time. It is logically possible that you might live a very long time, and have lived during the construction of the pyramids and still be alive to tell the tale in the 20th century A.D. But it is *not* logically possible to be in one century of time and in another century of time at the same time.

"But," one may object, "this is not the situation we are imagining. What we are imagining is being one day in the 20th century and then moving backward in time so that the next day we are in the year 3000 B.C.—and on that day we are no

From *An Introduction to Philosophical Analysis,* by Hospers, John, © 1953, 1967. Reprinted by permission of Pearson Education Inc, Upper Saddle River. NJ.

[1]Even here there is a question: Would it still be *you* if you were born in 3000 B.C.?

longer in the 20th century A.D." But let us be careful: suppose the day you are talking about is January 1, 1969, and that on January 2, 1969, you use the time machine and go back to some day in 3000 B.C. Isn't there a contradiction here again? For the next day after January 1, 1969, is January 2, 1969. The day after Tuesday is Wednesday (this is analytic—"Wednesday" is defined as the day that follows Tuesday), and the day after January 1 is January 2 (this also is analytic). So it is logically impossible to go from January 1 *to any other day* except January 2 of the same year. You may not live past January 1, but whether you do or don't, the next day (by definition) will be January 2. But to be living on January 2, 1969, *and* (at the same time) January 2, 3000 B.C., is a contradiction in terms, and hence logically impossible.

"That's true, but you still miss the point. The point is that we go *backward* in time, *not to the next day*, but to a day almost 5,000 years earlier. (It doesn't matter whether this is by means of a time machine, a magic wand, touching a crystal ball, or some means unknown to us.) So we don't go to the *next* day (if we did, it *would* be January 2), but to a *previous* day."

This argument presents a more difficult challenge, but there is still a confusion in it. Here is something we all *can* imagine easily: On January 1, 1969, you wake up and find that you are surrounded, not by modern streets and houses and automobiles, but by the environment of the 19th century (say Victorian England—horses and carriages, London streets as depicted by Dickens, women wearing hobble-skirts, and so on). This would be very strange, and you would probably not be able to explain the sudden change of environment, but you can easily imagine it happening. Then when you wake up on January 2, 1969, you find yourself surrounded by the environment of the 18th century, such as depicted in Fielding's *Tom Jones*. On the morning of January 3, the environment changes again—now it is the 17th century; and so on. On each successive day, you find yourself in a different environment, which fulfills the description of the historical period of a century earlier. While it would be most bizarre and unaccountable, this *is* logically possible—there is no contradiction in it, for the days would still be January 1, January 2, January 3, and so on. You could still mark them off on the calendar, and write in your diary for January 3, "Today I lived in the environment of the 17th century; I wonder what tomorrow will bring." Time would still be *going forward*, only the environment would be changing in unexplained ways; but each day you would still be getting *one day older*.

And here is the point: isn't "Time goes forward" analytic? "What else can it do but go forward?" we are tempted to ask. People can walk backward in space, but what would "going backward in time" literally mean? And if you continue to live, what can you do but get one day older every day? Isn't "getting younger every day" a contradiction in terms—unless, of course, it is meant figuratively, as in "My dear, you're getting younger every day," where it is still taken for granted that the person, while *looking* younger every day, is still *getting older* every day? In the description we have just given, you are still going from January 2 to January 3 (and so on) and getting a day older every day (analytic); so we have not been guilty of any contradiction. We have not said that you ever become younger or literally *go* backward in time. By definition we assign *numerically* later time to *successively* later events, no matter what characteristics these later events have.

"I'm still not convinced. The situation I am speaking of is that of going from January 1, 1969, *not* to January 2 but to 3000 B.C. And I still don't see how this is *logically* impossible, though it may be empirically impossible."

Let us try once again. Many centuries B.C., the pyramids were built, and when all this happened you were not there—you weren't even born. It all happened long before you were born, and it all happened without your assistance or even your observation. This is an unchangeable fact: *you can't change the past.* That is the crucial point: the past is what has happened, and you can't make what has happened not have happened. Not all the king's horses or all the king's men could make what *has* happened *not* have happened, for this is a logical impossibility. When you say that it is logically possible for you (literally) to go back to 3000 B.C. and help build the pyramids, you are faced with the question: Did you help them build the pyramids or did you not? The first time it happened, you did *not:* you weren't there, you weren't yet born, it was all over before you came on the scene. All you could say, then, would be that the *second* time it happened, you *were* there—and there was at least a difference between the first time and the second time: the first time you weren't there, and the second time you were. But now we are speaking of *two* times, the first time being 3000 B.C. and the second time being A.D. 1969.

Now it *is* logically possible that history might suddenly start repeating itself: that on January 1, 1969, all of our modern buildings and machinery would disappear and we would find ourselves among sand and pyramids and the world of 3000 B.C. This repetition *is* logically possible (though not empirically, to the best of our present knowledge), but it would be a repetition with a difference: the first time you were there (3000 B.C.), you weren't there; and the second time (A.D. 1969), you were. This would not be a case of literally *going back* in time to 3000 B.C.: it would be a case of history repeating itself (with a slight difference), with the world of 1969 suddenly vanishing and the world of 3000 B.C. suddenly replacing it. But time would still be going forward (if you want to use that expression), and the day *after* the sudden transformation would *not* be a day in 3000 B.C. (*that* day is long past and gone, and irrecoverable like everything else in the past), but January 2, 1969.

Once you are convinced of the logical impossibility of changing the past (or making what has happened un-happen), you will doubtless see the logical impossibility of literally "going back in time" to 3000 B.C. We are inclined to be misled into thinking that it is logically possible because we see movies like *The Time Machine* in which a person in 1900 pulls a lever on a machine and suddenly is surrounded by the world of many centuries earlier. What doesn't occur to the viewer is that he is in the world of many centuries earlier *after* he has pressed the lever. The inventors of these tales are involved in other logical difficulties as well: for example, our hero in 1900 pulls the lever in the other direction and finds himself in an unrecognizable world of many centuries in the future. There he meets a girl, marries her, and takes her back with him in the time machine to the year 1900. The girl wasn't born until A.D. 40,000, yet she gave birth to his child in 1900, long before she was born. One is tempted to speculate: What if he had decided, in the year 40,000, *not* to marry her and bring her back after all? Then her child (born in 1900, though the mother wasn't born until 40,000) wouldn't have been born either; and yet after 1900 he had already been born. Indeed, that child might have become the prime minister of Britain, and affected the course of the world in such a way that no human beings would have existed on the earth in the year 40,000. What if there had been a nuclear explosion in 1990 that obliterated life forever from the earth? What then would have happened to the charming hypothesis that he "went into the year 40,000" and brought the girl "back into 1900"—an event that the events of 1990 would have rendered impossible? The whole alleged situation is riddled with contradictions. When we say we can imagine it, we are only uttering the words, but there is nothing in fact even logically possible for the words to describe.

60. The Problem of the Criterion

Sextus Empiricus

Sextus Empiricus (c. 200 C.E.) was the codifier of ancient Greek scepticism and a physician. About his life practically nothing is known. He seems to have been a Greek. It is not known whether his Latin name "Empiricus" is a proper name or a designation of him as an "empirical" medical doctor. His extant works constitute the only lucid, complete, and firsthand summary of ancient Greek scepticism available to us and have exerted a significant influence on Western philosophizing.

But the dogmatists, conceited as they are, do not yield the judgment of the truth to others but claim truth as their own exclusive discovery. All right, let us base our argument on them[1] and show that not even in this way can any criterion of truth possibly be discovered.

Now, each one of those who claim to have discovered the truth either declares this by mere assertion only or else uses a proof. But he will not say it by mere assertion, for one of those on the opposing side will bring forward an assertion that claims the contrary, and in this way the former will be "no more" credible than the latter, one bare assertion being equal to another. If, on the other hand, he has proof for his declaration of himself as the criterion, it must in any case be a sound one. But in order to ascertain the soundness of the proof he uses in declaring himself the criterion, we must have a criterion, and moreover one that is agreed on beforehand. But we possess no generally accepted criterion, that being what is sought after. It is impossible, therefore, to discover a criterion.

Again, since those who call themselves criteria of the truth derive from different philosophical schools, and for this reason disagree with one another, we need to have at our disposal some criterion which we can use to decide their dispute for the purpose of giving our assent to some and withholding it from others. Now, this criterion is either in disagreement with all the parties disagreeing or it is in agreement with one only. But if in disagreement with all, it will itself also become a party to the disagreement, and as a party to it will not be a criterion but will itself be in need of judgement, like the disagreement as a whole. For it is an impossibility for the same thing to be at once both the examiner and the thing examined. And if it is not in disagreement with all views but is in agreement with one of them, this one with which it agrees, since it is involved in the disagreement, has need of an examiner. And hence the criterion agreeing with that view will

[1]That is, on their arguments. (—Tr.) (All other footnotes are by the editor, Philip P. Hallie.)

require judgement, as it is no different from it; and if it requires judgement it will not be a criterion.

But—what is most important of all—if we say that any one dogmatist is the judge of truth and that he alone is the repository of truth, we shall be saying this either because we fix our gaze on his age, or not on his age but on his hard work, or not on this but on his sagacity and intellect, or not on his sagacity but on the testimony of the multitude. But it is not appropriate in an investigation concerned with the truth to pay attention either to age or industry or any other of the factors mentioned, as we shall show. One should not, therefore, say that any one of the philosophers is the criterion of truth.[2] Indeed, the consideration of age is excluded by the fact that most of the dogmatists were more or less equal in age when they declared themselves criteria of the truth. . . . Also, it is not unreasonable to suppose that, just as in ordinary life and common intercourse we observe that young men are often more intelligent than older men, so also in philosophy young men may be shrewder than old men. . . . Therefore one must not say that any one dogmatist, by reason of his age, is the criterion. Nor indeed by reason of his industry either: for all are equally industrious, and there is none whose behaviour is sluggish once he has entered the contest for truth and claims to have found it. And when equality in this respect is ascribed to all, it is an injustice to incline towards one only.

And likewise one could not very well select one philosopher as superior to another on account of his intelligence. In the first place, they are all intelligent; they are not classed as dullards and non-dullards. Further, men who are considered intelligent often are advocates not of truth but of falsehood. For example, we call those orators powerful and intellectual who nobly come to the aid of the false and raise it to a level of credibility equal to the true; and conversely, those who are not of this class we call dull and unintelligent. Perhaps in philosophy too, then, those inquirers after truth who are the most ingenious seem to be convincing even if they plead the cause of falsehood, because they are naturally gifted, while the untalented are considered unconvincing even if they are allied with the truth. Therefore neither by reason of age nor of industry nor of intelligence is it proper to give the preference to any one person over anybody else and say that this man has discovered the truth and that man has not.

There remains, then, the alternative of listening to the agreement of the majority, for possibly someone will say that he is the best judge of truth whom the majority agree in approving. But this is foolish, and would be a worse criterion than those we have already discredited. . . . [J]ust as in the affairs of daily life it is

---

[2]This is a typical form of Sceptical argument against such notions as that of the Sage, or Wise Man, who is the arbiter of all knowledge and value to the Stoics. Nowadays this seems like a rather obvious "conclusion," but in the Middle Ages, for instance, it was to be by no means obvious, and this little sequence of arguments is one of the most potent attacks upon the notion of one-man authoritarianism to be found in Western civilization. The authority in question is an authority on intellectual matters, but this attack could be and was to be also extended to political authority. Neo-Sceptics like Petrarch, Erasmus, and Montaigne were to knock down the authority of the Philosopher, Aristotle, toward the end of the Middle Ages, but they were also to invade political thought, with arguments similar to the ones given by Sextus here and in the *Outlines*.

not impossible for one intelligent person to be better than many unintelligent ones, so also in philosophy it is not unreasonable to suppose that there is one man who is sensible, and hence reliable, and many who are like geese and for this reason unreliable, even if they are in agreement in their testimony in favour of somebody; for the intelligent man is rare, while the thoughtless are common. Also, even if we do give heed to agreement and to the testimony of the majority, we are brought round again to the opposite of the end in view, for of necessity those disagreeing about a thing out-number those who agree about it. . . .

But now if the discoverer of truth in philosophy is said to owe his success either to his age, or his industry, or his intelligence, or to the fact that he has large numbers to speak for him, while we, on the other hand, have shown that one can for none of these reasons say that he is the criterion of truth, then it is manifest that the criterion in philosophy is undiscoverable.

Also, the philosopher who declares himself to be the criterion is saying nothing more than what appears to himself. Therefore, since each of the other philosophers also says what appears to himself, and what is contrary to the statement of the former, it is plain that, as he is on an equal basis with all the others, we shall not be able to say definitely that any one of them is the criterion. For if this man is trustworthy because it appears to him that he himself is the criterion, the second man too will be trustworthy, since it appears to him also that he himself is the criterion, and so on with the third and all the rest. From this it follows that no one is definitely[3] the criterion of truth.

In addition to this, it is either by mere assertion that a man claims to be the criterion, or it is because he is using a criterion. But if it is by mere assertion, he will be checked by mere assertion, and if he is using a criterion, he will refute himself. For this criterion either disagrees or agrees with him. And if it disagrees it is untrustworthy, since it is in disagreement with him who believes himself to be the criterion, while if it agrees it will have need of a judge. For just as this man who declares himself the criterion was seen to be untrustworthy, so also the criterion which agrees with him, since it is in a way possessed of the same function[4] as he, will require some other criterion. And if this is so, then we must not say that each philosopher is the criterion, for everything that requires judging is of itself untrustworthy.— Again, whoever declares himself the criterion makes this claim either by mere assertion or by virtue of a proof. He cannot, for the reasons already urged, do so by mere assertion. And if he does so by virtue of a proof, it must at any rate be a sound one. But his declaration of the soundness of this proof is made either by assertion or by virtue of proof, and so on *ad infinitum*. And so this is one reason more why we must declare that the criterion of truth is undiscoverable.

Another argument is this. Those who profess to be able to judge the truth are bound to have a criterion of truth. Now, this criterion is either untested or tested.

---

[3]This does not necessarily mean that all of them are speaking falsely; it means only that we have no way of deciding whether one and one only is speaking truly. Sextus is here suspending judgment, not making an adverse judgment on the basis of the previous argument.
[4]The man and the criterion are both personal standards for making a decision about truth and falsity.

And if it is untested, how can it be trustworthy? No subject of dispute is without judging trustworthy. But if it is tested, than that which adjudges it is in turn either untested or tested. And if untested, it is untrustworthy; if tested, that which tests it is again either tested or not tested, and so on *ad infinitum*.—Again, since the criterion is a subject of dispute, it requires some proof. But since some proofs are true and some false, the proof employed for confirming the criterion must itself be confirmed by means of some criterion. The result is that we fall into the mode of circular reasoning, since the criterion is awaiting confirmation by the proof while the proof is waiting for confirmation from the criterion, and neither of them is able to show confirmation by the other. Besides, the same thing becomes both trustworthy and untrustworthy. The criterion is trustworthy because it judges the proof, and the proof because it proves the criterion; and the criterion is untrustworthy because it undergoes proof at the hand of the proof, and the proof because it undergoes judgement at the hand of the criterion.

Suggestions for Further Reading

Anthologies

Klemke, E. D., Robert Hollinger, and David Wijss Rudge, with A. David Kline, eds. *Introductory Readings in the Philosophy of Science*. Third Revised Edition. Amherst, N.Y.: Prometheus, 1998. This popular collection includes ten new readings on such topics as the natural and social sciences, feminism, postmodernism, relativism, confirmation acceptance, and science and value.

Landesman, Charles, and Robin Meeks, eds. *Skepticism: From Plato to Rorty*. Malden, Mass., and Oxford, U.K.: Blackwell, 2002. This volume presents a selection of texts in the Western philosophical tradition from ancient times to the present. It includes readings by proponents and opponents of skepticism and emphasizes the influence of skepticism on epistemology.

Moser, Paul K., ed. *The Oxford Handbook of Epistemology*. New York: Oxford Univ. Press, 2002. An up-to-date survey of current thinking and research in epistemology. This anthology contains nineteen previously unpublished chapters by some of the leading philosophers in the field. A work for the more advanced student.

Moser, Paul K., and Arnold Vander Nat. *Human Knowledge: Classical and Contemporary Approaches*. New York: Oxford Univ. Press, 1987. This anthology provides an informative selection of readings in the philosophical field of epistemology.

Schick Jr., Theodore, ed. *Readings in the Philosophy of Science: From Positivism to Postmodernism*. New York: McGraw-Hill, 1999. A particular merit of this anthology is that subsequent readings often clarify or critique preceding ones. This arrangement enables students to acquire an understanding of how philosophic theories develop in response to one another.

Sosa, Ernest, and Jaegwon Kim, eds. *Epistemology: An Anthology*. Malden, Mass., and Oxford, U.K.: Blackwell, 1999. This volume offers many of the most important contributions to the field in recent years. It is recommended for the more advanced student.

Individual Works

Annas, Julia, and Jonathan Barnes. *The Modes of Scepticism: Ancient Texts and Modern Interpretations*. Cambridge: Cambridge Univ. Press, 1985. This is an excellent example of recent scholarship concerning ancient skepticism and its subsequent influence.

Audi, Robert. *Epistemology: A Contemporary Introduction (Routledge Contemporary Introductions to Philosophy)*. New York: Routledge, 2003. This comprehensive exposition introduces the concepts and theories central for understanding knowledge.

Aune, Bruce A. *Rationalism, Empiricism & Pragmatism: An Introduction*. New York: Random House, 1970. This book gives a good general discussion of the problems of knowledge.

Ayer, A. J. *The Problem of Knowledge*. Baltimore: Penguin, 1956. A more advanced yet clearly written philosophical investigation of the nature, scope, and limits of human knowledge. This book was designed not only for the professional philosopher but for the general reader as well. Particular attention is called to Chapter 2, "Skepticism and Certainty."

Blanshard, Brand. *Reason and Analysis*. La Salle, Ill.: Open Court, The Paul Carus Lectures, 1964. A leading American philosopher defends his version of rationalism in terms of a lucid and comprehensive critique of British analytic philosophy.

Casti, John L. *Paradigms Lost: Images of Man in the Mirror of Science*. New York: William Morrow, 1989. This book offers a thoroughly informed and charmingly written account of the nature of science as actually practiced by scientists today. The author critically discusses some of the solutions to philosophic problems contemporary science allegedly has to offer.

Chisholm, Roderick. *Theory of Knowledge*. 3d ed. Englewood Cliffs, N.J.: Prentice Hall, 1989. This work is a short and clearly written introduction to epistemology. The first two chapters attempt to refute skepticism.

Cohen, Morris R. *Reason and Nature*. 2d ed. New York: Free Press, 1964. A classic work by an American philosopher who was a champion of the supremacy of critical reason in human life. Cohen devotes considerable attention to the ethical, legal, religious, and historical implications of scientific knowledge and method. A scholarly work, yet written so lucidly that the beginning student can read it with pleasure.

Dennett, Daniel C. *Darwin's Dangerous Idea: Evolution and the Meanings of Life*. New York: Simon and Schuster, 1995. In this gracefully written and often witty book the author, an American philosopher, shows how Darwin's idea of natural selection and its real implications transform not only our traditional religious conceptions but also our inherited view of our place in the universe and our understanding of our own human nature.

Gardner, Martin. *Fads and Fallacies in the Name of Science*. 2d ed. New York: Dover, 1957. A fascinating examination of extrasensory perception, the hollow earth hypothesis, dianetics, orgone boxes, and other theories and devices that the author criticizes as being pseudoscience.

Gardner, Martin. *Science: Good, Bad, and Bogus*. Buffalo, N.Y.: Prometheus Books, 1981. A collection of Gardner's essays, book reviews, and other writings that attack fraud, hoax, and self-delusion when practiced in the name of science.

Gardner, Martin. *The WHYS of a Philosophical Scrivener*. New York: Quill, a Division of William Morrow & Company, 1983. Learned in science, mathematics, and philosophy, the author imaginatively and wittily defends his own views on the fundamental issues of classical philosophy.

Grayling, A. C. *The Refutation of Scepticism*. Chicago, Ill.: Open Court, 1985. This is an example of contemporary responses to skepticism.

Hempel, Carl G. *Philosophy of Natural Science*. Englewood Cliffs, N.J.: Prentice Hall, Foundations of Philosophy Series, 1966. This is a classic study in the philosophy of science.

Hospers, John. *An Introduction to Philosophical Analysis*. 2d ed. Englewood Cliffs, N.J.: Prentice Hall, 1967. This expository text contains a clear, contemporary, and elementary discussion of rationalism and empiricism for the beginning student.

Johnson, Oliver. *Skepticism and Cognitivism*. Berkeley: Univ. of California Press, 1978. The author thoroughly examines nearly every argument for skepticism.

Kenny, Anthony. *Descartes*. New York: Random House, 1968. This book provides a good study of Descartes and his methods.

Kuhn, Thomas S. *The Structure of Scientific Revolutions*. 2d enlarged ed. Chicago: Univ. of Chicago Press, 1970. This very influential and controversial study rejects the view of the history of science as a steady, cumulative growth of knowledge in favor of an interpretation of that history as a series of peaceful interludes punctuated by revolutionary changes from one conceptual worldview to another.

Morris, Henry M. *Scientific Creationism*. Green Forest, Ark.: Master Books, 1986. Many creationists consider this work to be the best documented case for scientific creationism.

Nagel, Ernest. *The Structure of Science*. New York: Harcourt, 1961. A comprehensive treatment of the nature of explanation in the natural and social sciences by an outstanding American philosopher of science. A book for the more advanced student.

Poundstone, William. *Labyrinths of Reason: Paradox, Puzzles and the Frailty of Knowledge*. New York: Anchor, Doubleday, 1988. Wittily and provocatively the author explores various paradoxes to raise the philosophical question, How do we know what we know? In his epistemological journey, he ranges from ancient Greek philosophers like Zeno to such contemporary American philosophers as John Searle.

Russell, Bertrand. *Problems of Philosophy*. London: Oxford Univ. Press, 1912. For over 75 years of reprintings, this brief book has remained a popular and highly readable introduction to the problems of knowledge.

Stapledon, Olaf. *Last and First Men and Star Maker*. New York: Dover, 1968. Two science fiction novels by a philosopher, which convey the haunting beauty and disturbing strangeness of the world revealed by science better than most abstract treatises. These powerfully imaginative works reveal why many people find the scientific understanding and manipulation of the world and humankind so fascinating and hopeful and many others find them so appalling and depressing.

Unger, Peter K. *Ignorance: A Case for Scepticism*. New York: Oxford Univ. Press, 1975. The author presents a challenging defense of modern skepticism.

Encyclopedias

Dictionary of the History of Ideas: Studies of Selected Pivotal Ideas. Philip P. Wiener, editor-in-chief. New York: Scribners, 1973. Substantial and clearly written essays emphasizing the historical development of topics discussed in this part. Designed to inform the nonspecialist, each essay concludes with a select bibliography.

Encyclopedia of Philosophy. Paul Edwards, editor-in-chief. New York: Macmillan, 1967. The beginning student will find many worthwhile articles on the subjects treated in this part and excellent bibliographies.

Philosophy and Public Affairs. Princeton, N.J.: Princeton Univ. Press. A quarterly journal. Philosophers and philosophically inclined writers from various disciplines bring their methods to bear on problems that concern everyone interested in social and political issues.

Routledge Encyclopedia of Philosophy. Edward Craig, general editor. New York: Routledge, 1998. This ten-volume encyclopedia contains articles on all areas of philosophy and up-to-date bibliographies.

Internet Web Sites

RESEARCH NAVIGATOR (*http://www.researchnavigator.com*). This web site offers three research data bases: Ebsco Academic Journal and Abstract Data Base, *New York Times* Search by Subject Archive, and "Best of the Web" Link Library. In addition, this site provides helpful advice on how to conduct efficient and productive research from choosing a topic to polishing the final draft. Beginning philosophy students probably will find the "Best of the Web" Link Library the most appropriate place to start their research. The free access code necessary to employ Research Navigator can be found in the Prentice Hall Guide to Evaluating Online Resources. If your text did not come with this guide, please go to *www.prenhall.com/contentselect* for information on how you can purchase an access code.

EpistemeLinks (*http://www.epistemelinks.com*). This site provides many links to philosophical resources on the web.

Epilogue

This book will have accomplished all it can do if it not only has acquainted the student with some philosophy but also has encouraged the seeker to philosophize, to strive for genuine freedom of thought. The U.S. Constitution may guarantee freedom of expression; it cannot ensure freedom of thought. To achieve freedom of thought, one must practice the ceaseless questioning that is philosophy. In the simple but powerful words of the philosopher John Stuart Mill, without philosophizing, human beings

> are condemned to live second-hand. Their views on life's greatest questions come from sources other than themselves. Their character, their life, their *being* is shaped and controlled by philosophical views that are not their own. They believe what other men want them to believe, for other men's reasons. They never know the joy of living one's own life, which Plato likened to being released from lifelong imprisonment in a cave. They never know freedom of thought—though they may know freedom of expression.

It is not enough to express oneself. One also must have the Socratic wisdom to know and be oneself.

Glossary

A posteriori A way of knowing that a statement is true in which a person does refer to facts, experiments, or past experiences.

A priori A way of knowing that a statement is true in which one does not refer to facts, experiments, or past experiences. One just figures out or "sees" that the statement is true.

Absolute (1) In contexts concerning questions of knowledge, this term refers to being completely certain. (2) In the context of ethics, the term refers to the view that contrasts with ethical relativism. It is the view that there are principles of morality that should be binding on everyone, even if no one actually follows them. (3) In contexts of discussions of reality, the term refers to some thing that is beyond mere nature and that is a kind of goal that everything is striving toward.

Aesthetics The branch of philosophy that examines questions concerning beauty and art.

Agnosticism The view that there is no way of knowing whether or not God exists.

Altruism The view that one should aim at performing actions that benefit others whether or not they benefit oneself.

Analytic statement A statement that is true solely because of the meanings of the constituent words, such as, "All widows were once married."

Anarchy In philosophical contexts the form of society in which there is no government and no official laws. It is hoped that all members voluntarily keep themselves from violating others' rights.

Argument A series of statements in which one of the statements is to be accepted as true because the other statements are supposed to be true. Arguments are the means that people use to convince others through reason.

Argument from analogy A kind of argument in which two things are compared and found to be generally similar. Then, since one of the things has a feature that is of interest, the conclusion is that the other thing probably has the same feature.

Argument from design A way of arguing that God exists based on the premise that the world that we experience has many examples of complicated order which could not have occurred without a designer, who is held to be God.

Artificial intelligence A branch of technology that attempts to make machines and computer programs that simulate behavior that we usually call intelligent.

Atheism The view that God does not exist.

Capitalism An economic system in which ideally the important decisions of what should be produced and how it should be distributed are determined by individuals making their own separate decisions of how to spend their time and money.

Causal explanation A way of explaining why an event happened. The explanation that is offered is in terms of the causes that led to the event.

Cause and effect Two events are related as cause and effect if one, the cause, comes before the other, the effect, and furthermore, the cause *makes* the effect happen. These are the traditional and also the ordinary definitions; they play a major role in the debate concerning freedom and determinism.

Conclusion The part of an argument that is to be accepted on the basis of the reasons and evidence presented in the other part of the argument.

Consciousness The quality of being aware of the world and one's own mental states.

Consistency Two or more statements that can be true at the same time. In matters of rationality consistency refers to making similar judgments in similar situations.

Contingency The view that some events just occur randomly and accidentally, and not because they fit any pattern or fulfill any purpose.

Deduction A kind of argument in which the premises present absolutely conclusive reasons for accepting the conclusion. The standard example of deduction is that the premises "All men are mortal" and "Socrates is a man" require one to accept the conclusion "Socrates is mortal."

Deism The view that God does exist and did create the universe and set it into motion, but that this God is not particularly concerned about the actions of human beings.

Democracy The form of government in which the people participate in the important decisions that affect their lives.

Desert The concept that everyone deserves a particular kind of treatment. There are different standards for determining what people deserve. Among them are merit, effort, achievement, and need.

Determinism The view that *every* event in the universe is caused by the events that came before it.

Dilemma A situation in which a person faces two choices and both of them are undesirable.

Dualism The view that two basic kinds of things exist—one that is material and one that is nonmaterial.

Duty An action that a person ought to perform for moral reasons.

Empirical Having to do with factual matters, or matters that can be discovered by experiment.

Empiricism The view that the ultimate source of every true belief about the world is sense-experience. For a belief to be true according to this view, it must be confirmed in some way by sense-experience.

Epiphenomenalism The view that mental activities are not just material processes, but are the by-products, or mere accompaniments, of material processes. On this view mental events and processes can never cause changes in the physical world.

Epistemology The branch of philosophy that examines questions concerning knowledge. The major questions are: What is the nature of knowledge? Do we know anything? And if we do, how do we gain this knowledge?

Essence The really important features of a thing that make it what it is, and if it did not have them, it would not be what it is. A standard view used to be that part of the essence of human beings was rationality.

Ethical egoism The view that a person should always and only aim at improving his or her own welfare.

Ethics The branch of philosophy that deals with questions of what is good and what we should do.

Evolution A scientific theory that claims that complicated life-forms developed as the result of an accumulation of accidents.

External world What exists outside one's own mind, including one's own body.

Faith A kind of belief that is not supported by evidence. It is common in religious contexts.

Fatalism The view that the future is already set and cannot be changed by anything that is done in the present. The future is thus as set as is the past.

First cause argument An argument that concludes that God exists based on the premise that everything, including the universe, must have a cause.

Free will (1) The feeling that people have when they perform an action that they think is up to them. (2) The theory that at least some of our actions actually are up to us.

Hard determinism The variety of determinism that claims that no actions are due to free will. Hard determinists usually claim that the concept of free will makes no sense and as a result, people are not responsible for their actions.

Hypothesis A proposed answer to some question. William James used this term to mean any possible belief.

Idealism (1) The view that matter does not exist—that nothing material causes our sensations. (2) The view that the most important forces that cause effects in the human world are not physical ones.

Indetermination The philosophical view that some events have no cause at all. They just occur.

Induction A kind of argument in which the premises provide evidence for the conclusion but do not absolutely require that the conclusion be accepted. The conclusion is only more likely to be true than false. A standard example of induction: the premise that every known human being so far has been less than 100 feet tall provides evidence for the conclusion that no human beings are over 100 feet tall. The evidence makes the conclusion only probably true.

Instrumental good The kind of good thing that is desired just for what it leads to and not simply for itself, such as a trip to the dentist.

Intentionality The property of being about something. Sentences in a language, beliefs, thoughts, wishes, and other mental states all have this property. For example, one does not just have beliefs; one's beliefs are always about something.

Interactionism The view that mind and body are two different kinds of things that can cause changes in each other.

Intrinsic good The kind of good thing that is desired just for itself and not simply for what it leads to, such as happiness.

Introspection The ability to focus and report on one's own mental states.

Intuition A belief that one considers to be obviously and clearly correct. This term is often used in ethics.

Knowledge A highly valued state in which one has a true belief that can be defended against criticisms.

Law of contradiction A fundamental law of logic. According to this law, a statement and its contradiction cannot both be true and cannot both be false at the same time. Two statements that illustrate this law are "Elvis is alive" and "Elvis is not alive."

Law of the excluded middle A fundamental law of logic. According to this law, any statement is either true or false. Thus, "There is intelligent life on other planets" is either true or false. There is no third alternative.

Libertarianism Another name for the theory of free will, the theory that at least some of our actions are up to us.

Materialism The view that matter is the only kind of thing that exists, and so-called mental acts and entities are really just material things and processes.

Matter What takes up space and would exist even if there were no one to perceive it.

Metaphysics The branch of philosophy that deals with questions of reality—of what really exists.

Mind A nonphysical thing that is supposed to be the place where thinking, sensing, and feeling take place. A particular mind is considered to be accessible only to the particular person to whom it belongs.

Monism The view that only one kind of thing exists. This one kind of thing may be just material or nonmaterial.

Morality A system of rules or guidelines that set forth the most important features of how we should treat other people.

Mysticism The view that there are fundamental truths about the world that are not known through our senses or by our reason.

Naturalism The view that everything that is real is either part of nature or is built out of things found in nature.

Necessary condition A requirement for something else to occur. Water is a necessary condition for life as we know it.

Necessity The condition in which what happens or what is true has to be that way.

Objective A point of view in which no individual's biases or perspectives are allowed to distort the reality of the matter.

Obligation An action that a person ought to perform.

Occam's razor A guideline for correct thinking that states that one should not invent entities to explain something if it is not necessary to do so. What this amounts to is that one should make as few assumptions as possible and that one should try to keep one's explanations as simple as possible.

Ontology The branch of philosophy that attempts to determine what are the basic kinds of things that exist.

Paradox (1) An apparently sound argument that conflicts with what is generally believed to be true. Zeno's arguments against the possibility of motion are famous examples of this type of paradox. (2) A statement that seems to be neither true nor false. A famous example of this kind of paradox is "This statement is false."

Paternalism The view that restrictions on individual liberty are legitimate when they are justified by appealing to the values and the welfare of the person being restricted.

Personal identity What remains the same throughout one's life that makes one the person one is. There are debates about whether one's identity can be found in something material or something mental. Some argue that there is no such thing as personal identity at all.

Phenomenology Having to do with the qualities of a kind of experience. A phenomenological examination of religion would focus on the characteristics of religious experience without consideration of what, if anything, it is an experience of.

Possible A state of affairs that could exist. There are three different types of possibility commonly considered in philosophy. (1) Technically possible—states of affairs that could exist given the current state of technology. Examples: Sending a rocket to the moon is technically possible, but flying from New York to London in 5 minutes is not. (2) Physically possible—states of affairs that could exist given the current understanding of scientific theory. Examples: Flying from London to New York in 5 minutes is physically possible, but going the same distance faster than the speed of light is not. (3) Logically possible—states of affairs that could exist given our current understanding of logical consistency. Examples: Going from New York to London faster than the speed of light is logically possible, but the same small object being in both places at the same time is not.

Pragmatism The view that statements should be judged as true according to the value they have for us in believing them. Thus, if it is valuable for us to believe that we have free will, then we should consider it to be true that we do have free will.

Premise The part of an argument that provides the reasons and the evidence that are the basis for accepting the conclusion.

Proposition A statement that is true or false and in which everything is clearly specified.

Psychological egoism The view that all people, as a matter of fact, always and only aim at improving their own welfare. This view is just a description of what people do. It implies no judgment about whether or not this is the right way to act.

Rationalism The view that the source of at least some true beliefs about the world is not the senses. This source is sometimes called reason or the understanding. An often used example of a belief that is true although not confirmed by sense-experience is that flexible objects can be put into an infinite number of different shapes.

Rationality (1) The characteristic of adopting beliefs only when they are adequately supported by evidence. (2) The characteristic of selecting an efficient way to achieve one's ends.

Realism The view that certain things or qualities exist independently of human beings. These things or qualities would exist even if all human beings disappeared or had never existed in the first place.

Reason (1) A faculty of human beings that is contrasted with the emotions. (2) The disposition of accepting beliefs only when they are supported by evidence. (3) The disposition of using arguments to decide what to believe.

Reductio ad absurdum A commonly used strategy in philosophy in which one tries to show that a view is mistaken because it leads to a conclusion that is absurd, ridiculous, or obviously false.

Relativism In ethics the view that moral principles are just the teaching of certain groups, and that there is no principle that should be considered binding on all groups. Sometimes relativism is used to mean there is *no way to show* that a principle would be binding on all groups, and sometimes this term is used to mean that it *makes no sense* to say that a moral principle should be binding on all groups.

Retribution A theory of punishment that those who commit crimes deserve a certain amount of suffering proportional to the harm caused by the crime.

Rights In ethics the view that there are certain domains in which every person can act as he or she wishes without interference, such as the right to free speech and the right to own property.

Semantics The subject that studies the interpretations of symbols. In language semantics refers to the meanings of words.

Sensation The final result of processes of sight, touch, smell, taste, and hearing. Sensations are generally considered to occur in the mind.

Sense-data The information that our senses provide to us.

Skepticism The philosophical view that knowledge does not exist. Usually there is a reference in the context to a particular kind of knowledge, such as knowledge of what the world is like or knowledge about whether God exists.

Socialism An economic system in which ideally a publically chosen group makes the important decisions of what will be produced and how it will be distributed.

Soft determinism The variety of determinism that claims that determinism is compatible with free will. That means that the very same action can be the result of causes and also be called "free." This view of determinism does not eliminate the possibility of moral responsibility.

Sound argument An argument in which the premises are true and the reasoning is valid. This is the best kind of argument and provides the best grounds for accepting the conclusion.

Sovereignty In political philosophy the group that holds supreme political power. In a democracy, the people are sovereign. In a monarchy, the king or queen is the sovereign.

Spiritual A vague word that is often used to refer to anything that is not physical.

State In political philosophy the organization that has political control over a certain territory. The usual functions of the state are to make the laws, enforce them, and interpret them when necessary.

Subjective A personal point of view, or how matters appear to an individual.

Substance A philosophical term that refers to whatever it is that has properties, such as a table that has color, shape, and size. Some use substance to refer to whatever it is that has a body and a mind.

Sufficient condition An adequate ground for the occurrence of something, but not a requirement. A gunshot is sufficient to kill someone, but it is not a requirement because there are other ways to kill people.

Supernaturalism The view that there are real things besides what occurs in nature. This other kind of real thing is considered more powerful than nature.

Syntax The subject that studies the capacity to manipulate symbols according to rules. Syntax is often used to refer to the grammar of a language.

Synthetic statement A statement that is true, but the truth of which is not based solely on the meanings of the constituent words. An example of such a statement is "The dinosaurs are extinct."

Teleology The view that a thing has a predetermined purpose. Sometimes the word is used in connection with the universe as a whole. In ethics the view that what makes an act right is the results the act leads to. Utilitarianism is an example of a teleological theory in ethics.

Theism The view that there is a God who created the universe and who also has a personal interest in the well-being of humanity.

Theodicy A way of reconciling God's goodness, knowledge, and power with the fact of human suffering.

Universal (1) A statement that refers to all the members of some group. For example, "All men are mortal." (2) Qualities that all items of a particular group share. For example, all monkeys share in the universal of mortality.

Utilitarianism The view in ethics that acts are right to the extent that they increase happiness and wrong to the extent that they increase suffering.

Valid argument An argument in which the reasoning is good, but the premises are not necessarily all true. Valid arguments have one of the features of sound arguments, but they do not always have the other important feature—true premises.

Value What is important. Values involve comparison and ranking.